This boo
the Librar

COUNTY COURT DISTRICTS
(England & Wales)
INDEX OF PLACE NAMES

ELEVENTH EDITION

Compiled by the County Courts Branch

Lord Chancellor's Department

LONDON: HER MAJESTY'S STATIONERY OFFICE

1971

Published by
HER MAJESTY'S STATIONERY OFFICE

To be purchased from
49 High Holborn, London WC1V 6HB
13a Castle Street, Edinburgh EH2 3AR
109 St. Mary Street, Cardiff CF1 1JW
Brazennose Street, Manchester M60 8AS
50 Fairfax Street, Bristol BS1 3DE
258 Broad Street, Birmingham B1 2HE
7 Linenhall Street, Belfast BT2 8AY
or through booksellers

Printed in England for Her Majesty's Stationery Office
by Hobbs the Printers Ltd. Southampton

PREFATORY NOTE

This Index has been compiled by the County Courts Branch of the Lord Chancellor's Department from information furnished by the Officers of County Courts. It is requested that when a mistake or an omission is discovered, information thereof may be forwarded at once by unpaid post to Head of the County Courts Branch, Lord Chancellor's Department, 3 Deans Yard, Westminster, London SW1.

COUNTY COURT DISTRICTS
(England & Wales)

INDEX OF PLACE NAMES

A - ABE

Abbas Combe	*Somerset* - Yeovil
Abberley	*Worcester* - Kidderminster
Abberley Common	*Worcester* - Kidderminster
Abberton	*Essex* - Colchester
Abberton	*Worcester* - Evesham
Abberwick	*Northumberland* - Alnwick
Abbess End	*Essex* - Chelmsford
Abbess Roding	*Essex* - Chelmsford
Abbey	*Cumberland* - Workington
Abbey Bradwell	*Bucks* - Bletchley and Leighton Buzzard
Abbey Combe	*Warwick* - Rugby
Abbey Cowper	*Cumberland* - Carlisle
Abbey Crofts	*Dorset* - Blandford
Abbey Cwnhir	*Radnor* - Llandrindod Wells
Abbeydale	*Worcester* - Redditch
Abbeydale	*York, W.R.* - Sheffield
Abbeydore	*Hereford* - Hereford
Abbey Green	*Stafford* - Leek
Abbey Hey	*Lancaster* - Manchester
Abbey Hills	*Lancaster* - Oldham
Abbey House	*Cumberland* - Carlisle
Abbey Hulton	*Stafford* - Stoke-on-Trent
Abbey Lands	*Northumberland* - Alnwick
Abbey Town	*Cumberland* - Carlisle
Abbey Village	*Lancaster* - Chorley
Abbey Wood (part)	*London, S.E.2.* - Dartford
Abbey Wood (part)	*London, S.E.2* - Woolwich
Abbots Ann	*Hants* - Andover
Abbots Bickington	*Devon* - Bideford
Abbots Bromley	*Stafford* - Uttoxeter
Abbotsbury	*Dorset* - Weymouth
Abbotsham	*Devon* - Bideford
Abbotskerswell	*Devon* - Newton Abbot
Abbots Langley	*Herts* - Watford
Abbots Leigh	*Somerset* - Bristol
Abbots Lench	*Worcester* - Evesham
Abbotsley	*Hunts* - Biggleswade
Abbotsmead	*Lancaster* - Barrow-in-Furness
Abbots Morton	*Worcester* - Redditch
Abbots Ripton	*Hunts* - Huntingdon
Abbots Salford	*Warwick* - Redditch
Abbotstone	*Hants* - Winchester
Abbotswood	*Hants* - Southampton
Abbotswood	*Surrey* - Guildford
Abbots Wood	*Worcester* - Evesham
Abbots Worthy	*Hants* - Winchester
Abbots Wootton	*Dorset* - Axminster and Chard
Abcott	*Salop* - Ludlow
Abdon	*Salop* - Ludlow
Abdy	*York W.R.* - Rotherham
Abenbury	*Denbigh* - Wrexham
Abenhall	*Gloucester* - Gloucester
Aber	*Caernarvon* - Bangor
Aberaeron	*Cardigan* - Aberystwyth
Aberaman	*Glamorgan* - Aberdare
Aberangell	*Merioneth* - Dolgellau
Aberarth	*Cardigan* - Aberystwyth
Aberavon	*Glamorgan* - Neath
Aberbaiden	*Glamorgan* - Bridgend
Aber Bargoed	*Monmouth* - Blackwood
Aberbechan	*Montgomery* - Newtown
Aberbeeg	*Monmouth* - Blackwood
Aber Canaid, Lower	*Glamorgan* - Merthyr Tydfil
Aber Canaid, Upper	*Glamorgan* - Merthyr Tydfil
Abercarn	*Monmouth* - Blackwood
Abercastle	*Pembroke* - Haverfordwest
Abercegir	*Montgomery* - Machynlleth
Abercrave	*Brecon* - Neath

ABE - ABY

Abercregan	*Glamorgan* - Neath
Abercwmboi	*Glamorgan* - Aberdare
Abercych	*Pembroke* - Cardigan
Abercynon	*Glamorgan* - Aberdare
Aberdare	*Glamorgan* - Aberdare
Aberdaron	*Caernarvon* - Portmadoc
Aberdeen	*York, W.R.* - Keighley
Aberdovy	*Merioneth* - Machynlleth
Aberdulais	*Glamorgan* - Neath
Aberedw	*Radnor* - Builth
Abereiddy	*Pembroke* - Haverfordwest
Abererch	*Caernarvon* - Portmadoc
Aberfan	*Glamorgan* - Merthyr Tydfil
Aberffraw	*Anglesey* - Llangefni
Aberford	*York, W.R.* - Leeds
Abergarw	*Glamorgan* - Bridgend
Abergavenny	*Monmouth* - Pontypool and Abergavenny
Abergeirw	*Merioneth* - Dolgellau
Abergele	*Denbigh* - Rhyl
Aberglaslyn	*Caernarvon* - Portmadoc
Abergorlech	*Cardigan* - Lampeter
Abergwili	*Carmarthen* - Carmarthen
Abergwynfi	*Glamorgan* - Neath
Abergynolwyn	*Merioneth* - Dolgellau
Aberhafesp	*Montgomery* - Newtown
Aberhosan	*Montgomery* - Machynlleth
Aberhowy	*Brecon* - Pontypool and Abergavenny
Aberkenfig	*Glamorgan* - Bridgend
Aberllefeni	*Merioneth* - Dolgellau
Abermarchnant	*Montgomery* - Oswestry
Abermeurig	*Cardigan* - Aberystwyth
Abermeurig	*Cardigan* - Lampeter
Abermorddu	*Flint* - Wrexham
Abermule	*Montgomery* - Newtown
Abernant	*Carmarthen* - Carmarthen
Abernant	*Glamorgan* - Aberdare
Aberpergwm	*Glamorgan* - Neath
Aberporth	*Cardigan* - Cardigan
Abersoch	*Caernarvon* - Portmadoc
Abersychan	*Monmouth* - Pontypool and Abergavenny
Aberthaw, West	*Glamorgan* - Bridgend
Aberthin	*Glamorgan* - Bridgend
Abertillery	*Monmouth* - Blackwood
Abertridwr	*Glamorgan* - Caerphilly
Abertysswg	*Monmouth* - Blackwood
Aberyscir	*Brecon* - Brecknock
Aberystwyth	*Cardigan* - Aberystwyth
Abingdon	*Berks* - Oxford
Abinger	*Surrey* - Dorking
Abinger Common	*Surrey* - Dorking
Abinger Hammer	*Surrey* - Dorking
Abington	*Northampton* - Northampton
Abington, Great	*Cambridge* - Cambridge
Abington, Little	*Cambridge* - Cambridge
Abington Pigotts	*Cambridge* - Hitchin
Ab Kettleby	*Leicester* - Melton Mowbray
Ableton	*Gloucester* - Thornbury
Ablington	*Gloucester* - Cheltenham
Ablington	*Wilts* - Salisbury
Abney	*Derby* - Buxton
Abney Grange	*Derby* - Buxton
Abram	*Lancaster* - Wigan
Abridge	*Essex* - Ilford
Abshott	*Hants* - Portsmouth
Abson	*Gloucester* - Bristol
Abthorpe	*Northampton* - Northampton
Aby with Greenfield	*Lincoln* - Louth

ACA - ADS

Acaster Malbis	*York, W.R.* - York
Acaster Selby	*York, W.R.* - York
Accrington	*Lancaster* - Accrington
Ackenthwaite	*Westmorland* - Kendal
Acklam	*York, E.R.* - Malton
Ackleton	*Salop* - Bridgnorth
Acklington	*Northumberland* - Alnwick
Acklington Park	*Northumberland* - Alnwick
Ackton	*York, W.R.* - Pontefract
Ackworth	*York, W.R.* - Pontefract
Acle	*Norfolk* - Norwich
Acock's Green	*Warwick* - Birmingham
Acol	*Kent* - Margate
Acomb	*Northumberland* - Hexham
Acomb	*York, E.R.* - York
Aconbury	*Hereford* - Hereford
Acre	*Lancaster* - Rawtenstall
Acrefair	*Denbigh* - Wrexham
Acresford	*Leicester* - Ashby-de-la-Zouch
Acres Nook	*Stafford* - Stoke-on-Trent
Acrise	*Kent* - Folkestone
Acthorpe	*Lincoln* - Louth
Acton	*Cheshire* - Crewe
Acton	*Denbigh* - Wrexham
Acton	*Dorset* - Swanage
Acton	*London, W.3* - Brentford
Acton	*Northumberland* - Alnwick
Acton	*Salop* - Ludlow
Acton	*Stafford* - Stoke-on-Trent
Acton	*Suffolk* - Sudbury
Acton	*Worcester* - Worcester
Acton Beauchamp	*Worcester* - Worcester
Acton Bridge	*Cheshire* - Northwich
Acton Burnell	*Salop* - Shrewsbury
Acton Grange	*Cheshire* - Warrington
Acton Hill	*Stafford* - Stafford
Acton Piggott	*Salop* - Shrewsbury
Acton Reynold	*Salop* - Shrewsbury
Acton Round	*Salop* - Bridgnorth
Acton Scott	*Salop* - Ludlow
Acton Trussell	*Stafford* - Stafford
Acton Turville	*Gloucester* - Bristol
Adbaston	*Stafford* - Market Drayton
Adber	*Dorset* - Yeovil
Adbolton	*Notts* - Nottingham
Adbury	*Hants* - Newbury
Adderbury, East	*Oxford* - Banbury
Adderbury, West	*Oxford* - Banbury
Adderley	*Salop* - Market Drayton
Adderley Green	*Stafford* - Stoke-on-Trent
Adderley Park	*Warwick* - Birmingham
Addingham	*York, W.R.* - Skipton
Addington	*Bucks* - Aylesbury
Addington	*Kent* - Maidstone
Addington	*Surrey* - Croydon
Addington, Great	*Northampton* - Wellingborough
Addington, Little	*Northampton* - Wellingborough
Addiscombe	*Surrey* - Croydon
Addison Colliery	*Durham* - Newcastle-upon-Tyne
Addlestone	*Surrey* - Kingston-upon-Thames
Addlethorpe	*Lincoln* - Skegness
Adel	*York, W.R.* - Leeds
Adelaide Bridge	*Cambridge* - Ely
Aden	*York, W.R.* - Keighley
Adeney	*Salop* - Wellington (Salop)
Adeyfield	*Herts* - Hemel Hempstead
Adfa	*Montgomery* - Newtown
Adfarton	*Hereford* - Knighton
Adgestone	*I. of W.* - Newport (I.W.)
Adisham	*Kent* - Canterbury
Adlestrop	*Gloucester* - Cheltenham
Adlingfleet	*York, W.R.* - Goole
Adlington	*Cheshire* - Macclesfield
Adlington	*Lancaster* - Chorley
Admaston	*Salop* - Wellington (Salop)
Admaston	*Stafford* - Uttoxeter
Admington	*Warwick* - Stratford on Avon
Admistone	*Dorset* - Dorchester
Adesborough	*Somerset* - Taunton
Adsclean	*Sussex* - Chichester

ADS - ALB

Adsett	*Gloucester* - Gloucester
Adstock	*Bucks* - Aylesbury
Adstone	*Northampton* - Northampton
Adstone	*Salop* - Shrewsbury
Adswood	*Cheshire* - Stockport
Advent	*Cornwall* - Bodmin
Adversane	*Sussex* - Horsham
Adwalton	*York, W.R.* - Dewsbury
Adwell	*Oxford* - Thame
Adwick-le-Street	*York, W.R.* - Doncaster
Adwick Sidings	*York, W.R.* - Rotherham
Adwick-upon-Dearne	*York, W.R.* - Doncaster
Adwy'r Clawdd	*Denbigh* - Wrexham
Affetside	*Lancaster* - Bury
Afflington	*Dorset* - Swanage
Affpuddle	*Dorset* - Dorchester
Afoneitha	*Denbigh* - Wrexham
Afonwen	*Caernarvon* - Portmadoc
Afonwen	*Flint* - Holywell
Agbrigg	*York, W.R.* - Wakefield
Agden	*Cheshire* - Altrincham
Agden	*Cheshire* - Whitchurch
Agecroft	*Lancaster* - Salford
Aglionby	*Cumberland* - Carlisle
Aigburth	*Lancaster* - Liverpool
Aigburth Vale	*Lancaster* - Liverpool
Aikbank	*Cumberland* - Carlisle
Aike	*York, E.R.* - Beverley
Aiketgate	*Cumberland* - Penrith
Aikhead	*Cumberland* - Carlisle
Aikton	*Cumberland* - Carlisle
Ailby	*Lincoln* - Skegness
Ailstone	*Warwick* - Stratford on Avon
Ailsworth	*Northampton* - Peterborough and Oundle
Aimshaugh	*Cumberland* - Hexham
Ainderby Quernhow	*York, N.R.* - Northallerton
Ainderby Steeple	*York, N.R.* - Northallerton
Ainley Top	*York, W.R.* - Halifax
Ainsdale	*Lancaster* - Southport
Ainstable	*Cumberland* - Penrith
Ainsworth	*Lancaster* - Bury
Ainthorpe	*York, N.R.* - Whitby
Aintree	*Lancaster* - Liverpool
Airedale	*York, W.R.* - Pontefract
Airmyn	*York, W.R.* - Goole
Airton	*York, W.R.* - Skipton
Aisby	*Lincoln* - Gainsborough
Aisby	*Lincoln* - Grantham
Aisgill Moor	*Westmorland* - Penrith
Aish	*Devon* - Torquay
Aisholt, Higher	*Somerset* - Bridgwater
Aisholt, Lower	*Somerset* - Bridgwater
Aiskew	*York, N.R.* - Northallerton
Aislaby	*Durham* - Stockton on Tees
Aislaby	*York, N.R.* - Malton
Aislaby	*York, N.R.* - Whitby
Aisthorpe	*Lincoln* - Lincoln
Akeld	*Northumberland* - Berwick-on-Tweed
Akeley	*Bucks* - Aylesbury
Akenham	*Suffolk* - Ipswich
Aketon	*York, W.R.* - Harrogate
Aketon	*York, W.R.* - Pontefract
Akroyden	*York, W.R.* - Halifax
Albany Park (part)	*Kent* - Bromley
Albany Park (part)	*Kent* - Dartford
Albaston	*Cornwall* - Plymouth
Alberbury	*Salop & Mont.* - Shrewsbury
Albert Village	*Leicester* - Ashby-de-la-Zouch
Albion	*Stafford* - West Bromwich
Albourne	*Sussex* - Haywards Heath
Albrightlee	*Salop* - Shrewsbury
Albrighton	*Salop* - Shrewsbury
Albrighton	*Salop* - Wolverhampton
Alburgh	*Norfolk* - Norwich
Albury	*Herts* - Bishop's Stortford
Albury	*Oxford* - Thame
Albury	*Surrey* - Guildford
Alby	*Norfolk* - Norwich
Albyfield	*Cumberland* - Carlisle

Alby Top	*Cumberland* - Carlisle
Alcaston	*Salop* - Ludlow
Alcester	*Warwick* - Redditch
Alcester Lanes End	*Warwick* - Birmingham
Alciston	*Sussex* - Lewes
Alcombe	*Somerset* - Minehead
Alcombe	*Wilts* - Bath
Alconbury	*Hunts* - Huntingdon
Alconbury Weston	*Hunts* - Huntingdon
Aldborough	*Essex* - Ilford
Aldborough	*Norfolk* - Norwich
Aldborough	*York, W.R.* - Harrogate
Aldbourne	*Wilts* - Swindon
Aldbrough	*York, E.R.* - Kingston-upon-Hull
Aldbrough St. John	*York, N.R.* - Darlington
Aldbury	*Herts* - Hemel Hempstead
Aldcliffe	*Lancaster* - Lancaster
Aldeburgh	*Suffolk* - Woodbridge
Aldeby	*Norfolk* - Lowestoft
Aldenham	*Herts* - Watford
Aldenham	*Salop* - Bridgnorth
Alderbury	*Wilts* - Salisbury
Aldercar	*Derby* - Ilkeston
Aldercar Hall	*Derby* - Ilkeston
Alderford	*Norfolk* - Norwich
Alderholt	*Dorset* - Wimborne Minster
Alderley	*Gloucester* - Bristol
Alderley Edge	*Cheshire* - Macclesfield
Alderman's Green	*Warwick* - Coventry
Aldermaston	*Berks* - Newbury
Alderminster	*Warwick* - Stratford on Avon
Aldermoor	*Hants* - Southampton
Aldersey	*Cheshire* - Chester
Aldershaw	*Stafford* - Lichfield
Aldershot	*Hants* - Aldershot and Farnham
Aldersley	*Stafford* - Wolverhampton
Alderton	*Gloucester* - Cheltenham
Alderton	*Northampton* - Northampton
Alderton	*Salop* - Shrewsbury
Alderton	*Suffolk* - Woodbridge
Alderton	*Wilts* - Malmesbury
Alderwasley	*Derby* - Matlock
Aldfield	*York, W.R.* - Harrogate
Aldford	*Cheshire* - Chester
Aldgate	*London, E.1* - Mayor's and City of London
Aldham	*Essex* - Colchester
Aldham	*Suffolk* - Ipswich
Aldingbourne	*Sussex* - Chichester
Aldingham	*Lancaster* - Barrow-in-Furness
Aldin Grange	*Durham* - Durham
Aldington	*Kent* - Ashford
Aldington	*Worcester* - Evesham
Aldon	*Salop* - Ludlow
Aldoth	*Cumberland* - Carlisle
Aldreth	*Cambridge* - Ely
Aldridge	*Stafford* - Walsall
Aldringham with Thorpe	*Suffolk* - Woodbridge
Aldrington	*Sussex* - Brighton
Aldsworth	*Gloucester* - Cheltenham
Aldsworth	*Sussex* - Chichester
Aldwark	*Derby* - Matlock
Aldwark	*York, N.R.* - York
Aldwarke	*York, W.R.* - Rotherham
Aldwick	*Sussex* - Chichester
Aldwinckle All Saints	*Northampton* - Peterborough
Aldwinckle St. Peter	*Northampton* - Peterborough
Aldwincle	*Northants* - Kettering
Aldworth	*Berks* - Didcot
Aldworth	*Sussex* - Chichester
Alethorpe	*Norfolk* - King's Lynn
Alexandra Park	*Lancaster* - Manchester
Alexandra Park	*London, N.10* - Clerkenwell
Aley Green	*Beds* - Luton
Alfington	*Devon* - Exeter
Alfold	*Surrey* - Guildford
Alfold Bars	*Sussex* - Chichester
Alford	*Lincoln* - Skegness
Alford	*Somerset* - Yeovil
Alfred's Well	*Worcester* - Bromsgrove

Alfreton	*Derby* - Alfreton
Alfrick	*Worcester* - Worcester
Alfriston	*Sussex* - Eastbourne
Algarkirk	*Lincoln* - Boston
Algarkirk Fen	*Lincoln* - Boston
Alhampton	*Somerset* - Wells
Alice Holt	*Hants* - Aldershot and Farnham
Alkborough	*Lincoln* - Scunthorpe
Alkerton	*Gloucester* - Stroud
Alkerton	*Oxford* - Banbury
Alkham	*Kent* - Dover
Alkham, West	*Kent* - Dover
Alkington	*Gloucester* - Stroud
Alkington	*Salop* - Whitchurch
Alkmonton	*Derby* - Derby
Alkrington	*Lancaster* - Oldham
Allaleigh	*Devon* - Torquay
Alland Grange	*Kent* - Ramsgate
Allans Green	*Northumberland* - Hexham
Allbrook	*Hants* - Southampton
All Cannings	*Wilts* - Devizes
Allendale	*Northumberland* - Hexham
Allendale Cottages	*Durham* - Consett
Allen End	*Warwick* - Tamworth
Allenheads	*Northumberland* - Hexham
Allensford	*Durham* - Consett
Allen's Green	*Herts* - Bishop's Stortford
Allensmore	*Hereford* - Hereford
Allenton	*Derby* - Derby
Allen, West	*Northumberland* - Hexham
Aller	*Somerset* - Bridgwater
Allerby	*Cumberland* - Workington
Allerdean	*Northumberland* - Berwick-upon-Tweed
Allerford	*Devon* - Plymouth
Allerford	*Somerset* - Taunton
Allerston	*York, N.R.* - Malton
Allerthorpe	*York, E.R.* - York
Allerton	*Lancaster* - Liverpool
Allerton	*York, W.R.* - Bradford
Allerton	*York, W.R.* - Harrogate
Allerton Bywater	*York, W.R.* - Pontefract
Allesley	*Warwick* - Coventry
Allestree	*Derby* - Derby
Allet	*Cornwall* - Truro
Allexton	*Leicester* - Leicester
Allfield	*Salop* - Shrewsbury
Allgreave	*Cheshire* - Macclesfield
Allhallows	*Cumberland* - Carlisle
Allhallows	*Kent* - Rochester
Allimore Green	*Stafford* - Stafford
Allington	*Denbigh* - Wrexham
Allington	*Kent* - Maidstone
Allington	*Lincoln* - Grantham
Allington	*Wilts* - Chippenham
Allington	*Wilts* - Devizes
Allington	*Wilts* - Salisbury
Allington, East	*Devon* - Kingsbridge
Allington, South	*Devon* - Kingsbridge
Allithwaite, Lower	*Lancaster* - Barrow-in-Furness
Allithwaite, Upper	*Lancaster* - Barrow-in-Furness
Allonby	*Cumberland* - Carlisle
Allostock	*Chester* - Northwich
Allotment, The (Shiremoor)	*Northumberland* -North Shields
Allowenshay	*Somerset* - Yeovil
Allscote	*Salop* - Bridgnorth
Allscott	*Salop* - Wellington (Salop)
All Stretton	*Salop* - Shrewsbury
Alltami	*Flint* - Mold
Alltwen	*Glamorgan* - Neath
Alltywalis	*Carmarthen* - Carmarthen
Allum Green	*Hants* - Southampton
Almeley	*Hereford* - Hereford
Almeley Wootton	*Hereford* - Hereford
Almer	*Dorset* - Wimborne Minster
Almington	*Stafford* - Market Drayton
Almodington	*Sussex* - Chichester
Almond Brook	*Lancaster* - Wigan
Almondbury	*York, W.R.* - Huddersfield

ALM - ALW

Almond Park	*Salop* - Shrewsbury
Almondsbury, Lower	*Gloucester* - Thornbury
Almondsbury, Upper	*Gloucester* - Thornbury
Almsford	*Somerset* - Yeovil
Almshoebury	*Herts* - Hitchin
Almshoe, Little	*Herts* - Hitchin
Alne	*York, N.R.* - York
Alne, Great	*Warwick* - Redditch
Alne Hills	*Warwick* - Redditch
Alnham	*Northumberland* - Alnwick
Alnmouth	*Northumberland* - Alnwick
Alnwick	*Northumberland* - Alnwick
Alperton	*Middlesex* - Willesden
Alphamstone	*Essex* - Sudbury
Alpheton	*Suffolk* - Sudbury
Alpington	*Norfolk* - Norwich
Alport	*Derby* - Matlock
Alpraham	*Cheshire* - Crewe
Alresford	*Essex* - Colchester
Alresford, New	*Hants* - Winchester
Alresford, Old	*Hants* - Winchester
Alrewas	*Stafford* - Lichfield
Alrewas Hayes	*Stafford* - Lichfield
Alsager	*Cheshire* - Crewe
Alsagers Bank	*Stafford* - Stoke-on-Trent
Alsop-en-le-Dale	*Derby* - Buxton
Alston	*Cumberland* - Carlisle
Alston (Axminster)	*Devon* - Axminster and Chard
Alston	*Lancaster* - Preston
Alstonby	*Cumberland* - Carlisle
Alstone	*Gloucester* - Cheltenham
Alstone	*Stafford* - Stafford
Alstonefield	*Stafford* - Buxton
Alt	*Lancaster* - Ashton-under-Lyne
Alt	*Lancaster* - Oldham
Altarnum	*Cornwall* - Launceston
Altbough	*Hereford* - Hereford
Altcar	*Lancaster* - Southport
Altcar, Little	*Lancaster* - Southport
Alteryn	*Monmouth* - Newport (Mon.)
Altham	*Lancaster* - Accrington
Alt Hill	*Lancaster* - Ashton-under-Lyne
Althorne	*Essex* - Maldon
Althorpe	*Lincoln* - Scunthorpe
Althorpe	*Northampton* - Northampton
Altofts	*York, W.R.* - Wakefield
Alton	*Derby* - Chesterfield
Alton	*Hants* - Aldershot and Farnham
Alton	*Stafford* - Uttoxeter
Alton Barnes	*Wilts* - Devizes
Alton Pancras	*Dorset* - Dorchester
Alton Park	*Stafford* - Uttoxeter
Alton Priors	*Wilts* - Devizes
Alton Towers	*Stafford* - Uttoxeter
Altrincham	*Cheshire* - Altrincham
Alum Bay	*I. of W.* - Newport (I.W.)
Alum Rock	*Warwick* - Birmingham
Alvanley	*Cheshire* - Runcorn
Alvaston	*Derby* - Derby
Alvechurch	*Worcester* - Redditch
Alvecote	*Stafford* - Tamworth
Alveley	*Salop* - Bridgnorth
Alverdiscott	*Devon* - Bideford
Alverley	*York, W.R.* - Doncaster
Alverstoke	*Hants* - Portsmouth
Alverstone	*I. of W.* - Newport (I.W.)
Alverthorpe	*York, W.R.* - Wakefield
Alverton	*Notts* - Newark
Alvescot	*Oxford* - Witney
Alvesdiston	*Wilts* - Shaftesbury
Alveston	*Gloucester* - Thornbury
Alveston	*Warwick* - Stratford on Avon
Alvingham	*Lincoln* - Louth
Alvingham Fen	*Lincoln* - Louth
Alvington	*Gloucester* - Chepstow
Alvington, West	*Devon* - Kingsbridge
Alwalton	*Hunts* - Peterborough
Alweston	*Dorset* - Yeovil
Alwinton	*Northumberland* - Morpeth
Alwoodley	*York, W.R.* - Leeds

AMA - ANN

Amaston	*Salop* - Shrewsbury
Ambaston	*Derby* - Derby
Ambergate	*Derby* - Alfreton
Amber Hill	*Lincoln* - Boston
Amberley	*Gloucester* - Stroud
Amberley	*Sussex* - Chichester
Ambersham, North	*Sussex* - Petersfield
Ambersham, South	*Sussex* - Chichester
Amberswood Common	*Lancaster* - Wigan
Amble	*Cornwall* - Bodmin
Amble	*Northumberland* - Alnwick
Amblecote (Stourbridge)	*Worcester* - Stourbridge
Ambler Thorn	*York, W.R.* - Halifax
Ambleside	*Westmorland* - Kendal
Ambleston	*Pembroke* - Haverfordwest
Ambrosden	*Oxford* - Oxford
Amcotts	*Lincoln* - Scunthorpe
America	*Cornwall* - St. Austell
Amersham	*Bucks* - Amersham
Amersham-on-the-Hill	*Bucks* - Amersham
Amerton	*Stafford* - Stafford
Amesbury	*Wilts* - Salisbury
Amington	*Stafford* - Tamworth
Amlwch	*Anglesey* - Llangefni
Ammanford	*Carmarthen* - Ammanford
Ammerham	*Somerset* - Axminster and Chard
Amotherby	*York, N.R.* - Malton
Ampfield	*Hants* - Winchester
Ampleforth	*York, N.R.* - Malton
Ampney Crucis	*Gloucester* - Swindon
Ampney St. Mary	*Gloucester* - Swindon
Ampney St. Peter	*Gloucester* - Swindon
Amport	*Hants* - Andover
Ampton	*Suffolk* - Bury St. Edmunds
Amroth	*Pembroke* - Haverfordwest
Amthill	*Beds* - Bedford
Amwell	*Herts* - St. Albans
Amwell, Great	*Herts* - Hertford
Amwell, Little	*Herts* - Hertford
Ancaster	*Lincoln* - Grantham
Ancoats	*Lancaster* - Manchester
Ancroft	*Northumberland* - Berwick-upon-Tweed
Ancton	*Sussex* - Chichester
Anderby	*Lincoln* - Skegness
Andersea	*Somerset* - Bridgwater
Anderson	*Dorset* - Wimborne Minster
Anderton	*Cheshire* - Northwich
Anderton	*Lancaster* - Chorley
Andover	*Hants* - Andover
Andover Aerodrome	*Hants* - Andover
Andover Down	*Hants* - Andover
Andoversford	*Gloucester* - Cheltenham
Andwell	*Hants* - Basingstoke
Anerley (part)	*London, S.E.20* - Bromley
Anerley (part)	*London, S.E.20* - Croydon
Anfield	*Lancaster* - Liverpool
Angarrack	*Cornwall* - Redruth
Angarrick	*Cornwall* - Truro
Angel Bank	*Salop* - Ludlow
Angelton	*Glamorgan* - Bridgend
Angerton	*Cumberland* - Carlisle
Angerton, High	*Northumberland* - Morpeth
Angerton, Low	*Northumberland* - Morpeth
Angle	*Pembroke* - Haverfordwest
Anglesea	*Hants* - Portsmouth
Anglezarke	*Lancaster* - Chorley
Angmering	*Sussex* - Worthing
Angmering-on-Sea	*Sussex* - Worthing
Angram	*York, E.R.* - York
Angram	*York, W.R.* - Harrogate
Ankerdine Hills	*Worcester* - Worcester
Anlaby	*York, E.R.* - Kingston upon Hull
Anmer	*Norfolk* - King's Lynn
Annaside	*Cumberland* - Whitehaven
Anna Valley	*Hants* - Andover
Annesley	*Notts* - Mansfield
Annesley Woodhouse	*Notts* - Mansfield
Annfield Plain	*Durham* - Consett
Annington	*Sussex* - Worthing

Annitsford	*Northumberland* - Newcastle upon Tyne
Ann, Little	*Hants* - Andover
Annscroft	*Salop* - Shrewsbury
Ann's Hill	*Cumberland* - Workington
Ann's Hill	*Hants* - Portsmouth
Annstead	*Northumberland* - Alnwick
Annwell	*Derby* - Ashby-de-la-Zouch
Ansdell	*Lancaster* - Blackpool
Ansford	*Somerset* - Yeovil
Ansley	*Warwick* - Nuneaton
Ansley Common	*Warwick* - Nuneaton
Anslow	*Stafford* - Burton-upon-Trent
Anson Estate	*Lancaster* - Manchester
Anstey	*Herts* - Bishop's Stortford
Anstey	*Leicester* - Leicester
Anstey	*Warwick* - Coventry
Anstey	*Wilts* - Shaftesbury
Anstey, East	*Devon* - Tiverton
Anstey, West	*Devon* - Tiverton
Anston, North	*York, W.R.* - Worksop
Anston, South	*York, W.R.* - Worksop
Ansty	*Dorset* - Dorchester
Ansty	*Sussex* - Haywards Heath
Anthorn	*Cumberland* - Carlisle
Antingham	*Norfolk* - Norwich
Antons Gowt	*Lincoln* - Boston
Antony	*Cornwall* - Plymouth
Antonys Crosse	*Gloucester* - Gloucester
Antrobus	*Cheshire* - Northwich
Antron	*Cornwall* - Truro
Anty Cross	*Lancaster* - Barrow-in-Furness
Anwick	*Lincoln* - Sleaford
Anwick Fen	*Lincoln* - Sleaford
Apedale	*Stafford* - Stoke-on-Trent
Apes Hall	*Cambridge* - Ely
Apethorpe	*Northampton* - Peterborough
Apethorpe	*Northants* - Stamford
Apeton	*Stafford* - Stafford
Apley	*Lincoln* - Lincoln
Apley	*Salop* - Wellington (Salop)
Apley, New	*Lincoln* - Lincoln
Apley Park	*Salop* - Bridgnorth
Apperknowle	*Derby* - Chesterfield
Apperley	*Gloucester* - Cheltenham
Apperley Bridge (part)	*York, W.R.* - Bradford
Apperley Bridge (part)	*York, W.R.* - Otley
Appleby	*Lincoln* - Scunthorpe
Appleby	*Westmorland* - Penrith
Appleby Magna	*Leicester* - Ashby-de-la-Zouch
Appledore	*Devon* - Bideford
Appledore	*Devon* - Tiverton
Appledore	*Kent* - Cranbrook
Appledore, Little	*Kent* - Cranbrook
Appledram	*Sussex* - Chichester
Appleford	*Berks* - Didcot
Applesham	*Sussex* - Worthing
Appleshaw	*Hants* - Andover
Applethwaite	*Cumberland* - Workington
Appleton	*Berks* - Oxford
Appleton	*Cheshire* - Warrington
Appleton	*Kent* - Dover
Appleton	*Norfolk* - King's Lynn
Appleton	*York, N.R.* - Darlington
Appleton-le-Moors	*York, N.R.* - Malton
Appleton-le-Street	*York, N.R.* - Malton
Appleton Nun	*York, W.R.* - York
Appleton Roebuck	*York, W.R.* - York
Appleton Wiske	*York, N.R.* - Northallerton
Appletree	*Northampton* - Banbury
Appley	*Somerset* - Taunton
Appley Bridge	*Lancaster* - Wigan
Apse Heath	*I. of W.* - Newport (I.W.)
Apsley End	*Beds* - Hitchin
Apsley End	*Herts* - Hemel Hempstead
Aqualate	*Stafford* - Wellington (Salop)
Aquamoor	*Stafford* - Stafford
Aqueduct	*Salop* - Wellington
Arborfield	*Berks* - Reading
Arbourthorne	*York, W.R.* - Sheffield

Archdeacon Newton	*Durham* - Darlington
Arclid	*Cheshire* - Congleton
Arddleen	*Montgomery* - Oswestry
Ardeley	*Herts* - Hitchin
Ardens Grafton	*Warwick* - Stratford on Avon
Ardingly	*Sussex* - Haywards Heath
Ardington	*Berks* - Didcot
Ardleigh	*Essex* - Colchester
Ardleigh Green	*Essex* - Ilford
Ardley	*Oxford* - Banbury
Ardsley	*York, W.R.* - Barnsley
Ardsley, East	*York, W.R.* - Dewsbury
Ardsley, West	*York, W.R.* - Dewsbury
Ardwick	*Lancaster* - Manchester
Areley Kings	*Worcester* - Kidderminster
Arenig	*Merioneth* - Dolgellau
Arford	*Hants* - Aldershot and Farnham
Argal	*Cornwall* - Truro
Argoed	*Flint* - Mold
Argoed	*Monmouth* - Blackwood
Argoed	*Salop* - Shrewsbury
Arkendale	*York, W.R.* - Harrogate
Arkengarthdale	*York, N.R.* - Darlington
Arkesden	*Essex* - Bishop's Stortford
Arkholme with Cawood	*Lancaster* - Lancaster
Arkleby	*Cumberland* - Workington
Arkley	*Herts* - Barnet
Arksey	*York, W.R.* - Doncaster
Arkwright Town	*Derby* - Chesterfield
Arle	*Gloucester* - Cheltenham
Arlecdon	*Cumberland* - Whitehaven
Arlescot	*Warwick* - Banbury
Arlescott	*Salop* - Bridgnorth
Arlesey	*Beds* - Biggleswade
Arlesford	*Essex* - Colchester
Arleston	*Derby* - Derby
Arleston	*Salop* - Wellington (Salop)
Arleston Brook	*Salop* - Wellington (Salop)
Arley	*Cheshire* - Northwich
Arley	*Warwick* - Nuneaton
Arley, New	*Warwick* - Nuneaton
Arley, Old	*Warwick* - Nuneaton
Arley, Upper	*Worcester* - Kidderminster
Arlingham	*Gloucester* - Gloucester
Arlington	*Devon* - Barnstaple
Arlington	*Gloucester* - Cheltenham
Arlington	*Sussex* - Eastbourne
Armathwaite	*Cumberland* - Penrith
Armboth	*Cumberland* - Workington
Arminghall	*Norfolk* - Norwich
Armitage	*Stafford* - Lichfield
Armitage Bridge	*York, W.R.* Huddersfield
Armley	*York, W.R.* - Leeds
Armscote	*Warwick* - Stratford on Avon
Armshead	*Stafford* - Stoke-on-Trent
Armston	*Northampton* - Peterborough
Armsworth	*Hants* - Winchester
Armthorpe	*York, W.R.* - Doncaster
Arncliffe	*York, W.R.* - Skipton
Arncott, Lower	*Oxford* - Oxford
Arncott, Upper	*Oxford* - Oxford
Arne	*Dorset* - Swanage
Arnesby	*Leicester* - Leicester
Arnewood	*Hants* - Lymington
Arnold	*Notts* - Nottingham
Arnold	*York, E.R.* - Beverley
Arnside	*Westmorland* - Kendal
Arrad Foot	*Lancaster* - Barrow-in-Furness
Arram	*York, E.R.* - Beverley
Arreton	*I. of W.* - Newport (I.W.)
Arrington	*Cambridge* - Cambridge
Arrow	*Warwick* - Redditch
Arrowfield Top	*Worcester* - Redditch
Arrow Valley Park	*Worcester* - Redditch
Arrunden	*York, W.R.* - Huddersfield
Arscott	*Salop* - Shrewsbury
Arthington	*York, W.R.* - Otley
Arthingworth	*Northampton* - Northampton
Arthog	*Merioneth* - Dolgellau
Arthuret	*Cumberland* - Carlisle

Artington	*Surrey* - Guildford
Arundel	*Sussex* - Chichester
Asby	*Cumberland* - Whitehaven
Asby, Great	*Westmorland* - Penrith
Asby, Little	*Westmorland* - Penrith
Ascot	*Berks* - Slough
Ascot	*Bucks* - Bletchley and Leighton Buzzard
Ascot	*Oxford* - Thame
Ascott	*Salop* - Shrewsbury
Ascott	*Warwick* - Stratford on Avon
Ascott-under-Wychwood	*Oxford* - Banbury
Asenby	*York, N.R.* - Harrogate
Asfordby	*Leicester* - Melton Mowbray
Asfordby Hill	*Leicester* - Melton Mowbray
Asfordby Valley	*Leicester* - Melton Mowbray
Asgarby	*Lincoln* - Skegness
Asgarby	*Lincoln* - Sleaford
Ash	*Derby* - Derby
Ash	*Dorset* - Blandford
Ash	*Kent* - Deal
Ash	*Somerset* - Yeovil
Ash	*Surrey* - Aldershot and Farnham
Ashampstead	*Berks* - Reading
Ashbocking	*Suffolk* - Ipswich
Ashborne	*Derby* - Derby
Ashborne Green	*Derby* - Ashborne
Ashbrittle	*Somerset* - Taunton
Ashbrook	*Gloucester* - Swindon
Ashbrook	*Herts* - Hitchin
Ashburnham	*Sussex* - Hastings
Ashburton	*Devon* - Newton Abbot
Ashbury	*Berks* - Swindon
Ashbury	*Devon* - Okehampton
Ashby	*Lincoln* - Scunthorpe
Ashby-by-Partney	*Lincoln* - Skegness
Ashby	*Suffolk* - Lowestoft
Ashby-cum-Fenby	*Lincoln* - Great Grimsby
Ashby-de-la-Launde	*Lincoln* - Sleaford
Ashby-de-la-Zouch	*Leicester* - Ashby-de-la-Zouch
Ashby Folville	*Leicester* - Melton Mowbray
Ashby Magna	*Leicester* - Leicester
Ashby Parva	*Leicester* - Leicester
Ashby Pastures	*Leicester* - Melton Mowbray
Ashby Puerorum	*Lincoln* - Skegness
Ashby St. Ledgers	*Northampton* - Rugby
Ashby St. Mary	*Norfolk* - Norwich
Ashby, West	*Lincoln* - Lincoln
Ashby with Oby	*Norfolk* - Great Yarmouth
Ashchurch	*Gloucester* - Cheltenham
Ashcombe	*Devon* - Exeter
Ashcombe	*Somerset* - Weston Super Mare
Ashcombe	*Somerset* - Yeovil
Ashcombe	*Stafford* - Leek
Ashcombe	*Sussex* - Lewes
Ashcombe	*Wilts* - Shaftesbury
Ashcott	*Somerset* - Bridgwater
Ashcott Corner	*Somerset* - Wells
Ash-cum-Ridley	*Kent* - Dartford
Ashdon	*Essex* - Cambridge
Ashe	*Hants* - Basingstoke
Asheldham	*Essex* - Maldon
Ashen	*Essex* - Sudbury
Ashendon	*Bucks* - Aylesbury
Ashey	*I. of W.* - Newport (I.W.)
Ashfield	*Cornwall* - Truro
Ashfield	*Hants* - Southampton
Ashfield	*Hereford* - Monmouth
Ashfield Green	*Suffolk* - Halesworth
Ashfield with Thorpe	*Suffolk* - Ipswich
Ash Flats	*Stafford* - Stafford
Ashford	*Devon* - Barnstaple
Ashford	*Devon* - Kingsbridge
Ashford	*Hants* - Petersfield
Ashford	*Kent* - Ashford
Ashford	*Middlesex* - Slough
Ashford Bowdler	*Salop* - Ludlow
Ashford Carbonell	*Salop* - Ludlow
Ashford Common	*Middlesex* - Kingston upon Thames
Ashford Hill	*Berks* - Newbury

Ashford in the Water	*Derby* - Buxton
Ashford Newtown	*Kent* - Ashford
Ash Furlong	*Warwick* - Birmingham
Ashgate	*Derby* - Chesterfield
Ashgill	*Cumberland* - Carlisle
Ash Green	*Surrey* - Aldershot and Farnham
Ashgrove	*Wilts* - Shaftesbury
Ashill	*Devon* - Tiverton
Ashill	*Norfolk* - King's Lynn
Ashill (Ilminster)	*Somerset* - Axminster and Chard
Ashingdon	*Essex* - Southend
Ashington	*Dorset* - Wimborne Minster
Ashington	*Northumberland* - Morpeth
Ashington	*Somerset* - Yeovil
Ashington	*Sussex* - Worthing
Ashleworth	*Gloucester* - Gloucester
Ashley	*Cheshire* - Altrincham
Ashley	*Dorset* - Dorchester
Ashley	*Hants* - Lymington
Ashley	*Hants* - Bournemouth
Ashley	*Hants* - Winchester
Ashley	*Kent* - Deal
Ashley	*Northampton* - Corby
Ashley	*Stafford* - Market Drayton
Ashley	*Wilts* - Bath
Ashley	*Wilts* - Malmesbury
Ashley	*Cambridge* - Newmarket
Ashley Green	*Bucks* - Amersham
Ashleyhay	*Derby* - Matlock
Ashley Heath	*Hants* - Bournemouth
Ashley Walk	*Hants* - Bournemouth
Ashling, East	*Sussex* - Chichester
Ashling, West	*Sussex* - Chichester
Ash Magna	*Salop* - Whitchurch
Ashmanhaugh	*Norfolk* - Norwich
Ashmansworth	*Hants* - Newbury
Ashmead	*Gloucester* - Stroud
Ashmoor Common	*Worcester* - Worcester
Ashmore	*Dorset* - Shaftesbury
Ashmore Green	*Berks* - Newbury
Asholme	*Northumberland* - Hexham
Ashopton	*Derby* - Sheffield
Ashorne	*Warwick* - Stratford on Avon
Ashover	*Derby* - Chesterfield
Ashow	*Warwick* - Warwick
Ash Parva	*Salop* - Whitchurch
Ashperton	*Hereford* - Hereford
Ashprington	*Devon* - Torquay
Ash Priors	*Somerset* - Taunton
Ashreigney	*Devon* - Barnstaple
Ashridge	*Bucks* - Amersham
Ashtead	*Surrey* - Epsom
Ash Thomas	*Devon* - Tiverton
Ashton	*Cheshire* - Chester
Ashton	*Cornwall* - Penzance
Ashton	*Devon* - Exeter
Ashton	*Dorset* - Dorchester
Ashton	*Hants* - Winchester
Ashton	*Hereford* - Leominster
Ashton	*Lancaster* - Preston
Ashton	*Northampton* - Northampton
Ashton	*Northampton* - Peterborough
Ashton	*Huntingdon and Peterborough* - Stamford
Ashton	*Somerset* - Bristol
Ashton	*Wilts* - Trowbridge
Ashton Common	*Wilts* - Trowbridge
Ashton Gifford	*Wilts* - Warminster
Ashton Heath	*Lancaster* - Wigan
Ashton-in-Makerfield	*Lancaster* - Wigan
Ashton Keynes	*Wilts* - Swindon
Ashton, Long	*Somerset* - Bristol
Ashton Mill	*Wilts* - Trowbridge
Ashton-under-Hill	*Gloucester* - Evesham
Ashton-under-Lyne	*Lancaster* - Ashton-under-Lyne
Ashton-upon-Mersey	*Cheshire* - Altrincham
Ashton, West	*Wilts* - Trowbridge
Ashton with Stodday	*Lancaster* - Lancaster
Ashurst	*Kent* - Tunbridge Wells
Ashurst	*Sussex* - Brighton

ASH - AST

Ashurst Bridge	*Hants* - Southampton
Ashurst Wood	*Sussex* - East Grinstead
Ashvale	*Monmouth* - Blackwood
Ash Vale	*Surrey* - Aldershot and Farnham
Ashwater	*Devon* - Launceston
Ashwell	*Herts* - Hitchin
Ashwell	*Rutland* - Melton Mowbray
Ashwellthorpe	*Norfolk* - Norwich
Ashwicken	*Norfolk* - King's Lynn
Ashwood	*Stafford* - Stoke-on-Trent
Ashwood Dale	*Derby* - Buxton
Ashworth	*Lancaster* - Bury
Askam-in-Furness	*Lancaster* - Barrow-in-Furness
Aske	*York, N.R.* - Darlington
Askern	*York, W.R.* - Doncaster
Askerswell	*Dorset* - Dorchester
Askerton	*Cumberland* - Carlisle
Askett	*Bucks* - High Wycombe
Askham	*Notts* - East Retford
Askham	*Westmorland* - Penrith
Askham Bryan	*York, E.R.* - York
Askham Richard	*York, W.R.* - York
Askrigg	*York, N.R.* - Northallerton
Askwith	*York, W.R.* - Otley
Aslackby	*Lincoln* - Sleaford
Aslackby Fen	*Lincoln* - Sleaford
Aslacton	*Norfolk* - Norwich
Aslockton	*Notts* - Nottingham
Aspall	*Suffolk* - Stowmarket
Aspatria	*Cumberland* - Carlisle
Aspenden	*Herts* - Hertford
Asperton	*Lincoln* - Boston
Aspley	*Stafford* - Stafford
Aspley Guise	*Beds* - Bletchley and Leighton Buzzard
Aspley Heath	*Beds* - Bletchley and Leighton Buzzard
Aspley Heath	*Warwick* - Birmingham
Asps, The	*Warwick* - Warwick
Aspull	*Lancaster* - Wigan
Aspull Moor	*Lancaster* - Wigan
Asselby	*York, E.R.* - Goole
Assenden, Lower	*Oxford* - Reading
Assenden, Middle	*Oxford* - Reading
Assenden, Upper	*Oxford* - Reading
Asserby	*Lincoln* - Skegness
Assington	*Suffolk* - Sudbury
Astbury	*Cheshire* - Congleton
Astbury	*Salop* - Bridgnorth
Astcote	*Northampton* - Northampton
Asterby	*Lincoln* - Louth
Asterleigh	*Oxford* - Oxford
Asterley	*Salop* - Shrewsbury
Asterton	*Salop* - Shrewsbury
Asthall	*Oxford* - Witney
Asthall Leigh	*Oxford* - Witney
Astley	*Lancaster* - Leigh
Astley	*Salop* - Shrewsbury
Astley	*Warwick* - Nuneaton
Astley	*Worcester* - Kidderminster
Astley	*York, W.R.* - Pontefract
Astley Abbots	*Salop* - Bridgnorth
Astley Bridge	*Lancaster* - Bolton
Astley Burf	*Worcester* - Kidderminster
Astley Cross	*Worcester* - Kidderminster
Astley Green	*Lancaster* - Leigh
Astley Moss	*Lancaster* - Leigh
Astmoor	*Cheshire* - Runcorn
Aston	*Berks* - Reading
Aston	*Cheshire* - Runcorn
Aston	*Derby* - Buxton
Aston	*Derby* - Uttoxeter
Aston	*Flint* - Chester
Aston (Wigmore)	*Hereford* - Ludlow
Aston	*Herts* - Hertford
Aston	*Montgomery* - Welshpool
Aston (Claverley)	*Salop* - Bridgnorth
Aston (Munslow)	*Salop* - Ludlow
Aston	*Salop* - Oswestry
Aston	*Salop* - Shrewsbury

AST - ATT

Aston	*Salop* - Wellington (Salop)
Aston	*Stafford* - Market Drayton
Aston (Maer)	*Stafford* - Stoke-on-Trent
Aston	*Stafford* - Stafford
Aston	*Warwick* - Birmingham
Aston	*York, W.R.* - Rotherham
Aston Abbots	*Bucks* - Aylesbury
Aston Bampton	*Oxford* - Witney
Aston Blank	*Gloucester* - Cheltenham
Aston Botterell	*Salop* - Bridgnorth
Aston Bury	*Herts* - Hertford
Aston-by-Budworth	*Cheshire* - Northwich
Aston-by-Newhall	*Cheshire* - Crewe
Aston-by-Stone	*Stafford* - Stafford
Aston Cantlow	*Warwick* - Stratford on Avon
Aston Cliff	*Stafford* - Stoke-on-Trent
Aston Clinton	*Bucks* - Aylesbury
Aston Crews	*Hereford* - Gloucester
Aston Cross	*Gloucester* - Cheltenham
Aston Down	*Gloucester* - Stroud
Aston End	*Herts* - Hertford
Aston Eyre	*Salop* - Bridgnorth
Aston Fields	*Worcester* - Bromsgrove
Aston Flamville	*Leicester* - Hinckley
Aston Holdings	*Warwick* - Stratford on Avon
Aston Ingham	*Hereford* - Gloucester
Aston-le-Walls	*Northampton* - Banbury
Aston, Little (part)	*Stafford* - Lichfield
Aston Magna	*Gloucester* - Evesham
Aston Manor	*Warwick* - Birmingham
Aston, Middle	*Oxford* - Banbury
Aston Mullins	*Bucks* - Aylesbury
Aston Netherthorpe	*York, W.R.* - Rotherham
Aston, North	*Oxford* - Banbury
Aston-on-Carrant	*Gloucester* - Cheltenham
Aston-on-Clun	*Salop* - Ludlow
Aston Rowant	*Oxford* - Thame
Aston Sandford	*Bucks* - Thame
Aston Somerville	*Gloucester* - Evesham
Aston Subedge	*Gloucester* - Evesham
Aston Tirrold	*Berks* - Didcot
Aston-upon-Trent	*Derby* - Derby
Aston Upthorpe	*Berks* - Didcot
Aston-with-Aughton	*York, W.R.* - Rotherham
Astrop	*Herts* - Aylesbury
Astrop	*Northampton* - Banbury
Astwell with Falcutt	*Northampton* - Northampton
Astwick	*Beds* - Biggleswade
Astwick	*Northampton* - Banbury
Astwith	*Derby* - Chesterfield
Astwood	*Bucks* - Bedford
Astwood Bank	*Worcester* - Redditch
Astwood Lane	*Worcester* - Redditch
Astwood-under-Hill	*Worcester* - Redditch
Aswarby	*Lincoln* - Sleaford
Aswardby	*Lincoln* - Skegness
Atcham	*Salop* - Shrewsbury
Atch Lench	*Worcester* - Evesham
Atchley	*Salop* - Bridgnorth
Athelhampton	*Dorset* - Dorchester
Athelington	*Suffolk* - Halesworth
Athelney	*Somerset* - Taunton
Atherfield	*I. of W.* - Newport (I.W.)
Atherington	*Devon* - Barnstable
Athersley	*York, W.R.* - Barnsley
Atherstone	*Somerset* - Yeovil
Atherstone	*Warwick* - Nuneaton
Atherstone on Stour	*Warwick* - Stratford on Avon
Atherton	*Lancaster* - Leigh
Atherton Moor	*York, W.R.* - Dewsbury
Atlow	*Derby* - Derby
Atlow Winn	*Derby* - Derby
Attenborough	*Notts* - Nottingham
Atterby	*Lincoln* - Scunthorpe
Attercliffe	*York, W.R.* - Sheffield
Atterley	*Salop* - Bridgnorth
Atterton	*Leicester* - Nuneaton
Atthill	*Cornwall* - Launceston
Attleborough	*Norfolk* - Norwich
Attleborough	*Warwick* - Nuneaton

Attlebridge	*Norfolk* - Norwich
Atwick	*York, E.R.* - Beverley
Atworth	*Wilts* - Trowbridge
Aubourn	*Lincoln* - Lincoln
Auckland	*Durham* - Bishop Auckland
Auckland Park	*Durham* - Bishop Auckland
Auckland St. Andrew	*Durham* - Bishop Auckland
Auckland St. Helen	*Durham* - Bishop Auckland
Auckland, West	*Durham* - Bishop Auckland
Audenshaw	*Lancaster* - Ashton-under-Lyne
Audleby	*Lincoln* - Great Grimsby
Audlem	*Cheshire* - Crewe
Audley	*Stafford* - Stoke-on-Trent
Audley Brow	*Salop* - Market Drayton
Audley End	*Essex* - Bishop's Stortford
Audmore	*Stafford* - Stafford
Audnam	*Stafford* - Stourbridge
Aughton	*Lancaster* - Lancaster
Aughton	*Lancaster* - Southport
Aughton	*York, E.R.* - Selby
Aughton	*York, W.R.* - Rotherham
Aulden	*Hereford* - Leominster
Aulis Hill	*Northumberland* - Carlisle
Ault Hucknall	*Derby* - Chesterfield
Aunby	*Lincoln* - Stamford
Aunsby	*Lincoln* - Sleaford
Aust	*Gloucester* - Thornbury
Austcliffe	*Worcester* - Kidderminster
Austen Wood	*Bucks* - Amersham
Austerfield	*York, W.R.* - Doncaster
Austerlands	*Lancaster* - Oldham
Austerlands	*York, W.R.* - Oldham
Austhorpe	*York, W.R.* - Leeds
Austin Fen	*Lincoln* - Louth
Auston	*Salop* - Shrewsbury
Austonley	*York, W.R.* - Huddersfield
Austrey	*Warwick* - Tamworth
Austwick	*York, W.R.* - Skipton
Authorpe	*Lincoln* - Louth
Auton Style	*Durham* - Durham
Avebury	*Wilts* - Swindon
Aveley	*Essex* - Grays Thurrock
Avenbury	*Hereford* - Hereford
Avening	*Gloucester* - Stroud
Averham	*Notts* - Newark
Aveton Gifford	*Devon* - Kingsbridge
Avington	*Berks* - Newbury
Avington	*Hants* - Winchester
Avisford	*Sussex* - Chichester
Avishays	*Somerset* - Axminster and Chard
Avon	*Hants* - Bournemouth
Avon	*Wilts* - Chippenham
Avoncliff	*Wilts* - Trowbridge
Avon Dassett	*Warwick* - Banbury
Avonmouth	*Gloucester* - Bristol
Avon Tyrrell	*Hants* - Bournemouth
Avon Wick	*Devon* - Torquay
Awbridge	*Hants* - Southampton
Awkley	*Gloucester* - Thornbury
Awkley	*Notts & York, W.R.* - Doncaster
Awliscombe	*Devon* - Exeter
Awre	*Gloucester* - Gloucester
Awsworth	*Notts* - Ilkeston
Axbridge	*Somerset* - Wells
Axford	*Hants* - Basingstoke
Axford	*Wilts* - Swindon
Axham Wood	*Lincoln* - Gainsborough
Axminster	*Devon* - Axminster and Chard
Axmouth	*Devon* - Axminster and Chard
Axton	*Flint* - Holywell
Aychley (part)	*Salop* - Market Drayton
Aychley (part)	*Salop* - Whitchurch
Aycliffe, Great	*Durham* - Darlington
Aydon	*Northumberland* - Hexham
Aylburton	*Gloucester* - Chepstow
Ayle	*Northumberland* - Carlisle
Ayleford	*Gloucester* - Gloucester
Aylesbeare	*Devon* - Exeter
Aylesbury	*Bucks* - Aylesbury
Aylesbury End	*Bucks* - High Wycombe

Aylesby	*Lincoln* - Great Grimsby
Aylesford	*Kent* - Maidstone
Aylesham	*Kent* - Canterbury
Aylmerton	*Norfolk* - Norwich
Aylsham	*Norfolk* - Norwich
Aylton	*Hereford* - Hereford
Aymestry	*Hereford* - Leominster
Aynho	*Northampton* - Banbury
Aynho Station	*Northampton* - Banbury
Ayot Green	*Herts* - Hertford
Ayot St. Lawrence	*Herts* - Hertford
Ayot St. Peter	*Herts* - Hertford
Aysgarth	*York, N.R.* - Northallerton
Ayside	*Lancaster* - Barrow-in-Furness
Ayston	*Rutland* - Corby
Aythorpe Roding	*Essex* - Chelmsford
Ayton, East	*York, N.R.* - Scarborough
Ayton, Great	*York, N.R.* - Middlesbrough
Ayton, Little	*York, N.R.* - Middlesbrough
Ayton, West	*York, N.R.* - Scarborough
Azerley	*York, W.R.* - Harrogate

B

Baal Hill	*Durham* - Durham
Babbacombe	*Devon* - Torquay
Babbington	*Notts* - Nottingham
Babbs Green	*Herts* - Hertford
Babcary	*Somerset* - Yeovil
Babell	*Flint* - Holywell
Babingley	*Norfolk* - King's Lynn
Babington	*Somerset* - Frome
Bablock Hythe	*Oxford* - Witney
Babraham	*Cambridge* - Cambridge
Babworth	*Notts* - East Retford
Bache	*Cheshire* - Chester
Bacheldre	*Montgomery* - Welshpool
Bachelor Gardens	*York, W.R.* - Harrogate
Bache Mill	*Salop* - Ludlow
Bache, The	*Salop* - Ludlow
Bachie	*Montgomery* - Oswestry
Backbarrow	*Lancaster* - Barrow-in-Furness
Backford	*Cheshire* - Chester
Back Lane	*Stafford* - West Bromwich
Backmoor	*York, W.R.* - Sheffield
Backwell	*Somerset* - Bristol
Backworth	*Northumberland* - North Shields
Bacon's End	*Warwick* - Birmingham
Baconsthorpe	*Norfolk* - Norwich
Bacton	*Hereford* - Hereford
Bacton	*Norfolk* - Norwich
Bacton	*Suffolk* - Stowmarket
Bacup	*Lancaster* - Rawtenstall
Badbury	*Wilts* - Swindon
Badby	*Northampton* - Northampton
Baddeley Edge	*Stafford* - Stoke-on-Trent
Baddeley Green	*Stafford* - Stoke-on-Trent
Baddesley Clinton	*Warwick* - Warwick
Baddesley Ensor	*Warwick* - Nuneaton
Baddesley, North	*Hants* - Southampton
Baddesley, South	*Hants* - Lymington
Baddiley	*Cheshire* - Crewe
Baddow, Great	*Essex* - Chelmsford
Baddow, Little	*Essex* - Chelmsford
Badenhall	*Stafford* - Stafford
Badenhill	*Gloucester* - Thornbury
Badgemore	*Oxford* - Reading
Badger	*Salop* - Bridgnorth
Badgers Hill	*Worcester* - Evesham
Badgeworth	*Gloucester* - Cheltenham
Badgworth	*Somerset* - Weston Super Mare
Badharlick	*Cornwall* - Launceston
Badingham	*Suffolk* - Woodbridge
Badlesmere	*Kent* - Canterbury

BAD - BAL

Badley	*Suffolk* - Stowmarket	
Badley Moor	*Norfolk* - East Dereham	
Badley Wood	*Hereford* - Worcester	
Badmington	*Monmouth* - Blackwood	
Badminton	*Gloucester* - Bristol	
Badminton, Great	*Gloucester* - Bristol	
Badminton, Little	*Gloucester* - Bristol	
Badsey	*Worcester* - Evesham	
Badshot Lea	*Surrey* - Aldershot and Farnham	
Badsworth	*York, W.R.* - Pontefract	
Badwell Ash	*Suffolk* - Bury St. Edmunds	
Bagaton	*Devon* - Axminster and Chard	
Bagber	*Dorset* - Shaftesbury	
Bagborough, East	*Somerset* - Taunton	
Bagborough, West	*Somerset* - Taunton	
Bagby	*York, N.R.* - Northallerton	
Bag Enderby	*Lincoln* - Skegness	
Bagendon	*Gloucester* - Cheltenham	
Baggeridge	*Somerset* - Bath	
Bagginswood	*Salop* - Bridgnorth	
Baggrave	*Leicester* - Leicester	
Baggrow	*Cumberland* - Carlisle	
Baghill	*York, W.R.* - Pontefract	
Bagillt	*Flint* - Holywell	
Baginton	*Warwick* - Coventry	
Baglan	*Glamorgan* - Neath	
Bagley	*Salop* - Oswestry	
Bagley	*York, W.R.* - Doncaster	
Bagnall	*Stafford* - Stoke-on-Trent	
Bagnam	*Hants* - Bournemouth	
Bagnor	*Berks* - Newbury	
Bagpath	*Gloucester* - Stroud	
Bagshaw	*Derby* - Buxton	
Bagshot	*Surrey* - Aldershot and Farnham	
Bagshot	*Wilts* - Marlborough	
Bagstone	*Gloucester* - Bristol	
Bagthorpe	*Norfolk* - King's Lynn	
Bagthorpe (Bulwell)	*Notts* - Nottingham	
Bagthorpe (Jacksdale)	*Notts* - Alfreton	
Baguley	*Cheshire* - Manchester	
Bagworth	*Leicester* - Ashby-de-la-Zouch	
Bailbrook	*Somerset* - Bath	
Baildon	*York, W.R.* - Bradford	
Baildon Bridge	*York, W.R.* - Bradford	
Baildon Green	*York, W.R.* - Bradford	
Baildon, Low	*York, W.R.* - Bradford	
Baildon Woodbottom	*York, W.R.* - Bradford	
Bailes	*Cumberland* - Carlisle	
Bailey	*Cumberland* - Carlisle	
Bailey Brook	*Gloucester* - Ross	
Bailey, North	*Durham* - Durham	
Bailey, South	*Durham* - Durham	
Bailiff Bridge (part)	*York, W.R.* - Bradford	
Bailiff Bridge (part)	*York, W.R.* - Halifax	
Bailing Hill	*Sussex* - Horsham	
Bainbridge	*York, N.R.* - Northallerton	
Bainton	*Huntingdon and Peterborough* - Stamford	
Bainton	*Oxford* - Banbury	
Bainton	*York, E.R.* - Beverley	
Baker's End	*Herts* - Hertford	
Bakestone Moor	*Derby* - Worksop	
Bakewell	*Derby* - Matlock	
Bala	*Merioneth* - Dolgellau	
Balaams Heath	*Salop* - Ludlow	
Balby	*York, W.R.* - Doncaster	
Balcombe	*Sussex* - Haywards Heath	
Balcombe Forest	*Sussex* - Haywards Heath	
Baldersby	*York, N.R.* - Harrogate	
Balderstone	*Lancaster* - Blackburn	
Balderstone (Rochdale)	*Lancaster* - Rochdale	
Balderton	*Cheshire* - Chester	
Balderton	*Notts* - Newark	
Balderton	*Salop* - Shrewsbury	
Baldhu	*Cornwall* - Truro	
Baldingstone	*Lancaster* - Bury	
Baldock	*Herts* - Hitchin	
Baldslow	*Sussex* - Hastings	
Baldwinholme	*Cumberland* - Carlisle	
Baldwins Gate	*Stafford* - Stoke-on-Trent	

BAL - BAN

Bale	*Norfolk* - King's Lynn	
Balham	*London, S.W.12* - Wandsworth	
Balk	*York, N.R.* - Northallerton	
Balkholme	*York, E.R.* - Goole	
Balkwell	*Northumberland* - North Shields	
Ballam	*Lancaster* - Blackpool	
Ballam Hill	*Worcester* - Redditch	
Ball Green	*Stafford* - Stoke-on-Trent	
Ballidon	*Derby* - Matlock	
Ballingdon	*Essex* - Sudbury	
Ballingham	*Hereford* - Hereford	
Ball O'Ditton	*Lancaster* - St. Helens	
Balls	*Cornwall* - Truro	
Ball's Cross	*Sussex* - Chichester	
Ball's Pond (part)	*London, N.1* - Clerkenwell	
Ball's Pond (part)	*London, N.1* - Shoreditch	
Balmer	*Salop* - Oswestry	
Balne	*York, W.R.* - Pontefract	
Balsall	*Warwick* - Coventry	
Balsall Common	*Warwick* - Coventry	
Balsall Heath	*Warwick* - Birmingham	
Balsall Temple	*Warwick* - Coventry	
Balscote	*Oxford* - Banbury	
Balsham	*Cambridge* - Cambridge	
Balterley	*Stafford* - Crewe	
Baltonsborough	*Somerset* - Wells	
Balwest	*Cornwall* - Penzance	
Bamber Bridge	*Lancaster* - Preston	
Bambers Green	*Essex* - Bishop's Stortford	
Bamburgh	*Northumberland* - Berwick-upon-Tweed	
Bamford	*Derby* - Buxton	
Bamford (part)	*Lancaster* - Rochdale	
Bamfurlong	*Gloucester* - Cheltenham	
Bamfurlong	*Lancaster* - Wigan	
Bampton	*Devon* - Tiverton	
Bampton	*Oxford* - Witney	
Bampton	*Westmorland* - Penrith	
Bampton Grange	*Westmorland* - Penrith	
Bampton, Little	*Cumberland* - Carlisle	
Bampton, New	*Cumberland* - Carlisle	
Banbury	*Oxford* - Banbury	
Banbury Lane	*Northampton* - Northampton	
Bancffosfelin	*Carmarthen* - Carmarthen	
Bancroft Estate	*London, E.2* - Shoreditch	
Banc-y-Capal	*Carmarthen* - Carmarthen	
Banc-y-Darren	*Cardigan* - Aberystwyth	
Bancyduffryn	*Cardigan* - Cardigan	
Bancyfelin	*Carmarthen* - Carmarthen	
Bancyplas	*Cardigan* - Cardigan	
Bandley Hill	*Herts* - Hitchin	
Bandon Hill	*Surrey* - Croydon	
Bangley	*Stafford* - Tamworth	
Bangor	*Caernarvon* - Bangor	
Bangor	*Cardigan* - Cardigan	
Bangor Isycoed	*Flint* - Wrexham	
Bangor on Dee	*Flint* - Wrexham	
Bangrove	*Gloucester* - Cheltenham	
Banhadlauchaf	*Denbigh* - Oswestry	
Bank	*Hants* - Southampton	
Bank End	*York, W.R.* - Barnsley	
Bankfoot	*Northumberland* - Hexham	
Bankhead	*Durham* - Durham	
Bankland	*Somerset* - Bridgwater	
Bank Newton	*York, W.R.* - Skipton	
Banks	*Cumberland* - Carlisle	
Banks	*Lancaster* - Southport	
Banks Green	*Worcester* - Redditch	
Bankshead	*Salop* - Shrewsbury	
Bank Top	*Lancaster* - Bury	
Banktop	*Northumberland* - Carlisle	
Bank Top	*Stafford* - Stoke-on-Trent	
Bannel	*Flint* - Mold	
Banner Cross	*York, W.R.* - Sheffield	
Bannerdown	*Somerset* - Bath	
Banningham	*Norfolk* - Norwich	
Bannister Hall	*Lancaster* - Preston	
Banstead	*Surrey* - Epsom	
Bantham	*Devon* - Kingsbridge	

Banwell	*Somerset* - Weston Super Mare
Banweln	*Glamorgan* - Neath
Bapchild	*Kent* - Sittingbourne
Baptist End	*Worcester* - Dudley
Barber Green	*Lancaster* - Barrow-in-Furness
Barbers Bridge	*Gloucester* - Gloucester
Barbon	*Westmorland* - Kendal
Barbrook	*Devon* - Barnstaple
Barby	*Northampton* - Rugby
Barcelona	*Cornwall* - Liskeard
Barcheston	*Warwick* - Stratford on Avon
Barcombe	*Northumberland* - Hexham
Barcombe	*Sussex* - Lewes
Barcombe Mills	*Sussex* - Lewes
Barcote	*Berks* - Didcot
Barden	*York, N.R.* - Northallerton
Barden	*York, W.R.* - Skipton
Bardfield, Great	*Essex* - Braintree
Bardfield, Little	*Essex* - Braintree
Bardfield Saling	*Essex* - Braintree
Bardney	*Lincoln* - Lincoln
Bardney Dairies	*Lincoln* - Lincoln
Bardolph Fen	*Norfolk* - King's Lynn
Bardon	*Leicester* - Loughborough
Bardon Hill	*Leicester* - Ashby-de-la-Zouch
Bardon Mill	*Northumberland* - Hexham
Bardsea	*Lancaster* - Barrow-in-Furness
Bardsey	*York, W.R.* - Leeds
Bardsey, Isle of	*Caernarvon* - Portmadoc
Bardsley	*Lancaster* - Oldham
Bardwell	*Suffolk* - Bury St. Edmunds
Bare	*Lancaster* - Lancaster
Bareppa	*Cornwall* - Truro
Barewood (Eardisland)	*Hereford* - Leominster
Barewood (Pembridge)	*Hereford* - Leominster
Barford	*Norfolk* - Norwich
Barford	*Surrey* - Aldershot and Farnham
Barford	*Warwick* - Warwick
Barford, Great	*Beds* - Bedford
Barford, Little	*Beds* - Biggleswade
Barford St. John	*Oxford* - Banbury
Barford St. Martin	*Wilts* - Salisbury
Barford St. Michael	*Oxford* - Banbury
Barforth Camp	*York, N.R.* - Bishop Auckland
Barfrestone	*Kent* - Dover
Bargate	*Derby* - Derby
Bargoed	*Glamorgan* - Bargoed
Barham	*Hunts* - Huntingdon
Barham	*Kent* - Canterbury
Barham	*Suffolk* - Ipswich
Barhaugh	*Northumberland* - Haltwhistle
Bar Hill	*Cambridge* - Cambridge
Bar Hill	*Stafford* - Stoke-on-Trent
Barholm	*Lincoln* - Stamford
Baripper	*Cornwall* - Redruth
Barkby	*Leicester* - Leicester
Barkby Holt	*Leicester* - Leicester
Barkby Thorpe	*Leicester* - Leicester
Barkers Green	*Salop* - Shrewsbury
Barkers Hill	*Dorset* - Shaftesbury
Barkers Hill	*Wilts* - Shaftesbury
Barkers Square	*Salop* - Shrewsbury
Barkestone le Vale	*Leicester* - Melton Mowbray
Barkham	*Berks* - Reading
Barkhouse	*Cumberland* - Workington
Barking	*Essex* - Ilford
Barking	*Suffolk* - Stowmarket
Barkingside	*Essex* - Ilford
Barkisland	*York, W.R.* - Halifax
Barkston	*Lincoln* - Grantham
Barkston Ash	*York, W.R.* - Leeds
Barkway	*Herts* - Hitchin
Barkwith, East	*Lincoln* - Louth
Barkwith, West	*Lincoln* - Lincoln
Barlaston	*Stafford* - Stoke-on-Trent
Barlavington	*Sussex* - Chichester
Barlborough	*Derby* - Worksop
Barlby	*York, E.R.* - York
Barleston	*Leicester* - Ashby-de-la-Zouch
Barley	*Herts* - Hitchin

Barley	*Lancaster* - Nelson
Barley Green	*Suffolk* - Halesworth
Barley Mow and Picktree	*Durham* - Gateshead
Barleythorpe	*Rutland* - Melton Mowbray
Barley with Wheatley Booth	*Lancaster* - Nelson
Barling	*Essex* - Southend
Barlings	*Lincoln* - Lincoln
Barlow	*Derby* - Chesterfield
Barlow	*Durham* - Newcastle upon Tyne
Barlow	*York, W.R.* -York
Barlow Fold	*Lancaster* - Bury
Barmby Moor	*York, E.R.* - York
Barmby-on-the-Marsh	*York, E.R.* - Goole
Barmer	*Norfolk* - King's Lynn
Barming	*Kent* - Maidstone
Barmoor	*Durham* - Newcastle upon Tyne
Barmoor	*Northumberland* - Berwick-upon-Tweed
Barmoor	*Northumberland* - Morpeth
Barmouth	*Merioneth* - Dolgellau
Barmston	*York, E.R.* - Bridlington
Barmston, High	*Durham* - Gateshead
Barmston, Low	*Durham* - Gateshead
Barnaby Moor	*York, N.R.* - Middlesbrough
Barnack	*Huntingdon and Peterborough* - Stamford
Barnacle	*Warwick* - Coventry
Barnacre	*Lancaster* - Preston
Barnard Castle	*Durham* - Bishop Auckland
Barnard Gate	*Oxford* - Witney
Barnardiston	*Suffolk* - Bury St. Edmunds
Barnard's Green	*Worcester* - Great Malvern
Barnard's Hill	*Pembroke* - Haverfordwest
Barn Bank	*Stafford* - Stafford
Barnbow	*York, W.R.* - Leeds
Barnbrough	*York, W.R.* - Doncaster
Barnby	*Notts* - Newark
Barnby	*Suffolk* - Lowestoft
Barnby	*York, N.R.* - Whitby
Barnby Moor	*Notts* - East Retford
Barnby-upon-Don	*York, W.R.* - Doncaster
Barncoose	*Cornwall* - Redruth
Barnehurst	*Kent* - Dartford
Barnes	*London, S.E.13* - Wandsworth
Barnes Green	*Lancaster* - Manchester
Barnes Hall Green	*York, W.R.* - Sheffield
Barnes Hill	*Warwick* - Birmingham
Barnet	*Herts* - Barnet
Barnetby-le-Wold	*Lincoln* - Scunthorpe
Barnet, East	*Herts* - Barnet
Barnet Gate	*Herts* - Barnet
Barnet, New	*Herts* - Barnet
Barnet Vale	*Herts* - Barnet
Barney	*Norfolk* - King's Lynn
Barn Green Close (Denmead)	*Hants* - Portsmouth
Barnham	*Suffolk* - Thetford
Barnham	*Sussex* - Chichester
Barnham Broom	*Norfolk* - Norwich
Barn Hill	*Worcester* - Birmingham
Barnhurst	*Stafford* - Wolverhampton
Barningham	*Suffolk* - Thetford
Barningham	*York, N.R.* - Darlington
Barningham, Little	*Norfolk* - Norwich
Barningham Norwood	*Norfolk* - Norwich
Barningham Parva	*Norfolk* - Norwich
Barningham Town	*Norfolk* - Norwich
Barningham Winter	*Norfolk* - Norwich
Barnoldby-le-Beck	*Lincoln* - Great Grimsby
Barnoldswick	*York, W.R.* - Skipton
Barns	*Northumberland* - Haltwhistle
Barnsbury	*London, N.1.* - Clerkenwell
Barnsbury	*London, N.7* - Clerkenwell
Barnsdale	*York, W.R.* - Doncaster
Barnsdale Hill	*Rutland* - Melton Mowbray
Barn's Green	*Sussex* - Horsham
Barnshaw	*Cheshire* - Congleton
Barnside	*York, W.R.* - Huddersfield

BAR

Barnsley	*Gloucester* - Cheltenham
Barnsley	*Salop* - Bridgnorth
Barnsley	*York, W.R.* - Barnsley
Barnsole	*Kent* - Deal
Barnstaple	*Devon* - Barnstaple
Barnston	*Cheshire* - Birkenhead
Barnston	*Essex* - Braintree
Barnstone	*Notts* - Nottingham
Barnt Green (part)	*Worcester* - Bromsgrove
Barnt Green (part)	*Worcester* - Redditch
Barnton	*Cheshire* - Northwich
Barnwell	*Northants* - Peterborough
Barnwell All Saints	*Northampton* - Peterborough
Barnwell St. Andrew	*Northampton* - Peterborough
Barnwood	*Gloucester* - Gloucester
Baron's Cross	*Hereford* - Leominster
Baron Wood	*Cumberland* - Penrith
Barras	*Westmorland* - Penrith
Barrasford	*Northumberland* - Hexham
Barras Green	*Warwick* - Coventry
Barr Beacon	*Stafford* - Walsall
Barr Common	*Stafford* - Walsall
Barrel Lane	*Hereford* - Ross
Barren Clough	*Derby* - Buxton
Barr, Great (part)	*Stafford* - Birmingham
Barr, Great (part)	*Stafford* - Walsall
Barrington	*Cambridge* - Cambridge
Barrington	*Somerset* - Axminster and Chard
Barrington, Great	*Gloucester* - Cheltenham
Barrington, Little	*Gloucester* - Cheltenham
Barrington	*Northumberland* - Blyth
Barrow	*Cheshire* - Chester
Barrow	*Gloucester* - Cheltenham
Barrow	*Lancaster* - Blackburn
Barrow	*Northumberland* - Morpeth
Barrow	*Rutland* - Melton Mowbray
Barrow	*Salop* - Bridgnorth
Barrow	*Suffolk* - Bury St. Edmunds
Barrow Bridge	*Lancaster* - Bolton
Barrowby	*Lincoln* - Grantham
Barrowby	*York, W.R.* - Leeds
Barrow Common	*Somerset* - Bristol
Barrowden	*Rutland* - Stamford
Barrowford Booth	*Lancaster* - Nelson
Barrow, Great	*Cheshire* - Chester
Barrow Gurney	*Somerset* - Bristol
Barrow Hill	*Derby* - Chesterfield
Barrow Hill	*Stafford* - Uttoxeter
Barrow-in-Furness	*Lancaster* - Barrow-in-Furness
Barrow Nook (part)	*Lancaster* - Southport
Barrow, North	*Somerset* - Yeovil
Barrow, Old	*Lancaster* - Barrow-in-Furness
Barrow-on-Humber	*Lincoln* - Scunthorpe
Barrow-on-Soar	*Leicester* - Loughborough
Barrow-on-Trent	*Derby* - Derby
Barrows Green	*Westmorland* - Kendal
Barrow, South	*Somerset* - Yeovil
Barry	*Glamorgan* - Barry
Barsby	*Leicester* - Melton Mowbray
Barsham	*Suffolk* - Lowestoft
Barsham, East	*Norfolk* - King's Lynn
Barsham, North	*Norfolk* - King's Lynn
Barsham, West	*Norfolk* - King's Lynn
Barston	*Warwick* - Birmingham
Bartestree	*Hereford* - Hereford
Barthomley	*Cheshire* - Crewe
Barthorpe	*York, E.R.* - Malton
Bartington	*Cheshire* - Northwich
Bartle	*Lancaster* - Preston
Bartley	*Hants* - Southampton
Bartley Green	*Warwick* - Birmingham
Bartlow	*Cambridge* - Cambridge
Barton	*Cambridge* - Cambridge
Barton	*Cheshire* - Chester
Barton	*Devon* - Torquay
Barton	*Gloucester* - Cheltenham
Barton	*Lancaster* - Preston
Barton	*Lancaster* - Salford
Barton	*Notts* - Nottingham
Barton	*Oxford* - Oxford

BAR - BAT

Barton	*Somerset* - Weston Super Mare
Barton	*Stafford* - Stafford
Barton	*Warwick* - Stratford on Avon
Barton	*York, N.R.* - Darlington
Barton Bendish	*Norfolk* - King's Lynn
Barton Blount	*Derby* - Burton-upon-Trent
Barton-in-Fabis	*Notts* - Nottingham
Barton-in-the-Beans	*Leicester* - Ashby-de-la-Zouch
Barton-in-the-Clay	*Beds* - Luton
Barton-le-Street	*York, N.R.* - Malton
Barton-le-Willows	*York, N.R.* - Malton
Barton, Middle	*Oxford* - Banbury
Barton Mills	*Suffolk* - Bury St. Edmunds
Barton-on-Humber	*Lincoln* - Scunthorpe
Barton-on-Sea	*Hants* - Lymington
Barton-on-the-Heath	*Warwick* - Banbury
Barton St. David	*Somerset* - Yeovil
Barton Seagrave	*Northampton* - Kettering
Barton Stacey	*Hants* - Andover
Barton Steeple	*Oxford* - Banbury
Barton Turf	*Norfolk* - Norwich
Barton Turns	*Stafford* - Burton-upon-Trent
Barton-under-Needwood	*Stafford* - Burton-upon-Trent
Barton-upon-Irwell	*Lancaster* - Salford
Barton Westcott	*Oxford* - Banbury
Barton Woodhouses	*Stafford* - Burton-upon-Trent
Barugh	*Cumberland* - Carlisle
Barugh	*York, W.R.* - Barnsley
Barugh, Great	*York, N.R.* - Malton
Barugh Green	*York, W.R.* - Barnsley
Barugh, Little	*York, N.R.* - Malton
Barughsyke	*Cumberland* - Carlisle
Barway	*Cambridge* - Ely
Barwell	*Leicester* - Hinckley
Barwick	*Herts* - Hertford
Barwick	*Norfolk* - King's Lynn
Barwick	*Somerset* - Yeovil
Barwick-in-Elmet	*York, W.R.* - Leeds
Barwood	*York, W.R.* - Halifax
Baschurch	*Salop* - Shrewsbury
Bascote	*Warwick* - Warwick
Bascote Heath	*Warwick* - Warwick
Basegreen	*Derby* - Sheffield
Basford	*Cheshire* - Crewe
Basford	*Salop* - Ludlow
Basford (part)	*Stafford* - Stoke-on-Trent
Basford (part)	*Stafford* - Leek
Basford (part)	*Stafford* - Stoke-on-Trent
Basford Bridge	*Stafford* - Leek
Bashall Eaves	*York, W.R.* - Blackburn
Bashley	*Hants* - Lymington
Basildon	*Essex* - Brentwood
Basildon, Lower	*Berks* - Reading
Basildon, Upper	*Berks* - Reading
Basingfield	*Notts* - Nottingham
Basing, Little	*Hants* - Basingstoke
Basing, Old	*Hants* - Basingstoke
Basing Park	*Hants* - Petersfield
Basingstoke	*Hants* - Basingstoke
Baslow	*Derby* - Chesterfield
Basmead	*Beds* - Biggleswade
Bason Bridge (part)	*Somerset* - Bridgwater
Bason Bridge (part)	*Somerset* - Weston Super Mare
Bassaleg	*Monmouth* - Newport (Mon)
Bassenthwaite	*Cumberland* - Workington
Bassett	*Hants* - Southampton
Bassetts Green	*Herts* - Hitchin
Bassetts Pole	*Warwicks* - Tamworth
Bassingbourn	*Cambridge* - Cambridge
Bassingham	*Lincoln* - Newark
Bassingthorpe	*Lincoln* - Grantham
Bassington	*Northumberland* - Alnwick
Basted	*Kent* - Sevenoaks
Baston	*Lincoln* - Spalding
Baston Common	*Lincoln* - Spalding
Baston Fen	*Lincoln* - Spalding
Baswich	*Stafford* - Stafford
Baswick Steer	*York, E.R.* - Beverley
Batchacre	*Stafford* - Stafford
Batchcott	*Salop* - Ludlow

BAT - BAY

Batchelors Farm Estate	*Warwick* - Birmingham
Batchley	*Worcester* - Redditch
Batchmere	*Sussex* - Chichester
Batchworth	*Herts* - Watford
Batchworth Heath	*Herts* - Watford
Batcombe	*Dorset* - Dorchester
Batcombe	*Somerset* - Frome
Bateman's Green	*Worcester* - Birmingham
Batemoor	*York, W.R.* - Sheffield
Bates Cottages	*Northumberland* - North Shields
Bates Hill	*Northumberland* - Hexham
Batford	*Herts* - St. Albans
Bath	*Somerset* - Bath
Bathampton	*Somerset* - Bath
Bathampton	*Wilts* - Salisbury
Bathealton	*Somerset* - Taunton
Batheaston	*Somerset* - Bath
Bathford	*Somerset* - Bath
Bathley	*Notts* - Newark
Bathpool	*Cornwall* - Launceston
Bathpool	*Somerset* - Taunton
Batlers Green	*Herts* - Watford
Batley	*York, W.R.* - Dewsbury
Batley Carr	*York, W.R.* - Dewsbury
Batley, Upper	*York, W.R.* - Dewsbury
Batman's Hill	*Stafford* - Wolverhampton
Batsford	*Gloucester* - Evesham
Batson, Higher	*Devon* - Kingsbridge
Batson, Lower	*Devon* - Kingsbridge
Batten	*Devon* - Plymouth
Battersby	*York, N.R.* - Middlesbrough
Battersby Junction	*York, N.R.* - Middlesbrough
Battersea	*London, S.W.11* - Wandsworth
Battersea Park	*London, S.W.8* - Wandsworth
Battersea Park	*London, S.W.11* - Wandsworth
Battisford	*Suffolk* - Stowmarket
Battle	*Brecon* - Brecknock
Battle	*Sussex* - Hastings
Battledown	*Gloucester* - Cheltenham
Battlefield	*Salop* - Shrewsbury
Battle Flat	*Leicester* - Ashby-de-la-Zouch
Battlesbridge (part)	*Essex* - Chelmsford
Battlesbridge (part)	*Essex* - Southend
Battlesden	*Beds* - Bletchley and Leighton Buzzard
Battlesea Green	*Suffolk* - Halesworth
Battramsley	*Hants* - Lymington
Batts	*Durham* - Bishop Auckland
Batts Place	*Kent* - Gravesend
Battyeford	*York, W.R.* - Dewsbury
Baucott	*Salop* - Ludlow
Baughton Hill	*Worcester* - Worcester
Baughurst	*Hants* - Basingstoke
Baulking	*Berks* - Didcot
Baumber	*Lincoln* - Lincoln
Baunton	*Gloucester* - Cheltenham
Bausley	*Montgomery* - Shrewsbury
Baveney Wood	*Worcester* - Kidderminster
Baverstock	*Wilts* - Salisbury
Bavington, Great	*Northumberland* - Hexham
Bavington, Little	*Northumberland* - Hexham
Bawburgh	*Norfolk* - Norwich
Bawdeswell	*Norfolk* - East Dereham
Bawdrip	*Somerset* - Bridgwater
Bawdsey	*Suffolk* - Woodbridge
Bawsey	*Norfolk* - King's Lynn
Bawtry	*York, W.R.* - Doncaster
Baxenden (part)	*Lancaster* - Accrington
Baxenden (part)	*Lancaster* - Rawtenstall
Baxterley	*Warwick* - Nuneaton
Baybridge	*Hants* - Winchester
Baycliff	*Lancaster* - Barrow-in-Furness
Baydon	*Wilts* - Swindon
Bayfield	*Norfolk* - Norwich
Bayford	*Herts* - Hertford
Bayford (Wincanton)	*Somerset* - Yeovil
Bay Horse	*York, W.R.* - Lancaster
Bayles	*Cumberland* - Carlisle
Baylham	*Suffolk* - Ipswich

BAY - BEA

Baynards	*Surrey* - Guildford
Baynards Green	*Oxford* - Banbury
Baynton, Lower	*Wilts* - Trowbridge
Baynton, Upper	*Wilts* - Trowbridge
Bay of Biscay	*York, W.R.* - Bradford
Bayons Manor	*Lincoln* - Lincoln
Baysale	*York, N.R.* - Middlesbrough
Baysham	*Hereford* - Monmouth
Bayston	*Salop* - Shrewsbury
Bayston Hill	*Salop* - Shrewsbury
Bayswater	*London, W.2* - Bloomsbury and Marylebone
Bayswater	*Oxford* - Oxford
Bayton	*Worcester* - Kidderminster
Bayvil	*Pembroke* - Cardigan
Bayworth	*Berks* - Oxford
Beach	*Gloucester* - Bristol
Beach	*Salop* - Shrewsbury
Beachampton	*Bucks* - Bletchley and Leighton Buzzard
Beach Cwmago	*Salop* - Shrewsbury
Beachley	*Gloucester* - Chepstow
Beachy Head	*Sussex* - Eastbourne
Beacon	*Cornwall* - Redruth
Beacon Bank	*Stafford* - Stafford
Beacon Hill	*Bucks* - High Wycombe
Beacon Hill	*Lincoln* - Louth
Beacon Hill	*Stafford* - Stafford
Beacon's Bottom	*Bucks* - High Wycombe
Beaconsfield	*Bucks* - High Wycombe
Beacon The	*Kent* - Cranbrook
Beacontree	*Essex* - Ilford
Beacontree Heath	*Essex* - Ilford
Beacontree Heath	*Salop* - Shrewsbury
Beadlam	*York, N.R.* - Malton
Beadlow	*Beds* - Bedford
Beadnell	*Northumberland* - Alnwick
Beaford	*Devon* - Bideford
Beal	*Northumberland* - Berwick-upon-Tweed
Beal	*York, W.R.* - Pontefract
Beales Green Farm	*Kent* - Cranbrook
Bealings, Great	*Suffolk* - Ipswich
Bealings, Little	*Suffolk* - Ipswich
Beambridge	*Salop* - Ludlow
Beamhouse	*Salop* - Shrewsbury
Beamhurst	*Stafford* - Uttoxeter
Beaminster	*Dorset* - Yeovil
Beamish Pit	*Durham* - Gateshead
Beamish Village	*Durham* - Gateshead
Beamsley	*York, W.R.* - Skipton
Bean	*Kent* - Dartford
Beanacre	*Wilts* - Chippenham
Beanlands	*Cumberland* - Carlisle
Beanley	*Northumberland* - Alnwick
Beara	*Cornwall* - Launceston
Bear Cross	*Hants* - Bournemouth
Beare Green	*Surrey* - Dorking
Bearle	*Northumberland* - Hexham
Bearley	*Warwick* - Stratford on Avon
Bear Park	*Durham* - Durham
Bear Place	*Berks* - Reading
Bearsted	*Kent* - Maidstone
Bearstone	*Salop* - Market Drayton
Bearwardcote	*Derby* - Derby
Bearwood	*Berks* - Reading
Bear Wood	*Dorset* - Wimborne Minster
Bearwood	*Stafford* - West Bromwich
Beauchamp Roding	*Essex* - Chelmsford
Beauchief	*York, W.R.* - Sheffield
Beaudesert	*Warwick* - Stratford on Avon
Beaufort	*Brecon and Monmouth* - Blackwood
Beaulieu	*Hants* - Southampton
Beaumanor	*Leicester* - Loughborough
Beaumaris	*Anglesey* - Llangefni
Beaumont	*Cumberland* - Carlisle
Beaumont Chase	*Rutland* - Corby
Beaumont with Moze	*Essex* - Harwich
Beaurepaire	*Hants* - Basingstoke
Beausale	*Warwick* - Warwick

Beauvale	*Notts* - Nottingham
Beauworth	*Hants* - Winchester
Beaver	*Kent* - Ashford
Beaworthy	*Devon* - Okehampton
Bebington	*Cheshire* - Birkenhead
Bebington, Higher	*Cheshire* - Birkenhead
Bebington, Lower	*Cheshire* - Birkenhead
Bebside	*Northumberland* - Blyth
Beccles	*Suffolk* - Lowestoft
Beckbury	*Salop* - Bridgnorth
Beckenham	*Kent* - Bromley
Beckenham, New	*Kent* - Bromley
Beckering	*Lincoln* - Lincoln
Beckermet	*Cumberland* - Whitehaven
Beckermonds	*York, W.R.* - Skipton
Beckfoot	*Cumberland* - Carlisle
Beckfoot	*Westmorland* - Kendal
Beckford	*Worcs* - Cheltenham
Beckham, East	*Norfolk* - Norwich
Beckhampton	*Wilts* - Swindon
Beckham, West	*Norfolk* - Norwich
Beck Hill Shelf	*York, W.R.* - Bradford
Beckhole	*York, N.R.* - Whitby
Beckhouse	*Cumberland* - Workington
Beckingham	*Lincoln* - Newark
Beckingham	*Notts* - Gainsborough
Beckington	*Somerset* - Frome
Beckjay	*Salop* - Ludlow
Beckley	*Hants* - Bournemouth
Beckley	*Oxford* - Oxford
Beckley	*Sussex* - Hastings
Beckminstor	*Stafford* - Wolverhampton
Beck Row	*Suffolk* - Bury St. Edmunds
Beckside	*Lancaster* - Barrow-in-Furness
Beckton	*London, E.6* - Bow
Beckwith	*York W.R.* - Harrogate
Beckwithshaw	*York, W.R.* - Harrogate
Becontree	*Essex* - Ilford
Becontree Heath	*Essex* - Ilford
Bedale	*York, N.R.* - Northallerton
Bedburn, North	*Durham* - Bishop Auckland
Bedburn, South	*Durham* - Bishop Auckland
Bedchester	*Dorset* - Shaftesbury
Beddau	*Glamorgan* - Pontypridd
Beddgelert	*Caernarvon* - Portmadoc
Beddingham	*Sussex* - Lewes
Beddington	*Surrey* - Croydon
Bedfield	*Suffolk* - Halesworth
Bedfont	*Middlesex* - Brentford
Bedfont, West	*Middlesex* - Slough
Bedford	*Beds* - Bedford
Bedgebury	*Kent* - Cranbrook
Bedgrove	*Bucks* - Aylesbury
Bedham	*Sussex* - Chichester
Bedhampton	*Hants* - Portsmouth
Bedingfield	*Suffolk* - Norwich
Bedingham	*Norfolk* - Norwich
Bedlam	*Salop* - Ludlow
Bedlars Green	*Essex* - Bishop's Stortford
Bedlington	*Northumberland* - Blyth
Bedlinog	*Glamorgan* - Bargoed
Bedminster	*Somerset* - Bristol
Bedmond	*Herts* - Watford
Bednall	*Stafford* - Stafford
Bedstone	*Salop* - Knighton
Bedwas	*Monmouth* - Newport (Mon)
Bedwell Park	*Herts* - Hertford
Bedwell Plash	*Herts* - Hitchin
Bedwellty	*Monmouth* - Blackwood
Bedwellty Pits	*Monmouth* - Blackwood
Bedworth	*Warwick* - Nuneaton
Bedworth Heath	*Warwick* - Nuneaton
Bedwyn, Great	*Wilts* - Swindon
Bedwyn, Little	*Wilts* - Swindon
Beeby	*Leicester* - Leicester
Beeby Grange	*Leicester* - Leicester
Beech	*Hants* - Aldershot and Farnham
Beech	*Stafford* - Stoke-on-Trent
Beechamwell	*Norfolk* - King's Lynn
Beechburn Grange	*Durham* - Bishop Auckland

Beechburn, Low	*Durham* - Bishop Auckland
Beechburn, North	*Durham* - Bishop Auckland
Beeches Estate	*Stafford* - Birmingham
Beech, High	*Essex* - Edmonton
Beech Hill	*Berks* - Reading
Beech Hill	*Lancaster* - Wigan
Beechingstoke	*Wilts* - Devizes
Beech Lanes	*Worcester* - West Bromwich
Beech Pike	*Gloucester* - Swindon
Beechwood	*Warwick* - Coventry
Beeding, Lower	*Sussex* - Horsham
Beeding, Upper	*Sussex* - Brighton
Beedon	*Berks* - Newbury
Beeford	*York, E.R.* - Bridlington
Beeleigh	*Essex* - Maldon
Beeley	*Derby* - Matlock
Beelsby	*Lincoln* - Great Grimsby
Beeney	*Cornwall* - Launceston
Beenham Heath	*Berks* - Slough
Beer	*Devon* - Axminster and Chard
Beer Crocombe	*Somerset* - Taunton
Beer Hackett (Sherbourne)	*Dorset* - Yeovil
Beerhall	*Devon* - Axminster and Chard
Beesands	*Devon* - Kingsbridge
Beesby	*Lincoln* - Great Grimsby
Beesby-in-the-Marsh	*Lincoln* - Louth
Beeson	*Devon* - Kingsbridge
Beeston	*Beds* - Biggleswade
Beeston	*Cheshire* - Crewe
Beeston	*Norfolk* - East Dereham
Beeston	*Notts* - Nottingham
Beeston	*York, W.R.* - Leeds
Beeston Regis	*Norfolk* - Norwich
Beeston St. Andrew	*Norfolk* - Norwich
Beeston St. Lawrence	*Norfolk* - Norwich
Beetham	*Westmorland* - Kendal
Beetley	*Norfolk* - East Dereham
Beevers Bridge, Cowick	*York, W.R.* - Goole
Befcote	*Stafford* - Stafford
Begbroke	*Oxford* - Oxford
Begdale	*Cambridge* - Wisbech
Begelly	*Pembroke* - Haverfordwest
Beggarbush Hill	*Oxford* - Didcot
Beggarlee	*Notts* - Nottingham
Beggary	*Beds* - Biggleswade
Beguildy	*Radnor* - Knighton
Beighterton	*Salop* - Wolverhampton
Beighterton	*Stafford* - Wellington
Beighton	*Derby* - Sheffield
Beighton	*Norfolk* - Norwich
Bekesbourne	*Kent* - Canterbury
Belan	*Montgomery* - Welshpool
Belaugh	*Norfolk* - Norwich
Belbins	*Hants* - Southampton
Belbroughton	*Worcester* - Bromsgrove
Belby	*York, E.R.* - Goole
Belchalwell	*Dorset* - Dorchester
Belchamp Otten	*Essex* - Sudbury
Belchamp St. Paul	*Essex* - Sudbury
Belchamp Walter	*Essex* - Sudbury
Belchford	*Lincoln* - Louth
Beldy	*Cumberland* - Carlisle
Belford	*Northumberland* - Berwick-upon-Tweed
Belgrave	*Cheshire* - Chester
Belgrave	*Stafford* - Tamworth
Belgravia (part)	*London, S.W.1* - West London
Belgravia (part)	*London, S.W.1* - Westminster
Bellaport	*Salop* - Market Drayton
Bellbar	*Herts* - St. Albans
Bell Busk	*York, W.R.* - Skipton
Bell Common	*Essex* - Harlow
Belleau	*Lincoln* - Louth
Bell End	*Worcester* - Bromsgrove
Bellevale	*Lancaster* - Liverpool
Belle Vue	*Cumberland* - Carlisle
Belle Vue	*York, W.R.* - Wakefield
Bell Green	*London S.E.26* - Bromley
Bell Green	*Warwick* - Coventry
Bell Green	*Worcester* - Birmingham

BEL - BEN

Bell Hagg	*York, W.R.* - Sheffield
Belle Isle	*York, W.R.* - Leeds
Bellerby	*York, N.R.* - Northallerton
Bell Heath	*Worcester* - Bromsgrove
Bellingham	*London, S.E.6* - Bromley
Bellingham	*Northumberland* - Hexham
Bellington	*Worcester* - Kidderminster
Bellister	*Northumberland* - Hexham
Bell's Close	*Northumberland* - Newcastle upon Tyne
Belluton	*Somerset* - Bristol
Belmisthorpe	*Rutland* - Stamford
Belmont	*Durham* - Durham
Belmont	*Hereford* - Hereford
Belmont	*Lancaster* - Bolton
Belmont	*Surrey* - Epsom
Belmore (Upham)	*Hants* - Winchester
Belnie	*Lincoln* - Spalding
Belowda	*Cornwall* - St. Austell
Belper	*Derby* - Derby
Belph	*Derby* - Worksop
Belsay	*Northumberland* - Newcastle upon Tyne
Belsize Park	*London, N.W.3* - Bloomsbury and Marylebone
Belstead	*Suffolk* - Ipswich
Belstone	*Devon* - Okehampton
Belswardine	*Salop* - Shrewsbury
Belthorn (part)	*Lancaster* - Accrington
Belthorn (part)	*Lancaster* - Blackburn
Belthorpe	*York, E.R.* - York
Belthorpe, Low	*York, E.R.* - York
Beltinge	*Kent* - Canterbury
Beltingham	*Northumberland* - Hexham
Beltoft	*Lincoln* - Thorne
Belton	*Leicester* - Loughborough
Belton	*Lincoln* - Grantham
Belton	*Lincoln* - Thorne
Belton	*Rutland* - Leicester
Belton	*Suffolk* - Great Yarmouth
Beltring	*Kent* - Maidstone
Belvedere	*Kent* - Dartford
Belvoir	*Leicester* - Grantham
Bembridge	*I. of W.* - Newport (I.W.)
Bemersley	*Stafford* - Stoke-on-Trent
Bemerton	*Wilts* - Salisbury
Bempton	*York, E.R.* - Bridlington
Benacre	*Suffolk* - Lowestoft
Bendish	*Herts* - Hitchin
Bendor	*Northumberland* - Berwick-upon-Tweed
Benefield	*Northampton* - Kettering
Benefield, Lower	*Northampton* - Corby
Benefield, Upper	*Northampton* - Corby
Benenden	*Kent* - Cranbrook
Benfieldside	*Durham* - Consett
Benfleet, North	*Essex* - Southend
Benfleet, South	*Essex* - Southend
Bengeo	*Herts* - Hertford
Benges, The	*Sussex* - Chichester
Bengeworth	*Worcester* - Evesham
Benhall	*Suffolk* - Woodbridge
Beningbrough	*York, N.R.* - York
Benington	*Lincoln* - Boston
Benington Ings	*Lincoln* - Boston
Benllech	*Anglesey* - Llangefni
Bennacott	*Cornwall* - Launceston
Bennet Head	*Cumberland* - Penrith
Bennetland	*York, E.R.* - Goole
Bennett End	*Bucks* - High Wycombe
Bennett's End	*Herts* - Hemel Hempstead
Bennett's End	*Salop* - Ludlow
Bennetts Green	*Surrey* - Dorking
Benningholme	*York, E.R.* - Kingston-upon-Hull
Bennington	*Herts* - Hertford
Bennington, Long	*Lincoln* - Newark
Benniworth	*Lincoln* - Louth
Ben Rhydding	*York, W.R.* - Otley

BEN - BER

Benridge	*Northumberland* - Morpeth
Bensham St. Cuthbert	*Durham* - Gateshead
Bensington	*Oxford* - Didcot
Benson	*Oxford* - Didcot
Benson's Lane	*Sussex* - Horsham
Bentfield	*Essex* - Bishop's Stortford
Bentfield End	*Essex* - Bishop's Stortford
Bentfield Green	*Essex* - Bishop's Stortford
Benthall	*Salop* - Bridgnorth
Bentham	*Gloucester* - Cheltenham
Bentham, High	*York, W.R.* - Lancaster
Bentham, Low	*York, W.R.* - Lancaster
Bentilee	*Stafford* - Stoke-on-Trent
Bentley	*Hants* - Aldershot and Farnham
Bentley (Mottisfont)	*Hants* - Southampton
Bentley	*Salop* - Bridgnorth
Bentley	*Stafford* - Walsall
Bentley	*Suffolk* - Ipswich
Bentley	*Warwick* - Nuneaton
Bentley	*York, E.R.* - Beverley
Bentley	*York, W.R.* - Doncaster
Bentley Heath	*Herts* - Barnet
Bentley Heath	*Warwick* - Birmingham
Bentley, Lower	*Worcester* - Redditch
Bentley, Upper	*Worcester* - Redditch
Benton	*Northumberland* - Newcastle upon Tyne
Benton Green	*Warwick* - Coventry
Benton, Little	*Northumberland* - Newcastle upon Tyne
Benton, Long	*Northumberland* - Newcastle upon Tyne
Bents	*Lancaster* - Nelson
Bents	*Northumberland* - Haltwhistle
Bents Green	*York, W.R.* - Sheffield
Bentwaters	*Suffolk* - Woodbridge
Bentwitchen	*Devon* - Barnstaple
Bentworth	*Hants* - Basingstoke
Benwell	*Northumberland* - Newcastle upon Tyne
Benwick	*Cambridge* - March
Benwick Fen	*Cambridge* - March
Beobridge	*Salop* - Bridgnorth
Beoley	*Worcester* - Redditch
Beoley Cross	*Worcester* - Redditch
Bepton	*Sussex* - Chichester
Berden	*Essex* - Bishop's Stortford
Berea	*Pembroke* - Haverfordwest
Bere Alston	*Devon* - Plymouth
Bere Chapel	*Somerset* - Yeovil
Berechurch	*Essex* - Colchester
Bere Ferrers	*Devon* - Plymouth
Bere Heath	*Dorset* - Swanage
Berepper	*Cornwall* - Penzance
Bere Regis	*Dorset* - Swanage
Bergh-Apton	*Norfolk* - Norwich
Berghill, Lower	*Salop* - Oswestry
Bergholt, East	*Suffolk* - Ipswich
Bericote	*Warwick* - Warwick
Berinsfield	*Oxford* - Didcot
Berkeley	*Gloucester* - Stroud
Berkhamsted	*Herts* - Hemel Hempstead
Berkhamsted, Great	*Herts* - Hemel Hempstead
Berkhamsted, Little	*Herts* - Hertford
Berkley	*Somerset* - Frome
Berkswell	*Warwick* - Coventry
Bermondsey	*London, S.E.1* - Southwark
Bermondsey	*London, S.E.16* - Southwark
Bermuda	*Warwick* - Nuneaton
Berners Roothing	*Essex* - Chelmsford
Berrick	*Oxford* - Didcot
Berrick Prior	*Oxford* - Didcot
Berrick Salome	*Oxford* - Didcot
Berrier	*Cumberland* - Penrith
Berriew	*Montgomery* - Welshpool
Berrington	*Salop* - Shrewsbury
Berrington	*Worcester* - Ludlow
Berrington and Eye	*Hereford* - Leominster
Berrow	*Somerset* - Weston Super Mare
Berrow	*Worcester* - Great Malvern

BER - BET

Berrow Green	*Worcester* - Worcester
Berrow, Lower	*Worcester* - Redditch
Berrow, Upper	*Worcester* - Redditch
Berry Brow	*York, W.R.* - Huddersfield
Berry-Croft	*York, W.R.* - Huddersfield
Berryfield	*Wilts* - Chippenham
Berry Hill	*Gloucester* - Monmouth
Berry Hill	*Stafford* - Stoke-on-Trent
Berry Hill	*Stafford* - Stafford
Berrynarbor	*Devon* - Barnstaple
Berry Pomeroy	*Devon* - Torquay
Berry Wood	*Northampton* - Northampton
Berse	*Denbigh* - Wrexham
Bersham	*Denbigh* - Wrexham
Bersted, North	*Sussex* - Chichester
Bersted, South	*Sussex* - Chichester
Berthengam	*Flint* - Holywell
Berthlwyd	*Glamorgan* - Swansea
Bertie Fen	*Lincoln* - Spalding
Berwick	*Gloucester* - Thornbury
Berwick	*Salop* - Shrewsbury
Berwick	*Sussex* - Lewes
Berwick Bassett	*Wilts* - Swindon
Berwick Hill	*Northumberland* - Newcastle upon Tyne
Berwick St. James	*Wilts* - Salisbury
Berwick St. John	*Wilts* - Shaftesbury
Berwick St. Leonard	*Wilts* - Shaftesbury
Berwick-upon-Tweed	*Northumberland* - Berwick-upon-Tweed
Berwick Wharf	*Salop* - Shrewsbury
Berwood	*Warwick* - Birmingham
Berwyn	*Denbigh* - Wrexham
Bescaby	*Leicester* - Melton Mowbray
Bescar	*Lancaster* - Southport
Bescot	*Stafford* - Walsall
Besford	*Salop* - Shrewsbury
Besford	*Worcester* - Worcester
Bessacar	*York, W.R.* - Doncaster
Bessel's Green	*Kent* - Sevenoaks
Besselsleigh	*Berks* - Oxford
Besses o' th' Barn	*Lancaster* - Bury
Bessingby	*York E.R.* - Bridlington
Bessingham	*Norfolk* - Norwich
Besthorpe	*Norfolk* - Norwich
Besthorpe	*Notts* - Newark
Bestwood Park	*Notts* - Nottingham
Beswick	*Lancaster* - Manchester
Beswick	*York, E.R.* - Beverley
Betchcott	*Salop* - Shrewsbury
Betchetts Green	*Surrey* - Dorking
Betchton	*Cheshire* - Crewe
Betchworth (part)	*Surrey* - Dorking
Betchworth (part)	*Surrey* - Reigate
Bethania	*Cardigan* - Aberystwyth
Bethel	*Anglesey* - Llangefni
Bethel	*Caernarvon* - Caernarvon
Bethel	*Cornwall* - St. Austell
Bethel	*Merioneth* - Dolgellau
Bethel	*Montgomery* - Oswestry
Bethersden	*Kent* -Ashford
Bethesda	*Caernarvon* - Bangor
Bethlehem	*Carmarthen* - Llandovery
Bethnal Green	*London, E.2* - Shoreditch
Betley	*Stafford* - Crewe
Betsham	*Kent* - Dartford
Betterton	*Berks* - Didcot
Betteshanger	*Kent* - Deal
Bettiscombe	*Dorset* - Axminster & Chard
Bettisfield	*Flint* - Whitchurch
Betton	*Salop* - Market Drayton
Betton	*Salop* - Shrewsbury
Betton Strange	*Salop* - Shrewsbury
Betton Wood	*Salop* - Market Drayton
Bettws	*Glamorgan* - Bridgend
Bettws	*Monmouth* - Pontypool and Abergavenny
Bettws	*Monmouth* - Newport (Mon)
Bettws	*Montgomery* - Newtown
Bettws Bleddrws	*Cardigan* - Lampeter

BET - BID

Bettws Evan	*Cardigan* - Cardigan
Bettws Garmon	*Caernarvon* - Caernarvon
Bettws Gwerfilgoch	*Merioneth* - Wrexham
Bettws Leiki	*Cardigan* - Lampeter
Bettws Newydd	*Monmouth* - Pontypool and Abergavenny
Bettws-y-Crwyn	*Salop* - Knighton
Bettys Grave	*Gloucester* - Swindon
Betws	*Carmarthen* - Ammandford
Betws y Coed	*Caernarvon* - Conway
Betws yn Rhos	*Denbigh* - Rhyl
Beulah	*Brecon* - Builth
Beulah	*Cardigan* - Cardigan
Beveley	*Salop* - Wellington (Salop)
Bevendean	*Sussex* - Brighton
Bevercoates	*Notts* - East Retford
Bevere	*Worcester* - Worcester
Beverley	*York, E.R.* - Beverley
Beverley Parks	*York, E.R.* - Beverley
Beverstone	*Gloucester* - Malmesbury
Bevington	*Gloucester* - Stroud
Bevington	*Warwick* - Redditch
Bevois Valley	*Hants* - Southampton
Bewaldeth	*Cumberland* - Carlisle
Bewaldeth	*Cumberland* - Workington
Bewbush	*Sussex* - Horsham
Bewcastle	*Cumberland* - Carlisle
Bewdley	*Worcester* - Kidderminster
Bewell Head	*Worcester* - Bromsgrove
Bewerley	*York, W.R.* - Harrogate
Bewholme	*York, E.R.* - Beverley
Bewicke Main	*Durham* - Gateshead
Bewsey	*Lancaster* - Warrington
Bexhill	*Sussex* - Hastings
Bexington, East	*Dorset* - Weymouth
Bexington, West	*Dorset* - Dorchester
Bexley	*Kent* - Dartford
Bexleyheath	*Kent* - Dartford
Bexley Hill (Fernhurst)	*Sussex* - Petersfield
Bexley Hill (North Ambersham)	*Sussex* - Petersfield
Bexley Hill (South Ambersham)	*Sussex* - Chichester
Bexton Knutsford	*Cheshire* - Altrincham
Bexwell	*Norfolk* - King's Lynn
Beyton	*Suffolk* - Bury St. Edmunds
Biana	*Stafford* - Stafford
Bibury	*Gloucester* - Cheltenham
Bicester	*Oxford* - Oxford
Bickenhill	*Somerset* - Taunton
Bickenhill	*Warwick* - Birmingham
Bickenhill, Middle	*Warwick* - Birmingham
Bicker	*Lincoln* - Boston
Bicker Fen	*Lincoln* - Boston
Bickershaw	*Lancaster* - Wigan
Bickerstaffe	*Lancaster* - Southport
Bickerton	*Cheshire* - Crewe
Bickerton	*Northumberland* - Morpeth
Bickerton	*York, W.R.* - York
Bickford	*Stafford* - Stafford
Bickington	*Devon* - Barnstaple
Bickington	*Devon* - Newton Abbot
Bickleigh	*Devon* - Plymouth
Bickleigh	*Devon* - Tiverton
Bickley	*Cheshire* - Whitchurch
Bickley	*Kent* - Bromley
Bickley	*Worcester* - Kidderminster
Bickley	*York, N.R.* - Scarborough
Bickmarsh	*Warwick* - Evesham
Bicknacre	*Essex* - Maldon
Bicknoller	*Somerset* - Minehead
Bicknor	*Kent* - Sittingbourne
Bickton	*Hants* - Salisbury
Bickwell	*Devon* - Exeter
Bicton	*Devon* - Exeter
Bicton (Clun)	*Salop* - Ludlow
Bicton	*Salop* - Shrewsbury
Bicton Heath	*Salop* - Shrewsbury
Bidborough	*Kent* - Tonbridge

BID - BIL

Biddenden	*Kent* - Cranbrook
Biddenham	*Beds* - Bedford
Biddesden	*Wilts* - Andover
Biddestone	*Wilts* - Chippenham
Biddick, North	*Durham* - Gateshead
Biddick, South	*Durham* - Durham
Biddisham	*Somerset* - Weston Super Mare
Biddlesden	*Bucks* - Bangor
Biddlestone	*Hereford* - Monmouth
Biddlestone	*Northumberland* - Morpeth
Biddlestone Edge	*Northumberland* - Morpeth
Biddulph	*Stafford* - Congleton
Biddulph Moor	*Stafford* - Congleton
Biddulph Park	*Stafford* - Congleton
Bideford	*Devon* - Bideford
Bidford-on-Avon	*Warwick* - Stratford on Avon
Bidston	*Cheshire* - Birkenhead
Bidwell	*Beds* - Luton
Bielby	*York, E.R.* - York
Biergate	*Lincoln* - Louth
Bierley (Tintinhull)	*Somerset* - Yeovil
Bierley, East	*York, W.R.* - Bradford
Bierley, North	*York, W.R.* - Bradford
Bierton	*Bucks* - Aylesbury
Bigbury	*Devon* - Kingsbridge
Bigbury-on-Sea	*Devon* - Kingsbridge
Bigby	*Lincoln* - Scunthorpe
Biggar	*Lancaster* - Barrow-in-Furness
Bigges Quarter	*Northumberland* - Morpeth
Biggin	*Northampton* - Peterborough
Biggin	*Warwick* - Rugby
Biggin	*York, W.R.* - York
Biggin-by-Hulland	*Derby* - Derby
Biggin-by-Newhaven	*Derby* - Buxton
Biggin Hill	*Kent* - Bromley
Biggleswade	*Beds* - Biggleswade
Bighton	*Hants* - Winchester
Biglands	*Cumberland* - Carlisle
Bigmoore Common	*Oxford* - High Wycombe
Bignall End	*Stafford* - Stoke-on-Trent
Bignell	*Oxford* - Oxford
Bignor	*Sussex* - Chichester
Bigrigg	*Cumberland* - Whitehaven
Bilberry	*Cornwall* - St. Austell
Bilborough	*Notts* - Nottingham
Bilbrook	*Somerset* - Minehead
Bilbrough	*York, W.R.* - York
Bilby	*Notts* - East Retford
Bildershaw Bank	*Durham* - Bishop Auckland
Bildeston	*Suffolk* - Stowmarket
Bilham	*York, W.R.* - Doncaster
Billacombe	*Devon* - Plymouth
Billbrook	*Stafford* - Wolverhampton
Billericay	*Essex* - Brentwood
Billesdon	*Leicester* - Leicester
Billesley	*Warwick* - Stratford on Avon
Billesley Common	*Warwick* - Birmingham
Billincoat	*Lancaster* - Barrow-in-Furness
Billingborough	*Lincoln* - Sleaford
Billingborough Fen	*Lincoln* - Sleaford
Billinge	*Lancaster* - Wigan
Billinge Chapel End	*Lancaster* - Wigan
Billinge Higher End	*Lancaster* - Wigan
Billingford	*Norfolk* - East Dereham
Billingford	*Norfolk* - Norwich
Billing, Great	*Northampton* - Northampton
Billingham	*Durham* - Stockton on Tees
Billinghay	*Lincoln* - Sleaford
Billinghay Dales	*Lincoln* - Seaford
Billinghay Fen	*Lincoln* - Sleaford
Billinghay Fields	*Lincoln* - Sleaford
Billingley	*York, W.R.* - Barnsley
Billing, Little	*Northampton* - Northampton
Billingshurst	*Sussex* - Horsham
Billingsley	*Salop* - Bridgnorth
Billington	*Lancaster* - Blackburn
Billington	*Stafford* - Stafford
Billington, Great	*Beds* - Bletchley and Leighton Buzzard

BIL - BIR

Billington Little	*Beds* - Bletchley and Leighton Buzzard
Billockby	*Norfolk* - Great Yarmouth
Bill Quay	*Durham* Gateshead
Billy Hill	*Durham* - Bishop Auckland
Billy Mill	*Northumberland* - North Shields
Billy Row	*Durham* - Bishop Auckland
Billy Row Green	*Durham* - Bishop Auckland
Bilney, East	*Norfolk* - East Dereham
Bilney, West	*Norfolk* - King's Lynn
Bilsborough	*Lancaster* - Preston
Bilsby	*Lincoln* - Skegness
Bilsdale West Side	*York, N.R.* - Malton
Bilsham	*Sussex* - Chichester
Bilsington	*Kent* - Ashford
Bilsom	*Gloucester* - Thornbury
Bilson Green	*Gloucester* - Gloucester
Bilsthorpe	*Notts* - Mansfield
Bilston	*Stafford* - Wolverhampton
Bilstone	*Leicester* - Ashby-de-la-Zouch
Bilton	*Northumberland* - Alnwick
Bilton	*Warwick* - Rugby
Bilton	*York, E.R.* - Kingston-upon-Hull
Bilton	*York, W.R.* - Harrogate
Bilton	*York, W.R.* - York
Bilton, New	*Warwick* - Rugby
Binbrook	*Lincoln* - Louth
Binbrook Aerodrome	*Lincoln* - Louth
Binchester	*Durham* - Bishop Auckland
Bincombe	*Dorset* - Weymouth
Binderton	*Sussex* - Chichester
Bindon	*Dorset* - Dorchester
Binegar	*Somerset* - Wells
Binfield	*Berks* - Reading
Binfield Heath	*Oxford* - Reading
Bingfield	*Northumberland* - Hexham
Bingham	*Dorset* - Dorchester
Bingham	*Notts* - Nottingham
Bingham Melcombe	*Dorset* - Dorchester
Bingley	*York, W.R.* - Keighley
Bingley Lane	*York, W.R.* - Sheffield
Binham	*Norfolk* - King's Lynn
Binley	*Hants* - Andover
Binley	*Warwick* - Coventry
Binley Woods	*Warwick* - Coventry
Binnegar	*Dorset* - Swanage
Binnington	*York, E.R.* - Scarborough
Binnington Wold	*York, E.R.* - Scarborough
Binscombe	*Surrey* - Guildford
Binsey	*Oxford* - Oxford
Binstead	*I. of W.* - Newport (I.W.)
Binsted	*Hants* - Aldershot and Farnham
Binsted	*Sussex* - Chichester
Binton	*Warwick* - Stratford on Avon
Bintree	*Norfolk* - East Dereham
Birch	*Essex* - Colchester
Birch (Hopwood)	*Lancaster* - Bury
Birch (Middleton)	*Lancaster* - Oldham
Birch	*Salop* - Oswestry
Birch	*Salop* - Shrewsbury
Bircham, Great	*Norfolk* - King's Lynn
Bircham Newton	*Norfolk* - King's Lynn
Bircham Tofts	*Norfolk* - King's Lynn
Birchanger	*Essex* - Bishop's Stortford
Birchen Bridge	*Sussex* - Horsham
Birchencliffe	*York, W.R.* - Huddersfield
Bircher	*Hereford* - Leominster
Bircher Common	*Hereford* - Leominster
Birches	*Salop* - Ludlow
Birches Green	*Warwick* - Birmingham
Birches Head	*Stafford* - Stoke-on-Trent
Birchfield	*Warwick* - Birmingham
Birchgate	*Stafford* - Stoke-on-Trent
Birch Green	*Herts* - Hertford
Birch Green	*Sussex* - Haywards Heath
Birch Green	*Worcester* - Worcester
Birch Grove (Swansea)	*Glamorgan* - Swansea
Birchgrove (Whitchurch)	*Glamorgan* - Cardiff
Birchgrove	*Sussex* - East Grinstead
Birchill	*Derby* - Matlock

BIR - BIS

Birchills	*Stafford* - Walsall
Birchington-on-Sea	*Kent* - Margate
Birchley	*Lancaster* - Wigan
Birchley Heath	*Warwick* - Nuneaton
Birch, Little	*Hereford* - Hereford
Birchmoor	*Warwick* - Tamworth
Birchmoor Green (Woburn)	*Bedford* - Bletchley and Leighton Buzzard
Birch, Much	*Hereford* - Hereford
Birchover	*Derby* - Matlock
Birchwood	*Derby* - Alfreton
Birchwood	*Kent* - Dartford
Birchwood, Lower	*Derby* - Alfreton
Birchwood Park	*Stafford* - Uttoxeter
Birchwood, Upper	*Derby* - Alfreton
Bircle	*Lancaster* - Bury
Bircotes	*Notts* - Worksop
Birdbrook	*Essex* - Sudbury
Bird End	*Stafford* - West Bromwich
Birdforth	*York, N.R.* - Northallerton
Birdham	*Sussex* - Chichester
Birdholme	*Derby* - Chesterfield
Birdingbury	*Warwick* - Rugby
Birdlip	*Gloucester* - Cheltenham
Birdoswald	*Cumberland* - Carlisle
Birdsall	*York, E.R.* - Malton
Birds Drove	*Lincoln* - Spalding
Birds Edge	*York, W.R.* - Huddersfield
Birds Green	*Essex* - Chelmsford
Birds Green	*Salop* - Bridgnorth
Birdsmoregate	*Dorset* - Axminster and Chard
Birdwell	*York, W.R.* - Barnsley
Birdwood	*Gloucester* - Gloucester
Birkby	*Cumberland* - Workington
Birkby	*York, W.R.* - Huddersfield
Birkby Nab	*York, N.R.* - Harrogate
Birkdale	*Lancaster* - Southport
Birkenhead	*Cheshire* - Birkenhead
Birkenshaw	*York, W.R.* - Dewsbury
Birkenshaw Bottoms	*York, W.R.* - Dewsbury
Birket Bank	*Cumberland* - Workington
Birkin	*York, W.R.* - Pontefract
Birkshaw	*Northumberland* - Hexham
Birley	*Derby* - Sheffield
Birley	*Hereford* - Leominster
Birley Carr	*York, W.R.* - Sheffield
Birley Moor	*Derby* - Sheffield
Birley Spa	*Derby* - Sheffield
Birley Spa	*York, W.R.* - Sheffield
Birley Vale	*York, W.R.* - Sheffield
Birling	*Kent* - Maidstone
Birling	*Northumberland* - Alnwick
Birling Gap	*Sussex* - Eastbourne
Birlingham	*Worcester* - Worcester
Birmingham	*Warwick* - Birmingham
Birstall	*Leicester* - Leicester
Birstall	*York, W.R.* - Dewsbury
Birstwith	*York, W.R.* - Harrogate
Birtenshaw	*Lancaster* - Bolton
Birthop	*Lincoln* - Sleaford
Birthwaite	*Westmorland* - Kendal
Birtle	*Lancaster* - Bury
Birtle Dene	*Lancaster* - Bury
Birtles	*Cheshire* - Macclesfield
Birtley	*Durham* - Gateshead
Birtley	*Hereford* - Knighton
Birtley	*Northumberland* - Hexham
Birtsmorton	*Worcester* - Great Malvern
Bisbrooke	*Rutland* - Corby
Biscathorpe	*Lincoln* - Louth
Biscovey	*Cornwall* - St. Austell
Bisham	*Berks* - High Wycombe
Bishampton	*Worcester* - Evesham
Bishmill	*Devon* - Barnstaple
Bishop Auckland	*Durham* - Bishop Auckland
Bishopbridge	*Lincoln* - Lincoln
Bishop Burton	*York, E.R.* - Beverley
Bishop Middleham	*Durham* - Durham
Bishop Monkton	*York, W.R.* - Harrogate
Bishop Norton	*Lincoln* - Scunthorpe

BIS - BIX

Bishopsbourne	*Kent* - Canterbury
Bishop's Cannings	*Wilts* - Devizes
Bishop's Castle	*Salop* - Shrewsbury
Bishop's Caundle	*Dorset* - Yeovil
Bishop's Cleeve	*Gloucester* - Cheltenham
Bishop's Frome	*Hereford* - Hereford
Bishop's Green	*Berks* - Newbury
Bishop's Hull	*Somerset* - Taunton
Bishopside, High	*York, W.R.* - Harrogate
Bishopside, Low	*York, W.R.* - Harrogate
Bishop's Itchington	*Warwick* - Warwick
Bishop's Lavington	*Wilts* - Devizes
Bishops Lydeard	*Somerset* - Taunton
Bishops Nympton	*Devon* - Barnstaple
Bishop's Offley	*Stafford* - Market Drayton
Bishop's Stortford	*Herts* - Bishop's Stortford
Bishop's Sutton	*Hants* - Winchester
Bishop's Tachbrook	*Warwick* - Warwick
Bishop's Tawton	*Devon* - Barnstaple
Bishopsteignton	*Devon* - Newton Abbot
Bishopstoke	*Hants* - Southampton
Bishopston	*Gloucester* - Bristol
Bishopstone	*Bucks* - Aylesbury
Bishopstone	*Glamorgan* - Swansea
Bishopstone	*Hereford* - Hereford
Bishopstone	*Sussex* - Lewes
Bishopstone	*Wilts* - Salisbury
Bishopstone	*Wilts* - Swindon
Bishopstrow	*Wilts* - Warminster
Bishop Sutton	*Somerset* - Bristol
Bishop's Waltham	*Hants* - Winchester
Bishopswood	*Hereford* - Monmouth
Bishopswood	*Somerset* - Taunton
Bishopswood	*Stafford* - Wolverhampton
Bishopswood	*Worcester* - Kidderminster
Bishopsworth	*Somerset* - Bristol
Bishop Thornton	*York, W.R.* - Harrogate
Bishop Thorpe	*Lincoln* - Great Grimsby
Bishopthorpe	*York, W.R.* - York
Bishopton	*Durham* - Stockton on Tees
Bishopton	*Warwick* - Stratford on Avon
Bishopton	*York, W.R.* - Harrogate
Bishopwearmouth	*Durham* - Sunderland
Bishop Wilton	*York, E.R.* - York
Bishpool	*Monmouth* - Newport (Mon.)
Bishport	*Somerset* - Bristol
Bishton	*Monmouth* - Newport (Mon.)
Bishton	*Stafford* - Stafford
Bisley	*Gloucester* - Stroud
Bisley	*Surrey* - Guildford
Bisley Camp	*Surrey* - Guildford
Bismore	*Gloucester* - Stroud
Bispham	*Lancaster* - Wigan
Bispham Green	*Lancaster* - Wigan
Bispham Hall	*Lancaster* - Wigan
Bissick	*Cornwall* - Truro
Bissoe (part)	*Cornwall* - Redruth
Bissoe (part)	*Cornwall* - Truro
Bissoe Bridge	*Cornwall* - Truro
Bisterne	*Hants* - Bournemouth
Bisterne Close	*Hants* - Bournemouth
Bitchburn Colliery	*Durham* - Bishop Auckland
Bitchburn, North	*Durham* - Bishop Auckland
Bitchett Common	*Kent* - Sevenoaks
Bitchfield	*Lincoln* - Grantham
Bitchfield	*Northumberland* - Newcastle upon Tyne
Biteabout	*Northumberland* - Berwick-upon-Tweed
Bittaford	*Devon* - Plymouth
Bittell, Lower	*Worcester* - Redditch
Bittell, Upper	*Worcester* - Redditch
Bittering	*Norfolk* - East Dereham
Bitterley	*Salop* - Ludlow
Bitterne	*Hants* - Southampton
Bitterscote	*Stafford* - Tamworth
Bittesby	*Leicester* - Rugby
Bitteswell	*Leicester* - Rugby
Bitton	*Gloucester* - Bristol
Bix	*Oxford* - Reading

Bixley	*Norfolk* - Norwich
Blabbs, The	*Warwick* - Birmingham
Blaby	*Leicester* - Leicester
Blackawton	*Devon* - Kingsbridge
Blackawton Forces	*Devon* - Kingsbridge
Black Bank	*Cambridge* - Ely
Black Bank	*Warwick* - Nuneaton
Blackbeck	*Cumberland* - Whitehaven
Blackborough	*Devon* - Tiverton
Blackbourton	*Oxford* - Witney
Blackboys	*Sussex* - Lewes
Black Brook	*Derby* - Buxton
Blackbrook	*Derby* - Derby
Blackbrook	*Lancaster* - St. Helens
Blackbrook (Garswood)	*Lancaster* - Wigan
Blackbrook	*Leicester* - Loughborough
Blackbrook (Weeford)	*Stafford* - Lichfield
Blackbrook	*Stafford* - Stoke-on-Trent
Blackbrook	*Surrey* - Dorking
Blackbrook	*Worcester* - Redditch
Black Bull	*Stafford* - Congleton
Blackburn	*Lancaster* - Blackburn
Blackburn	*York, W.R.* - Rotherham
Blackburn Meadows	*York, W.R.* - Sheffield
Blackbushe	*Hants* - Aldershot and Farnham
Black Callerton	*Northumberland* - Newcastle upon Tyne
Black Carts and Rye Hill	*Northumberland* - Hexham
Black Cleugh	*Northumberland* - Hexham
Black Dean, East	*Durham* - Bishop Auckland
Black Dean, West	*Durham* - Bishop Auckland
Blackden	*Cheshire* - Congleton
Black Dog	*Devon* - Tiverton
Black Dog	*Lancaster* - Barrow-in-Furness
Blackdown	*Devon* - Plymouth
Black Down	*Dorset* - Yeovil
Blackdown	*Surrey* - Aldershot and Farnham
Blackdown	*Sussex* - Chichester
Blackdown	*Warwick* - Warwick
Black Dyke	*Cumberland* - Carlisle
Black Dyke Lane	*York, W.R.* - Bradford
Blacker	*York, W.R.* - Barnsley
Blackerwyke	*Northants* - Stamford
Blackett Terrace	*Northumberland* - Hexham
Black Fell	*Durham* - Gateshead
Black Fen	*Kent* - Dartford
Blackfield	*Hants* - Southampton
Blackford	*Cumberland* - Carlisle
Blackford	*Salop* - Ludlow
Blackford	*Somerset* - Wells
Blackford (Wincanton)	*Somerset* - Yeovil
Blackford Bridge	*Lancaster* - Bury
Blackfordby	*Leicester* - Ashby-de-la-Zouch
Blackfords	*Stafford* - Walsall
Blackfriars	*London, E.C.4* - Mayor's and City of London
Blackfriars	*London, S.E.1* - Southwark
Blackgang	*I. of W.* - Newport (I.W.)
Black Gate	*Durham* - Durham
Black Gates	*York, W.R.* - Dewsbury
Black Green	*Herts* - St. Albans
Blackhall	*Durham* - Hartlepool
Blackhall Mill	*Durham* - Newcastle upon Tyne
Blackhall Rocks	*Durham* - Hartlepool
Blackham	*Sussex* - East Grinstead
Blackheath (part)	*London, S.E.3* - Bromley
Blackheath (part)	*London, S.E.3* - Woolwich
Blackheath	*Stafford* - Dudley
Blackheath	*Surrey* - Guildford
Blackheath (part)	*Worcester* - Stourbridge
Black Heddon	*Northumberland* - Newcastle upon Tyne
Black Hill	*Durham* - Consett
Black Hole Drove	*Lincoln* - Spalding
Black Horse	*Durham* - Durham
Black Horse Drove	*Cambridge* - Ely
Black House	*Durham* - Durham
Black House	*Hereford* - Monmouth
Black Ladies	*Stafford* - Wolverhampton

Black Lake	*Stafford* - Stoke-on-Trent
Blacklands	*Kent* - Rochester
Blacklands	*Wilts* - Chippenham
Black Lane	*Lancaster* - Bury
Blackley	*Lancaster* - Manchester
Blackley	*York, W.R.* - Halifax
Blackmanstone	*Kent* - Ashford
Blackmill	*Glamorgan* - Bridgend
Blackmoor	*Hants* - Aldershot and Farnham
Blackmoor	*Lancaster* - Leigh
Blackmoor	*Lincoln* - Lincoln
Blackmoorfoot	*York, W.R.* - Huddersfield
Blackmore	*Essex* - Brentwood
Blackmore End	*Herts* - Hitchin
Blacknest	*Hants* - Aldershot and Farnham
Blacknoll	*Dorset* - Swanage
Black Notley	*Essex* - Braintree
Blacko	*Lancaster* - Nelson
Blackoe	*Salop* - Whitchurch
Black Park	*Denbigh* - Wrexham
Black Park	*Salop* - Whitchurch
Blackpill	*Glamorgan* - Swansea
Blackpool	*Devon* - Kingsbridge
Blackpool	*Devon* - Plymouth
Blackpool	*Lancaster* - Blackpool
Blackrock	*Brecon* - Pontypool and Abergavenny
Black Rock	*Cornwall* - Redruth
Blackrock	*Lancaster* - Ashton-under-Lyne
Blackrod	*Lancaster* - Wigan
Blackshaw	*York, W.R.* - Todmorden
Blackshaw Moor	*Stafford* - Leek
Blackstone	*Worcester* - Kidderminster
Blackstone	*Sussex* - Brighton
Blackthorn	*Oxford* - Oxford
Blacktoft	*York, E.R.* - Goole
Blacktoft Grange	*York, E.R.* - Goole
Black Torrington	*Devon* - Bideford
Blackwall	*London, E.14* - Bow
Blackwater	*Cornwall* - Truro
Blackwater (Christchurch)	*Hants* - Bournemouth
Blackwater	*Hants* - Aldershot and Farnham
Blackwater	*I. of W.* - Newport (I.W.)
Blackwell	*Cumberland* - Carlisle
Blackwell	*Derby* - Alfreton
Blackwell	*Derby* - Buxton
Blackwell	*Warwick* - Stratford on Avon
Blackwell	*Worcester* - Bromsgrove
Blackwell Mill	*Derby* - Buxton
Blackwells End	*Gloucester* - Gloucester
Blackwood	*Monmouth* - Blackwood
Blackwood	*Stafford* - Leek
Blacky Boy	*Durham* - Durham
Blacon	*Cheshire* - Chester
Bladon	*Oxford* - Oxford
Bladon Heath	*Oxford* - Oxford
Blaenanerch	*Cardigan* - Cardigan
Blaenau Festiniog	*Merioneth* - Portmadoc
Blaenaugwent	*Monmouth* - Blackwood
Blaenavon	*Monmouth* - Pontypool and Abergavenny
Blaencaerau	*Glamorgan* - Bridgend
Blaenclydach	*Glamorgan* - Pontypridd
Blaencwm	*Glamorgan* - Pontypridd
Blaenduar	*Brecon* - Pontypool and Abergavenny
Blaenffos	*Pembroke* - Cardigan
Blaengarw	*Glamorgan* - Bridgend
Blaengwynfi	*Glamorgan* - Neath
Blaenllechau	*Glamorgan* - Pontypridd
Blaenogwr	*Glamorgan* - Bridgend
Blaenpennal	*Cardigan* - Lampeter
Blaenplwyf	*Cardigan* - Aberystwyth
Blaenorth	*Cardigan* - Cardigan
Blaenrhondda	*Glamorgan* - Pontypridd
Blaenwaun	*Carmarthen* - Carmarthen
Blaenycoed	*Carmarthen* - Carmarthen
Blaenymaes	*Glamorgan* - Swansea
Blagdon	*Cornwall* - Launceston

BLA - BLE

Blagdon	*Northumberland* - Morpeth
Blagdon	*Somerset* - Wells
Blagdon Hill	*Somerset* - Taunton
Blagill	*Cumberland* - Carlisle
Blagill Head	*Cumberland* - Carlisle
Blaina	*Monmouth* - Blackwood
Blaisdon	*Gloucester* - Gloucester
Blaithwaite	*Cumberland* - Carlisle
Blaize Bailey	*Gloucester* - Gloucester
Blakedown	*Worcester* - Kidderminster
Blakehurst	*Sussex* - Chichester
Blakelaw	*Northumberland* - Newcastle upon Tyne
Blakely Hal	*Stafford* - West Bromwich
Blakelow	*Stafford* - Stoke-on-Trent
Blakemere	*Hereford* - Hereford
Blakenall	*Stafford* - Walsall
Blakeney	*Gloucester* - Gloucester
Blakeney	*Norfolk* - Norwich
Blakeney Hill	*Gloucester* - Gloucester
Blakenhall	*Leicester* - Rugby
Blakenhall	*Stafford* - Wolverhampton
Blakenham, Great	*Suffolk* - Ipswich
Blakenham, Little	*Suffolk* - Ipswich
Blakenham Magna	*Suffolk* - Ipswich
Blakenham Parva	*Suffolk* - Ipswich
Blakeshall	*Worcester* - Kidderminster
Blakesley	*Northampton* - Northampton
Blakesley Hall (Yardley)	*Warwick* - Birmingham
Blakesware	*Hertford* - Hertford
Blakeway	*Salop* - Shrewsbury
Blakey	*York, N.R.* - Malton
Blanchland	*Northumberland* - Consett
Blandford	*Dorset* - Wimborne Minster
Blandford Camp	*Dorset* - Wimborne Minster
Blandford Forum	*Dorset* - Wimborne Minster
Blandford St. Mary	*Dorset* - Wimborne Minster
Blankney	*Lincoln* - Sleaford
Blankney Fen	*Lincoln* - Sleaford
Blashenwell	*Dorset* - Swanage
Blashford	*Hants* - Salisbury
Blaston	*Leicester* - Corby
Blatchbridge	*Somerset* - Frome
Blatchington West	*Sussex* - Brighton
Blatherwycke	*Northampton* - Peterborough
Blawith	*Lancaster* - Barrow-in-Furness
Blaxhall	*Suffolk* - Woodbridge
Blaxton	*York, W.R.* - Doncaster
Blaydon	*Durham* - Newcastle upon Tyne
Blaydon Burn	*Durham* - Newcastle upon Tyne
Blaydon Haughs	*Durham* - Newcastle upon Tyne
Blayney Row	*Northumberland* - Newcastle upon Tyne
Blazefield	*York, W.R.* - Harrogate
Bleach Green	*Durham* - Newcastle upon Tyne
Bleadney	*Somerset* - Wells
Bleadon	*Somerset* - Weston Super Mare
Bleak Hill	*Hants* - Salisbury
Bleak Hill	*Lancaster* - St. Helens
Blean	*Kent* - Canterbury
Bleasby	*Lincoln* - Louth
Bleasby	*Notts* - Newark
Bleasby Moor	*Lincoln* - Louth
Bleasdale	*Lancaster* - Lancaster
Bleatarn	*Westmorland* - Penrith
Bleathwood	*Hereford* - Ludlow
Bleddfa	*Radnor* - Knighton
Bledington	*Gloucester* - Cheltenham
Bledlow	*Bucks* - High Wycombe
Bledlow Ridge	*Bucks* - High Wycombe
Blencarn	*Cumberland* - Penrith
Blencogo	*Cumberland* - Carlisle
Blencow	*Cumberland* - Penrith
Blendworth	*Hants* - Petersfield
Blenheim	*Oxford* - Oxford
Blenheim, Little	*Oxford* - Oxford
Blenheim Park	*Oxford* - Oxford
Blennerhasset	*Cumberland* - Carlisle
Bletchingdon	*Oxford* - Oxford
Bletchingley	*Surrey* - Reigate

BLE - BOA

Bletchley	*Bucks* - Bletchley and Leighton Buzzard
Bletchley	*Salop* - Market Drayton
Bletherstone	*Pembroke* - Haverfordwest
Bletsoe	*Beds* - Bedford
Blewbury	*Berks* - Didcot
Blickling	*Norfolk* - Norwich
Blidworth	*Notts* - Mansfield
Blidworth Bottoms	*Notts* - Mansfield
Blindbothel	*Cumberland* - Workington
Blindcrake	*Cumberland* - Workington
Blindley Heath	*Surrey* - Reigate
Blisland	*Cornwall* - Bodmin
Blissford	*Hants* - Salisbury
Bliss Gate	*Worcester* - Kidderminster
Blisworth	*Northampton* - Northampton
Blithbury	*Stafford* - Lichfield
Blithfield	*Stafford* - Uttoxeter
Blitterlees	*Cumberland* - Carlisle
Blockhouse	*Worcester* - Worcester
Blockley	*Gloucester* - Evesham
Blodwell	*Salop* - Oswestry
Blofield	*Norfolk* - Norwich
Blo'Norton	*Norfolk* - Norwich
Bloomfield	*Stafford* - Dudley
Bloomfield	*Stafford* - West Bromwich
Blooming Heather	*Cumberland* - Carlisle
Bloomsbury (part)	*London, W.C.1* - Bloomsbury and Marylebone
Bloomsbury (part)	*London, W.C.1* - Clerkenwell
Bloomsbury (part)	*London, W.C.1* - Westminster
Bloomsbury (part)	*London, W.C.2* - Westminster
Bloomsbury	*Salop* - Wellington (Salop)
Bloomsbury	*Warwick* - Birmingham
Blore	*Stafford* - Leek
Blore	*Stafford* - Market Drayton
Blore Pipe	*Stafford* - Stafford
Blossomfield	*Warwick* - Birmingham
Blounts Green	*Stafford* - Uttoxeter
Blowers Green	*Worcester* - Dudley
Blowty	*Montgomery* - Welshpool
Bloxham	*Oxford* - Banbury
Bloxholme	*Lincoln* - Sleaford
Bloxwich	*Stafford* - Walsall
Bloxwich, Little	*Stafford* - Walsall
Bloxworth	*Dorset* - Swanage
Blubberhouses	*York, W.R.* - Otley
Blue Anchor	*Cornwall* - Truro
Blue Anchor	*Somerset* - Minehead
Blue Ball	*Somerset* - Taunton
Blue Bell	*Montgomery* - Welshpool
Blue Bell	*Salop* - Wellington
Bluebell Hill	*Kent* - Rochester
Blue Hill	*Herts* - Hertford
Blue Town (Sheerness)	*Kent* - Sheerness
Blundellsands	*Lancaster* - Liverpool
Blundeston	*Suffolk* - Lowestoft
Blunham	*Beds* - Biggleswade
Blunsdon	*Wilts* - Swindon
Bluntington	*Worcester* - Kidderminster
Bluntisham	*Hunts* - Huntingdon
Blunts	*Cornwall* - Liskeard
Blurton	*Stafford* - Stoke-on-Trent
Blyborough	*Lincoln* - Gainsborough
Blyford	*Suffolk* - Halesworth
Blymhill	*Stafford* - Stafford
Blymhill Common	*Stafford* - Stafford
Blymhill Lawn	*Stafford* - Stafford
Blymhill Marsh	*Stafford* - Stafford
Blyth	*Northumberland* - Blyth
Blyth	*Notts* - Worksop
Blythburgh	*Suffolk* - Halesworth
Blythe Bridge	*Stafford* - Stoke-on-Trent
Blythe Bridge (Kingston)	*Stafford* - Uttoxeter
Blythe Marsh	*Stafford* - Stoke-on-Trent
Blythfield	*Stafford* - Uttoxeter
Blyth, South	*Northumberland* - Blyth
Blyton	*Lincoln* - Gainsborough
Boak End	*York, N.R.* - Scarborough

BOA - BOL

Boarded Barns	*Essex* - Chelmsford
Boarhunt	*Hants* - Portsmouth
Boarhunt, North	*Hants* - Portsmouth
Boarshaw	*Lancaster* - Oldham
Boars Head	*Kent* - Tunbridge Wells
Boars Head	*Lancaster* - Wigan
Boar's Hill	*Berks* - Oxford
Boarstall	*Bucks* - Thame
Bobbing	*Kent* - Sittingbourne
Bobbington	*Stafford* - Stourbridge
Bobbingworth	*Essex* - Harlow
Bobs Smithy	*Lancaster* - Bolton
Bockenfield	*Northumberland* - Morpeth
Bockhampton	*Dorset* - Dorchester
Bockhampton	*Hants* - Bournemouth
Bocking	*Essex* - Braintree
Bocking	*York, W.R.* - Keighley
Bockleton	*Worcester* - Leominster
Boconnoc	*Cornwall* - Liskeard
Bodaioch	*Montgomery* - Newtown
Boddington	*Gloucester* - Cheltenham
Boddington, Lower	*Northampton* - Banbury
Boddington, Upper	*Northampton* - Banbury
Bodedern	*Anglesey* - Llangefni
Bodelva	*Cornwall* - St. Austell
Bodelwyddan	*Flint* - Rhyl
Bodenham	*Hereford* - Leominster
Bodenham	*Wilts* - Salisbury
Bodfach	*Montgomery* - Oswestry
Bodfari	*Flint* - Denbigh
Bodferin	*Caernarvon* - Portmadoc
Bodham	*Norfolk* - Norwich
Bodiam	*Sussex* - Hastings
Bodicote	*Oxford* - Banbury
Bodilly	*Cornwall* - Penzance
Bodinnick	*Cornwall* - Liskeard
Bodle Street Green	*Sussex* - Eastbourne
Bodlith	*Denbigh* - Oswestry
Bodmin	*Cornwall* - Bodmin
Bodnant	*Denbigh* - Conway
Bodran	*Montgomery* - Oswestry
Bodvean	*Caernarvon* - Portmadoc
Bodwrog	*Anglesey* - Llangefni
Bodyddon	*Montgomery* - Oswestry
Bodymoor Heath	*Warwick* - Tamworth
Bodynfol	*Montgomery* - Oswestry
Bog Head	*Northumberland* - Hexham
Bogmoor	*Stafford* - Stafford
Bognor Regis	*Sussex* - Chichester
Bog, The	*Salop* - Shrewsbury
Bohetherick	*Cornwall* - Liskeard
Bojewyan	*Cornwall* - Penzance
Bolam	*Durham* - Bishop Auckland
Bolam	*Northumberland* - Newcastle upon Tyne
Bolam Vicarage	*Northumberland* - Newcastle upon Tyne
Bolas, Great	*Salop* - Market Drayton
Bolas, Great	*Salop* - Wellington (Salop)
Bolas, Little	*Salop* - Market Drayton
Bolas Magna	*Salop* - Market Drayton
Bolas Magna	*Salop* - Wellington (Salop)
Bolas Parva	*Salop* - Market Drayton
Bolberry	*Devon* - Kingsbridge
Bold	*Lancaster* - St. Helens
Boldershaw	*Stafford* - Uttoxeter
Boldmere	*Warwick* - Birmingham
Boldon Colliery	*Durham* - South Shields
Boldon, East	*Durham* - South Shields
Boldon, South	*Durham* - South Shields
Boldre	*Hants* - Lymington
Boldre, East	*Hants* - Lymington
Boldron	*York, N.R.* - Bishop Auckland
Boldventure	*Cornwall* - St. Austell
Bole	*Notts* - Gainsborough
Bolehall	*Stafford* - Tamworth
Bole Hill	*Derby* - Matlock
Bolenowe	*Cornwall* - Redruth
Bolesworth	*Cheshire* - Chester
Bolham	*Devon* - Tiverton

BOL - BOO

Bolham	Notts - East Retford
Bolham Water	*Devon* - Taunton
Bolingbroke Fen	*Lincoln* - Skegness
Bolingbroke, New	*Lincoln* - Boston
Bolingey	*Cornwall* - Truro
Bollihope	*Durham* - Bishop Auckland
Bollington	*Cheshire* - Altrincham
Bollington	*Cheshire* - Macclesfield
Bollington Cross	*Cheshire* - Macclesfield
Bollow	*Gloucester* - Gloucester
Bolney	*Sussex* - Haywards Heath
Bolnhurst	*Beds* - Bedford
Bolsover	*Derby* - Chesterfield
Bolsterstone	*York, W.R.* - Sheffield
Bolstone	*Hereford* - Hereford
Boltby	*York, N.R.* - Northallerton
Bolt Head	*Devon* - Kingsbridge
Bolton	*Lancaster* - Bolton
Bolton	*Northumberland* - Alnwick
Bolton	*Westmorland* - Penrith
Bolton	*York, E.R.* - York
Bolton	*York, W.R.* - Bradford
Bolton Abbey	*York, W.R.* - Skipton
Bolton Bridge	*York, W.R.* - Skipton
Bolton-by-Bowland	*York, W.R.* - Blackburn
Boltonfell	*Cumberland* - Carlisle
Bolton Gate	*Cumberland* - Carlisle
Bolton Ground	*Lancaster* - Barrow-in-Furness
Bolton-le-Sands	*Lancaster* - Lancaster
Bolton Low Houses	*Cumberland* - Carlisle
Bolton New Houses	*Cumberland* - Carlisle
Bolton Park	*Cumberland* - Carlisle
Bolton Percy	*York, W.R.* - York
Boltons	*Cumberland* - Carlisle
Bolton-upon-Derne	*York, W.R.* - Doncaster
Bolton-upon-Swale	*York, N.R.* - Darlington
Bolton with Redmire	*York, N.R.* - Northallerton
Bolton Woods	*York, W.R.* - Bradford
Bolventor (Part)	*Cornwall* - Launceston
Bolventor (Part)	*Cornwall* - Liskeard
Bomarsund	*Northumberland* - Blyth
Bomere Heath	*Salop* - Shrewsbury
Bonby	*Lincoln* - Scunthorpe
Boncath	*Pembroke* - Cardigan
Bonchurch	*I. of W.* - Newport (I.W.)
Bondleigh	*Devon* - Okehampton
Bonds	*Lancaster* - Preston
Bondsmain	*Derby* - Chesterfield
Bonehill	*Stafford* - Tamworth
Boney Hay	*Stafford* - Litchfield
Bonfire Hill	*Sussex* - Horsham
Boningale	*Salop* - Wolverhampton
Bonnington	*Kent* - Ashford
Bonsall	*Derby* - Matlock
Bonson	*Somerset* - Bridgwater
Bont	*Montgomery* - Machynlleth
Bontddu	*Merioneth* - Dolgellau
Bontdolgadfan	*Montgomery* - Machynlleth
Bontgoch	*Cardigan* - Aberystwyth
Bonthorpe	*Lincoln* - Skegness
Bontnewydd	*Caernarvon* - Caernarvon
Bontnewydd	*Denbigh* - Denbigh
Bontnewydd	*Merioneth* - Dolgellau
Bontuchel	*Denbigh* - Denbigh
Bonvilston	*Glamorgan* - Barry
Bonymaen	*Glamorgan* - Swansea
Boode	*Devon* - Barnstaple
Booker	*Bucks* - High Wycombe
Bookham, Great	*Surrey* - Epsom
Bookham, Little	*Surrey* - Epsom
Booley	*Salop* - Shrewsbury
Boon Hill	*Stafford* - Stoke-on-Trent
Boorley Green	*Hants* - Southampton
Boosbeck	*York, N.R.* - Middlesbrough
Boot	*Cumberland* - Whitehaven
Boothby	*Cumberland* - Carlisle
Boothby	*Lincoln* - Skegness
Boothby Graffoe	*Lincoln* - Lincoln
Boothby Pagnell	*Lincoln* - Grantham
Booth Dean	*York, W.R.* - Halifax

BOO - BOT

Booth Gate	*Derby* - Alfreton
Boothorpe	*Leicester* - Ashby-de-la-Zouch
Boothouse	*York, W.R.* - Huddersfield
Boothroydon	*Lancaster* - Manchester
Booths Farm	*Stafford* - Birmingham
Boothstown (Part)	*Lancs* - Leigh
Boothstown (Part)	*Lancaster* - Salford
Boothtown	*York, W.R.* - Halifax
Bootle	*Cumberland* - Whitehaven
Bootle	*Lancaster* - Liverpool
Booton	*Norfolk* - Norwich
Boozer Pit (Merriott)	*Somerset* - Yeovil
Boraston	*Salop* - Ludlow
Bordean	*Hants* - Petersfield
Borde Hill	*Sussex* - Haywards Heath
Borden	*Kent* - Sittingbourne
Borden Wood	*Sussex* - Petersfield
Border	*Cumberland* - Carlisle
Bordesley	*Warwick* - Birmingham
Bordesley	*Worcester* - Redditch
Bordesley Green	*Warwick* - Birmingham
Bordley	*York, W.R.* - Skipton
Bordon	*Hants* - Aldershot and Farnham
Boreatton	*Salop* - Shrewsbury
Boreham	*Essex* - Chelmsford
Boreham	*Wilts* - Warminster
Boreham Street	*Sussex* - Eastbourne
Boreham Wood	*Herts* - Barnet
Boreley	*Worcester* - Worcester
Boresford	*Hereford* - Knighton
Boresisle	*Kent* - Cranbrook
Boreton	*Salop* - Shrewsbury
Borley	*Essex* - Sudbury
Borley Green	*Herts* - Bishop's Stortford
Borough	*London, S.E.1* - Southwark
Boroughbridge	*York, W.R.* - Harrogate
Borough Fen	*Northampton* - Peterborough
Borough Green	*Kent* - Sevenoaks
Borras	*Denbigh* - Wrexham
Borrowash	*Derby* - Derby
Borrow Bridge	*Westmorland* - Kendal
Borrowby	*York, N.R.* - Northallerton
Borrowby	*York, N.R.* - Whitby
Borrowdale	*Cumberland* - Workington
Borstal	*Kent* - Rochester
Borth	*Cardigan* - Aberystwyth
Borthygest	*Caernarvon* - Portmadoc
Borwick	*Lancaster* - Lancaster
Bosbury	*Hereford* - Hereford
Boscastle	*Cornwall* - Launceston
Boscaswell	*Cornwall* - Penzance
Boscobel	*Salop* - Wolverhampton
Boscombe	*Hants* - Bournemouth
Boscombe	*Wilts* - Salisbury
Boscomoor	*Stafford* - Stafford
Boscoppa	*Cornwall* - St. Austell
Bosham	*Sussex* - Chichester
Bosherston	*Pembroke* - Haverfordwest
Bosleake	*Cornwall* - Redruth
Bosley	*Cheshire* - Macclesfield
Bosmere and Claydon	*Suffolk* - Ipswich
Bosom's End	*Stafford* - West Bromwich
Bosparva	*Cornwall* - Redruth
Bossall	*York, N.R.* - York
Bossiney	*Cornwall* - Launceston
Bossingham	*Kent* - Canterbury
Bossington	*Hants* - Winchester
Bossington	*Somerset* - Minehead
Bostall Heath (Part)	*London, S.E.2* - Dartford
Bostall Heath (Part)	*London, S.E.2* - Woolwich
Bostock	*Chester* - Northwich
Boston	*Lincoln* - Boston
Boston Longhedges	*Lincoln* - Boston
Boston Spa	*York, W.R.* - Leeds
Boston, West	*Lincoln* - Boston
Boswell	*Lincoln* - Louth
Boswin	*Cornwall* - Penzance
Botallack	*Cornwall* - Penzance
Botany	*Lancaster* - Chorley
Botany Bay	*Derby* - Burton-upon-Trent

BOT - BOU

Botany Bay	*Stafford* - Litchfield
Botcherby	*Cumberland* - Carlisle
Botcheston	*Leicester* - Leicester
Botesdale	*Suffolk* - Norwich
Bothal Demesne	*Northumberland* - Morpeth
Bothampstead	*Berks* - Newbury
Bothamsall	*Notts* - East Retford
Bothel	*Cumberland* - Workington
Bothenhampton	*Dorset* - Dorchester
Botley	*Berks* - Oxford
Botley	*Hants* - Southampton
Botley Hill	*Warwick* - Stratford-on-Avon
Botloes Green	*Gloucester* - Gloucester
Botolph Clayton	*Bucks* - Aylesbury
Botolphs	*Brighton* - Sussex
Bottesford	*Leicester* - Grantham
Bottesford	*Lincoln* - Scunthorpe
Bottisham	*Cambridge* - Cambridge
Bottlebrook	*Derby* - Ilkeston
Bottlesford	*Wilts* - Devizes
Bottom Boat	*York, W.R.* - Wakefield
Bottom, East	*Kent* - Dover
Bottom House	*Stafford* - Leek
Bottom, Old	*Kent* - Dover
Bottom o' the Moor	*Lancaster* - Bolton
Bottoms	*Lancaster* - Ashton-under-Lyne
Botton	*Lancaster* - Lancaster
Bottreaux Mill	*Devon* - Barnstaple
Botts Green	*Warwick* - Birmingham
Botusfleming	*Devon* - Plymouth
Botwell	*Middlesex* - Uxbridge
Botwnnog	*Caernarvon* - Portmadoc
Bough Beech	*Kent* - Tonbridge
Boughrood	*Radnor* - Brecknock
Boughton	*Cheshire* - Chester
Boughton	*Kent* - Canterbury
Boughton	*Lincoln* - Sleaford
Boughton	*Norfolk* - King's Lynn
Boughton	*Northampton* - Northampton
Boughton	*Notts* - Mansfield
Boughton	*Worcester* - Worcester
Boughton Aluph	*Kent* - Ashford
Boughton, Great	*Chester* - Chester
Boughton Lees	*Kent* - Ashford
Boughton Malherbe	*Kent* - Maidstone
Boughton Monchelsea	*Kent* - Maidstone
Boughton under Blean	*Kent* - Canterbury
Boulby	*York, N.R.* - Whitby
Boulby Barns	*York, N.R.* - Whitby
Bould	*Oxford* - Banbury
Boulder Clough	*York, W.R.* - Halifax
Bouldnor	*I. of W.* - Newport (I.W.)
Bouldon	*Salop* - Ludlow
Boulge	*Suffolk* - Woodbridge
Boulmer	*Northumberland* - Alnwick
Boulsbury	*Wilts* - Bournemouth
Boulsdon	*Gloucester* - Gloucester
Boulston	*Pembroke* - Haverfordwest
Boulter End	*Bucks* - High Wycombe
Boultham	*Lincoln* - Lincoln
Boundary	*Derby and Leicester* - Ashby-de-la-Zouch
Boundary	*Stafford* - Stoke-on-Trent
Bounds Cross	*Kent* - Cranbrook
Bounds Green	*London, N.11* - Edmonton
Bourn	*Cambridge* - Cambridge
Bournbrook	*Warwick* - Birmingham
Bourne	*Gloucester* - Stroud
Bourne	*Lincoln* - Spalding
Bourne End, Cranfield	*Beds* - Bedford
Bourne End	*Bucks* - High Wycombe
Bourne End	*Herts* - Hemel Hempstead
Bourneheath	*Worcester* - Bromsgrove
Bourne, Lower	*Surrey* - Aldershot and Farnham
Bournemouth	*Hants* - Bournemouth
Bournes Green	*Gloucester* - Stroud
Bournes Green	*Worcester* - Kidderminster
Bourne South Fen	*Lincoln* - Spalding
Bourne, Upper	*Surrey* - Aldershot and Farnham
Bournville	*Warwick* - Birmingham

BOU - BOW

Bourton	*Berks* - Swindon
Bourton	*Dorset* - Shaftesbury
Bourton	*Salop* - Bridgnorth
Bourton	*Somerset* - Bristol
Bourton	*Warwick* - Rugby
Bourton	*Wilts* - Devizes
Bourton, Great	*Oxford* - Banbury
Bourton, Little	*Oxford* - Banbury
Bourton, Lower	*Berks* - Swindon
Bourton-on-the-Hill	*Gloucester* - Evesham
Bourton, West	*Dorset* - Shaftesbury
Boustead Hill	*Cumberland* - Carlisle
Bouthrop	*Gloucester* - Cirencester
Bouthwaite	*York, W.R.* - Harrogate
Boveney	*Bucks* - Slough
Boveridge	*Dorset* - Wimborne Minster
Boverton	*Glamorgan* - Bridgend
Boveton on the Water	*Gloucester* - Cheltenham
Bovey, North	*Devon* - Newton Abbot
Bovey Tracey	*Devon* - Newton Abbot
Bovingdon	*Herts* - Hemel Hempstead
Bovingdon's Green	*Bucks* - High Wycombe
Bovington	*Dorset* - Dorchester
Bovisand	*Devon* - Plymouth
Bow	*Devon* - Exeter
Bow	*London, E.3* - Bow
Bow Brickill	*Bucks* - Bletchley and Leighton Buzzard
Bow Bridge	*Devon* - Torquay
Bowbridge	*Gloucester* - Stroud
Bowburn	*Durham* - Durham
Bowcombe	*Devon* - Kingsbridge
Bowd	*Devon* - Exeter
Bowden	*Somerset* - Yeovil
Bowden Edge	*Derby* - Buxton
Bowden, Great	*Leicester* - Kettering
Bowden Head	*Derby* - Buxton
Bowden Hill	*Wilts* - Chippenham
Bowden, Little	*Northampton* - Kettering
Bowdon	*Cheshire* - Altrincham
Bower Ashton	*Somerset* - Bristol
Bower Chalke	*Wilts* - Salisbury
Bower, East	*Somerset* - Bridgwater
Bower End	*Stafford* - Stoke-on-Trent
Bower Heath	*Herts* - St. Albans
Bowerhill	*Wilts* - Chippenham
Bower Hinton	*Somerset* - Yeovil
Bowers	*Stafford* - Stoke-on-Trent
Bowers Gifford	*Essex* - Brentwood
Bowers' Row	*York, W.R.* - Pontefract
Bower, West	*Somerset* - Bridgwater
Bowes	*York, N.R.* - Bishop Auckland
Bowes Park	*London, N.11* - Edmonton
Bowes Park	*London, N.22* - Edmonton
Bowford	*Sussex* - Chichester
Bowithick	*Cornwall* - Launceston
Bowland Bridge	*Westmorland* - Kendal
Bowland Forest High	*York, W.R.* - Preston
Bowland with Leagram	*Lancaster* - Preston
Bowlee	*Lancaster* - Oldham
Bowlees	*Durham* - Bishop Auckland
Bowley Lane	*Hereford* - Leominster
Bowling Bank	*Denbigh* - Wrexham
Bowling, East	*York, W.R.* - Bradford
Bowling Green	*Stafford* - Dudley
Bowling, West	*York, W.R.* - Bradford
Bowness-on-Solway	*Cumberland* - Carlisle
Bowness-on-Windermere	*Westmorland* - Kendal
Bownham	*Gloucester* - Stroud
Bowood	*Derby* - Matlock
Bowood	*Wilts* - Chippenham
Bowring Park (part)	*Lancaster* - Liverpool
Bowring Park (part)	*Lancaster* - St. Helens
Bowscar	*Cumberland* - Penrith
Bowsden	*Northumberland* - Berwick-upon-Tweed
Bowsell Green	*Kent* - Sevenoaks
Bowsey Hill	*Berks* - Reading
Bowsey Wood	*Stafford* - Stoke-on-Trent
Bow Street	*Cardigan* - Aberystwyth

BOW - BRA

Bowthorpe	*Lincoln* - Spalding
Bowthorpe	*Norfolk* - Norwich
Bowthorpe	*York, E.R.* - York
Box	*Gloucester* - Stroud
Box	*Wilts* - Bath
Box End, Kempston	*Beds* - Bedford
Boxford	*Berks* - Newbury
Boxford	*Suffolk* - Sudbury
Boxgrove	*Sussex* - Chichester
Box Hill	*Surrey* - Dorking
Box Hill	*Wilts* - Bath
Boxley	*Kent* - Maidstone
Boxmoor	*Herts* - Hemel Hempstead
Boxted	*Essex* - Colchester
Boxted	*Suffolk* - Sudbury
Boxwell	*Gloucester* - Malmesbury
Boxworth	*Cambridge* - Cambridge
Boycott	*Salop* - Shrewsbury
Boylestone	*Derby* - Uttoxeter
Boyne Colliery	*Durham* - Durham
Boyne Hill	*Berks* - Slough
Boyne's Wood	*Hants* - Aldershot and Farnham
Boynton	*York, E.R.* - Bridlington
Boythorpe	*Derby* - Chesterfield
Boythorpe	*York, E.R.* - Beverley
Boyton	*Cornwall* - Launceston
Boyton	*Suffolk* - Woodbridge
Boyton	*Wilts* - Warminster
Boyton Cross	*Essex* - Chelmsford
Bozeat	*Northampton* - Wellingborough
Bozen Green	*Herts* - Bishop's Stortford
Bozenham Mill	*Northampton* - Northampton
Brabourne	*Kent* - Ashford
Brabourne Lees	*Kent* - Ashford
Brabourne Street	*Kent* - Ashford
Brabourne, West	*Kent* - Ashford
Braceborough	*Lincoln* - Stamford
Bracebridge	*Lincoln* - Lincoln
Bracebridge Heath	*Lincoln* - Lincoln
Braceby	*Lincoln* - Grantham
Bracewell	*York, W.R.* - Skipton
Bracken	*York, E.R.* - Beverley
Brackenborough	*Lincoln* - Louth
Brackenfield	*Derby* - Alfreton
Brackenhill	*Cumberland* - Carlisle
Bracken Hill	*York, W.R.* - Sheffield
Brackenhill	*York, W.R.* - Pontefract
Brackenhill	*York, W.R.* - York
Brackenholme with Woodhall	*York, E.R.* - York
Brackenlands	*Cumberland* - Carlisle
Bracken Moor	*York, W.R.* - Sheffield
Brackenthwaite	*Cumberland* - Carlisle
Brackenthwaite	*Cumberland* - Workington
Bracklesham	*Sussex* - Chichester
Brackley	*Northampton* - Banbury
Brackley Hatch	*Northampton* - Banbury
Bracknell	*Berks* - Reading
Bracon Ash	*Norfolk* - Norwich
Bradbury	*Durham* - Stockton on Tees
Bradden	*Northampton* - Northampton
Braddock	*Cornwall* - Liskeard
Bradeley	*Stafford* - Stoke-on-Trent
Bradenham	*Bucks* - High Wycombe
Bradenham, East	*Norfolk* - East Dereham
Bradenham, West	*Norfolk* - East Dereham
Braden Heath (part)	*Salop* - Oswestry
Braden Heath (part)	*Salop* - Whitchurch
Bradenstoke	*Wilts* - Chippenham
Bradestone	*Norfolk* - Norwich
Brades Village	*Worcester* - Dudley
Bradfield	*Berks* - Reading
Bradfield	*Essex* - Harwich
Bradfield	*Norfolk* - Norwich
Bradfield	*York, W.R.* - Sheffield
Bradfield Combust	*Suffolk* - Bury St. Edmunds
Bradfield Green	*Cheshire* - Crewe
Bradfield St. Clare	*Suffolk* - Bury St. Edmunds
Bradfield St. George	*Suffolk* - Bury St. Edmunds
Bradford	*Cornwall* - Bodmin

Bradford	*Devon* - Bideford
Bradford	*Lancaster* - Manchester
Bradford	*Northumberland* - Newcastle-upon-Tyne
Bradford	*York, W.R.* - Bradford
Bradford Abbas	*Dorset* - Yeovil
Bradford Leigh	*Wilts* - Trowbridge
Bradford-on-Avon	*Wilts* - Trowbridge
Bradford-on-Tone	*Somerset* - Taunton
Bradford Peverell	*Dorset* - Dorchester
Bradford, West	*York, W.R.* - Blackburn
Bradgate	*York, W.R.* - Rotherham
Bradiford	*Devon* - Barnstaple
Brading	*I. of W.* - Newport (I.W.)
Bradley	*Cheshire* - Whitchurch
Bradley	*Denbigh* - Wrexham
Bradley	*Derby* - Derby
Bradley	*Gloucester* - Stroud
Bradley	*Hants* - Basingstoke
Bradley	*Lincoln* - Great Grimsby
Bradley (Coseley)	*Stafford* - Wolverhampton
Bradley	*Stafford* - Stafford
Bradley (Bilston)	*Stafford* - Wolverhampton
Bradley	*Worcester* - Redditch
Bradley	*York, W.R.* - Huddersfield
Bradley Burn	*Durham* - Bishop Auckland
Bradley Fold	*Lancaster* - Bury
Bradley, Great	*Suffolk* - Newmarket
Bradley Green	*Cheshire* - Whitchurch
Bradley Green	*Worcester* - Redditch
Bradley High	*York, W.R.* - Skipton
Bradley Hill	*Gloucester* - Gloucester
Bradley-in-the-Moors	*Stafford* - Uttoxeter
Bradley, Little	*Suffolk* - Newmarket
Bradley, Low	*York, W.R.* - Skipton
Bradley, North	*Wilts* - Trowbridge
Bradley, West	*Somerset* - Wells
Bradmore	*Notts* - Nottingham
Bradmore	*Stafford* - Wolverhampton
Bradney	*Somerset* - Bridgwater
Bradninch	*Devon* - Tiverton
Bradnocks Marsh	*Warwick* - Coventry
Bradnop	*Stafford* - Leek
Bradon, South	*Somerset* - Axminster and Chard
Bradshaw	*Lancaster* - Bolton
Bradshaw	*York, W.R.* - Barnsley
Bradshaw	*York, W.R.* - Halifax
Bradshaw Edge	*Derby* - Buxton
Bradshott	*Hants* - Aldershot and Farnham
Bradstone	*Cornwall* - Launceston
Bradwall	*Cheshire* - Crewe
Bradway	*York, W.R.* - Sheffield
Bradwell	*Derby* - Buxton
Bradwell	*Stafford* - Stoke-on-Trent
Bradwell	*Suffolk* - Great Yarmouth
Bradwell Abbey	*Bucks* - Bletchley and Leighton Buzzard
Bradwell, New	*Bucks* - Bletchley and Leighton Buzzard
Bradwell next Coggeshall	*Essex* - Braintree
Bradwell, Old	*Bucks* - Bletchley and Leighton Buzzard
Bradwell-on-Sea	*Essex* - Maldon
Bradworthy	*Devon* - Bideford
Brafferton	*Durham* - Darlington
Brafferton	*York, N.R.* - York
Braffords	*York, E.R.* - Kingston-upon-Hull
Brafield-on-the-Green	*Northampton* - Northampton
Bragbury End	*Herts* - Hertford
Bragenham	*Bucks* - Bletchley and Leighton Buzzard
Braichmelyn	*Caernarvon* - Bangor
Brailes	*Warwick* - Banbury
Brailes, Lower	*Warwick* - Banbury
Brailes under Sutton	*Warwick* - Banbury
Brailes, Upper	*Warwick* - Banbury
Brailsford	*Derby* - Derby
Brains Green	*Gloucester* - Gloucester
Braintree	*Essex* - Braintree

Braiseworth	*Suffolk* - Norwich
Braishfield	*Hants* - Winchester
Braishfield, Lower	*Hants* - Winchester
Braistywoods	*York, W.R.* - Harrogate
Braithwaite	*Cumberland* - Workington
Braithwaite	*York, W.R.* - Doncaster
Braithwaite	*York, W.R.* - Harrogate
Braithwaite	*York, W.R.* - Keighley
Braithwaite, Low	*Cumberland* - Penrith
Braithwell	*York, W.R.* - Doncaster
Bramber	*Sussex* - Brighton
Bramber (Chichester)	*Sussex* - Chichester
Brambling	*Kent* - Canterbury
Brambridge	*Hants* - Winchester
Bramcote	*Notts* - Nottingham
Bramcote	*Warwick* - Tamworth
Bramcote	*Warwick* - Nuneaton
Bramdean	*Hants* - Winchester
Bramerton	*Norfolk* - Norwich
Bramfield	*Herts* - Hertford
Bramfield	*Suffolk* - Halesworth
Bramford	*Suffolk* - Ipswich
Bramhall	*Chester* - Stockport
Bramham	*York, W.R.* - Leeds
Bramhope	*York, W.R.* - Otley
Bramley	*Hants* - Basingstoke
Bramley	*Surrey* - Guildford
Bramley	*York, W.R.* - Leeds
Bramley	*York, W.R.* - Rotherham
Bramley Grange	*York, W.R.* - Harrogate
Bramley Lane	*York, W.R.* - Halifax
Bramley Vale	*Derby* - Chesterfield
Brampford Speke	*Devon* - Exeter
Brampton	*Cumberland* - Carlisle
Brampton	*Derby* - Chesterfield
Brampton	*Hereford* - Hereford
Brampton	*Hunts* - Huntingdon
Brampton	*Lincoln* - Gainsborough
Brampton	*Norfolk* - Norwich
Brampton	*Suffolk* - Halesworth
Brampton	*Westmorland* - Penrith
Brampton Abbotts	*Hereford* - Monmouth
Brampton Ash	*Northampton* - Corby
Brampton Bierlow	*York, W.R.* - Rotherham
Brampton Bryan	*Hereford* - Knighton
Brampton-en-le-Morthen	*York, W.R.* - Rotherham
Brampton, Little	*Salop* - Ludlow
Brampton, Old	*Derby* - Chesterfield
Bramshall	*Stafford* - Uttoxeter
Bramshaw	*Hants and Wilts* - Southampton
Bramshill	*Hants* - Basingstoke
Bramshott	*Hants* - Petersfield
Bramwith, South	*York, W.R.* - Thorne
Bramwith Woodhouse	*York, W.R.* - Doncaster
Brancaster	*Norfolk* - King's Lynn
Brancepeth	*Durham* - Durham
Brancepeth Colliery	*Durham* - Durham
Brancepeth, New	*Durham* - Durham
Branch End	*York, W.R.* - Middlesbrough
Brandesburton	*York, E.R.* - Beverley
Brandeston	*Suffolk* - Woodbridge
Brandfold	*Kent* - Cranbrook
Brand Green	*Glos* - Gloucester
Brand Hill	*Salop* - Ludlow
Brandiscorner	*Devon* - Bideford
Brandiston	*Norfolk* - Norwich
Brandlee	*Salop* - Wellington (Salop)
Brandlesholme	*Lancaster* - Bury
Brandon	*Durham* - Durham
Brandon	*Lincoln* - Grantham
Brandon	*Suffolk* - Thetford
Brandon	*Northumberland* - Alnwick
Brandon	*Warwick* - Rugby
Brandon Parva	*Norfolk* - Norwich
Brandon Walls	*Durham* - Bishop Auckland
Brandon, West	*Durham* - Durham
Brandsby	*York, N.R.* - York
Brands Hill	*Bucks* - Slough
Brand Side	*Derby* - Buxton
Brand, The	*Salop* - Market Drayton

BRA - BRE

Brand Top	*Derby* - Buxton
Brandwood	*Salop* - Shrewsbury
Brandwood End	*Warwick* - Birmingham
Brandy Carr	*York, W.R.* - Wakefield
Brandy Wharf	*Lincoln* - Scunthorpe
Branksome	*Dorset* - Poole
Branksome Park	*Dorset* - Poole
Bransbury	*Hants* - Andover
Bransby	*Lincoln* - Gainsborough
Branscombe	*Devon* - Axminster
Bransdale	*York, N.R.* - Malton
Bransford	*Worcester* - Great Malvern
Bransgore	*Hants* - Bournemouth
Branston	*Leicester* - Melton Mowbray
Branston	*Lincoln* - Lincoln
Branston Booths	*Lincoln* - Lincoln
Branstone	*Stafford* - Burton-upon-Trent
Branston Fen	*Lincoln* - Lincoln
Branston Moor	*Lincoln* - Lincoln
Brant Broughton	*Lincoln* - Newark
Brantham	*Suffolk* - Ipswich
Branthwaite	*Cumberland* - Workington
Brantingham	*York, E.R.* - Beverley
Brantley	*Salop* - Bridgnorth
Branton	*Northumberland* - Alnwick
Branton	*York, W.R.* - Doncaster
Branton Green	*York, W.R.* - Harrogate
Branxton	*Northumberland* - Berwick-upon-Tweed
Brasside	*Durham* - Durham
Brassington Moor	*Derby* - Derby
Brasted	*Kent* - Sevenoaks
Brasted Chart	*Kent* - Sevenoaks
Bratch	*Stafford* - Wolverhampton
Brathay	*Lancaster* - Kendal
Brathay Hill	*Cumberland* - Workington
Bratoft	*Lincoln* - Skegness
Brattleby	*Lincoln* - Lincoln
Bratton	*Salop* - Wellington (Salop)
Bratton	*Wilts* - Trowbridge
Bratton Clovelly	*Devon* - Okehampton
Bratton Fleming	*Devon* - Barnstaple
Bratton Seymour	*Somerset* - Yeovil
Braughing	*Herts* - Bishop's Stortford
Braughing Friars	*Essex* - Bishop's Stortford
Brauncewell	*Lincoln* - Sleaford
Braunston	*Northampton* - Rugby
Braunston	*Rutland* - Melton Mowbray
Braunstone	*Leicester* - Leicester
Braunstone Frith	*Leicester* - Leicester
Braunton	*Devon* - Barnstaple
Brawby	*York, N.R.* - Malton
Brawdy	*Pembroke* - Haverfordwest
Braxted, Great	*Essex* - Maldon
Braxted, Little	*Essex* - Maldon
Bray	*Berks* - Slough
Braybrooke	*Northampton* - Kettering
Braydon	*Wilts* - Swindon
Brayfield	*Northampton* - Northampton
Brayfield, Cold	*Bucks* - Northampton
Brayford	*Devon* - Barnstaple
Bray Shop (part)	*Cornwall* - Launceston
Bray Shop (part)	*Cornwall* - Liskeard
Braystones	*Cumberland* - Whitehaven
Brayton	*Cumberland* - Carlisle
Brayton	*York, W.R.* - Selby
Bray Wick	*Berks* - Slough
Braziers Park	*Oxford* - Didcot
Brea	*Cornwall* - Redruth
Breach Hill	*Somerset* - Bristol
Breachwood Green	*Herts* - Hitchin
Breadsall	*Derby* - Derby
Breadstone	*Gloucester* - Stroud
Breage	*Cornwall* - Penzance
Bream	*Gloucester* - Monmouth
Breamfield	*Derby* - Matlock
Breamore	*Hants* - Salisbury
Bream's Eaves	*Gloucester* - Monmouth
Brean	*Somerset* - Weston Super Mare
Brearley	*York, W.R.* - Todmorden

BRE - BRI

Brearton	*York, W.R.* - Harrogate
Breaston	*Derby* - Derby
Brechfa (Part)	*Carmarthen* - Lampeter
Brechfa (Part)	*Carmarthen* - Carmarthen
Breckles	*Norfolk* - Thetford
Breckney Hill	*Northumberland* - Newcastle-upon-Tyne
Brecon	*Brecon* - Brecknock
Brecon Hill	*Durham* - Durham
Bredbury	*Cheshire* - Stockport
Brede	*Sussex* - Hastings
Bredenbury	*Hereford* - Hereford
Bredfield	*Suffolk* - Woodbridge
Bredgar	*Kent* - Sittingbourne
Bredhurst	*Kent* - Maidstone
Bredicot	*Worcester* - Worcester
Bredon	*Worcester* - Cheltenham
Bredon's Hardwicke	*Worcester* - Cheltenham
Bredon's Norton	*Worcester* - Cheltenham
Bredwardine	*Hereford* - Hereford
Bredy, Little	*Dorset* - Dorchester
Bredy, Long	*Dorset* - Dorchester
Breedon Brand	*Leicester* - Ashby-de-la-Zouch
Breedon-on-the-Hill	*Leicester* - Ashby-de-la-Zouch
Breedons Cross	*Warwick* - Birmingham
Breightmet (part)	*Lancaster* - Bolton
Breightmet (part)	*Lancaster* - Bury
Breightmet Fold	*Lancaster* - Bolton
Breighton and Gunby	*York, E.R.* - York
Breinton	*Hereford* - Hereford
Brelston Green	*Hereford* - Monmouth
Bremhill	*Wilts* - Chippenham
Brenchley	*Kent* - Tonbridge Wells
Brendon	*Devon* - Barnstaple
Brendon Hill	*Somerset* - Minehead
Brenkley	*Northumberland* - Newcastle upon Tyne
Brent	*London, N.W.11* - Willesden
Brent, East	*Somerset* - Weston Super Mare
Brent Eleigh	*Suffolk* - Sudbury
Brentfield	*London, N.W.10* - Willesden
Brentford	*Middlesex* - Brentford
Brentingby	*Leicester* - Melton Mowbray
Brent Knoll	*Somerset* - Weston Super Mare
Brentor	*Devon* - Plymouth
Brent Pelham	*Herts* - Bishop's Stortford
Brentry	*Gloucester* - Bristol
Brent, South	*Devon* - Torquay
Brent, South	*Somerset* - Weston Super Mare
Brentwater Estate	*London, N.W.2* - Willesden
Brentwater Estate	*London, N.W.10* - Willesden
Brentwood	*Essex* - Brentwood
Brenzett	*Kent* - Ashford
Brereton	*Cheshire* - Congleton
Brereton	*Stafford* - Stafford
Brereton Colliery	*Stafford* - Stafford
Bressingham	*Norfolk* - Norwich
Bretby	*Derby* - Burton-upon-Trent
Bretford	*Warwick* - Rugby
Bretforton	*Worcester* - Evesham
Bretherdale	*Westmorland* - Penrith
Bretherton	*Lancaster* - Chorley
Brettenham	*Norfolk* - Thetford
Brettenham	*Suffolk* - Stowmarket
Bretton	*Derby* - Buxton
Bretton	*Flint* - Chester
Bretton Clough	*Derby* - Buxton
Bretton, West	*York, W.R.* - Wakefield
Brewham, North	*Somerset* - Yeovil
Brewham, South	*Somerset* - Yeovil
Brewood	*Stafford* - Wolverhampton
Briants Puddle	*Dorset* - Dorchester
Briardene	*Northumberland* - North Shields
Briary Brook	*Stafford* - Stoke-on-Trent
Bricett, Great	*Suffolk* - Stowmarket
Bricett, Little	*Suffolk* - Stowmarket
Brickendon	*Herts* - Hertford
Bricket Wood	*Herts* - St. Albans
Brickhill, Great	*Bucks* - Bletchley and Leighton Buzzard

Brickhill, Little	*Bucks* - Bletchley and Leighton Buzzard
Brickhouse Farm Estate	*Stafford* - Dudley
Bricklehampton	*Worcester* - Evesham
Bridekirk	*Cumberland* - Workington
Bridell	*Pembroke* - Cardigan
Bridestowe	*Devon* - Okehampton
Bridford	*Devon* - Exeter
Bridge	*Cornwall* - Redruth
Bridge	*Kent* - Canterbury
Bridge End	*Cumberland* - Carlisle
Bridge End	*Cumberland* - Workington
Bridge End (Levens)	*Westmorland* - Kendal
Bridgegate	*Lancaster* - Barrow-in-Furness
Bridgehall	*Cheshire* - Stockport
Bridgehampton	*Somerset* - Yeovil
Bridge Hewick	*York, W.R.* - Harrogate
Bridge Hill	*Durham* - Consett
Bridgehouse Gate	*York, W.R.* - Harrogate
Bridgemarsh Island	*Essex* - Maldon
Bridgemere	*Cheshire* - Crewe
Bridgemont	*Derby* - Buxton
Bridgend	*Glamorgan* - Bridgend
Bridgend (Stonehouse)	*Gloucester* - Stroud
Bridgend	*Worcester* - Cheltenham
Bridgerule, East	*Devon* - Launceston
Bridgerule, West	*Devon* - Launceston
Bridges	*Cornwall* - Bodmin
Bridges	*Salop* - Shrewsbury
Bridge Sollars	*Hereford* - Hereford
Bridge Town	*Cornwall* - Launceston
Bridgetown	*Devon* - Launceston
Bridgetown	*Somerset* - Tiverton
Bridge Trafford	*Cheshire* - Chester
Bridge Yate	*Gloucester* - Bristol
Bridgford, East	*Notts* - Nottingham
Bridgford, Great	*Stafford* - Stafford
Bridgford, Little	*Stafford* - Stafford
Bridgford, West	*Notts* - Nottingham
Bridgham	*Norfolk* - Thetford
Bridgmary	*Hants* - Portsmouth
Bridgnorth	*Salop* - Bridgnorth
Bridgtown	*Stafford* - Walsall
Bridgwater	*Somerset* - Bridgwater
Bridlington	*York, E.R.* - Bridlington
Bridport	*Dorset* - Dorchester
Bridstow	*Hereford* - Monmouth
Briercliffe	*Lancaster* - Burnley
Brierfield	*Lancaster* - Nelson
Brierley	*Gloucester* - Gloucester
Brierley	*Hereford* - Leominster
Brierley	*York, W.R.* - Barnsley
Brierley Hill	*Hereford* - Knighton
Brierley Hill	*Stafford* - Stourbridge
Briery	*Cumberland* - Workington
Briestfield	*York, W.R.* - Dewsbury
Brigg	*Lincoln* - Scunthorpe
Briggswath	*York, N.R.* - Whitby
Brigham	*Cumberland* - Workington
Brigham	*York, E.R.* - Beverley
Brighouse	*York, W.R.* - Halifax
Brighstone	*I. of W.* - Newport (I.W.)
Brighthampton	*Oxford* - Witney
Brightholmlee	*York, W.R.* - Sheffield
Brightley	*Devon* - Okehampton
Brightley	*Devon* - Barnstaple
Brightling	*Sussex* - Hastings
Brightlingsea	*Essex* - Colchester
Brighton	*Cornwall* - Truro
Brighton	*Sussex* - Brighton
Brighton, New	*Cheshire* - Birkenhead
Brighton, New	*Hants* - Portsmouth
Brighton, New	*York, W.R.* - Bradford
Brightside	*York, W.R.* - Sheffield
Brightwalton	*Berks* - Didcot
Brightwell	*Berks* - Didcot
Brightwell	*Suffolk* - Woodbridge
Brightwell Baldwin	*Oxford* - Didcot
Brignall	*York, N.R.* - Darlington
Brigmerston	*Wilts* - Salisbury

Brigsley	*Lincoln* - Great Grimsby
Brigsteer	*Westmorland* - Kendal
Brigstock	*Northampton* - Kettering
Brill	*Bucks* - Thame
Brill	*Cornwall* - Truro and Falmouth
Brilley	*Hereford* - Hereford
Brimfield	*Hereford* - Ludlow
Brimham Rocks	*York, W.R.* - Harrogate
Brimington	*Derby* - Chesterfield
Brimmington Common	*Derby* - Chesterfield
Brimington, New	*Derby* - Chesterfield
Brimpsfield	*Gloucester* - Cheltenham
Brimpton	*Berks* - Newbury
Brimpton	*Oxford* - Thame
Brimpts	*Devon* - Plymouth
Brimscombe	*Gloucester* - Stroud
Brimsdown	*Middlesex* - Edmonton
Brimstage	*Cheshire* - Birkenhead
Brind	*York, E.R.* - Goole
Brindle	*Lancaster* - Chorley
Brindley	*Cheshire* - Crewe
Brindley Ford	*Stafford* - Stoke-on-Trent
Brindley Heath	*Stafford* - Stafford
Brindleys	*York, E.R.* - Goole
Brindley Village	*Stafford* - Stafford
Brineton	*Stafford* - Stafford
Bringhurst	*Leicester* - Kettering
Bringsty Common	*Hereford* - Worcester
Brington	*Hunts* - Huntingdon
Brington	*Hunts* - Peterborough
Brington, Great	*Northampton* - Northampton
Brington, Little	*Northampton* - Northampton
Brinkburn High Ward	*Northumberland* - Morpeth
Brinkburn Low Ward	*Northumberland* - Morpeth
Brinkburn, South	*Northumberland* - Morpeth
Brinkhill	*Lincoln* - Skegness
Brinkin	*Montgomery* - Welshpool
Brinkley	*Cambridge* - Newmarket
Brinkley Hill	*Hereford* - Hereford
Brinklow	*Warwick* - Rugby
Brinkmarsh	*Gloucester* - Thornbury
Brinkworth	*Wilts* - Malmesbury
Brinningham	*Norfolk* - King's Lynn
Brinnington	*Cheshire* - Stockport
Brinscall	*Lancaster* - Chorley
Brinscombe	*Somerset* - Wells
Brinsley (Plain Spot)	*Notts* - Alfreton
Brinsley	*Notts* - Nottingham
Brinsop	*Hereford* - Hereford
Brinsworth	*York, W.R.* - Rotherham
Brinton	*Norfolk* - King's Lynn
Brisco	*Cumberland* - Carlisle
Briscoe	*York, N.R.* - Bishop Auckland
Brisington	*Oxford* - Thame
Brisley	*Norfolk* - East Dereham
Brislington	*Somerset* - Bristol
Bristnall Fields	*Worcester* - West Bromwich
Bristol	*Gloucester* - Bristol
Briston	*Norfolk* - King's Lynn
Britannia	*Lancaster* - Rawtenstall
Britford	*Wilts* - Salisbury
Brithdir	*Denbigh and Montgomery* - Oswestry
Brithdir	*Glamorgan* - Bargoed
Brithdir	*Merioneth* - Dolgellau
Brithdir	*Montgomery* - Newtown
Brithdir	*Montgomery* - Welshpool
Brithembottom	*Devon* - Tiverton
British	*Monmouth* - Pontypool and Abergavenny
British Camp	*Hereford* - Great Malvern
Briton Ferry	*Glamorgan* - Neath
Britwell Prior	*Oxford* - Didcot
Britwell Salome	*Oxford* - Didcot
Briw	*Denbigh* - Oswestry
Brixham	*Devon* - Torquay
Brixton	*Devon* - Plymouth
Brixton (part)	*London, S.W.2* - Lambeth
Brixton (part)	*London, S.W.2* - Wandsworth
Brixton Deverill	*Wilts* - Warminster

Brixton, North	*London, S.W.9* - Lambeth
Brixworth	*Northampton* - Northampton
Brize Norton	*Oxford* - Witney
Broad Blunsdon	*Wilts* - Swindon
Broadbottom	*Cheshire* - Hyde
Broad Bridge Heath	*Sussex* - Horsham
Broad Campden	*Gloucester* - Evesham
Broad Carr	*York, W.R.* - Halifax
Broad Chalke	*Wilts* - Salisbury
Broad Clyst	*Devon* - Exeter
Broad Colney	*Herts* - St. Albans
Broadenham	*Somerset* - Axminster and Chard
Broadfield	*Cumberland* - Penrith
Broadfield	*Herts* - Hitchin
Broadfield	*Lancaster* - Bury
Broadford Bridge	*Sussex* - Chichester
Broad Green	*Lancaster* - Liverpool
Broad Green	*Worcester* - Redditch
Broadham Green	*Surrey* - Reigate
Broad Haven	*Pembroke* - Haverfordwest
Broadheath	*Cheshire* - Altrincham
Broadheath	*Hereford* - Leominster
Broadheath	*Worcester* - Worcester
Broadhembury	*Devon* - Exeter
Broadhempston	*Devon* - Newton Abbot
Broad Hinton	*Wilts* - Swindon
Broadholme	*Notts* - Lincoln
Broadlands	*Hants* - Southampton
Broadlane	*Cornwall* - Redruth
Broad Lanes	*Salop* - Bridgnorth
Broad Lanes	*Stafford* - Wolverhampton
Broadleas	*Kent* - Dover
Broad Lee	*Northumberland* - Hexham
Broadley Common	*Essex* - Harlow
Broad Marston	*Gloucester* - Evesham
Broadmayne	*Dorset* - Dorchester
Broadmoor	*Berks* - Reading
Broadmoor	*Somerset* - Bath
Broadmoor	*Surrey* - Dorking
Broadmoor Common	*Hereford* - Hereford
Broadoak	*Cornwall* - Liskeard
Broadoak	*Dorset* - Dorchester
Broadoak	*Gloucester* - Gloucester
Broad Oak	*Kent* - Canterbury
Broad Oak	*Lancaster* - St. Helens
Broad Oak	*Northumberland* - Hexham
Broad Oak	*Salop* - Bridgnorth
Broadoak	*Salop* - Shrewsbury
Broad Oak	*Sussex* - Eastbourne
Broads Green	*Essex* - Chelmsford
Broads Green	*Wilts* - Devizes
Broadside	*Northumberland* - Hexham
Broadstone	*Dorset* - Poole
Broadstone Hill	*Oxford* - Banbury
Broadstreet	*Wilts* - Devizes
Broadstruther	*Northumberland* - Alnwick
Broad, The	*Hereford* - Leominster
Broad Town	*Wilts* - Swindon
Broadward	*Hereford* - Leominster
Broadwas	*Worcester* - Worcester
Broadwater	*Herts* - Hitchin
Broadwater	*Sussex* - Worthing
Broadwath	*Cumberland* - Carlisle
Broadway	*Carmarthen* - Carmarthen
Broadway	*Hants* - Petersfield
Broadway	*Montgomery* - Welshpool
Broadway	*Somerset* - Axminster and Chard
Broadway	*Worcester* - Evesham
Broadway Capland	*Somerset* - Axminster and Chard
Broadwell	*Gloucester* - Cheltenham
Broadwell	*Oxford* - Witney
Broadwell	*Warwick* - Rugby
Broadwell	*Worcester* - Dudley
Broadwindsor	*Dorset* - Yeovil
Broadwood	*Durham* - Durham
Broadwoodkelly	*Devon* - Okehampton
Broadwood Widger	*Devon* - Launceston
Brobury	*Hereford* - Hereford
Brock	*Lancaster* - Preston
Brockamin	*Worcester* - Great Malvern

Brockdish	*Norfolk* - Norwich
Brockencote	*Worcester* - Kidderminster
Brockenhurst	*Hants* - Lymington
Brockeridge	*Gloucester* - Cheltenham
Brockford	*Suffolk* - Stowmarket
Brockhall	*Northampton* - Northampton
Brockham	*Surrey* - Dorking
Brockham Green	*Surrey* - Dorking
Brockhampton	*Dorset* - Dorchester
Brockhampton	*Gloucester* - Cheltenham
Brockhampton	*Hants* - Portsmouth
Brockhampton	*Hereford* - Hereford
Brockhampton, Great	*Gloucester* - Cheltenham
Brockhampton, Little	*Gloucester* - Cheltenham
Brockhill, Lower	*Worcester* - Redditch
Brockhill, Upper	*Worcester* - Redditch
Brockholes	*Lancaster* - Preston
Brockholes	*York, W.R.* - Huddersfield
Brockhurst	*Hants* - Portsmouth
Brockhurst	*Salop* - Shrewsbury
Brockhurst	*Warwick* - Rugby
Brockhurst, Lower	*Stafford* - Stafford
Brockhurst Moats	*Stafford* - Stafford
Brocklebank	*Cumberland* - Carlisle
Brocklesby	*Lincoln* - Great Grimsby
Brocklesby Station	*Lincoln* - Great Grimsby
Brockley (part)	*London, S.E.4* - Bromley
Brockley (part)	*London, S.E.4* - Lambeth
Brockley	*Somerset* - Bristol
Brockley	*Suffolk* - Bury St.Edmunds
Brockley Hill	*Middlesex* - Willesden
Brockley Warren	*Hants* - Andover
Brockley Whins	*Durham* - South Shields
Brockmanton	*Hereford* - Leominster
Brockmoor	*Stafford* - Stourbridge
Brockbridge	*Gloucester* - Bristol
Brockton (Much Wenlock)	*Salop* - Bridgnorth
Brockton (Shifnal)	*Salop* - Bridgnorth
Brockton	*Salop* - Ludlow
Brockton	*Salop* - Shrewsbury
Brockton (Newport)	*Salop* - Wellington (Salop)
Brockton	*Stafford* - Stafford
Brockton Grange (Shifnal)	*Salop* - Stafford
Brockton Grange (Newport)	*Salop* - Wellington (Salop)
Brockweir	*Glos* - Chepstow
Brockworth	*Gloucester* - Gloucester
Brocton	*Stafford* - Stafford
Brodsworth	*York, W.R.* - Doncaster
Brogden	*York, W.R.* - Skipton
Brokenborough	*Wilts* - Malmesbury
Broken Cross	*Cheshire* - Macclesfield
Broken Green	*Herts* - Hertford
Brokers Wood	*Wilts* - Trowbridge
Bromborough	*Cheshire* - Birkenhead
Brome	*Suffolk* - Norwich
Bromeswell	*Suffolk* - Woodbridge
Bromfield	*Cumberland* - Carlisle
Bromfield	*Salop* - Ludlow
Bromford	*Warwick* - Birmingham
Bromham	*Beds* - Bedford
Bromham	*Wilts* - Devizes
Bromham Common	*Wilts* - Devizes
Bromley	*Hereford* - Hereford
Bromley	*Kent* - Bromley
Bromley	*London, E.3* - Bow
Bromley	*London, E.14* - Bow
Bromley	*Salop* - Bridgnorth
Bromley	*Stafford* - Stourbridge
Bromley Common	*Kent* - Bromley
Bromley Cross	*Lancaster* - Bolton
Bromley Green	*Kent* - Ashford
Bromley Hurst	*Stafford* - Uttoxeter
Bromley Park	*Stafford* - Uttoxeter
Bromley Wood	*Stafford* - Uttoxeter
Brompton (Berrington)	*Salop* - Shrewsbury
Brompton (Chirbury)	*Salop* - Welshpool
Brompton	*York, N.R.* - Northallerton

Brompton	*York, N.R.* - Scarborough
Brompton, Old	*Kent* - Rochester
Brompton Ralph	*Somerset* - Minehead
Brompton Regis	*Somerset* - Tiverton
Brompton-upon-Swale	*York, N.R.* - Darlington
Brompton, West	*London, S.W.10* - West London
Bromsash	*Hereford* - Gloucester
Bromsberrow	*Gloucester* - Gloucester
Bromsberrow Heath	*Gloucester* - Gloucester
Bromsgrove	*Worcester* - Bromsgrove
Bromson Hill	*Warwick* - Stratford on Avon
Bromstead	*Stafford* - Stafford
Bromwich, Little	*Warwick* - Birmingham
Bromyard	*Hereford* - Hereford
Bronaber (Trawsfyndd)	*Merioneth* - Portmadoc
Bronant	*Cardigan* - Aberystwyth
Broncroft	*Salop* - Ludlow
Brondesbury (part)	*London, N.W.6* - Broomsbury and Marylebone
Brondesbury (part)	*London, N.W.6* - Willesden
Brondesbury Park	*London, N.W.6* - Willesden
Brongest	*Cardigan* - Cardigan
Brongwyn	*Cardigan* - Cardigan
Bronington	*Flint* - Whitchurch
Bronllys	*Brecon* - Brecknock
Bronwydd Arms	*Carmarthen* - Carmarthen
Bronygarth	*Salop* - Oswestry
Brook	*Hants* - Southampton
Brook (Kings Somborne)	*Hants* - Winchester
Brook	*I. of W.* - Newport (I.W.)
Brook	*Kent* - Ashford
Brook	*Surrey* - Guildford
Brooke	*Norfolk* - Norwich
Brooke	*Rutland* - Melton Mowbray
Brook End	*Essex* - Chelmsford
Brookend	*Gloucester* - Stroud
Brook End	*Stafford* - Lichfield
Brookend, New	*Gloucester* - Stroud
Brookfield	*Cumberland* - Carlisle
Brookfield	*Derby* - Hyde
Brookfield	*Lancaster* - Bolton
Brookfields	*Warwick* - Birmingham
Brookfoot	*York, W.R.* - Halifax
Brookhampton	*Salop* - Ludlow
Brookhampton	*Somerset* - Yeovil
Brookhouse	*Lancaster* - Lancaster
Brookhouse	*York, W.R.* - Rotherham
Brookhouse Green	*Stafford* - Stoke-on-Trent
Brookhouses	*Stafford* - Stoke-on-Trent
Brooking	*Devon* - Torquay
Brookland	*Kent* - Ashford
Brooklands (part)	*Cheshire* - Altrincham
Brooklands (part)	*Cheshire* - Manchester
Brooklands	*Salop* - Wellington (Salop)
Brookman's Park	*Herts* - St. Albans
Brooksbottoms	*Lancaster* - Bury
Brooksby	*Leicester* - Melton Mowbray
Brooksend	*Kent* - Margate
Brooks Green	*Sussex* - Horsham
Brooks's Bar (part)	*Lancaster* - Manchester
Brooks's Bar (part)	*Lancaster* - Salford
Brook Street	*Kent* - Cranbrook
Brookthorpe	*Gloucester* - Gloucester
Brookvale	*Warwick* - Birmingham
Brookwood	*Kent* - Cranbrook
Brookwood	*Surrey* - Guildford
Broom	*Beds* - Biggleswade
Broom	*Devon* - Axminster and Chard
Broom	*Durham* - Durham
Broom	*Warwick* - Stratford on Avon
Broom	*Worcester* - Stourbridge
Broom Court	*Warwick* - Stratford on Avon
Broome	*Salop* - Ludlow
Broome	*Norfold* - Norwich
Broome Park	*Northumberland* - Alnwick
Broomers Corner	*Sussex* - Horsham
Broomfield	*Essex* - Chelmsford
Broomfield	*Kent* - Canterbury
Broomfield	*Somerset* - Bridgwater

BRO

Broomfields	*Salop* - Shrewsbury
Broomfleet	*York, E.R.* - Goole
Broomford	*Northumberland* - Alnwick
Broomhall	*Cheshire* - Crewe
Broomhall	*York, W.R.* - Sheffield
Broomhaugh	*Northumberland* - Hexham
Broom Hill	*Dorset* - Wimborne Minster
Broom Hill	*Durham* - Consett
Broomhill	*Durham* - Durham
Broomhill	*Hereford* - Hereford
Broomhill	*Kent and Sussex* - Hastings
Broomhill	*Norfolk* - Thetford
Broomhill	*Northumberland* - Morpeth
Broomhill	*Stafford* - Walsall
Broom Hill	*Worcester* - Bromsgrove
Broomhill	*York, W.R.* - Barnsley
Broomhill	*Cumberland* - Carlisle
Broomhill	*York, W.R.* - Sheffield
Broomhill Colliery	*Northumberland* - Morpeth
Broomhouses	*Notts* - East Retford
Broomley	*Northumberland* - Hexham
Broom Park	*Cumberland* - Carlisle
Broompark	*Durham* - Durham
Brooms Green	*Gloucester* - Gloucester
Broomside	*Durham* - Durham
Broomsthorpe	*Norfolk* - King's Lynn
Broomston	*Lincoln* - Gainsborough
Broseley	*Salop* - Wellington (Salop)
Brotherhouse Bar	*Lincoln* - Spalding
Brotheridge Green	*Worcester* - Great Malvern
Brotherlee	*Durham* - Bishop Auckland
Brothertoft	*Lincoln* - Boston
Brotherton	*York, W.R.* - Pontefract
Brotherwick	*Northumberland* - Alnwick
Brotton	*York, N.R.* - Middlesbrough
Brough	*Derby* - Buxton
Brough	*Notts* - Newark
Brough	*Westmorland* - Penrith
Brough	*York, E.R.* - Beverley
Broughall	*Salop* - Whitchurch
Brougham	*Westmorland* - Penrith
Brough Sowerby	*Westmorland* - Penrith
Broughton	*Bucks* - Aylesbury
Broughton	*Bucks* - Bletchley and Leighton Buzzard
Broughton	*Denbigh* - Wrexham
Broughton	*Flint* - Chester
Broughton	*Hants* - Andover
Broughton	*Hunts* - Huntingdon
Broughton	*Lancaster* - Preston
Broughton	*Lancaster* - Salford
Broughton	*Lincoln* - Scunthorpe
Broughton	*Northampton* - Kettering
Broughton	*Oxford* - Banbury
Broughton	*Salop* - Bridgnorth
Broughton	*Salop* - Shrewsbury
Broughton	*Stafford* - Stafford
Broughton	*York, N.R.* - Malton
Broughton	*York, W.R.* - Skipton
Broughton Astley	*Leicester* - Hinckley
Broughton Beck	*Lancaster* - Barrow-in-Furness
Broughton Cross	*Cumberland* - Workington
Broughton, East	*Lancaster* - Barrow-in-Furness
Broughton Gifford	*Wilts* - Trowbridge
Broughton, Great	*Cumberland* - Workington
Broughton, Great	*York, N.R.* - Middlesbrough
Broughton Green	*Worcester* - Bromsgrove
Broughton Hackett	*Worcester* - Worcester
Broughton, Higher	*Lancaster* - Salford
Broughton-in-Cartmel	*Lancaster* - Barrow-in-Furness
Broughton-in-Furness	*Lancaster* - Barrow-in-Furness
Broughton, Little	*Cumberland* - Workington
Broughton, Little	*York, N.R.* - Middlesbrough
Broughton, Lower	*Lancaster* - Salford
Broughton Mills	*Lancaster* - Barrow-in-Furness

BRO - BRY

Broughton Moor	*Cumberland* - Workington
Broughton Moss	*Denbigh* - Wrexham
Broughton, Nether	*Leicester* - Melton Mowbray
Broughton, New	*Denbigh* - Wrexham
Broughton Poggs	*Oxford* - Witney
Broughton, Upper	*Notts* - Melton Mowbray
Broughton, West	*Lancaster* - Barrow-in-Furness
Broughton Wick	*Glamorgan* - Bridgend
Brown Candover	*Hants* - Winchester
Brown Clee Hill	*Salop* - Ludlow
Browndown	*Hants* - Portsmouth
Brownedge	*Lancaster* - Preston
Brown Edge	*Stafford* - Stoke-on-Trent
Browney Colliery	*Durham* - Durham
Brown Gill	*Cumberland* - Carlisle
Brown Heath	*Salop* - Shrewsbury
Brown Heath	*Worcester* - Worcester
Brownhill	*Lancaster* - Blackburn
Brownhills (Tunstall)	*Stafford* - Stoke-on-Trent
Brownhills	*Stafford* - Walsall
Brownlees	*Stafford* - Congleton
Brownley Green (part)	*Cheshire* - Manchester
Brownley Green	*Warwick* - Warwick
Brownley Hill	*Cumberland* - Haltwhistle
Brownlow	*Cheshire* - Congleton
Brownlow Fold	*Lancaster* - Bolton
Brownrigg	*Cumberland* - Carlisle
Brown's Buildings	*Durham* - Gateshead
Brownsea Island	*Dorset* - Poole
Brown's Green	*Warwick* - Birmingham
Brownshill	*Gloucester* - Stroud
Brownshill Green	*Warwick* - Coventry
Brownside	*Cumberland* - Carlisle
Brownside	*Derby* - Buxton
Brownside	*Lancaster* - Burnley
Brownslow	*Salop* - Ludlow
Brownsover	*Warwick* - Rugby
Brownston	*Devon* - Kingsbridge
Brownwick	*Hants* - Portsmouth
Browston	*Suffolk* - Great Yarmouth
Broxa	*York, N.R.* - Scarborough
Broxbourne	Herts - Hertford
Broxfield	*Northumberland* - Alnwick
Broxholme	*Lincoln* - Lincoln
Broxmore	*Hants* - Southampton
Broxmore	*Wilts* - Salisbury
Broxted	*Essex* - Braintree
Broxton	*Cheshire* - Chester
Broxwood	*Hereford* - Leominster
Bruen Stapleford	*Cheshire* - Chester
Bruern	*Oxford* - Banbury
Bruisyard	*Suffolk* - Woodbridge
Brumby, New	*Lincoln* - Scunthorpe
Brumby, Old	*Lincoln* - Scunthorpe
Brumstead	*Norfolk* - Great Yarmouth
Brundall	*Norfolk* - Norwich
Brundish	*Suffolk* - Halesworth
Brund Lane	*Stafford* - Leek
Brunshaw	*Lancaster* - Burnley
Brunstock	*Cumberland* - Carlisle
Brunswick Park	*London, N.11* - Barnet
Brunswick Village	*Northumberland* - Newcastle-upon-Tyne
Bruntcliffe	*York, W.R.* - Dewsbury
Brunthwaite	*York, W.R.* - Skipton
Bruntingthorpe	*Leicester* - Leicester
Brunton	*Northumberland* - Alnwick
Brunton	*Northumberland* - Hexham
Brunton, East	*Northumberland* - Newcastle-upon-Tyne
Brunton, West	*Northumberland* - Newcastle-upon-Tyne
Brushford	*Devon* - Okehampton
Brushford	*Somerset* - Tiverton
Brusselton Cottages	*Durham* - Bishop Auckland
Bruton	*Somerset* - Yeovil
Bryanston	*Dorset* - Blandford
Bryant's Bottom	*Bucks* - High Wycombe

BRY - BUC

Bryher	*Scilly Isles* - Penzance
Brymbo	*Denbigh* - Wrexham
Brympton	*Somerset* - Yeovil
Bryn	*Carmarthen* - Llanelli
Bryn	*Glamorgan* - Neath
Bryn	*Lancaster* - Wigan
Bryn	*Salop* - Ludlow
Brynamman	*Carmarthen* - Ammanford
Brynbachau	*Caernarvon* - Portmadoc
Bryn Barkud	*Denbigh* - Bangor
Brynberian	*Pembroke* - Cardigan
Bryncelyn	*Flint* - Holywell
Bryncethin	*Glamorgan* - Bridgend
Bryncoch	*Glamorgan* - Bridgend
Bryncoch	*Glamorgan* - Neath
Bryncroes	*Caernarvon* - Portmadoc
Bryncrug	*Merioneth* - Machynlleth
Bryndu	*Anglesey* - Llangefni
Bryndu	*Glamorgan* - Bridgend
Bryneglwys	*Denbigh* - Denbigh
Brynford	*Flint* - Holywell
Bryn Gates	*Lancaster* - Wigan
Bryngwran	*Anglesey* - Llangefni
Bryngwyn	*Caernarvon* - Caernarvon
Bryngwyn	*Monmouth* - Pontypool and Abergavenny
Bryngwyn	*Montgomery* - Oswestry
Bryngwyn	*Radnor* - Builth
Bryngwynedd	*Cardigan* - Cardigan
Bryngwyneth	*Cardigan* - Cardigan
Brynhafod	*Carmarthen* - Lampeter
Brynhoffnant	*Cardigan* - Cardigan
Brynhyfryd	*Glamorgan* - Swansea
Bryning	*Lancaster* - Preston
Brynkir	*Caernarvon* - Portmadoc
Brynmawr	*Brecon* - Blackwood
Brynmelin	*Glamorgan* - Swansea
Brynmenin	*Glamorgan* - Bridgend
Brynmill	*Glamorgan* - Swansea
Brynna	*Glamorgan* - Bridgend
Brynpeylan	*Denbigh* - Wrexham
Brynrhydyrarian	*Denbigh* - Denbigh
Brynsadler	*Glamorgan* - Pontypridd
Brynsiencyn	*Anglesey* - Llangefni
Bryntail	*Montgomery* - Newtown
Brynteg	*Anglesey* - Llangefni
Brynteg	*Denbigh* - Wrexham
Brynteg Bethesda	*Caernarvon* - Bangor
Brynteifi	*Carmarthen* - Lampeter
Bryntirion	*Glamorgan* - Bridgend
Brynwith	*Glamorgan* - Bridgend
Brynybaal	*Flint* - Mold
Bryn-y-maen	*Denbigh* - Conway
Brynyrefail	*Caernarvon* - Caernarvon
Buan	*Caernarvon* - Portmadoc
Bubbenhall	*Warwick* - Coventry
Bubnell	*Derby* - Chesterfield
Bubwith	*York, E. R.* - Selby
Buckabank	*Cumberland* - Carlisle
Buck Barn	*Sussex* - Horsham
Buckby, Long	*Northampton* - Northampton
Buckcastle	*Hereford* - Monmouth
Buckden	*Hunts* - Huntingdon
Buckden	*York, W. R.* - Skipton
Buckenham	*Norfolk* - Norwich
Buckenham, New	*Norfolk* - Norwich
Buckenham, Old	*Norfolk* - Norwich
Buckenham Tofts	*Norfolk* - Thetford
Buckerell	*Devon* - Exeter
Buckeridge	*Worcester* - Kidderminster
Buckfast	*Devon* - Newton Abbot
Buckfastleigh	*Devon* - Newton Abbot
Buckham	*Dorset* - Dorchester
Buckholt	*Hants* - Salisbury
Buckholt	*Monmouth* - Monmouth
Buckhorn Weston	*Dorset* - Yeovil
Buckhurst	*Kent* - Cranbrook
Buckhurst Hill	*Essex* - Bow
Buckingham	*Bucks* - Aylesbury
Buckland	*Bucks* - Aylesbury

BUC - BUL

Place	County	Post Town
Buckland	*Gloucester*	Cheltenham
Buckland	*Hants*	Portsmouth
Buckland	*Hereford*	Leominster
Buckland	*Herts*	Hitchin
Buckland	*Kent*	Sittingbourne
Buckland	*Surrey*	Reigate
Buckland Brewer	*Devon*	Bideford
Buckland Common	*Bucks*	Aylesbury
Buckland Dinham	*Somerset*	Frome
Buckland, East	*Devon*	Kingsbridge
Buckland, East	*Devon*	Barnstaple
Buckland, Great	*Kent*	Gravesend
Buckland Hollow	*Derby*	Alfreton
Buckland Marsh	*Berks*	Oxford
Buckland Milton	*Devon*	Plymouth
Buckland Monachorum	*Devon*	Plymouth
Buckland Newton	*Dorset*	Dorchester
Buckland Ripers	*Dorset*	Weymouth
Buckland St. Mary	*Somerset*	Axminster and Chard
Bucklands End	*Warwick*	Birmingham
Buckland Tout Saints	*Devon*	Kingsbridge
Buckland, West	*Devon*	Kingsbridge
Buckland, West	*Devon*	Barnstaple
Buckland, West	*Somerset*	Taunton
Bucklebury	*Berks*	Newbury
Bucklegate	*Lincoln*	Boston
Buckler's Hard	*Hants*	Southampton
Bucklesham	*Suffolk*	Woodbridge
Buckley	*Flint*	Mold
Bucklow Hill	*Cheshire*	Altrincham
Buckman's Corner	*Sussex*	Horsham
Buckminster	*Leicester*	Melton Mowbray
Bucknall	*Lincoln*	Lincoln
Bucknall	*Stafford*	Stoke-on-Trent
Bucknell	*Oxford*	Banbury
Bucknell	*Salop*	Knighton
Buckover	*Gloucester*	Thornbury
Buckpool	*Stafford*	Stourbridge
Bucks Bottom	*Herts*	Watford
Bucks Cross	*Devon*	Bideford
Bucks Green	*Sussex*	Horsham
Bucks Hill	*Herts*	Watford
Bucks Mills	*Devon*	Bideford
Buckton	*Hereford*	Knighton
Buckton	*York, E.R.*	Bridlington
Buckwood Stubbs	*Beds*	Luton
Buckworth	*Hunts*	Huntingdon
Budbrooke	*Warwick*	Warwick
Budby	*Notts*	Worksop
Buddicom Park	*Cheshire*	Chester
Bude	*Cornwall*	Bideford
Budleigh, East	*Devon*	Exeter
Budleigh Salterton	*Devon*	Exeter
Budna	*Beds*	Biggleswade
Budock	*Cornwall*	Truro
Budock Water	*Cornwall*	Truro
Budworth, Great	*Cheshire*	Northwich
Budworth, Little	*Cheshire*	Northwich
Buerton	*Cheshire*	Chester
Buerton	*Cheshire*	Crewe
Bufferland	*Pembroke*	Haverfordwest
Buffery	*Worcester*	Dudley
Bugbrooke	*Northampton*	Northampton
Bugford	*Devon*	Kingsbridge
Buglawton	*Cheshire*	Congleton
Bugle	*Cornwall*	St. Austell
Bugley	*Dorset*	Shaftesbury
Bugthorpe	*York, E.R.*	York
Buildwas	*Salop*	Shrewsbury
Builth Wells	*Brecon*	Builth
Bulborne	*Herts*	Aylesbury
Bulby	*Lincoln*	Grantham
Bulcamp	*Suffolk*	Halesworth
Bulcote	*Notts*	Nottingham
Bulford	*Wilts*	Salisbury
Bulk	*Lancaster*	Lancaster
Bulkeley	*Cheshire*	Crewe
Bulkington	*Warwick*	Nuneaton
Bulkington	*Wilts*	Trowbridge
Bulkington Lane	*Warwick*	Nuneaton

BUL - BUR

Place	County	Post Town
Bullaford	*Devon*	Barnstaple
Bull Bay	*Anglesey*	Llangefni
Bull Bridge	*Derby*	Alfreton
Bullen, High	*Stafford*	Dudley
Buller Donns	*Cornwall*	Redruth
Bullers Green	*Northumberland*	Morpeth
Bulley	*Gloucester*	Gloucester
Bull Fort	*Lincoln*	Great Grimsby
Bullgill	*Cumberland*	Workington
Bullingham, Lower	*Hereford*	Hereford
Bullingham, Upper	*Hereford*	Hereford
Bullington	*Hants*	Andover
Bullington	*Lincoln*	Lincoln
Bullock's Hall	*Northumberland*	Morpeth
Bullo Pill	*Gloucester*	Gloucester
Bull Point	*Devon*	Plymouth
Bull's Bridge	*Middlesex*	Uxbridge
Bull's Cross	*Gloucester*	Stroud
Bull's Green	*Herts*	Hertford
Bull's Hill	*Hereford*	Monmouth
Bull's Mill	*Herts*	Hertford
Bulmer	*Essex*	Sudbury
Bulmer	*York, N.R.*	Malton
Bulphan	*Essex*	Grays Thurrock
Bulthey	*Salop*	Shrewsbury
Bulverhythe	*Sussex*	Hastings
Bulwark	*Monmouth*	Chepstow
Bulwell	*Notts*	Nottingham
Bulwick	*Northants*	Stamford
Bulwick	*Northampton*	Peterborough
Bulwick Lodges	*Northampton*	Peterborough
Bumble Hole	*Worcester*	Dudley
Bumbles Green	*Essex*	Harlow
Bunbury	*Cheshire*	Crewe
Buncefield	*Herts*	St. Albans
Buncton, Lower	*Sussex*	Worthing
Buncton, Upper	*Sussex*	Worthing
Bungay	*Suffolk*	Norwich
Bungay Lake	*Worcester*	Bromsgrove
Bunker's Hill	*Cumberland*	Carlisle
Bunkers Hill	*Lincoln*	Gainsborough
Bunker's Hill	*Lincoln*	Boston
Bunker's Hill	*Norfolk*	King's Lynn
Bunker's Hill	*Stafford*	Wolverhampton
Bunny	*Notts*	Nottingham
Bunstye (Gayhurst)	*Bucks*	Bletchley and Leighton Buzzard
Buntingford	*Herts*	Hitchin
Buntingsdale	*Salop*	Market Drayton
Bunwell	*Norfolk*	Norwich
Burbage	*Derby*	Buxton
Burbage	*Leicester*	Hinckley
Burbage	*Wilts*	Swindon
Burcher	*Hereford*	Leominster
Burchett's Green	*Berks*	Reading
Burcot	*Oxford*	Oxford
Burcot	*Salop*	Wellington (Salop)
Burcot	*Worcester*	Bromsgrove
Burcote	*Salop*	Bridgnorth
Burcote Field	*Northampton*	Northampton
Burcote Wood	*Northampton*	Northampton
Burcott	*Bucks*	Aylesbury
Burcott	*Bucks*	Bletchley and Leighton Buzzard
Burderop	*Wilts*	Swindon
Burdon	*Durham*	Sunderland
Burdon, Great	*Durham*	Darlington
Burdon, Old	*Durham*	Sunderland
Burdon Village	*Durham*	Sunderland
Burdrop	*Oxford*	Banbury
Bures Hamlet	*Essex*	Sudbury
Bures St. Mary	*Suffolk*	Sudbury
Burford	*Oxford*	Witney
Burford	*Salop*	Ludlow
Burgate	*Hants*	Salisbury
Burgate	*Suffolk*	Norwich
Burge End	*Herts*	Hitchin
Burgess Hill	*Sussex*	Haywards Heath
Burgh	*Norfolk*	Norwich
Burgh (Aylsham)	*Norfolk*	Norwich

BUR

Burgh	*Suffolk* - Woodbridge
Burgh by Sands	*Cumberland* - Carlisle
Burgh Castle	*Suffolk* - Great Yarmouth
Burghclere	*Hants* - Newbury
Burghfield	*Berks* - Reading
Burghfield Common	*Berks* - Reading
Burgh Heath	*Surrey* - Epsom
Burghill	*Hereford* - Hereford
Burgh-le-Marsh	*Lincoln* - Skegness
Burgh-on-Bain	*Lincoln* - Louth
Burgh St. Margaret	*Norfolk* - Great Yarmouth
Burgh St. Mary	*Norfolk* - Great Yarmouth
Burgh St. Peter	*Norfolk* - Lowestoft
Burghwallis	*York, W.R.* - Doncaster
Burham	*Kent* - Rochester
Buriton	*Hants* - Petersfield
Burland	*Cheshire* - Crewe
Burleigh	*Gloucester* - Stroud
Burleigh	*Salop* - Wellington (Salop)
Burlescombe	*Devon* - Tiverton
Burlestone	*Devon* - Kingsbridge
Burlestone	*Dorset* - Dorchester
Burley	*Hants* - Bournemouth
Burley	*Hereford* - Worcester
Burleydam	*Cheshire* - Whitchurch
Burley Gate	*Hereford* - Worcester
Burley-in-Wharfedale	*York, W.R.* - Otley
Burley on the Hill	*Rutland* - Melton Mowbray
Burley Street	*Hants* - Bournemouth
Burley Woodhead	*York, W.R.* - Otley
Burlingham, North	*Norfolk* - Norwich
Burlingham, South	*Norfolk* - Norwich
Burlington	*Salop* - Wellington (Salop)
Burlinjobb	*Radnor* - Knighton
Burlton	*Salop* - Shrewsbury
Burmarsh	*Kent* - Ashford
Burmington	*Warwick* - Stratford on Avon
Burmos	*Cornwall* - Penzance
Burn	*York, W.R.* - Pontefract
Burnage	*Lancaster* - Manchester
Burnaston	*Derby* - Derby
Burn Bank	*Westmorland* - Penrith
Burn Bridge	*York, W.R.* - Harrogate
Burn Butts	*York, E.R.* - Beverley
Burnby	*York, E.R.* - York
Burncoose	*Cornwall* - Redruth
Burncross	*York, W.R.* - Sheffield
Burnden	*Lancaster* - Bolton
Burnedge	*Lancaster* - Rochdale
Burneside	*Westmorland* - Kendal
Burneston	*York, W.R.* - Harrogate
Burnett	*Somerset* - Bath
Burneville	*Durham* - Gateshead
Burnfoot	*Cumberland* - Carlisle
Burngullow	*Cornwall* - St. Austell
Burnham	*Bucks* - Slough
Burnham	*Lincoln* - Gt. Grimsby
Burnham Beeches	*Bucks* - Slough
Burnham Deepdale	*Norfolk* - King's Lynn
Burnham, East	*Bucks* - Slough
Burnham Green	*Herts* - Hertford
Burnham, High	*Lincoln* - Gainsborough
Burnham, Low	*Lincoln* - Gainsborough
Burnham Market	*Norfolk* - King's Lynn
Burnham Norton	*Norfolk* - King's Lynn
Burnham-on-Crouch	*Essex* - Maldon
Burnham-on-Sea	*Somerset* - Weston Super Mare
Burnham Overy	*Norfolk* - King's Lynn
Burnham Sutton	*Norfolk* - King's Lynn
Burnham Thorpe	*Norfolk* - King's Lynn
Burnham Ulph	*Norfolk* - King's Lynn
Burnham Westgate	*Norfolk* - King's Lynn
Burnhill	*Durham* - Durham
Burnhill Green	*Stafford* - Wolverhampton
Burnhope	*Durham* - Bishop Auckland
Burnhope	*Durham* - Durham
Burnigill	*Durham* - Durham
Burnipside	*Durham* - Durham
Burniston	*York, N.R.* - Scarborough
Burn Lee	*York, W.R.* - Huddersfield

BUR

Burnley	*Lancaster* - Burnley
Burn, Little	*Durham* - Durham
Burn Moor	*Durham* - Durham
Burn Naze	*Lancaster* - Blackpool
Burnopfield	*Durham* - Consett
Burns	*Cumberland* - Workington
Burnsall	*York, W.R.* - Skipton
Burns Green	*Herts* - Hertford
Burnstones	*Northumberland* - Carlisle
Burnt Ash	*London, S.E.12* - Bromley
Burnt Chimney Drove	*Cambridge* - Ely
Burnt Fen	*Suffolk* - Bury St. Edmunds
Burnt Fen Bank	*Cambridge* - Ely
Burnt Hill	*Berks* - Reading
Burnt House	*Cornwall* - Truro
Burnt Oak	*Middlesex* - Willesden
Burnt Tree	*Stafford* - Dudley
Burntwood	*Stafford* - Lichfield
Burnt Yates	*York, W.R.* - Harrogate
Burpham	*Surrey* - Guildford
Burpham	*Sussex* - Chichester
Burradon	*Northumberland* - Morpeth
Burradon	*Northumberland* - Newcastle-upon-Tyne
Burraton	*Cornwall* - Plymouth
Burrator	*Devon* - Plymouth
Burrel with Cowling	*York, N.R.* - Northallerton
Burringham	*Lincoln* - Scunthorpe
Burrington	*Devon* - Barnstaple
Burrington	*Hereford* - Ludlow
Burrington	*Somerset* - Weston Super Mare
Burrough Green	*Cambridge* - Newmarket
Burrough-on-the-Hill	*Leicester* - Melton Mowbray
Burrow	*Lancaster* - Lancaster
Burrowbridge (part)	*Somerset* - Bridgwater
Burrowbridge (part)	*Somerset* - Taunton
Burrow Hill	*Surrey* - Guildford
Burrows Hill (Stembridge)	*Somerset* - Yeovil
Burrows, Nether	*Derby* - Derby
Burr's Green	*Herts* - Hertford
Burry Green	*Glamorgan* - Swansea
Burry Port	*Carmarthen* - Llanelli
Burscough	*Lancaster* - Southport
Burscough Bridge	*Lancaster* - Southport
Bursea	*York, E.R.* - Goole
Burshill	*York, E.R.* - Beverley
Bursledon	*Hants* - Southampton
Burslem	*Stafford* - Stoke-on-Trent
Burstall	*Suffolk* - Ipswich
Burstock	*Dorset* - Yeovil
Burston	*Norfolk* - Norwich
Burston	*Stafford* - Stafford
Burstow	*Surrey* - Reigate
Burstwick	*York, E.R.* - Kingston-upon-Hull
Burtholme	*Cumberland* - Carlisle
Burthwaite	*Cumberland* - Carlisle
Burton	*Cheshire* - Birkenhead
Burton	*Denbigh* - Wrexham
Burton	*Hants* - Bournemouth
Burton	*Lincoln* - Lincoln
Burton	*Pembroke* - Haverfordwest
Burton	*Somerset* - Bridgwater
Burton	*Sussex* - Chichester
Burton	*Wilts* - Chippenham
Burton (Mere)	*Wilts* - Shaftesbury
Burton Agnes	*York, E.R.* - Bridlington
Burton Beck	*Durham* - Bishop Auckland
Burton Bower	*Essex* - Bishop's Stortford
Burton Bradstock	*Dorset* - Dorchester
Burton-by-Tarvin	*Cheshire* - Chester
Burton Carr	*Lincoln* - Gainsborough
Burton Coggles	*Lincoln* - Grantham
Burton Constable	*York, E.R.* - Kingston-upon-Hull
Burton Dassett	*Warwick* - Banbury
Burton, East	*Dorset* - Dorchester
Burton End	*Essex* - Bishop's Stortford
Burton Fen	*Lincoln* - Lincoln
Burton Fleming	*York, E.R.* - Bridlington
Burton Green	*Warwick* - Coventry

Burton Hastings	*Warwick* - Nuneaton
Burton-in-Kendal	*Westmorland* - Kendal
Burton-in-Lonsdale	*Westmorland* - Lancaster
Burton Joyce	*Notts* - Nottingham
Burton Latimer	*Northampton* - Kettering
Burton Lazars	*Leicester* - Melton Mowbray
Burton Leonard	*York, W.R.* - Harrogate
Burton, Long	*Dorset* - Yeovil
Burton Manor	*Stafford* - Stafford
Burton-on-the-Wolds	*Leicester* - Loughborough
Burton Overy	*Leicester* - Leicester
Burton Pedwardine	*Lincoln* - Sleaford
Burton Pidsea	*York, E.R.* - Kingston-upon-Hull
Burton Salmon	*York, W.R.* - Pontefract
Burton-upon-Stather	*Lincoln* - Scunthorpe
Burton-upon-Trent	*Stafford* - Burton-upon-Trent
Burton-upon-Yore	*York, N.R.* - Harrogate
Burton, West	*Notts* - Gainsborough
Burton, West	*Sussex* - Chichester
Burtonwood	*Lancaster* - Warrington
Burtreeford	*Durham* - Bishop Auckland
Burwardsley	*Cheshire* - Chester
Burwarton	*Salop* - Bridgnorth
Burwash	*Kent* - Tunbridge Wells
Burwell	*Cambridge* - Newmarket
Burwell	*Lincoln* - Louth
Burwood	*Salop* - Ludlow
Bury	*Hants* - Portsmouth
Bury	*Hunts* - Chichester
Bury	*Lancaster* - Bury
Bury	*Somerset* - Tiverton
Buryas Bridge	*Cornwall* - Penzance
Bury Green	*Herts* - Bishop's Stortford
Bury, New	*Lancaster* - Bolton
Bury St. Edmunds	*Suffolk* - Bury St. Edmunds
Burythorpe	*York, E.R.* - Malton
Busbridge	*Surrey* - Guildford
Busby, Great	*York, N.R.* - Middlesbrough
Busby, Little	*York, N.R.* - Middlesbrough
Buscot	*Berks* - Swindon
Buscot Wick	*Berks* - Swindon
Bushbury	*Stafford* - Wolverhampton
Bushby	*Leicester* - Leicester
Bushey	*Dorset* - Swanage
Bushey	*Herts* - Watford
Bushey Heath	*Herts* - Watford
Bush Hill Park	*Middlesex* - Edmonton
Bushley	*Worcester* - Cheltenham
Bush Mead	*Beds* - Biggleswade
Bushton	*Wilts* - Swindon
Bushwood	*Warwick* - Warwick
Busk	*Cumberland* - Penrith
Buslingthorpe	*Lincoln* - Lincoln
Bussage	*Gloucester* - Stroud
Bussex	*Somerset* - Bridgwater
Bustleholme Mill	*Stafford* - West Bromwich
Busveal	*Cornwall* - Redruth
Butcombe	*Somerset* - Bristol
Buteland	*Northumberland* - Hexham
Bute Town	*Glamorgan* - Bargoed
Butlass	*Devon* - Plymouth
Butleigh	*Somerset* - Wells
Butler Green	*Lancaster* - Oldham
Butlers Bank	*Salop* - Shrewsbury
Butler's Cross	*Bucks* - Aylesbury
Butler's Green	*Sussex* - Haywards Heath
Butler's Hill	*Notts* - Nottingham
Butlers Marston	*Warwick* - Stratford on Avon
Butley	*Suffolk* - Woodbridge
Butley Lanes	*Cheshire* - Macclesfield
Butley Town	Cheshire - Macclesfield
Butlocks Heath	*Hants* - Southampton
Butsfield	*Durham* - Durham
Butsfield Abbey	*Durham* - Durham
Butsfield, East	*Durham* - Durham
Butsfield, West	*Durham* - Durham
Butterbank	*Stafford* - Stafford
Butterby	*Durham* - Durham
Buttercrambe	*York, N.R.* - York
Butterfield Green	*Beds* - Luton

Butter Hill	*Stafford* - Stafford
Butterhill Bank	*Stafford* - Stafford
Butterknowle	*Durham* - Bishop Auckland
Butterlaw	*Northumberland* - Newcastle-upon-Tyne
Butterleigh	*Devon* - Tiverton
Butterley (Ripley)	*Derby* - Alfreton
Butterley (Ashover)	*Derby* - Chesterfield
Butterley	*Hereford* - Leominster
Buttermere	*Cumberland* - Workington
Buttermere	*Wilts* - Newbury
Butterow	*Gloucester* - Stroud
Butters Bank	*Stafford* - Stafford
Butters Green	*Stafford* - Stoke-on-Trent
Buttershaw	*York, W.R.* - Bradford
Butterthwaite	*York, W.R.* - Sheffield
Butterton	*Stafford* - Leek
Butterton	*Stafford* - Stoke-on-Trent
Butterwick	*Durham* - Stockton-on-Tees
Butterwick	*Lincoln* - Boston
Butterwick	*Westmorland* - Penrith
Butterwick	*York, E.R.* - Beverley
Butterwick	*York, N.R.* - Malton
Butterwick, East	*Lincoln* - Scunthorpe
Butterwick Ings	*Lincoln* - Boston
Butterwick, West	*Lincoln* - Scunthorpe
Buttery	*Salop* - Wellington (Salop)
Buttington	*Montgomery* - Welshpool
Butt Lane	*Stafford* - Stoke-on-Trent
Button Oak	*Salop* - Kidderminster
Buttris Gate	*Cornwall* - Penzance
Butt's Ash	*Hants* - Southampton
Buttsbury	*Essex* - Brentwood
Butts Green	*Essex* - Chelmsford
Butts Green	*Hants* - Salisbury
Buxhall	*Suffolk* - Stowmarket
Buxted	*Sussex* - Lewes
Buxton	*Derby* - Buxton
Buxton with Lammas	*Norfolk* - Norwich
Buxworth	*Derby* - Buxton
B. Winning	*Derby* - Alfreton
Bwlch (part)	*Brecon* - Pontypool and Abergavenny
Bwlch (part)	*Brecon* - Brecknock
Bwlchderwyn	*Caernarvon* - Caernarvon
Bwlchgwyn	*Denbigh* - Wrexham
Bwlchnewydd	*Carmarthen* - Carmarthen
Bwlch Trewyn	*Monmouth* - Pontypool and Abergavenny
Bwlchycibau	*Montgomery* - Oswestry
Bwlchyddar	*Denbigh* - Oswestry
Bwlchyffrydd	*Montgomery* - Newtown
Bwlchygroes	*Pembroke* - Cardigan
Bwlch y Sarnau	*Radnor* - Llandrindod Wells
Byanna	*Stafford* - Stafford
Byeness	*Northumberland* - Hexham
Byer Moor Colliery	*Durham* - Gateshead
Byers Garth	*Durham* - Durham
Byers Green	*Durham* - Bishop Auckland
Byfield	*Northampton* - Banbury
Byfleet	*Surrey* - Guildford
Byfleet, West	*Surrey* - Guildford
Byford	*Hereford* - Hereford
Bygrave	*Herts* - Hitchin
Byker	*Northumberland* - Newcastle-upon-Tyne
Byland, Old	*York, N.R.* - Malton
Bylaugh	*Norfolk* - East Dereham
Bylchau	*Denbigh* - Denbigh
Byley	*Cheshire* - Northwich
Bynea	*Carmarthen* - Llanelli
Byram-cum-Sutton	*York, W.R.* - Pontefract
Byshottles	*Durham* - Durham
Bytham, Little	*Lincoln* - Stamford
Bythom	*Hunts and Peterborough* - Huntingdon
Bythorn	*Hereford* - Knighton
Bythorn	*Hunts* - Peterborough
Byton	*Hereford* - Leominster
Byton Hill	*Hereford* - Leominster

Bywell	*Northumberland* - Hexham
Byworth	*Sussex* - Chichester

C

Cabin	*Salop* - Shrewsbury
Cabourn	*Lincoln* - Great Grimsby
Cabus	*Lancaster* - Lancaster
Cacca Dutton	*Denbigh* - Wrexham
Cacklebury	*Sussex* - Eastbourne
Cacrsws	*Montgomery* - Newtown
Cadbury	*Devon* - Tiverton
Cadbury	*Somerset* - Bristol
Cadbury Camp	*Somerset* - Bristol
Cadbury Heath	*Gloucester* - Bristol
Cadbury, North	*Somerset* - Yeovil
Cadbury, South	*Somerset* - Yeovil
Caddecroft	*Worcester* - Evesham
Caddington	*Beds* - Luton
Cadeby	*Leicester* - Hinckley
Cadeby	*Lincoln* - Louth
Cadeby	*York, W.R.* - Doncaster
Cadeleigh	*Devon* - Tiverton
Cade Street	*Sussex* - Eastbourne
Cadgerford	*Northumberland* - Hexham
Cadgwith	*Cornwall* - Penzance
Cadishead	*Lancaster* - Salford
Cadlands	*Hants* - Southampton
Cadleigh	*Devon* - Plymouth
Cadley	*Lancaster* - Preston
Cadley	*Wilts* - Swindon
Cadley Hill	*Derby* - Burton-upon-Trent
Cadmore End	*Bucks* - High Wycombe
Cadnam	*Hants* - Southampton
Cadney-cum-Howsham	*Lincoln* - Scunthorpe
Cadoxton	*Glamorgan* - Neath
Cadster Woods	*Derby* - Buxton
Cadwell	*Herts* - Hitchin
Cadwell	*Lincoln* - Louth
Caeharris	*Glamorgan* - Merthyr Tydfil
Caemawr	*Glamorgan* - Swansea
Caenby	*Lincoln* - Lincoln
Caen Hill	*Wilts* - Devizes
Caepantwyll	*Glamorgan* - Merthyr Tydfil
Caeracca	*Glamorgan* - Merthyr Tydfil
Caerau (Ely)	*Glamorgan* - Cardiff
Caerau (Maesteg)	*Glamorgan* - Bridgend
Caerestyn	*Flint* - Wrexham
Caergeiliog	*Anglesey* - Llangefni
Caergwrle	*Flint* - Wrexham
Caerhowel	*Montgomery* - Welshpool
Caerhun	*Caernarvon* - Conway
Caerhun	*Caernarvon* - Bangor
Caerleon	*Monmouth* - Newport (Mon)
Caernarvon	*Caernarvon* - Caernarvon
Caerneddau	*Salop* - Oswestry
Caerphilly	*Glamorgan* - Caerphilly
Caersws	*Montgomery* - Newtown
Caerwent	*Monmouth* - Chepstow
Caerwys	*Flint* - Holywell
Cagebrook	*Hereford* - Hereford
Cainscross	*Gloucester* - Stroud
Caio	*Carmarthen* - Llandovery
Caister-on-Sea	*Norfolk* - Great Yarmouth
Caistor	*Lincoln* - Great Grimsby
Caistor St. Edmunds	*Norfolk* - Norwich
Caistron	*Northumberland* - Morpeth
Cakebole	*Worcester* - Kidderminster
Calbourne	*I. of W.* - Newport (I.W.)
Calceby	*Lincoln* - Skegness
Calcethorpe	*Lincoln* - Louth
Calcot	*Berks* - Reading
Calcot	*Flint* - Holywell
Calcott	*Salop* - Shrewsbury
Calcut	*Warwick* - Rugby

Calcut	*Wilts* - Swindon
Calcutt	*Gloucester* - Swindon
Caldbeck	*Cumberland* - Carlisle
Caldecote	*Bucks* - Bletchley and Leighton Buzzard
Caldecote	*Cambridge* - Cambridge
Caldecote	*Herts* - Hitchin
Caldecote	*Hunts* - Peterborough
Caldecote	*Norfolk* - King's Lynn
Caldecote	*Warwick* - Nuneaton
Caldecote, Lower	*Beds* - Biggleswade
Caldecote, Upper	*Beds* - Biggleswade
Caldecott	*Cheshire* - Chester
Caldecott	*Cheshire* - Whitchurch
Caldecott	*Rutland* - Corby
Calder Bridge	*Cumberland* - Whitehaven
Calderbrook	*Lancaster* - Rochdale
Calder Grove	*York, W.R.* - Wakefield
Calderstones	*Lancaster* - Liverpool
Calder Vale	*Lancaster* - Preston
Caldicot	*Monmouth* - Chepstow
Caldicote	*Northampton* - Northampton
Caldicott (Bow Brickhill)	*Bucks* - Bletchley and Leighton Buzzard
Caldmore	*Stafford* - Walsall
Caldwell	*York, N.R.* - Darlington
Caldy	*Cheshire* - Birkenhead
Caldy Island	*Pembroke* - Haverfordwest
Calenick	*Cornwall* - Truro
Caletwr	*Merioneth* - Dolgellau
Calf Heath	*Stafford* - Stafford
California	*Cambridge* - Ely
California	*Durham* - Gateshead
California	*Norfolk* - Great Yarmouth
California	*Stafford* - Market Drayton
California	*Warwick* - Birmingham
California	*York, N.R.* - Middlesbrough
Calke	*Derby* - Ashby-de-la-Zouch
Callaly	*Northumberland* - Alnwick
Callaughton	*Salop* - Bridgnorth
Callerton	*Northumberland* - Newcastle upon Tyne
Callerton, High	*Northumberland* - Newcastle upon Tyne
Callerton, Little	*Northumberland* - Newcastle upon Tyne
Callestick	*Cornwall* - Truro
Callington	*Cornwall* - Liskeard
Callingwood	*Stafford* - Burton-upon-Trent
Callow	*Derby* - Ashborne
Callow	*Derby* - Matlock
Callow	*Hereford* - Hereford
Callow Brook	*Warwick* - Birmingham
Callow End	*Worcester* - Worcester
Callow Hill	*Worcester* - Kidderminster
Callow Hill (Alvechurch)	*Worcester* - Redditch
Callow Hill (Hunts End)	*Worcester* - Redditch
Calmore	*Hants* - Southampton
Calmsden	*Gloucester* - Cheltenham
Calne	*Wilts* - Chippenham
Calow	*Derby* - Chesterfield
Calrows	*Lancaster* - Bury
Calshot	*Hants* - Southampton
Calstock	*Cornwall* - Plymouth
Calstone	*Wilts* - Chippenham
Calthorpe	*Norfolk* - Norwich
Calthwaite	*Cumberland* - Penrith
Calton	*Stafford* - Leek
Calton	*York, W.R.* - Skipton
Calton-in-Blore	*Derby* - Leek
Calveley	*Cheshire* - Crewe
Calver	*Derby* - Chesterfield
Calverleigh	*Devon* - Tiverton
Calverley	*York, W.R.* - Bradford
Calverley Bridge (part)	*York, W.R.* - Bradford
Calverley Bridge (part)	*York, W.R.* - Leeds
Calvert	*Bucks* - Aylesbury
Calverton	*Bucks* - Bletchley and Leighton Buzzard
Calverton	*Notts* - Nottingham

CAL - CAN

Calvington	*Salop* - Wellington (Salop)
Calvo	*Cumberland* - Carlisle
Calwich	*Stafford* - Uttoxeter
Cam	*Gloucester* - Stroud
Camber	*Sussex* - Hastings
Camberley	*Surrey* - Aldershot and Farnham
Camberwell	*London, S.E.5* - Lambeth
Camblesforth	*York, W.R.* - Goole
Cambo	*Northumberland* - Morpeth
Cambois	*Northumberland* - Blyth
Camborne	*Cornwall* - Redruth
Cambridge	*Cambridge* - Cambridge
Cambridge	*Gloucester* - Stroud
Cambridge Heath	*London, E.2* - Shoreditch
Cambridge Heath	*London, E.8* - Shoreditch
Camden	*Kent* - Cranbrook
Camden Town	*London, N.W.1* - Bloomsbury and Marylebone
Came	*Dorset* - Dorchester
Cameley	*Somerset* - Bristol
Camelford	*Cornwall* - Bodmin
Camels	*Cornwall* - Truro
Camelsdale	*Sussex* - Petersfield
Camel's Head	*Devon* - Plymouth
Camel, West	*Somerset* - Yeovil
Camen	*Montgomery* - Oswestry
Camers Green	*Worcester* - Great Malvern
Camerton	*Cumberland* - Workington
Camerton (part)	*Somerset* - Bath
Camerton (part)	*Somerset* - Bristol
Camerton	*York, E.R.* - Kingston-upon-Hull
Camley Corner	*Berks* - High Wycombe
Cam, Lower	*Gloucester* - Stroud
Cammeringham	*Lincoln* - Lincoln
Camomile Green	*Gloucester* - Monmouth
Camomile Green	*Warwick* - Birmingham
Camp	*Gloucester* - Stroud
Campden	*Gloucester* - Evesham
Camperdown	*Northumberland* - Newcastle-upon-Tyne
Camp Hill	*I. of W.* - Newport (I.W.)
Camp Hill	*Warwick* - Birmingham
Camp Lane	*Somerset* - Bristol
Campsall	*York, W.R.* - Doncaster
Campsea Ash	*Suffolk* - Woodbridge
Campsfield	*Oxford* - Oxford
Camps Heath	*Suffolk* - Lowestoft
Campton	*Beds* - Biggleswade
Camrose	*Pembroke* - Haverfordwest
Cam, Upper	*Gloucester* - Stroud
Canada	*Hants* - Southampton
Canadia	*Sussex* - Hastings
Candlesby	*Lincoln* - Skegness
Candlestone	*Glamorgan* - Bridgend
Cane End	*Oxford* - Reading
Cane Heath	*Sussex* - Eastbourne
Canewdon	*Essex* - Southend
Canfield, Great	*Essex* - Braintree
Canfield, Little	*Essex* - Braintree
Canford	*Dorset* - Poole
Canford Cliffs	*Dorset* - Poole
Canklow	*York, W.R.* - Rotherham
Canley	*Warwick* - Coventry
Canley Gardens	*Warwick* - Coventry
Cann	*Dorset* - Shaftesbury
Cann Common	*Dorset* - Shaftesbury
Canney Hill	*Durham* - Bishop Auckland
Cannington	*Somerset* - Bridgwater
Canning Town	*London, E.16* - Bow
Cannock	*Stafford* - Walsall
Cannock Wood	*Stafford* - Walsall
Cannon Hill	*Warwick* - Birmingham
Cannons Green	*Herts* - Hitchin
Cannop	*Gloucester* - Monmouth
Canonbury (part)	*London, N.1* - Clerkenwell
Canonbury (part)	*London, N.1* - Shoreditch
Canon Frome	*Hereford* - Hereford
Canon Pyon	*Hereford* - Hereford
Canons Ashby	*Northampton* - Bambury

CAN - CAR

Canonstown	*Cornwall* - Penzance
Canterbury	*Kent* - Canterbury
Canterton, Lower	*Hants* - Southampton
Canterton, Upper	*Hants* - Southampton
Cantley	*Norfolk* - Norwich
Cantley	*York, W.R.* - Doncaster
Cantlop	*Salop* - Shrewsbury
Cantre	*Brecon* - Brecknock
Cantril Farm (part)	*Lancaster* - St. Helens
Cantsfield	*Lancaster* - Lancaster
Canvey Island	*Essex* - Southend
Canwell	*Stafford* - Tamworth
Canwick	*Lincoln* - Lincoln
Canworthywater	*Cornwall* - Launceston
Canycoed	*Montgomery* - Newtown
Cape Hill	*Stafford* - West Bromwich
Capel	*Kent* - Tonbridge
Capel	*Surrey* - Dorking
Capel Bangor	*Cardigan* - Aberystwyth
Capel Celyn	*Merioneth* - Dolgellau
Capel Coch	*Anglesey* - Llangefni
Capel Colman	*Pembroke* - Cardigan
Capel Curig	*Caernarvon* - Conway
Capel Cynon	*Cardigan* - Cardigan
Capel Dewi	*Cardigan* - Aberystwyth
Capel Dewi	*Carmarthen* - Carmarthen
Capel Evan	*Carmarthen* - Cardigan
Capel Garmon	*Denbigh* - Conway
Capel Garnedd	*Denbigh* - Denbigh
Capel Gwilym	*Glamorgan* - Cardiff
Capel Gwyn	*Anglesey* - Llangefni
Capel Hendre	*Carmarthen* - Ammanford
Capel Isaac (part)	*Carmarthen* - Ammanford
Capel Isaac (part)	*Carmarthen* - Carmarthen
Capel-le-Ferne	*Kent* - Dover
Capel Madog	*Cardigan* - Aberystwyth
Capel St. Andrew	*Suffolk* - Woodbridge
Capel St. Mary	*Suffolk* - Ipswich
Capel Seion	*Cardigan* - Aberystwyth
Capel Sion	*Caernarvon* - Caernarvon
Capelulo	*Caernarvon* - Conway
Capenhurst	*Cheshire* - Chester
Capernwray	*Lancaster* - Lancaster
Capesthorne	*Cheshire* - Macclesfield
Capheaton	*Northumberland* - Newcastle-upon-Tyne
Capland	*Somerset* - Taunton
Captain Fold	*Lancaster* - Bury
Capton	*Devon* - Torquay
Caradon Town	*Cornwall* - Liskeard
Carbean	*Cornwall* - St. Austell
Carbis	*Cornwall* - St. Austell
Carbis Bay	*Cornwall* - Penzance
Carbrooke	*Norfolk* - Swaffham
Carburton	*Notts* - Worksop
Carclaze	*Cornwall* - St. Austell
Carclew	*Cornwall* - Truro
Car Colston	*Notts* - Nottingham
Carcroft	*York, W.R.* - Doncaster
Carden	*Cheshire* - Chester
Cardeston	*Salop* - Shrewsbury
Cardew	*Cumberland* - Carlisle
Cardewlees	*Cumberland* - Carlisle
Cardiff	*Glamorgan* - Cardiff
Cardigan	*Cardigan* - Cardigan
Cardington	*Beds* - Bedford
Cardington	*Salop* - Shrewsbury
Cardinham	*Cornwall* - Bodmin
Cardrew	*Cornwall* - Redruth
Cardurnock	*Cumberland* - Carlisle
Careby	*Lincoln* - Stamford
Careless Green	*Worcester* - Stourbridge
Carew	*Pembroke* - Haverfordwest
Carey	*Hereford* - Ross
Carey Fitzpaine	*Somerset* - Yeovil
Cargentle	*Cornwall* - Launceston
Cargenwyn	*Cornwall* - Redruth
Cargo	*Cumberland* - Carlisle
Cargo Fleet	*York, N.R.* - Middlesbrough
Cargreen	*Cornwall* - Plymouth

Carham	*Northumberland* - Berwick-upon-Tweed
Carhampton	*Somerset* - Minehead
Carharrack	*Cornwall* - Redruth
Carisbrooke	*I. of W.* - Newport (I.W.)
Cark	*Lancaster* - Barrow-in-Furness
Carkeel	*Cornwall* - Plymouth
Carkettle	*Lancaster* - Barrow-in-Furness
Carlatton	*Cumberland* - Carlisle
Carlby	*Lincoln* - Stamford
Carleen	*Cornwall* - Penzance
Carle's Moor	*York, W.R.* - Ripon
Carleton	*Cumberland* - Carlisle
Carleton	*Cumberland* - Penrith
Carleton (Bootle)	*Cumberland* - Whitehaven
Carleton (Egremont)	*Cumberland* - Whitehaven
Carleton	*Lancaster* - Blackpool
Carleton	*York, W.R.* - Pontefract
Carleton	*York, W.R.* - Skipton
Carleton, East	*Norfolk* - Norwich
Carleton Forehoe	*Norfolk* - Norwich
Carleton, Little	*Lancaster* - Blackpool
Carleton Rode	*Norfolk* - Norwich
Carleton St. Peter	*Norfolk* - Norwich
Carlingcott	*Somerset* - Bath
Carlinghow	*York, W.R.* - Dewsbury
Carlin How	*York, N.R.* - Middlesbrough
Carlisle	*Cumberland* - Carlisle
Carlisle, Old	*Cumberland* - Carlisle
Carlisles Quarter	*Northumberland* - Morpeth
Carloggas	*Cornwall* - St. Austell
Carl's Moor	*York, W.R.* - Harrogate
Carlton	*Beds* - Bedford
Carlton	*Cambridge* - Newmarket
Carlton	*Durham* - Stockton-on-Tees
Carlton	*Leicester* - Ashby-de-la-Zouch
Carlton	*Notts* - Nottingham
Carlton	*Suffolk* - Woodridge
Carlton	*York, E.R.* - Kingston-upon-Hull
Carlton	*York, W.R.* - Barnsley
Carlton (Rothwell)	*York, W.R.* - Leeds
Carlton (Wharfedale)	*York, W.R.* - Otley
Carlton	*York, W.R.* - Goole
Carlton Colville	*Suffolk* - Lowestoft
Carlton Curlieu	*Leicester* - Leicester
Carlton, East	*Northampton* - Corby
Carlton Fossam	*York, E.R.* - Kingston-upon-Hull
Carlton, Great	*Lincoln* - Louth
Carlton Husthwaite	*York, N.R.* - York
Carlton-in-Cleveland	*York, N.R.* - Middlesbrough
Carlton-in-Coverdale	*York, N.R.* - Northallerton
Carlton in Lindrick	*Notts* - Worksop
Carlton le Moorland	*Lincoln* - Newark
Carlton, Little	*Lincoln* - Louth
Carlton Miniott	*York, N.R.* - Northallerton
Carlton, North	*Lincoln* - Lincoln
Carlton North	*Notts* - Worksop
Carlton Scroop	*Lincoln* - Grantham
Carlton, South	*Lincoln* - Lincoln
Carlton, South	*Notts* - Worksop
Carlton upon Trent	*Notts* - Newark
Carluddon	*Cornwall* - St. Austell
Carmarthen	*Carmarthen* - Carmarthen
Carmel	*Anglesey* - Llangefni
Carmel	*Carmarthen* - Ammanford
Carmel	*Caernarvon* - Caernarvon
Carmel	*Flint* - Holywell
Carmount Side	*Stafford* - Stoke-on-Trent
Carnaby	*York, E.R.* - Bridlington
Carnanton	*Cornwall* - Truro
Carn Brea	*Cornwall* - Redruth
Carneddi	*Caernarvon* - Bangor
Carneles Green	*Herts* - Hertford
Carnetown	*Glamorgan* - Aberdare
Carnforth	*Lancaster* - Lancaster
Carngiwch	*Caernarvon* - Portmadoc
Carn Grey	*Cornwall* - St. Austell
Carnhell	*Cornwall* - Redruth
Carnkie	*Cornwall* - Penzance
Carnkie	*Cornwall* - Redruth

Carnkief	*Cornwall* - Truro
Carnmarth	*Cornwall* - Redruth
Carnmenellis	*Cornwall* - Penzance
Carno	*Montgomery* - Newtown
Carnon Downs	*Cornwall* - Truro
Carnsnerry	*Cornwall* - St. Austell
Carn Stents	*Cornwall* - St. Austell
Carnyorth	*Cornwall* - Penzance
Carpella	*Cornwall* - St. Austell
Carpenders Park	*Middlesex* - Watford
Carperby	*York, N.R.* - Northallerton
Carr	*York, W.R.* - Rotherham
Carrbrook	*Cheshire* - Ashton-under-Lyne
Carreghofa	*Montgomery* - Oswestry
Carreglefn	*Anglesey* - Llangefni
Carregwen	*Pembroke* - Cardigan
Carr Gate (part)	*York, W.R.* - Dewsbury
Carr Gate (part)	*York, W.R.* - Wakefield
Carr Green	*York, W.R.* - Barnsley
Carrick Roads	*Cornwall* - Truro
Carrington	*Cheshire* - Altrincham
Carrington	*Lincoln* - Boston
Carrington	*Lincoln* - Skegness
Carrington	*Notts* - Nottingham
Carr Mill	*Lancaster* - St. Helens
Carrog	*Merioneth* - Wrexham
Carron, Lower	*Cardigan* - Lampeter
Carron, Upper	*Cardigan* - Lampeter
Carrs	*Lancaster* - Rawtenstall
Carrsgate	*Northumberland* - Hexham
Carr Shield	*Northumberland* - Hexham
Carr's Hill	*Durham* - Gateshead
Carr Vale	*Derby* - Chesterfield
Carrville	*Durham* - Durham
Carrycoats	*Northumberland* - Hexham
Carshalton	*Surrey* - Croydon
Carshalton Beeches	*Surrey* - Croydon
Carshalton-on-the-Hill	*Surrey* - Croydon
Carsington	*Derby* - Matlock
Carswell	*Berks* - Didcot
Carswell Marsh	*Berks* - Didcot
Cartaway Heads	*Northumberland* - Consett
Cartbridge	*Surrey* - Guildford
Carters Clay	*Hants* - Southampton
Carters Green	*Essex* - Harlow
Carters Green	*Stafford* - West Bromwich
Carterside Farm	*Northumberland* - Morpeth
Carterton	*Oxford* - Witney
Carthew	*Cornwall* - St. Austell
Carthorpe	*York, N.R.* - Harrogate
Cartington	*Northumberland* - Morpeth
Cartland Estate	*Warwick* - Birmingham
Cart Lane	*Lancaster* - Barrow-in-Furness
Cartmel	*Lancaster* - Barrow-in-Furness
Cartmel, Lower	*Lancaster* - Barrow-in-Furness
Cartworth	*York, W.R.* - Huddersfield
Carville	*Northumberland* - Durham
Carway	*Carmarthen* - Llanelli
Carwinlay	*Cumberland* - Carlisle
Carwood	*Salop* - Ludlow
Carzantic	*Cornwall* - Launceston
Cascade	*Glamorgan* - Bargoed
Cascob	*Radnor* - Knighton
Casewick	*Lincoln* - Stamford
Cashes Green	*Gloucester* - Stroud
Cash Moor	*Dorset* - Salisbury
Cassington	*Oxford* - Oxford
Cassop Colliery	*Durham* - Durham
Cassop, New	*Durham* - Durham
Cassop, Old	*Durham* - Durham
Castellian	*Pembroke* - Cardigan
Castell Coch	*Glamorgan* - Cardiff
Castelldwyran	*Carmarthen* - Haverfordwest
Castern	*Stafford* - Leek
Casterton	*Westmorland* - Kendal
Casterton, Great	*Rutland* - Stamford
Casterton, Little	*Rutland* - Stamford
Casthorpe	*Lincoln* - Grantham
Castle	*Cheshire* - Northwich
Castleacre	*Norfolk* - King's Lynn

CAS - CAT

Castle Ashby	*Northampton* - Northampton
Castle Bromwich	*Warwick* - Birmingham
Castle Bytham	*Lincoln* - Stamford
Castlebythe	*Pembroke* - Haverfordwest
Castle Caerinion	*Montgomery* - Welshpool
Castle Camps	*Cambridge* - Cambridge
Castle Carlton	*Lincoln* - Louth
Castle Carrock	*Cumberland* - Carlisle
Castle Cary	*Somerset* - Yeovil
Castle Combe	*Wilts* - Chippenham
Castle Coote	*Kent* - Canterbury
Castlecroft	*Stafford* - Wolverhampton
Castledene	*Durham* - Durham
Castle Donington	*Leicester* - Loughborough
Castle Door	*Cornwall* - St. Austell
Castle Eaton	*Wilts* - Swindon
Castle Eden	*Durham* - Hartlepool
Castleford	*York, W.R.* - Pontefract
Castle Frome	*Hereford* - Hereford
Castle Gate	*Cornwall* - Penzance
Castle Gresley	*Derby* - Burton-upon-Trent
Castle Hedingham	*Essex* - Braintree
Castle Hill	*Lancaster* - Bolton
Castle Leavington	*York, N.R.* - Stockton on Tees
Castle Liberty	*Warwick* - Tamworth
Castlemartin	*Pembroke* - Haverfordwest
Castle Morris	*Pembroke* - Haverfordwest
Castlemorton	*Worcester* - Great Malvern
Castle Nook	*Northumberland* - Carlisle
Castle Park	*Northumberland* - North Shields
Castle Pulberbatch	*Salop* - Shrewsbury
Castle Rigg	*Cumberland* - Workington
Castle Rising	*Norfolk* - King's Lynn
Castleshaw	*York, W.R.* - Oldham
Castleside	*Durham* - Consett
Castle Sowerby	*Cumberland* - Penrith
Castle Thorpe	*Bucks* - Bletchley and Leighton Buzzard
Castle Thorpe	*Lincoln* - Scunthorpe
Castleton	*Derby* - Buxton
Castleton (Sherborne)	*Dorset* - Yeovil
Castleton	*Lancaster* - Rochdale
Castleton	*Monmouth* - Newport (Mon.)
Castleton	*York, N.R.* - Whitby
Castleton's Cak	*Kent* - Cranbrook
Castle Town	*Cheshire* - Whitchurch
Castle Town	*Durham* - Sunderland
Castle Tump	*Gloucester* - Gloucester
Castle-upon-Alum	*Glamorgan* - Bridgend
Castle Vale	*Warwick* - Birmingham
Castlewright	*Montgomery* - Welshpool
Castley	*York, W.R.* - Otley
Caston	*Norfolk* - Thetford
Castor	*Northampton* - Peterborough
Caswell	*Somerset* - Bristol
Caswell Bay	*Glamorgan* - Swansea
Catbrain	*Gloucester* - Thornbury
Catcastle	*York, N.R.* - Bishop Auckland
Catchburn	*Northumberland* - Morpeth
Catcherside	*Northumberland* - Hexham
Catchgate	*Durham* - Consett
Catleugh	*Northumberland* - Hexham
Catcliffe	*York, W.R.* - Rotherham
Catcombe	*Wilts* - Chippenham
Catcott	*Somerset* - Bridgwater
Catcott Burtle	*Somerset* - Bridgwater
Caterham	*Surrey* - Croydon
Catesby	*Northampton* - Rugby
Catfield	*Norfolk* - Great Yarmouth
Catford	*London, S.E.6* - Bromley
Catforth	*Lancaster* - Preston
Catfoss	*York, E.R.* - Beverley
Cathedine	*Brecon* - Brecknock
Catherine de Barnes	*Warwick* - Birmingham
Catherine Slack	*York, W.R.* - Halifax
Catherington	*Hants* - Petersfield
Catherston Leweston	*Dorset* - Axminster and Chard
Catisfield	*Hants* - Portsmouth
Catlands	*Cumberland* - Carlisle
Catlow	*Lancaster* - Nelson

CAT - CAY

Catlowdy, High	*Cumberland* - Carlisle
Catlowdy, Low	*Cumberland* - Carlisle
Catmere End	*Essex* - Bishop's Stortford
Catmore	*Berks* - Didcot
Caton	*Lancaster* - Lancaster
Cat's Ash	*Monmouth* - Newport (Mon.)
Catsclough	*Cheshire* - Northwich
Catsedge	*Stafford* - Leek
Catsfield	*Sussex* - Hastings
Catshill	*Stafford* - Walsall
Catshill	*Warwick* - Birmingham
Catshill	*Worcester* - Bromsgrove
Catstree	*Salop* - Bridgnorth
Cattal	*York, W.R.* - Harrogate
Cattawade	*Suffolk* - Ipswich
Catterall	*Lancaster* - Preston
Catterick	*York, N.R.* - Darlington
Catterick Aerodrome	*York, N.R.* - Darlington
Catterick Camp	*York, N.R.* - Darlington
Catterlen	*Cumberland* - Penrith
Catterton	*York, W.R.* - York
Cat, The	*Oxford* - Reading
Catthorpe	*Leicester* - Rugby
Cattistock	*Dorset* - Dorchester
Cattleholmes	*York, E.R.* - Beverley
Catton	*Derby* - Burton-upon-Trent
Catton	*Norfolk* - Norwich
Catton	*Northumberland* - Hexham
Catton	*York, N.R.* - Northallerton
Catton, High	*York, E.R.* - York
Catton, Low	*York, E.R.* - York
Catton, New	*Norfolk* - Norwich
Catton, Old	*Norfolk* - Norwich
Catwick	*Yorks, E.R.* - Beverley
Catworth, Great	*Hunts* - Huntingdon
Catworth, Little	*Hunts* - Huntingdon
Caudledown	*Cornwall* - St. Austell
Caudle Green	*Gloucester* - Cheltenham
Caudworthy	*Devon* - Launceston
Caughall	*Cheshire* - Chester
Caughley	*Salop* - Bridgnorth
Caulcott	*Oxford* - Banbury
Cauldon	*Stafford* - Leek
Cauldon, Low	*Stafford* - Leek
Cauldwell	*Derby* - Burton-upon-Trent
Caundle Marsh	*Dorset* - Yeovil
Caunsall	*Worcester* - Kidderminster
Caunton	*Notts* - Newark
Cause Mountain	*Salop* - Shrewsbury
Causeway End	*Lancaster* - Barrow-in-Furness
Causeway Foot	*York, W.R.* - Halifax
Causeway Green	*Worcester* - West Bromwich
Causeway Head	*Cumberland* - Carlisle
Causey Park	*Northumberland* - Morpeth
Cautley	*York, W.R.* - Kendal
Cavendish	*Suffolk* - Sudbury
Cavenham	*Suffolk* - Bury St. Edmunds
Caversfield	*Oxford* - Oxford
Caversham	*Oxford* - Reading
Caverswall	*Stafford* - Stoke-on-Trent
Cave, North	*York, E.R.* - Beverley
Cave, South	*York, E.R.* - Beverley
Cawfields	*Northumberland* - Hexham
Cawkell	*York, E.R.* - Beverley
Cawkwell	*Lincoln* - Louth
Cawney Hill	*Worcester* - Dudley
Cawood	*Lancaster* - Lancaster
Cawood	*York, W.R.* - York
Cawsand	*Cornwall* - Plymouth
Cawston	*Norfolk* - Norwich
Cawston	*Warwick* - Rugby
Cawthorne	*York, W.R.* - Barnsley
Cawthorpe	*Lincoln* - Spalding
Cawthorpe, Little	*Lincoln* - Louth
Cawton	*York, N.R.* - Malton
Caxton	*Cambridge* - Cambridge
Caynham	*Salop* - Ludlow
Caynton (Shifnal)	*Salop* - Bridgnorth
Caynton (Newport)	*Salop* - Wellington (Salop)

Caythorpe	*Lincoln* - Newark
Caythorpe	*Notts* - Nottingham
Cayton	*York, N.R.* - Scarborough
Cayton Bay	*York, N.R.* - Scarborough
Cayton, High	*York, W.R.* - Harrogate
Cefn (St. Asaph)	*Denbigh* - Rhyl
Cefn (Ruabon)	*Denbigh* - Wrexham
Cefnbrith	*Denbigh* - Denbigh
Cefnbychan	*Denbigh* - Wrexham
Cefncaeau	*Carmarthen* - Llanelli
Cefn Carnau	*Glamorgan* - Cardiff
Cefncawse	*Glamorgan* - Bridgend
Cefncleisiog	*Montgomery* - Oswestry
Cefncoch	*Denbigh* - Conway
Cefncoch	*Montgomery* - Oswestry
Cefncoch	*Montgomery* - Newtown
Cefn Coed	*Glamoragn* - Merthyr Tydfil
Cefncribbwr	*Glamorgan* - Bridgend
Cefnddwygraig	*Merioneth* - Dolgellau
Cefnddwysarn	*Merioneth* - Dolgellau
Cefn Einion	*Salop* - Ludlow
Cefneithin	*Carmarthen* - Carmarthen
Cefn Forest	*Monmouth* - Blackwood
Cefngolau	*Monmouth* - Blackwood
Cefngorwydd	*Brecon* - Builth
Cefnhafodau	*Montgomery* - Newtown
Cefn Hengoed	*Glamorgan* - Bargoed
Cefn Hirgoed	*Glamorgan* - Bridgend
Cefnllyfnog	*Montgomery* - Oswestry
Cefnllys	*Montgomery* - Oswestry
Cefnllys	*Radnor* - Llandrindod Wells
Cefnllys Hirgoed	*Montgomery* - Oswestry
Cefn Mably	*Glamorgan* - Cardiff
Cefn Mawr	*Denbigh* - Wrexham
Cefn Meriadog	*Denbigh* - Rhyl
Cefn On	*Glamorgan* - Cardiff
Cefnpennar	*Glamorgan* - Aberdare
Cefnybedd	*Flint* - Wrexham
Cefnycoed	*Montgomery* - Oswestry
Cefn-y-coed	*Montgomery* - Newtown
Cefnycrib	*Monmouth* - Pontypool and Abergavenny
Cefnygroes	*Denbigh* - Denbigh
Ceidio	*Caernarvon* - Portmadoc
Cellan	*Cardigan* - Lampeter
Cellar Head	*Stafford* - Leek
Cemaes Bay	*Anglesey* - Llangefni
Cemlyn	*Anglesey* - Llangefni
Cemmaes	*Montgomery* - Machynlleth
Cemmaes Road	*Montgomery* - Machynlleth
Cenarth	*Carmarthen* - Cardigan
Cerne Abbas	*Dorset* - Dorchester
Cerne, Nether	*Dorset* - Dorchester
Cerne, Up	*Dorset* - Dorchester
Cerney	*Denbigh* - Wrexham
Cerney, North	*Gloucester* - Cheltenham
Cerney, South	*Gloucester* - Malmesbury
Cerney Wick	*Gloucester* - Swindon
Cerrigceinwen	*Anglesey* - Llangefni
Cerrigydruidion	*Denbigh* - Denbigh
Cerrist	*Montgomery* - Newtown
Ceserea	*Caernarvon* - Caernarvon
Ceunant	*Caernarvon* - Caernarvon
Chaceley	*Worcester* - Gloucester
Chackmore	*Bucks* - Aylesbury
Chacombe	*Northampton* - Banbury
Chadbury	*Worcester* - Evesham
Chadden Wicke	*Wilts* - Shaftsbury
Chadderton	*Lancaster* - Oldham
Chadderton Fold	*Lancaster* - Oldham
Chaddesden	*Derby* - Derby
Chaddesley Corbett	*Worcester* - Kidderminster
Chaddleworth	*Berks* - Didcot
Chadkirk	*Cheshire* - Stockport
Chadlington	*Oxford* - Banbury
Chadnor	*Hereford* - Leominster
Chadshunt	*Warwick* - Warwick
Chadsmoor	*Stafford* - Walsall
Chadstone	*Northampton* - Northampton
Chadwell	*Leicester* - Melton Mowbray

Chadwell Heath	*Essex* - Ilford
Chadwell St. Mary	*Essex* - Grays Thurrock
Chadwich	*Worcester* - Bromsgrove
Chadwick End	*Warwick* - Coventry
Chaffcombe	*Somerset* - Axminster and Chard
Chafford	*Kent* - Tonbridge
Chagford	*Devon* - Okehampton
Chaigley	*Lancaster* - Blackburn
Chailey	*Sussex* - Lewes
Chain Causeway	*Cambridge* - Ely
Chalbury	*Dorset* - Wimborne Minster
Chaldon	*Surrey* - Reigate
Chaldon Herring	*Dorset* - Weymouth
Chale	*I. of W.* - Newport (I.W.)
Chale Green	*I. of W.* - Newport (I.W.)
Chalfield, Great	*Wilts* - Trowbridge
Chalfield, Little	*Wilts* - Trowbridge
Chalfont, Little	*Bucks* - Amersham
Chalfont St. Giles	*Bucks* - Amersham
Chalfont St. Peter	*Bucks* - Amersham
Chalford	*Gloucester* - Stroud
Chalford	*Oxford* - Banbury
Chalford	*Oxford* - Thame
Chalford	*Wilts* - Trowbridge
Chalford Hill	*Gloucester* - Stroud
Chalgrave	*Beds* - Luton
Chalgrove	*Oxford* - Thame
Chalk	*Kent* - Gravesend
Chalk Hill	*Beds* - Luton
Chalkley	*Gloucester* - Bristol
Challaborough	*Devon* - Kingsbridge
Challacombe	*Devon* - Barnstaple
Challock	*Kent* - Ashford
Challock Lees	*Kent* - Ashford
Challow, East	*Berks* - Didcot
Challow Station	*Berks* - Didcot
Challow, West	*Berks* - Didcot
Chalmington	*Dorset* - Dorchester
Chalton	*Beds* - Biggleswade
Chalton	*Beds* - Luton
Chalton	*Hants* - Petersfield
Chalvey	*Bucks* - Slough
Chalvington	*Sussex* - Lewes
Chancery	*Cardigan* - Aberystwyth
Chances Pitch	*Hereford* - Great Malvern
Chandlers Cross	*Herts* - Watford
Chandlersford	*Hants* - Southampton
Chantry	*Somerset* - Frome
Chapel Allerton	*Somerset* - Wells
Chapel Allerton	*York, W.R.* - Leeds
Chapel Amble	*Cornwall* - Bideford
Chapel Ascote	*Warwick* - Warwick
Chapel Bassenthwaite	*Cumberland* - Workington
Chapel Brampton	*Northampton* - Northampton
Chapel Brow	*Cumberland* - Workington
Chapel Chorlton	*Stafford* - Stoke-on-Trent
Chapel End	*Essex* - Bishop's Stortford
Chapel End	*Warwick* - Nuneaton
Chapel-en-le-Frith	*Derby* - Buxton
Chapelfield	*Lancaster* - Bury
Chapel Fields	*Warwick* - Coventry
Chapel Foot	*Herts* - Hitchin
Chapel Gate	*Lincoln* - Spalding
Chapel Haddlesey	*York, W.R.* - Pontefract
Chapel Hill	*Lincoln* - Sleaford
Chapel House (Uldale)	*Cumberland* - Carlisle
Chapel House	*Northumberland* - Newcastle-upon-Tyne
Chapel House	*Oxford* - Banbury
Chapel Knapp	*Wilts* - Chippenham
Chapel Lawn	*Salop* - Ludlow
Chapel-le-Dale	*York, W.R.* - Lancaster
Chapel Leigh	*Somerset* - Taunton
Chapel Milton	*Derby* - Buxton
Chapel, North	*Sussex* - Chichester
Chapel St. Leonards	*Lincoln* - Skegness
Chapel Stile	*Westmorland* - Kendal
Chapelthorpe	*York, W.R.* - Wakefield

Chapelton	*Devon* - Barnstaple
Chapeltown	*Lancaster* - Bolton
Chapeltown	*York, W.R.* - Sheffield
Chapel Tumps	*Hereford* - Hereford
Chapels	*Lancaster* - Barrow-in-Furness
Chapman's Hill	*Worcester* - Bromsgrove
Chapmanslade	*Wilts* - Warminster
Chapmans Pool	*Dorset* - Swanage
Chapmanswell	*Devon* - Launceston
Chapmore End	*Herts* - Hertford
Chappel	*Essex* - Colchester
Charborough	*Dorset* - Swanage
Charcott	*Kent* - Tonbridge
Chard	*Somerset* - Axminster and Chard
Chard Junction	*Somerset* - Axminster and Chard
Chardstock	*Devon* - Axminster and Chard
Charfield	*Gloucester* - Thornbury
Charford	*Worcester* - Bromsgrove
Charford, North	*Hants* - Salisbury
Charford, South	*Hants* - Salisbury
Charing	*Kent* - Ashford
Charingworth	*Gloucester* - Evesham
Charlaw	*Durham* - Durham
Charlbury	*Oxford* - Banbury
Charlcombe	*Somerset* - Bath
Charlcutt	*Wilts* - Chippenham
Charlecote	*Warwick* - Stratford on Avon
Charlemont	*Stafford* - West Bromwich
Charles	*Devon* - Barnstaple
Charlestown	*Cornwall* - St. Austell
Charlestown (Baildon)	*York, W.R.* - Bradford
Charlestown	*York, W.R.* - Todmorden
Charlesworth	*Derby* - Hyde
Charleton	*Devon* - Kingsbridge
Charley	*Leicester* - Loughborough
Charlinch	*Somerset* - Bridgwater
Charlton	*Berks* - Didcot
Charlton	*Gloucester* - Thornbury
Charlton	*Hants* - Andover
Charlton	*Herts* - Hitchin
Charlton	*London, S.E.7* - Woolwich
Charlton	*Middlesex* - Kingston-upon-Thames
Charlton	*Northampton* - Banbury
Charlton	*Salop* - Wellington (Salop)
Charlton	*Sussex* - Chichester
Charlton	*Wilts* - Malmesbury
Charlton	*Worcester* - Evesham
Charlton	*Worcester* - Kidderminster
Charlton Abbots	*Gloucester* - Cheltenham
Charlton Adam	*Somerset* - Yeovil
Charlton All Saints	*Wilts* - Salisbury
Charltonbrook	*York, W.R.* - Sheffield
Charlton Down	*Hants* - Andover
Charlton, East	*Northumberland* - Hexham
Charlton Horethorne	*Somerset* - Yeovil
Charlton Kings	*Gloucester* - Cheltenham
Charlton Mackrell	*Somerset* - Yeovil
Charlton Marshall	*Dorset* - Wimborne Minster
Charlton Musgrove	*Somerset* - Yeovil
Charlton-on-Otmoor	*Oxford* - Oxford
Charltons	*York, N.R.* - Middlesbrough
Charlton St. Peter	*Wilts* - Devizes
Charlton, West	*Northumberland* - Hexham
Charlwood	*Surrey* - Reigate
Charmey Down	*Somerset* - Bath
Charminster	*Dorset* - Dorchester
Charminster	*Hants* - Bournemouth
Charmouth	*Dorset* - Axminster and Chard
Charndon	*Bucks* - Aylesbury
Charnes	*Stafford* - Stafford
Charney Bassett	*Berks* - Didcot
Charnock	*Derby* - Sheffield
Charnock Richard	*Lancaster* - Chorley
Charsfield	*Suffolk* - Woodbridge
Charter Alley	*Hants* - Basingstoke
Charterhouse	*Somerset* - Wells
Chart, Great	*Kent* - Ashford
Chartham	*Kent* - Canterbury
Chartham Hatch	*Kent* - Canterbury

Chartley	*Stafford* - Stafford
Chart, Little	*Kent* - Ashford
Chartridge	*Bucks* - Amersham
Chart Sutton	*Kent* - Maidstone
Chartwell	*Kent* - Sevenoaks
Charwelton	*Northampton* - Northampton
Chase Cross	*Essex* - Ilford
Chase Terrace	*Stafford* - Lichfield
Chasetown	*Stafford* - Lichfield
Chastleton	*Oxford* - Banbury
Chatburn	*Lancaster* - Blackburn
Chatcull	*Stafford* - Stafford
Chatershaugh	*Durham* - Gateshead
Chatford	*Salop* - Shrewsbury
Chatham	*Kent* - Rochester
Chatham Green	*Essex* - Chelmsford
Chathill	*Northumberland* - Alnwick
Chatley	*Essex* - Braintree
Chatley	*Worcester* - Worcester
Chat Moss (Astley)	*Lancaster* - Leigh
Chatsworth	*Derby* - Matlock
Chattenden	*Kent* - Rochester
Chatteris	*Cambridge* - March
Chatterley	*Stafford* - Stoke-on-Trent
Chatterton	*Lancaster* - Bury
Chattisham	*Suffolk* - Ipswich
Chatton (part)	*Northumberland* - Alnwick
Chatton (part)	*Northumberland* - Berwick-upon-Tweed
Chatwall	*Salop* - Shrewsbury
Chatwell	*Stafford* - Stafford
Chatwell, Great	*Stafford* - Stafford
Chatwell, Little	*Stafford* - Stafford
Chaulden	*Herts* - Hemel Hempstead
Chaul End	*Bedford* - Luton
Chavenage	*Gloucester* - Malmesbury
Chavey Down	*Berks* - Slough
Chawleigh	*Devon* - Barnstaple
Chawley	*Berks* - Oxford
Chawson	*Dorset* - Dorchester
Chawston	*Beds* - Bedford
Chawton	*Hants* - Aldershot and Farnham
Chaxhill	*Gloucester* - Gloucester
Chazey Heath	*Oxford* - Reading
Cheadle	*Cheshire* - Stockport
Cheadle	*Stafford* - Stoke-on-Trent
Cheadle Heath	*Cheshire* - Stockport
Cheadle Hulme	*Cheshire* - Stockport
Cheam	*Surrey* - Epsom
Cheapside	*Lancaster* - Burnley
Chearsley	*Bucks* - Thame
Chebsey	*Stafford* - Stafford
Checkendon	*Oxford* - Didcot
Checker House	*Notts* - East Retford
Checkley	*Stafford* - Uttoxeter
Checkley cum Wrinehill	*Cheshire* - Crewe
Chedburgh	*Suffolk* - Bury St. Edmunds
Cheddar	*Somerset* - Wells
Cheddington	*Bucks* - Bletchley and Leighton Buzzard
Cheddington	*Dorset* - Yeovil
Cheddleton	*Stafford* - Leek
Cheddon Fitzpaine	*Somerset* - Taunton
Cheddon, Upper	*Somerset* - Taunton
Chedgrave	*Norfolk* - Norwich
Chediston	*Suffolk* - Halesworth
Chedworth	*Gloucester* - Cheltenham
Chedworth Laines	*Gloucester* - Cheltenham
Chedzoy	*Somerset* - Bridgwater
Cheeseburn Grange	*Northumberland* - Newcastle-upon-Tyne
Cheeseman's Green	*Kent* - Ashford
Cheetham	*Lancaster* - Manchester
Chelborough, East	*Dorset* - Yeovil
Chelborough, West	*Dorset* - Yeovil
Cheldon	*Devon* - Barnstaple
Chelford	*Cheshire* - Macclesfield
Chell	*Stafford* - Stoke-on-Trent

Chellaston	*Derby* - Derby
Chell Green	*Stafford* - Stoke-on-Trent
Chell Heath	*Stafford* - Stoke-on-Trent
Chellington	*Beds* - Bedford
Chellow Dean	*York, W.R.* - Bradford
Chells	*Herts* - Hitchin
Chelmarsh	*Salop* - Bridgnorth
Chelmarsh Common	*Salop* - Bridgnorth
Chelmick	*Salop* - Ludlow
Chelmondiston	*Suffolk* - Ipswich
Chelmorton	*Derby* - Buxton
Chelmsford	*Essex* - Chelmsford
Chelmsley Wood	*Warwicks* - Birmingham
Chelsea	*London, S.W.3* - West London
Chelsfield	*Kent* - Bromley
Chelsham	*Surrey* - Croydon
Chelsing	*Herts* - Hitchin
Chelston	*Devon* - Torquay
Chelston	*Somerset* - Taunton
Chelston Heathfield	*Somerset* - Taunton
Chelsworth	*Suffolk* - Sudbury
Cheltenham	*Brecon* - Pontypridd and Abergavenny
Cheltenham	*Gloucester* - Cheltenham
Chelveston	*Northampton* - Wellingborough
Chelvey	*Somerset* - Bristol
Chelwood	*Somerset* - Bristol
Chelwood Common	*Sussex* - East Grinstead
Chelwood Gate	*Sussex* - East Grinstead
Chelworth	*Wilts* - Malmesbury
Chelworth	*Wilts* - Swindon
Cheney Longville	*Salop* - Ludlow
Chenies	*Bucks* - Amersham
Chennell's Brook	*Sussex* - Horsham
Chepping Wycombe	*Bucks* - High Wycombe
Chepstow	*Monmouth* - Chepstow
Chequerbent	*Lancaster* - Bolton
Cherhill	*Wilts* - Chippenham
Cherington	*Gloucester* - Malmesbury
Cherington	*Warwick* - Stratford on Avon
Cheriton	*Glamorgan* - Swansea
Cheriton	*Hants* - Winchester
Cheriton	*Kent* - Folkestone
Cheriton Bishop	*Devon* - Exeter
Cheriton Cross	*Devon* - Exeter
Cheriton Fitzpaine	*Devon* - Tiverton
Cheriton, North	*Somerset* - Yeovil
Cheriton, South	*Somerset* - Yeovil
Cherrington	*Salop* - Wellington (Salop)
Cherry Brook	*Devon* - Plymouth
Cherry Burton	*York, E.R.* - Beverley
Cherry Cob Sands	*York, E.R.* - Kingston-upon-Hull
Cherry Garden	*Kent* - Cranbrook
Cherry Hinton	*Cambridge* - Cambridge
Cherry Tree	*Herts* - St. Albans
Cherry Tree	*Lancaster* - Blackburn
Cherry Willingham	*Lincoln* - Lincoln
Chertsey	*Surrey* - Kingston upon Thames
Chesham	*Bucks* - Amersham
Chesham	*Lancaster* - Bury
Chesham Bois	*Bucks* - Amersham
Cheshire Coppice	*Salop* - Wellington (Salop)
Cheshunt	*Herts* - Edmonton
Chesilbourne	*Dorset* - Dorchester
Cheslyn-Hay	*Stafford* - Walsall
Chessington	*Surrey* - Kingston-upon-Thames
Chester	*Cheshire* - Chester
Chesterblade	*Somerset* - Wells
Chester Burns	*Durham* - Durham
Chester Castle	*Cheshire* - Chester
Chesterfield	*Derby* - Chesterfield
Chesterfield	*Stafford* - Lichfield
Chesterford, Great	*Essex* - Cambridge
Chesterford, Little	*Essex* - Cambridge
Chester Green	*Derby* - Derby
Chesterhope	*Northumberland* - Hexham
Chester-le-Street	*Durham* - Durham
Chester Moor	*Durham* - Durham
Chester Road	*Warwick* - Birmingham
Chesters	*Northumberland* - Hexham

Chesterton	*Cambridge* - Cambridge
Chesterton	*Gloucester* - Stroud
Chesterton	*Hunts* - Peterborough
Chesterton	*Oxford* - Oxford
Chesterton	*Salop* - Bridgnorth
Chesterton	*Stafford* - Stoke-on-Trent
Chesterton	*Warwick* - Warwick
Chesterton, Little	*Oxford* - Oxford
Chesterwood	*Northumberland* - Hexham
Chestnut Street	*Kent* - Sittingbourne
Cheston	*Devon* - Plymouth
Cheswardine	*Salop* - Market Drayton
Cheswell	*Salop* - Wellington (Salop)
Chetnole	*Dorset* - Yeovil
Chettiscombe	*Devon* - Tiverton
Chettisham	*Cambridge* - Ely
Chettle	*Dorset* - Salisbury
Chetton	*Salop* - Bridgnorth
Chetwode	*Bucks* - Oxford
Chetwynd	*Salop* - Wellington (Salop)
Chetwynd Aston	*Salop* - Wellington (Salop)
Chetwynd End	*Salop* - Wellington (Salop)
Chetwynd Firs	*Salop* - Wellington (Salop)
Chetwynd Grange	*Salop* - Wellington (Salop)
Chetwynd Heath	*Salop* - Wellington (Salop)
Chetwynd Rural	*Salop* - Wellington (Salop)
Cheveley	*Cambridge* - Newmarket
Chevening	*Kent* - Sevenoaks
Cheverell, Great	*Wilts* - Devizes
Cheverell, Little	*Wilts* - Devizes
Cheverell's Green (part)	*Beds* - Luton
Cheverell's Green (part)	*Herts* - St. Albans
Chevet	*York, W.R.* - Wakefield
Chevin	*Derby* - Derby
Chevin End	*York, W.R.* - Otley
Chevington	*Suffolk* - Bury St. Edmunds
Chevington Colliery	*Northumberland* - Morpeth
Chevington, East	*Northumberland* - Morpeth
Chevington, West	*Northumberland* - Morpeth
Chevithorne	*Devon* - Tiverton
Chew Magna	*Somerset* - Bristol
Chew Moor	*Lancaster* - Bolton
Chew Stoke	*Somerset* - Bristol
Chewton	*Hants* - Bournemouth
Chewton Common	*Hants* - Bournemouth
Chewton Keynsham	*Somerset* - Bristol
Chewton Mendip	*Somerset* - Wells
Cheylesmore	*Warwick* - Coventry
Chicheley	*Bucks* - Bletchley and Leighton Buzzard
Chichester	*Sussex* - Chichester
Chickenley	*York, W.R.* - Dewsbury
Chickenley Heath	*York, W.R.* - Dewsbury
Chickerell	*Dorset* - Weymouth
Chicklade	*Wilts* - Shaftesbury
Chickney	*Essex* - Braintree
Chicksands Priory	*Beds* - Biggleswade
Chicksgrove	*Wilts* - Shaftesbury
Chidden	*Hants* - Petersfield
Chiddingfold	*Surrey* - Guildford
Chiddingly	*Sussex* - Eastbourne
Chiddingstone	*Kent* - Tonbridge
Chiddingstone Causeway	*Kent* - Tonbridge
Chiddingstone Hoath	*Kent* - Tonbridge
Chideock	*Dorset* - Axminster and Chard
Chidham	*Sussex* - Chichester
Chidswell	*York, W.R.* - Dewsbury
Chieveley	*Berks* - Newbury
Chignal St. James	*Essex* - Chelmsford
Chignal Smealy	*Essex* - Chelmsford
Chigwell	*Essex* - Ilford
Chigwell Row	*Essex* - Ilford
Chilbolton	*Hants* - Andover
Chilcomb	*Hants* - Winchester
Chilcombe	*Dorset* - Dorchester
Chilcompton	*Somerset* - Wells
Chilcote	*Leicester* - Ashby-de-la-Zouch
Childerditch	*Essex* - Brentwood
Childerley	*Cambridge* - Cambridge

CHI

Childer Thornton	*Cheshire* - Ellesmere Port
Child Okeford	*Dorset* - Shaftesbury
Childrey	*Berks* - Didcot
Childs Ercall	*Salop* - Market Drayton
Childs Ercall Heath	*Salop* - Market Drayton
Child's Hill (Part)	*London, N.W.2* - Bloomsbury and Marylebone
Child's Hill (part)	*London, N.W.2* - Willesden
Childs Wickham	*Gloucester* - Evesham
Childwall	*Lancaster* - Liverpool
Childwick Green	*Herts* - St. Albans
Chilfrome	*Dorset* - Dorchester
Chilgrove	*Sussex* - Chichester
Chilham	*Kent* - Canterbury
Chilland	*Hants* - Winchester
Chillaton	*Cornwall* - Plymouth
Chillenden	*Kent* - Canterbury
Chillerton	*I. of W.* - Newport (I.W.)
Chillesford	*Suffolk* - Woodbridge
Chillingham	*Northumberland* - Alnwick
Chillington	*Devon* - Kingsbridge
Chillington	*Somerset* - Yeovil
Chillington	*Stafford* - Wolverhampton
Chilmark	*Wilts* - Shaftesbury
Chilson	*Oxford* - Banbury
Chilson	*Somerset* - Axminster and Chard
Chilswell	*Berks* - Oxford
Chilsworthy	*Cornwall* - Plymouth
Chiltern Green	*Beds* - Luton
Chilthorne Domer	*Somerset* - Yeovil
Chiltington, East	*Sussex* - Lewes
Chiltington, West	*Sussex* - Chichester
Chilton	*Berks* - Didcot
Chilton	*Bucks* - Thame
Chilton	*Durham* - Durham
Chilton	*Salop* - Shrewsbury
Chilton Burtle	*Somerset* - Bridgwater
Chilton Candover	*Hants* - Winchester
Chilton Cantelo	*Somerset* - Yeovil
Chilton Colliery	*Durham* - Durham
Chilton Foliat	*Wilts* - Swindon
Chilton, Little	*Durham* - Durham
Chilton Moor	*Durham* - Durham
Chilton-on-Polden	*Somerset* - Bridgeater
Chilton Trinity	*Somerset* - Bridgwater
Chilvers Coton	*Warwick* - Nuneaton
Chilwell	*Notts* - Nottingham
Chilworth	*Hants* - Southampton
Chilworth	*Oxford* - Thame
Chilworth	*Surrey* - Guildford
Chimney	*Oxford* - Witney
Chimney, Long	*Devon* - Axminster and Chard
Chimney Mills	*Suffolk* - Bury St. Edmunds
China Downs	*Cornwall* - Bideford
Chineham	*Hants* - Basingstoke
Chingford	*London, E.4* - Edmonton
Chinley	*Derby* - Buxton
Chinnell	*Salop* - Whitchurch
Chinnock, East	*Somerset* - Yeovil
Chinnock, Middle	*Somerset* - Yeovil
Chinnock, West	*Somerset* - Yeovil
Chinnor	*Oxford* - Thame
Chinnor Hill	*Oxford* - Thame
Chipchase	*Northumberland* - Hexham
Chipley	*Somerset* - Taunton
Chipnal	*Salop* - Market Drayton
Chippenham	*Bucks* - Slough
Chippenham	*Cambridge* - Newmarket
Chippenham	*Wilts* - Chippenham
Chipperfield	*Herts* - Hemel Hempstead
Chipping	*Herts* - Hitchin
Chipping	*Lancaster* - Preston
Chipping Barnet	*Herts* - Barnet
Chipping Campden	*Gloucester* - Evesham
Chipping Hill	*Essex* - Braintree
Chippinghurst	*Oxford* - Oxford
Chipping Norton	*Oxford* - Banbury
Chipping Ongar	*Essex* - Brentwood
Chipping Sodbury	*Gloucester* - Bristol
Chipping Warden	*Northampton* - Banbury

CHI - CHR

Chipshop	*Cornwall* - Plymouth
Chipstable	*Somerset* - Taunton
Chipstead	*Kent* - Sevenoaks
Chipstead	*Surrey* - Reigate
Chipstead	*Surrey* - Croydon
Chirbury	*Salop* - Welshpool
Chirdon	*Northumberland* - Hexham
Chirk	*Denbigh* - Wrexham
Chirk Bank	*Salop* - Oswestry
Chirk, Lower	*Denbigh* - Wrexham
Chirk, Upper	*Denbigh* - Wrexham
Chirton	*Northumberland* - North Shields
Chirton	*Wilts* - Devizes
Chisbury	*Wilts* - Swindon
Chiselborough	*Somerset* - Yeovil
Chiseldon	*Wilts* - Swindon
Chiselhampton	*Oxford* - Didcot
Chisenbury	*Wilts* - Devizes
Chishill, Great	*Essex* - Cambridge
Chishill, Little	*Essex* - Cambridge
Chislehurst	*Kent* - Bromley
Chislet	*Kent* - Canterbury
Chiswell Green	*Herts* - St. Albans
Chiswick	*London, W.4* - Brentford
Chisworth	*Derby* - Hyde
Chithurst	*Sussex* - Petersfield
Chithurst Marsh	*Sussex* - Petersfield
Chittering	*Cambridge* - Cambridge
Chitterne	*Wilts* - Warminster
Chittlehamholt	*Devon* - Barnstaple
Chittlehampton	*Devon* - Barnstaple
Chittoe	*Wilts* - Devizes
Chivelstone	*Devon* - Kingsbridge
Chivery	*Bucks* - Aylesbury
Chivingstone, East	*Northumberland* - Morpeth
Chivingstone, West	*Northumberland* - Morpeth
Chobham	*Surrey* - Guildford
Cholderton	*Wilts* - Salisbury
Cholderton, East	*Hants* - Andover
Cholesbury	*Bucks* - Amersham
Cholesbury Common	*Bucks* - Amersham
Cholesbury cum St. Leonards	*Bucks* - Amersham
Chollerton	*Northumberland* - Hexham
Cholmondeley	*Cheshire* - Crewe
Cholmondeston	*Cheshire* - Crewe
Cholsey	*Berks* - Didcot
Cholstrey	*Hereford* - Leominster
Cholwell	*Somerset* - Bristol
Chop Gate	*York, N.R.* - Malton
Choppards	*York, W.R.* - Huddersfield
Choppington	*Northumberland* - Blyth
Chopwell	*Durham* - Newcastle upon Tyne
Chopwell Colliery	*Durham* - Newcastle upon Tyne
Chorley	*Cheshire* - Macclesfield
Chorley	*Lancaster* - Chorley
Chorley	*Salop* - Bridgnorth
Chorley	*Stafford* - Lichfield
Chorley Wood	*Herts* - Watford
Chorlton	*Cheshire* - Whitchurch
Chorlton	*Stafford* - Stoke-on-Trent
Chorlton-by-Backford	*Cheshire* - Chester
Chorlton-cum-Hardy	*Lancaster* - Manchester
Chorlton-upon-Medlock	*Lancaster* - Manchester
Chorlton Ville	*Lancs* - Manchester
Choseley	*Norfolk* - King's Lynn
Choulton	*Salop* - Shrewsbury
Chowley	*Cheshire* - Chester
Chrishall	*Essex* - Bishop's Stortford
Christchurch	*Cambridge* - Wisbech
Christchurch	*Hants* - Bournemouth
Christchurch	*Kent* - Canterbury
Christchurch	*Monmouth* - Newport (Mon.)
Christian Malford	*Wilts* - Chippenham
Christleton	*Cheshire* - Chester
Christmas Common	*Oxford* - Thame
Christon	*Somerset* - Weston Super Mare
Christon Bank	*Northumberland* - Alnwick
Christow	*Devon* - Exeter
Christ's Hospital	*Sussex* - Horsham

Chudleigh	*Devon* - Newton Abbot
Chudleigh Knighton	*Devon* - Newton Abbot
Chulmleigh	*Devon* - Barnstaple
Chunal	*Derby* - Hyde
Church	*Lancaster* - Accrington
Churcham	*Gloucester* - Gloucester
Church Aston	*Salop* - Wellington (Salop)
Church Bank	*Salop* - Ludlow
Church Bickenhill	*Warwick* - Birmingham
Church Brampton	*Northampton* - Northampton
Churchbridge	*Stafford* - Walsall
Church Bridge	*Worcester* - Dudley
Church Brough	*Westmorland* - Penrith
Church Broughton	*Derby* - Burton-upon-Trent
Church Coniston	*Lancaster* - Kendal
Church Crookham	*Hants* - Aldershot and Farnham
Churchdown	*Gloucester* - Gloucester
Church Eaton	*Stafford* - Stafford
Church End	*Essex* - Bishop's Stortford
Church End	*Gloucester* - Cheltenham
Church End	*Lincoln* - Spalding
Church End	*London, N.W.10* - Willesden
Church End	*Warwick* - Birmingham
Church Enstone	*Oxford* - Banbury
Church Fenton	*York, W.R.* - York
Churchfield	*Northampton* - Peterborough
Churchfield	*Stafford* - West Bromwich
Church Gresley	*Derby* - Burton-upon-Trent
Church Handborough	*Oxford* - Witney
Church Hill	*Cumberland* - Carlisle
Church Honeybourne	*Worcester* - Evesham
Church Hulme	*Cheshire* - Congleton
Churchill	*Devon* - Axminster and Chard
Churchill	*Devon* - Barnstaple
Churchill	*Oxford* - Banbury
Churchill	*Somerset* - Weston Super Mare
Churchill	*Warwick* - Birmingham
Churchill	*Worcester* - Kidderminster
Church Hill	*Worcester* - Redditch
Churchill	*Worcester* - Worcester
Churchingford	*Devon* - Taunton
Church Knowle	*Dorset* - Swanage
Church Laneham	*Notts* - East Retford
Church Langton	*Leicester* - Leicester
Church Lawford	*Warwick* - Rugby
Church Lawton	*Cheshire* - Congleton
Church Lench	*Worcester* - Evesham
Church Merrington	*Durham* - Bishop Auckland
Church Minshull	*Cheshire* - Crewe
Church Moor	*Salop* - Ludlow
Church Norton	*Sussex* - Chichester
Church Oakley	*Hants* - Basingstoke
Churchover	*Warwick* - Rugby
Church Preen	*Salop* - Shrewsbury
Church Pulverbatch	*Salop* - Shrewsbury
Church Road	*Monmouth* - Newport (Mon.)
Churchstanton	*Somerset* - Taunton
Church Stoke	*Montgomery* - Welshpool
Church Stoke, Old	*Montgomery* - Welshpool
Churchstow	*Devon* - Kingsbridge
Church Stowe	*Northampton* - Northampton
Church Stretton	*Salop* - Shrewsbury
Church Style	*Northumberland* - Carlisle
Churchtown	*Lancaster* - Preston
Churchtown	*Lancaster* - Southport
Church Town	*Somerset* - Bristol
Church Village	*Glamorgan* - Pontypridd
Church Warsop	*Notts* - Mansfield
Churston Ferrers	*Devon* - Torquay
Churt, Lower	*Surrey* - Guildford
Churton	*Cheshire* - Chester
Churton	*Salop* - Shrewsbury
Churton Heath	*Cheshire* - Chester
Churt, Upper	*Surrey* - Guildford
Churwell	*York, W.R.* - Dewsbury
Chute	*Wilts* - Andover
Chute Forest	*Wilts* - Andover
Chwilog	*Caernarvon* - Portmadoc
Chyknell	*Salop* - Bridgnorth
Chyvelah	*Cornwall* - Truro

Chyvogue	*Cornwall* - Redruth
Ciffig	*Carmarthen* - Haverfordwest
Cilcain	*Flint* - Mold
Cilcennin	*Cardigan* - Aberystwyth
Cilfrew	*Glamorgan* - Neath
Cilfynydd	*Glamorgan* - Pontypridd
Cilgerran	*Pembroke* - Cardigan
Cilgwyn	*Pembroke* - Cardigan
Ciliau Aeron	*Cardigan* - Aberystwyth
Cilmery	*Brecon* - Builth
Cilrledyn, East	*Pembroke* - Cardigan
Cilrledyn, West	*Pembroke* - Cardigan
Ciltalgarth	*Merioneth* - Bala
Cilybebyll	*Glamorgan* - Neath
Cilycwm	*Carmarthen* - Llandovery
Cilymaenllwyd	*Carmarthen* - Haverfordwest
Cimla	*Glamorgan* - Neath
Cinder Bank	*Worcester* - Dudley
Cinderford	*Gloucester* - Gloucester
Cinderhill	*Notts* - Nottingham
Cinder Hill	*Stafford* - Wolverhampton
Cinder Hill	*Stafford* - Stoke-on-Trent
Cinder Hill	*York, W.R.* - Sheffield
Cippin	*Pembroke* - Cardigan
Cirencester	*Gloucester* - Swindon
City (Upper Tividale)	*Stafford* - Dudley
City Llasannor	*Glamorgan* - Bridgend
Clack	*Wilts* - Chippenham
Clacton-on-Sea	*Essex* - Colchester
Claife	*Lancaster* - Kendal
Claines	*Worcester* - Worcester
Clandon, East	*Surrey* - Guildford
Clandon, West	*Surrey* - Guildford
Clandown	*Somerset* - Frome
Clanfield	*Hants* - Petersfield
Clanfield	*Oxford* - Witney
Clannaborough	*Devon* - Exeter
Clanville	*Hants* - Andover
Clanville	*Somerset* - Yeovil
Clapcot	*Berks* - Didcot
Clapgate	*Hants* - Andover
Clapgate	*Herts* - Bishop's Stortford
Claphall	*Kent* - Gravesend
Clapham	*Beds* - Bedford
Clapham (part)	*London, S.W.4* - Lambeth
Clapham (part)	*London, S.W.4* - Wandsworth
Clapham	*Sussex* - Worthing
Clapham Common	*London, S.W.4* - Wandsworth
Clapham-cum-Newby	*York, W.R.* - Skipton
Clapham Park	*London, S.W.4* - Wandsworth
Clapper Hill	*Kent* - Cranbrook
Clappersgate	*Westmorland* - Kendal
Clapton	*Berks* - Newbury
Clapton	*Gloucester* - Stroud
Clapton	*London, E.5* - Shoreditch
Clapton	*Somerset* - Wells
Clapton	*Somerset* - Yeovil
Clapton Common	*London, E.5* - Shoreditch
Clapton-in-Gordano	*Somerset* - Bristol
Clapton, Lower	*London, E.5* - Shoreditch
Clapton on the Hill	*Gloucester* - Cheltenham
Clapton Park	*London, E.5* - Shoreditch
Clapton, Upper	*London, E.5* - Shoreditch
Clarach	*Cardigan* - Aberystwyth
Clara Vale	*Durham* - Newcastle upon Tyne
Clarbeston	*Pembroke* - Haverfordwest
Clarbeston Road	*Pembroke* - Haverfordwest
Clarborough	*Notts* - East Retford
Clare	*Suffolk* - Sudbury
Claremount	*York, W.R.* - Halifax
Clarendon	*Wilts* - Salisbury
Clarendon Park	*Leicester* - Leicester
Clareton	*York, W.R.* - Harrogate
Clarewood	*Northumberland* - Hexham
Clarghyll	*Cumberland* - Carlisle
Clargill	*Cumberland* - Haltwhistle
Clarkenwater	*Cornwall* - Bodmin
Clark's Green	*Surrey* - Dorking
Clase	*Glamorgan* - Swansea
Clatford	*Wilts* - Swindon

Clatford Goodworth	*Hants* - Andover
Clatford Oakcutts	*Hants* - Andover
Clatford, Upper	*Hants* - Andover
Clatter	*Montgomery* - Newtown
Clatterbridge	*Cheshire* - Birkenhead
Clattercote	*Oxford* - Banbury
Clatterford End	*Essex* - Chelmsford
Clatworthy	*Somerset* - Minehead
Claughton	*Lancaster* - Lancaster
Claughton	*Lancaster* - Preston
Claughton	*Cheshire* - Birkenhead
Clavelshay	*Somerset* - Bridgwater
Claverdon	*Warwick* - Warwick
Claverham	*Somerset* - Weston Super Mare
Clavering	*Essex* - Bishop's Stortford
Claverley	*Salop* - Bridgnorth
Claverton	*Cheshire* - Chester
Claverton	*Somerset* - Bath
Clawddnewydd	*Denbigh* - Denbigh
Clawson	*Leicester* - Melton Mowbray
Clawson, Long	*Leicester* - Melton Mowbray
Clawthorpe	*Westmorland* - Kendal
Clawton	*Devon* - Launceston
Claxby	*Lincoln* - Great Grimsby
Claxby	*Lincoln* - Skegness
Claxby Pluckacre	*Lincoln* - Boston
Claxton	*Norfolk* - Norwich
Claxton	*York, N.R.* - York
Claybrooke Magna	*Leicester* - Hinckley
Claybrooke Parva	*Leicester* - Hinckley
Claybury	*Essex* - Ilford
Claycoton	*Northampton* - Rugby
Clay Cross	*Derby* - Chesterfield
Claydon	*Gloucester* - Cheltenham
Claydon	*Oxford* - Banbury
Claydon	*Suffolk* - Ipswich
Claygate	*Surrey* - Kingston-upon-Thames
Claygate Cross	*Kent* - Sevenoaks
Clayhall	*Hants* - Portsmouth
Clayhanger	*Devon* - Tiverton
Clayhanger	*Stafford* - Walsall
Clayhiddon	*Devon* - Taunton
Clayhill	*Kent* - Cranbrook
Clay Hills	*Stafford* - Stoke-on-Trent
Clayhithe	*Cambridge* - Cambridge
Clay Lane	*Lincoln* - Spalding
Clay Mills	*Stafford* - Burton-upon-Trent
Claypits	*Gloucester* - Stroud
Claypole	*Lincoln* - Newark
Claythorpe	*Lincoln* - Louth
Clayton	*Lancaster* - Manchester
Clayton	*Stafford* - Stoke-on-Trent
Clayton	*Sussex* - Hayward's Heath
Clayton	*York, W.R.* - Bradford
Clayton Bridge	*Lancaster* - Manchester
Clayton-cum-Frickley	*York, W.R.* - Doncaster
Clayton Green	*Lancaster* - Chorley
Clayton Heights	*York, W.R.* - Bradford
Clayton-in-le-Clay	*York, W.R.* - Doncaster
Clayton-le-Dale	*Lancaster* - Blackburn
Clayton-le-Moors	*Lancaster* - Accrington
Clayton-le-Woods	*Lancaster* - Chorley
Clayton, West	*York, W.R.* - Huddersfield
Clayton Wickham	*Sussex* - Haywards Heath
Clayway	*Cambridge* - Ely
Clayworth	*Notts* - East Retford
Cleadon	*Durham* - South Shields
Cleadon Park Estate	*Durham* - South Shields
Clearbrook	*Devon* - Plymouth
Clearwell	*Gloucester* - Monmouth
Cleasby	*York, N.R.* - Darlington
Cleatham	*Lincoln* - Scunthorpe
Cleatlam	*Durham* - Darlington
Cleatlam, South	*Durham* - Darlington
Cleator	*Cumberland* - Whitehaven
Cleator Moor	*Cumberland* - Whitehaven
Cleavancy	*Wilts* - Swindon
Cleavewater	*Sussex* - Haywards Heath
Cleckheaton	*York, W.R.* - Dewsbury
Clee Downton	*Salop* - Ludlow

Clee Hill	*Salop* - Ludlow
Clee St. Margaret	*Salop* - Ludlow
Clee Stanton	*Salop* - Ludlow
Cleethorpes	*Lincoln* - Great Grimsby
Cleeton St. Mary	*Salop* - Ludlow
Cleeve	*Gloucester* - Bristol
Cleeve	*Gloucester* - Cheltenham
Cleeve	*Gloucester* - Gloucester
Cleeve	*Oxford* - Didcot
Cleeve	*Somerset* - Weston Super Mare
Cleeve Hill	*Gloucester* - Cheltenham
Cleevelode	*Worcester* - Great Malvern
Cleeve, Old	*Somerset* - Minehead
Cleeve Prior	*Worcester* - Evesham
Clehonger	*Hereford* - Hereford
Clench Common	*Wilts* - Swindon
Clenchwarton	*Norfolk* - King's Lynn
Clennell	*Northumberland* - Morpeth
Clent	*Worcester* - Stourbridge
Cleobury Mortimer	*Salop* - Kidderminster
Cleobury, North	*Salop* - Bridgnorth
Clerkenwell	*London, E.C.1* - Clerkenwell
Clerk Green	*York, W.R.* - Dewsbury
Cletterwood	*Montgomery* - Welshpool
Clevedon	*Somerset* - Weston Super Mare
Cleveley	*Oxford* - Banbury
Cleveleys	*Lancaster* - Blackpool
Cleverton	*Wilts* - Malmesbury
Clewer	*Berks* - Slough
Clewer Green	*Berks* - Slough
Cley-next-the-Sea	*Norfolk* - Norwich
Cliburn	*Westmorland* - Penrith
Cliddesden	*Hants* - Basingstoke
Cliff	*York, E.R.* - York
Cliff Ash	*Derby* - Matlock
Cliffe	*Kent* - Rochester
Cliffe	*York, E.R.* - York
Cliffe End	*Kent* - Ramsgate
Cliffe Marshes	*Kent* - Rochester
Cliffe, North	*York, E.R.* - Beverley
Cliffe, South	*York, E.R.* - Beverley
Clifford	*Hereford* - Hereford
Clifford	*York, W.R.* - Leeds
Clifford Chambers	*Warwick* - Stratford on Avon
Cliffords Mesne	*Gloucester* - Gloucester
Cliff Vale	*Stafford* - Stoke-on-Trent
Clifton	*Beds* - Biggleswade
Clifton	*Cheshire* - Runcorn
Clifton	*Derby* - Derby
Clifton	*Gloucester* - Bristol
Clifton	*Lancaster* - Preston
Clifton	*Lancaster* - Salford
Clifton	*Oxford* - Banbury
Clifton	*Westmorland* - Penrith
Clifton	*Worcester* - Worcester
Clifton	*York, W.R.* - Doncaster
Clifton	*York, W.R.* - Halifax
Clifton	*York, W.R.* - Otley
Clifton Campville	*Stafford* - Tamworth
Clifton cum Glapton	*Notts* - Nottingham
Clifton Dykes	*Westmorland* - Penrith
Clifton, Great	*Cumberland* - Workington
Clifton Hampden	*Oxford* - Didcot
Clifton Heath	*Oxford* - Oxford
Clifton, Little	*Cumberland* - Workington
Clifton Maybank	*Dorset* - Yeovil
Clifton, North	*Notts* - Newark
Clifton Reynes	*Bucks* - Northampton
Clifton, South	*Notts* - Newark
Clifton-upon-Dunsmore	*Warwick* - Rugby
Clifton-upon-Teme	*Worcester* - Worcester
Cliftonville	*Kent* - Margate
Climping	*Sussex* - Chichester
Clinch	*Northumberland* - Alnwick
Clink	*Somerset* - Frome
Clinkham Wood	*Lancaster* - St. Helens
Clint	*York, W.R.* - Harrogate
Clippesby	*Norfolk* - Great Yarmouth
Clipsham	*Rutland* - Stamford
Clipston	*Northampton* - Northampton

CLI - COA

Clipstone	*Beds* - Bletchley and Leighton Buzzard
Clipstone	*Notts* - Mansfield
Clipstone (Near Cotgrave)	*Notts* - Nottingham
Clipstone, Old	*Notts* - Mansfield
Clissold Park	*London, N.16* - Shoreditch
Clitheroe	*Cumberland* - Carlisle
Clitheroe	*Lancaster* - Blackburn
Clitters	*Cornwall* - Launceston
Clive	*Cheshire* - Northwich
Clive	*Salop* - Shrewsbury
Clive Vale	*Sussex* - Hastings
Cliviger	*Lancaster* - Burnley
Clixby	*Lincoln* - Scunthorpe
Clocaenog	*Denbigh* - Denbigh
Clock Face	*Lancaster* - St. Helens
Clodock	*Hereford* - Pontypridd and Abergavenny
Cloford	*Somerset* - Frome
Clophill	*Beds* - Bedford
Clopton	*Gloucester* - Stratford on Avon
Clopton	*Northampton* - Kettering
Clopton	*Suffolk* - Woodbridge
Clopton	*Warwick* - Stratford on Avon
Closeaburns	*Northumberland* - Hexham
Close Booth, West	*Lancaster* - Burnley
Close, High	*Cumberland* - Workington
Close House	*Durham* - Bishop Auckland
Close House	*Northumberland* - Newcastle upon Tyne
Closworth	*Somerset* - Yeovil
Clothall	*Herts* - Hitchin
Clotherholme	*York, W.R.* - Harrogate
Clotton Hoofield	*Cheshire* - Chester
Cloudesley Bush	*Warwick* - Rugby
Clough Fold	*Lancaster* - Rawtenstall
Cloughfoot	*Lancaster* - Todmorden
Cloughton	*York, N.R.* - Scarborough
Clousden Hill	*Northumberland* - Newcastle upon Tyne
Clovelly	*Devon* - Bideford
Clowbridge	*Lancaster* - Burnley
Clowne	*Derby* - Worksop
Clows Top	*Worcester* - Kidderminster
Clubworthy	*Devon* - Launceston
Cluddley	*Salop* - Wellington (Salop)
Clumber	*Notts* - Worksop
Clun	*Salop* - Ludlow
Clunbury	*Salop* - Ludlow
Clungunford	*Salop* - Ludlow
Clunton	*Salop* - Ludlow
Clutton	*Cheshire* - Chester
Clutton	*Somerset* - Bristol
Clwydyfagwr	*Glamorgan* - Merthyr Tydfil
Clydach	*Brecon* - Pontypridd and Abergavenny
Clydach	*Glamorgan* - Neath
Clydach Vale	*Glamorgan* - Pontypridd
Clydey	*Pembroke* - Cardigan
Clyffe Pypard	*Wilts* - Swindon
Clynderwen	*Carmarthen* - Haverfordwest
Clyne	*Glamorgan* - Neath
Clynnog	*Caernarvon* - Caernarvon
Clyro	*Radnor* - Brecknock
Clyst Honiton	*Devon* - Exeter
Clyst Hydon	*Devon* - Exeter
Clyst St. George	*Devon* - Exeter
Clyst St. Lawrence	*Devon* - Exeter
Clyst St. Mary	*Devon* - Exeter
Clytha	*Monmouth* - Pontypool and Abergavenny
Cnwchcoch	*Cardigan* - Aberystwyth
Coads Green	*Cornwall* - Launceston
Coal Aston	*Derby* - Chesterfield
Coalbrookdale	*Salop* - Wellington (Salop)
Coalburn	*Northumberland* - Morpeth
Coalburns	*Durham* - Newcastle upon Tyne
Coalcleugh	*Northumberland* - Hexham

COA - COD

Coaley	*Gloucester* - Stroud
Coalfell	*Cumberland* - Carlisle
Coal Houses	*Northumberland* - Morpeth
Coalmoor	*Salop* - Wellington (Salop)
Coalmouth Creek	*Kent* - Rochester
Coalpit Heath	*Gloucester* - Bristol
Coalpit Hill	*Stafford* - Stoke-on-Trent
Coalpool	*Stafford* - Walsall
Coalport	*Salop* - Wellington (Salop)
Coalville	*Leicester* - Ashby-de-la-Zouch
Coalway	*Gloucester* - Monmouth
Coanwood	*Northumberland* - Hexham
Coanwood, East	*Northumberland* - Hexham
Coat	*Somerset* - Yeovil
Coate	*Wilts* - Devizes
Coate	*Wilts* - Swindon
Coates	*Cambridge* - Peterborough
Coates	*Gloucester* - Stroud
Coates	*Sussex* - Chichester
Coates by Stow	*Lincoln* - Gainsborough
Coates Cottam	*Notts* - East Retford
Coates Grange	*Lincoln* - Louth
Coates, Great	*Lincoln* - Great Grimsby
Coates Mill	*Gloucester* - Cheltenham
Coates, North	*Lincoln* - Louth
Coates Park	*Derby* - Alfreton
Coatham	*York, N.R.* - Middlesbrough
Coatham Mundeville	*Durham* - Darlington
Coatham Stob	*Durham* - Stockton on Tees
Coatyards	*Northumberland* - Morpeth
Cobbaton	*Devon* - Barnstaple
Coberley	*Gloucester* - Cheltenham
Cobham	*Kent* - Gravesend
Cobham	*Surrey* - Kingston-upon-Thames
Cobley	*Worcester* - Redditch
Cobnash	*Hereford* - Leominster
Cobridge	*Stafford* - Stoke-on-Trent
Cockayne Hatley	*Beds* - Biggleswade
Cockbridge	*Cumberland* - Carlisle
Cockbrook	*Lancaster* - Ashton-under-Lyne
Cockbury	*Gloucester* - Cheltenham
Cock Clarks	*Essex* - Maldon
Cocken	*Durham* - Durham
Cockerham	*Lancaster* - Lancaster
Cockerington, North	*Lincoln* - Louth
Cockerington, South	*Lincoln* - Louth
Cockermouth	*Cumberland* - Workington
Cockernhoe	*Herts* - Hitchin
Cockersdale	*York, W.R.* - Dewsbury
Cockett	*Glamorgan* - Swansea
Cockeymoor	*Lancaster* - Bury
Cockfield	*Durham* - Bishop Auckland
Cockfield	*Suffolk* - Bury St. Edmunds
Cockfosters (part)	*Middlesex* - Barnet
Cockfosters (part)	*Middlesex* - Edmonton
Cockhampstead	*Herts* - Bishop's Stortford
Cocking	*Sussex* - Chichester
Cockington	*Devon* - Torquay
Cocklake	*Somerset* - Wells
Cocklakes	*Cumberland* - Carlisle
Cocklaw	*Northumberland* - Hexham
Cockleford	*Gloucester* - Cheltenham
Cockle Park	*Northumberland* - Morpeth
Cockley Beck	*Lancaster* - Barrow-in-Furness
Cockley Cley	*Norfolk* - King's Lynn
Cockmannings	*Kent* - Bromley
Cockmount Hill	*Northumberland* - Hexham
Cocknage	*Stafford* - Stoke-on-Trent
Cockpole	*Berks* - Reading
Cocks	*Cornwall* - Truro
Cockshutford	*Salop* - Ludlow
Cockshutt	*Salop* - Oswestry
Cockthorpe	*Norfolk* - King's Lynn
Cockwells	*Cornwall* - Penzance
Cockwood (part)	*Devon* - Exeter
Cockyard	*Derby* - Buxton
Coddenham	*Suffolk* - Ipswich
Coddington	*Cheshire* - Chester
Coddington	*Hereford* - Hereford
Coddington	*Notts* - Newark

Codford St. Mary	*Wilts* - Warminster
Codford St. Peter	*Wilts* - Warminster
Codicote	*Herts* - Hitchin
Codmore Hill	*Sussex* - Chichester
Codnor	*Derby* - Ilkeston
Codnor Gate (Ripley)	*Derby* - Alfreton
Codnor Gate (Codnor)	*Derby* - Ilkeston
Codnor Park (Alfreton)	*Derby* - Alfreton
Codnor Park (Codnor)	*Derby* - Ilkeston
Codrington	*Gloucester* - Bristol
Codsall	*Stafford* - Wolverhampton
Codsall Wood	*Stafford* - Wolverhampton
Coedana	*Anglesey* - Llangefni
Coedcae (Nantyglo)	*Monmouth* - Blackwood
Coedcanlas	*Pembroke* - Haverfordwest
Coedely	*Glamorgan* - Pontypridd
Coedkernew	*Monmouth* - Newport (Mon.)
Coedmawr	*Caernarvon* - Bangor
Coedpoeth	*Denbigh* - Wrexham
Coed y Bryn	*Cardigan* - Cardigan
Coed Ymwstwr	*Glamorgan* - Bridgend
Coedyrallt	*Salop* - Oswestry
Coffinswell	*Devon* - Newton Abbot
Cofton	*Devon* - Newton Abbot
Cofton Hackett	*Worcester* - Bromsgrove
Cogan	*Glamorgan* - Cardiff
Coganhoe	*Northampton* - Northampton
Cogges	*Oxford* - Witney
Coggeshall, Great	*Essex* - Braintree
Coggeshall, Little	*Essex* - Braintree
Cogshall	*Cheshire* - Northwich
Coity, Higher	*Glamorgan* - Bridgend
Coity, Lower	*Glamorgan* - Bridgend
Cokeham	*Sussex* - Worthing
Coker, East	*Somerset* - Yeovil
Coker Hill	*Somerset* - Yeovil
Coker, North	*Somerset* - Yeovil
Coker, West	*Somerset* - Yeovil
Colan	*Cornwall* - Truro
Colaton Raleigh	*Devon* - Exeter
Colbren	*Brecon* - Neath
Colburn	*York, N.R.* - Darlington
Colbury	*Hants* - Southampton
Colby	*Norfolk* - Norwich
Colby	*Westmorland* - Penrith
Colchester	*Essex* - Colchester
Cold Ash	*Berks* - Newbury
Cold Ashby	*Northampton* - Northampton
Cold Ashton	*Gloucester* - Bath
Cold Ashton	*Wilts* - Bath
Cold Aston	*Gloucester* - Cheltenham
Cold Blow	*Kent* - Cranbrook
Coldblow	*Pembroke* - Haverfordwest
Cold Brayfield	*Bucks* - Northampton
Coldcoats	*Northumberland* - Newcastle-upon-Tyne
Cold Comfort	*Gloucester* - Cheltenham
Coldean	*Sussex* - Brighton
Cold Eaton	*Derby* - Matlock
Cold Edge	*York, W.R.* - Halifax
Colden	*York, W.R.* - Todmorden
Colden Common	*Hants* - Winchester
Coldham	*Cambridge* - Wisbech
Cold Hanworth	*Lincoln* - Lincoln
Cold Harbour	*Bucks* - Thame
Cold Harbour	*Herts* - Hertford
Cold Harbour	*Herts* - St. Albans
Cold Harbour (Wye)	*Kent* - Ashford
Cold Harbour	*Kent* - Cranbrook
Cold Harbour	*Kent* - Deal
Cold Harbour	*Oxford* - Banbury
Cold Harbour	*Oxford* - Oxford
Cold Harbour	*Somerset* - Yeovil
Coldharbour	*Surrey* - Dorking
Cold Harbour	*Sussex* - Haywards Heath
Cold Hatton	*Salop* - Wellington (Salop)
Cold Henley	*Hants* - Andover
Cold Hesledon	*Durham* - Sunderland
Cold Higham	*Northampton* - Northampton
Coldhill	*York, W.R.* - Leeds

Cold Kirby	*York, N.R.* - Malton
Cold Martin	*Northumberland* - Alnwick
Cold Meece	*Stafford* - Stafford
Coldmoorholm	*Bucks* - High Wycombe
Cold Newton	*Leicester* - Leicester
Cold Northcott	*Cornwall* - Launceston
Cold Norton	*Essex* - Maldon
Cold Norton	*Stafford* - Stafford
Cold Overton	*Leicester* - Melton Mowbray
Coldred	*Kent* - Dover
Coldrewick	*Cornwall* - Liskeard
Coldridge	*Devon* - Okehampton
Coldrife	*Northumberland* - Morpeth
Coldside	*Northumberland* - Morpeth
Coldsmouth	*Northumberland* - Berwick-upon-Tweed
Coldwatham	*Sussex* - Chichester
Coldwell	*Lancaster* - Nelson
Coldwell	*Northumberland* - Hexham
Coldwell	*Stafford* - Uttoxeter
Cold Weston	*Salop* - Ludlow
Cole (Bruton)	*Somerset* - Yeovil
Colebatch	*Salop* - Shrewsbury
Colebrook	*Devon* - Plymouth
Colebrooke	*Devon* - Exeter
Coleby	*Lincoln* - Lincoln
Coleby	*Lincoln* - Scunthorpe
Coleby Heath	*Lincoln* - Lincoln
Coledale	*Cumberland* - Workington
Cole End	*Warwick* - Birmingham
Coleford	*Devon* - Exeter
Coleford	*Gloucester* - Monmouth
Coleford	*Somerset* - Frome
Coleford	*Warwick* - Birmingham
Coleford Water	*Somerset* - Minehead
Cole Green	*Herts* - Hertford
Colehill	*Dorset* - Wimborne Minster
Colehurst	*Salop* - Market Drayton
Coleman Green	*Herts* - St. Albans
Coleman's Hatch	*Sussex* - East Grinstead
Colemere	*Salop* - Oswestry
Colemore	*Hants* - Petersfield
Colemore Green	*Salop* - Bridgnorth
Coleorton	*Leicester* - Ashby-de-la-Zouch
Colerne	*Wilts* - Bath
Colesbourne	*Gloucester* - Cheltenham
Coles Cross	*Devon* - Kingsbridge
Colesdon	*Beds* - Bedford
Coles Green	*Worcester* - Great Malvern
Coleshill	*Berks* - Swindon
Coleshill	*Bucks* - Amersham
Coleshill	*Warwick* - Birmingham
Colestay	*Salop* - Ludlow
Colestocks	*Devon* - Exeter
Colethrop	*Glos* - Gloucester
Coley	*Stafford* - Stafford
Coley	*York, W.R.* - Halifax
Coley, High	*Stafford* - Stafford
Coley Lane	*York, W.R.* - Rotherham
Colgate	*Sussex* - Horsham
Colham Green	*Middlesex* - Uxbridge
Colhook Common	*Sussex* - Chichester
Colindale	*London, N.W.9* - Willesden
Colkirk	*Norfolk* - King's Lynn
Collafield	*Glos* - Gloucester
Collaton	*Devon* - Torquay
College Fields	*Salop* - Market Drayton
College Park (part)	*London, N.W.10* - Bloomsbury and Marylebone
College Park (part)	*London, N.W.10* - Willesden
Colletts Bridge	*Norfolk* - Wisbech
Collett's Brook	*Warwick* - Birmingham
Colley Gate	*Worcester* - Stourbridge
Collfryn	*Montgomery* - Oswestry
Collier Row	*Essex* - Ilford
Collier's End	*Herts* - Hertford
Collier's Green	*Kent* - Cranbrook
Colliers Hatch	*Essex* - Harlow
Colliers Row, Lower	*Glamorgan* - Merthyr Tydfil
Colliers Row, Upper	*Glamorgan* - Merthyr Tydfil

Collier's Wood	*London, S.W.19* - Croydon
Colliery Dykes	*Durham* - Durham
Colliery Row	*Durham* - Durham
Collingbourne Ducis	*Wilts* - Andover
Collingbourne Kingston	*Wilts* - Andover
Collingham	*York, W.R.* - Leeds
Collingham, North	*Notts* - Newark
Collingham, South	*Notts* - Newark
Collington	*Hereford* - Hereford
Collingtree	*Northampton* - Northampton
Collins Green	*Lancaster* - Warrington
Collycroft	*Warwick* - Nuneaton
Collyhurst	*Lancaster* - Manchester
Collyweston	*Northampton* - Stamford
Colmworth	*Beds* - Bedford
Colnbrook	*Bucks* - Uxbridge
Colne	*Hunts* - Huntingdon
Colne	*Lancaster* - Nelson
Colne Bridge	*York, W.R.* - Huddersfield
Colne Engaine	*Essex* - Colchester
Colney	*Norfolk* - Norwich
Colney Hatch	*London, N.11* - Barnet
Colney Heath	*Herts* - St. Albans
Colney Street	*Herts* - St. Albans
Coln Rogers	*Gloucester* - Cheltenham
Coln St. Aldwyn	*Gloucester* - Cheltenham
Coln St. Dennis	*Gloucester* - Cheltenham
Colsterdale	*York, N.R.* - Harrogate
Colsterworth	*Lincoln* - Grantham
Colston Bassett	*Notts* - Nottingham
Colthouse	*Lancaster* - Kendal
Coltishall	*Norfolk* - Norwich
Colton	*Lancaster* - Barrow-in-Furness
Colton	*Norfolk* - Norwich
Colton	*Stafford* - Stafford
Colton	*York, W.R.* - Leeds
Colton	*York, W.R.* - York
Colva	*Radnor* - Builth Wells
Colveston	*Norfolk* - King's Lynn
Colwall	*Hereford* - Great Malvern
Colwall Green	*Hereford* - Great Malvern
Colwall, Old	*Hereford* - Great Malvern
Colwell	*Devon* - Axminster
Colwell	*Northumberland* - Hexham
Colwell Bay	*I. of W.* - Newport (I.W.)
Colwich	*Stafford* - Stafford
Colwick	*Notts* - Nottingham
Colwinstone	*Glamorgan* - Bridgend
Colwith	*Westmorland* - Kendal
Colwood	*Sussex* - Haywards Heath
Colworth	*Sussex* - Chichester
Colwyn Bay	*Denbigh* - Conway
Colyford	*Devon* - Axminster and Chard
Colyton	*Devon* - Axminster and Chard
Combe	*Berks* - Newbury
Combe	*Dorset* - Yeovil
Combe	*Hereford* - Leominster
Combe	*Oxford* - Oxford
Combe	*Wilts* - Devizes
Combe Almer	*Dorset* - Wimborne Minster
Combe Down	*Somerset* - Bath
Combe East	*Somerset* - Taunton
Combe Fields	*Oxford* - Oxford
Combe Fields	*Warwick* - Rugby
Combe Florey	*Somerset* - Taunton
Combe Hay	*Somerset* - Bath
Combe Martin	*Devon* - Barnstaple
Combe Moor	*Hereford* - Leominster
Combend	*Gloucester* - Gloucester
Combepyne	*Devon* - Axminster and Chard
Combe Raleigh	*Devon* - Exeter
Comberbach	*Cheshire* - Northwich
Comberford	*Stafford* - Tamworth
Comberton	*Cambridge* - Cambridge
Comberton	*Hereford* - Leominster
Comberton, Great	*Worcester* - Evesham
Comberton, Little	*Worcester* - Evesham
Combe St. Nicholas	*Somerset* - Axminster and Chard
Combe, South	*Devon* - Axminster and Chard
Comb Hill	*Northumberland* - Hexham

Combhill	*Northumberland* - Morpeth
Combourne	*Kent* - Cranbrook
Combridge	*Stafford* - Uttoxeter
Combroke	*Warwick* - Stratford on Avon
Combs	*Derby* - Buxton
Combs	*Suffolk* - Stowmarket
Combs Edge	*Derby* - Buxton
Combwich	*Somerset* - Bridgwater
Comeytrowe	*Somerset* - Taunton
Comford	*Cornwall* - Redruth
Comins	*Denbigh* - Oswestry
Comley	*Salop* - Shrewsbury
Commercial	*Pembroke* - Haverfordwest
Comminscoch	*Cardigan* - Aberystwyth
Comminscoch	*Montgomery* - Machynlleth
Commondale	*York, N.R.* - Whitby
Common House	*Northumberland* - Hexham
Common, Little	*York, W.R.* - Sheffield
Common Moor	*Cornwall* - Liskeard
Commonwood	*Denbigh* - Wrexham
Common Wood	*Herts* - Watford
Common Wood	*Salop* - Shrewsbury
Comp	*Kent* - Sevenoaks
Compstall	*Cheshire* - Stockport
Compton	*Berks* - Didcot
Compton	*Derby* - Derby
Compton	*Devon* - Torquay
Compton	*Hants* - Winchester
Compton (Kinver)	*Stafford* - Stourbridge
Compton	*Stafford* - Wolverhampton
Compton	*Surrey* - Guildford
Compton	*Sussex* - Chichester
Compton	*Wilts* - Devizes
Compton Abbas	*Dorset* - Dorchester
Compton Abbas	*Dorset* - Shaftesbury
Compton Abdale	*Gloucester* - Cheltenham
Compton Bassett	*Wilts* - Swindon
Compton Beauchamp	*Berks* - Swindon
Compton Bishop	*Somerset* - Weston Super Mare
Compton Chamberlayne	*Wilts* - Salisbury
Compton Dando	*Somerset* - Bath
Compton Dundon	*Somerset* - Wells
Compton Durville	*Somerset* - Yeovil
Compton, East	*Dorset* - Dorchester
Compton, East	*Somerset* - Wells
Compton Gifford	*Devon* - Plymouth
Compton Greenfield	*Gloucester* - Thornbury
Compton, Little	*Warwick* - Banbury
Compton, Long	*Stafford* - Stafford
Compton, Long	*Warwick* - Stratford on Avon
Compton Martin	*Somerset* - Bristol
Compton, Nether	*Dorset* - Yeovil
Compton, Over	*Dorset* - Yeovil
Compton Pauncefoot	*Somerset* - Yeovil
Compton Scorpion	*Warwick* - Stratford on Avon
Compton Vallance	*Dorset* - Dorchester
Compton Verney	*Warwick* - Stratford on Avon
Compton, West	*Dorset* - Dorchester
Compton, West	*Somerset* - Wells
Compton Wynyates	*Warwick* - Banbury
Conder Green	*Lancaster* - Lancaster
Conderton	*Worcester* - Evesham
Condicote	*Gloucester* - Cheltenham
Condover	*Salop* - Shrewsbury
Condurrow	*Cornwall* - Redruth
Coney Hall	*Kent* - Bromley
Coney Hill	*Glos* - Gloucester
Coneyhurst Corner	*Sussex* - Horsham
Coneysthorpe	*York, N.R.* - Malton
Coneythorpe	*York, W.R.* - Harrogate
Coney Weston	*Suffolk* - Thetford
Conford	*Hants* - Petersfield
Congerstone	*Leicester* - Ashby-de-la-Zouch
Congham	*Norfolk* - King's Lynn
Congleton	*Cheshire* - Congleton
Congresbury	*Somerset* - Weston Super Mare
Congreve	*Stafford* - Stafford
Conham	*Gloucester* - Bristol
Coningsby	*Lincoln* - Boston

Coningsby Fen Allotment	*Lincoln* - Boston
Coningsby Moor	*Lincoln* - Boston
Conington	*Cambridge* - Huntingdon
Conington	*Hunts* - Huntingdon
Conisbrough	*York, W.R.* - Doncaster
Coniscliffe,	*Durham* - Darlington
Conisholme	*Lincoln* - Louth
Coniston	*Lancaster* - Kendal
Coniston	*York, E.R.* - Kingston-upon-Hull
Coniston Cold	*York, W.R.* - Skipton
Conistone with Kilnsey	*York, W.R.* - Skipton
Conkwell	*Wilts* - Trowbridge
Connah's Quay	*Flint* - Holywell
Connor Downs	*Cornwall* - Redruth
Conock	*Wilts* - Devizes
Cononley	*York, W.R.* - Skipton
Consall	*Stafford* - Leek
Consett	*Durham* - Consett
Constable Burton	*York, N.R.* - Northallerton
Constantine	*Cornwall* - Truro and Falmouth
Conway	*Caernarvon* - Conway
Conwil	*Carmarthen* - Carmarthen
Conwil Gaio	*Carmarthen* - Llandovery
Conyer	*Kent* - Sittingbourne
Cooden	*Sussex* - Hastings
Cookbury	*Devon* - Bideford
Cookham	*Berks* - Slough
Cookham Dean	*Berks* - Slough
Cookham Rise	*Berks* - Slough
Cookhay	*Stafford* - West Bromwich
Cookhill	*Warwick* - Redditch
Cookley	*Oxford* - Reading
Cookley	*Suffolk* - Halesworth
Cookley	*Worcester* - Kidderminster
Cookridge	*York, W.R.* - Leeds
Cooksbridge	*Sussex* - Lewes
Cooksey Green	*Worcester* - Bromsgrove
Cookshill	*Stafford* - Stoke-on-Trent
Cooks Mill Green	*Essex* - Chelmsford
Cookworthy	*Cornwall* - Launceston
Coolham	*Sussex* - Horsham
Cooling	*Kent* - Rochester
Coombe (St. Stephen)	*Cornwall* - St. Austell
Coombe (Kea)	*Cornwall* - Truro
Coombe (Malborough)	*Devon* - Kingsbridge
Coombe (Bigbury)	*Devon* - Kingsbridge
Coombe (Swannaton)	*Devon* - Kingsbridge
Coombe	*Hants* - Petersfield
Coombe (Crewkerne)	*Somerset* - Yeovil
Coombe	*Surrey* - Kingston-upon-Thames
Coombe Almer	*Dorset* - Wimborne Minster
Coombe Bissett	*Wilts* - Salisbury
Coombe, Higher	*Wilts* - Shaftesbury
Coombe Hill	*Gloucester* - Cheltenham
Coombe in Teignhead	*Devon* - Newton Abbot
Coombe Keynes	*Dorset* - Dorchester
Coombe, Lower	*Wilts* - Shaftesbury
Coombe, Middle	*Wilts* - Shaftesbury
Coombes	*Sussex* - Worthing
Coombes Wood	*Worcester* - Stourbridge
Coombses	*Somerset* - Axminster and Chard
Cooper, New	*Cumberland* - Carlisle
Coppersale	*Essex* - Harlow
Coppersale Common	*Essex* - Harlow
Coopers Bank	*Stafford* - Dudley
Coopers Corner	*Kent* - Sevenoaks
Cooper's Green	*Herts* - St. Albans
Coopers Hill	*Worcester* - Redditch
Cootham	*Sussex* - Worthing
Copalder	*Cambridge* - March
Copcourt	*Oxford* - Thame
Copcut Elm	*Worcester* - Worcester
Copdock	*Suffolk* - Ipswich
Copely Hill	*Warwick* - Birmingham
Copford	*Essex* - Colchester
Copgrove	*York, W.R.* - Harrogate
Cophall	*Cambridge* - Ely
Cople	*Beds* - Bedford
Copley	*Cheshire* - Ashton-under-Lyne

Copley	*Durham* - Bishop Auckland
Copley	*York, W.R.* - Halifax
Copley Lane	*Durham* - Bishop Auckland
Copmanthorpe	*York, W.R.* - York
Copmere End	*Stafford* - Stafford
Copnor	*Hants* - Portsmouth
Copped Hall	*Essex* - Harlow
Coppenhall	*Stafford* - Stafford
Copperhouse	*Cornwall* - Redruth
Coppett Hill	*Hereford* - Monmouth
Coppice	*Lancaster* - Oldham
Coppice	*Stafford* - Dudley
Coppingford	*Hunts* - Huntingdon
Copping Syke	*Lincoln* - Boston
Copplestone	*Devon* - Exeter
Coppull	*Lancaster* - Chorley
Copsale	*Sussex* - Horsham
Copsewood	*Warwick* - Coventry
Copston Magna	*Warwick* - Hinckley
Copthall Green	*Essex* - Harlow
Copt Hewick	*York, W.R.* - Harrogate
Copthill	*Durham* - Durham
Copthorne	*Salop* - Shrewsbury
Copthorne (part)	*Surrey* - Reigate
Copthorne	*Sussex* - East Grinstead
Copt Oak	*Leicester* - Leicester
Coptwiney	*Salop* - Oswestry
Copy Bottom	*Lancaster* - Burnley
Copythorne	*Hants* - Southampton
Corbets Tey	*Essex* - Ilford
Corbridge	*Northumberland* - Hexham
Corby	*Lincoln* - Grantham
Corby	*Northampton* - Corby
Corby, Great	*Cumberland* - Carlisle
Corby Hill	*Cumberland* - Carlisle
Corby, Little	*Cumberland* - Carlisle
Corbyn's Hall	*Stafford* - Stourbridge
Cordley	*Stafford* - West Bromwich
Coreley	*Salop* - Ludlow
Cores End	*Bucks* - High Wycombe
Corey's Mill	*Herts* - Hitchen
Corfe	*Somerset* - Taunton
Corfe Castle	*Dorset* - Swanage
Corfe Mullen	*Dorset* - Wimborne Minster
Corfton	*Salop* - Ludlow
Corhampton	*Hants* - Petersfield
Corley	*Warwick* - Coventry
Corley Ash	*Warwick* - Coventry
Corley Moor	*Warwick* - Coventry
Corley Rock	*Warwick* - Coventry
Cornbrook	*Lancaster* - Salford
Cornbury	*Oxford* - Oxford
Corndean	*Gloucester* - Cheltenham
Corndon Marsh	*Montgomery* - Welshpool
Corneldu	*Glamorgan* - Bridgend
Cornelly	*Cornwall* - Truro
Cornelly, North	*Glamorgan* - Bridgend
Cornelly, South	*Glamorgan* - Bridgend
Corney	*Cumberland* - Whitehaven
Cornforth	*Durham* - Durham
Cornforth, New	*Durham* - Durham
Cornforth, Old	*Durham* - Durham
Cornforth, West	*Durham* - Durham
Corngreaves	*Stafford* - Dudley
Cornhill	*Northumberland* - Berwick-upon-Tweed
Corn Howe	*Cumberland* - Workington
Cornish Hall End	*Essex* - Braintree
Cornley	*Lincoln* - Gainsborough
Cornsay	*Durham* - Durham
Cornsay Colliery	*Durham* - Durham
Corntown	*Glamorgan* - Bridgend
Cornwell	*Oxford* - Banbury
Cornwood	*Devon* - Plymouth
Cornworthy	*Devon* - Torquay
Coronation	*Durham* - Bishop Auckland
Corpslanding	*York, E.R.* - Beverley
Corpusty	*Norfolk* - Norwich
Corra	*Salop* - Whitchurch
Corridge	*Northumberland* - Morpeth

COR - COT

Corringham	*Essex* - Grays Thurrock
Corringham	*Lincoln* - Gainsborough
Corris	*Merioneth* - Dolgellau
Corry Hill	*Northumberland* - Hexham
Corscombe	*Dorset* - Yeovil
Corse	*Gloucester* - Gloucester
Corse Lawn	*Worcester* - Cheltenham
Corsenside	*Northumberland* - Hexham
Corse Wood	*Worcester* - Cheltenham
Corsham	*Wilts* - Chippenham
Corsham Side	*Wilts* - Chippenham
Corsley	*Wilts* - Warminster
Corston	*Somerset* - Bath
Corston	*Wilts* - Malmesbury
Cortington	*Wilts* - Warminster
Corton	*Suffolk* - Lowestoft
Corton	*Wilts* - Swindon
Corton	*Wilts* - Warminster
Corton Denham	*Somerset* - Yeovil
Cortonwood	*York, W.R.* - Rotherham
Cortworth	*York, W.R.* - Rotherham
Corwen	*Merioneth* - Wrexham
Corwen Parish	*Merioneth* - Wrexham
Coryates	*Dorset* - Weymouth
Coryton	*Devon* - Plymouth
Coryton	*Essex* - Grays Thurrock
Coryton	*Glamorgan* - Cardiff
Cosby	*Leicester* - Leicester
Coscomb, Lower	*Gloucester* - Cheltenham
Coscomb, Upper	*Gloucester* - Cheltenham
Coseley (part)	*Stafford* - Dudley
Coseley (part)	*Stafford* - Wolverhampton
Cosford	*Warwick* - Rugby
Cosgrove	*Northampton* - Northampton
Cosham	*Hants* - Portsmouth
Cosheston	*Pembroke* - Haverfordwest
Cosmore Green	*Dorset* - Dorchester
Cossall	*Notts* - Ilkeston
Cossington	*Leicester* - Leicester
Cossington	*Somerset* - Bridgwater
Costessy	*Norfolk* - Norwich
Costhorpe	*Notts* - Worksop
Costock	*Notts* - Loughborough
Coston	*Leicester* - Melton Mowbray
Coston	*Norfolk* - Norwich
Cote	*Oxford* - Witney
Cotebrook	*Cheshire* - Crewe
Cotehele Quay	*Cornwall* - Plymouth
Cotehill	*Cumberland* - Carlisle
Cotehill	*York, W.R.* - Halifax
Cotes	*Leicester* - Loughborough
Cotesbach	*Leicester* - Rugby
Cotes-de-Val	*Leicester* - Rugby
Cotes Heath	*Stafford* - Stafford
Cotgrave	*Notts* - Nottingham
Cotham	*Notts* - Newark
Cothelstone	*Somerset* - Taunton
Cothercott	*Salop* - Shrewsbury
Cotheridge	*Worcester* - Worcester
Cotherstone	*York, N.R.* - Bishop Auckland
Cothill	*Berks* - Oxford
Cothi Bridge	*Carmarthen* - Carmarthen
Cotleigh	*Devon* - Axminster
Cotmanhay	*Derby* - Ilkeston
Cotman's Ash	*Kent* - Sevenoaks
Cotness	*York, E.R.* - Goole
Coton	*Cambridge* - Cambridge
Coton	*Derby* - Burton-on-Trent
Coton	*Northampton* - Northampton
Coton	*Oxford* - Banbury
Coton	*Salop* - Bridgnorth
Coton	*Salop* - Shrewsbury
Coton (Gnosall)	*Stafford* - Stafford
Coton (Stone)	*Stafford* - Stafford
Coton	*Stafford* - Tamworth
Coton Clanford	*Stafford* - Stafford
Coton, Far	*Leicester* - Hinckley
Coton Hayes	*Stafford* - Stafford
Coton-in-the-Elms	*Derby* - Burton-upon-Trent
Coton, Near	*Leicester* - Hinckley

COT - COV

Coton Park	*Derby* - Burton-upon-Trent
Cotsbrook	*Salop* - Bridgnorth
Cottage End	*Hants* - Andover
Cottam	*Lancaster* - Preston
Cottam	*Notts* - East Retford
Cottam	*York, E.R.* - Beverley
Cottenham	*Cambridge* - Cambridge
Cottenworth	*Hants* - Andover
Cotterbury	*Devon* - Kingsbridge
Cottered	*Herts* - Hitchin
Cotteridge	*Warwick* - Birmingham
Cotterills Farm Estate	*Stafford* - Dudley
Cotterstock	*Northampton* - Corby
Cottesbrook	*Northampton* - Northampton
Cottesloe	*Bucks* - Bletchley and Leighton Buzzard
Cottesmore	*Rutland* - Melton Mowbray
Cottingham	*Northampton* - Corby
Cottingham	*York, E.R.* - Kingston-upon-Hull
Cottingley	*York, W.R.* - Keighley
Cottington	*Kent* - Deal
Cottingwith, East	*York, E.R.* - Selby
Cottingwith, West	*York, E.R.* - Selby
Cottingwood	*Northumberland* - Morpeth
Cottisford	*Oxford* - Banbury
Cotton	*Cheshire* - Congleton
Cotton	*Salop* - Market Drayton
Cotton	*Stafford* - Leek
Cotton	*Suffolk* - Stowmarket
Cotton Abbotts	*Cheshire* - Chester
Cotton Edmunds	*Cheshire* - Chester
Cotton End	*Beds* - Bedford
Cotton End	*Northampton* - Northampton
Cotton Stones	*York, W.R.* - Halifax
Cotton Tree	*Lancaster* - Nelson
Cotts	*Devon* - Plymouth
Cotwall	*Salop* - Wellington (Salop)
Cotwalton	*Stafford* - Stafford
Couches Mill	*Cornwall* - Liskeard
Coughton	*Hereford* - Monmouth
Coughton	*Warwick* - Redditch
Coulderton	*Cumberland* - Whitehaven
Coulsdon	*Surrey* - Croydon
Coulston, East	*Wilts* - Trowbridge
Coulston, West	*Wilts* - Trowbridge
Coultershaw	*Sussex* - Chichester
Coultings	*Somerset* - Bridgwater
Coulton	*York, N.R.* - Malton
Cound	*Salop* - Shrewsbury
Coundon	*Durham* - Bishop Auckland
Coundon	*Warwick* - Coventry
Coundon Gate	*Durham* - Bishop Auckland
Coundon Grange	*Durham* - Bishop Auckland
Coundon, New	*Durham* - Bishop Auckland
Coundon, Old	*Durham* - Bishop Auckland
Counter Drain	*Lincoln* - Spalding
Countesthorpe	*Leicester* - Leicester
Counthorpe	*Lincoln* - Stamford
Countisbury	*Devon* - Barnstaple
Country, North	*Cornwall* - Redruth
County Bridge	*Stafford* - Walsall
County End	*York, W.R.* - Oldham
Coupe Green	*Lancaster* - Preston
Court Colman	*Glamorgan* - Bridgend
Courteenhall	*Northampton* - Northampton
Court House	*Montgomery* - Welshpool
Courthouse Green	*Warwick* - Coventry
Cove	*Devon* - Tiverton
Cove	*Hants* - Aldershot and Farnham
Covehithe	*Suffolk* - Lowestoft
Coven	*Stafford* - Wolverhampton
Coveney	*Cambridge* - Ely
Covenham St.	*Lincoln* - Louth
Coven Heath	*Stafford* - Wolverhampton
Covenhope	*Hereford* - Leominster
Coven Lawn	*Stafford* - Wolverhampton
Covent Garden	*London, W.C.2* - Westminster
Coventry	*Warwick* - Coventry
Coverack	*Cornwall* - Penzance
Coverack Bridges	*Cornwall* - Penzance

Coverham	*York, N.R.* - Northallerton
Covington	*Hunts* - Huntingdon
Cowan Bridge	*Lancaster* - Lancaster
Cowarch	*Merioneth* - Dolgellau
Cowark	*Lancaster* - Blackburn
Cowarne, Little	*Hereford* - Worcester
Cowbeech	*Sussex* - Eastbourne
Cowbit	*Lincoln* - Spalding
Cowbridge	*Glamorgan* - Bridgend
Cow Brow	*Westmorland* - Kendal
Cowburn Rigg	*Northumberland* - Haltwhistle
Cowcliffe	*York, W.R.* - Huddersfield
Cowcombe Hill	*Gloucester* - Stroud
Cowdale	*Derby* - Buxton
Cowden	*Dorset* - Dorchester
Cowden	*Kent* - East Grinstead
Cowden, Great	*York, E.R.* - Kingston-upon-Hull
Cowden, Little	*York, E.R.* - Kingston-upon-Hull
Cowdray Park	*Sussex* - Chichester
Cowes	*I. of W.* - Newport (I.W.)
Cowfield	*Gloucester* - Cheltenham
Cowfield Gould	*Lincs* - Spalding
Cowfold	*Sussex* - Horsham
Cowgate	*Northumberland* - Newcastle upon Tyne
Cowgrove	*Dorset* - Wimborne Minster
Cowhill	*Gloucester* - Thornbury
Cowhirne	*Lincoln* - Spalding
Cow Honeybourne	*Gloucester* - Evesham
Cowick, East	*York, W.R.* - Goole
Cowick, West	*York, W.R.* - Goole
Cowlam	*York, E.R.* - Beverley
Cowlersley	*York, W.R.* - Huddersfield
Cowlesmead	*Gloucester* - Cheltenham
Cowley	*Derby* - Chesterfield
Cowley	*Gloucester* - Cheltenham
Cowley	*Middlesex* - Uxbridge
Cowley	*Oxford* - Oxford
Cowley	*Stafford* - Stafford
Cowling	*York, W.R.* - Skipton
Cowlinge	*Suffolk* - Newmarket
Cowlishaw	*Lancaster* - Oldham
Cowlow	*Derby* - Buxton
Cowpe	*Lancaster* - Rawtenstall
Cowpen	*Northumberland* - Blyth
Cowpen Bewley	*Durham* - Stockton-on-Tees
Cowplain	*Hants* - Portsmouth
Cowsden	*Worcester* - Worcester
Cowshill	*Durham* - Bishop Auckland
Cowshot	*Surrey* - Guildford
Cowthorpe	*York, W.R.* - York
Cowton, East	*York, N.R.* - Northallerton
Cowton, North	*York, N.R.* - Darlington
Cowton, South	*York, N.R.* - Northallerton
Cox Bank	*Cheshire* - Crewe
Coxbench	*Derby* - Derby
Coxford	*Hants* - Southampton
Cox Green	*Berks* - Slough
Coxgreen	*Durham* - Durham
Cox Green	*Herts* - Hitchin
Cox Green	*Lancaster* - Bolton
Coxheath	*Kent* - Maidstone
Cox Hill	*Cornwall* - Truro
Coxhoe	*Durham* - Durham
Coxley	*Somerset* - Wells
Coxley	*York, W.R.* - Wakefield
Coxlodge	*Northumberland* - Newcastle-upon-Tyne
Coxpark	*Cornwall* - Plymouth
Coxtie Green	*Essex* - Brentwood
Coxwell, Great	*Berks* - Swindon
Coxwell, Little	*Berks* - Swindon
Coxwold	*York, N.R.* - York
Coychurch, Higher	*Glamorgan* - Bridgend
Coychurch, Lower	*Glamorgan* - Bridgend
Coytrahen	*Glamorgan* - Bridgend
Crabb's Cross	*Worcester* - Redditch
Crabbs Green	*Essex* - Harlow

Crabley	*York, E.R.* - Beverley
Crabtree	*Devon* - Plymouth
Crabtree	*Sussex* - Horsham
Crabtree	*York, W.R.* - Sheffield
Crabwall	*Cheshire* - Chester
Crabwood	*Hants* - Winchester
Crackenthorpe	*Westmorland* - Penrith
Crackington Haven	*Cornwall* - Launceston
Crackley	*Stafford* - Stoke-on-Trent
Crackley	*Warwick* - Warwick
Cracknore Hard	*Hants* - Southampton
Cracoe	*York, W.R.* - Skipton
Craddock	*Devon* - Tiverton
Cradley	*Hereford* - Worcester
Cradley (Halesowen)	*Worcester* - Stourbridge
Cradley Heath	*Stafford* - Dudley
Cradoc	*Brecon* - Brecknock
Crafthole	*Cornwall* - Plymouth
Crafton	*Bucks* - Bletchley and Leighton Buzzard
Cragend Farm	*Northumberland* - Morpeth
Cragg	*Cumberland* - Workington
Cragg Top	*York, W.R.* - Skipton
Cragg Vale	*York, W.R.* - Todmorden
Craghead	*Durham* - Consett
Cragside Cottages	*Northumberland* - Morpeth
Cragside Hall	*Northumberland* - Morpeth
Cragwood Colliery	*Durham* - Bishop Auckland
Craig	*Cumberland* - Haltwhistle
Craig - Hengoed	*Glamorgan* - Bargoed
Cragweil	*Sussex* - Chichester
Craigydon	*Caernarvon* - Conway
Craig-y-nos	*Brecon* - Neath
Crakehall	*York, N.R.* - Northallerton
Crakemarsh	*Stafford* - Uttoxeter
Crambe	*York, N.R.* - Malton
Cramlington	*Northumberland* - North Shields
Cramlington, East	*Northumberland* - North Shields
Cramlington, South	*Northumberland* - North Shields
Cramlington Village	*Northumberland* - North Shields
Cramlington, West	*Northumberland* - North Shields
Crampmoor	*Hants* - Southampton
Cranage	*Cheshire* - Congleton
Cranage	*Cheshire* - Northwich
Cranberry	*Stafford* - Stafford
Cranborne	*Dorset* - Wimborne Minster
Cranbourne	*Berks* - Slough
Cranbrook	*Essex* - Ilford
Cranbrook	*Kent* - Cranbrook
Cranbrook Common	*Kent* - Cranbrook
Cranbury	*Hants* - Winchester
Crane Moor	*York, W.R.* - Barnsley
Crane Row	*Durham* - Bishop Auckland
Cranesmoor	*Hants* - Bournemouth
Cranfield	*Beds* - Bedford
Cranford (part)	*Middlesex* - Brentford
Cranford (part)	*Middlesex* - Uxbridge
Cranford	*Northampton* - Corby
Cranham (part)	*Essex* - Ilford
Cranham (part)	*Essex* - Grays Thurrock
Cranham	*Gloucester* - Stroud
Cranhill	*Warwick* - Stratford on Avon
Crank	*Lancaster* - St. Helens
Crank	*Lancaster* - Wigan
Crankhall Lane	*Stafford* - West Bromwich
Cranleigh	*Surrey* - Guildford
Cranmore	*I. of W.* - Newport (I.W.)
Cranmore	*Lincoln* - Spalding
Cranmore	*Somerset* - Wells
Cranoe	*Leicester* - Kettering
Cransford	*Suffolk* - Woodbridge
Cransley	*Northampton* - Kettering
Crantock	*Cornwall* - Truro
Cranwell	*Bucks* - Aylesbury
Cranwell	*Lincoln* - Sleaford
Cranwich	*Norfolk* - Thetford
Cranworth	*Norfolk* - East Dereham
Craster	*Northumberland* - Alnwick
Craswall	*Hereford* - Hereford

CRA - CRI

Crateford	*Salop* - Bridgnorth
Crateford	*Stafford* - Wolverhampton
Cratfield	*Suffolk* - Halesworth
Crathorne	*York, N.R.* - Middlesbrough
Crave	*Montgomery* - Oswestry
Craven Arms	*Salop* - Ludlow
Crawcrook	*Durham* - Newcastle upon Tyne
Crawford	*Lancaster* - Wigan
Crawley	*Devon* - Axminster and Chard
Crawley	*Hants* - Winchester
Crawley	*Northumberland* - Alnwick
Crawley	*Oxford* - Witney
Crawley	*Sussex* - Horsham
Crawley Down	*Sussex* - East Grinstead
Crawley, North	*Bucks* - Bletchley and Leighton Buzzard
Crawleyside	*Durham* - Bishop Auckland
Crawshawbooth	*Lancaster* - Rawtenstall
Cray	*Brecon* - Brecknock
Craycombe	*Worcester* - Evesham
Crayford	*Kent* - Dartford
Crayke	*York, N.R.* - York
Cray, North	*Kent* - Bromley
Crays Pond	*Oxford* - Didcot
Crazies Hill	*Berks* - Reading
Creacombe	*Devon* - Tiverton
Creake, North	*Norfolk* - King's Lynn
Creake, South	*Norfolk* - King's Lynn
Crean	*Cornwall* - Penzance
Creaton	*Northampton* - Northampton
Credenhill	*Hereford* - Hereford
Crediton	*Devon* - Exeter
Creech Heathfield	*Somerset* - Taunton
Creech St. Michael	*Somerset* - Taunton
Creed	*Cornwall* - St. Austell
Creegbrause	*Cornwall* - Truro
Creeksea	*Essex* - Maldon
Creeksea Ferry	*Essex* - Southend
Creeting All Saints	*Suffolk* - Stowmarket
Creeting St. Mary	*Suffolk* - Stowmarket
Creeting St. Olave	*Suffolk* - Stowmarket
Creeting St. Peter	*Suffolk* - Stowmarket
Creeton	*Lincoln* - Stamford
Cregrina	*Radnor* - Builth
Creighton	*Stafford* - Uttoxeter
Creigiau	*Glamorgan* - Cardiff
Cremyll	*Cornwall* - Plymouth
Crendle	*Dorset* - Wimborne Minster
Crendon, Long	*Bucks* - Thame
Creslow	*Bucks* - Aylesbury
Cressage	*Salop* - Shrewsbury
Cressbrook	*Derby* - Buxton
Cresselly	*Pembroke* - Haverfordwest
Cressing	*Essex* - Braintree
Cressingham, Great	*Norfolk* - King's Lynn
Cressingham, Little	*Norfolk* - King's Lynn
Cresswell	*Northumberland* - Morpeth
Cresswell	*Stafford* - Stoke-on-Trent
Cresswell Quay	*Pembroke* - Haverfordwest
Creswell	*Derby* - Worksop
Creswell	*Stafford* - Stafford
Cretingham	*Suffolk* - Ipswich
Crewe	*Cheshire* - Crewe
Crewe-by-Farndon	*Cheshire* - Chester
Crewes	*Cumberland* - Carlisle
Crew Green	*Montgomery* - Shrewsbury
Crewkerne	*Somerset* - Yeovil
Crewkerne, West	*Somerset* - Yeovil
Crewton	*Derby* - Derby
Cribbs Causeway	*Gloucester* - Thornbury
Cribyn	*Cardigan* - Lampeter
Criccieth	*Caernarvon* - Portmadoc
Crich	*Derby* - Alfreton
Crich Carr	*Derby* - Alfreton
Crichel, Long	*Dorset* - Wimborne Minster
Crichel More	*Dorset* - Wimborne Minster
Crick	*Monmouth* - Chepstow
Crick	*Northampton* - Rugby
Crickadarn	*Brecon* - Builth
Cricket Malherbie	*Somerset* - Axminster and Chard

CRI - CRO

Cricket St. Thomas	*Somerset* - Axminster and Chard
Crickett	*Salop* - Oswestry
Crickheath	*Salop* - Oswestry
Crickhowell	*Brecon* - Pontypool and Abergavenny
Cricklade	*Wilts* - Swindon
Cricklewood (part)	*London, N.W.2* - Bloomsbury and Marylebone
Cricklewood (part)	*London, N.W.2* - Willesden
Crickley Hill	*Gloucester* - Cheltenham
Crickmerry	*Salop* - Market Drayton
Criddon	*Salop* - Bridgnorth
Cridling Stubbs	*York, W.R.* - Pontefract
Criftin	*Salop* - Shrewsbury
Criftins	*Salop* - Oswestry
Criggan	*Cornwall* - St. Austell
Criggion	*Montgomery* - Shrewsbury
Crigglestone	*York, W.R.* - Wakefield
Crill	*Cornwall* - Truro
Crimble	*Lancaster* - Bury
Crimble	*York, W.R.* - Huddersfield
Crimdon	*Durham* - Hartlepool
Crimplesham	*Norfolk* - King's Lynn
Crimscote	*Warwick* - Stratford on Avon
Crimsworth	*York, W.R.* - Todmorden
Crindledike	*Cumberland* - Carlisle
Cringleford	*Norfolk* - Norwich
Cringles	*York, W.R.* - Skipton
Crinnis	*Cornwall* - St. Austell
Crinow	*Pembroke* - Haverfordwest
Crippetts, The	*Gloucester* - Cheltenham
Cripplegate	*Sussex* - Horsham
Cripple's Ease	*Cornwall* - Penzance
Cripplestyle	*Dorset* - Wimborne Minster
Cripps Corner	*Sussex* - Hastings
Crithall	*Kent* - Cranbrook
Croasdale	*Cumberland* - Whitehaven
Crockenhill	*Kent* - Dartford
Crocker End	*Oxford* - Reading
Crocker Hill	*Hants* - Portsmouth
Crocker Hill	*Sussex* - Chichester
Crockernwell	*Devon* - Exeter
Crockerton	*Wilts* - Warminster
Crockerton Furze	*Dorset* - Shaftesbury
Crockham Hill	*Kent* - Sevenoaks
Crocks Top	*Somerset* - Bristol
Croeserw	*Glamorgan* - Neath
Croesgoch	*Pembroke* - Haverfordwest
Croesllwybir	*Montgomery* - Newtown
Croesor	*Merioneth* - Portmadoc
Croespenmain	*Monmouth* - Blackwood
Croesyceilog	*Carmarthen* - Carmarthen
Croesyceilog	*Monmouth* - Newport (Mon)
Croford	*Somerset* - Taunton
Croft	*Cornwall* - Bodmin
Croft	*Hereford* - Leominster
Croft	*Lancaster* - Warrington
Croft	*Leicester* - Leicester
Croft	*Lincoln* - Skegness
Croft	*York, N.R.* - Darlington
Croft Handy	*Cornwall* - Redruth
Crofton	*Cumberland* - Carlisle
Crofton	*Hants* - Portsmouth
Crofton	*Lincoln* - Sleaford
Crofton	*Wilts* - Swindon
Crofton	*York, W.R.* - Wakefield
Crofton, New	*York, W.R.* - Wakefield
Croft, West	*Stafford* - Wolverhampton
Crofty	*Glamorgan* - Swansea
Croglin	*Cumberland* - Penrith
Cromer	*Herts* - Hitchin
Cromer	*Norfolk* - Norwich
Cromer Hyde	*Herts* - St. Albans
Cromford	*Derby* - Matlock
Cromford Station	*Derby* - Matlock
Cromhall	*Gloucester* - Thornbury
Crompton	*Lancaster* - Oldham
Crompton, High	*Lancaster* - Oldham
Crompton, Low	*Lancaster* - Oldham
Cromwell	*Notts* - Newark

Cromwell Bottom	*York, W.R.* - Halifax
Crondall	*Hants* - Aldershot and Farnham
Cronkhill	*Salop* - Shrewsbury
Cronkley	*Northumberland* - Hexham
Cronton	*Lancaster* - St. Helens
Crook	*Durham* - Bishop Auckland
Crook	*Westmorland* - Kendal
Crookdake	*Cumberland* - Carlisle
Crookdean	*Northumberland* - Hexham
Crooke	*Lancaster* - Wigan
Crookgate	*Durham* - Consett
Crookhall	*Durham* - Consett
Crookham	*Berks* - Newbury
Crookham	*Northumberland* - Berwick-upon-Tweed
Crookham Heath	*Berks* - Newbury
Crookham Village	*Hants* - Aldershot and Farnham
Crookhay	*Stafford* - West Bromwich
Crooklands	*Cumberland* - Carlisle
Crooklands	*Westmorland* - Kendal
Crookmoor	*Salop* - Whitchurch
Crooks March	*Gloucester* - Thornbury
Crooks, The	*Northumberland* - Hexham
Croome	*York, E.R.* - Beverley
Croome D'Abitot	*Worcester* - Worcester
Cropredy	*Oxford* - Banbury
Cropstone	*Leicester* - Leicester
Cropthorne	*Worcester* - Evesham
Cropton	*York, N.R.* - Malton
Cropwell Bishop	*Notts* - Nottingham
Cropwell Butler	*Notts* - Nottingham
Crosby	*Cumberland* - Workington
Crosby	*Lancaster* - Liverpool
Crosby	*Lincoln* - Scunthorpe
Crosby Garrett	*Westmorland* - Penrith
Crosby, High	*Cumberland* - Carlisle
Crosby, Low	*Cumberland* - Carlisle
Crosby Moor	*Cumberland* - Carlisle
Crosby on Eden	*Cumberland* - Carlisle
Crosby Ravensworth	*Westmorland* - Penrith
Crosby Villa	*Cumberland* - Workington
Croscombe	*Somerset* - Wells
Crosemere	*Salop* - Oswestry
Crosland Moor	*York, W.R.* - Huddersfield
Crosland, South	*York, W.R.* - Huddersfield
Cross	*Somerset* - Weston Super Mare
Cross Acres (part)	*Cheshire* - Manchester
Cross-a-Moor	*Lancaster* - Barrow-in-Furness
Cross Bank	*Northumberland* - Haltwhistle
Crossbarrow	*Cumberland* - Workington
Cross Bush	*Sussex* - Chichester
Crosscanonby	*Cumberland* - Workington
Cross Cwtta	*Glamorgan* - Bridgend
Crossens	*Lancaster* - Southport
Cross Flatts	*York, W.R.* - Keighley
Crossgate	*Lincs* - Spalding
Cross Gate	*Stafford* - Stoke-on-Trent
Crossgates	*Lancaster* - Barrow-in-Furness
Crossgates	*Northumberland* - Carlisle
Crossgates	*Radnor* - Llandrindod Wells
Cross Gates	*York, W.R.* - Leeds
Cross Green	*Salop* - Wellington (Salop)
Crossgreens	*Cumberland* - Carlisle
Crosshall	*Beds* - Biggleswade
Crosshall	*Hunts* - Huntingdon
Cross Hands (part)	*Carmarthen* - Carmarthen
Cross Hands (part)	*Carmarthen* - Llanelli
Cross Heath	*Stafford* - Stoke-on-Trent
Crosshill	*Cumberland* - Carlisle
Crosshills	*York, W.R.* - Skipton
Cross Houses	*Salop* - Shrewsbury
Crossings	*Cumberland* - Carlisle
Cross-in-Hand	*Sussex* - Eastbourne
Cross-in-Hand	*Warwick* - Rugby
Cross Inn (Llanon)	*Cardigan* - Aberystwyth
Cross Inn	*Glamorgan* - Pontypridd
Cross Keys	*Kent* - Sevenoaks
Cross Keys	*Monmouth* - Newport (Mon.)
Cross Lanes	*Denbigh* - Wrexham
Crossley Estate	*Lancaster* - Oldham

Cross Oak	*Brecon* - Brecknock
Crosspool	*York, W.R.* - Sheffield
Cross Roads	*Berks* - High Wycombe
Cross Roads	*York, W.R.* - Keighley
Cross Stone	*Lancaster* - Todmorden
Crossway Green	*Worcester* - Kidderminster
Crossways	*Dorset* - Dorchester
Crossways	*Gloucester* - Thornbury
Crosswood	*Cardigan* - Aberystwyth
Crosthwaite	*Cumberland* - Workington
Crosthwaite	*Westmorland* - Kendal
Crosthwaite, Great	*Cumberland* - Workington
Crosthwaite, Little	*Cumberland* - Workington
Croston	*Lancaster* - Chorley
Crostwick	*Norfolk* - Norwich
Crostwight	*Norfolk* - Norwich
Crouch	*Kent* - Sevenoaks
Crouch End	*London, N.8* - Clerkenwell
Crouch Field	*Herts* - St. Albans
Crouch Hill	*London, N.4* - Clerkenwell
Croughton	*Cheshire* - Chester
Croughton	*Northampton* - Banbury
Crow	*Hants* - Bournemouth
Crowan	*Cornwall* - Redruth
Crowborough	*Stafford* - Congleton
Crowborough	*Sussex* - Tunbridge Wells
Crowcombe	*Somerset* - Minehead
Crowdecote	*Derby* - Buxton
Crowden	*Derby* - Hyde
Crowd Hill	*Hants* - Winchester
Crowdleham	*Kent* - Sevenoaks
Crow Edge	*York, W.R.* - Barnsley
Crowell	*Oxford* - Thame
Crowfield	*Northampton* - Banbury
Crowfield	*Suffolk* - Ipswich
Crowgreaves	*Salop* - Bridgnorth
Crow Hill	*Hereford* - Gloucester
Crowhurst	*Kent* - Sevenoaks
Crowhurst (part)	*Surrey* - Reigate
Crowhurst	*Sussex* - Hastings
Crowland	*Lincoln* - Spalding
Crowland Common	*Lincoln* - Spalding
Crowlas	*Cornwall* - Penzance
Crowle	*Lincoln* - Thorne
Crowle	*Worcester* - Worcester
Crowley	*Cheshire* - Northwich
Crowmarsh	*Oxford* - Didcot
Crowmarsh Gifford	*Oxford* - Didcot
Crowndale	*Devon* - Plymouth
Crown Dale	*London, S.E.19* - Croydon
Crown Hill	*Devon* - Plymouth
Crown Hill	*London, S.E.19* - Croydon
Crown Point	*Kent* - Sevenoaks
Crown Point	*Lancaster* - Bolton
Crownthorpe	*Norfolk* - Norwich
Crowntown	*Cornwall* - Penzance
Crows-an-Wra	*Cornwall* - Penzance
Crowsley	*Oxford* - Reading
Crows Nest	*Cornwall* - Liskeard
Crowthorne	*Berks* - Reading
Crowton	*Cheshire* - Northwich
Crow Wood	*Lancaster* - St. Helens
Croxall	*Derby* - Tamworth
Croxby	*Lincoln* - Great Grimsby
Croxdale	*Durham* - Durham
Croxden	*Stafford* - Uttoxeter
Croxden Common	*Stafford* - Uttoxeter
Croxley Green	*Herts* - Watford
Croxteth	*Lancaster* - Liverpool
Croxton	*Cambridge* - Huntingdon
Croxton	*Cheshire* - Northwich
Croxton	*Lincoln* - Scunthorpe
Croxton	*Norfolk* - King's Lynn
Croxton	*Norfolk* - Thetford
Croxton	*Stafford* - Stafford
Croxton Kerrial	*Leicester* - Melton Mowbray
Croxton, South	*Leicester* - Leicester
Croyde	*Devon* - Barnstaple
Croydon	*Surrey* - Croydon
Croydon	*Cambridge* - Cambridge

CRU - CUM

Place	County - Post town
Cruckmeole	*Salop* - Shrewsbury
Cruckton	*Salop* - Shrewsbury
Crudgington	*Salop* - Wellington (Salop)
Crudwell	*Wilts* - Malmesbury
Crug-y-Car	*Carmarthen* - Llandovery
Crumlin	*Monmouth* - Blackwood
Crummock Bank	*Cumberland* - Carlisle
Crumpsall	*Lancaster* - Manchester
Crumpsall, Higher	*Lancaster* - Manchester
Crundale	*Kent* - Ashford
Crundale	*Pembroke* - Haverfordwest
Crunnells Green	*Herts* - Hitchin
Crunwear	*Pembroke* - Haverfordwest
Crutchmoor	*Herts* - Hitchin
Cruwys Morchard	*Devon* - Tiverton
Crux Easton	*Hants* - Newbury
Cruxton	*Dorset* - Dorchester
Crwbin	*Carmarthen* - Carmarthen
Crymmych	*Pembroke* - Cardigan
Crynant	*Glamorgan* - Neath
Cubberley	*Hereford* - Monmouth
Cubbington	*Warwick* - Warwick
Cubert	*Cornwall* - Truro
Cubley	*Derby* - Uttoxeter
Cublington	*Bucks* - Aylesbury
Cuckfield	*Sussex* - Haywards Heath
Cuckingstool End	*Essex* - Bishop's Stortford
Cucklington	*Somerset* - Yeovil
Cuckney	*Notts* - Worksop
Cuckoo	*Pembroke* - Haverfordwest
Cuckoo Bridge	*Lincoln* - Spalding
Cuckoorstone	*Derby* - Matlock
Cuckoo's Holt	*Oxford* - Banbury
Cuddesden	*Oxford* - Oxford
Cuddington	*Bucks* - Aylesbury
Cuddington	*Cheshire* - Northwich
Cuddington	*Cheshire* - Whitchurch
Cuddington	*Surrey* - Epsom
Cuddra	*Cornwall* - St. Austell
Cudham	*Kent* - Bromley
Cudliptown	*Devon* - Plymouth
Cudworth	*Somerset* - Yeovil
Cudworth	*York, W.R.* - Barnsley
Cuerdale	*Lancaster* - Preston
Cuerden	*Lancaster* - Chorley
Cuerdley	*Lancaster* - Warrington
Cuffley	*Herts* - Barnet
Culbone	*Somerset* - Minehead
Culcheth	*Lancaster* - Leigh
Culford	*Suffolk* - Bury St. Edmunds
Culgaith	*Cumberland* - Penrith
Culham	*Berks* - Reading
Culham	*Oxford* - Didcot
Culkerton	*Gloucester* - Stroud
Cullamoor	*Stafford* - Stafford
Culland	*Derby* - Derby
Cullercoats	*Northumberland* - North Shields
Cullingworth (part)	*York, W.R.* - Keighley
Cullompton	*Devon* - Tiverton
Culm Davey	*Somerset* - Taunton
Culmhead	*Somerset* - Taunton
Culmington	*Salop* - Ludlow
Culmstock	*Devon* - Taunton
Culpho	*Suffolk* - Ipswich
Culverley	*Hants* - Southampton
Culverstone	*Kent* - Gravesend
Culverthorpe	*Lincoln* - Sleaford
Culworth	*Northampton* - Banbury
Cumberwell	*Wilts* - Trowbridge
Cumberworth	*Lincoln* - Skegness
Cumberworth	*York, W.R.* - Huddersfield
Cumberworth, Lower	*York, W.R.* - Huddersfield
Cumberworth, Upper	*York, W.R.* - Huddersfield
Cumboots	*York, N.R.* - Scarborough
Cumdivock	*Cumberland* - Carlisle
Cumhampton	*Worcester* - Worcester
Cummersdale, High	*Cumberland* - Carlisle
Cummersdale, Low	*Cumberland* - Carlisle
Cumnor	*Berks* - Oxford
Cumrew	*Cumberland* - Carlisle

CUM - CWM

Place	County - Post town
Cumwhinton	*Cumberland* - Carlisle
Cumwhitton	*Cumberland* - Carlisle
Cundall with Leckby	*York, W.R.* - Harrogate
Cundy Cross	*York, W.R.* - Barnsley
Cunsey	*Lancaster* - Kendal
Cupernham	*Hants* - Southampton
Cupid Green	*Herts* - Hemel Hempstead
Curbar	*Derby* - Chesterfield
Curborough	*Stafford* - Lichfield
Curbridge	*Hants* - Portsmouth
Curbridge	*Oxford* - Witney
Curdridge	*Hants* - Southampton
Curdworth	*Warwick* - Birmingham
Curland	*Somerset* - Taunton
Curridge	*Berks* - Newbury
Currock	*Cumberland* - Carlisle
Curry Mallet	*Somerset* - Taunton
Curry, North	*Somerset* - Taunton
Curry Rivel	*Somerset* - Taunton
Curscombe	*Devon* - Exeter
Curthwaite, East	*Cumberland* - Carlisle
Curthwaite, West	*Cumberland* - Carlisle
Curtisden Green	*Kent* - Cranbrook
Cury	*Cornwall* - Penzance
Cury Cross Lanes	*Cornwall* - Penzance
Cusgarne	*Cornwall* - Redruth
Cushuish	*Somerset* - Taunton
Cusop	*Hereford* - Hereford
Custom House	*London, E.16* - Bow
Cusworth	*York, W.R.* - Doncaster
Cutcombe	*Somerset* - Minehead
Cutmere	*Cornwall* - Liskeard
Cut Mill	*Dorset* - Shaftesbury
Cutnall Green (part)	*Worcester* - Bromsgrove
Cutnall Green (part)	*Worcester* - Kidderminster
Cutridge	*Devon* - Exeter
Cutsdean	*Worcester* - Cheltenham
Cutsdean Hill	*Worcester* - Cheltenham
Cutsyke	*York, W.R.* - Pontefract
Cutteridge	*Wilts* - Trowbridge
Cutteslowe	*Oxford* - Oxford
Cutthorpe	*Derby* - Chesterfield
Cuxham	*Oxford* - Didcot
Cuxton	*Kent* - Rochester
Cuxwold	*Lincoln* - Great Grimsby
Cwm	*Flint* - Rhyl
Cwm	*Monmouth* - Blackwood
Cwm	*Montgomery* - Welshpool
Cwm	*Salop* - Ludlow
Cwmaman	*Glamorgan* - Aberdare
Cwmavon	*Glamorgan* - Neath
Cwmavon	*Monmouth* - Pontypool and Abergavenny
Cwmbach	*Carmarthen* - Carmarthen
Cwmbach	*Glamorgan* - Aberdare
Cwmbargoed,	*Glamorgan* - Merthyr Tydfil
Cwmbelan	*Montgomery* - Newtown
Cwmblacks	*Glamorgan* - Merthyr Tydfil
Cwmblaenglyn	*Merioneth* - Dolgellau
Cwmbran	*Monmouth* - Newport (Mon.)
Cwmbran, Upper	*Monmouth* - Newport (Mon.)
Cwmbrwyno	*Cardigan* - Aberystwyth
Cwmbwria	*Glamorgan* - Swansea
Cwmcarn	*Monmouth* - Blackwood
Cwmcarvan	*Monmouth* - Monmouth
Cwmcelyn	*Monmouth* - Blackwood
Cwmcewydd	*Merioneth* - Dolgellau
Cwm Coy	*Cardigan* - Cardigan
Cwmdare	*Glamorgan* - Aberdare
Cwmdauddwr	*Radnor* - Llandrindod Wells
Cwmddu	*Brecon* - Pontypool and Abergavenny
Cwmdu	*Carmarthen* - Ammanford
Cwmdu	*Glamorgan* - Bridgend
Cwmdu	*Glamorgan* - Swansea
Cwmdu	*Montgomery* - Oswestry
Cwmduad	*Carmarthen* - Carmarthen
Cwmdwr	*Carmarthen* - Llandovery
Cwmerfin	*Cardigan* - Aberystwyth

Cwmfelin	*Glamorgan* - Bargoed
Cwmfelin	*Glamorgan* - Bridgend
Cwmfelinfach	*Monmouth* - Blackwood
Cwmffrwdoer	*Monmouth* - Pontypool and Abergavenny
Cwmgarn	*Glamorgan* - Bridgend
Cwmgiedd	*Brecon* - Neath
Cwmgorse	*Glamorgan* - Ammanford
Cwmgwaun	*Pembroke* - Cardigan
Cwmgwili	*Carmarthen* - Carmarthen
Cwmgwili	*Carmarthen* - Llanelli
Cwmgwrach	*Glamorgan* - Neath
Cwmgwyn	*Radnor* - Knighton
Cwm Head	*Salop* - Ludlow
Cwm Llanellen	*Monmouth* - Pontypool and Abergavenny
Cwmllinau	*Montgomery* - Machynlleth
Cwmllynfell	*Glamorgan* - Ammanford
Cwmmawr	*Carmarthen* - Llanelli
Cwm Morgan	*Carmarthen* - Cardigan
Cwmnantgam	*Brecon* - Pontypool and Abergavenny
Cwmogwr	*Glamorgan* - Bridgend
Cwmpadarn	*Cardigan* - Aberystwyth
Cwmparc	*Glamorgan* - Pontypridd
Cwm Pengraig	*Carmarthen* - Carmarthen
Cwm Penmachno	*Caernarvon* - Conway
Cwmpennar	*Glamorgan* - Aberdare
Cwmprysor	*Merioneth* - Portmadoc
Cwmrheidol	*Cardigan* - Aberystwyth
Cwmrhydyceirw	*Glamorgan* - Swansea
Cwmriscla	*Glamorgan* - Bridgend
Cwmsifiog	*Monmouth* - Blackwood
Cwmsymlog	*Cardigan* - Aberystwyth
Cwmtaf (part)	*Brecon* - Aberdare
Cwmtaf	*Brecon* - Merthyr Tydfil
Cwmtillery	*Monmouth* - Blackwood
Cwmtirmynach	*Merioneth* - Dollegau
Cwmtwrch	*Glamorgan* - Neath
Cwm Victoria	*Monmouth* - Blackwood
Cwmwhitton	*Radnor* - Knighton
Cwmyglo	*Caernarvon* - Caernarvon
Cwmynys Coy	*Monmouth* - Pontypool and Abergavenny
Cwmyoy	*Monmouth* - Ponytpool and Abergavenny
Cwmyreglwys	*Cardigan* - Cardigan
Cwmystwyth	*Cardigan* - Aberystwyth
Cwrt	*Montgomery* - Machynlleth
Cwrtnewydd	*Cardigan* - Lampeter
Cyffic	*Carmarthen* - Haverfordwest
Cyfronydd	*Montgomery* - Welshpool
Cymau	*Flint* - Wrexham
Cymdda	*Glamorgan* - Bridgend
Cymdy	*Montgomery* - Oswestry
Cymmer	*Glamorgan* - Neath
Cymmer (Porth)	*Glamorgan* - Pontypridd
Cynghordy	*Carmarthen* - Llandovery
Cynheidre	*Carmarthen* - Llanelli
Cynllwyd	*Merioneth* - Wrexham
Cyntwell	*Glamorgan* - Cardiff
Cynwyd	*Merioneth* - Wrexham
Cynynion	*Salop* - Oswestry

D

Dabbs Place	*Kent* - Gravesend
Daccombe	*Devon* - Newton Abbot
Dacre	*Cumberland* - Penrith
Dacre	*York, W.R.* - Harrogate
Daddlebrook	*Salop* - Bridgnorth
Daddryshield	*Durham* - Bishop Auckland
Dadford	*Bucks* - Aylesbury
Dadlington	*Leicester* - Hinckley
Defarn Newydd	*Denbigh* - Conway
Defarnyfedw	*Denbigh* - Conway

Dafen	*Carmarthen* - Llanelli
Daffaluke	*Hereford* - Ross
Daffy Green	*Norfolk* - East Dereham
Dagenham	*Essex* - Ilford
Daggons	*Dorset* - Wimborne Minster
Daglingworth	*Gloucester* - Cheltenham
Dagnall	*Bucks* - Bletchley and Leighton Buzzard
Dagnell End	*Worcester* - Redditch
Dag Tail End	*Worcester* - Redditch
Dagnorth	*Suffolk* - Stowmarket
Dairyfields	*Stafford* - Stoke-on-Trent
Daisy Bank (part)	*Stafford* - Dudley
Daisy Bank (part)	*Staffs* - Wolverhampton
Daisy Hill	*Durham* - Durham
Daisy Hill	*Lancaster* - Bolton
Daisy Hill	*York, W.R.* - Bradford
Daisy Hill (Morley)	*York, W.R.* - Dewsbury
Dalbury	*Derby* - Derby
Dalbury Lees	*Derby* - Derby
Dalby	*Lincoln* - Skegness
Dalby	*York, N.R.* - York
Dalby, Great	*Leicester* - Melton Mowbray
Dalby, Little	*Leicester* - Melton Mowbray
Dalby, Old	*Leicester* - Melton Mowbray
Dalderby	*Lincoln* - Lincoln
Dale	*Pembroke* - Haverfordwest
Dale Abbey	*Derby* - Ilkeston
Dale Bottom	*Cumberland* - Workington
Dale Garth	*Cumberland* - Whitehaven
Dale Park	*Sussex* - Chichester
Dales Green	*Stafford* - Stoke-on-Trent
Dalham	*Suffolk* - Newmarket
Dallam	*Lancaster* - Warrington
Dallicott	*Salop* - Bridgnorth
Dallinghoo	*Suffolk* - Woodbridge
Dallington	*Northampton* - Northampton
Dallington	*Sussex* - Hastings
Dallowgill	*York, W.R.* - Harrogate
Dalmonds	*Herts* - Hertford
Dalscote	*Northampton* - Northampton
Dalston	*Cumberland* - Carlisle
Dalston	*London, E.8* - Shoreditch
Dalton	*Lancaster* - Kendal
Dalton	*Lancaster* - Wigan
Dalton	*Northumberland* - Hexham
Dalton	*Northumberland* - Newcastle upon Tyne
Dalton	*York, N.R.* - Darlington
Dalton	*York, W.R.* - Huddersfield
Dalton	*York, W.R.* - Rotherham
Dalton Brook	*York, W.R.* - Rotherham
Dalton Holme	*York, E.R.* - Beverley
Dalton-in-Furness	*Lancaster* - Barrow-in-Furness
Dalton-le-Dale	*Durham* - Sunderland
Dalton Lees	*Lancaster* - Wigan
Dalton Magna	*York, W.R.* - Rotherham
Dalton, North	*York, E.R.* - Beverley
Dalton-on-Tees	*York, N.R.* - Darlington
Dalton Parva	*York, W.R.* - Rotherham
Dalton Piercy	*Durham* - Hartlepool
Dalton Sessay	*York, N.R.* - Northallerton
Dalton, South	*York, E.R.* - Beverley
Dalwood	*Devon* - Axminster and Chard
Damask Green	*Herts* - Hitchin
Damens	*York, W.R.* - Keighley
Damerham, North	*Hants* - Salisbury
Damerham, South	*Hants* - Salisbury
Damflask	*York, W.R.* - Sheffield
Dam, The	*Hereford* - Monmouth
Danaway	*Kent* - Sittingbourne
Danbury	*Essex* - Chelmsford
Danby	*York, N.R.* - Whitby
Danby Coombs	*York, N.R.* - Whitby
Danby Dale	*York, N.R.* - Whitby
Danby End	*York, N.R.* - Whitby
Danby Wiske	*York, N.R.* - Northallerton
Dancer's End	*Bucks* - Aylesbury
Dancing Green	*Gloucester* - Ross
Dane End	*Herts* - Hertford

DAN - DAW

Danehill	*Sussex* - East Grinstead
Dane-in-Shaw	*Cheshire* - Congleton
Danescombe	*Cornwall* - Plymouth
Danesdale	*York, E.R.* - Beverley
Danesford	*Salop* - Bridgnorth
Danesmoor	*Derby* - Chesterfield
Danes Moss	*Cheshire* - Macclesfield
Dane Street	*Beds* - Luton
Danethorpe	*Notts* - Newark
Dangstein	*Sussex* - Petersfield
Daniel's Water	*Kent* - Ashford
Danthorpe	*York, E.R.* - Kingston-upon-Hull
Danygraig	*Glamorgan* - Swansea
Dapple Heath	*Stafford* - Uttoxeter
Darby End	*Worcester* - Dudley
Darby Green	*Surrey* - Aldershot and Farnham
Darbys Hill	*Stafford* - Dudley
Darcy Lever	*Lancaster* - Bolton
Darenth	*Kent* - Dartford
Darenth, South	*Kent* - Dartford
Daresbury	*Cheshire* - Warrington
Darfield	*York, W.R.* - Barnsley
Darfoulds	*Notts* - Worksop
Dargate	*Kent* - Canterbury
Darite	*Cornwall* - Liskeard
Darlaston	*Stafford* - Stafford
Darlaston	*Stafford* - Walsall
Darlescote	*Northampton* - Northampton
Darley	*Derby* - Matlock
Darley	*York, W.R.* - Harrogate
Darley Abbey	*Derby* - Derby
Darley Dale	*Derby* - Matlock
Darleyford	*Cornwall* - Liskeard
Darley Hall	*Herts* - Hitchin
Darley Moor	*Derby* - Derby
Darley, North	*Derby* - Matlock
Darley, South	*Derby* - Matlock
Darlingscott	*Warwick* - Stratford on Avon
Darlington	*Durham* - Darlington
Darliston	*Cheshire* - Whitchurch
Darlton	*Notts* - East Retford
Darmsden	*Suffolk* - Stowmarket
Darnall	*York, W.R.* - Sheffield
Darnford	*Stafford* - Lichfield
Darnhall	*Cheshire* - Northwich
Darn Hill	*Lancaster* - Bury
Darnholme	*York, N.R.* - Whitby
Darowen	*Montgomery* - Machynlleth
Darras Hall	*Northumberland* - Newcastle upon Tyne
Darrenfelin	*Brecon* - Pontypool and Abergavenny
Darrington	*York, W.R.* - Pontefract
Darrington Leys	*York, W.R.* - Pontefract
Darsham	*Suffolk* - Halesworth
Dartford	*Kent* - Dartford
Dartington	*Devon* - Torquay
Dartmeet	*Devon* - Plymouth
Dartmoor Forest	*Devon* - Plymouth
Dartmouth	*Devon* - Torquay
Dartmouth Park	*Stafford* - West Bromwich
Darton	*York, W.R.* - Barnsley
Darwen, Lower	*Lancaster* - Blackburn
Dassels	*Herts* - Bishop's Stortford
Datchet	*Bucks* - Slough
Datchet Common	*Bucks* - Slough
Datchworth	*Herts* - Hertford
Daubhill	*Lancaster* - Bolton
Dauntsey	*Wilts* - Malmesbury
Davenham	*Cheshire* - Northwich
Davenport	*Cheshire* - Congleton
Davenport	*Cheshire* - Stockport
Davenport Green	*Cheshire* - Macclesfield
Daventry	*Northampton* - Northampton
Daveylands	*Cheshire* - Macclesfield
Davidstow	*Cornwall* - Launceston
Davids Town	*Durham* - Durham
Davington	*Kent* - Canterbury
Davyhulme	*Lancaster* - Salford
Dawdon	*Durham* - Sunderland

DAW - DEE

Dawdon Colliery	*Durham* - Sunderland
Dawes Heath	*Essex* - Southend
Daw Green	*York, W.R.* - Dewsbury
Daw Green	*York, W.R.* - Wakefield
Dawley	*Middlesex* - Uxbridge
Dawley	*Salop* - Wellington (Salop)
Dawley Bank	*Salop* - Wellington (Salop)
Dawley Green	*Salop* - Wellington (Salop)
Dawley, Little	*Salop* - Wellington (Salop)
Dawley Magna	*Salop* - Wellington (Salop)
Dawley Parva	*Salop* - Wellington (Salop)
Dawlish	*Devon* - Newton Abbot
Dawlish Warren	*Devon* - Newton Abbot
Dawn	*Denbigh* - Conway
Daws Bridge	*Essex* - Harlow
Daws House	*Cornwall* - Launceston
Dawsmere	*Lincs* - Spalding
Daybrook	*Notts* - Nottingham
Day Hills	*Stafford* - Stafford
Dayhouse Bank	*Worcester* - Bromsgrove
Daylesford	*Gloucester* - Cheltenham
Daywell	*Salop* - Oswestry
Ddol (St. Asaph)	*Denbigh* - Rhyl
Ddol	*Flint* - Holywell
Deadman's Cross	*Beds* - Bedford
Deaf Hill Colliery	*Durham* - Durham
Deal	*Kent* - Deal
Dean	*Cumberland* - Workington
Dean	*Dorset* - Blandford
Dean	*Oxford* - Banbury
Deanbank	*Durham* - Durham
Dean Bridge Colliery	*Durham* - Durham
Dean Court	*Berks* - Oxford
Deane	*Hants* - Basingstoke
Deane	*Lancaster* - Bolton
Dean, East	*Hants* - Salisbury
Dean, East	*Sussex* - Chichester
Dean, East	*Sussex* - Eastbourne
Dean Hall	*York, N.R.* - Whitby
Deanham	*Northumberland* - Morpeth
Deanhead	*York, W.R.* - Huddersfield
Dean House	*York, W.R.* - Huddersfield
Deanlane End	*Sussex* - Chichester
Dean, Little	*Gloucester* - Gloucester
Dean, Lower	*Beds* - Bedford
Dean Moor	*Cumberland* - Workington
Dean, North	*Bucks* - High Wycombe
Dean Prior	*Devon* - Newton Abbot
Dean Row	*Cheshire* - Macclesfield
Dean, Upper	*Beds* - Bedford
Deans	*Durham* - South Shields
Deanscales	*Cumberland* - Workington
Deanshanger	*Northampton* - Northampton
Dean, West	*Sussex* - Chichester
Dean, West	*Sussex* - Eastbourne
Dean, West	*Wilts* - Salisbury
Deards Green	*Herts* - Hitchin
Dearham	*Cumberland* - Workington
Dearnley	*Lancaster* - Rochdale
Dearnsdale	*Stafford* - Stafford
Debach	*Suffolk* - Woodbridge
Debden (Saffron Walden)	*Essex* - Bishop's Stortford
Debden	*Warwick* - Warwick
Debden Cross	*Essex* - Bishop's Stortford
Debden Green	*Essex* - Bishop's Stortford
Debdon	*Northumberland* - Morpeth
De Beauvoir Town	*London, N.1* - Shoreditch
Debenham	*Suffolk* - Ipswich
Deddington	*Oxford* - Banbury
Dedham	*Essex* - Colchester
Dedisham	*Sussex* - Horsham
Dedworth	*Berks* - Slough
Deene	*Northampton* - Corby
Deenethorpe	*Northampton* - Corby
Deep Car	*York, W.R.* - Sheffield
Deepcut	*Surrey* - Aldershot and Farnham
Deepdale	*Beds* - Biggleswade
Deepdale-in-Dent	*York, W.R.* - Kendal
Deepfields (part)	*Stafford* - Dudley

DEE - DEN

Deepfields (part)	*Staffs* - Wolverhampton
Deeping Common	*Lincoln* - Spalding
Deeping Fen	*Lincoln* - Spalding
Deeping Gate	*Northampton* - Peterborough
Deeping High Bank	*Lincoln* - Spalding
Deeping St. James	*Lincoln* - Spalding
Deeping St. James Fen	*Lincoln* - Spalding
Deeping St. Nicholas	*Lincoln* - Spalding
Deeping, West	*Lincoln* - Stamford
Deeplish	*Lancaster* - Rochdale
Deeply Vale	*Lancaster* - Bury
Deep Pits	*York, W.R.* - Sheffield
Deerbolt Camp	*York, N.R.* - Bishop Auckland
Deerfold (part)	*Hereford* - Ludlow
Deerfold (part)	*Hereford* - Knighton
Deerhurst	*Gloucester* - Cheltenham
Deerhurst Walton	*Gloucester* - Cheltenham
Defford	*Worcester* - Worcester
Defynock	*Brecon* - Brecknock
Deganwy	*Caernarvon* - Conway
Dehewid	*Cardigan* - Lampeter
Deighton	*York, E.R.* - York
Deighton	*York, W.R.* - Huddersfield
Deighton Kirk	*York, W.R.* - Harrogate
Deighton, North	*York, W.R.* - Harrogate
Deiniolen	*Caernarvon* - Caernarvon
Delabole	*Cornwall* - Bideford
Delamere	*Cheshire* - Northwich
Delamore	*Devon* - Plymouth
Delank	*Cornwall* - Bideford
Delaware	*Cornwall* - Plymouth
Dell Quay	*Sussex* - Chichester
Dell's Common	*Bucks* - High Wycombe
Delmonden (part)	*Kent* - Cranbrook
Delph	*Stafford* - Stourbridge
Delph	*York, W.R.* - Oldham
Delves	*Durham* - Consett
Delves	*Stafford* - Walsall
Dembleby	*Lincoln* - Sleaford
Denaby Main	*York, W.R.* - Doncaster
Denbigh	*Denbigh* - Denbigh
Denbury	*Devon* - Newton Abbot
Denby	*Derby* - Ilkeston
Denby	*York, W.R.* - Huddersfield
Denby Common	*Derby* - Ilkeston
Denby Dale	*York, W.R.* - Huddersfield
Denby Grange	*York, W.R.* - Huddersfield
Denchworth	*Berks* - Didcot
Dendron	*Lancaster* - Barrow-in-Furness
Denford	*Berks* - Newbury
Denford	*Northampton* - Kettering
Denford	*Stafford* - Leek
Dengie	*Essex* - Maldon
Denham	*Bucks* - Aylesbury
Denham	*Bucks* - Uxbridge
Denham	*Suffolk* - Bury St. Edmunds
Denham	*Suffolk* - Norwich
Denham Bridge	*Devon* - Plymouth
Denham New-Town	*Bucks* - Uxbridge
Denham, Upper	*Bucks* - Uxbridge
Denholme	*York, W.R.* - Bradford
Denholme Clough	*York, W.R.* - Bradford
Denholme Gate	*York, W.R.* - Bradford
Denio	*Caernarvon* - Portmadoc
Denland	*Dorset* - Salisbury
Denmead	*Hants* - Portsmouth
Denne Park	*Sussex* - Horsham
Denner Hill	*Bucks* - High Wycombe
Dennington	*York, W.R.* - Wakefield
Denny	*Somserset* - Bristol
Denny Lodge	*Hants* - Southampton
Denshaw	*York, W.R.* - Oldham
Denston	*Suffolk* - Bury St. Edmunds
Denstone	*Stafford* - Uttoxeter
Denstroude	*Kent* - Canterbury
Dent	*York, W.R.* - Kendal
Denton	*Hunts* - Peterborough
Denton	*Kent* - Dover
Denton	*Kent* - Gravesend
Denton	*Lancaster* - Hyde

DEN - DID

Denton	*Lincoln* - Grantham
Denton	*Norfolk* - Norwich
Denton	*Northampton* - Northampton
Denton	*Oxford* - Oxford
Denton	*Sussex* - Lewes
Denton	*York, W.R.* - Otley
Denton Bridge	*York, W.R.* - Halifax
Denton, East	*Northumberland* - Newcastle upon Tyne
Denton Holme	*Cumberland* - Carlisle
Denton, Nether	*Cumberland* - Carlisle
Dentons Green	*Lancaster* - St. Helens
Denton, Upper	*Cumberland* - Carlisle
Denton, West	*Northumberland* - Newcastle upon Tyne
Denver	*Norfolk* - Kings Lynn
Denver Sluice	*Norfolk* - Kings Lynn
Denvilles	*Hants* - Portsmouth
Denwick	*Northumberland* - Alnwick
Deopham	*Norfolk* - Norwich
Depden	*Suffolk* - Bury St. Edmunds
Depper's Bridge	*Warwick* - Warwick
Deptford	*Durham* - Sunderland
Deptford (part)	*London, S.E.8* - Southwark
Deptford (part)	*London, S.E.8* - Woolwich
Deptford	*Wilts* - Salisbury
Derby	*Derby* - Derby
Derbyshire Hill	*Lancaster* - St. Helens
Derby, West	*Lancaster* - Liverpool
Dereham, East	*Norfolk* - East Dereham
Dereham, West	*Norfolk* - Kings Lynn
Deri	*Glamorgan* - Bargoed
Deritend	*Warwick* - Birmingham
Derker	*Lancaster* - Oldham
Derringstone	*Kent* - Canterbury
Derrington	*Stafford* - Stafford
Derry Hill	*Wilts* - Chippenham
Derrythorpe	*Lincoln* - Scunthorpe
Dersingham	*Norfolk* - King's Lynn
Derwen	*Denbigh* - Denbigh
Derwen Fawr	*Glamorgan* - Swansea
Derwenlas	*Montgomery* - Machynlleth
Derwent	*Derby* - Sheffield
Derwent Cottages	*Durham* - Consett
Derwenthaugh	*Durham* - Newcastle upon Tyne
Derwydd Road	*Carmarthen* - Ammanford
Desborough	*Northampton* - Kettering
Desford	*Leicester* - Leicester
De Soglin	*Cumberland* - Carlisle
Dethick	*Derby* - Matlock
Detling	*Kent* - Maidstone
Deuxhill	*Salop* - Bridgnorth
Devauden	*Monmouth* - Chepstow
Devil's Bridge	*Cardigan* - Aberystwyth
Devil's Dyke	*Sussex* - Brighton
Devizes	*Wilts* - Devizes
Devonport	*Devon* - Plymouth
Devoran	*Cornwall* - Truro
Dewchurch, Little	*Hereford* - Hereford
Dewchurch, Much	*Hereford* - Hereford
Dewlish	*Dorset* - Dorchester
Dewsall	*Hereford* - Hereford
Dewsbury	*York, W.R.* - Dewsbury
Dewsbury Moor	*York, W.R.* - Dewsbury
Deytheur	*Montgomery* - Oswestry
Dial Post	*Gloucester* - Cheltenham
Dial Post	*Sussex* - Horsham
Diamond End	*Herts* - Hitchin
Dibdale Bank	*Stafford* - Dudley
Dibden	*Hants* - Southampton
Dibden	*Kent* - Sevenoaks
Dibden Purlieu	*Hants* - Southampton
Dicken House	*Durham* - Bishop Auckland
Dicker, Lower	*Sussex* - Eastbourne
Dicker, Upper	*Sussex* - Eastbourne
Dickleburgh	*Norfolk* - Norwich
Dicklow Cob	*Cheshire* - Macclesfield
Didbrook	*Gloucester* - Cheltenham
Didcot	*Berks* - Didcot

Didcote Pastures	*Gloucester* - Cheltenham
Diddington	*Hunts* - Huntingdon
Diddlebury	*Salop* - Ludlow
Didley	*Hereford* - Hereford
Didling	*Sussex* - Chichester
Didlington	*Dorset* - Wimborne Minster
Didlington	*Norfolk* - King's Lynn
Didmarton	*Gloucester* - Malmesbury
Didsbury	*Lancaster* - Manchester
Didsbury, West	*Lancaster* - Manchester
Digby	*Lincoln* - Sleaford
Digby Fen	*Lincoln* - Sleaford
Diggle	*York, W.R.* - Oldham
Digmoor	*Lancaster* - Wigan
Digswell	*Herts* - Hertford
Dilham	*Norfolk* - Norwich
Dilhorne	*Stafford* - Stoke-on-Trent
Dillicar	*Westmorland* - Kendal
Dillington	*Hunts* - Huntingdon
Dillington	*Norfolk* - East Dereham
Dilston	*Northumberland* - Hexham
Dilton	*Hants* - Lymington
Dilton	*Wilts* - Trowbridge
Dilton Marsh	*Wilts* - Trowbridge
Dilworth	*Lancaster* - Preston
Dilwyn	*Hereford* - Leominster
Dilwyn, Little	*Hereford* - Leominster
Dimlington	*York, E.R.* - Kingston-upon-Hull
Dimma	*Cornwall* - Launceston
Dimmer	*Somerset* - Yeovil
Dimsdale	*Stafford* - Stoke-on-Trent
Dimson	*Cornwall* - Plymouth
Dinas	*Caernarvon* - Caernarvon
Dinas	*Caernarvon* - Portmadoc
Dinas	*Glamorgan* - Pontypridd
Dinas	*Pembroke* - Cardigan
Dinas Cross	*Pembroke* - Cardigan
Dinas Dinlle	*Caernarvon* - Caernarvon
Dinas Mawddwy	*Merioneth* - Dolgellau
Dinas Powis	*Glamorgan* - Barry
Dinaton	*Cornwall* - Plymouth
Dinchope	*Salop* - Ludlow
Dinder	*Somerset* - Wells
Dinedor	*Hereford* - Hereford
Dingestow	*Monmouth* - Monmouth
Dingle	*Lancaster* - Liverpool
Dingleden	*Kent* - Cranbrook
Dingley	*Northampton* - Corby
Dinhams Bridge	*Cornwall* - Bodmin
Dinkley	*Lancaster* - Blackburn
Dinmore	*Hereford* - Hereford
Dinnington	*Northumberland* - Newcastle upon Tyne
Dinnington	*Somerset* - Yeovil
Dinnington	*York, W.R.* - Worksop
Dinorwic	*Caernarvon* - Caernarvon
Dinsdale	*Durham* - Darlington
Dinthill	*Salop* - Shrewsbury
Dinting	*Derby* - Hyde
Dinton	*Bucks* - Aylesbury
Dinton	*Wilts* - Salisbury
Dipford	*Somerset* - Taunton
Dipley	*Hants* - Basingstoke
Dippenhall	*Surrey* - Aldershot and Farnham
Diptford	*Devon* - Kingsbridge
Dipton	*Durham* - Consett
Discoyd	*Radnor* - Knighton
Diseworth	*Leicester* - Loughborough
Dishforth	*York, N.R.* - Harrogate
Dishley	*Leicester* - Loughborough
Disley	*Cheshire* - Stockport
Diss	*Norfolk* - Norwich
Disserth	*Radnor* - Builth
Diss-Heywood	*Norfolk* - Norwich
Dissington	*Northumberland* - Newcastle upon Tyne
Dissington, North	*Northumberland* - Newcastle upon Tyne

Dissington, South	*Northumberland* - Newcastle upon Tyne
Distington	*Cumberland* - Whitehaven
Ditcham	*Hants* - Petersfield
Ditchburn	*Northumberland* - Alnwick
Ditcheat	*Somerset* - Wells
Ditches	*Salop* - Shrewsbury
Ditchingham	*Norfolk* - Norwich
Ditchley	*Oxford* - Banbury
Ditchling	*Sussex* - Haywards Heath
Ditherington	*Salop* - Shrewsbury
Ditteridge	*Wilts* - Bath
Dittisham	*Devon* - Torquay
Ditton	*Bucks* - Slough
Ditton	*Kent* - Maidstone
Ditton	*Lancaster* - St. Helens
Ditton, Long	*Surrey* - Kingston-upon-Thames
Ditton Priors	*Salop* - Bridgnorth
Dixons Green	*Worcester* - Dudley
Dixton	*Gloucester* - Cheltenham
Dizzard	*Cornwall* - Launceston
Dobb Brow	*Lancaster* - Bolton
Dobbs Weir	*Essex* - Harlow
Dob Cross	*York, W.R.* - Oldham
Dobholes	*Derby* - Ilkeston
Dobs Hill	*Cheshire* - Chester
Dobwalls	*Cornwall* - Liskeard
Doccombe	*Devon* - Newton Abbot
Dockenfield	*Surrey* - Aldershot and Farnham
Docker	*Lancaster* - Lancaster
Docker	*Westmorland* - Kendal
Docking	*Norfolk* - King's Lynn
Docklow	*Hereford* - Leominster
Dockray	*Cumberland* - Penrith
Dockray	*Cumberland* - Carlisle
Dodbrooke	*Devon* - Kingsbridge
Dodcot	*Cheshire* - Whitchurch
Doddenham	*Worcester* - Worcester
Dodderhill	*Worcester* - Bromsgrove
Doddershall	*Bucks* - Aylesbury
Doddinghurst	*Essex* - Brentwood
Doddington	*Cambridge* - March
Doddington	*Cheshire* - Crewe
Doddington	*Kent* - Sittingbourne
Doddington	*Lincoln* - Lincoln
Doddington	*Northumberland* - Berwick-upon-Tweed
Doddington	*Salop* - Kidderminster
Doddington Fen	*Cambridge* - March
Doddington, Great	*Northampton* - Wellingborough
Doddiscombsleigh	*Devon* - Exeter
Dodford	*Northampton* - Northampton
Dodford	*Worcester* - Bromsgrove
Doddington	*Gloucester* - Bristol
Dodington	*Salop* - Whitchurch
Dodington	*Somerset* - Minehead
Dodington Ash	*Gloucester* - Bristol
Dod Lea	*York, W.R.* - Huddersfield
Dodleston	*Cheshire* - Chester
Dodnor	*I. of W.* - Newport (I.W.)
Dodsleigh	*Stafford* - Uttoxeter
Dodwell	*Warwick* - Stratford-upon-Avon
Dodworth	*York, W.R.* - Barnsley
Doe Bank	*Warwick* - Birmingham
Doe Hill	*Derby* - Alfreton
Doe Lea	*Derby* - Chesterfield
Doe Royd	*York, W.R.* - Sheffield
Doffcocker	*Lancaster* - Bolton
Dogbarking	*Sussex* - Horsham
Dogdyke	*Lincoln* - Sleaford
Dog Kennells	*Sussex* - Chichester
Dogley Bar	*York, W.R.* - Huddersfield
Dogmersfield	*Hants* - Basingstoke
Dogs Hill	*Sussex* - Hastings
Dog Town	*Durham* - Durham
Doithie Camddwr	*Cardigan* - Lampeter
Doithie Pysgottwr	*Cardigan* - Lampeter
Dolan	*Radnor* - Knighton
Dolanog (part)	*Montgomery* - Oswestry
Dolanog (part)	*Montgomery* - Welshpool

Dolbenmaen	*Caernarvon* - Portmadoc
Dolberry	*Somerset* - Weston Super Mare
Dolborough	*Somerset* - Weston Super Mare
Doldowlod	*Radnor* - Llandrindod Wells
Doley	*Stafford* - Market Drayton
Doley Common	*Stafford* - Stafford
Dolfor	*Montgomery* - Newtown
Dolforwyn	*Montgomery* - Newtown
Dolgadfan	*Montgomery* - Machynlleth
Dolgarrog	*Caernarvon* - Conway
Dolgellau	*Merioneth* - Dolgellau
Dolgwden	*Montgomery* - Newtown
Dolley Green	*Radnor* - Knighton
Dollis Hill	*London, N.W.2* - Willesden
Dolphinholme	*Lancaster* - Lancaster
Dolton	*Devon* - Bideford
Dolwar	*Montgomery* - Oswestry
Dolwen	*Denbigh* - Conway
Dolwen	*Montgomery* - Newtown
Dolwyd	*Denbigh* - Conway
Dolwyddelan	*Caernarvon* - Conway
Dolybont	*Cardigan* - Aberystwyth
Dolygaer	*Glamorgan* - Merthyr Tydfil
Dolyhir	*Radnor* - Knighton
Dolywern	*Denbigh* - Wrexham
Domgay	*Montgomery* - Oswestry
Donaldson's Lodge	*Northumberland* - Berwick-upon-Tweed
Doncaster	*York, W.R.* - Doncaster
Donhead St. Andrew	*Wilts* - Shaftesbury
Donhead St. Mary	*Wilts* - Shaftesbury
Donington	*Lincoln* - Spalding
Donington	*Salop* - Wolverhampton
Donington Eaudyke	*Lincoln* - Spalding
Donington-le-Heath	*Leicester* - Ashby-de-la-Zouch
Donington North Ing.	*Lincoln* - Spalding
Donington Northorpe	*Lincs* - Spalding
Donington-on-Bain	*Lincoln* - Louth
Donington South Ing.	*Lincoln* - Spalding
Donington Westdale	*Lincoln* - Spalding
Donisthorpe	*Leicester* - Ashby-de-la-Zouch
Donkley Wood	*Northumberland* - Hexham
Donnerville	*Salop* - Wellington (Salop)
Donnington	*Berks* - Newbury
Donnington	*Gloucester* - Cheltenham
Donnington	*Hereford* - Hereford
Donnington	*Salop* - Wellington (Salop)
Donnington	*Sussex* - Chichester
Donnington (Near Wroxeter)	*Salop* - Shrewsbury
Donnington Wood	*Salop* - Wellington (Salop)
Donyatt	*Somerset* - Axminster and Chard
Doomsday Green	*Sussex* - Horsham
Doors	*Northumberland* - Haltwhistle
Dorchester	*Dorset* - Dorchester
Dorchester	*Oxford* - Didcot
Dordale	*Worcester* - Bromsgrove
Dordon	*Warwick* - Tamworth
Dore	*York, W.R.* - Sheffield
Dorhall	*Worcester* - Kidderminster
Dorking	*Surrey* - Dorking
Dormans Land	*Surrey* - East Grinstead
Dormans Park	*Surrey* - East Grinstead
Dormanstown	*York, N.R.* - Middlesbrough
Dormer Leys	*Oxford* - Thame
Dormington	*Hereford* - Hereford
Dormston	*Worcester* - Redditch
Dorn	*Gloucester* - Evesham
Dorney	*Bucks* - Slough
Dorridge	*Warwick* - Birmingham
Dorrington	*Lincoln* - Sleaford
Dorrington	*Salop* - Market Drayton
Dorrington	*Salop* - Shrewsbury
Dorrington Fen	*Lincoln* - Sleaford
Dorsington	*Warwick* - Stratford on Avon
Dorsington, Little	*Warwick* - Stratford on Avon
Dorstone	*Hereford* - Hereford
Dorton	*Bucks* - Thame
Doseley	*Salop* - Wellington (Salop)

Dosthill	*Warwick* - Tamworth
Dothill	*Salop* - Wellington (Salop)
Dotton	*Devon* - Exeter
Double Hill	*Somerset* - Bath
Doughton	*Norfolk* - King's Lynn
Doulting	*Somerset* - Wells
Dousland	*Devon* - Plymouth
Douthwaite Dale	*York, N.R.* - Malton
Dovaston	*Salop* - Oswestry
Dovecliffe	*York, W.R.* - Barnsley
Dove Cot	*Lancaster* - Liverpool
Dovecote Colliery	*Northumberland* - Morpeth
Doveholes	*Derby* - Buxton
Dovenby	*Cumberland* - Workington
Dover	*Kent* - Dover
Dovercourt	*Essex* - Harwich
Doverdale	*Worcester* - Kidderminster
Doverhay	*Somerset* - Minehead
Doveridge	*Derby* - Uttoxeter
Dovey Bridge	*Merioneth* - Machynlleth
Doward	*Hereford* - Monmouth
Dowbiggin	*York, W.R.* - Kendal
Dowdeswell	*Gloucester* - Cheltenham
Dowfold (Crook)	*Durham* - Bishop Auckland
Dowgas	*Cornwall* - St. Austell
Dowlais	*Glamorgan* - Merthyr Tydfil
Dowlais Top	*Glamorgan* - Merthyr Tydfil
Dowles	*Worcester* - Kidderminster
Dowle Street	*Kent* - Ashford
Dowlish Wake	*Somerset* - Axminster and Chard
Dowlish, West	*Somerset* - Axminster and Chard
Downall Green	*Lancaster* - Wigan
Down Ampney	*Gloucester* - Swindon
Downderry	*Cornwall* - Liskeard
Downderry	*Cornwall* - St. Austell
Downe	*Kent* - Bromley
Down End	*Berks* - Newbury
Downend	*Gloucester* - Bristol
Downend	*Gloucester* - Stroud
Down Gate	*Cornwall* - Launceston
Down Gate (Linkinhorne)	*Cornwall* - Liskeard
Down Hall	*Cumberland* - Carlisle
Downham	*Essex* - Brentwood
Downham	*Lancaster* - Blackburn
Downham	*Northumberland* - Berwick-upon-Tweed
Downham Common	*Cambridge* - Ely
Downham Estate	*Kent* - Bromley
Downham Fen, Little	*Cambridge* - Ely
Downham Hythe	*Cambridge* - Ely
Downham, Little	*Cambridge* - Ely
Downham Market	*Norfolk* - King's Lynn
Down Hatherley	*Gloucester* - Gloucester
Downhayne, Colyton	*Devon* - Axminster and Chard
Downhead	*Somerset* - Frome
Downhead (West Camel)	*Somerset* - Yeovil
Downholland	*Lancaster* - Southport
Downholme	*York, N.R.* - Darlington
Downing	*Flint* - Holywell
Downing	*Gloucester* - Cheltenham
Downinney	*Cornwall* - Launceston
Downley	*Bucks* - High Wycombe
Down, Lower	*Salop* - Shrewsbury
Down, Old	*Gloucester* - Thornbury
Down St. Mary	*Devon* - Exeter
Downs, High	*Durham* - Durham
Downside	*Somerset* - Bristol
Downs Lane	*Durham* - Durham
Downs, Low	*Durham* - Durham
Down Stonebeck	*York, W.R.* - Harrogate
Down, The	*Salop* - Bridgnorth
Down Thomas	*Devon* - Plymouth
Downton	*Hants* - Lymington
Downton	*Salop* - Shrewsbury
Downton	*Wilts* - Salisbury
Downton Castle	*Hereford* - Ludlow

Downton on the Rock	*Salop* - Ludlow
Dowsby	*Lincoln* - Spalding
Dowsby Fen	*Lincoln* - Spalding
Dowsby, Little	*Lincoln* - Spalding
Dowsdale	*Lincoln* - Spalding
Dowthwaitehead	*Cumberland* - Penrith
Doxey	*Stafford* - Stafford
Doxey Wood	*Stafford* - Stafford
Doxford	*Northumberland* - Alnwick
Doynton	*Gloucester* - Bristol
Draetnen, The	*Monmouth* - Newport (Mon.)
Dragonby	*Lincoln* - Scunthorpe
Dragon's Green	*Sussex* - Horsham
Dragonville	*Durham* - Durham
Drakeholes	*Notts* - East Retford
Drakelow	*Cheshire* - Northwich
Drakelow	*Derby* - Burton-upon-Trent
Drakelow	*Worcester* - Kidderminster
Drakes Broughton	*Worcester* - Evesham
Drakes Cross	*Worcester* - Birmingham
Drakewalls	*Cornwall* - Plymouth
Draughton	*Northampton* - Northampton
Draughton	*York, W.R.* - Skipton
Drax	*York, W.R.* - Goole
Drax, Long	*York, W.R.* - Goole
Draycot	*Oxford* - Thame
Draycot Cerne	*Wilts* - Chippenham
Draycote	*Warwick* - Rugby
Draycot Foliatt	*Wilts* - Swindon
Draycott	*Derby* - Derby
Draycott	*Somerset* - Wells
Draycott	*Gloucester* - Evesham
Draycott-in-the-Clay	*Stafford* - Uttoxeter
Draycott-in-the-Moors	*Stafford* - Stoke on Trent
Drayford	*Devon* - Tiverton
Draynes	*Cornwall* - Liskeard
Drayton	*Berks* - Didcot
Drayton	*Hants* - Portsmouth
Drayton	*Leicester* - Kettering
Drayton (Swineshead)	*Lincoln* - Boston
Drayton	*Norfolk* - Norwich
Drayton	*Northampton* - Northampton
Drayton	*Oxford* - Banbury
Drayton	*Somerset* - Taunton
Drayton	*Stafford* - Stafford
Drayton	*Sussex* - Chichester
Drayton	*Warwick* - Stratford on Avon
Drayton	*Worcester* - Kidderminster
Drayton Bassett	*Stafford* - Tamworth
Drayton Beauchamp	*Bucks* - Aylesbury
Drayton, East	*Notts* - East Retford
Drayton, Moor	*Berks* - Oxford
Drayton Park	*London, N.5* - Clerkenwell
Drayton Parslow	*Bucks* - Bletchley and Leighton Buzzard
Drayton St. Leonards	*Oxford* - Didcot
Drayton, West	*Middlesex* - Uxbridge
Drayton, West	*Notts* - East Retford
Dreepwood	*Salop* - Shrewsbury
Drefach	*Carmarthen* - Carmarthen
Drellingore	*Kent* - Dover
Dresden	*Stafford* - Stoke-on-Trent
Drewsteignton	*Devon* - Okehampton
Drewton	*York, E.R.* - Beverley
Driby	*Lincoln* - Skegness
Driffield	*Gloucester* - Cirencester
Driffield, Great	*York, E.R.* - Beverley
Driffield, Little	*York. E.R.* - Beverley
Driffold	*Warwick* - Birmingham
Drift	*Cornwall* - Penzance
Drigg	*Cumberland* - Whitehaven
Drightlington	*York, W.R.* - Dewsbury
Drimpton	*Dorset* - Yeovil
Dringhoe	*York, E.R.* - Bridlington
Dringhouses	*York, W.R.* - York
Drinkstone	*Suffolk* - Stowmarket
Drointon	*Stafford* - Stafford
Droitwich	*Worcester* - Worcester
Dronfield	*Derby* - Chesterfield
Dronfield Woodhouses	*Derby* - Chesterfield

Droop	*Dorset* - Dorchester
Drope	*Glamorgan* - Cardiff
Dropmore	*Bucks* - Slough
Droppingwell	*York, W.R.* - Rotherham
Drove End	*Lincs* - Spalding
Droxford	*Hants* - Petersfield
Droylsden	*Lancaster* - Ashton-under-Lyne
Drub	*York, W.R.* - Dewsbury
Druid	*Merioneth* - Wrexham
Druids Heath	*Warwick* - Birmingham
Drumburgh	*Cumberland* - Carlisle
Drumleaning	*Cumberland* - Carlisle
Drungewick	*Sussex* - Petworth
Drury Lane	*Salop* - Shrewsbury
Druxton	*Devon* - Launceston
Drwsycoed	*Caernarvon* - Caernarvon
Drwsynant	*Merioneth* - Dolgellau
Drybeck	*Westmorland* - Penrith
Drybrook	*Gloucester* - Gloucester
Dry Doddington	*Lincoln* - Newark
Dry Drayton	*Cambridge* - Cambridge
Dry Gill	*York, W.R.* - Skipton
Dry Hill	*Kent* - Sevenoaks
Drynham	*Wilts* - Trowbridge
Dry Pool	*Gloucester* - Cheltenham
Dry Sandford	*Berks* - Oxford
Drysllwyn	*Carmarthen* - Carmarthen
Dryton	*Salop* - Shrewsbury
Dubmire	*Durham* - Durham
Dubwath	*Cumberland* - Workington
Duck Hole	*Gloucester* - Thornbury
Duckington	*Cheshire* - Whitchurch
Ducklington	*Oxford* - Witney
Duckmanton	*Derby* - Chesterfield
Duckthorpe	*Lincoln* - Louth
Dudbridge	*Gloucester* - Stroud
Dudden Hill	*London, N.W.10* - Willesden
Duddenhoe End	*Essex* - Bishop's Stortford
Duddeston	*Warwick* - Birmingham
Duddington	*Northampton* - Stamford
Duddle	*Dorset* - Dorchester
Duddlestone	*Somerset* - Taunton
Duddleswell	*Sussex* - Lewes
Duddo	*Northumberland* - Berwick-upon-Tweed
Duddon	*Cheshire* - Chester
Duddon Bridge	*Lancaster* - Barrow-in-Furness
Dudgrove	*Gloucester* - Swindon
Dudleston	*Salop* - Oswestry
Dudleston Heath	*Salop* - Oswestry
Dudley	*Northumberland* - Newcastle upon Tyne
Dudley	*Worcester* - Dudley
Dudley Hill	*York, W.R.* - Bradford
Dudley Port	*Stafford* - Dudley
Dudley Wood	*Worcester* - Dudley
Dudmaston	*Salop* - Bridgnorth
Dueshill	*Northumberland* - Morpeth
Duffan Foots	*Northumberland* - Hexham
Duffield	*Derby* - Derby
Duffield, North	*York, E.R.* - York
Duffield, South	*York, E.R.* - York
Duffryn	*Glamorgan* - Barry
Duffryn	*Glamorgan* - Merthyr Tydfil
Duffryn (Cymmer)	*Glamorgan* - Neath
Duffryn	*Monmouth* - Newport (Mon.)
Duffryn Ceri	*Cardigan* - Cardigan
Duffryn Clydach	*Glamorgan* - Neath
Dufton	*Westmorland* - Penrith
Duggleby	*York, E.R.* - Malton
Duke End	*Warwick* - Birmingham
Duker's Hagg	*Northumberland* - Hexham
Dukesfield	*Northumberland* - Berwick-upon-Tweed
Dukestown	*Monmouth* - Blackwood
Dukinfield	*Cheshire* - Ashton-under-Lyne
Dulas	*Anglesey* - Llangefni
Dulas	*Hereford* - Hereford
Dulcote	*Somerset* - Wells
Dulford	*Devon* - Exeter

DUL - DUN

Dullingham	*Cambridge* - Newmarket
Dully	*Kent* - Sittingbourne
Dully, Little	*Kent* - Sittingbourne
Duloe	*Beds* - Biggleswade
Duloe	*Cornwall* - Liskeard
Dulverton	*Somerset* - Tiverton
Dulwich	*London, S.E.21* - Lambeth
Dulwich, East	*London, S.E.22* - Lambeth
Dulwich, North	*London, S.E.24* - Lambeth
Dulwich Village	*London, S.E.21* - Lambeth
Dulwich, West	*London, S.E.21* - Lambeth
Dumbleton	*Gloucester* - Cheltenham
Dummer	*Hants* - Basingstoke
Dummer Clump	*Hants* - Basingstoke
Dunball	*Somerset* - Bridgwater
Dunbridge	*Hants* - Southampton
Dunces Houses	*Northumberland* - Morpeth
Dunchideock	*Devon* - Exeter
Dunchurch	*Warwick* - Rugby
Dunclent	*Worcester* - Kidderminster
Duncot	*Salop* - Shrewsbury
Duncote	*Northampton* - Northampton
Duncott	*Salop* - Shrewsbury
Duncton	*Sussex* - Chichester
Dundas	*Wilts* - Trowbridge
Dundraw	*Cumberland* - Carlisle
Dundridge	*Hants* - Winchester
Dundry, East	*Somerset* - Bristol
Dundry West	*Somerset* - Bristol
Dunfield	*Gloucester* - Cirencester
Dunford	*Sussex* - Chichester
Dunford Bridge	*York, W.R.* - Barnsley
Dungeness	*Kent* - Ashford
Dungworth	*York, W.R.* - Sheffield
Dunham	*Notts* - East Retford
Dunham, Great	*Norfolk* - King's Lynn
Dunham, Little	*Norfolk* - King's Lynn
Dunham	*Cheshire* - Altrincham
Dunham-on-the-Hill	*Cheshire* - Chester
Dunhampton	*Hereford* - Leominster
Dunhampton	*Worcester* - Worcester
Dunhamstead	*Worcester* - Worcester
Dunholme	*Lincoln* - Lincoln
Dunkerton	*Somerset* - Bath
Dunkeswell	*Devon* - Exeter
Dunkeswell Abbey	*Devon* - Exeter
Dunkeswick	*York, W.R.* - Otley
Dunkirk	*Cambridge* - Ely
Dunkirk	*Cheshire* - Chester
Dunkirk	*Gloucester* - Stroud
Dunkirk	*Kent* - Canterbury
Dunkirk	*Notts* - Nottingham
Dunkirk	*Stafford* - Stoke-on-Trent
Dunkirk	*Stafford* - West Bromwich
Dunkirk	*Wilts* - Devizes
Dunks Green	*Kent* - Sevenoaks
Dunley	*Hants* - Newbury
Dunley	*Worcester* - Kidderminster
Dunmere	*Cornwall* - Bodmin
Dunmow	*Essex* - Braintree
Dunmow, Great	*Essex* - Braintree
Dunmow, Little	*Essex* - Braintree
Dunnerdale	*Lancaster* - Barrow-in-Furness
Dunnerholme	*Lancaster* - Barrow-in-Furness
Dunnington	*Warwick* - Redditch
Dunnington	*York, E.R.* - Beverley
Dunnington	*York, E.R.* - York
Dunnockshaw	*Lancaster* - Burnley
Dunsby	*Lincoln* - Spalding
Dunsby Fen	*Lincoln* - Spalding
Dunscroft	*York, W.R.* - Thorne
Dunsdale	*York, N.R.* - Middlesbrough
Dunsden	*Oxford* - Reading
Dunsfold	*Surrey* - Guildford
Dunsford	*Devon* - Exeter
Dunsforth, Lower	*York, W.R.* - Harrogate
Dunsforth, Upper	*York, W.R.* - Harrogate
Dunsley	*Stafford* - Stourbridge

DUN - DYK

Dunsley	*York, N.R.* - Whitby
Dunsmore	*Bucks* - Aylesbury
Dunsmore Green	*Gloucester* - Cheltenham
Dunsop Bridge	*Lancaster* - Preston
Dunstable	*Beds* - Luton
Dunstall	*Lincoln* - Gainsborough
Dunstall	*Stafford* - Burton-upon-Trent
Dunstall	*Stafford* - Wolverhampton
Dunstall	*Worcester* - Worcester
Dunstan	*Northumberland* - Alnwick
Dunster	*Somerset* - Minehead
Duns Tew	*Oxford* - Banbury
Dunston	*Lincoln* - Lincoln
Dunston	*Norfolk* - Norwich
Dunston	*Stafford* - Stafford
Dunstone	*Devon* - Kingsbridge
Dunstone	*Devon* - Plymouth
Dunston Fen	*Lincoln* - Lincoln
Dunston Heath	*Lincoln* - Lincoln
Dunston Heath	*Stafford* - Stafford
Dunston-on-Tyne	*Durham* - Gateshead
Dunsville	*York, W.R.* - Thorne
Dunswell	*York, E.R.* - Kingston-upon-Hull
Dunterton	*Cornwall* - Launceston
Dunthrop	*Oxford* - Banbury
Duntisbourne Abbotts	*Gloucester* - Cheltenham
Duntisbourne Leer	*Gloucester* - Cheltenham
Duntisbourne Rouse	*Gloucester* - Cheltenham
Duntish	*Dorset* - Dorchester
Dunton	*Beds* - Biggleswade
Dunton	*Bucks* - Aylesbury
Dunton	*Essex* - Brentwood
Dunton	*Norfolk* - King's Lynn
Dunton	*Warwick* - Birmingham
Dunton Bassett	*Leicester* - Leicester
Dunton Green	*Kent* - Sevenoaks
Dunvant	*Glamorgan* - Swansea
Dunwear	*Somerset* - Bridgwater
Dunwich	*Suffolk* - Halesworth
Dunwood	*Hants* - Southampton
Duporth	*Cornwall* - St. Austell
Durdar	*Cumberland* - Carlisle
Durfold	*Surrey* - Guildford
Durfold Wood	*Sussex* - Chichester
Durham	*Durham* - Durham
Durham, New	*Durham* - Durham
Durham, Old	*Durham* - Durham
Durkar	*York, W.R.* - Wakefield
Durleigh	*Somerset* - Bridgwater
Durleighmarsh	*Sussex* - Petersfield
Durley	*Hants* - Southampton
Durley	*Wilts* - Swindon
Durlock (part)	*Kent* - Deal
Durlow Common	*Hereford* - Hereford
Durndale	*Kent* - Gravesend
Durnford	*Wilts* - Salisbury
Durranhill	*Cumberland* - Carlisle
Durrants	*Hants* - Petersfield
Durrington	*Sussex* - Worthing
Durrington	*Wilts* - Salisbury
Dursley	*Gloucester* - Stroud
Dursley Cross	*Gloucester* - Gloucester
Durston	*Somerset* - Taunton
Durweston	*Dorset* - Shaftesbury
Duston	*Northampton* - Northampton
Duston, New	*Northampton* - Northampton
Duthlas	*Radnor* - Knighton
Dutton	*Cheshire* - Northwich
Dutton	*Lancaster* - Preston
Dutton Diffeth	*Denbigh* - Wrexham
Duxbury	*Lancaster* - Chorley
Duxford	*Berks* - Oxford
Duxford	*Cambridge* - Cambridge
Dwrbach	*Pembroke* - Haverfordwest
Dwygyfylchi	*Caernarvon* - Conway
Dwyran	*Anglesey* - Llangefni
Dyffryn Ardudwy	*Merioneth* - Dolgellau
Dyffryn Crawnon	*Brecon* - Pontypool and Abergavenny
Dyke	*Lincoln* - Spalding

Dyke Fen	*Lincoln* - Spalding
Dylife	*Montgomery* - Machynlleth
Dymchurch	*Kent* - Ashford
Dymock	*Gloucester* - Gloucester
Dyrham and Hinton	*Gloucester* - Bristol
Dyserth	*Flint* - Rhyl
Dyson Lane	*York, W.R.* - Halifax

E

Eachwick	*Northumberland* - Newcastle upon Tyne
Eagle	*Lincoln* - Lincoln
Eagle Barnsdale	*Lincoln* - Lincoln
Eagle Moor	*Lincoln* - Lincoln
Eaglescliffe	*Durham* - Stockton on Tees
Eaglesfield	*Cumberland* - Workington
Eagletor	*Derby* - Matlock
Eagle Woodhouse	*Lincoln* - Lincoln
Eagley	*Lancaster* - Bolton
Eakley Lanes	*Bucks* - Northampton
Eakring	*Notts* - Newark
Ealand	*Lincoln* - Thorne
Ealing	*London, W.5* - Brentford
Ealing Common	*London, W.5* - Brentford
Ealinghearth	*Lancaster* - Barrow-in-Furness
Ealing, West	*London, W.13* - Brentford
Eals	*Northumberland* - Carlisle
Eamont Bridge	*Westmorland* - Penrith
Earby	*York, W.R.* - Skipton
Eardington	*Salop* - Bridgnorth
Eardisland	*Hereford* - Leominster
Eardisley	*Hereford* - Hereford
Eardiston	*Salop* - Oswestry
Eardiston	*Worcester* - Kidderminster
Eardley End	*Stafford* - Stoke-on-Trent
Earith	*Hunts* - Huntingdon
Earith Gravel Drove	*Cambridge* - Ely
Earith Hermitage	*Cambridge* - Ely
Earle	*Northumberland* - Alnwick
Earlestown	*Lancaster* - Warrington
Earley	*Berks* - Reading
Earley, Lower	*Berks* - Reading
Earls Barton	*Northampton* - Wellingborough
Earl's Colne	*Essex* - Colchester
Earls Common	*Worcester* - Worcester
Earl's Court	*London, S.W.5* - West London
Earl's Croome	*Worcester* - Worcester
Earlsdon	*Warwick* - Coventry
Earlsfield	*London, S.W.18* - Wandsworth
Earlsheaton	*York, W.R.* - Dewsbury
Earl Shilton	*Leicester* - Hinckley
Earl Soham	*Suffolk* - Ipswich
Earl Sterndale	*Derby* - Buxton
Earl Stonham	*Suffolk* - Stowmarket
Earlswood	*Monmouth* - Chepstow
Earlswood	*Surrey* - Reigate
Earlswood	*Warwick* - Birmingham
Earnley	*Sussex* - Chichester
Earnshill	*Somerset* - Taunton
Earnstrey Park	*Salop* - Ludlow
Earsdon	*Northumberland* - Morpeth
Earsdon	*Northumberland* - North Shields
Earsdon Forest	*Northumberland* - Morpeth
Earsham	*Norfolk* - Norwich
Earswick, New	*York, N.R.* - York
Earswick, Old	*York, N.R.* - York
Eartham	*Sussex* - Chichester
Earthcott Green	*Gloucester* - Thornbury
Easby	*York, N.R.* - Middlesbrough
Easby, Great	*Cumberland* - Carlisle
Easby, Little	*Cumberland* - Carlisle
Easebourne	*Sussex* - Chichester
Easenhall	*Warwick* - Rugby
Eashing	*Surrey* - Guildford
Easington	*Durham* - Sunderland
Easington	*Northumberland* - Berwick-upon-Tweed
Easington	*Oxford* - Thame

Easington	*Oxford* - Didcot
Easington	*York, E.R.* - Kingston-upon-Hull
Easington	*York, N.R.* - Whitby
Easington	*York, W.R.* - Blackburn
Easington Colliery	*Durham* - Sunderland
Easington Lane	*Durham* - Durham
Easington Village	*Durham* - Sunderland
Easingwold	*York, N.R.* - York
Easole Street	*Kent* - Canterbury
East Aberthaw	*Glamorgan* - Barry
Eastacombe	*Devon* - Barnstaple
Eastacott	*Devon* - Barnstaple
East Adderbury	*Oxford* - Banbury
East Allington	*Devon* - Kingsbridge
East Anstey	*Devon* - Tiverton
Eastanton	*Hants* - Andover
East Ardsley	*York, W.R.* - Dewsbury
East Ashling	*Sussex* - Chichester
East Ayton	*York, N.R.* - Scarborough
East Bagborough	*Somerset* - Taunton
East Barkwith	*Lincoln* - Louth
East Barnet	*Herts* - Barnet
East Barsham	*Norfolk* - Fakenham
East Beckham	*Norfolk* - Norwich
East Bergholt	*Suffolk* - Ipswich
East Bierley	*York, W.R.* - Dewsbury
East Bilney	*Norfolk* - East Dereham
East Black Dean	*Durham* - Bishop Auckland
East Boldon	*Durham* - South Shields
East Boldre	*Hants* - Lymington
East Bottom	*Kent* - Dover
Eastbourne	*Sussex* - Eastbourne
East Bower	*Somerset* - Bridgwater
East Bowling	*York, W.R.* - Bradford
East Bradenham	*Norfolk* - East Dereham
East Brent	*Somerset*- Weston Super Mare
Eastbridge	*Kent* - Ashford
Eastbridge	*Suffolk* - Woodbridge
East Bridgford	*Notts* - Nottingham
East Brunton	*Northumberland* - Newcastle upon Tyne
East Buckland	*Devon* - Kingsbridge
East Buckland	*Devon* - Banstaple
East Budleigh	*Devon* - Exeter
Eastburn	*York, E.R.* - Beverley
Eastburn	*York, W.R.* - Keighley
East Burnham	*Bucks* - Slough
East Burton	*Dorset* - Dorchester
Eastbury	*Berks* - Newbury
Eastbury	*Dorset* - Blandford
Eastbury	*Herts* - Watford
East Butsfield	*Durham* - Durham
East Butterwick	*Lincoln* - Scunthorpe
Eastby	*York, W.R.* - Skipton
East Cams (Fareham)	*Hants* - Portsmouth
East Carleton	*Norfolk* - Norwich
East Carlton	*Northampton* - Corby
East Castle	*Durham* - Consett
East Chaldon	*Dorset* - Weymouth
East Challow	*Berks* - Didcot
East Charlton	*Northumberland* - Hexham
East Chelborough	*Dorset* - Yeovil
East Chettle	*Dorset* - Salisbury
East Chevington	*Northumberland* - Morpeth
East Chiltington	*Sussex* - Lewes
East Chinnock	*Somerset* - Yeovil
East Chivingstone	*Northumberland* - Morpeth
East Cholderton	*Hants* - Andover
Eastchurch	*Kent* - Sheerness
East Cilrledyn	*Pembroke* - Cardigan
East Claydon	*Bucks* - Aylesbury
East Cliff	*Cumberland* - Carlisle
East Coanwood	*Northumberland* - Hexham
East Coker	*Somerset* - Yeovil
Eastcombe	*Gloucester* - Stroud
East Combe	*Somerset* - Taunton
East Compton	*Dorset* - Dorchester
East Compton	*Somerset* - Wells
Eastcote	*Middlesex* - Uxbridge

Eastcote	*Northampton* - Northampton
Eastcote	*Warwick* - Birmingham
Eastcott	*Wilts* - Devizes
East Cottingwith	*York, E.R.* - York
Eastcotts	*Beds* - Bedford
East Coulston	*Wilts* - Trowbridge
Eastcourt	*Wilts* - Malmesbury
Eastcourt	*Wilts* - Newbury
East Cowes	*I. of W.* - Newport (I.W.)
East Cowick	*York, W.R.* - Goole
East Cranmore	*Somerset* - Wells
East Creech	*Dorset* - Swanage
East Curthwaite	*Cumberland* - Carlisle
East Dean	*Hants* - Salisbury
East Dean	*Sussex* - Chichester
East Dean	*Sussex* - Eastbourne
Eastdene	*York, W.R.* - Rotherham
East Denton	*Northumberland* - Newcastle upon Tyne
East Dereham	*Norfolk* - East Dereham
East Donyland	*Essex* - Colchester
East Down	*Devon* - Kingsbridge
East Drayton	*Notts* - East Retford
East Dulwich	*London, S.E.22* - Lambeth
East Dundry	*Somerset* - Bristol
East End	*Bucks* - Bletchley and Leighton Buzzard
East End	*Hants* - Lymington
East End	*Herts* - Bishop's Stortford
East End (Benenden)	*Kent* - Cranbrook
East End Green	*Herts* - Hertford
East End, Roydon	*Essex* - Harlow
Easter Compton	*Gloucester* - Thornbury
Eastergate	*Sussex* - Chichester
Easter, High	*Essex* - Braintree
Eastern Green	*Warwick* - Coventry
Eastern Green, Lower	*Warwick* - Coventry
Easterton	*Wilts* - Devizes
East Farleigh	*Kent* - Maidstone
East Farndon	*Northampton* - Kettering
Eastfield	*York, N.R.* - Scarborough
Eastfield	*York, W.R.* - Doncaster
Eastfields	*Berks* - Newbury
East Finchley (part)	*London, N.2* - Barnet
East Finchley (part)	*London, N.2* - Clerkenwell
East Firsby	*Lincoln* - Lincoln
East Freshwater	*Pembroke* - Haverfordwest
East Garston	*Berks* - Newbury
Eastgate	*Durham* - Bishop Auckland
Eastgate (Bourne)	*Lincoln* - Spalding
East Goscote	*Leics* - Leicester
East Grafton	*Wilts* - Swindon
East Grinstead	*Wilts* - Salisbury
East Grinstead	*Sussex* - East Grinstead
East Guldeford	*Sussex* - Hastings
East Haddon	*Northampton* - Northampton
East Hagbourne	*Berks* - Didcot
East Halsham	*York, E.R.* - Kingston-upon-Hull
East Halton	*Lincoln* - Great Grimsby
Eastham	*Cheshire* - Birkenhead
East Ham	*London, E.6* - Bow
Eastham	*Worcester* - Kidderminster
East Hamlet	*Salop* - Ludlow
East Hampnett	*Sussex* - Chichester
Easthampstead	*Berks* - Reading
East Hanney	*Berks* - Didcot
East Hanningfield	*Essex* - Chelmsford
East Hardwick	*York, W.R.* - Pontefract
East Harling	*Norfolk* - Thetford
East Harptree	*Somerset* - Wells
East Hartford	*Northumberland* - North Shields
East Harting	*Sussex* - Petersfield
East Hatley	*Cambridge* - Biggleswade
East Heddon	*Northumberland* - Newcastle upon Tyne
East Hendred	*Berks* - Didcot
East Herrington	*Durham* - Sunderland
East Heslerton	*York, E.R.* - Malton
East Hetton	*Durham* - Durham

East Hill (part)	*Kent* - Sevenoaks
East Hillingdon	*Middlesex* - Uxbridge
East Hoathly	*Sussex* - Lewes
East Hoe (Hambledon)	*Hants* - Portsmouth
Easthope	*Salop* - Shrewsbury
East Horndon	*Essex* - Brentwood
Easthorpe	*Essex* - Colchester
Easthorpe	*Leicester* - Grantham
Easthorpe	*York, E.R.* - Malton
Easthorpe	*York, W.R.* - Dewsbury
East Horrington	*Somerset* - Wells
East Horsley	*Surrey* - Guildford
East Howdon	*Northumberland* - North Shields
East Howe	*Hants* - Bournemouth
East Howle	*Durham* - Durham
East Huntspill	*Somerset* - Bridgwater
East Hyde	*Beds* - Luton
East Ilsley	*Berks* - Didcot
Eastington	*Devon* - Exeter
Eastington	*Gloucester* - Cheltenham
Eastington	*Gloucester* - Stroud
Eastington	*Worcester* - Cheltenham
East Jarrow	*Durham* - South Shields
East Keal	*Lincoln* - Skegness
East Kelfield	*Lincoln* - Gainsborough
East Kennett	*Wilts* - Swindon
East Keswick	*York, W.R.* - Leeds
East Kirkby	*Lincoln* - Skegness
East Knighton	*Dorset* - Dorchester
East Knowle	*Devon* - Exeter
East Knoyle	*Wilts* - Shaftesbury
East Kyo	*Durham* - Consett
East Lambrook	*Somerset* - Yeovil
East Langdon	*Kent* - Dover
East Langton	*Leicester* - Leicester
East Lavant	*Sussex* - Chichester
East Lavington	*Sussex* - Chichester
East Lavington	*Wilts* - Devizes
East Layton	*York, N.R.* - Darlington
Eastleach	*Gloucester* - Cheltenham
East Leake	*Notts* - Loughborough
Eastleigh	*Devon* - Bideford
East Leigh	*Devon* - Kingsbridge
Eastleigh	*Hants* - Southampton
East Lexham	*Norfolk* - King's Lynn
East Lilburn	*Northumberland* - Alnwick
Eastling	*Kent* - Sittingbourne
East Linton	*York, E.R.* - Goole
East Liss	*Hants* - Petersfield
East Lockinge	*Berks* - Didcot
East Looe	*Cornwall* - Liskeard
East Lound	*Lincoln* - Gainsborough
East Lulworth	*Dorset* - Dorchester
East Lutton	*York, E.R.* - Beverley
East Lydford	*Somerset* - Wells
East Lyng	*Somerset* - Bridgwater
East Malling	*Kent* - Maidstone
East Marden	*Sussex* - Chichester
East Markham	*Notts* - East Retford
East Martin	*Wilts* - Salisbury
East Marton	*York, W.R.* - Skipton
East Matfen	*Northumberland* - Newcastle upon Tyne
East Melbury	*Dorset* - Shaftesbury
East Meon	*Hants* - Petersfield
East Mersea	*Essex* - Colchester
East Molesey	*Surrey* - Kingston-upon-Thames
East Moor	*Derby* - Chesterfield
Eastmoor	*Norfolk* - King's Lynn
East Morton	*York, W.R.* - Keighley
East Murton	*Durham* - Sunderland
East Newchurch	*Monmouth* - Chepstow
East Newton	*York, E.R.* - Kingston-upon-Hull
East Newton	*York, N.R.* - Malton
Eastney	*Hants* - Portsmouth
Eastnor	*Hereford* - Hereford
East Northdown	*Kent* - Margate
East Norton	*Leicester* - Leicester
East Nynehead	*Somerset* - Taunton
East Oakley	*Hants* - Basingstoke

EAS

Eastoft	*Lincoln* - Thorne
Eastoft	*York, W.R.* - Goole
East Ogwell	*Devon* - Newton Abbot
Eastoke (Hayling)	*Hants* - Portsmouth
Easton	*Berks* - Newbury
Easton	*Cumberland* - Carlisle
Easton	*Hants* - Winchester
Easton	*Hunts* - Huntingdon
Easton	*Lincoln* - Grantham
Easton	*Norfolk* - Norwich
Easton	*Somerset* - Wells
Easton	*Suffolk* - Woodbridge
Easton	*Wilts* - Devizes
Easton	*Wilts* - Swindon
Easton	*York, E.R.* - Bridlington
Easton Bavents	*Suffolk* - Halesworth
Easton Court	*Hereford* - Ludlow
Easton, Great	*Essex* - Braintree
Easton, Great	*Leicester* - Kettering
Easton Grey	*Wilts* - Malmesbury
Easton-in-Gordano	*Somerset* - Bristol
Easton, Little	*Essex* - Braintree
Easton Maudit	*Northampton* - Wellingborough
Easton Neston	*Northampton* - Northampton
Easton-on-the-Hill	*Northampton* - Stamford
East Orchard	*Dorset* - Shaftesbury
East Ord	*Northumberland* - Berwick-upon-Tweed
Eastover	*Hants* - Andover
East Panson	*Devon* - Launceston
East Park	*Durham* - Bishop Auckland
East Parley	*Hants* - Bournemouth
East Peckham	*Kent* - Maidstone
East Pennard	*Somerset* - Wells
East Perry	*Hunts* - Huntingdon
East Plain	*Lancaster* - Barrow-in-Furness
East Port Holland	*Cornwall* - St. Austell
East Portlemouth	*Devon* - Kingsbridge
East Prawle	*Devon* - Kingsbridge
East Preston	*Sussex* - Worthing
East Putney	*London, S.W.15* - Wandsworth
East Quantoxhead	*Somerset* - Minehead
East Rainton	*Durham* - Durham
East Ravendale	*Lincoln* - Great Grimsby
East Raynham	*Norfolk* - King's Lynn
Eastrea	*Cambridge* - Peterborough
East Retford	*Notts* - East Retford
Eastridge	*Wilts* - Swindon
Eastrington	*York, E.R.* - Goole
Eastrop	*Hants* - Basingstoke
Eastrop	*Wilts* - Swindon
East Row	*York, N.R.* - Whitby
East Rudham	*Norfolk* - King's Lynn
East Runton	*Norfolk* - Norwich
East Ruston	*Norfolk* - Norwich
Eastry	*Kent* - Deal
East Saltney	*Flint* - Chester
East Shaftoe	*Northumberland* - Newcastle upon Tyne
East Shalford	*Surrey* - Guildford
East Sheen	*London, S.W.14* - Wandsworth
East Shefford	*Berks* - Newbury
East Shield Hill	*Northumberland* - Morpeth
East Sleekburn	*Northumberland* - Blyth
East Somerton	*Norfolk* - Great Yarmouth
East Stanley	*Durham* - Consett
East Stannington	*Northumberland* - Morpeth
East Stannington	*York, W.R.* - Sheffield
East Stockwith	*Lincoln* - Gainsborough
East Stoke	*Dorset* - Swanage
East Stoke	*Notts* - Newark
East Stonehouses	*Devon* - Plymouth
East Stour	*Dorset* - Shaftesbury
East Stratton	*Hants* - Winchester
East Sutton	*Kent* - Maidstone
East Tanfield	*York, N.R.* - Harrogate
East Taphouse	*Cornwall* - Liskeard
East Thickley	*Durham* - Bishop Auckland
East Thirston	*Northumberland* - Morpeth
East Thorney	*Sussex* - Chichester

EAS - EBO

East Thornton	*Northumberland* - Morpeth
East Thorpe	*Lincoln* - Lincoln
East Tilbury	*Essex* - Grays Thurrock
East Tisbury	*Wilts* - Shaftesbury
East Tisted	*Hants* - Aldershot and Farnham
East Torrington	*Lincoln* - Louth
East Tuddenham	*Norfolk* - East Dereham
East Tytherley	*Hants* - Salisbury
East Tytherton	*Wilts* - Chippenham
East Vale	*Stafford* - Stoke-on-Trent
Eastville	*Lincoln* - Boston
East Wall	*Salop* - Ludlow
East Walton	*Norfolk* - King's Lynn
East Walton	*Pembroke* - Haverfordwest
Eastwell	*Kent* - Ashford
Eastwell	*Leicester* - Melton Mowbray
East Wellow	*Hants* - Southampton
East Whorlton	*Northumberland* - Newcastle upon Tyne
Eastwick	*Berks* - Newbury
Eastwick	*Herts* - Hertford
East Wick	*Wilts* - Swindon
East Wickham	*Kent* - Dartford
East Williamston	*Pembroke* - Haverfordwest
East Winch	*Norfolk* - King's Lynn
East Wittering	*Sussex* - Chichester
Eastwood	*Essex* - Southend
Eastwood	*Gloucester* - Thornbury
Eastwood	*Notts* - Ilkeston
Eastwood	*York, W.R.* - Rotherham
Eastwood	*Lancaster* - Todmorden
East Woodburn	*Northumberland* - Hexham
East Woodhay	*Hants* - Newbury
East Woodlands	*Somerset* - Frome
Eastwood, New	*Notts* - Ilkeston
East Woodside	*Cumberland* - Carlisle
East Woodyates	*Dorset* - Salisbury
East Worldham	*Hants* - Aldershot and Farnham
East Wretham	*Norfolk* - Thetford
Eathorpe	*Warwick* - Warwick
Eaton	*Berks* - Oxford
Eaton	*Cheshire* - Chester
Eaton	*Cheshire* - Congleton
Eaton	*Cheshire* - Crewe
Eaton	*Cheshire* - Northwich
Eaton	*Hereford* - Leominster
Eaton	*Leicester* - Melton Mowbray
Eaton	*Norfolk* - Norwich
Eaton	*Notts* - East Retford
Eaton	*Salop* - Shrewsbury
Eaton and Alsop	*Derby* - Matlock
Eaton Bishop	*Hereford* - Hereford
Eaton Bray	*Beds* - Bletchley and Leighton Buzzard
Eaton Constantine	*Salop* - Shrewsbury
Eaton Ford	*Beds* - Huntingdon
Eaton Green	*Herts* - Luton
Eaton Hastings	*Berks* - Swindon
Eaton, Long	*Derby* - Nottingham
Eaton Mascott	*Salop* - Shrewsbury
Eaton Socon	*Beds* - Huntingdon
Eaton-under-Heywood	*Salop* - Ludlow
Eaton-upon-Tern	*Salop* - Market Drayton
Eaves	*Lancaster* - Preston
Eavestone	*York, W.R.* - Harrogate
Ebbesbourne Wake	*Wilts* - Salisbury
Ebberston	*York, N.R.* - Malton
Ebbs Fleet	*Kent* - Ramsgate
Ebbw Bridge	*Monmouth* - Newport (Mon.)
Ebbw Vale	*Monmouth* - Blackwood
Ebchester	*Durham* - Consett
Ebernoe	*Sussex* - Chichester
Ebford	*Devon* - Exeter
Ebley	*Gloucester* - Stroud
Ebnal	*Hereford* - Leominster
Ebnal	*Salop* - Oswestry
Ebnal	*Cheshire* - Whitchurch
Ebony	*Kent* - Cranbrook

EBR - EDI

Ebrington	*Gloucester* - Evesham
Ebstree	*Stafford* - Wolverhampton
Ecchinswell	*Hants* - Newbury
Eccleriggs	*Lancaster* - Barrow-in-Furness
Eccles	*Kent* - Maidstone
Eccles	*Lancaster* - Salford
Eccles (Smallburgh)	*Norfolk* - Norwich
Eccles	*Norfolk* - Norwich
Ecclesall Bierlow	*York, W.R.* - Sheffield
Ecclesfield	*York, W.R.* - Sheffield
Eccleshall	*Stafford* - Stafford
Eccleshill	*Lancaster* - Blackburn
Eccleshill	*York, W.R.* - Bradford
Eccleston	*Cheshire* - Chester
Eccleston	*Lancaster* - Chorley
Eccleston	*Lancaster* - St. Helens
Eccleston, Great	*Lancaster* - Preston
Eccleston Hill	*Lancaster* - St. Helens
Eccleston, Little	*Lancaster* - Blackpool
Eccleston Park	*Lancaster* - St. Helens
Eccup	*York, W.R.* - Leeds
Eckington	*Derby* - Chesterfield
Eckington	*Worcester* - Worcester
Ecton	*Northampton* - Wellingborough
Ecton	*Stafford* - Leek
Edale	*Derby* - Buxton
Edburton	*Sussex* - Brighton
Edderside	*Cumberland* - Carlisle
Eddington	*Berks* - Newbury
Eddington	*Kent* - Canterbury
Eddisbury	*Cheshire* - Northwich
Eddlethorpe	*York, E.R.* - Malton
Edenbridge	*Kent* - Tonbridge
Edenfield	*Lancaster* - Bury
Edenhall	*Cumberland* - Penrith
Edenham	*Lincoln* - Spalding
Eden Lane	*Durham* - Hartlepool
Eden Park, South	*Kent* - Bromley
Eden Place	*Durham* - Gateshead
Edens Hill	*Gloucester* - Gloucester
Edensor	*Derby* - Matlock
Edenthorpe	*York, W.R.* - Doncaster
Edeyrn	*Caernarvon* - Portmadoc
Edgbaston	*Warwick* - Birmingham
Edgbold	*Salop* - Shrewsbury
Edgcott	*Bucks* - Aylesbury
Edgcott	*Northampton* - Banbury
Edgcumbe	*Cornwall* - Penzance
Edge	*Cheshire* - Whitchurch
Edge	*Durham* - Bishop Auckland
Edge	*Gloucester* - Stroud
Edge	*Salop* - Shrewsbury
Edgbolton	*Salop* - Shrewsbury
Edge End	*Salop* - Shrewsbury
Edgefield	*Norfolk* - Norwich
Edgefold	*Lancaster* - Bolton
Edge Green	*Cheshire* - Whitchurch
Edge Green	*Lancaster* - Leigh
Edge Hill	*Lancaster* - Liverpool
Edge Hill	*Warwick* - Banbury
Edgehills	*Gloucester* - Gloucester
Edgeley	*Cheshire* - Stockport
Edgeley	*Salop* - Whitchurch
Edge, Nether	*York, W.R.* - Sheffield
Edgerley	*Cheshire* - Chester
Edgerley	*Salop* - Oswestry
Edgerton	*York, W.R.* - Huddersfield
Edges Green	*Northumberland* - Hexham
Edgeside	*Lancaster* - Rawtenstall
Edgeworth	*Gloucester* - Stroud
Edgmond	*Salop* - Wellington (Salop)
Edgmond Marsh	*Salop* - Wellington (Salop)
Edgton	*Salop* - Ludlow
Edgware (part)	*Middlesex* - Watford
Edgware (part)	*Middlesex* - Willesden
Edgwarebury	*Middlesex* - Willesden
Edgworth	*Lancaster* - Bolton
Edial	*Stafford* - Lichfield
Edingale	*Stafford* - Tamworth
Edingley	*Notts* - Newark

EDI - EGR

Edingthorpe	*Norfolk* - Norwich
Edington	*Northumberland* - Morpeth
Edington	*Somerset* - Bridgwater
Edington	*Wilts* - Trowbridge
Edington Burtle	*Somerset* - Bridgwater
Edingworth	*Somerset* - Weston Super Mare
Edith Mead	*Somerset* - Weston Super Mare
Edith Weston	*Rutland* - Stamford
Edlaston	*Derby* - Derby
Eddlesborough	*Bucks* - Bletchley and Leighton Buzzard
Edlingham	*Northumberland* - Alnwick
Edlington	*Lincoln* - Lincoln
Edlington	*York, W.R.* - Doncaster
Edlington Moor	*Lincoln* - Lincoln
Edmondbyers	*Durham* - Consett
Edmond Castle	*Cumberland* - Carlisle
Edmondsham	*Dorset* - Wimborne Minster
Edmondsley	*Durham* - Durham
Edmondstown	*Glamorgan* - Pontypridd
Edmondthorpe	*Leicester* - Melton Mowbray
Edmonton	*Cornwall* - Bodmin
Edmonton	*London, N.9.* - Edmonton
Edmonton	*London, N.18* - Edmonton
Ednaston	*Derby* - Derby
Ednol	*Radnor* - Knighton
Edstaston	*Salop* - Shrewsbury
Edstone, Great	*York, N.R.* - Malton
Edstone, Little	*York, N.R.* - Malton
Edvin Loach	*Worcester* - Leominster
Edvin Ralph	*Hereford* - Leominster
Edwalton	*Notts* - Nottingham
Edwardstone	*Suffolk* - Sudbury
Edwinstowe	*Notts* - Mansfield
Edworth	*Beds* - Biggleswade
Efail Isaf	*Glamorgan* - Pontypridd
Efailnewydd	*Caernarvon* - Portmadoc
Efailwen	*Pembroke* - Haverfordwest
Efelrhyd	*Denbigh* - Oswestry
Efenechtyd	*Denbigh* - Denbigh
Effingham	*Surrey* - Dorking
Effingham Common	*Surrey* - Dorking
Effingham Junction	*Surrey* - Guildford
Efford	*Devon* - Plymouth
Egdean	*Sussex* - Chichester
Egdon	*Worcester* - Worcester
Egerton	*Cheshire* - Crewe
Egerton	*Kent* - Ashford
Egerton	*Lancaster* - Bolton
Egerton Forstal	*Kent* - Ashford
Egerton Green	*Cheshire* - Whitchurch
Egford	*Somerset* - Frome
Eggborough	*York, W.R.* - Pontefract
Egg Buckland	*Devon* - Plymouth
Eggbury	*Hants* - Andover
Eggesford	*Devon* - Barnstaple
Egginton	*Beds* - Bletchley and Leighton Buzzard
Egginton	*Derby* - Burton-upon-Trent
Egglestone	*Durham* - Bishop Auckland
Egglestone Abbey	*York, N.R.* - Bishop Auckland
Eggleton	*Hereford* - Hereford
Egham	*Surrey* - Slough
Egham Hythe	*Surrey* - Slough
Egham's Green	*Bucks* - High Wycombe
Egleton	*Rutland* - Melton Mowbray
Eglingham	*Northumberland* - Alnwick
Egloshayle	*Cornwall* - Bodmin
Egloskerry	*Cornwall* - Launceston
Eglwysbrewis	*Glamorgan* - Bridgend
Eglwys Cross	*Flint* - Whitchurch
Eglwyscymmyn	*Carmarthen* - Haverfordwest
Eglwysfach	*Cardigan* - Machynlleth
Eglwysfach	*Denbigh* - Conway
Eglwysfairacherrig	*Carmarthen* - Haverfordwest
Eglwyswrw	*Pembroke* - Cardigan
Egmanton	*Notts* - Newark
Egmere	*Norfolk* - King's Lynn
Egremont	*Carmarthen* - Haverfordwest

EGR - ELL

Egremont	*Cheshire* - Birkenhead
Egremont	*Cumberland* - Whitehaven
Egthorpe	*Bucks* - Aylesbury
Egton	*Lancaster* - Barrow-in-Furness
Egton	*York, N.R.* - Whitby
Egton Bridge	*York, N.R.* - Whitby
Egton Grange	*York, N.R.* - Whitby
Egypt	*Bucks* - Slough
Eight Ash Green	*Essex* - Colchester
Eithinog	*Caernarvon* - Bangor
Elan Valley	*Radnor* - Llandrindod Wells
Elan Village	*Brecon* - Llandrindod Wells
Elba	*Cumberland* - Haltwhistle
Elberton	*Gloucester* - Thornbury
Elbridge	*Sussex* - Chichester
Elburton	*Devon* - Plymouth
Elcocks Brook	*Worcester* - Redditch
Elcombe	*Wilts* - Swindon
Elcot	*Berks* - Newbury
Elcot	*Wilts* - Swindon
Eldersfield	*Worcester* - Cheltenham
Elder Street	*Essex* - Bishop's Stortford
Eldon	*Durham* - Bishop Auckland
Eldon Lane	*Durham* - Bishop Auckland
Eldon, Lower	*Hants* - Winchester
Eldon, Upper	*Hants* - Winchester
Eldwick	*York, W.R.* - Keighley
Elemore	*Durham* - Durham
Elevan Acreland (Kirton)	*Lincoln* - Boston
Elford	*Northumberland* - Alnwick
Elford	*Stafford* - Tamworth
Elham	*Kent* - Folkestone
Eling	*Hants* - Southampton
Eliza	*Durham* - Durham
Eliza Farm	*Durham* - Durham
Elizabethville	*Durham* - Gateshead
Elkington	*Northampton* - Rugby
Elkington, North	*Lincoln* - Louth
Elkington, South	*Lincoln* - Louth
Elksley	*Notts* - East Retford
Elkstone	*Gloucester* - Cheltenham
Elkstone, Lower	*Stafford* - Leek
Elkstone, Upper	*Stafford* - Leek
Ellacombe	*Devon* - Torquay
Elland	*York, W.R.* - Halifax
Ellastone	*Stafford* - Uttoxeter
Ella, West	*York, E.R.* - Kingston-upon-Hull
Ellel	*Lancaster* - Lancaster
Ellenborough	*Cumberland* - Workington
Ellenbrook	*Herts* - St. Albans
Ellenhall	*Stafford* - Stafford
Ellens Green	*Surrey* - Guildford
Ellenthorpe	*York, W.R.* - Harrogate
Ellen Villa	*Cumberland* - Workington
Ellerby	*York, E.R.* - Kingston-upon-Hull
Ellerby	*York, N.R.* - Whitby
Ellerdine	*Salop* - Wellington (Salop)
Ellerdine Heath	*Salop* - Wellington (Salop)
Ellerker	*York, E.R.* - Beverley
Ellerton	*Salop* - Market Drayton
Ellerton Priory	*York, E.R.* - York
Ellerton-upon-Swale	*York, N.R.* - Darlington
Ellesborough	*Bucks* - Aylesbury
Ellesmere	*Salop* - Oswestry
Ellesmere Port	*Cheshire* - Ellesmere Port
Ellingham	*Hants* - Salisbury
Ellingham	*Norfolk* - Norwich
Ellingham	*Northumberland* - Alnwick
Ellingham, Great	*Norfolk* - Norwich
Ellingham, Little	*Norfolk* - Norwich
Ellingstring	*York, N.R.* - Harrogate
Ellington	*Hunts* - Huntingdon
Ellington	*Northumberland* - Morpeth
Ellington, High	*York, N.R.* - Harrogate
Ellington, Low	*York, N.R.* - Harrogate
Elliotts Town	*Monmouth* - Blackwood
Ellisfield	*Hants* - Basingstoke
Ellistown	*Leicester* - Ashby-de-la-Zouch
Ellonby	*Cumberland* - Penrith
Ellough	*Suffolk* - Lowestoft

ELL - ELT

Elloughton	*York, E.R.* - Beverley
Elm	*Cambridge* - Wisbech
Elm Park	*Essex* - Ilford
Elmbridge	*Worcester* - Bromsgrove
Elmdon	*Essex* - Bishop's Stortford
Elmdon	*Warwick* - Birmingham
Elmdon Heath	*Warwick* - Birmingham
Elmer	*Sussex* - Chichester
Elmer Sand	*Sussex* - Chichester
Elmer's End	*Kent* - Bromley
Elmers Green	*Lancaster* - Wigan
Elmesthorpe	*Leicester* - Hinckley
Elm, Great	*Somerset* - Frome
Elmham	*Norfolk* - East Dereham
Elmham All Saints, South	*Suffolk* - Halesworth
Elmham St. Cross, South	*Suffolk* - Halesworth
Elmham St. James, South	*Suffolk* - Halesworth
Elmham St. Margaret South	*Suffolk* - Halesworth
Elmham St. Mary, South	*Suffolk* - Halesworth
Elmham St. Michael, South	*Suffolk* - Halesworth
Elmham St. Nicholas, South	*Suffolk* - Halesworth
Elmham St. Peter, South	*Suffolk* - Halesworth
Elmhurst	*Stafford* - Lichfield
Elmington	*Northampton* - Peterborough
Elmley	*Kent* - Sheerness
Elmley Castle	*Worcester* - Evesham
Elmley Lovett	*Worcester* - Kidderminster
Elmore	*Gloucester* - Gloucester
Elm Park	*Essex* - Ilford
Elm Park Road Ends	*Durham* - Bishop Auckland
Elmsall, Little	*York, W.R.* - Pontefract
Elmsall, Long	*York, W.R.* - Pontefract
Elmsall, North	*York, W.R.* - Pontefract
Elmsall, South	*York, W.R.* - Pontefract
Elmsett	*Suffolk* - Ipswich
Elmstead	*Kent* - Folkstone
Elmstead Heath	*Essex* - Colchester
Elmstead Market	*Essex* - Colchester
Elmstead Woods	*Kent* - Bromley
Elmstone	*Kent* - Canterbury
Elmstone Hardwicke	*Gloucester* - Cheltenham
Elmswell	*Suffolk* - Stowmarket
Elmswell	*York, E.R.* - Beverley
Elmton	*Derby* - Worksop
Elm Tree	*York, W.R.* - Sheffield
Elsdon	*Northumberland* - Morpeth
Elsecar	*York, W.R.* - Barnsley
Elsenham	*Essex* - Bishop's Stortford
Elsfield	*Oxford* - Oxford
Elsham	*Lincoln* - Scunthorpe
Elsing	*Norfolk* - East Dereham
Elslack	*York, W.R.* - Skipton
Elson	*Hants* - Portsmouth
Elson	*Salop* - Oswestry
Elstead	*Surrey* - Guildford
Elsted	*Sussex* - Petersfield
Elsthorpe	*Lincoln* - Spalding
Elston	*Lancaster* - Preston
Elston	*Notts* - Newark
Elstone	*Devon* - Barnstaple
Elstow	*Beds* - Bedford
Elstree	*Herts* - Barnet
Elstronwick	*York, E.R.* - Kingston-upon-Hull
Elswick	*Lancaster* - Preston
Elswick	*Northumberland* - Newcastle upon Tyne
Elsworth	*Cambridge* - Cambridge
Elterwater	*Westmorland* - Kendal
Eltham	*London, S.E.9* - Woolwich
Eltham, New	*London, S.E.9* - Bromley
Eltisley	*Cambridge* - Huntingdon
Elton	*Cheshire* - Chester
Elton	*Cheshire* - Crewe

Elton	*Derby* - Matlock
Elton	*Durham* - Stockton on Tees
Elton	*Gloucester* - Gloucester
Elton	*Hereford* - Ludlow
Elton	*Hunts and Peterborough* - Peterborough
Elton	*Lancaster* - Bury
Elton	*Notts* - Nottingham
Eltringham	*Northumberland* - Hexham
Elvaston	*Derby* - Derby
Elvedon	*Suffolk* - Thetford
Elvetham	*Hants* - Basingstoke
Elvet Moor	*Durham* - Durham
Elvington	*Kent* - Dover
Elvington	*York, W.R.* - York
Elwick	*Durham* - Hartlepool
Elworth	*Cheshire* - Crewe
Elworthy	*Somerset* - Minehead
Ely	*Cambridge* - Ely
Ely	*Glamorgan* - Cardiff
Elyhaugh	*Northumberland* - Alnwick
Emberton	*Bucks* - Northampton
Embleton	*Cumberland* - Workington
Embleton	*Durham* - Stockton on Tees
Embleton	*Northumberland* - Alnwick
Embley	*Hants* - Southampton
Emborough	*Somerset* - Wells
Embridge	*Devon* - Kingsbridge
Embrook	*Berks* - Reading
Embsay	*York, W.R.* - Skipton
Emerson Park	*Essex* - Ilford
Emery Down	*Hants* - Southampton
Emley	*York, W.R.* - Huddersfield
Emley Moor	*York, W.R.* - Huddersfield
Emma Villa	*Durham* - Newcastle upon Tyne
Emmer Green	*Oxford* - Reading
Emmett Carr	*Derby* - Chesterfield
Emmington	*Oxford* - Thame
Emmotland	*York, E.R.* - Bridlington
Emneth	*Norfolk* - Wisbech
Emneth Hungate	*Norfolk* - Wisbech
Empingham	*Rutland* - Stamford
Empshott	*Hants* - Petersfield
Emscote	*Warwick* - Warwick
Emstrey	*Salop* - Shrewsbury
Emsworth	*Hants* - Portsmouth
Emsworth (Hermitage)	*Sussex* - Chichester
Enborne	*Berks* - Newbury
Enchmarsh	*Salop* - Shrewsbury
Encombe	*Dorset* - Swanage
Endcliffe	*York, W.R.* - Sheffield
Enderby	*Leicester* - Leicester
Endmoor	*Westmorland* - Kendal
Endon	*Stafford* - Leek
Enfield	*Gloucester* - Cheltenham
Enfield	*Middlesex* - Edmonton
Enfield Chase	*Middlesex* - Edmonton
Enfield Highway	*Middlesex* - Edmonton
Enfield Lock	*Middlesex* - Edmonton
Enfield Wash	*Middlesex* - Edmonton
Enford	*Wilts* - Devizes
Engelley	*Cornwall* - Truro
Englefield	*Berks* - Reading
Englefield Green	*Surrey* - Slough
English Batch	*Somerset* - Bath
English Bicknor	*Gloucester* - Monmouth
English Combe	*Somerset* - Bath
English Drove	*Northampton* - Peterborough
English Frankton	*Salop* - Oswestry
Englishtown	*Cumberland* - Carlisle
Enham Alamein	*Hants* - Andover
Enmore	*Somerset* - Bridgwater
Enmore Green (Shaftesbury)	*Dorset* - Shaftesbury
Ennerdale	*Cumberland* - Whitehaven
Ennerdale Bridge	*Cumberland* - Whitehaven
Enniscaven	*Cornwall* - St. Austell
Ensbury Park	*Hants* - Bournemouth
Ensdon	*Salop* - Shrewsbury
Ensford	*Kent* - Tonbridge

Enson	*Stafford* - Stafford
Enstone	*Oxford* - Banbury
Enthorpe	*York, E.R.* - Beverley
Entwistle	*Lancaster* - Bolton
Enville	*Stafford* - Stourbridge
Enys	*Cornwall* - Truro
Epney	*Gloucester* - Gloucester
Epperstone	*Notts* - Nottingham
Epping	*Essex* - Harlow
Epping Green	*Essex* - Harlow
Epping Upland	*Essex* - Harlow
Epple Bay	*Kent* - Margate
Eppleby	*York, N.R.* - Darlington
Eppleton, Great	*Durham* - Durham
Eppleton, Little	*Durham* - Durham
Epsom	*Surrey* - Epsom
Epsom Common	*Surrey* - Epsom
Epwell	*Oxford* - Banbury
Epworth	*Lincoln* - Thorne
Erbistock	*Denbigh* - Wrexham
Ercall, High	*Salop* - Wellington (Salop)
Ercall Magna	*Salop* - Wellington (Salop)
Ercall Park	*Salop* - Wellington (Salop)
Erdington	*Warwick* - Birmingham
Eresby	*Lincoln* - Skegness
Eridge	*Sussex* - Tunbridge Wells
Eriswell	*Suffolk* - Bury St. Edmunds
Erith	*Kent* - Dartford
Erlestoke	*Wilts* - Devizes
Ermington	*Devon* - Plymouth
Erpingham	*Norfolk* - Norwich
Erwarton	*Suffolk* - Ipswich
Erwood	*Brecon* - Builth
Eryholme	*York, N.R.* - Darlington
Eryrys	*Denbigh* - Mold
Esclusham Above	*Denbigh* - Wrexham
Esclusham Below	*Denbigh* - Wrexham
Escomb	*Durham* - Bishop Auckland
Escomb Bridge	*Durham* - Bishop Auckland
Escomb Lane Ends	*Durham* - Bishop Auckland
Escomb Low	*Durham* - Bishop Auckland
Escrick	*York, N.R.* - York
Esh	*Durham* - Durham
Esh Drift	*Durham* - Durham
Esher	*Surrey* - Kingston-upon-Thames
Esholt	*York, W.R.* - Otley
Eshott	*Northumberland* - Morpeth
Eshton	*York, W.R.* - Skipton
Esh Winning	*Durham* - Durham
Esh Winning Colliery	*Durham* - Durham
Eskdale	*Cumberland* - Whitehaven
Eskdaleside Cum Ugglebarnby	*York, N.R.* - Whitby
Eske	*York, E.R.* - Beverley
Eskett	*Cumberland* - Whitehaven
Eskham	*Lincoln* - Louth
Eskirieth	*Montgomery* - Newtown
Eskmeals	*Cumberland* - Whitehaven
Eskrigg	*Cumberland* - Carlisle
Esless	*Denbigh* - Wrexham
Esperley Lane	*Durham* - Bishop Auckland
Esperley Lane End	*Durham* - Bishop Auckland
Espersheels	*Northumberland* - Hexham
Espley	*Salop* - Market Drayton
Espley	*Northumberland* - Morpeth
Esprick	*Lancaster* - Preston
Esscroft	*York, W.R.* - Otley
Essendine	*Rutland* - Stamford
Essendon	*Herts* - Hertford
Essington	*Stafford* - Wolverhampton
Essington Sneyd	*Stafford* - Wolverhampton
Essington Wood	*Stafford* - Wolverhampton
Eston	*York, N.R.* - Middlesbrough
Etal	*Northumberland* - Berwick-upon-Tweed
Etchilhampton	*Wilts* - Devizes
Etchingham	*Sussex* - Tunbridge Wells
Etchinhill	*Kent* - Folkestone
Etching Hill	*Stafford* - Stafford
Etherley	*Durham* - Bishop Auckland

ETH - EXC

Etherley Dene	*Durham* - Bishop Auckland
Etherley High	*Durham* - Bishop Auckland
Etherley Moor	*Durham* - Bishop Auckland
Etling Green	*Norfolk* - East Dereham
Etloe	*Gloucester* - Gloucester
Eton	*Bucks* - Slough
Eton Wick	*Bucks* - Slough
Etruria	*Stafford* - Stoke-on-Trent
Etterby	*Cumberland* - Carlisle
Ettersgill	*Durham* - Bishop Auckland
Ettingshall	*Stafford* - Wolverhampton
Ettingshall Upper	*Stafford* - Dudley
Ettington	*Warwick* - Stratford on Avon
Etton	*Northampton* - Peterborough
Etton	*York, E.R.* - Beverley
Etwall	*Derby* - Derby
Eudon Burnell	*Salop* - Bridgnorth
Eudon George	*Salop* - Bridgnorth
Euston	*Suffolk* - Thetford
Euxton	*Lancaster* - Chorley
Evanstown (part)	*Glamorgan* - Bridgend
Evedon	*Lincoln* - Sleaford
Evelith	*Salop* - Wellington (Salop)
Evendine	*Hereford* - Great Malvern
Evening Hill	*Cumberland* - Carlisle
Evenjobb	*Radnor* - Knighton
Evenley	*Northampton* - Banbury
Evenlode	*Gloucester* - Cheltenham
Evenwood	*Durham* - Bishop Auckland
Evenwood	*Salop* - Shrewsbury
Everards	*Dorset* - Dorchester
Evercreech	*Somerset* - Wells
Everdon, Great	*Northampton* - Northampton
Everdon, Little	*Northampton* - Northampton
Everingham	*York, E.R.* - York
Everleigh	*Wilts* - Andover
Everley	*York, N.R.* - Scarborough
Eversden, Great	*Cambridge* - Cambridge
Eversden, Little	*Cambridge* - Cambridge
Eversholt	*Beds* - Bedford
Evershot	*Dorset* - Yeovil
Eversley	*Hants* - Basingstoke
Everthorpe	*York, E.R.* - Beverley
Everton	*Beds* - Biggleswade
Everton	*Hants* - Lymington
Everton	*Lancaster* - Liverpool
Everton	*Notts* - East Retford
Evesbatch	*Hereford* - Worcester
Evesham	*Worcester* - Evesham
Evington	*Gloucester* - Cheltenham
Evington	*Kent* - Ashford
Evington	*Leicester* - Leicester
Evington, North	*Leicester* - Leicester
Ewanrigg	*Cumberland* - Workington
Ewden	*York, W.R.* - Sheffield
Ewden Valley	*York, W.R.* - Sheffield
Ewdness	*Salop* - Bridgnorth
Ewe Cote	*York, N.R.* - Whitby
Ewell	*Kent* - Canterbury
Ewell	*Surrey* - Epsom
Ewell Minnis	*Kent* - Dover
Ewell, West	*Surrey* - Epsom
Ewelme	*Oxford* - Didcot
Ewen	*Gloucester* - Malmesbury
Ewenny	*Glamorgan* - Bridgend
Ewerby	*Lincoln* - Sleaford
Ewerby Fen	*Lincoln* - Sleaford
Ewerby Thorpe	*Lincoln* - Sleaford
Ewesley	*Northumberland* - Morpeth
Ewhurst	*Hants* - Basingstoke
Ewhurst	*Surrey* - Guildford
Ewhurst	*Sussex* - Hastings
Ewloe	*Flint* - Chester
Ewood Bridge	*Lancaster* - Rawtenstall
Ewshott	*Hants* - Aldershot and Farnham
Ewyas Harold	*Hereford* - Hereford
Exbourne	*Devon* - Okehampton
Exbury	*Hants* - Southampton
Exceat	*Sussex* - Eastbourne
Exceat Bridge	*Sussex* - Lewes

EXE - FAI

Exe	*Devon* - Tiverton
Exebridge	*Somerset* - Tiverton
Exelby	*York, N.R.* - Northallerton
Exeter	*Devon* - Exeter
Exfold	*Sussex* - Horsham
Exford	*Somerset* - Minehead
Exfords Green	*Salop* - Shrewsbury
Exhall	*Warwick* - Redditch
Exhall	*Warwick* - Nuneaton
Exley	*York, W.R.* - Halifax
Exmansford	*Hants* - Newbury
Exminster	*Devon* - Exeter
Exmoor	*Cambridge* - Wisbech
Exmouth	*Devon* - Exeter
Exning	*Suffolk* - Newmarket
Exton	*Devon* - Exeter
Exton	*Hants* - Petersfield
Exton	*Rutland* - Stamford
Exton	*Somerset* - Tiverton
Extwistle	*Lancaster* - Burnley
Exworthy	*Devon* - Plymouth
Eyam	*Derby* - Buxton
Eyam Woodlands	*Derby* - Sheffield
Eydon	*Northampton* - Banbury
Eye	*Hereford* - Leominster
Eye	*Northampton* - Peterborough
Eye	*Oxford* - Reading
Eye	*Suffolk* - Norwich
Eye Hill	*Cambridge* - Ely
Eye Kettleby	*Leicester* - Melton Mowbray
Eyeworth	*Beds* - Biggleswade
Eyeford	*Gloucester* - Cheltenham
Eyford	*Gloucester* - Cheltenham
Eyke	*Suffolk* - Woodbridge
Eymore Wood	*Worcester* - Kidderminster
Eynesbury	*Hunts* - Huntingdon
Eynesbury Harwicke	*Hunts* - Huntingdon
Eynsford	*Kent* - Dartford
Eynsham	*Oxford* - Witney
Eype	*Dorset* - Dorchester
Eysey	*Wilts* - Swindon
Eythorne	*Kent* - Dover
Eythrope	*Bucks* - Aylesbury
Eyton	*Denbigh* - Wrexham
Eyton	*Hereford* - Leominster
Eyton	*Salop* - Ludlow
Eyton	*Salop* - Shrewsbury
Eyton	*Salop* - Wellington (Salop)

F

Faccombe	*Hants* - Andover
Faceby	*York, N.R.* - Middlesbrough
Fachwen	*Caernarvon* - Caernarvon
Fachwen	*Montgomery* - Oswestry
Faddiley	*Cheshire* - Crewe
Fadmoor	*York, N.R.* - Malton
Fagley	*York, W.R.* - Bradford
Failand	*Somerset* - Bristol
Failsworth	*Lancaster* - Oldham
Faintree	*Salop* - Bridgnorth
Fairbourne	*Merioneth* - Dolgellau
Fairburn	*York, W.R.* - Pontefract
Fairfield	*Derby* - Buxton
Fairfield	*Durham* - Stockton on Tees
Fairfield	*Kent* - Ashford
Fairfield	*Lancaster* - Ashton-under-Lyne
Fairfield	*Lancaster* - Bury
Fairfield	*Lancaster* - Liverpool
Fairfield	*Worcester* - Bromsgrove
Fairfield	*Worcester* - Evesham
Fairfield Green	*Derby* - Buxton
Fairford	*Gloucester* - Swindon
Fairgreen	*Oxford* - Banbury
Fairhaugh	*Northumberland* - Morpeth
Fairhaven	*Lancaster* - Blackpool
Fair Head	*York, N.R.* - Whitby
Fair Hill	*Cumberland* - Carlisle
Fair Hill	*Northumberland* - Hexham
Fairlight	*Sussex* - Hastings

FAI - FAR

Fairlop	*Essex* - Ilford
Fair Mile	*Devon* - Exeter
Fairnley	*Northumberland* - Morpeth
Fair Oak	*Hants* - Winchester
Fair Oak	*Stafford* - Stafford
Fair Oak Colliery	*Stafford* - Stafford
Fair Oak Green	*Hants* - Basingstoke
Fairseat	*Kent* - Sevenoaks
Fairsted	*Essex* - Braintree
Fairthorn	*Kent* - Tonbridge
Fair View	*Monmouth* - Blackwood
Fairwater	*Glamorgan* - Cardiff
Fairweather Green	*York, W.R.* - Bradford
Fairwood	*Wilts* - Trowbridge
Fakenham	*Norfolk* - King's Lynn
Fakenham Heath	*Norfolk* - King's Lynn
Fakenham Magna	*Suffolk* - Thetford
Falcon, The	*Hereford* - Hereford
Falcutt	*Northampton* - Northampton
Faldingworth	*Lincoln* - Lincoln
Falfield	*Gloucester* - Thornbury
Falhouse	*York, W.R.* - Dewsbury
Falkenham	*Suffolk* - Ipswich
Fallibroome	*Cheshire* - Macclesfield
Fallings Park	*Stafford* - Wolverhampton
Fallodon	*Northumberland* - Alnwick
Fallowfield	*Durham* - Durham
Fallowfield	*Lancaster* - Manchester
Fallowfield	*Northumberland* - Hexham
Fallowlees	*Northumberland* - Morpeth
Falmer	*Sussex* - Brighton
Falmouth	*Cornwall* - Truro
Falsam Pitts	*Worcester* - Worcester
Falsgrave	*York, N.R.* - Scarborough
Falstone	*Northumberland* - Hexham
Fambridge, North	*Essex* - Maldon
Fambridge, South	*Essex* - Southend
Fancott	*Beds* - Luton
Fangfoss	*York, E.R.* - York
Fanners Green	*Essex* - Chelmsford
Far Bletchley	*Bucks* - Bletchley and Leighton Buzzard
Farcet	*Hunts* - Peterborough
Farcet Fen	*Hunts* - Peterborough
Far Coton	*Leicester* - Hinckley
Far Cotton	*Northampton* - Northampton
Farcroft Estate	*Warwick* - Birmingham
Fareham	*Hants* - Portsmouth
Farewell	*Stafford* - Lichfield
Far Forest	*Worcester* - Kidderminster
Farforth cum Maldenwell	*Lincoln* - Louth
Faringdon	*Berks* - Didcot
Faringdon, Great	*Berks* - Didcot
Faringdon, Little	*Oxford* - Witney
Farington	*Dorset* - Shaftesbury
Farington	*Lancaster* - Preston
Farlam	*Cumberland* - Carlisle
Farleigh	*Somerset* - Bristol
Farleigh	*Surrey* - Croydon
Farleigh, East	*Kent* - Maidstone
Farleigh Hungerford	*Somerset* - Frome
Farleigh Wallop	*Hants* - Basingstoke
Farleigh, West	*Kent* - Maidstone
Farleigh Wick	*Wilts* - Bath
Farlesthorpe	*Lincoln* - Skegness
Farleton	*Lancaster* - Lancaster
Farleton	*Westmorland* - Kendal
Farley	*Derby* - Matlock
Farley	*Kent* - Sevenoaks
Farley	*Salop* - Bridgnorth
Farley	*Stafford* - Stafford
Farley	*Stafford* - Uttoxeter
Farley	*Wilts* - Salisbury
Farley Chamberlayne	*Hants* - Winchester
Farley Green	*Surrey* - Guildford
Farley Hill	*Berks* - Reading
Farleys End	*Glos* - Gloucester
Farlington	*Hants* - Portsmouth
Farlington	*York, N.R.* - York

FAR - FAW

Farlow	*Salop* - Bridgnorth
Farlow	*Salop* - Ludlow
Farmborough	*Somerset* - Bristol
Farmcote, Little	*Gloucester* - Cheltenham
Farmcote, North	*Gloucester* - Cheltenham
Farmers	*Carmarthen* - Llandovery
Farmers Common	*Cornwall* - Penzance
Farmington	*Gloucester* - Cheltenham
Farm Town	*Leicester* - Ashby-de-la-Zouch
Farnah Green	*Derby* - Derby
Farnborough	*Berks* - Didcot
Farnborough	*Hants* - Aldershot and Farnham
Farnborough	*Kent* - Bromley
Farnborough	*Warwick* - Banbury
Farncombe	*Surrey* - Guildford
Farndale East Side	*York, N.R.* - Malton
Farndish	*Beds* - Wellingborough
Farndon	*Cheshire* - Chester
Farndon	*Notts* - Newark
Farndon, East	*Northampton* - Kettering
Farne Islands	*Northumberland* - Alnwick
Farneyshield	*Northumberland* - Hexham
Farneyside	*Northumberland* - Hexham
Farnham	*Dorset* - Salisbury
Farnham	*Essex* - Bishop's Stortford
Farnham	*Northumberland* - Morpeth
Farnham	*Suffolk* - Woodbridge
Farnham	*Surrey* - Aldershot and Farnham
Farnham	*York, W.R.* - Harrogate
Farnham Common	*Bucks* - Slough
Farnham Green	*Essex* - Bishop's Stortford
Farnham Royal	*Bucks* - Slough
Farnhill	*York, W.R.* - Skipton
Farnicombe	*Warwick* - Stratford-on-Avon
Farningham	*Kent* - Dartford
Farnley	*York, W.R.* - Leeds
Farnley	*York, W.R.* - Otley
Farnley Grange	*York, N.R.* - Harrogate
Farnley Tyas	*York, W.R.* - Huddersfield
Farnsfield	*Notts* - Mansfield
Farnworth	*Lancaster* - Bolton
Farringdon	*Devon* - Exeter
Farringdon	*Hants* - Aldershot and Farnham
Farringdon, Lower	*Hants* - Aldershot and Farnham
Farringdon, Upper	*Hants* - Aldershot and Farnham
Farrington Gurney	*Somerset* - Wells
Farsley	*York, W.R.* - Bradford
Farsley Beck Bottom (part)	*York, W.R.* - Bradford
Farsley Beck Bottom (part)	*York, W.R.* - Leeds
Farthinghoe	*Northampton* - Banbury
Farthinghoe Station	*Northampton* - Banbury
Farthingloe	*Kent* - Dover
Farthingstone	*Northampton* - Northampton
Farthing Street	*Kent* - Bromley
Far Thorpe	*Lincoln* - Lincoln
Far Town	*Northumberland* - Carlisle
Fartown	*York, W.R.* - Huddersfield
Farway	*Devon* - Exeter
Fatfield	*Durham* - Gateshead
Faugh	*Cumberland* - Carlisle
Fauld	*Stafford* - Burton-upon-Trent
Faulds	*Cumberland* - Carlisle
Faulkbourne	*Essex* - Braintree
Faulkland	*Somerset* - Frome
Fauls Green	*Salop* - Whitchurch
Faversham	*Kent* - Canterbury
Fawcettlees	*Cumberland* - Carlisle
Fawdon	*Northumberland* - Alnwick
Fawdon	*Northumberland* - Newcastle-upon-Tyne
Fawfield Head	*Stafford* - Leek
Fawke Common	*Kent* - Sevenoaks
Fawkham	*Kent* - Dartford
Fawler	*Oxford* - Oxford
Fawley	*Bucks* - Reading
Fawley	*Hants* - Southampton
Fawley	*Hereford* - Hereford

FAW - FEN

Fawley, Much	*Hereford* - Ross
Fawley, North	*Berks* - Didcot
Fawley, South	*Berks* - Didcot
Fawns	*Northumberland* - Hexham
Fawsley	*Northampton* - Northampton
Faxfleet	*York, E.R.* - Goole
Faxton	*Northampton* - Northampton
Faygate	*Sussex* - Horsham
Fazakerley	*Lancaster* - Liverpool
Fazeley	*Stafford* - Tamworth
Fearby	*York, N.R.* - Harrogate
Fearnhead	*Lancaster* - Warrington
Featherstone	*Northumberland* - Hexham
Featherstone	*Stafford* - Wolverhampton
Featherstone	*York, W.R.* - Pontefract
Featherstone, North	*York, W.R.* - Pontefract
Feckenham	*Worcester* - Redditch
Feering	*Essex* - Braintree
Fegg Hayes	*Stafford* - Stoke-on-Trent
Felbridge	*Sussex* - East Grinstead
Felbrigge	*Norfolk* - Norwich
Felday (part)	*Surrey* - Dorking
Felday (part)	*Surrey* - Guildford
Felden	*Herts* - Hemel Hempstead
Felhampton	*Salop* - Ludlow
Felindre	*Radnor* - Knighton
Felinfach	*Cardigan* - Lampeter
Felinfach	*Brecon* - Brecknock
Felinfoel	*Carmarthen* - Llanelli
Felingwn	*Carmarthen* - Carmarthen
Felinheli (part)	*Caernarvon* - Bangor
Felixkirk	*York, N.R.* - Northallerton
Felixstowe	*Suffolk* - Ipswich
Felkington	*Northumberland* - Berwick-upon-Tweed
Fell	*Durham* - Durham
Fell Beck	*York, W.R.* - Harrogate
Fell End	*Northumberland* - Hexham
Felley	*Notts* - Alfreton
Fellgate	*Durham* - South Shields
Felling	*Durham* - Gateshead
Felling, High	*Durham* - Gateshead
Felling, Low	*Durham* - Gateshead
Felling, Nether	*Durham* - Gateshead
Felling Shore	*Durham* - Gateshead
Felliscliffe	*York, W.R.* - Harrogate
Fell, Low	*Durham* - Gateshead
Fellside	*Cumberland* - Carlisle
Fellside	*Durham* - Gateshead
Felmersham	*Beds* - Bedford
Felmingham	*Norfolk* - Norwich
Felpham	*Sussex* - Chichester
Felsham	*Suffolk* - Stowmarket
Felstead	*Essex* - Braintree
Feltham	*Middlesex* - Brentford
Feltham	*Somerset* - Frome
Felthorpe	*Norfolk* - Norwich
Felton	*Hereford* - Hereford
Felton	*Northumberland* - Alnwick
Felton	*Somerset* - Bristol
Felton Butler	*Salop* - Shrewsbury
Felton, Old	*Somerset* - Bristol
Felton, West	*Salop* - Oswestry
Feltwell	*Norfolk* - Thetford
Fenay Bridge	*York, W.R.* - Huddersfield
Fence	*Lancaster* - Nelson
Fence	*York, W.R.* - Rotherham
Fence Houses	*Durham* - Durham
Fencote	*Hereford* - Leominster
Fencote, Little	*York, N.R.* - Northallerton
Fencott	*Oxford* - Oxford
Fen Ditton	*Cambridge* - Cambridge
Fen Drayton	*Cambridge* - Huntingdon
Fen End	*Lincoln* - Spalding
Fen End	*Warwick* - Coventry
Fenham	*Northumberland* - Newcastle-upon-Tyne
Feniscowles	*Lancaster* - Blackburn
Feniton	*Devon* - Exeter
Fen, Middle	*Cambridge* - Ely

FEN - FID

Fenneymere	*Salop* - Shrewsbury
Fenn Green	*Salop* - Bridgnorth
Fennington	*Somerset* - Taunton
Fen, North	*Cambridge* - Ely
Fenns	*Salop* - Whitchurch
Fenn St. Mary's	*Kent* - Rochester
Fenns Bank	*Salop* - Whitchurch
Fenny Bentley	*Derby* - Derby
Fenny Bridges	*Devon* - Exeter
Fenny Castle	*Somerset* - Wells
Fenny Compton	*Warwick* - Banbury
Fenny Drayton	*Leicester* - Nuneaton
Fenny Stratford	*Bucks* - Bletchley and Leighton Buzzard
Fenrother	*Northumberland* - Morpeth
Fenstanton	*Hunts* - Huntingdon
Fenterwanson	*Cornwall* - Bideford
Fenton	*Cumberland* - Carlisle
Fenton	*Hunts* - Huntingdon
Fenton	*Lincoln* - Gainsborough
Fenton	*Northumberland* - Berwick-upon-Tweed
Fenton	*Notts* - East Retford
Fenton	*Stafford* - Stoke-on-Trent
Fentonadle	*Cornwall* - Bideford
Fenton-by-Stubton	*Lincoln* - Newark
Fenton, Little	*York, W.R.* - Selby
Fenton Pitts	*Cornwall* - Bodmin
Fenwick	*Northumberland* - Berwick-upon-Tweed
Fenwick	*Northumberland* - Newcastle-upon-Tyne
Fenwick	*York, W.R.* - Doncaster
Ferndale	*Glamorgan* - Pontypridd
Ferndown	*Dorset* - Wimborne Minster
Ferneybeds	*Northumberland* - Morpeth
Ferney Hall	*Salop* - Ludlow
Ferney Hill	*Worcester* - Redditch
Fernham	*Berks* - Swindon
Fern Hill	*Gloucester* - Thornbury
Fernhill	*Pembroke* - Haverfordwest
Fern Hill	*Stafford* - Wellington (Salop)
Fernhill Heath	*Worcester* - Worcester
Fernhurst	*Sussex* - Petersfield
Fernilee	*Derby* - Buxton
Fernyhaigh	*Lancaster* - Preston
Ferny Hill	*Stafford* - Leek
Ferrensby	*York, W.R.* - Harrogate
Ferriby, North	*York, E.R.* - Kingston-upon-Hull
Ferriby Sluice	*Lincoln* - Scunthorpe
Ferriby, South	*Lincoln* - Scunthorpe
Ferring	*Sussex* - Worthing
Ferry	*Lancaster* - Kendal
Ferrybridge	*York, W.R.* - Pontefract
Ferry, East	*Lincoln* - Gainsborough
Ferry Fryston	*York, W.R.* - Pontefract
Ferryhill	*Durham* - Durham
Ferryside	*Carmarthen* - Carmarthen
Fersfield	*Norfolk* - Norwich
Festiniog	*Merioneth* - Portmadoc
Fetcham	*Surrey* - Epsom
Fewcott	*Oxford* - Banbury
Fewston	*York, W.R.* - Otley
Ffairfach	*Carmarthen* - Ammanford
Ffairrhos	*Cardigan* - Aberystwyth
Fforddgyfraith	*Glamorgan* - Bridgend
Fforestfach	*Glamorgan* - Swansea
Ffostrasol	*Cardigan* - Cardigan
Ffriddoedd	*Caernarvon* - Bangor
Ffrith	*Flint* - Wrexham
Ffrwd	*Denbigh* - Wrexham
Ffwddog	*Brecon* - Pontypool and Abergavenny
Ffynnongroew	*Flint* - Holywell
Ffynondrain	*Carmarthen* - Carmarthen
Ffynonpedr	*Carmarthen* - Carmarthen
Fiddington	*Gloucester* - Cheltenham
Fiddington	*Somerset* - Bridgwater
Fiddington	*Wilts* - Devizes
Fiddleford	*Dorset* - Shaftesbury

Fiddler's Green	*Cornwall* - Truro
Fiddlers Green	*Gloucester* - Cheltenham
Fiddlers Hamlet	*Essex* - Harlow
Field	*Stafford* - Uttoxeter
Field Aston	*Salop* - Wellington (Salop)
Field Broughton	*Lancaster* - Barrow-in-Furness
Field Burcote	*Northampton* - Northampton
Field Dalling	*Norfolk* - Norwich
Fieldhead	*Cumberland* - Carlisle
Fieldhead	*York, W.R.* - Dewsbury
Fifehead Magdalen	*Dorset* - Shaftesbury
Fifehead Neville	*Dorset* - Shaftesbury
Fifehead St. Quinton	*Dorset* - Shaftesbury
Fifield	*Berks* - Slough
Fifield	*Oxford* - Banbury
Fifield (Benson)	*Oxford* - Didcot
Fifield (Enford)	*Wilts* - Devizes
Fifield Bavant	*Wilts* - Salisbury
Figheldean	*Wilts* - Salisbury
Fighting Cocks	*Stafford* - Wolverhampton
Filby	*Norfolk* - Great Yarmouth
Filey	*York, E. and N.R.* - Scarborough
Filgrave	*Bucks* - Bletchley and Leighton Buzzard
Filkins	*Oxford* - Witney
Filleigh	*Devon* - Barnstaple
Fillingham	*Lincoln* - Gainsborough
Fillongley	*Warwick* - Coventry
Fillwood	*Somerset* - Bristol
Filly Close	*Lancaster* - Burnley
Filmer Hill	*Hants* - Petersfield
Filton	*Gloucester* - Bristol
Fimber	*York, E.R.* - Beverley
Finborough, Great	*Suffolk* - Stowmarket
Finborough, Little	*Suffolk* - Stowmarket
Finchale Abbey	*Durham* - Durham
Fincham	*Norfolk* - King's Lynn
Finchampstead	*Berks* - Reading
Finchdean	*Hants* - Petersfield
Finchfield	*Stafford* - Wolverhampton
Finchingfield	*Essex* - Braintree
Finchley, Church End	*London, N.3* - Barnet
Finchley, East (part)	*London, N.2* - Barnet
Finchley, East (part)	*London, N.2* - Clerkenwell
Finchley, North	*London, N.12* - Barnet
Finchley, West	*Middlesex* - Barnet
Findern	*Derby* - Derby
Findon	*Sussex* - Worthing
Findon Hill	*Durham* - Durham
Findon Valley	*Sussex* - Worthing
Finedon	*Northampton* - Wellingborough
Fineshade	*Northampton* - Stamford
Fingerpost	*Lancaster* - St. Helens
Fingest	*Bucks* - High Wycombe
Finghall	*York, N.R.* - Northallerton
Fingland	*Cumberland* - Carlisle
Finglesham	*Kent* - Deal
Fingringhoe	*Essex* - Colchester
Finham	*Warwick* - Coventry
Finkley	*Hants* - Andover
Finmere	*Oxford* - Banbury
Finney Green	*Cheshire* - Macclesfield
Finney Green	*Stafford* - Stoke-on-Trent
Finningham	*Suffolk* - Stowmarket
Finningley	*Notts and York, W.R.* - Doncaster
Finsbury (part)	*London, E.C.1* - Clerkenwell
Finsbury (part)	*London, E.C.1* - Mayor's and City of London
Finsbury (part)	*London, E.C.2* - Mayor's and City of London
Finsbury (part)	*London, E.C.2* - Shoreditch
Finsbury Park (part)	*London, N.4* - Clerkenwell
Finsbury Park (part)	*London, N.4* - Shoreditch
Finstall	*Worcester* - Bromsgrove
Finsthwaite	*Lancaster* - Barrow-in-Furness
Finstock	*Oxford* - Oxford
Finwood	*Warwick* - Warwick
Firbank	*Westmorland* - Kendal
Firbeck	*York, W.R.* - Worksop
Firby	*York, E.R.* - Malton

Firby	*York, N.R.* - Northallerton
Firle	*Sussex* - Lewes
Firsby	*Lincoln* - Skegness
Firsby, East	*Lincoln* - Lincoln
Firsby, West	*Lincoln* - Lincoln
Firswood	*Lancaster* - Salford
Firth Park	*York, W.R.* - Sheffield
Fir Tree	*Durham* - Bishop Auckland
Fir Vale	*York, W.R.* - Sheffield
Firwood	*Lancaster* - Bolton
Fishbourne	*I. of W.* - Newport (I.W.)
Fishbourne	*Sussex* - Chichester
Fishburn	*Durham* - Stockton on Tees
Fishergate	*Sussex* - Brighton
Fisher Lane	*Surrey* - Guildford
Fishers Green	*Herts* - Hitchin
Fishers Pond	*Hants* - Winchester
Fisher Street	*Sussex* - Chichester
Fisherton Anger	*Wilts* - Salisbury
Fisherton de la Mare	*Wilts* - Salisbury
Fisherwick	*Stafford* - Lichfield
Fishguard	*Pembroke* - Haverfordwest
Fishlake	*York, W.R.* - Thorne
Fishley	*Norfolk* - Norwich
Fishley	*Stafford* - Walsall
Fishmore	*Salop* - Ludlow
Fishponds	*Dorset* - Axminster and Chard
Fishpool	*Lancaster* - Bury
Fishpool	*Montgomery* - Welshpool
Fishpools	*Gloucester* - Gloucester
Fishtoft	*Lincoln* - Boston
Fiskerton	*Lincoln* - Lincoln
Fiskerton	*Notts* - Newark
Fitling	*York, E.R.* - Kingston-upon-Hull
Fittleton	*Wilts* - Salisbury
Fittleworth	*Sussex* - Chichester
Fitton Hill	*Lancaster* - Oldham
Fitz	*Cumberland* - Carlisle
Fitz	*Salop* - Shrewsbury
Fitzhead	*Somerset* - Taunton
Fitzwilliam	*York, W.R.* - Pontefract
Five Ash Down	*Sussex* - Lewes
Five Ashes	*Sussex* - Tunbridge Wells
Fivehead	*Somerset* - Taunton
Five Lanes	*Cornwall* - Launceston
Five Oak Green	*Kent* - Tonbridge
Five Oaks	*Sussex* - Horsham
Five Roads	*Carmarthen* - Llanelli
Five Turnings	*Salop* - Knighton
Five Ways (Tipton)	*Stafford* - Dudley
Five Ways (Cradley Heath)	*Stafford* - Dudley
Fixby (part)	*York, W.R.* - Halifax
Fixby (part)	*York, W.R.* - Huddersfield
Flacks Green	*Essex* - Chelmsford
Flackwell Heath	*Bucks* - High Wycombe
Fladbury	*Worcester* - Evesham
Flagg	*Derby* - Buxton
Flagg Moor	*Derby* - Buxton
Flaggoner's Green	*Hereford* - Hereford
Flamborough	*York, E.R.* - Bridlington
Flamborough Head	*York, E.R.* - Bridlington
Flamstead	*Herts* - St. Albans
Flanderwell	*York, W.R.* - Rotherham
Flansham	*Sussex* - Chichester
Flanshaw	*York, W.R.* - Wakefield
Flappit	*York, W.R.* - Keighley
Flasby	*York, W.R.* - Skipton
Flash	*Stafford* - Buxton
Flashbrook	*Stafford* - Market Drayton
Flash Dam	*Derby* - Matlock
Flask	*York, N.R.* - Whitby
Flatford	*Suffolk* - Ipswich
Flat Holm	*Glamorgan* - Cardiff
Flatt	*Cumberland* - Carlisle
Flatt, High	*Cumberland* - Workington
Flatts, High	*Durham* - Durham
Flatworth	*Northumberland* - North Shields
Flatworth, Low	*Northumberland* - North Shields
Flaunden	*Herts* - Amersham

FLA - FOL

Flawborough	*Notts* - Newark
Flawith	*York, N.R.* - York
Flax Bourton	*Somerset* - Bristol
Flaxby	*York, W.R.* - Harrogate
Flaxley	*Gloucester* - Gloucester
Flax Moss	*Lancaster* - Rawtenstall
Flaxton-on-the-Moor	*York, N.R.* - York
Fleckney	*Leicester* - Leicester
Flecknoe	*Warwick* - Rugby
Fledborough	*Notts* - East Retford
Fleet	*Dorset* - Weymouth
Fleet	*Hants* - Aldershot and Farnham
Fleet	*Lincoln* - Spalding
Fleet Bank	*Lincoln* - Spalding
Fleet Church End	*Lincoln* - Spalding
Fleet Fen	*Lincoln* - Spalding
Fleetham	*Northumberland* - Alnwick
Fleet Marston	*Bucks* - Aylesbury
Fleetville	*Herts* - St. Albans
Fleetwood	*Lancaster* - Blackpool
Flegg Burgh	*Norfolk* - Great Yarmouth
Fleming	*Kent* - Deal
Flemingstone	*Glamorgan* - Bridgend
Flempton	*Suffolk* - Bury St. Edmunds
Fletchers Bridge	*Cornwall* - Bodmin
Fletchertown	*Cumberland* - Carlisle
Fletching	*Sussex* - Lewes
Fletchwood	*Hants* - Southampton
Fletton, New	*Northampton* - Peterborough
Fletton, Old	*Hunts* - Peterborough
Fleur-de-Lis	*Monmouth* - Blackwood
Flexford	*Surrey* - Guildford
Flimby	*Cumberland* - Workington
Flimwell	*Sussex* - Tunbridge Wells
Flint	*Flint* - Holywell
Flintham	*Notts* - Newark
Flint Hill	*Durham* - Consett
Flint Hyde	*Beds* - Luton
Flint Mountain	*Flint* - Holywell
Flinton	*York, E.R.* - Kingston-upon-Hull
Flintsham	*Hereford* - Leominster
Flishinghurst	*Kent* - Cranbrook
Flitcham with Appleton	*Norfolk* - King's Lynn
Flitteris Park	*Rutland* - Melton Mowbray
Flitton	*Beds* - Bedford
Flitwick	*Beds* - Bedford
Flixborough	*Lincoln* - Scunthorpe
Flixton	*Lancaster* - Salford
Flixton	*Suffolk* - Halesworth
Flixton	*Suffolk* - Lowestoft
Flixton	*York, E.R.* - Scarborough
Flixton Wold	*York, E.R.* - Scarborough
Floater's Mill	*Durham* - Durham
Flockton	*York, W.R.* - Huddersfield
Flookburgh	*Lancaster* - Barrow-in-Furness
Flordon	*Norfolk* - Norwich
Flore	*Northampton* - Northampton
Florence	*Stafford* - Stoke-on-Trent
Floriston	*Cumberland* - Carlisle
Flotmanby	*York, E.R.* - Scarborough
Flotterton	*Northumberland* - Morpeth
Flower's Bottom	*Bucks* - High Wycombe
Flowton	*Suffolk* - Ipswich
Flush	*York, W.R.* - Dewsbury
Flushdyke	*York, W.R.* - Dewsbury
Flush House	*York, W.R.* - Huddersfield
Flushing	*Cornwall* - Truro
Flyford Flavel	*Worcester* - Worcester
Fobbing	*Essex* - Grays Thurrock
Fobdown	*Hants* - Winchester
Fochriw	*Glamorgan* - Bargoed
Fockerby	*York, W.R.* - Goole
Foel	*Montgomery* - Welshpool
Foelgastell	*Carmarthen* - Carmarthen
Foggerthorpe	*York, E.R.* - Selby
Foggintor	*Devon* - Plymouth
Fold, High	*York, W.R.* - Harrogate
Fold, Low	*York, W.R.* - Harrogate
Fole	*Stafford* - Uttoxeter
Foleshill	*Warwick* - Coventry

FOL - FOR

Foley	*Stafford* - Stoke-on-Trent
Folijon Park	*Berks* - Slough
Folke	*Dorset* - Yeovil
Folkestone	*Kent* - Folkestone
Folkingham	*Lincoln* - Sleaford
Folkington	*Sussex* - Eastbourne
Folksworth	*Hunts* - Peterborough
Folkton	*York, E.R.* - Scarborough
Follifoot	*York, W.R.* - Harrogate
Follingsby Colliery	*Durham* - Gateshead
Follingsby, North	*Durham* - Gateshead
Follingsby, South	*Durham* - Gateshead
Folly Gate	*Devon* - Okehampton
Folly Gill	*York, W.R.* - Harrogate
Folly Hall	*York, W.R.* - Huddersfield
Folly Hill	*Kent* - Cranbrook
Folly Point	*Worcester* - Kidderminster
Fonaby	*Lincoln* - Great Grimsby
Fonmon	*Glamorgan* - Barry
Fonthill Bishop	*Wilts* - Shaftesbury
Fonthill Giffors	*Wilts* - Shaftesbury
Fontmell Magna	*Dorset* - Shaftesbury
Fontmell Parva	*Dorset* - Shaftesbury
Fontwell	*Sussex* - Chichester
Foolow	*Derby* - Buxton
Fools Nook	*Cheshire* - Macclesfield
Footherley	*Stafford* - Lichfield
Foot's Cray	*Kent* - Bromley
Force Forge	*Lancaster* - Kendal
Forcett	*York, N.R.* - Darlington
Ford	*Bucks* - Aylesbury
Ford	*Derby* - Chesterfield
Ford	*Devon* - Kingsbridge
Ford	*Devon* - Plymouth
Ford	*Durham* - Sunderland
Ford	*Gloucester* - Cheltenham
Ford	*Lancaster* - Liverpool
Ford	*Northumberland* - Berwick-upon-Tweed
Ford	*Salop* - Shrewsbury
Ford	*Stafford* - Leek
Ford	*Sussex* - Chichester
Ford	*Wilts* - Chippenham
Ford	*Wilts* - Salisbury
Ford	*York, W.R.* - Halifax
Ford Bridge	*Hereford* - Leominster
Fordbridge	*Warks* - Birmingham
Fordcombe	*Kent* - Tonbridge
Forden	*Montgomery* - Welshpool
Ford End	*Beds* - Bedford
Ford End	*Essex* - Chelmsford
Forder	*Cornwall* - Plymouth
Ford Estate	*Cheshire* - Birkenhead
Ford Gate	*Somerset* - Bridgwater
Ford Green	*Stafford* - Stoke-on-Trent
Ford Hall	*Salop* - Market Drayton
Fordham	*Cambridge* - Newmarket
Fordham	*Essex* - Colchester
Fordham	*Norfolk* - King's Lynn
Ford Hill	*Gloucester* - Cheltenham
Ford Houses	*Stafford* - Wolverhampton
Fordingbridge	*Hants* - Salisbury
Fordington	*Dorset* - Dorchester
Fordington	*Lincoln* - Skegness
Fordon	*York, E.R.* - Bridlington
Ford Street	*Somerset* - Taunton
Fordton	*Devon* - Exeter
Ford Wells	*Oxford* - Oxford
Fordwich	*Kent* - Canterbury
Fore Hill	*Worcester* - Redditch
Foremark	*Derby* - Derby
Forest	*Carmarthen* - Llanelli
Forest (Coal Pit)	*Monmouth* - Pontypool and Abergavenny
Forest	*Salop* - Shrewsbury
Forest	*Wilts* - Chippenham
Forest and Frith	*Durham* - Bishop Auckland
Forest Gate	*London, E.7* - Bow
Forest Green	*Berks* - Slough
Forest Green	*Gloucester* - Stroud

FOR - FOU

Forest Green	*Surrey* - Dorking
Forest Hall	*Northumberland* - Newcastle upon Tyne
Forest Head	*Cumberland* - Carlisle
Forest, High	*Northumberland* - Hexham
Forest Hill (part)	*London, S.E.23* - Bromley
Forest Hill (part)	*London, S.E.23* - Lambeth
Forest Hill	*Oxford* - Oxford
Forest, Low	*Northumberland* - Hexham
Forest, Lower	*Wilts* - Chippenham
Forest Row	*Sussex* - East Grinstead
Forest Side	*Sussex* - Chichester
Forest Town	*Notts* - Mansfield
Forewoods Common	*Wilts* - Trowbridge
Forge	*Montgomery* - Machynlleth
Forge Hill	*Gloucester* - Gloucester
Forge Lane	*Stafford* - West Bromwich
Forge Mills	*Warwick* - Birmingham
Formby	*Lancaster* - Southport
Forncett St. Mary	*Norfolk* - Norwich
Forncett St. Peter	*Norfolk* - Norwich
Fornham All Saints	*Suffolk* - Bury St. Edmunds
Fornham St. Genevieve	*Suffolk* - Bury St. Edmunds
Fornham St. Martin	*Suffolk* - Bury St. Edmunds
Forsbrook	*Stafford* - Stoke-on-Trent
Forshaw Heath	*Warwick* - Birmingham
Forston	*Dorset* - Dorchester
Forthampton	*Gloucester* - Cheltenham
Fortis Green (part)	*London, N.2* - Barnet
Fortis Green (part)	*London, N.2* - Clerkenwell
Fortis Green	*London, N.10* - Clerkenwell
Forton	*Hants* - Andover
Forton	*Lancaster* - Lancaster
Forton	*Salop* - Shrewsbury
Forton (Chard)	*Somerset* - Axminster and Chard
Forton	*Stafford* - Wellington (Salop)
Fortyfoot Bank, North	*Lincs* - Boston
Forty Green	*Bucks* - High Wycombe
Forty Green	*Gloucester* - Gloucester
Forty Green Place	*Bucks* - High Wycombe
Forward Green	*Suffolk* - Stowmarket
Fosbury	*Wilts* - Andover
Foscote	*Northampton* - Northampton
Foscott	*Oxford* - Banbury
Fosdyke	*Lincoln* - Boston
Fosdyke Fen	*Lincoln* - Boston
Foss Bridge	*Gloucester* - Cheltenham
Fosten Green	*Kent* - Cranbrook
Fosterhouses	*York, W.R.* - Thorne
Fosters Booth	*Northampton* - Northampton
Foster Street	*Essex* - Harlow
Foston	*Derby* - Burton-upon-Trent
Foston	*Leicester* - Leicester
Foston	*Lincoln* - Grantham
Foston	*York, N.R.* - Malton
Foston-on-the-Wolds	*York, E.R.* - Bridlington
Foston's Ash	*Gloucester* - Stroud
Fotherby	*Lincoln* - Louth
Fotheringhay	*Northampton* - Peterborough
Fotherley, High	*Northumberland* - Hexham
Foul Anchor	*Cambridge* - Wisbech
Foulard	*Cumberland* - Carlisle
Foulby	*York, W.R.* - Pontefract
Foulden	*Norfolk* - King's Lynn
Foulk Stapleford	*Cheshire* - Chester
Foulmead	*Kent* - Deal
Foulness	*Essex* - Southend
Foulridge	*Lancaster* - Nelson
Foulsham	*Norfolk* - King's Lynn
Foulshaw, High	*Westmorland* - Kendal
Foulshaw, Low	*Westmorland* - Kendal
Foulshaw, Middle	*Westmorland* - Kendal
Foundry (Hayles)	*Cornwall* - Redruth
Fountain	*Glamorgan* - Bridgend
Fountain Dale	*Notts* - Mansfield
Fountains	*York, W.R.* - Ripon
Fountains Abbey	*York, N.R.* - Harrogate
Fountains Earth	*York, W.R.* - Harrogate
Four Ashes	*Stafford* - Stourbridge

FOU - FRA

Four Ashes	*Stafford* - Wolverhampton
Four Crosses	*Caernarvon* - Portmadoc
Four Crosses	*Montgomery* - Oswestry
Four Crosses	*Stafford* - Wolverhampton
Four Elms	*Kent* - Tonbridge
Four Forks	*Somerset* - Bridgwater
Four Gates	*Lancaster* - Bolton
Four Lane Ends	*Lancaster* - Bolton
Four Lane Ends	*Lancaster* - Bury
Four Lanes	*Cornwall* - Redruth
Four Marks	*Hants* - Winchester
Four Mile Bridge	*Anglesey* - Llangefni
Four Oaks	*Gloucester* - Gloucester
Four Oaks	*Warwick* - Birmingham
Four Oaks (Berkswell)	*Warwick* - Coventry
Fourstones	*Northumberland* - Hexham
Four Throws	*Kent* - Cranbrook
Four Ways (Cradley Heath)	*Stafford* - Dudley
Fovant	*Wilts* - Salisbury
Fowberry	*Northumberland* - Alnwick
Fowey	*Cornwall* - St. Austell
Fowl End	*Warwick* - Tamworth
Fowlmere	*Cambridge* - Cambridge
Fownhope	*Hereford* - Hereford
Foxcombe Hill	*Berks* - Oxford
Foxcote	*Bucks* - Bletchley and Leighton Buzzard
Foxcote	*Gloucester* - Cheltenham
Foxcote	*Hants* - Andover
Foxcote	*Somerset* - Frome
Foxcote	*Warwick* - Stratford on Avon
Foxearth	*Stafford* - Stoke-on-Trent
Foxearth	*Suffolk* - Sudbury
Foxfield	*Lancaster* - Barrow-in-Furness
Foxhall	*Suffolk* -Ipswich
Foxhall Park	*Hereford* - Hereford
Foxham	*Wilts* - Chippenham
Fox Hill	*Worcester* - Redditch
Fox Hill	*York, W.R.* - Sheffield
Fox Hills	*Hants* - Southampton
Foxhole	*Cornwall* - St. Austell
Foxholes	*Salop* - Shrewsbury
Foxholes	*York, E.R.* - Bridlington
Foxley	*Norfolk* - East Dereham
Foxley	*Northampton* - Northampton
Foxley	*Stafford* - Stoke-on-Trent
Foxley	*Stafford* - Stafford
Foxley	*Wilts* - Malmesbury
Foxlydiate	*Worcester* - Redditch
Fox Platt	*Lancaster* - Ashton-under-Lyne
Foxt	*Stafford* - Leek
Foxton	*Cambridge* - Cambridge
Foxton	*Leicester* - Leicester
Foxton	*Northumberland* - Alnwick
Foxton	*York, N.R.* - Northallerton
Foxup	*York, W.R.* - Skipton
Fox Yards	*Stafford* - Dudley
Foy	*Hereford* - Monmouth
Fraddam	*Cornwall* - Redruth
Fraddon	*Cornwall* - Truro
Fradley	*Stafford* - Lichfield
Fradley Junction	*Stafford* - Lichfield
Fradswell	*Stafford* - Stafford
Fradswell Heath	*Stafford* - Stafford
Fraisthorpe	*York, E.R.* - Bridlington
Framfield	*Sussex* - Lewes
Framilode	*Gloucester* - Gloucester
Framingham Earl	*Norfolk* - Norwich
Framingham Pigot	*Norfolk* - Norwich
Framlingham	*Suffolk* - Woodbridge
Frampton	*Dorset* - Dorchester
Frampton	*Gloucester* - Cheltenham
Frampton	*Lincoln* - Boston
Frampton Bank	*Lincoln* - Boston
Frampton Common	*Gloucester* - Bristol
Frampton Cotterell	*Gloucester* - Bristol
Frampton Fen	*Lincoln* - Boston
Frampton Mansell	*Gloucester* - Stroud
Frampton-on-Severn	*Gloucester* - Gloucester

FRA - FRI

Frampton Sandholme	*Lincoln* - Boston
Frampton West End	*Lincoln* - Boston
Framsden	*Suffolk* - Ipswich
Framwellgate Moor	*Durham* - Durham
France Lynch	*Gloucester* - Stroud
Franche	*Worcester* - Kidderminster
Frandley Brow	*Cheshire* - Northwich
Frankby	*Cheshire* - Birkenhead
Frankley	*Worcester* - Bromsgrove
Frankton	*Warwick* - Rugby
Fransham, Great	*Norfolk* - East Dereham
Fransham, Little	*Norfolk* - East Dereham
Frant	*Sussex* - Tunbridge Wells
Frating	*Essex* - Colchester
Fratton	*Hants* - Portsmouth
Freasley	*Warwick* - Tamworth
Freathy	*Cornwall* - Plymouth
Freechville	*Derby* - Sheffield
Freckenham	*Suffolk* - Newmarket
Freckleton	*Lancaster* - Preston
Free-Birch	*Derby* - Chesterfield
Freeby	*Leicester* - Melton Mowbray
Freefolk	*Hants* - Andover
Freeford	*Stafford* - Lichfield
Freehold	*Durham* - Durham
Freeholders Quarter	*Northumberland* - Morpeth
Freehold Land	*Monmouth* - Pontypool and Abergavenny
Freeland	*Oxford* - Witney
Freemantle	*Hants* - Southampton
Freethorpe	*Norfolk* - Great Yarmouth
Freight, The	*Kent* - Cranbrook
Freiston	*Lincoln* - Boston
Freiston Ings	*Lincoln* - Boston
Freiston Shore	*Lincoln* - Boston
Fremington	*Devon* - Barnstaple
Frenchay	*Gloucester* - Bristol
French Drove	*Northampton* - Peterborough
Frenchmoor	*Hants* - Salisbury
French Street	*Kent* - Sevenoaks
Frensham	*Surrey* - Aldershot and Farnham
Frenze	*Norfolk* - Norwich
Freshfield	*Lancaster* - Southport
Freshford	*Somerset* - Bath
Freshwater	*I. of W.* - Newport (I.W.)
Freshwater, East	*Pembroke* - Haverfordwest
Freshwater, West	*Pembroke* - Haverfordwest
Fressingfield	*Suffolk* - Halesworth
Freston	*Suffolk* - Ipswich
Fretherne	*Gloucester* - Gloucester
Frettenham	*Norfolk* - Norwich
Freystrop	*Pembroke* - Haverfordwest
Friar Park	*Stafford* - West Bromwich
Friar's Bay	*Sussex* - Brighton
Friars Cliff	*Hants* - Bournemouth
Friar's Goose	*Durham* - Gateshead
Friar's Ground	*Lancaster* - Barrow-in-Furness
Friar's Wash	*Herts* - St. Albans
Frickley	*York, W.R.* - Doncaster
Friday Bridge	*Cambridge* - Wisbech
Friday Street	*Surrey* - Dorking
Friday Street	*Sussex* - Eastbourne
Friday Street (Rusper)	*Sussex* - Horsham
Friday Street (Warnham)	*Sussex* - Horsham
Fridaythorpe	*York, E.R.* - Beverley
Friden Wharf	*Derby* - Buxton
Friends Green	*Herts* - Hitchin
Friern Barnet	*London, N.11* - Barnet
Friesthorpe	*Lincoln* - Lincoln
Frieston	*Lincoln* - Newark
Frieth	*Bucks* - Reading
Friggle Street	*Somerset* - Frome
Frilford	*Berks* - Oxford
Frilsham	*Berks* - Newbury
Frimley	*Surrey* - Aldershot and Farnham
Frimley Green	*Surrey* - Aldershot and Farnham
Frindsbury	*Kent* - Rochester
Fring	*Norfolk* - King's Lynn

FRI - FUL

Frinstead	*Kent* - Sittingbourne
Frinton-on-Sea	*Essex* - Colchester
Friog	*Merioneth* - Dolgellau
Frisby	*Leicester* - Leicester
Frisby-on-the-Wreake	*Leicester* - Melton Mowbray
Friskney	*Lincoln* - Skegness
Friston	*Suffolk* - Woodbridge
Friston	*Sussex* - Eastbourne
Fritchley	*Derby* - Alfreton
Frith	*Durham* - Bishop Auckland
Fritham	*Hants* - Salisbury
Fritham	*Hants* - Southampton
Frith Bank	*Lincoln* - Boston
Frith Common	*Worcester* - Kidderminster
Frithelstock	*Devon* - Bideford
Frithoedd	*Denbigh* - Denbigh
Frithsden	*Herts* - Hemel Hempstead
Frith Ville	*Lincoln* - Boston
Frittenden	*Kent* - Cranbrook
Frittiscombe	*Devon* - Kingsbridge
Fritton	*Norfolk* - Norwich
Fritton	*Suffolk* - Great Yarmouth
Fritwell	*Oxford* - Banbury
Frizinghall	*York, W.R.* - Bradford
Frizington	*Cumberland* - Whitehaven
Frocester	*Gloucester* - Stroud
Frodesley	*Salop* - Shrewsbury
Frodingham	*Lincoln* - Scunthorpe
Frodingham, North	*York, E.R.* - Bridlington
Frodingham, South	*York, E.R.* - Kingston upon-Hull
Frodsham	*Cheshire* - Runcorn
Frodsham Bridge	*Cheshire* - Runcorn
Frogall	*Stafford* - Leek
Frog Firle	*Sussex* - Eastbourne
Froggatt	*Derby* - Chesterfield
Frogham	*Hants* - Salisbury
Frogmore	*Devon* - Kingsbridge
Frogmore	*Dorset* - Dorchester
Frogmore (Camberley)	*Hants* - Aldershot and Farnham
Frogmore	*Herts* - Hertford
Frogmore	*Herts* - Hitchin
Frogmore	*Herts* - St. Albans
Frognall	*Lincoln* - Spalding
Frogpool	*Cornwall* - Redruth
Frogs Green	*Essex* - Bishop's Stortford
Frolesworth	*Leicester* - Hinckley
Frome	*Somerset* - Frome
Frome Billet	*Dorset* - Dorchester
Frome Bridge	*Gloucester* - Gloucester
Frome St. Quintin	*Dorset* - Dorchester
Frome Vauchurch	*Dorset* - Dorchester
Fron	*Denbigh* - Wrexham
Froncysyllte	*Denbigh* - Wrexham
Frongoch	*Merioneth* - Dolgellau
Froome's Hill	*Hereford* - Part Worcester Part Hereford
Frostenden	*Suffolk* - Lowestoft
Frosterley	*Durham* - Bishop Auckland
Frostra	*York, W.R.* - Kendal
Froxfield	*Beds* - Bedford
Froxfield	*Hants* - Petersfield
Froxfield	*Wilts* - Swindon
Froyle, Lower	*Hants* - Aldershot and Farnham
Froyle, Upper	*Hants* - Aldershot and Farnham
Fryerning	*Essex* - Chelmsford
Fryston	*York, W.R.* - Pontefract
Fryton	*York, N.R.* - Malton
Fryup, Great	*York, N.R.* - Whitby
Fryup, Little	*York, N.R.* - Whitby
Fulbeck	*Lincoln* - Newark
Fulbeck	*Northumberland* - Morpeth
Fulbourn	*Cambridge* - Cambridge
Fulbrook	*Oxford* - Witney
Fulbrook	*Warwick* - Stratford on Avon
Fulfen	*Stafford* - Lichfield
Fulflood	*Hants* - Winchester
Fulford	*Somerset* - Taunton
Fulford	*Stafford* - Stoke-on-Trent
Fulford	*York, E.R.* - York
Fulham	*London, S.W.6* - West London

FUL - GAL

Fulhope	*Northumberland* - Morpeth
Fulking	*Sussex* - Brighton
Fullbrook	*Stafford* - Walsall
Fullerton	*Hants* - Andover
Fulletby	*Lincoln* - Lincoln
Fullready	*Warwick* - Stratford on Avon
Full Sutton	*York, E.R.* - York
Fulmer	*Bucks* - Uxbridge
Fulmodestone	*Norfolk* - King's Lynn
Fulmodestone Common	*Norfolk* - King's Lynn
Fulneck	*York, W.R.* - Bradford
Fulnetby	*Lincoln* - Lincoln
Fulney	*Lincoln* - Spalding
Fulney, Low	*Lincoln* - Spalding
Fulshaw	*Cheshire* - Macclesfield
Fulstow	*Lincoln* - Louth
Fulwell	*Durham* - Sunderland
Fulwell	*Oxford* - Banbury
Fulwood	*Lancaster* - Preston
Fulwood	*York, W.R.* - Sheffield
Funden Hall	*Norfolk* - Norwich
Funtington	*Sussex* - Chichester
Funton	*Kent* - Sittingbourne
Furland	*Somerset* - Yeovil
Furley	*Devon* - Axminster and Chard
Furnace	*Cardigan* - Machynlleth
Furnace	*Carmarthen* - Llanelli
Furnace, Old	*Monmouth* - Pontypool and Abergavenny
Furnace Row	*Cumberland* - Workington
Furner's Green	*Sussex* - Lewes
Furness Abbey	*Lancaster* - Barrow-in-Furness
Furness Vale	*Derby* - Buxton
Furneux Pelham	*Herts* - Bishop's Stortford
Furtho	*Northampton* - Northampton
Furzebrook	*Dorset* - Swanage
Furze Down	*Hants* - Winchester
Furze Hill	*Devon* - Barnstaple
Furze Hill	*Worcs* - Evesham
Furzehill	*Hants* - Salisbury
Furze Hills	*Lincoln* - Lincoln
Furzley	*Hants* - Southampton
Fwdog	*Brecon* - Pontypool and Abergavenny
Fwthog	*Hereford* - Pontypool and Abergavenny
Fyfield	*Berks* - Oxford
Fyfield	*Essex* - Brentwood
Fyfield	*Gloucester* - Cirencester
Fyfield	*Hants* - Andover
Fyfield	*Wilts* - Swindon
Fyfield Wick	*Berks* - Oxford
Fylands	*Durham* - Bishop Auckland
Fylands Bridge	*Durham* - Bishop Auckland
Fylingdales	*York, N.R.* - Whitby
Fylingdales Moor	*York, N.R.* - Whitby
Fyning	*Sussex* - Petersfield
Fyrnwy	*Montgomery* - Oswestry

G

Gabalfa	*Glamorgan* - Cardiff
Gadbrook	*Surrey* - Reigate
Gaddesby	*Leicester* - Melton Mowbray
Gaddesden, Great	*Herts* - Hemel Hempstead
Gaddesden, Little	*Herts* - Hemel Hempstead
Gaddesden Row	*Herts* - Hemel Hempstead
Gadebridge	*Herts* - Hemel Hempstead
Gaerwen	*Anglesey* - Llangefni
Gagingwell	*Oxford* - Banbury
Gailey	*Stafford* - Stafford
Gailey End	*Essex* - Chelmsford
Gainford	*Durham* - Darlington
Gain, Little	*Salop* - Bridgnorth
Gainsborough	*Lincoln* - Gainsborough
Gainscross	*Dorset* - Shaftesbury
Gaisby	*York, W.R.* - Bradford
Gaisgill	*Westmorland* - Penrith
Gaitle Bridge	*Cumberland* - Carlisle
Gaitsgill	*Cumberland* - Carlisle
Galemire	*Cumberland* - Whitehaven

GAL - GAR

Galgate	*Lancaster* - Lancaster
Galhampton	*Somerset* - Yeovil
Galleys Bank	*Stafford* - Stoke-on-Trent
Galleywood	*Essex* - Chelmsford
Galligill	*Cumberland* - Carlisle
Gallowhill	*Northumberland* - Newcastle upon Tyne
Gallows Tree Common	*Oxford* - Reading
Galltegfa	*Denbigh* - Denbigh
Galmington	*Somerset* - Taunton
Galmpton	*Devon* - Kingsbridge
Galmpton	*Devon* - Torquay
Galon Uchaf	*Glamorgan* - Merthyr Tydfil
Galphay	*York, W.R.* - Harrogate
Gamblesby	*Cumberland* - Penrith
Gamblesby	*Cumberland* - Carlisle
Gamesley	*Derby* - Hyde
Gamlingay	*Cambridge* - Biggleswade
Gamston	*Notts* - East Retford
Gamston	*Notts* - Nottingham
Ganarew	*Hereford* - Monmouth
Gang	*Cornwall* - Liskeard
Gangsdown Hill	*Oxford* - Didcot
Ganllwyd	*Merioneth* - Dolgellau
Gannow Green	*Worcester* - Bromsgrove
Ganstead	*York, E.R.* - Kingston-upon-Hull
Ganton	*York, E.R.* - Scarborough
Ganton Wold	*York, E.R.* - Scarborough
Gaol Butts	*Stafford* - Stafford
Garboldisham	*Norfolk* - Norwich
Gardham	*York, E.R.* - Beverley
Gardner Street	*Sussex* - Eastbourne
Gare Hill	*Somerset* - Frome
Garendon	*Leicester* - Loughborough
Garesfield	*Durham* - Newcastle upon Tyne
Garford	*Berks* - Oxford
Garforth	*York, W.R.* - Pontefract
Gargrave	*York, W.R.* - Skipton
Garkar	*Cornwall* - St. Austell
Garlands	*Cumberland* - Carlisle
Garlinge	*Kent* - Margate
Garlinge Green	*Kent* - Canterbury
Garmelow	*Stafford* - Stafford
Garmondsway	*Durham* - Durham
Garnant	*Carmarthen* - Ammanford
Garndiffaith	*Monmouth* - Pontypool and Abergavenny
Garn Dolbenmaen	*Caernarvon* - Portmadoc
Garnett Bridge	*Westmorland* - Kendal
Garnswllt (part)	*Carmarthen* - Ammanford
Garn-y-Erw	*Monmouth* - Pontypool and Abergavenny
Garras	*Cornwall* - Penzance
Garreglefn	*Anglesey* - Llangefni
Garrett, High	*Essex* - Braintree
Garretts Green	*Warwick* - Birmingham
Garrigill	*Cumberland* - Carlisle
Garrowby	*York, E.R.* - York
Garsdale	*York, W.R.* - Kendal
Garsdale Head	*York, W.R.* - Kendal
Garsdon	*Wilts* - Malmesbury
Garshall Green	*Stafford* - Stafford
Garsington	*Oxford* - Oxford
Garstang	*Lancaster* - Preston
Garston	*Herts* - Watford
Garston	*Lancaster* - Liverpool
Garston, East	*Berks* - Newbury
Garswood	*Lancaster* - Wigan
Garth	*Brecon* - Builth
Garth	*Caernarvon* - Bangor
Garth	*Denbigh* - Wrexham
Garth	*Glamorgan* - Bridgend
Garth, Upper	*Denbigh* - Wrexham
Garthbeibio	*Montgomery* - Welshpool
Garthbrengy	*Brecon* - Brecknock
Gartheli	*Cardigan* - Lampeter
Gartherin	*Montgomery* - Oswestry
Garthmyl	*Montgomery* - Welshpool
Garthnewydd	*Glamorgan* - Merthyr Tydfil
Garthorpe	*Leicester* - Melton Mowbray

GAR - GED

Garthorpe	*Lincoln and York, W.R.* - Goole
Garthrow	*Westmorland* - Kendal
Garton	*York, E.R.* - Kingston-upon-Hull
Garton-on-the-Wold	*York, E.R.* - Beverley
Garvestone	*Norfolk* - East Dereham
Garway	*Hereford* - Monmouth
Garway Hill	*Hereford* - Hereford
Garw Valley	*Glamorgan* - Bridgend
Gascoigne Wood	*York, W.R.* - Pontefract
Gasper	*Dorset* - Shaftesbury
Gastard	*Wilts* - Chippenham
Gasthorpe	*Norfolk* - Thetford
Gaston Green	*Essex* - Bishop's Stortford
Gatcombe	*Gloucester* - Gloucester
Gatcombe	*I. of. W.* - Newport (I.W.)
Gate	*Lancs* - Kendal
Gateacre	*Lancaster* - Liverpool
Gatebeck	*Westmorland* - Kendal
Gate Burton	*Lincoln* - Gainsborough
Gateford	*Notts* - Worksop
Gateforth	*York, W.R.* - Pontefract
Gatehampton	*Oxford* - Didcot
Gate Helmsley	*York, N.R.* - York
Gatehouse	*Caernarvon* - Bangor
Gatehouse	*Northumberland* - Hexham
Gateley	*Norfolk* - King's Lynn
Gatenby	*York, N.R.* - Northallerton
Gatesend	*Norfolk* - King's Lynn
Gatesgarth	*Cumberland* - Workington
Gateshead	*Durham* - Gateshead
Gateshead Fell	*Durham* - Gateshead
Gatesheath	*Cheshire* - Chester
Gatfield Elm	*Worcester* - Cheltenham
Gatherwynd	*Stafford* - Stafford
Gathurst	*Lancaster* - Wigan
Gatley	*Cheshire* - Stockport
Gatsford	*Hereford* - Monmouth
Gatten	*Salop* - Shrewsbury
Gattertop	*Hereford* - Leominster
Gatton	*Surrey* - Reigate
Gatwick	*Surrey* - Reigate
Gaulby	*Leicester* - Leicester
Gaunts	*Dorset* - Wimborne Minster
Gaunts Earthcott	*Gloucester* - Thornbury
Gaunts End	*Essex* - Bishop's Stortford
Gautby	*Lincoln* - Lincoln
Gawber	*York, W.R.* - Barnsley
Gawcott	*Bucks* - Aylesbury
Gawsworth	*Cheshire* - Macclesfield
Gawthorpe	*York, W.R.* - Dewsbury
Gawthorp-in-Dent	*York, W.R.* - Kendal
Gawthwaite	*Lancaster* - Barrow-in-Furness
Gawton	*Devon* - Plymouth
Gaydon	*Warwick* - Warwick
Gay Hill	*Worcester* - Birmingham
Gayhurst	*Bucks* - Bletchley and Leighton Buzzard
Gayles	*York, N.R.* - Darlington
Gaynes	*Hunts* - Huntingdon
Gaystead	*Northumberland* - Hexham
Gay Street	*Sussex* - Chichester
Gayton	*Cheshire* - Birkenhead
Gayton	*Norfolk* - King's Lynn
Gayton	*Northampton* - Northampton
Gayton	*Stafford* - Stafford
Gayton-le-Marsh	*Lincoln* - Louth
Gayton-le-Wold	*Lincoln* - Louth
Gayton Thorpe	*Norfolk* - King's Lynn
Gaywood	*Norfolk* - King's Lynn
Gazeley	*Suffolk* - Newmarket
Gear	*Cornwall* - Truro
Gedding	*Suffolk* - Stowmarket
Geddinge	*Kent* - Dover
Geddington	*Northampton* - Kettering
Gedgrave	*Suffolk* - Woodbridge
Gedling	*Notts* - Nottingham
Gedney	*Lincoln* - Spalding
Gedney Broadgate	*Lincoln* - Spalding
Gedney Drove End	*Lincoln* - Spalding
Gedney Dyke	*Lincoln* - Spalding

GED - GIL

Gedney Fen	*Lincoln* - Spalding
Gedney Hill	*Lincoln* - Spalding
Gedney Marsh	*Lincoln* - Spalding
Gee Cross	*Cheshire* - Hyde
Geeston	*Rutland* - Stamford
Geldeston	*Norfolk* - Lowestoft
Gellifaelog	*Glamorgan* - Merthyr Tydfil
Gellifor	*Denbigh* - Denbigh
Gelligaer	*Glamorgan* - Bargoed
Gelligroes	*Monmouth* - Blackwood
Gellilas	*Glamorgan* - Bridgend
Gellilydan	*Merioneth* - Portmadoc
Gelliwen	*Carmarthen* - Carmarthen
Gellydeg	*Glamorgan* - Merthyr Tydfil
Gellygron	*Glamorgan* - Neath
Gellyswick	*Pembroke* - Haverfordwest
Gellyvelin	*Brecon* - Pontypool and Abergavenny
Gelston	*Lincoln* - Grantham
Gelt Bridge, Low	*Cumberland* - Carlisle
Gembling	*York, E.R.* - Bridlington
Gendros	*Glamorgan* - Swansea
Gentleshaw	*Stafford* - Lichfield
George Green	*Bucks* - Uxbridge
Georgeham	*Devon* - Barnstaple
George Nympton	*Devon* - Barnstaple
Georges Elm	*Warwick* - Stratford on Avon
Gerards Bridge	*Lancaster* - St. Helens
Gerlan	*Caernarvon* - Bangor
Germansweek	*Devon* - Okehampton
Germoe	*Cornwall* - Penzance
Gernick	*Cornwall* - Redruth
Gerrans	*Cornwall* - Truro
Gerrards Cross	*Bucks* - Uxbridge
Gestingthorpe	*Essex* - Sudbury
Geufron	*Radnor* - Llandrindod Wells
Giants Grave	*Glamorgan* - Neath
Giant's Seat	*Lancaster* - Bolton
Gib Heath	*Warwick* - Birmingham
Gibb	*Wilts* - Chippenham
Gibraltar	*Bucks* - Aylesbury
Gibraltar	*Oxford* - Oxford
Gibsey Bridge	*Lincoln* - Boston
Gibside	*Durham* - Gateshead
Gibsmere	*Notts* - Newark
Gidda Hall	*Wilts* - Chippenham
Gidding, Great	*Hunts* - Huntingdon
Gidding, Little	*Hunts* - Huntingdon
Gidea Park	*Essex* - Ilford
Gidleigh	*Devon* - Okehampton
Gidlow	*Lancaster* - Wigan
Gigg	*Lancaster* - Bury
Giggity	*Stafford* - Wolverhampton
Giggleswick	*York, W.R.* - Skipton
Gilberdyke	*York, E.R.* - Goole
Gilberts Cross	*Stafford* - Stourbridge
Gilcrux	*Cumberland* - Workington
Gildersber	*York, W.R.* - Skipton
Gildersome	*York, W.R.* - Dewsbury
Gildingwells	*York, W.R.* - Worksop
Gilesgate Moor	*Durham* - Durham
Gileston	*Glamorgan* - Bridgend
Gilfach	*Glamorgan* - Bargoed
Gilfach Goch (part)	*Glamorgan* - Bridgend
Gilfach Goch (part)	*Glamorgan* - Pontypridd
Gilfrachyrheda	*Cardigan* - Aberystwyth
Gilgal	*Cambridge* - Ely
Gilgarron	*Cumberland* - Whitehaven
Gill	*Cumberland* - Penrith
Gillam	*Cornwall* - Penzance
Gillamoor	*York, N.R.* - Malton
Gillbrow	*Cumberland* - Workington
Gillibrands	*Lancaster* - Wigan
Gilling	*York, N.R.* - Darlington
Gilling, East	*York, N.R.* - Malton
Gillingham	*Dorset* - Shaftesbury
Gillingham	*Kent* - Rochester
Gillingham	*Norfolk* - Lowestoft
Gillingstool	*Gloucester* - Thornbury
Gill Moss	*Lancaster* - Liverpool

GIL - GLA

Gills Green	*Kent* - Cranbrook
Gilmonby	*York, N.R.* - Darlington
Gilmorton	*Leicester* - Rugby
Gilroyd	*York, W.R.* - Barnsley
Gilsland (part)	*Northumberland* - Hexham
Gilsland (part)	*Cumberland* - Carlisle
Gilson	*Warwick* - Birmingham
Gilstead	*York, W.R.* - Keighley
Gilston	*Herts* - Hertford
Giltbrook	*Notts* - Nottingham
Gilwern	*Brecon* - Pontypool and Abergavenny
Gimingham	*Norfolk* - Norwich
Ginge	*Berks* - Didcot
Gin Pit Village	*Lancs* - Leigh
Gipping	*Suffolk* - Stowmarket
Girlington	*York, W.R.* - Bradford
Girrick	*York, N.R.* - Whitby
Girsby	*Lincoln* - Louth
Girsby	*York, N.R.* - Darlington
Girtford	*Beds* - Biggleswade
Girton	*Cambridge* - Cambridge
Girton	*Notts* - Newark
Gisburn	*York, W.R.* - Blackburn
Gisleham	*Suffolk* - Lowestoft
Gislingham	*Suffolk* - Norwich
Gissing	*Norfolk* - Norwich
Gittisham	*Devon* - Exeter
Givendale	*York, W.R.* - Harrogate
Givendale, Great	*York, E.R.* - York
Givendale, Little	*York, E.R.* - York
Gladestry	*Radnor* - Builth Wells
Glais (part)	*Glamorgan* - Neath
Glais (part)	*Glamorgan* - Swansea
Glaisdale	*York, N.R.* - Whitby
Glanadda	*Caernarvon* - Bangor
Glanamman	*Carmarthen* - Ammanford
Glan Conway	*Denbigh* - Conway
Glandford with Bayfield	*Norfolk* - Norwich
Glanduar	*Carmarthen* - Lampeter
Glandwr	*Pembroke* - Haverfordwest
Glandyfi	*Cardigan* - Machynlleth
Glangwili	*Carmarthen* - Carmarthen
Glanhafon	*Montgomery* - Oswestry
Glanhafron	*Montgomery* - Newtown
Glanrafon	*Anglesey* - Llangefni
Glanrafon	*Denbigh* - Oswestry
Glanrafon	*Flint* - Holywell
Glanrhyd	*Pembroke* - Cardigan
Glantlees	*Northumberland* - Alnwick
Glanton	*Northumberland* - Alnwick
Glanville	*Dorset* - Dorchester
Glanwydden	*Caernarvon* - Conway
Glanydon	*Flint* - Holywell
Glapthorne	*Northampton* - Corby
Glapton with Clifton	*Notts* - Nottingham
Glapwell	*Derby* - Chesterfield
Glasbury	*Brecon* - Brecknock
Glasbwll	*Montgomery* - Machynlleth
Glascoed	*Denbigh* - Rhyl
Glascoed	*Flint* - Wrexham
Glascoed	*Monmouth* - Pontypool and Abergavenny
Glascote	*Stafford* - Tamworth
Glascwm	*Radnor* - Builth
Glasfryn	*Denbigh* - Denbigh
Glasinfryn	*Caernarvon* - Bangor
Glasshampton	*Worcester* - Kidderminster
Glass Houghton	*York, W.R.* - Pontefract
Glass House	*Gloucester* - Gloucester
Glasshouses	*York, W.R.* - Harrogate
Glassmore	*Cambridge* - Peterborough
Glasson	*Cumberland* - Carlisle
Glassonby	*Cumberland* - Penrith
Glasson Dock	*Lancaster* - Lancaster
Glasthorpe Hills	*Northampton* - Northampton
Glaston	*Rutland* - Stamford
Glastonbury	*Somerset* - Wells
Glatton	*Hunts* - Peterborough

GLA - GOD

Glazebrook	*Lancaster* - Warrington
Glazebury	*Lancaster* - Leigh
Glazeley	*Salop* - Bridgnorth
Gleadless	*York, W.R.* - Sheffield
Gleadless Valley	*York, W.R.* - Sheffield
Gleaston	*Lancaster* - Barrow-in-Furness
Glebe Farm	*Warwick* - Birmingham
Gledhow	*York, W.R.* - Leeds
Gledrid	*Salop* - Oswestry
Gleiniant	*Montgomery* - Newtown
Glemham, Great	*Suffolk* - Woodbridge
Glemham, Little	*Suffolk* - Woodbridge
Glemsford	*Suffolk* - Sudbury
Glendale	*Northumberland* - Hexham
Glenfield	*Leicester* - Leicester
Glenfield Frith	*Leicester* - Leicester
Glen, Great	*Leicester* - Leicester
Glen, Little	*Leicester* - Leicester
Glen Magna	*Leicester* - Leicester
Glen Parva	*Leicester* - Leicester
Glenridding	*Westmorland* - Penrith
Glentham	*Lincoln* - Lincoln
Glentworth	*Lincoln* - Gainsborough
Glenwhelt	*Northumberland* - Hexham
Glevering	*Suffolk* - Woodbridge
Glewstone	*Hereford* - Monmouth
Glidden (Hambledon)	*Hants* - Portsmouth
Glinton	*Northampton* - Peterborough
Glodwick	*Lancaster* - Oldham
Glogue	*Pembroke* - Cardigan
Glooston	*Leicester* - Leicester
Glossop	*Derby* - Hyde
Gloster Hill	*Northumberland* - Alnwick
Gloucester	*Gloucester* - Gloucester
Glusburn	*York, W.R.* - Skipton
Glutton Bridge	*Derby* - Buxton
Gluvian	*Cornwall* - Newquay
Glympton	*Oxford* - Oxford
Glympton Assarts	*Oxford* - Oxford
Glynarthen	*Cardigan* - Cardigan
Glynbrochan	*Montgomery* - Newtown
Glynceiriog	*Denbigh* - Wrexham
Glyncoch	*Glamorgan* - Pontypridd
Glyncorrwg	*Glamorgan* - Neath
Glynde	*Sussex* - Lewes
Glyndyfrdwy	*Merioneth* - Wrexham
Glyngynwydd	*Montgomery* - Newtown
Glynhafren Lower	*Montgomery* - Newtown
Glynhafren Upper	*Montgomery* - Newtown
Glyn Morlas	*Salop* - Oswestry
Glyn Neath	*Glamorgan* - Neath
Glynogwr	*Glamorgan* - Bridgend
Glyntawe	*Brecon* - Brecknock
Glyntrefnant Lower	*Montgomery* - Newtown
Glyntrefnant Upper	*Montgomery* - Newtown
Gnosall	*Stafford* - Stafford
Goadby	*Leicester* - Leicester
Goadby Marwood	*Leicester* - Melton Mowbray
Goadsbarrow	*Lancaster* - Barrow-in-Furness
Goatacre	*Wilts* - Chippenham
Goathill	*Dorset* - Yeovil
Goathland	*York, N.R.* - Whitby
Goathorn	*Dorset* - Swanage
Goathurst	*Somerset* - Bridgwater
Goathurst Common	*Kent* - Sevenoaks
Gobowen	*Salop* - Oswestry
Godalming	*Surrey* - Guildford
Goddards Green	*Kent* - Cranbrook
Goddards Green	*Sussex* - Haywards Heath
Godden Green	*Kent* - Sevenoaks
Godington	*Oxford* - Oxford
Godley	*Cheshire* - Hyde
Godley Bridge	*York, W.R.* - Halifax
Godmanchester	*Hunts* - Huntingdon
Godmanstone	*Dorset* - Dorchester
Godmersham	*Kent* - Ashford
Godney	*Somerset* - Wells
Godolphin Cross	*Cornwall* - Penzance
Godreaman	*Glamorgan* - Aberdare
Godregraig	*Glamorgan* - Neath

GOD - GOO

Godrevey	*Cornwall* - Redruth
Godsfield	*Hants* - Winchester
Godshill	*Hants* - Salisbury
Godshill	*I. of W.* - Newport (I.W.)
Godstone	*Surrey* - Reigate
Godstone, South	*Surrey* - Reigate
Godstowe	*Oxford* - Oxford
Godwinscroft	*Hants* - Bournemouth
Goffs Hill	*Sussex* - Horsham
Goff's Oak	*Herts* - Edmonton
Goginan	*Cardigan* - Aberystwyth
Gogyan	*Cardigan* - Lampeter
Golant	*Cornwall* - St. Austell
Golberdon	*Cornwall* - Liskeard
Golborne	*Lancaster* - Leigh
Golborne Bellow	*Cheshire* - Chester
Golborne David	*Cheshire* - Chester
Golcar	*York, W.R.* - Huddersfield
Goldcliff	*Monmouth* - Newport (Mon.)
Golden Cross	*Sussex* - Eastbourne
Golden Green	*Kent* - Tonbridge
Golden Grove (part)	*Carmarthen* - Ammanford
Golden Grove (part)	*Carmarthen* - Carmarthen
Goldenhill	*Stafford* - Stoke-on-Trent
Golden Pot	*Hants* - Aldershot and Farnham
Golden Valley	*Derby* - Alfreton
Golden Valley	*Gloucester* - Cheltenham
Golderfield	*Hereford* - Leominster
Golders Green (part)	*London, N.W.11* - Watford
Golders Green (part)	*London, N.W.11* - Willesden
Goldhanger	*Essex* - Maldon
Gold Hill	*Bucks* - Amersham
Goldicote, Lower	*Warwick* - Stratford on Avon
Goldicote, Upper	*Warwick* - Stratford on Avon
Golding	*Salop* - Shrewsbury
Goldsborough	*York, W.R.* - Harrogate
Goldsbrough	*York, N.R.* - Whitby
Goldshaw Booth	*Lancaster* - Nelson
Golds Hill	*Stafford* - West Bromwich
Goldsithney	*Cornwall* - Penzance
Goldstone	*Salop* - Market Drayton
Goldsworth	*Surrey* - Guildford
Goldthorn Hill	*Stafford* - Wolverhampton
Goldthorn Hill Estate	*Stafford* - Wolverhampton
Goldthorn Park	*Stafford* - Wolverhampton
Goldthorpe	*York, W.R.* - Doncaster
Golford	*Kent* - Cranbrook
Golftyn	*Flint* - Holywell
Gollinrod	*Lancaster* - Bury
Goltho	*Lincoln* - Lincoln
Gomeldom	*Wilts* - Salisbury
Gomersal	*York, W.R.* - Dewsbury
Gomersal, Great	*York, W.R.* - Dewsbury
Gomersal, Little	*York, W.R.* - Dewsbury
Gomshall	*Surrey* - Guildford
Gonalston	*Notts* - Nottingham
Gonerby, Great	*Lincoln* - Grantham
Gonsall	*Salop* - Shrewsbury
Good Easter	*Essex* - Chelmsford
Gooderstone	*Norfolk* - King's Lynn
Goodleigh	*Devon* - Barnstaple
Goodmanham	*York, E.R.* - Beverley
Goodmayes	*Essex* - Ilford
Goodnestone	*Kent* - Canterbury
Goodrich	*Hereford* - Monmouth
Goodshaw Fold	*Lancaster* - Rawtenstall
Goodwick	*Pembroke* - Haverfordwest
Goodwood	*Sussex* - Chichester
Goodworth Clatford	*Hants* - Andover
Goodyers End	*Warwick* - Nuneaton
Goole	*York, W.R.* - Goole
Goole Fields	*York, W.R.* - Goole
Goonbell	*Cornwall* - Truro
Goongumpas	*Cornwall* - Redruth
Goonhavern	*Cornwall* - Truro
Goonlaze	*Cornwall* - Truro
Goonown	*Cornwall* - Truro
Goonvrea	*Cornwall* - Truro
Goose Eye	*York, W.R.* - Keighley
Goose Green	*Hants* - Southampton

GOO - GOT

Goose Green	*Herts* - Hertford
Goose Green	*Lancaster* -Wigan
Goose Green (Warnham)	*Sussex* - Horsham
Goose Green	*Sussex* - Chichester
Goosemoor	*Stafford* - Stafford
Goosepool	*Durham* - Stockton on Tees
Goosey	*Berks* - Didcot
Goosnargh	*Lancaster* - Preston
Goostrey	*Cheshire* - Congleton
Gopsall	*Leicester* - Ashby-de-la-Zouch
Garcott Hill	*Worcester* - Redditch
Gordon Gill Colliery	*Durham* - Bishop Auckland
Gore End	*Kent* - Margate
Gorefield	*Cambridge* - Wisbech
Gore, Old	*Hereford* - Ross
Gore, The	*Kent* - Cranbrook
Gorhambury	*Herts* - St. Albans
Goring	*Sussex* - Worthing
Goring Heath	*Oxford* - Reading
Goring-on-Thames	*Oxford* - Didcot
Gorleston-on-Sea	*Norfolk* - Great Yarmouth
Gorley, North	*Hants* - Salisbury
Gorley, South	*Hants* - Salisbury
Gornal, Lower	*Stafford* - Dudley
Gornal, Upper	*Stafford* - Dudley
Gornal Wood	*Stafford* - Dudley
Goronddu	*Montgomery* - Newtown
Gorran	*Cornwall* - St. Austell
Gorran Haven	*Cornwall* - St. Austell
Gorsedd	*Flint* - Holywell
Gorse Hill	*Lancaster* - Salford
Gorseinon	*Glamorgan* - Swansea
Gorses Mount	*Lancaster* - Bolton
Gorsey Bank	*Salop* - Market Drayton
Gorsey Bank (Shifnal)	*Stafford* - Wellington (Salop)
Gorsgoch	*Cardigan* - Lampeter
Gorslas (part)	*Carmarthen* - Ammanford
Gorslas (part)	*Carmarthen* - Carmarthen
Gorsley	*Gloucester* - Gloucester
Gorsley Common	*Hereford* - Gloucester
Gorsley, Little	*Gloucester* - Gloucester
Gorstage	*Cheshire* - Northwich
Gorstella	*Cheshire* - Chester
Gorsty Hill	*Stafford* - Dudley
Gorton	*Lancaster* - Manchester
Gorton, West	*Lancaster* - Manchester
Gorwydd	*Cardigan* - Lampeter
Gosbeck	*Suffolk* - Ipswich
Gosberton	*Lincoln* - Spalding
Gosberton Cheal	*Lincoln* - Spalding
Gosberton Fen	*Lincoln* - Spalding
Gosberton Risegate	*Lincoln* - Spalding
Goscote	*Stafford* - Walsall
Goscote, East	*Leics* - Leicester
Gosfield	*Essex* - Braintree
Gosford	*Oxford* - Oxford
Gosforth	*Cumberland* - Whitehaven
Gosforth, North	*Northumberland* - Newcastle upon Tyne
Gosforth Park	*Northumberland* - Newcastle upon Tyne
Gosforth, South	*Northumberland* - Newcastle upon Tyne
Gosmore	*Herts* - Hitchin
Gospel Ash	*Stafford* - Stourbridge
Gospel End	*Stafford* - Wolverhampton
Gospel Green	*Sussex* - Chichester
Gospel Oak	*London, N.W.5* - Bloomsbury and Marylebone
Gospel Oak	*Stafford* - Dudley
Gospel Oak	*Warwick* - Stratford on Avon
Gosport	*Hants* - Portsmouth
Gossoms End	*Herts* - Hemel Hempstead
Gosta Green	*Warwick* - Birmingham
Goswick	*Northumberland* - Berwick-upon-Tweed
Gotham	*Notts* - Nottingham
Gothelney	*Somerset* - Bridgwater
Gotherington	*Gloucester* - Cheltenham

Gotherington Fields	*Gloucester* - Cheltenham
Gothers	*Cornwall* - St. Austell
Gothersley	*Stafford* - Stourbridge
Gotton	*Somerset* - Taunton
Goudhurst	*Kent* - Cranbrook
Goulceby	*Lincoln* - Louth
Goulceby Top	*Lincoln* - Louth
Goulds Green	*Middlesex* - Uxbridge
Gouthwaite	*York, W.R.* - Harrogate
Gover	*Cornwall* - St. Austell
Goverseth	*Cornwall* - St. Austell
Goverton	*Notts* - Newark
Goveton	*Devon* - Kingsbridge
Govilon	*Monmouth* - Pontypool and Abergavenny
Gowdall	*York, W.R.* - Goole
Gowerton	*Glamorgan* - Swansea
Gowthorpe	*York, E.R.* - Goole
Gowthorpe	*York, E.R.* - York
Goxhill	*Lincoln* - Great Grimsby
Goxhill	*York, E.R.* - Beverley
Goytre	*Monmouth* - Pontypool and Abergavenny
Graby	*Lincoln* - Sleaford
Gracca	*Cornwall* - St. Austell
Gracedieu	*Leicester* - Loughborough
Grace Mary Estate	*Stafford* - Dudley
Gradbach	*Stafford* - Buxton
Grade	*Cornwall* - Penzance
Grade Ruan	*Cornwall* - Penzance
Graffham	*Sussex* - Chichester
Grafham	*Hunts* - Huntingdon
Grafton	*Cheshire* - Whitchurch
Grafton	*Gloucester* - Cheltenham
Grafton	*Hereford* - Hereford
Grafton	*Oxford* - Witney
Grafton	*Salop* - Shrewsbury
Grafton	*Warwick* - Stratford on Avon
Grafton	*Wilts* - Swindon
Grafton	*Worcester* - Bromsgrove
Grafton	*York, W.R.* - Harrogate
Grafton, East	*Wilts* - Swindon
Grafton Flyford	*Worcester* - Worcester
Grafton Regis	*Northampton* - Northampton
Grafton Underwood	*Northampton* - Kettering
Grafton, West	*Wilts* - Swindon
Grafty Green	*Kent* - Maidstone
Grahamsley	*Durham* - Bishop Auckland
Graig	*Denbigh* - Conway
Graigadwywynt	*Denbigh* - Denbigh
Graig Berthllwyd	*Glamorgan* - Merthyr Tydfil
Graigcefnparc	*Glamorgan* - Neath
Graigfechan	*Denbigh* - Denbigh
Grain Bridge	*Kent* - Rochester
Grainger Houses	*Cumberland* - Carlisle
Grainingfold	*Sussex* - Horsham
Grain St. James	*Kent* - Rochester
Grains Bar	*Lancaster* - Oldham
Grainsby	*Lincoln* - Great Grimsby
Grainthorpe	*Lincoln* - Louth
Graizelound	*Lincoln* - Gainsborough
Grampound	*Cornwall* - St. Austell
Grampound Road	*Cornwall* - Truro
Granby cum Sutton	*Notts* - Nottingham
Grandborough	*Bucks* - Aylesbury
Grandborough	*Warwick* - Rugby
Grandston	*Pembroke* - Haverfordwest
Grange	*Cumberland* - Carlisle
Grange	*Dorset* - Swanage
Grange-de-Lings	*Lincoln* - Lincoln
Grange Hill	*Durham* - Bishop Auckland
Grange Hill	*Essex* - Ilford
Grange-in-Borrowdale	*Cumberland* - Workington
Grange Lane	*York, W.R.* - Sheffield
Grange-over-Sands	*Lancaster* - Barrow-in-Furness
Grange Park	*Lancaster* - St. Helens
Grange Park	*London, N.21* - Edmonton
Grange Road	*Sussex* - East Grinstead
Grange, The	*Kent* - Cranbrook
Grange Town	*Durham* - Sunderland

Grange Town	*York, N.R.* - Middlesbrough
Grange Villa	*Durham* - Durham
Gransden, Great	*Hunts* - Biggleswade
Gransden, Little	*Cambridge* - Biggleswade
Gransmoor	*York, E.R.* - Bridlington
Grantchester	*Cambridge* - Cambridge
Grantham	*Lincoln* - Grantham
Grantley	*York, W.R.* - Harrogate
Grantsfield	*Hereford* - Leominster
Granville Buildings	*Salop* - Wellington (Salop)
Grappenhall	*Cheshire* - Warrington
Grasby	*Lincoln* - Scunthorpe
Grasless	*Northumberland* - Morpeth
Grasmere	*Westmorland* - Kendal
Grasscroft	*York, W.R.* - Oldham
Grassendale	*Lancaster* - Liverpool
Grassings	*Cumberland* - Carlisle
Grassington	*York, W.R.* - Skipton
Grasslot	*Cumberland* - Workington
Grassmoor	*Derby* - Chesterfield
Grassthorpe	*Notts* - Newark
Grasswell	*Durham* - Durham
Grately	*Hants* - Andover
Gratton	*Derby* - Matlock
Gratton	*Stafford* - Leek
Gratwich	*Stafford* - Uttoxeter
Graveley	*Cambridge* - Huntingdon
Graveley	*Herts* - Hitchin
Gravelly Hill	*Warwick* - Birmingham
Graveney	*Kent* - Canterbury
Gravenhunger	*Salop* - Market Drayton
Gravenhurst, Lower	*Beds* - Hitchin
Gravenhurst, Upper	*Beds* - Hitchin
Gravesend	*Kent* - Gravesend
Graves Park	*York, W.R.* - Sheffield
Grayingham	*Lincoln* - Gainsborough
Grayrigg	*Westmorland* - Kendal
Grays	*Essex* - Grays Thurrock
Grayshott	*Hants* - Aldershot and Farnham
Graythorpe	*Durham* - Hartlepool
Graythwaite	*Lancaster* - Kendal
Grazeley	*Berks* - Reading
Greasbrough	*York, W.R.* - Rotherham
Greasby	*Cheshire* - Birkenhead
Greasley	*Notts* - Nottingham
Great Abington	*Cambridge* - Cambridge
Great Addington	*Northampton* - Wellingborough
Great Alne	*Warwick* - Redditch
Great Amwell	*Herts* - Hertford
Great Ashfield	*Suffolk* - Bury St. Edmunds
Great Aycliffe	*Durham* - Darlington
Great Ayton	*York, N.R.* - Middlesbrough
Great Baddow	*Essex* - Chelmsford
Great Badminton	*Gloucester* - Bristol
Great Bardfield	*Essex* - Braintree
Great Barford	*Beds* - Bedford
Great Barr (part)	*Stafford* - Birmingham
Great Barr (part)	*Stafford* - Walsall
Great Barr (part)	*Stafford* - West Bromwich
Great Barrington	*Gloucester* - Cheltenham
Great Barrow	*Cheshire* - Chester
Great Barton	*Suffolk* - Bury St. Edmunds
Great Barugh	*York, N.R.* - Malton
Great Barwick	*Herts* - Hertford
Great Bavington	*Northumberland* - Hexham
Great Bealings	*Suffolk* - Ipswich
Great Bedwyn	*Wilts* - Swindon
Great Bentley	*Essex* - Colchester
Great Berkhamsted	*Herts* - Hemel Hempstead
Great Billing	*Northampton* - Northampton
Great Billington	*Beds.* - Bletchley and Leighton Buzzard
Great Birch	*Essex* - Colchester
Great Bircham	*Norfolk* - King's Lynn
Great Blakenham	*Suffolk* - Ipswich
Great Bolas	*Salop* - Market Drayton
Great Bolas	*Salop* - Wellington (Salop)
Great Bookham	*Surrey* - Epsom
Great Boughton	*Cheshire* - Chester
Great Bourton	*Oxford* - Banbury

Great Bowden	*Leicester* - Kettering
Great Braxted	*Essex* - Maldon
Great Bricett	*Suffolk* - Stowmarket
Great Brickhill	*Bucks* - Bletchley and Leighton Buzzard
Great Bridge	*Hants* - Southampton
Great Bridge (part)	*Stafford* - Dudley
Great Bridge (part)	*Stafford* - West Bromwich
Great Bridgford	*Stafford* - Stafford
Great Brington	*Northampton* - Northampton
Great Brockhampton	*Gloucester* - Cheltenham
Great Bromley	*Essex* - Colchester
Great Broughton	*Cumberland* - Workington
Great Broughton	*York, N.R.* - Middlesbrough
Great Buckland	*Kent* - Gravesend
Great Budworth	*Cheshire* - Northwich
Great Burdon	*Durham* - Darlington
Great Burstead	*Essex* - Brentwood
Great Busby	*York, N.R.* - Middlesbrough
Great Canfield	*Essex* - Braintree
Great Carlton	*Lincoln* - Louth
Great Casterton	*Rutland* - Stamford
Great Catworth	*Hunts* - Huntingdon
Great Chalfield	*Wilts* - Trowbridge
Great Chart	*Kent* - Ashford
Great Chatwell	*Stafford* - Stafford
Great Chesterford	*Essex* - Cambridge
Great Cheverell	*Wilts* - Devizes
Great Chishill	*Essex* - Cambridge
Great Clacton	*Essex* - Colchester
Great Clifton	*Cumberland* - Workington
Great Coates	*Lincoln* - Great Grimsby
Great Coggeshall	*Essex* - Braintree
Great Comberton	*Worcester* - Evesham
Great Corby	*Cumberland* - Carlisle
Great Cornard	*Suffolk* - Sudbury
Great Cowden	*York, E.R.* - Kingston-upon-Hull
Great Coxwell	*Berks* - Swindon
Great Cressingham	*Norfolk* - King's Lynn
Great Crosthwaite	*Cumberland* - Workington
Great Dalby	*Leicester* - Melton Mowbray
Great Dawley	*Salop* - Wellington (Salop)
Great Doddington	*Northampton* - Wellingborough
Great Driffield	*York, E.R.* - Beverley
Great Dunham	*Norfolk* - King's Lynn
Great Dunmow	*Essex* - Braintree
Great Easby	*Cumberland* - Carlisle
Great Easton	*Essex* - Braintree
Great Easton	*Leicester* - Market Harborough
Great Easton	*Northampton* - Kettering
Great Eccleston	*Lancaster* - Preston
Great Edstone	*York, N.R.* - Malton
Great Ellingham	*Norfolk* - Norwich
Great Elm	*Somerset* - Frome
Great Eppleton	*Durham* - Durham
Great Everdon	*Northampton* - Northampton
Great Eversden	*Cambridge* - Cambridge
Great Faringdon	*Berks* - Didcot
Great Finborough	*Suffolk* - Stowmarket
Greatford	*Lincoln* - Stamford
Great Fransham	*Norfolk* - East Dereham
Great Fryup	*York, N.R.* - Whitby
Great Gaddesden	*Herts* - Hemel Hempstead
Great Gate	*Stafford* - Uttoxeter
Great Gidding	*Hunts* - Huntingdon
Great Givendale	*York, E.R.* - York
Great Glemham	*Suffolk* - Woodbridge
Great Glen	*Leicester* - Leicester
Great Gomersal	*York, W.R.* - Dewsbury
Great Gonerby	*Lincoln* - Grantham
Great Gransden	*Hunts* - Biggleswade
Great Grimsby	*Lincoln* - Great Grimsby
Great Habton	*York, N.R.* - Malton
Great Hale	*Lincoln* - Sleaford
Great Hale Fen	*Lincoln* - Sleaford
Great Hallingbury	*Essex* - Bishop's Stortford
Greatham	*Durham* - Hartlepool
Greatham	*Hants* - Petersfield
Greatham	*Sussex* - Chichester
Great Hampden	*Bucks* - High Wycombe

GRE

Great Hampton	*Worcester* - Evesham
Great Hanwood	*Salop* - Shrewsbury
Great Harrowden	*Northampton* - Wellingborough
Great Harwood	*Lancaster* - Blackburn
Great Haseley	*Oxford* - Thame
Great Hatfield	*York, E.R.* - Beverley
Great Hautbois	*Norfolk* - Norwich
Great Haywood	*Stafford* - Stafford
Great Henny	*Essex* - Sudbury
Great Hinton	*Wilts* - Trowbridge
Great Holland	*Essex* - Colchester
Great Horkesley	*Essex* - Colchester
Great Horton	*York, W.R.* - Bradford
Great Horwood	*Bucks* - Bletchley and Leighton Buzzard
Great Houghton	*Northampton* - Northampton
Great Houghton	*York, W.R.* - Barnsley
Great Howarth	*Lancaster* - Rochdale
Great Hucklow	*Derby* - Buxton
Great Humby	*Lincoln* - Grantham
Great Ilford	*Essex* - Ilford
Great Kelk	*York, E.R.* - Bridlington
Great Kimble	*Bucks* - Aylesbury
Great Kineton	*Warwick* - Stratford on Avon
Great Kingshill	*Bucks* - High Wycombe
Great Langdale	*Westmorland* - Kendal
Great Langton	*York, N.R.* - Northallerton
Great Leighs	*Essex* - Braintree
Great Lever	*Lancaster* - Bolton
Great Limber	*Lincoln* - Great Grimsby
Great Linford	*Bucks* - Bletchley and Leighton Buzzard
Great Linstead	*Suffolk* - Halesworth
Great Livermere	*Suffolk* - Bury St. Edmunds
Great Longstone	*Derby* - Buxton
Great Lumley	*Durham* - Durham
Great Lyth	*Salop* - Shrewsbury
Great Malvern	*Worcester* - Great Malvern
Great Maplestead	*Essex* - Braintree
Great Marlow	*Bucks* - High Wycombe
Great Massingham	*Norfolk* - King's Lynn
Great Melton	*Norfolk* - Norwich
Great Milton	*Oxford* - Thame
Great Missenden	*Bucks* - Amersham
Great Mongeham	*Kent* - Deal
Great Moor	*Cheshire* - Stockport
Great Munden	*Herts* - Hertford
Great Musgrave	*Westmorland* - Penrith
Greatness	*Kent* - Sevenoaks
Great Ness	*Salop* - Shrewsbury
Great Oakley	*Essex* - Harwich
Great Oakley	*Northampton* - Kettering
Great Orme	*Caernarvon* - Conway
Great Ormesby	*Norfolk* - Great Yarmouth
Great Ormside	*Cumberland* - Penrith
Great Orton	*Cumberland* - Carlisle
Great Ouseburn	*York, W.R.* - Harrogate
Great Oxendon	*Northampton* - Northampton
Great Packington	*Warwick* - Coventry
Great Palgrave	*Norfolk* - King's Lynn
Great Paxton	*Hunts* - Huntingdon
Great Plumstead	*Norfolk* - Norwich
Great Ponton	*Lincoln* - Grantham
Great Preston	*York, W.R.* - Pontefract
Great Raveley	*Hunts* - Huntingdon
Great Raynham	*Norfolk* - King's Lynn
Great Ribston	*York, W.R.* - Harrogate
Great Rissington	*Gloucester* - Cheltenham
Great Rollright	*Oxford* - Banbury
Great Rudham	*Norfolk* - King's Lynn
Great Ryburgh	*Norfolk* - King's Lynn
Great Ryle	*Northumberland* - Alnwick
Great Saling	*Essex* - Braintree
Great Salkeld	*Cumberland* - Penrith
Great Sampford	*Essex* - Bishop's Stortford
Great Sankey	*Lancaster* - Warrington
Great Saredon	*Stafford* - Wolverhampton
Great Saxham	*Suffolk* - Bury St. Edmunds
Great Shefford	*Berks* - Newbury
Great Shelford	*Cambridge* - Cambridge

GRE

Great Shurdington	*Gloucester* - Cheltenham
Great Singleton	*Lancaster* - Blackpool
Great Smeaton	*York, N.R.* - Northallerton
Great Snoring	*Norfolk* - King's Lynn
Great Somerford	*Wilts* - Malmesbury
Great Stainton	*Durham* - Stockton on Tees
Great Stambridge	*Essex* - Southend
Great Stanmore	*Middlesex* - Watford
Great Stanney	*Cheshire* - Ellesmere Port
Great Staughton	*Hunts* - Huntingdon
Great Steeping	*Lincoln* - Skegness
Greatstone	*Kent* - Ashford
Great Stretton	*Leicester* - Leicester
Great Strickland	*Westmorland* - Penrith
Great Stukeley	*Hunts* - Huntingdon
Great Sturton	*Lincoln* - Lincoln
Great Sugnall	*Stafford* - Stafford
Great Sutton	*Cheshire* - Ellesmere Port
Great Swinburne	*Northumberland* - Hexham
Great Tew	*Oxford* - Banbury
Great Tey	*Essex* - Colchester
Great Tosson	*Northumberland* - Morpeth
Great Totham	*Essex* - Maldon
Great Tows	*Lincoln* - Louth
Great Urswick	*Lancaster* - Barrow-in-Furness
Great Usworth	*Durham* - Gateshead
Great Wadd	*Kent* - Maidstone
Great Wakering	*Essex* - Southend
Great Waldingfield	*Suffolk* - Sudbury
Great Walsingham	*Norfolk* - King's Lynn
Great Waltham	*Essex* - Chelmsford
Great Warford	*Cheshire* - Macclesfield
Great Warley	*Essex* - Brentwood
Great Washbourne	*Gloucester* - Gloucester
Great Welnetham	*Suffolk* - Bury St. Edmunds
Great Whittington	*Northumberland* - Hexham
Great Wigborough	*Essex* - Colchester
Great Wigston	*Leicester* - Leicester
Great Wilbraham	*Cambridge* - Cambridge
Great Witchingham	*Norfolk* - Norwich
Great Witcombe	*Gloucester* - Cheltenham
Great Witley	*Worcester* - Worcester
Great Wolford	*Warwick* - Stratford on Avon
Great Wollaston	*Salop* - Shrewsbury
Greatwood	*Stafford* - Stafford
Great Woolstone	*Bucks* - Bletchley and Leighton Buzzard
Greatworth	*Northampton* - Banbury
Great Wratting	*Suffolk* - Sudbury
Great Wymondley	*Herts* - Hitchin
Great Wyrley	*Stafford* - Walsall
Great Wytheford	*Salop* - Shrewsbury
Great Yarmouth	*Norfolk* - Great Yarmouth
Great Yeldham	*Essex* - Sudbury
Greave (Rochdale)	*Lancaster* - Rochdale
Grebby	*Lincoln* - Skegness
Gredditch	*Gloucester* - Thornbury
Green	*Denbigh* - Denbigh
Greenacombe Moor	*Devon* - Launceston
Greenacres	*Lancaster* - Oldham
Greenbank	*Cheshire* - Northwich
Green Bank	*Lancaster* - Barrow-in-Furness
Greenbooth	*Lancaster* - Rochdale
Greenbottom	*Cornwall* - Truro
Green Bottom	*Gloucester* - Gloucester
Greenclose (Whitchurch)	*Glamorgan* - Cardiff
Green End (Kempston)	*Beds* - Bedford
Greenend	*Bucks* - High Wycombe
Green End	*Herts* - Hertford
Greenend	*Herts* - Hitchin
Greenend (Hemel Hempstead)	*Herts* - St. Albans
Greeneys	*Lancaster* - Manchester
Greenfield	*Beds* - Bedford
Greenfield	*Flint* - Holywell
Greenfield	*Lincoln* - Louth
Greenfield	*York, W.R.* - Oldham
Greenfields	*Stafford* - Stoke-on-Trent
Greenford	*Middlesex* - Brentford

GRE

Greengate	*Lancaster* - Salford
Greengates	*York, W.R.* - Bradford
Greengill	*Cumberland* - Workington
Green Hailey	*Bucks* - High Wycombe
Greenhalgh	*Lancaster* - Preston
Greenham	*Berks* - Newbury
Greenham	*Somerset* - Taunton
Greenham	*Somerset* - Yeovil
Green Hammerton	*York, W.R.* - Harrogate
Green Haugh	*Northumberland* - Haltwhistle
Green Haugh	*Northumberland* - Hexham
Greenhaume	*Lancaster* - Barrow-in-Furness
Green Haworth	*Lancaster* - Accrington
Greenhead	*Northumberland* - Hexham
Green Heath	*Stafford* - Walsall
Greenhill	*Cumberland* - Carlisle
Greenhill	*York, W.R.* - Sheffield
Greenhill	*Glamorgan* - Swansea
Greenhill	*Gloucester* - Thornbury
Greenhill	*Hants* - Winchester
Greenhill	*Salop* - Oswestry
Greenhill	*Wilts* - Swindon
Greenhithe (part)	*Kent* - Dartford
Greenhithe (part)	*Kent* - Gravesend
Greenholme	*Westmorland* - Penrith
Greenhouses	*York, N.R.* - Whitby
Greenhow	*York, W.R.* - Harrogate
Greenhowe	*York, N.R.* - Whitby
Greenhurst	*Salop* - Market Drayton
Green Island	*Dorset* - Poole
Greenlands	*Worcester* - Redditch
Green Lane	*Dorset* - Shaftesbury
Green Lane	*Montgomery* - Newtown
Green Lane	*Salop* - Wellington (Salop)
Greenleighton	*Northumberland* - Morpeth
Greenley Cleugh	*Northumberland* - Hexham
Green Lowe	*Derby* - Matlock
Green Meadow	*Glamorgan* - Bridgend
Greenmeadow (Tongwynlais)	*Glamorgan* - Cardiff
Greenmount	*Lancaster* - Bury
Greenodd	*Lancaster* - Barrow-in-Furness
Green Quarries	*Cumberland* - Carlisle
Greens	*Northumberland* - Alnwick
Greenscoe	*Lancaster* - Barrow-in-Furness
Greenshaw Hill	*Northumberland* - Alnwick
Greenside	*Durham* - Newcastle-upon-Tyne
Green's Norton	*Northampton* - Northampton
Greensplat	*Cornwall* - St. Austell
Greenspot	*Cumberland* - Carlisle
Greenstead	*Essex* - Brentwood
Greenstead	*Essex* - Colchester
Greenstreet Green (Farnborough)	*Kent* - Bromley
Greenstreet Green	*Kent* - Dartford
Green, The	*Cumberland* - Whitehaven
Greenthorne	*Lancaster* - Bolton
Green Tye	*Herts* - Bishop's Stortford
Greenway	*Gloucester* - Gloucester
Greenwell	*Cumberland* - Carlisle
Greenwich	*Derby* - Alfreton
Greenwich	*London, S.E.10* - Woolwich
Greenwood House	*Cumberland* - Carlisle
Greet	*Gloucester* - Cheltenham
Greet	*Warwick* - Birmingham
Greete	*Salop* - Ludlow
Greetham	*Lincoln* - Lincoln
Greetham	*Rutland* - Melton Mowbray
Greetland	*York, W.R.* - Halifax
Greet's Green	*Stafford* - West Bromwich
Greetwell	*Lincoln* - Lincoln
Greetwell	*Lincoln* - Scunthorpe
Gregson Lane	*Lancaster* - Preston
Greinton	*Somerset* - Bridgwater
Grendon	*Northampton* - Wellingborough
Grendon	*Warwick* - Tamworth
Grendon Bishop	*Hereford* - Leominster
Grendon Underwood	*Bucks* - Aylesbury
Grendon Warren	*Hereford* - Hereford

GRE - GRI

Grenfell Park	*Glamorgan* - Swansea
Grenofen	*Devon* - Plymouth
Grenoside	*York, W.R.* - Sheffield
Grenowood Head	*York, W.R.* - Sheffield
Gresford	*Denbigh* - Wrexham
Gresham	*Norfolk* - Norwich
Gressenhall	*Norfolk* - East Dereham
Gressingham	*Lancaster* - Lancaster
Gresty	*Cheshire* - Crewe
Greta Bridge	*York, N.R.* - Darlington
Gretna Junction	*Cumberland* - Carlisle
Gretton	*Gloucester* - Cheltenham
Gretton	*Northampton* - Corby
Gretton	*Salop* - Shrewsbury
Gretton Fields	*Gloucester* - Cheltenham
Grewelthorpe	*York, W.R.* - Harrogate
Greylake	*Somerset* - Bridgwater
Grey's Forest	*Northumberland* - Berwick-upon-Tweed
Grey's Green	*Oxford* - Reading
Greysouthen	*Cumberland* - Workington
Greystead	*Northumberland* - Hexham
Greystoke	*Cumberland* - Penrith
Greystones	*York, W.R.* - Sheffield
Greywell	*Hants* - Basingstoke
Grianrhyd	*Denbigh* - Denbigh
Gribdale	*York, N.R.* - Middlesbrough
Griff	*Warwick* - Nuneaton
Griff Grange	*Derby* - Matlock
Griffins Hill	*Warwick* - Birmingham
Griffithstown	*Monmouth* - Pontypool and Abergavenny
Griffydam	*Leicester* - Ashby-de-la-Zouch
Griggs Green	*Hants* - Petersfield
Grillis Moor	*Cornwall* - Redruth
Grimblethorpe	*Lincoln* - Louth
Grimes Hill	*Worcester* - Birmingham
Grimesthorpe	*York, W.R.* - Sheffield
Grimethorpe	*York, W.R.* - Barnsley
Grimley	*Worcester* - Worcester
Grimoldby	*Lincoln* - Louth
Grimpo	*Salop* - Oswestry
Grimsargh	*Lancaster* - Preston
Grimsby, Great	*Lincoln* - Great Grimsby
Grimsby, Little	*Lincoln* - Louth
Grimscote	*Northampton* - Northampton
Grimstead, East	*Wilts* - Salisbury
Grimstead, West	*Wilts* - Salisbury
Grimsthorpe	*Lincoln* - Spalding
Grimston	*Leicester* - Melton Mowbray
Grimston	*Norfolk* - King's Lynn
Grimston	*York, E.R.* - Kingston-upon-Hull
Grimston	*York, E.R.* - York
Grimston	*York, N.R.* - Malton
Grimston	*York, W.R.* - York
Grimstone	*Dorset* - Dorchester
Grimston, Little	*York, W.R.* - York
Grimston, North	*York, E.R.* - Malton
Grimston Park	*York, W.R.* - York
Grimthorpe	*York, E.R.* - York
Grimwith	*York, W.R.* - Skipton
Grin	*Derby* - Buxton
Grindale	*York, E.R.* - Bridlington
Grindleford	*Derby* - Sheffield
Grindle in Ryton	*Salop* - Bridgnorth
Grindleton	*York, W.R.* - Blackburn
Grindley	*Stafford* - Stafford
Grindley Brook	*Salop* - Whitchurch
Grindlow	*Derby* - Buxton
Grindon	*Durham* - Stockton on Tees
Grindon	*Durham* - Sunderland
Grindon	*Northumberland* - Hexham
Grindon	*Stafford* - Leek
Gringley Carr	*Notts* - East Retford
Gringley Grange	*Notts* - East Retford
Gringley, Little	*Notts* - East Retford
Gringley Lock	*Notts* - East Retford
Gringley-on-the-Hill	*Notts* - East Retford
Grinkle Park	*York, N.R.* - Whitby
Grinsdale	*Cumberland* - Carlisle

GRI - GUI

Grinshill	*Salop* - Shrewsbury
Grinstead, East	*Sussex* - East Grinstead
Grinstead, West	*Sussex* - Horsham
Grinton	*York, N.R.* - Darlington
Grisedale	*Lancaster* - Kendal
Gristhorpe	*York, N.R.* - Scarborough
Griston	*Norfolk* - King's Lynn
Gritnam	*Hants* - Southampton
Grittenham	*Wilts* - Malmesbury
Grittleton	*Wilts* - Chippenham
Grizebeck	*Lancaster* - Barrow-in-Furness
Groby	*Leicester* - Leicester
Groes	*Denbigh* - Denbigh
Groes Faen	*Glamorgan* - Cardiff
Groesfaen	*Glamorgan* - Pontypridd
Groesfawr	*Denbigh* - Denbigh
Groesffordd	*Caernarvon* - Conway
Groesford	*Brecon* - Brecknock
Groeslon	*Caernarvon* - Caernarvon
Groeswen	*Glamorgan* - Caerphilly
Groeswen	*Glamorgan* - Pontypridd
Groesynydd	*Caernarvon* - Conway
Gromford	*Suffolk* - Woodbridge
Gronant	*Flint* - Holywell
Grondre	*Pembroke* - Haverfordwest
Groombridge	*Kent* - Tunbridge Wells
Groombridge	*Sussex* - Tunbridge Wells
Groombridge	*Sussex* - East Grinstead
Grosmont	*Monmouth* - Pontypool and Abergavenny
Grosmont	*York, N.R.* - Whitby
Groton	*Suffolk* - Sudbury
Grotton	*York, W.R.* - Oldham
Groundslow Fields	*Stafford* - Stoke-on-Trent
Grove	*Berks* - Didcot
Grove	*Bucks* - Bletchley and Leighton Buzzard
Grove	*Kent* - Canterbury
Grove	*Notts* - East Retford
Grove Common	*Hereford* - Monmouth
Grove Ferry	*Kent* - Canterbury
Grovehill	*Herts* - Hemel Hempstead
Grovehurst	*Kent* - Sittingbourne
Grovely	*Wilts* - Salisbury
Grove Park	*London, S.E.12* - Bromley
Grovesend	*Glamorgan* - Swansea
Grovesend	*Gloucester* - Thornbury
Grove, The	*Worcester* - Cheltenham
Grovetown	*York, W.R.* - Pontefract
Grubb's Farn	*Herts* - Hertford
Grubhill	*Lincoln* - Lincoln
Grumbla	*Cornwall* - Penzance
Grundisburgh	*Suffolk* - Ipswich
Grunty Fen	*Cambridge* - Ely
Grwynefechan	*Brecon* - Pontypool and Abergavenny
Grwyne-y-fawr	*Brecon* - Pontypool and Abergavenny
Guadaloupe, Old	*Leicester* - Melton Mowbray
Guards	*Cumberland* - Carlisle
Guarlford	*Worcester* - Great Malvern
Gubbershill	*Gloucester* - Cheltenham
Gubblecote	*Herts* - Aylesbury
Gubeon	*Northumberland* - Morpeth
Gubshill	*Gloucester* - Cheltenham
Guestling	*Sussex* - Hastings
Guestwick	*Norfolk* - Norwich
Guide Bridge	*Lancaster* - Ashton-under-Lyne
Guide Post	*Northumberland* - Blyth
Guildeford, East	*Sussex* - Hastings
Guilden Down	*Salop* - Ludlow
Guilden Morden	*Cambridge* - Hitchin
Guilden Sutton	*Cheshire* - Chester
Guildford	*Cornwall* - Redruth
Guildford	*Surrey* - Guildford
Guilsborough	*Northampton* - Northampton
Guilsfield	*Montgomery* - Welshpool
Guilthwaite	*York, W.R.* - Rotherham
Guilton	*Kent* - Deal
Guisborough	*York, N.R.* - Middlesbrough

GUI - GYR

Guiseley	*York, W.R.* - Otley
Guist	*Norfolk* - King's Lynn
Guiting Hill	*Gloucester* - Cheltenham
Guiting, Lower	*Gloucester* - Cheltenham
Guiting Power	*Gloucester* - Cheltenham
Gulval	*Cornwall* - Penzance
Gulworthy	*Devon* - Plymouth
Gumfreston	*Pembroke* - Haverfordwest
Gumley	*Leicester* - Leicester
Gunby	*Lincoln* - Grantham
Gunby	*Lincoln* - Skegness
Gunby	*York, E.R.* - York
Gundenham	*Somerset* - Taunton
Gun Green	*Kent* - Cranbrook
Gunheath	*Cornwall* - St. Austell
Gunnerside	*York, N.R.* - Darlington
Gunnerton	*Northumberland* - Hexham
Gunness	*Lincoln* - Scunthorpe
Gunnislake	*Cornwall* - Plymouth
Gunston	*Stafford* - Wolverhampton
Gunters Bridge	*Sussex* - Chichester
Gunthorpe	*Lincoln* - Gainsborough
Gunthorpe	*Norfolk* - King's Lynn
Gunthorpe	*Notts* - Nottingham
Gunthorpe	*Rutland* - Melton Mowbray
Gunton	*Norfolk* - Norwich
Gunville	*I. of W.* - Newport (I.W.)
Gunwalloe	*Cornwall* - Penzance
Gupworthy	*Somerset* - Tiverton
Gurnard	*I. of W.* - Newport (I.W.)
Gurnett	*Cheshire* - Macclesfield
Gurney Slade	*Somerset* - Wells
Gurney Valley	*Durham* - Bishop Auckland
Gussage All Saints	*Dorset* - Wimborne Minster
Gussage St. Andrew	*Dorset* - Salisbury
Gussage St. Michael	*Dorset* - Wimborne Minster
Gustard Wood	*Herts* - St. Albans
Guston	*Kent* - Dover
Gutch Common	*Dorset* - Shaftesbury
Guthram Court	*Lincoln* - Spalding
Guthram Gowt	*Lincoln* - Spalding
Guyhirne	*Cambridge* - Wisbech
Guys Cliffe	*Warwick* - Warwick
Guyzance	*Northumberland* - Alnwick
Gwaelodygarth	*Glamorgan* - Cardiff
Gwaenysgor	*Flint* - Holywell
Gwalchmai	*Anglesey* - Llangefni
Gwaun-cae-Gurwen	*Glamorgan* - Ammanford
Gwaun Valley	*Cardigan* - Cardigan
Gwbert-on-Sea	*Cardigan* - Cardigan
Gweek (part)	*Cornwall* - Truro and Falmouth
Gweek (part)	*Cornwall* - Penzance
Gwehelog	*Monmouth* - Pontypool and Abergavenny
Gwenddwr	*Brecon* - Builth
Gwennap	*Cornwall* - Redruth
Gwernaffield	*Flint* - Mold
Gwernesney	*Monmouth* - Pontypool and Abergavenny
Gwernogle	*Carmarthen* - Lampeter
Gwernymynydd	*Flint* - Mold
Gwersyllt	*Denbigh* - Wrexham
Gwespyr	*Flint* - Holywell
Gwinear	*Cornwall* - Redruth
Gwithian	*Cornwall* - Redruth
Gwddelwern	*Merioneth* - Denbigh
Gwyddgrug	*Carmarthen* - Carmarthen
Gwynfe	*Carmarthen* - Llandovery
Gwynfil	*Cardigan* - Lampeter
Gwynfryn	*Denbigh* - Wrexham
Gwynfryn Llanbedr	*Merioneth* - Portmadoc
Gwystre	*Radnor* - Llandrindod Wells
Gwytherin	*Denbigh* - Conway
Gyfelia	*Denbigh* - Wrexham
Gyffin	*Caernarvon* - Conway
Gyffylliog	*Denbigh* - Denbigh
Gyrngoch	*Caernarvon* - Caernarvon
Gyrt	*Denbigh* - Denbigh

H - HAG

Habberley	*Salop* - Shrewsbury
Habberley	*Worcester* - Kidderminster
Habblesthorpe	*Notts* - East Retford
Habergham Eaves	*Lancaster* - Burnley
Habertoft	*Lincoln* - Skegness
Habin Fyning	*Sussex* - Petersfield
Habrough	*Lincoln* - Great Grimsby
Habton, Great	*York, N.R.* - Malton
Habton, Little	*York, N.R.* - Malton
Hacconby	*Lincoln* - Spalding
Hacconby Fen	*Lincoln* - Spalding
Haceby	*Lincoln* - Sleaford
Hacheston	*Suffolk* - Woodbridge
Hackbridge	*Surrey* - Croydon
Hackenthorpe	*Derby* - Sheffield
Hackets	*Herts* - Hertford
Hackett, The	*Gloucester* - Thornbury
Hackford	*Norfolk* - Norwich
Hackforth	*York, N.R.* - Northallerton
Hackington	*Kent* - Canterbury
Hackleton	*Northampton* - Northampton
Hackman's Gate	*Worcester* - Stourbridge
Hackness	*York, N.R.* - Scarborough
Hackney	*London, E.8* - Shoreditch
Hackney, South	*London, E.9* - Shoreditch
Hackney, Upper	*Derby* - Matlock
Hackney, West	*London, E.8* - Shoreditch
Hackney Wick	*London, E.9* - Shoreditch
Hackthorne	*Lincoln* - Lincoln
Hackthorpe	*Westmorland* - Penrith
Haddenham	*Bucks* - Thame
Haddenham	*Cambridge* - Ely
Haddenham, Low	*Bucks* - Thame
Haddens	*York, W.R.* - Ashton-under-Lyne
Haddington	*Lincoln* - Lincoln
Haddiscoe	*Norfolk* - Great Yarmouth
Haddlesey, West	*York, W.R.* - Pontefract
Haddon	*Derby* - Matlock
Haddon	*Hunts* - Peterborough
Haddon, East	*Northampton* - Northampton
Haddon Lane	*Stafford* - Stoke-on-Trent
Haddon, West	*Northampton* - Rugby
Hade Edge	*York, W.R.* - Huddersfield
Hademore	*Stafford* - Lichfield
Haden Hill	*Stafford* - Dudley
Hadfield	*Derby* - Hyde
Hadham, Little	*Herts* - Bishop's Stortford
Hadham, Much	*Herts* - Bishop's Stortford
Hadleigh	*Essex* - Southend
Hadleigh	*Suffolk* - Ipswich
Hadley	*Herts* - Barnet
Hadley	*Salop* - Wellington (Salop)
Hadley	*Worcester* - Worcester
Hadley End (Yoxall)	*Stafford* - Lichfield
Hadley Lodge	*Salop* - Wellington (Salop)
Hadley, New	*Salop* - Wellington (Salop)
Hadlow	*Kent* - Tonbridge
Hadlow Common	*Kent* - Tonbridge
Hadlow Down	*Sussex* - Lewes
Hadnall	*Salop* - Shrewsbury
Hadspen	*Somerset* - Yeovil
Hadstock	*Essex* - Cambridge
Hadstone	*Northumberland* - Morpeth
Hadzor	*Worcester* - Worcester
Hafod	*Denbigh* - Wrexham
Hafod	*Glamorgan* - Swansea
Hafodelwy	*Denbigh* - Denbigh
Hafodyrynys (part)	*Monmouth* - Blackwood
Hafodyrynys (part)	*Monmouth* - Pontypool and Abergavenny
Hagbourne, East	*Berks* - Didcot
Hagbourne, West	*Berks* - Didcot
Hag Fold	*Lancs* - Leigh
Hagg	*York, W.R.* - Huddersfield
Haggate	*Lancaster* - Burnley
Haggerleazes	*Durham* - Bishop Auckland
Haggerston	*London, E.8* - Shoreditch
Haggerston	*Northumberland* - Berwick-upon-Tweed
Haggoufields	*Notts* - Worksop

HAG - HAL

Haggs	*Cumberland* - Carlisle
Hagg, Upper	*York, W.R.* - Huddersfield
Hagley	*Hereford* - Hereford
Hagley	*Worcester* - Stourbridge
Hagnaby	*Lincoln* - Louth
Hagnaby	*Lincoln* - Skegness
Hague Bar	*Derby* - Buxton
Hagworthingham	*Lincoln* - Skegness
Haigh	*Lancaster* - Wigan
Haigh	*York, W.R.* - Barnsley
Haighton	*Lancaster* - Preston
Haile	*Cumberland* - Whitehaven
Hailes	*Gloucester* - Cheltenham
Hailey	*Herts* - Hertford
Hailey (Ipsden)	*Oxford* - Didcot
Hailey	*Oxford* - Witney
Haileybury	*Herts* - Hertford
Hailsham	*Sussex* - Eastbourne
Hail Weston	*Hunts* - Huntingdon
Hainault	*Essex* - Ilford
Haine	*Kent* - Ramsgate
Haines Hill	*Berks* - Reading
Hainford	*Norfolk* - Norwich
Hainworth	*York, W.R.* - Keighley
Hainton	*Lincoln* - Louth
Haisthorpe	*York, E.R.* - Bridlington
Hakin	*Pembroke* - Haverfordwest
Halam	*Notts* - Newark
Halamanning	*Cornwall* - Penzance
Halberton	*Devon* - Tiverton
Halden, High	*Kent* - Cranbrook
Haldenby	*York, W.R.* - Goole
Halden Place	*Kent* - Cranbrook
Hale	*Cheshire* - Altrincham
Hale	*Lancaster* - St. Helens
Hale	*Surrey* - Aldershot and Farnham
Hale	*Westmorland* - Kendal
Hale	*Wilts* - Salisbury
Halebank	*Lancaster* - St. Helens
Hale Barns	*Cheshire* - Altrincham
Halecote (Witherslack)	*Westmorland* - Kendal
Hale Fen, Great	*Lincoln* - Sleaford
Hale Fen, Little	*Lincoln* - Sleaford
Hale, Great	*Lincoln* - Sleaford
Hale, Little	*Lincoln* - Sleaford
Hales	*Norfolk* - Norwich
Hales	*Stafford* - Market Drayton
Halesfield	*Salop* - Wellington (Salop)
Halesowen	*Worcester* - Stourbridge
Halesworth	*Suffolk* - Halesworth
Hale, The	*London, N.W.7* - Willesden
Hale, Upper	*Surrey* - Aldershot and Farnham
Halewood	*Lancaster* - St. Helens
Half Key	*Worcester* - Great Malvern
Halford	*Warwick* - Stratford on Avon
Halfpenny Green	*Stafford* - Stourbridge
Halfway	*Carmarthen* - Llandovery
Halfway	*Carmarthen* - Llanelli
Halfway	*Derby* - Sheffield
Halfway Bridge	*Caernarvon* - Bangor
Halfway Bridge	*Sussex* - Chichester
Halfway House	*Salop* - Shrewsbury
Halghton	*Flint* - Whitchurch
Halifax	*York, W.R.* - Halifax
Halkyn	*Flint* - Holywell
Hallam Fields	*Derby* - Ilkeston
Hallam, Little	*Derby* - Ilkeston
Hallam, Nether	*York, W.R.* - Sheffield
Hallam, Upper	*York, W.R.* - Sheffield
Hallam, West	*Derby* - Ilkeston
Halland	*Sussex* - Lewes
Hallas Bridge	*York, W.R.* - Keighley
Hallaton	*Leicester* - Corby
Hallatrow	*Somerset* - Bristol
Hall Bank	*Cumberland* - Workington
Hallbankgate	*Cumberland* - Carlisle
Hall Bower	*York, W.R.* - Huddersfield
Hallburn	*Cumberland* - Carlisle
Hall Carr	*Lancaster* - Rawtenstall
Hallen	*Gloucester* - Thornbury

HAL - HAM

Hall End	*Stafford* - West Bromwich
Hall End	*Warwick* - Tamworth
Hallfield Gate	*Derby* - Alfreton
Hall Green	*Lancaster* - Wigan
Hall Green	*Stafford* - Wolverhampton
Hall Green	*Stafford* - West Bromwich
Hall Green	*Warwick* - Birmingham
Hall Green	*York, W.R.* - Wakefield
Hall Green, Old	*Herts* - Hertford
Halliford	*Middlesex* - Kingston-upon-Thames
Hallingbury Great	*Essex* - Bishop's Stortford
Hallingbury, Little	*Essex* - Bishop's Stortford
Halling, Lower	*Kent* - Rochester
Hallington	*Lincoln* - Louth
Hallington	*Northumberland* - Hexham
Halling, Upper	*Kent* - Rochester
Hall-i-th-Wood	*Lancaster* - Bolton
Halliwell	*Lancaster* - Bolton
Halloughton	*Notts* - Newark
Hallow	*Worcester* - Worcester
Hallsands	*Devon* - Kingsbridge
Halls Green	*Herts* - Hitchin
Hall's Green	*Kent* - Sevenoaks
Hallthwaites	*Cumberland* - Whitehaven
Hallwood Green	*Gloucester* - Gloucester
Hallworthy	*Cornwall* - Launceston
Halmerend	*Stafford* - Stoke-on-Trent
Halmore	*Gloucester* - Stroud
Halnaby	*York, N.R.* - Darlington
Halnaker	*Sussex* - Chichester
Halsall	*Lancaster* - Southport
Halse	*Northampton* - Banbury
Halse	*Somerset* - Taunton
Halsetown	*Cornwall* - Penzance
Halsham, East	*York, E.R.* - Kingston-upon-Hull
Halsham, West	*York, E.R.* - Kingston-upon-Hull
Halshaw Moor	*Lancaster* - Bolton
Halstead	*Essex* - Braintree
Halstead	*Kent* - Sevenoaks
Halstead	*Leicester* - Leicester
Halstock	*Dorset* - Yeovil
Halstock Leigh	*Dorset* - Yeovil
Halston	*Salop* - Oswestry
Halston	*Salop* - Shrewsbury
Halstow	*Kent* - Sittingbourne
Halstow, High	*Kent* - Rochester
Halstow, Lower	*Kent* - Sittingbourne
Haltcliffe Bridge	*Cumberland* - Penrith
Halterworth	*Hants* - Southampton
Haltham	*Lincoln* - Boston
Haltham Fen Allotment	*Lincoln* - Boston
Halton	*Bucks* - Aylesbury
Halton	*Cheshire* - Runcorn
Halton	*Lancaster* - Lancaster
Halton	*Northumberland* - Hexham
Halton	*Sussex* - Hastings
Halton	*York, W.R.* - Leeds
Halton, East	*Lincoln* - Great Grimsby
Halton, East	*York, W.R.* - Skipton
Halton Gill	*York, W.R.* - Skipton
Halton Holegate	*Lincoln* - Skegness
Halton-Lea-Gate	*Northumberland* - Carlisle
Halton Quay	*Cornwall* - Liskeard
Halton Shields	*Northumberland* - Hexham
Halton Skitter	*Lincoln* - Great Grimsby
Halton View	*Lancaster* - St. Helens
Halton, West	*Lincoln* - Scunthorpe
Halton, West	*York, W.R.* - Skipton
Haltwhistle	*Northumberland* - Hexham
Halvergate	*Norfolk* - Great Yarmouth
Halvosso	*Cornwall* - Truro
Halwell	*Devon* - Kingsbridge
Halwill	*Devon* - Launceston
Halwill Junction	*Devon* - Launceston
Halwin	*Cornwall* - Penzance
Halworthy	*Cornwall* - Launceston
Ham	*Bucks* - High Wycombe
Ham	*Gloucester* - Cheltenham
Ham	*Gloucester* - Stroud
Ham	*Kent* - Deal

Ham	*Kent* - Canterbury
Ham	*Somerset* - Taunton
Ham	*Surrey* - Kingston-upon-Thames
Ham	*Wilts* - Newbury
Hamble	*Hants* - Southampton
Hambleden	*Bucks* - Reading
Hambledon	*Hants* - Portsmouth
Hambledon	*Surrey* - Guildford
Hambleton	*Lancaster* - Blackpool
Hambleton	*York, N.R.* - Malton
Hambleton	*York, W.R.* - York
Hambleton, Higher	*Rutland* - Melton Mowbray
Hambleton, Lower	*Rutland* - Melton Mowbray
Hambleton, Middle	*Rutland* - Melton Mowbray
Hambridge	*Somerset* - Taunton
Hambrook	*Gloucester* - Bristol
Hambrook	*Sussex* - Chichester
Ham, Coombe St. Nicholas	*Somerset* - Axminster and Chard
Ham, East	*London, E.6* - Bow
Hameringham	*Lincoln* - Skegness
Hamerton	*Hunts* - Huntingdon
Hamfallow	*Gloucester* - Stroud
Ham Green	*Kent* - Sittingbourne
Ham Green	*Somerset* - Bristol
Ham Green	*Worcester* - Redditch
Ham, High	*Somerset* - Bridgwater
Hamilton Row	*Durham* - Durham
Hamlet, East	*Salop* - Ludlow
Hamlet of St. Martin	*Pembroke* - Haverfordwest
Hamlet of St. Thomas	*Pembroke* - Haverfordwest
Hamley Heath	*Stafford* - Stafford
Ham, Low	*Somerset* - Bridgwater
Hammer	*Hants* - Petersfield
Hammer	*Sussex* - Petersfield
Hammerfield	*Herts* - St. Albans
Hammersmith	*Derby* - Alfreton
Hammersmith (part)	*London, W.6* - Brentford
Hammersmith (part)	*London, W.6* - West London
Hammerwich	*Stafford* - Lichfield
Hammerwood	*Sussex* - East Grinstead
Hammill	*Kent* - Deal
Hammonds Green	*Salop* - Ludlow
Hammoon	*Dorset* - Shaftesbury
Hamnish Clifford	*Hereford* - Leominster
Hampden, Great	*Bucks* - High Wycombe
Hampden, Little	*Bucks* - High Wycombe
Hampden Park	*Sussex* - Eastbourne
Hampen	*Gloucester* - Cheltenham
Hampen Hill	*Gloucester* - Cheltenham
Hampeth Colliery	*Northumberland* - Alnwick
Hampnett	*Gloucester* - Cheltenham
Hampole	*York, W.R.* - Doncaster
Hampreston	*Dorset* - Wimborne Minster
Hampstead	*London, N.W.3* - Bloomsbury and Marylebone
Hampstead Garden Suburb (part)	*London, N.W.11* - Barnet
Hampstead Garden Suburb (part)	*London, N.W.11* - Willesden
Hampstead Marshall	*Berks* - Newbury
Hampstead Norris	*Berks* - Newbury
Hampsthwaite	*York, W.R.* - Harrogate
Ham, Stockland	*Devon* - Axminster and Chard
Hampt	*Cornwall* - Launceston
Hampton	*Cheshire* - Whitchurch
Hampton	*Kent* - Canterbury
Hampton	*Middlesex* - Kingston-upon-Thames
Hampton	*Wilts* - Swindon
Hampton Bank	*Salop* - Oswestry
Hampton Bishop	*Hereford* - Hereford
Hampton Charles	*Hereford* - Leominster
Hampton Court	*Middlesex* - Kingston-upon-Thames
Hampton Fields	*Gloucester* - Stroud
Hampton Gay	*Oxford* - Oxford
Hampton, Great	*Worcester* - Evesham
Hampton Heath	*Cheshire* - Whitchurch
Hampton Hill	*Middlesex* - Kingston-upon-Thames
Hampton in Arden	*Warwick* - Birmingham
Hampton, Little	*Worcester* - Evesham

Hampton Load	*Salop* - Bridgnorth
Hampton Lovett	*Worcester* - Bromsgrove
Hampton Lucy	*Warwick* - Stratford on Avon
Hampton Magna	*Warwick* - Warwick
Hampton-on-the-Hill	*Warwick* - Warwick
Hampton Park	*Hereford* - Hereford
Hampton Poyle	*Oxford* - Oxford
Hampton Wafer	*Hereford* - Leominster
Hampton Wick	*Middlesex* - Kingston-upon-Thames
Hampton Wood	*Salop* - Oswestry
Hamptworth	*Wilts* - Salisbury
Hamstall Ridware	*Stafford* - Lichfield
Hamstead	*Stafford* - West Bromwich
Hamsteels	*Durham* - Durham
Hamsterley	*Durham* - Bishop Auckland
Hamsterley Colliery	*Durham* - Consett
Hamsterley Mill	*Durham* - Consett
Ham Street	*Kent* - Ashford
Hamswell	*Gloucester* - Bath
Ham, West	*London, E.15* - Bow
Hamworthy	*Dorset* - Poole
Hanbury	*Stafford* - Burton-upon-Trent
Hanbury	*Worcester* - Bromsgrove
Hanbury Woodend	*Stafford* - Burton-upon-Trent
Hanby	*Lincoln* - Grantham
Hanch	*Stafford* - Lichfield
Hanchurch	*Stafford* - Stoke-on-Trent
Handborough, Long	*Oxford* - Witney
Handbridge	*Cheshire* - Chester
Handcross	*Sussex* - Haywards Heath
Handford	*Dorset* - Shafetsbury
Handford	*Stafford* - Stoke-on-Trent
Handforth	*Cheshire* - Macclesfield
Hand-in-Hold	*Durham* - Durham
Handley	*Cheshire* - Chester
Handley	*Derby* - Alfreton
Handley	*Dorset* - Salisbury
Handley	*Northampton* - Northampton
Handley Green	*Essex* - Chelmsford
Handley, Middle	*Derby* - Chesterfield
Handley, Nether	*Derby* - Chesterfield
Handley, West	*Derby* - Chesterfield
Handsacre	*Stafford* - Lichfield
Handsworth	*Warwick* - Birmingham
Handsworth	*York, W.R.* - Sheffield
Handy Cross	*Bucks* - High Wycombe
Hanger	*Wilts* - Chippenham
Hangerberry	*Glos* - Gloucester
Hanging Bridge	*Derby* - Derby
Hanging Grimston	*York, E R.* - York
Hanging Heaton	*York, W.R.* - Dewsbury
Hanging Houghton	*Northampton* - Northampton
Hanging Langford	*Wilts* - Salisbury
Hanging Shaw	*Northumberland* - Carlisle
Hangleton	*Sussex* - Brighton
Hangleton	*Sussex* - Worthing
Hankelow	*Cheshire* - Crewe
Hankerton	*Wilts* - Malmesbury
Hankham	*Sussex* - Eastbourne
Hanley	*Stafford* - Stoke-on-Trent
Hanley Castle	*Worcester* - Great Malvern
Hanley Child	*Worcester* - Kidderminster
Hanley Swan	*Worcester* - Great Malvern
Hanley William	*Worcester* - Kidderminster
Hanlith	*York, W.R.* - Skipton
Hanmer	*Flint* - Whitchurch
Hannah	*Lincoln* - Louth
Hanney, East	*Berks* - Didcot
Hanney, West	*Berks* - Didcot
Hanningfield, East	*Essex* - Chelmsford
Hanningfield, West	*Essex* - Chelmsford
Hannington	*Hants* - Newbury
Hannington	*Northampton* - Northampton
Hannington	*Wilts* - Swindon
Hanslope	*Bucks* - Northampton
Hanthorpe	*Lincoln* - Spalding
Hanwell	*London, W.7* - Brentford
Hanwell	*Oxford* - Banbury
Hanwell Mental Hospital	*Middlesex* - Uxbridge
Hanwood, Great	*Salop* - Shrewsbury

HAN - HAR

Hanworth	*Middlesex* - Brentford
Hanworth	*Norfolk* - Norwich
Happerton	*Somerset* - Bristol
Happisburgh	*Norfolk* - Norwich
Hapsford	*Cheshire* - Chester
Hapstead	*Sussex* - Haywards Heath
Hapton	*Lancaster* - Burnley
Hapton	*Norfolk* - Norwich
Harbarrow	*Lancaster* - Barrow-in-Furness
Harberton	*Devon* - Kingsbridge
Harberton Ford	*Devon* - Kingsbridge
Harbledown	*Kent* - Canterbury
Harborne	*Warwick* - Birmingham
Harborough	*Worcester* - Kidderminster
Harborough Magna	*Warwick* - Rugby
Harborough Parva	*Warwick* - Rugby
Harbottle	*Northumberland* - Morpeth
Harbourne	*Kent* - Cranbrook
Harbridge	*Hants* - Salisbury
Harbury	*Warwick* - Warwick
Harbury Heath	*Warwick* - Warwick
Harby	*Leicester* - Melton Mowbray
Harby	*Notts* - Lincoln
Harcombe	*Devon* - Exeter
Harcombe Bottom	*Devon* - Axminster and Chard
Harcourt	*Salop* - Shrewsbury
Hardcake Hall	*Cumberland* - Carlisle
Hardcastle	*York, W.R.* - Harrogate
Hard Edge	*Cumberland* - Haltwhistle
Harden	*Stafford* - Walsall
Harden	*York, W.R.* - Keighley
Hardendale	*Westmorland* - Penrith
Hardenhuish	*Wilts* - Chippenham
Harden Park	*Cheshire* - Macclesfield
Hardham	*Sussex* - Chichester
Hardhaugh	*Northumberland* - Hexham
Hardingham	*Norfolk* - Norwich
Hardingstone	*Northampton* - Northampton
Hardings Wood	*Stafford* - Stoke-on-Trent
Hardington	*Somerset* - Frome
Hardington Mandeville	*Somerset* - Yeovil
Hardington Marsh	*Somerset* - Yeovil
Hardiwicke	*Stafford* - Stafford
Hardley	*Hants* - Southampton
Hardley	*Norfolk* - Norwich
Hardman's Green	*Lancaster* - Bury
Hardmead	*Bucks* - Bedford
Hardres, Lower	*Kent* - Canterbury
Hardres, Upper	*Kent* - Canterbury
Hard Riding	*Northumberland* - Hexham
Hardstoft	*Derby* - Chesterfield
Hardway	*Hants* - Portsmouth
Hardway	*Somerset* - Yeovil
Hardwick	*Bucks* - Aylesbury
Hardwick	*Cambridge* - Cambridge
Hardwick	*Derby* - Chesterfield
Hardwick	*Lincoln* - Lincoln
Hardwick	*Monmouth* - Pontypool and Abergavenny
Hardwick	*Northampton* - Wellingborough
Hardwick	*Notts* - Worksop
Hardwick	*Salop* - Oswestry
Hardwick	*Salop* - Shrewsbury
Hardwick	*York, W.R.* - Rotherham
Hardwicke	*Gloucester* - Gloucester
Hardwicke	*Hereford* - Hereford
Hardwicke	*Norfolk* - Norwich
Hardwicke	*Oxford* - Witney
Hardwick, East	*York, W.R.* - Pontefract
Hardwick Hill	*Lincoln* - Gainsborough
Hardwick, West	*York, W.R.* - Pontefract
Hardwick with Tusmore	*Oxford* - Banbury
Harebreaks	*Herts* - Watford
Hareby	*Lincoln* - Skegness
Hareby Fen	*Lincoln* - Skegness
Harecrag	*Northumberland* - Alnwick
Harefield	*Middlesex* - Uxbridge
Hare Hatch	*Berks* - Reading
Harehill	*Derby* - Uttoxeter
Hareholme	*Lancaster* - Rawtenstall

HAR

Harehope	*Northumberland* - Alnwick
Harehope Gill	*Durham* - Bishop Auckland
Harescombe	*Gloucester* - Gloucester
Haresfield	*Gloucester* - Gloucester
Haresfinch	*Lancaster* - St. Helens
Hareshawhead Colliery	*Northumberland* - Hexham
Harestock	*Hants* - Winchester
Hare Street	*Herts* - Hitchin
Harewood	*York, W.R.* - Otley
Harewood End	*Hereford* - Hereford
Harewood Grange	*Derby* - Matlock
Harford	*Devon* - Plymouth
Hargham	*Norfolk* - Norwich
Hargrave	*Cheshire* - Chester
Hargrave	*Northampton* - Wellingborough
Hargrave	*Suffolk* - Bury St. Edmunds
Hargreaves	*Cheshire* - Ellesmere Port
Hargreavesfold	*Lancaster* - Rawtenstall
Harker	*Cumberland* - Carlisle
Harker Lodge	*Cumberland* - Workington
Harker Marsh	*Cumberland* - Workington
Harkstead	*Suffolk* - Ipswich
Harlackden	*Kent* - Cranbrook
Harlaston	*Stafford* - Tamworth
Harlaxton	*Lincoln* - Grantham
Harlech	*Merioneth* - Portmadoc
Harle, Little	*Northumberland* - Hexham
Harlescott	*Salop* - Shrewsbury
Harlesden	*London, N.W.10* - Willesden
Harleston	*Norfolk* - Norwich
Harleston	*Suffolk* - Stowmarket
Harlestone	*Northampton* - Northampton
Harle Syke	*Lancaster* - Burnley
Harle, West	*Northumberland* - Hexham
Harley	*Salop* - Shrewsbury
Harley	*York, W.R.* - Rotherham
Harleyford	*Bucks* - High Wycombe
Harlington	*Bedford* - Luton
Harlington	*Middlesex* - Uxbridge
Harlington	*York, W.R.* - Doncaster
Harlow	*Essex* - Harlow
Harlow Hill	*Northumberland* - Newcastle upon Tyne
Harlow Hill	*York, W.R.* - Harrogate
Harlsey	*York, N.R.* - Northallerton
Harlthorpe	*York, E.R.* - York
Harlton	*Cambridge* - Cambridge
Harlyn Bay	*Cornwall* - Bodmin
Harmans Cross	*Dorset* - Swanage
Harmer Green	*Herts* - Hertford
Harmer Hill	*Salop* - Shrewsbury
Harmondsworth	*Middlesex* - Uxbridge
Harmston	*Lincoln* - Lincoln
Harnage	*Salop* - Shrewsbury
Harnden	*Kent* - Deal
Harnham	*Northumberland* - Newcastle upon Tyne
Harnhill	*Gloucester* - Swindon
Harold Bridge	*Cambridge* - Wisbech
Harold Hill	*Essex* - Ilford
Haroldston St. Issells	*Pembroke* - Haverfordwest
Haroldston West	*Pembroke* - Haverfordwest
Harold Wood	*Essex* - Ilford
Harome	*York, N.R.* - Malton
Harpenden	*Herts* - St. Albans
Harperley	*Durham* - Bishop Auckland
Harperridge	*Northumberland* - Berwick-upon-Tweed
Harper Town	*Northumberland* - Carlisle
Harpford	*Devon* - Exeter
Harpham	*York, E.R.* - Bridlington
Harp Hill	*Gloucester* - Cheltenham
Harpley	*Norfolk* - King's Lynn
Harpole	*Northampton* - Northampton
Harpsden	*Oxford* - Reading
Harpsford	*Salop* - Bridgnorth
Harpswell	*Lincoln* - Gainsborough
Harpswood	*Salop* - Bridgnorth
Harpton	*Radnor* - Knighton

Harpton, Lower	*Hereford* - Leominster
Harpton, Upper	*Radnor* - Knighton
Harptree	*Somerset* - Wells
Harptree, East	*Somerset* - Wells
Harptree, West	*Somerset* - Wells
Harpurhey	*Lancaster* - Manchester
Harpur Hill	*Derby* - Buxton
Harraby	*Cumberland* - Carlisle
Harraton	*Devon* - Kingsbridge
Harraton	*Durham* - Gateshead
Harrietsham	*Kent* - Maidstone
Harriets Hayes	*Salop* - Wolverhampton
Harringay (part)	*London, N.4* - Clerkenwell
Harringay (part)	*London, N.4* - Edmonton
Harringay (part)	*London, N.8* - Clerkenwell
Harringay (part)	*London, N.8* - Edmonton
Harrington	*Cumberland* - Workington
Harrington	*Lincoln* - Skegness
Harrington	*Northampton* - Kettering
Harrington	*Salop* - Bridgnorth
Harringworth	*Northampton* - Corby
Harriseahead	*Stafford* - Stoke-on-Trent
Harriston	*Cumberland* - Carlisle
Harrogate	*York, W.R.* - Harrogate
Harrogate, High	*York, W.R.* - Harrogate
Harrogate, Low	*York, W.R.* - Harrogate
Harrold	*Beds* - Bedford
Harrop Green	*York, W.R.* - Oldham
Harrow (part)	*Middlesex* - Watford
Harrow (part)	*Middlesex* - Willesden
Harrowbarrow	*Cornwall* - Plymouth
Harrowby	*Lincoln* - Grantham
Harrowden	*Beds* - Bedford
Harrowden, Great	*Northampton* - Wellingborough
Harrowden, Little	*Northampton* - Wellingborough
Harrow Garden Village	*Middlesex* - Watford
Harrow Hill	*Glos* - Gloucester
Harrow, North (part)	*Middlesex* - Watford
Harrow, North (part)	*Middlesex* - Willesden
Harrow-on-the-Hill	*Middlesex* - Willesden
Harrow, South	*Middlesex* - Willesden
Harrow Weald	*Middlesex* - Watford
Harrow, West	*Middlesex* - Willesden
Harsley	*Northumberland* - Hexham
Harston	*Cambridge* - Cambridge
Harston	*Leicester* - Grantham
Harswell	*York, E.R.* - York
Hart	*Durham* - Hartlepool
Hartburn	*Durham* - Stockton on Tees
Hartburn	*Northumberland* - Morpeth
Hartburn Grange	*Northumberland* - Morpeth
Hart Common	*Lancaster* - Bolton
Hartest	*Suffolk* - Sudbury
Hartfield	*Sussex* - East Grinstead
Hartford	*Cheshire* - Northwich
Hartford	*Hunts* - Huntingdon
Hartford	*Northumberland* - North Shields
Hartford Bridge	*Hants* - Basingstoke
Hartford Bridge	*Northumberland* - Blyth
Hartford Colliery	*Northumberland* - North Shields
Hartford, East	*Northumberland* - North Shields
Hartford End	*Essex* - Chelmsford
Hartford, West	*Northumberland* - North Shields
Hartforth	*York, N.R.* - Darlington
Hartgrove	*Dorset* - Shaftesbury
Harthill	*Cheshire* - Chester
Harthill	*Derby* - Matlock
Harthill	*York, W.R.* - Worksop
Harting, East	*Sussex* - Petersfield
Harting, South	*Sussex* - Petersfield
Hartington	*Northumberland* - Morpeth
Hartington Hall	*Northumberland* - Morpeth
Hartington Middle Quarter	*Derby* - Buxton
Hartington Nether Quarter	*Derby* - Buxton
Hartington Town Quarter	*Derby* - Buxton
Hartington Upper Quarter	*Derby* - Buxton

Harting, West	*Sussex* - Petersfield
Hartland	*Devon* - Bideford
Hartle Moor	*Derby* - Matlock
Hartlebury	*Salop* - Bridgnorth
Hartlebury	*Worcester* - Kidderminster
Hartlepool	*Durham* - Hartlepool
Hartleton	*Hereford* - Gloucester
Hartley (Cranbrook)	*Kent* - Cranbrook
Hartley	*Kent* - Dartford
Hartley	*Northumberland* - North Shields
Hartley	*Westmorland* - Penrith
Hartley Brook	*York, W.R.* - Sheffield
Hartley Burn	*Northumberland* - Carlisle
Hartley Cleugh	*Northumberland* - Hexham
Hartley Green	*Stafford* - Stafford
Hartley Mauditt	*Hants* - Aldershot and Farnham
Hartley, New	*Northumberland* - North Shields
Hartley Wespall	*Hants* - Basingstoke
Hartley Wintney	*Hants* - Basingstoke
Hartlington	*York, W.R.* - Skipton
Hartlington Raikes	*York, W.R.* - Skipton
Hartlip	*Kent* - Sittingbourne
Hartoft	*York, N.R.* - Malton
Harton	*Durham* - South Shields
Harton	*York, N.R.* - York
Harton Colliery	*Durham* - South Shields
Harton Green Lane	*Durham* - South Shields
Harton, West	*Durham* - South Shields
Hartpury	*Gloucester* - Gloucester
Hartsdown	*Kent* - Margate
Harts Grounds	*Lincoln* - Boston
Hartshay, Lower	*Derby* - Alfreton
Hartshay, Upper	*Derby* - Alfreton
Hartshead	*Lancaster* - Ashton-under-Lyne
Hartshead	*York, W.R.* - Dewsbury
Harts Hill (part)	*Stafford* - Dudley
Hartshill	*Stafford* - Stoke-on-Trent
Harts Hill (part)	*Stafford* - Stourbridge
Hartshill	*Warwick* - Nuneaton
Hartsholme	*Lincoln* - Lincoln
Hartshorne	*Derby* - Ashby-de-la-Zouch
Hartside	*Northumberland* - Alnwick
Hartsop	*Westmorland* - Penrith
Hart Station	*Durham* - Hartlepool
Hartwell	*Bucks* - Aylesbury
Hartwell	*Northampton* - Northampton
Hartwell	*Stafford* - Stafford
Hartwith	*York, W.R.* - Harrogate
Harty	*Kent* - Sheerness
Harty Ferry	*Kent* - Canterbury
Harvel	*Kent* - Gravesend
Harvest Hill	*Warwick* - Coventry
Harvills Hawthorn	*Stafford* - West Bromwich
Harvington	*Worcester* - Evesham
Harvington	*Worcester* - Kidderminster
Harwell	*Berks* - Didcot
Harwich	*Essex* - Harwich
Harwood	*Durham* - Bishop Auckland
Harwood	*Lancaster* - Bolton
Harwood	*Northumberland* - Morpeth
Harwood Dale	*York, N.R.* - Scarborough
Harwood, Great	*Lancaster* - Blackburn
Harwood, Little	*Lancaster* - Blackburn
Harworth	*Notts* - Worksop
Hasbury	*Worcester* - Stourbridge
Hascombe	*Surrey* - Guildford
Haselbech	*Northampton* - Northampton
Haselbury Plucknett	*Somerset* - Yeovil
Haseley	*Warwick* - Warwick
Haselor	*Warwick* - Redditch
Haselour	*Stafford* - Tamworth
Hasfield	*Gloucester* - Gloucester
Hasguard	*Pembroke* - Haverfordwest
Haskayne	*Lancaster* - Southport
Hasketon	*Suffolk* - Woodbridge
Hasland	*Derby* - Chesterfield
Haslar	*Hants* - Portsmouth
Haslemere	*Surrey* - Guildford
Haslingbourne	*Sussex* - Chichester
Haslingden	*Lancaster* - Rawtenstall

HAS - HAU

Haslingden Grane	*Lancaster* - Rawtenstall
Haslingfield	*Cambridge* - Cambridge
Haslington	*Cheshire* - Crewe
Hassage	*Somerset* - Bath
Hassell Green	*Kent* - Ashford
Hassingham	*Norfolk* - Norwich
Hassocks	*Sussex* - Haywards Heath
Hassop	*Derby* - Matlock
Hasthorpe	*Lincoln* - Skegness
Hastingleigh	*Kent* - Ashford
Hastings	*Sussex* - Hastings
Hastoe	*Herts* - Aylesbury
Haston	*Salop* - Shrewsbury
Haswell Colliery	*Durham* - Durham
Haswell, High	*Durham* - Durham
Haswell Lane	*Durham* - Durham
Haswell, Low	*Durham* - Durham
Haswell Moor	*Durham* - Durham
Haswell Plough	*Durham* - Durham
Hatch	*Beds* - Biggleswade
Hatch (Tisbury)	*Wilts* - Shaftesbury
Hatch Beauchamp	*Somerset* - Taunton
Hatch End	*Middlesex* - Watford
Hatches Green	*Cornwall* - Plymouth
Hatchmere	*Cheshire* - Runcorn
Hatch, West	*Somerset* - Taunton
Hatcliffe	*Lincoln* - Great Grimsby
Hateley Heath	*Stafford* - West Bromwich
Hatfield	*Hereford* - Leominster
Hatfield	*Herts* - St. Albans
Hatfield	*York, W.R.* - Thorne
Hatfield Broad Oak	*Essex* - Bishop's Stortford
Hatfield, Great	*York, E.R.* - Beverley
Hatfield Green	*Essex* - Chelmsford
Hatfield Heath	*Essex* - Bishop's Stortford
Hatfield Hyde (Welwyn Garden City)	*Herts* - Hertford
Hatfield Hyde (Hatfield)	*Herts* - St. Albans
Hatfield Peverel	*Essex* - Chelmsford
Hatfield Regis	*Essex* - Bishop's Stortford
Hatfield Woodhouse	*York, W.R.* - Thorne
Hatfield Woodside	*Herts* - St. Albans
Hatford	*Berks* - Didcot
Hatherden	*Hants* - Andover
Hatherleigh	*Devon* - Okehampton
Hatherley, Up	*Gloucester* - Cheltenham
Hatherlow	*Cheshire* - Stockport
Hathern	*Leicester* - Loughborough
Hatherop	*Gloucester* - Cheltenham
Hathersage	*Derby* - Sheffield
Hathershaw	*Lancaster* - Oldham
Hatherton	*Cheshire* - Crewe
Hatherton	*Stafford* - Walsall
Hathow	*Lincoln* - Lincoln
Hatley, East	*Cambridge* - Biggleswade
Hatley St. George	*Cambridge* - Biggleswade
Hatt	*Cornwall* - Plymouth
Hattersley	*Cheshire* - Hyde
Hattingley	*Hants* - Winchester
Hatton	*Cheshire* - Chester
Hatton	*Cheshire* - Warrington
Hatton	*Derby* - Burton-upon-Trent
Hatton	*Lincoln* - Lincoln
Hatton	*Salop* - Wellington (Salop)
Hatton	*Salop* - Shrewsbury
Hatton	*Stafford* - Stoke-on-Trent
Hatton	*Warwick* - Warwick
Hatton, High	*Salop* - Market Drayton
Hattons	*Stafford* - Wolverhampton
Haugh	*Lincoln* - Louth
Haugham	*Lincoln* - Louth
Haugh End	*York, W.R.* - Halifax
Haughley	*Suffolk* - Stowmarket
Haugh, Lower	*York, W.R.* - Rotherham
Haughurst Hill	*Hants* - Basingstoke
Haughmond Demesne	*Salop* - Shrewsbury
Haugh, Nether	*York, W.R.* - Rotherham
Haughton	*Cheshire* - Crewe
Haughton	*Montgomery* - Oswestry

HAU - HAW

Haughton	*Northumberland* - Hexham
Haughton	*Notts* - East Retford
Haughton	*Salop* - Bridgnorth
Haughton	*Salop* - Wellington (Salop)
Haughton	*Salop* - Oswestry
Haughton	*Salop* - Shrewsbury
Haughton	*Stafford* - Stafford
Haughton Green	*Lancaster* - Hyde
Haugh, Upper	*York, W.R.* - Rotherham
Haulgh	*Lancaster* - Bolton
Haultwick	*Herts* - Hertford
Haunton	*Stafford* - Tamworth
Hautbois, Great	*Norfolk* - Norwich
Hautbois, Little	*Norfolk* - Norwich
Hauxley	*Northumberland* - Alnwick
Hauxton	*Cambridge* - Cambridge
Hauxwell	*York, N.R.* - Northallerton
Havant	*Hants* - Portsmouth
Haven Bank	*Lincoln* - Boston
Haven, Broad	*Pembroke* - Haverfordwest
Havengore	*Essex* - Southend
Haven, Little	*Pembroke* - Haverfordwest
Haven's Lee	*Bucks* - High Wycombe
Haven Street	*I. of W.* - Newport (I.W.)
Haven, The	*Sussex* - Horsham
Haverah Park	*York, W.R.* - Harrogate
Haverbrack	*Westmorland* - Kendal
Havercroft	*York, W.R.* - Barnsley
Haverfordwest	*Pembroke* - Haverfordwest
Haverhill	*Suffolk* - Cambridge
Haverigg	*Cumberland* - Whitehaven
Havering	*Essex* - Ilford
Havering-atte-Bower	*Essex* - Ilford
Haveringland	*Norfolk* - Norwich
Haversham	*Bucks* - Bletchley and Leighton Buzzard
Haverthwaite	*Lancaster* - Barrow-in-Furness
Haverton Hill	*Durham* - Stockton-on-Tees
Havyatt	*Somerset* - Weston Super Mare
Havyatt Green	*Somerset* - Weston Super Mare
Hawarden	*Flint* - Chester
Haw Bridge	*Gloucester* - Cheltenham
Hawbush	*Stafford* - Stourbridge
Hawcoat	*Lancaster* - Barrow-in-Furness
Hawcross	*Gloucester* - Gloucester
Hawden	*Kent* - Tonbridge
Hawerby	*Lincoln* - Great Grimsby
Hawes	*York, N.R.* - Northallerton
Hawford	*Worcester* - Worcester
Hawick	*Northumberland* - Hexham
Hawkbatch	*Worcester* - Kidderminster
Hawkchurch	*Devon* - Axminster and Chard
Hawkedon	*Suffolk* - Bury St. Edmunds
Hawkenbury	*Kent* - Tunbridge Wells
Hawkenbury (Headcorn)	*Kent* - Maidstone
Hawkeridge	*Wilts* - Trowbridge
Hawkesbury	*Gloucester* - Bristol
Hawkesbury Common	*Gloucester* - Bristol
Hawkesbury Lane (part)	*Warwick* - Coventry
Hawkesbury Lane (part)	*Warwick* - Nuneaton
Hawkesbury Upton	*Gloucester* - Bristol
Hawkesdale	*Cumberland* - Carlisle
Hawkes Tor	*Cornwall* - Bodmin
Hawkesworth	*York, W.R.* - Leeds
Hawk Green	*Cheshire* - Stockport
Hawkhill	*Northumberland* - Alnwick
Hawkhouse Green	*York, W.R.* - Doncaster
Hawkhurst	*Kent* - Cranbrook
Hawkhurst	*Sussex* - Chichester
Hawkinge	*Kent* - Folkestone
Hawkins Pill	*Glos* - Gloucester
Hawkley	*Hants* - Petersfield
Hawkridge	*Somerset* - Tiverton
Hawkshaw	*Lancaster* - Bury
Hawkshead	*Lancaster* - Kendal
Hawksted	*Northumberland* - Hexham
Hawkstone (part)	*Salop* - Market Drayton
Hawkstone (part)	*Salop* - Whitchurch
Hawkswick	*York, W.R.* - Skipton

HAW - HAZ

Hawksworth	*Notts* - Nottingham
Hawksworth	*York, W.R.* - Otley
Hawkup Lee	*Northumberland* - Hexham
Hawkwell	*Essex* - Southend
Hawkwell	*Northumberland* - Newcastle-upon-Tyne
Hawkwell Green	*Glos* - Gloucester
Hawley	*Hants* - Aldershot and Farnham
Hawley	*Kent* - Dartford
Hawling	*Gloucester* - Cheltenham
Hawnby	*York, N.R.* - Malton
Hawne	*Stafford* - Stourbridge
Haw, New	*Surrey* - Kingston-upon-Thames
Haworth	*York, W.R.* - Keighley
Hawridge	*Bucks* - Amersham
Hawsker-with-Stainsacre	*York, N.R.* - Whitby
Hawsley	*Gloucester* - Gloucester
Hawstead	*Suffolk* - Bury St. Edmunds
Haw, The	*Gloucester* - Cheltenham
Hawthorn	*Durham* - Sunderland
Hawthorn (part)	*Wilts* - Bath
Hawthorn (part)	*Wilts* - Chippenham
Hawthorn Hill	*Lincoln* - Boston
Hawthorpe	*Lincoln* - Grantham
Hawton	*Notts* - Newark
Haxby	*York, E.R.* - York
Haxey	*Lincoln* - Gainsborough
Haxey Turbery	*Lincoln* - Gainsborough
Haxton	*Wilts* - Salisbury
Hay	*Brecon* - Brecknock
Hay-a-Park	*York, W.R.* - Harrogate
Hayborough	*Cumberland* - Workington
Haybridge	*Salop* - Wellington (Salop)
Haybridge	*Somerset* - Wells
Hayburn Wyke	*York, N.R.* - Scarborough
Hayden	*Gloucester* - Cheltenham
Hayden Elm	*Gloucester* - Cheltenham
Haydock	*Lancaster* - St. Helens
Haydon	*Dorset* - Yeovil
Haydon	*Northumberland* - Hexham
Haydon	*Somerset* - Taunton
Haydon Bridge	*Northumberland* - Hexham
Haydon Wick	*Wilts* - Swindon
Hayes	*Kent* - Bromley
Hayes	*Middlesex* - Uxbridge
Hayes Common	*Kent* - Bromley
Hayesden	*Kent* - Tonbridge
Hayes Hill	*Sussex* - Horsham
Hayes, The	*Stafford* - Stafford
Haye, The	*Salop* - Shrewsbury
Hay-Gate	*Salop* - Wellington (Salop)
Hayle	*Cornwall* - Redruth
Hayley Green	*Worcester* - Stourbridge
Hayling, North	*Hants* - Portsmouth
Hayling, South	*Hants* - Portsmouth
Hay, Little	*Stafford* - Lichfield
Hay Mills	*Warwick* - Birmingham
Haynes	*Beds* - Bedford
Hayscastle	*Pembroke* - Haverfordwest
Hayseech	*Stafford* - Dudley
Hay, South	*Hants* - Aldershot and Farnham
Hayton	*Cumberland* - Carlisle
Hayton	*Notts* - East Retford
Hayton	*Salop* - Ludlow
Hayton	*York, E.R.* - York
Hayton, Lower	*Salop* - Ludlow
Hayton's Bent	*Salop* - Ludlow
Hayton, Upper	*Salop* - Ludlow
Haywards Heath	*Sussex* - Haywards Heath
Haywood	*Hereford* - Hereford
Haywood	*York, W.R.* - Doncaster
Haywood, Great	*Stafford* - Stafford
Haywood, Little	*Stafford* - Stafford
Haywood Oaks	*Notts* - Mansfield
Hazelbeach	*Pembroke* - Haverfordwest
Hazelbury Bryan	*Dorset* - Dorchester
Hazelden	*Kent* - Cranbrook
Hazeleigh	*Essex* - Maldon

HAZ - HEA

Hazel End	*Essex* - Bishop's Stortford
Hazeley	*Hants* - Winchester
Hazeley Heath	*Hants* - Basingstoke
Hazel Grove	*Cheshire* - Stockport
Hazel Head	*York, N.R.* - Whitby
Hazel Hill	*Gloucester* - Gloucester
Hazelhurst	*Hereford* - Monmouth
Hazelhurst	*Lancaster* - Ashton-under-Lyne
Hazelor, Lower	*Worcester* - Evesham
Hazelor, Upper	*Worcester* - Evesham
Hazelrigg Colliery	*Northumberland* - Newcastle upon Tyne
Hazel Slade	*Stafford* - Walsall
Hazelstrine	*Stafford* - Stafford
Hazelwell	*Warwick* - Birmingham
Hazelwood	*Derby* - Derby
Hazelwood	*Devon* - Kingsbridge
Hazelwood	*York, W.R.* - Leeds
Hazlehead	*York, W.R.* - Barnsley
Hazle, Lower	*Gloucester* - Thornbury
Hazlemere	*Bucks* - High Wycombe
Hazleton	*Gloucester* - Cheltenham
Hazle, Upper	*Gloucester* - Thornbury
Hazlewood	*Suffolk* - Woodbridge
Hazlewood	*York, W.R.* - Skipton
Hazon	*Northumberland* - Alnwick
Heacham	*Norfolk* - King's Lynn
Headbourne Worthy	*Hants* - Winchester
Headcorn	*Kent* - Maidstone
Headingley	*York, W.R.* - Leeds
Headington	*Oxford* - Oxford
Headington, New	*Oxford* - Oxford
Headington Quarry	*Oxford* - Oxford
Headlam	*Durham* - Darlington
Headless Cross	*Worcester* - Redditch
Headley	*Hants* - Aldershot and Farnham
Headley	*Hants* - Newbury
Headley Heath	*Worcester* - Birmingham
Headon-cum-Upton	*Notts* - East Retford
Headsnook	*Cumberland* - Carlisle
Headstone	*Middlesex* - Watford
Heady Hill	*Lancaster* - Bury
Heage	*Derby* - Alfreton
Heage, Nether	*Derby* - Alfreton
Heage, Upper	*Derby* - Alfreton
Healaugh	*York, N.R.* - Darlington
Healaugh	*York, W.R.* - York
Heald Green (part)	*Cheshire* - Stockport
Heald Green (part)	*Cheshire* - Manchester
Healey	*Lancaster* - Rochdale
Healey	*Northumberland* - Hexham
Healey (Batley)	*York, W.R.* - Dewsbury
Healey (Ossett)	*York, W.R.* - Dewsbury
Healey and Combhill	*Northumberland* - Morpeth
Healey Field	*Durham* - Consett
Healey House	*York, W.R.* - Huddersfield
Healey-with-Sutton	*York, N.R.* - Harrogate
Healing	*Lincoln* - Great Grimsby
Heamies	*Stafford* - Stafford
Heamoor	*Cornwall* - Penzance
Heanor	*Derby* - Ilkeston
Heanton Punchardon	*Devon* - Barnstaple
Heap	*Lancaster* - Bury
Heap Bridge	*Lancaster* - Bury
Heapey	*Lancaster* - Chorley
Heapham	*Lincoln* - Gainsborough
Heasley	*Devon* - Barnstaple
Heath	*Beds* - Bletchley and Leighton Buzzard
Heath	*Derby* - Chesterfield
Heath	*Salop* - Ludlow
Heath	*York, W.R.* - Wakefield
Heath and Reach	*Beds* - Bletchley and Leighton Buzzard
Heath Charnock	*Lancaster* - Chorley
Heath Common	*Sussex* - Worthing
Heath Common	*Worcester* - Ludlow
Heathcote	*Derby* - Buxton
Heathcote	*Warwick* - Warwick
Heathencote	*Northampton* - Northampton

HEA - HED

Heath End	*Bucks* - Amersham
Heath End (Flackwell Heath)	*Bucks* - High Wycombe
Heath End (Great Kingshill)	*Bucks* - High Wycombe
Heath End	*Hants* - Basingstoke
Heath End	*Leicester* - Ashby-de-la-Zouch
Heath End	*Surrey* - Aldershot and Farnham
Heath End	*Sussex* - Chichester
Heather	*Leicester* - Ashby-de-la-Zouch
Heathercleugh	*Durham* - Bishop Auckland
Heatherstone Green	*Cheshire* - Whitchurch
Heatherton Park	*Somerset* - Taunton
Heathery	*Northumberland* - Alnwick
Heathfield	*Devon* - Newton Abbot
Heathfield	*Devon* - Plymouth
Heathfield	*Gloucester* - Stroud
Heathfield	*Hants* - Bournemouth
Heath Field	*Lancaster* - Bolton
Heathfield	*Somerset* - Taunton
Heathfield	*Sussex* - Eastbourne
Heathfield	*York, W.R.* - Harrogate
Heathfield, Old	*Sussex* - Eastbourne
Heath Green	*Hants* - Winchester
Heath Hayes	*Stafford* - Walsall
Heath, High	*Worcester* - Birmingham
Heath, Higher	*Salop* - Whitchurch
Heath Hill	*Salop* - Wellington (Salop)
Heath House Lane	*Stafford* - Leek
Heath, Little	*Essex* - Ilford
Heath, Little	*Herts* - St. Albans
Heath, Little	*Warwick* - Birmingham
Heath, Lower	*Salop* - Whitchurch
Heathon	*Salop* - Bridgnorth
Heathrow	*Middlesex* - Uxbridge
Heathstock	*Devon* - Axminster and Chard
Heath, The	*Gloucester* - Gloucester
Heathtop	*Derby* - Burton-upon-Trent
Heath Town	*Stafford* - Wolverhampton
Heathwaite	*Lancaster* - Barrow-in-Furness
Heath, West	*Hants* - Basingstoke
Heath, West	*Warwick* - Birmingham
Heathy Lee	*Stafford* - Leek
Heatley	*Cheshire* - Altrincham
Heatley	*Stafford* - Uttoxeter
Heaton	*Lancaster* - Bolton
Heaton	*Northumberland* - Newcastle upon Tyne
Heaton	*Stafford* - Leek
Heaton	*York, W.R.* - Bradford
Heaton Chapel	*Lancaster* - Stockport
Heaton High	*Northumberland* - Newcastle upon Tyne
Heaton Mersey	*Lancaster* - Stockport
Heaton Moor	*Lancaster* - Stockport
Heaton Mount	*Lancashire* - Leigh
Heaton Norris	*Lancaster* - Stockport
Heaton North	*Northumberland* - Newcastle upon Tyne
Heaton Park	*Lancaster* - Salford
Heaton Shay	*York, W.R.* - Bradford
Heaton with Oxcliffe	*Lancaster* - Lancaster
Heaviley	*Cheshire* - Stockport
Heavygate	*Durham* - Newcastle upon Tyne
Hebden	*York, W.R.* - Skipton
Hebden Bridge	*York, W.R.* - Todmorden
Hebers	*Lancaster* - Oldham
Hebingend	*Herts* - Hertford
Hebron	*Carmarthen* - Haverfordwest
Hebron	*Northumberland* - Morpeth
Heck	*York, W.R.* - Pontefract
Heckdyke	*Lincoln* - Gainsborough
Heckfield	*Hants* - Basingstoke
Heckfield Green	*Suffolk* - Norwich
Heckingham	*Norfolk* - Norwich
Heckington	*Lincoln* - Sleaford
Heckington Fen	*Lincoln* - Sleaford
Heckley	*Northumberland* - Alnwick
Heckmondwike	*York, W.R.* - Dewsbury
Heddington	*Wilts* - Devizes

HED - HEM

Heddington Wick	*Wilts* - Devizes
Heddon	*Devon* - Barnstaple
Heddon, East	*Northumberland* - Newcastle upon Tyne
Heddon-on-the-Wall	*Northumberland* - Newcastle upon Tyne
Heddon, West	*Northumberland* - Newcastle upon Tyne
Hedenham	*Norfolk* - Norwich
Hedge End	*Hants* - Southampton
Hedgeley	*Northumberland* - Alnwick
Hedgerley	*Bucks* - Uxbridge
Hedgerley Dean	*Bucks* - Uxbridge
Hedging	*Somerset* - Bridgwater
Hedley Hall	*Durham* - Gateshead
Hedley Hill	*Durham* - Durham
Hednesford	*Stafford* - Walsall
Hedon	*York, E.R.* - Kingston-upon-Hull
Hedsor	*Bucks* - High Wycombe
Hedworth	*Durham* - South Shields
Heeley	*York, W.R.* - Sheffield
Heeley, Green	*York, W.R.* - Sheffield
Heene	*Sussex* - Worthing
Heighholme	*York, E.R.* - Beverley
Heighington	*Durham* - Darlington
Heighington	*Lincoln* - Lincoln
Heighington Fen	*Lincoln* - Lincoln
Heighley Gate	*Northumberland* - Morpeth
Heighley, High	*Northumberland* - Morpeth
Heighley, Low	*Northumberland* - Morpeth
Height	*Cumberland* - Carlisle
Heightington	*Worcester* - Kidderminster
Heighton, South	*Sussex* - Lewes
Heights	*York, W.R.* - Oldham
Heldre	*Montgomery* - Welshpool
Hele	*Devon* - Barnstaple
Hele	*Devon* - Tiverton
Hele	*Devon* - Torquay
Hele	*Somerset* - Taunton
Helford	*Cornwall* - Penzance
Helhoughton	*Norfolk* - King's Lynn
Heligan	*Cornwall* - St. Austell
Helions Bumpstead	*Essex* - Cambridge
Hellaby	*York, W.R.* - Rotherham
Helland	*Cornwall* - Bodmin
Helland Bridge	*Cornwall* - Bodmin
Hellesdon	*Norfolk* - Norwich
Hellidon	*Northampton* - Rugby
Hellifield	*York, W.R.* - Skipton
Hellingly	*Sussex* - Eastbourne
Hellington	*Norfolk* - Norwich
Helmdon	*Northampton* - Banbury
Helme Cottages	*Durham* - Bishop Auckland
Helme Park	*Durham* - Bishop Auckland
Helmingham	*Suffolk* - Ipswich
Helmington	*Durham* - Bishop Auckland
Helmington Row	*Durham* - Bishop Auckland
Helmshore	*Lancaster* - Rawtenstall
Helmsley	*York, N.R.* - Malton
Helmsley, Upper	*York, N.R.* - York
Helperby	*York, N.R.* - York
Helperthorpe	*York, E.R.* - Beverley
Helpringham	*Lincoln* - Sleaford
Helpringham Fen	*Lincoln* - Sleaford
Helpston	*Northampton* - Peterborough
Helsby	*Cheshire* - Runcorn
Helshaw	*Salop* - Market Drayton
Helsington	*Westmorland* - Kendal
Helston	*Cornwall* - Penzance
Helstone	*Cornwall* - Bideford
Helston Water	*Cornwall* - Truro
Helton	*Westmorland* - Penrith
Hemblington	*Norfolk* - Norwich
Hemel Hempstead	*Herts* - Hemel Hempstead
Hemerdon	*Devon* - Plymouth
Hemford	*Salop* - Shrewsbury
Hemheath	*Stafford* - Stoke-on-Trent
Hemingborough	*York, E.R.* - York
Hemingby	*Lincoln* - Lincoln
Hemingfield	*York, W.R.* - Barnsley

HEM - HEN

Hemingford Abbots	*Hunts* - Huntingdon
Hemingford Grey	*Hunts* - Huntingdon
Hemingstone	*Suffolk* - Ipswich
Hemington	*Leicester* - Loughborough
Hemington	*Northampton* - Peterborough
Hemington	*Somerset* - Frome
Hemington Fields	*Leicester* - Loughborough
Hemley	*Suffolk* - Ipswich
Hemlington	*York, N.R.* - Middlesbrough
Hempholme	*York, E.R.* - Beverley
Hempnall	*Norfolk* - Norwich
Hempshill	*Notts* - Nottingham
Hempstead	*Essex* - Bishop's Stortford
Hempstead	*Kent* - Rochester
Hempstead	*Norfolk* - Norwich
Hempstead with Eccles	*Norfolk* - Norwich
Hempsted	*Glos* - Gloucester
Hempton	*Gloucester* - Thornbury
Hempton	*Norfolk* - King's Lynn
Hempton	*Oxford* - Banbury
Hemsby	*Norfolk* - Great Yarmouth
Hemsted	*Kent* - Cranbrook
Hemswell	*Lincoln* - Gainsborough
Hemsworth	*York, W.R.* - Sheffield
Hemsworth	*Dorset* - Wimborne Minster
Hemsworth	*York, W.R.* - Pontefract
Hemyock	*Devon* - Taunton
Henbury	*Cheshire* - Macclesfield
Hencote	*Salop* - Shrewsbury
Hendham Vale	*Lancaster* - Manchester
Hendon	*Berks* - Oxford
Hendon	*Durham* - Sunderland
Hendon	*London, N.W.4* - Willesden
Hendra	*Cornwall* - St. Austell
Hendra	*Cornwall* - Truro
Hendre	*Caernarvon* - Conway
Hendre	*Glamorgan* - Bridgend
Hendred, East	*Berks* - Didcot
Hendred, West	*Berks* - Didcot
Hendrerwydd	*Denbigh* - Denbigh
Hendre, The	*Hereford* - Monmouth
Hendy	*Carmarthen* - Llanelli
Heneglwys	*Anglesey* - Llangefni
Henfache	*Denbigh* - Oswestry
Henfield	*Gloucester* - Bristol
Henfield	*Sussex* - Brighton
Henfynyw	*Cardigan* - Aberystwyth
Hengoed	*Carmarthen* - Llanelli
Hengoed	*Glamorgan* - Bargoed
Hengoed	*Radnor* - Builth Wells
Hengoed	*Salop* - Oswestry
Hengrave	*Suffolk* - Bury St. Edmunds
Hengrove	*Kent* - Margate
Hengynwydd Fach	*Montgomery* - Newtown
Henham	*Essex* - Bishop's Stortford
Henham	*Suffolk* - Halesworth
Henhurst	*Stafford* - Burton-on-Trent
Henlade	*Somerset* - Taunton
Henley	*Dorset* - Dorchester
Henley	*Salop* - Ludlow
Henley (Crewkerne)	*Somerset* - Yeovil
Henley	*Suffolk* - Ipswich
Henley	*Wilts* - Bath
Henley Common	*Salop* - Ludlow
Henley Down	*Sussex* - Hastings
Henley Hill (part)	*Sussex* - Chichester
Henley Hill (part)	*Sussex* - Petersfield
Henley-in-Arden	*Warwick* - Stratford on Avon
Henley-on-Thames	*Oxford* - Reading
Henllan	*Cardigan* - Cardigan
Henllan	*Denbigh* - Denbigh
Henllan Amgoed	*Carmarthen* - Haverfordwest
Henllys	*Monmouth* - Newport (Mon.)
Henlow	*Beds* - Biggleswade
Hennock	*Devon* - Newton Abbot
Hennor	*Hereford* - Leominster
Henryd	*Caernarvon* - Conway
Henry's Moat	*Pembroke* - Haverfordwest
Hensall	*York, W.R.* - Pontefract
Hensbarrow	*Cornwall* - St. Austell

HEN - HES

Hensborough Hill	*Warwick* - Rugby
Henshaw	*Northumberland* - Hexham
Hensingham	*Cumberland* - Whitehaven
Hensington Within	*Oxford* - Oxford
Hensington Without	*Oxford* - Oxford
Henstead	*Suffolk* - Lowestoft
Hensting	*Hants* - Winchester
Henstridge	*Somerset* - Yeovil
Hentland	*Hereford* - Hereford
Henton	*Somerset* - Wells
Henwick	*Berks* - Newbury
Henwood	*Berks* - Oxford
Henwood	*Cornwall* - Liskeard
Heolgerrig	*Glamorgan* - Merthyr Tydfil
Heollaethog	*Glamorgan* - Bridgend
Heol Las	*Glamorgan* - Bridgend
Heol Las	*Glamorgan* - Swansea
Heol Las Wick	*Glamorgan* - Bridgend
Heol Senni	*Brecon* - Brecknock
Heolycyw	*Glamorgan* - Bridgend
Heol-y-March	*Glamorgan* - Cardiff
Heolymynydd	*Glamorgan* - Bridgend
Hepburn	*Northumberland* - Alnwick
Hepple	*Northumberland* - Morpeth
Hepple Demesne	*Northumberland* - Morpeth
Hepscott	*Northumberland* - Morpeth
Hepthorne Lane	*Derby* - Chesterfield
Heptonstall	*York, W.R.* - Todmorden
Hepworth	*Suffolk* - Thetford
Hepworth	*York, W.R.* - Huddersfield
Herberts Town	*Monmouth* - Pontypool and Abergavenny
Herbrandston	*Pembroke* - Haverfordwest
Herding Hill	*Northumberland* - Hexham
Herdley Bank	*Northumberland* - Haltwhistle
Hereford	*Hereford* - Hereford
Hereford, Little	*Hereford* - Ludlow
Hergest Camp	*Hereford* - Hereford
Hergest, Lower	*Hereford* - Hereford
Hergest, Upper	*Hereford* - Hereford
Herland Cross	*Cornwall* - Penzance
Hermitage	*Berks* - Newbury
Hermitage	*Dorset* - Yeovil
Hermitage	*Durham* - Durham
Hermitage	*Sussex* - Chichester
Hermitage Hill	*Stafford* - Tamworth
Hermit Hole	*York, W.R.* - Keighley
Hermon	*Anglesey* - Llangefni
Hermon	*Carmarthen* - Carmarthen
Hermon	*Pembroke* - Cardigan
Hermongers	*Sussex* - Horsham
Herne	*Kent* - Canterbury
Herne Bay	*Kent* - Canterbury
Herne Hill	*London, S.E.24* - Lambeth
Hernhill	*Kent* - Canterbury
Herniss	*Cornwall* - Redruth
Hernstone	*Glamorgan* - Bridgend
Herodsfoot	*Cornwall* - Liskeard
Heron Cross	*Stafford* - Stoke-on-Trent
Heronden	*Kent* - Cranbrook
Herongate	*Essex* - Brentwood
Heronsgate	*Herts* - Watford
Herriard	*Hants* - Basingstoke
Herringbroom	*Sussex* - Chichester
Herringby	*Norfolk* - Great Yarmouth
Herringfleet	*Suffolk* - Lowestoft
Herringstone	*Dorset* - Dorchester
Herringswell	*Suffolk* - Newmarket
Herringthorpe	*York, W.R.* - Rotherham
Herrington, East	*Durham* - Sunderland
Herrington, Middle	*Durham* - Sunderland
Herrington, West	*Durham* - Durham
Hersham	*Surrey* - Kingston-upon-Thames
Herstmonceux	*Sussex* - Eastbourne
Herston	*Dorset* - Swanage
Hertford	*Herts* - Hertford
Hertford Heath	*Herts* - Hertford
Hertingfordbury	*Herts* - Hertford
Hesketh Bank	*Lancaster* - Southport
Hesket, High	*Cumberland* - Penrith

Hesket, Low	*Cumberland* - Penrith
Hesket Newmarket	*Cumberland* - Carlisle
Heskin	*Lancaster* - Chorley
Hesleden	*Durham* - Hartlepool
Hesleden, High	*Durham* - Hartlepool
Hesledon, New	*Durham* - Sunderland
Heslerton, East	*York, E.R.* - Malton
Heslerton, West	*York, E.R.* - Malton
Hesley Bar	*York, W.R.* - Sheffield
Hesley Hall	*Notts* - Worksop
Hesleyhurst	*Northumberland* - Morpeth
Hesley Lane	*York, W.R.* - Sheffield
Heslington	*York, N.R.* - York
Hessay	*York, N.R.* - York
Hessenford	*Cornwall* - Liskeard
Hessett	*Suffolk* - Bury St. Edmunds
Hessle	*York, E.R.* - Kingston-upon-Hull
Hessle	*York, W.R.* - Pontefract
Hessle Common	*York, E.R.* - Kingston-upon-Hull
Hessle Mount	*York, E.R.* - Kingston-upon-Hull
Hest	*Lancaster* - Lancaster
Hest Bank	*Lancaster* - Lancaster
Hester's Way	*Gloucester* - Cheltenham
Heswall	*Cheshire* - Birkenhead
Hethe	*Oxford* - Banbury
Hethel	*Norfolk* - Norwich
Hethelpit Cross	*Gloucester* - Gloucester
Hethersett	*Norfolk* - Norwich
Hethersgill	*Cumberland* - Carlisle
Hett	*Durham* - Durham
Hetton	*Durham* - Durham
Hetton	*York, W.R.* - Skipton
Hetton, East	*Durham* - Durham
Hetton-le-Hole	*Durham* - Durham
Hetton-on-the-Hill	*Durham* - Durham
Hetton, South	*Durham* - Durham
Heugh	*Northumberland* - Newcastle upon Tyne
Heveningham	*Suffolk* - Halesworth
Hever	*Kent* - Tonbridge
Heverham	*Kent* - Sevenoaks
Heversham	*Westmorland* - Kendal
Hevingham	*Norfolk* - Norwich
Hewas Water	*Cornwall* - St. Austell
Hewell	*Worcester* - Redditch
Hewell Grange	*Worcester* - Redditch
Hewelsfield	*Gloucester* - Chepstow
Hewenden	*York, W.R.* - Keighley
Hewer Hill	*Cumberland* - Penrith
Hewish	*Somerset* - Weston Super Mare
Hewish (Crewkerne)	*Somerset* - Yeovil
Hewood	*Dorset* - Axminster and Chard
Heworth	*Durham* - Gateshead
Heworth	*York, N.R.* - York
Heworth Colliery	*Durham* - Gateshead
Heworth Shore	*Durham* - Gateshead
Hewstock	*Dorset* - Blandford
Hewton	*Devon* - Plymouth
Hexden	*Kent* - Cranbrook
Hexham	*Northumberland* - Hexham
Hextable	*Kent* - Dartford
Hexthorpe	*York, W.R.* - Doncaster
Hexton	*Herts* - Hitchin
Hey (Marsden)	*York, W.R.* - Huddersfield
Heybridge	*Essex* - Maldon
Heybridge Basin	*Essex* - Maldon
Heydon	*Essex* - Cambridge
Heydon	*Norfolk* - Norwich
Heydour	*Lincoln* - Grantham
Heyford, Lower	*Northampton* - Northampton
Heyford, Lower	*Oxford* - Banbury
Heyford, Upper	*Northampton* - Northampton
Heyford, Upper	*Oxford* - Banbury
Hey Green	*York, W.R.* - Huddersfield
Hey Heads	*Lancaster* - Ashton-under-Lyne
Heyhouses	*Lancaster* - Burnley
Heyop	*Radnor* - Knighton
Heyrod	*Lancaster* - Ashton-under-Lyne
Heysham	*Lancaster* - Lancaster
Heyshaw	*York, W.R.* - Harrogate

Heyshott	*Sussex* - Chichester
Heyside	*Lancaster* - Oldham
Heytesbury	*Wilts* - Warminster
Heythrop	*Oxford* - Banbury
Heywood	*Lancaster* - Bury
Heywood	*Wilts* - Trowbridge
Hibaldstowe	*Lincoln* - Scunthorpe
Hickleton	*York, W.R.* - Doncaster
Hickling	*Norfolk* - Great Yarmouth
Hickling	*Notts* - Nottingham
Hickling Pastures	*Notts* - Melton Mowbray
Hicks Mill (part)	*Cornwall* - Truro
Hicks Mill (part)	*Cornwall* - Redruth
Hickstead	*Sussex* - Haywards Heath
Hidcote	*Gloucester* - Evesham
Higford	*Salop* - Bridgnorth
Higginshaw	*Lancaster* - Oldham
Higham	*Cumberland* - Workington
Higham	*Derby* - Alfreton
Higham	*Suffolk* - Ipswich
Higham	*Suffolk* - Newmarket
Higham	*York, W.R.* - Barnsley
Higham Dykes	*Northumberland* - Newcastle upon Tyne
Higham Ferrers	*Northampton* - Wellingborough
Higham Gobion	*Beds* - Hitchin
Higham Gobion Lane	*Beds* - Hitchin
Higham, Lower	*Kent* - Rochester
Higham-on-the-Hill	*Leicester* - Hinckley
Highampton	*Devon* - Okehampton
Highams Park	*London, E.4* - Edmonton
Higham, Upper	*Kent* - Rochester
Higham with West Close Booth	*Lancaster* - Burnley
High Angerton	*Northumberland* - Morpeth
High Barnston	*Durham* - Gateshead
High Beech	*Essex* - Edmonton
High Bentham	*York, W.R.* - Lancaster
High Bishopside	*York, W.R.* - Harrogate
High Bonwick	*York, E.R.* - Beverley
High Bradley	*York, W.R.* - Skipton
Highbridge	*Cumberland* - Carlisle
Highbridge	*Hants* - Winchester
Highbridge	*Somerset* - Weston Super Mare
High Brinkburn	*Northumberland* - Morpeth
Highbrook	*Sussex* - East Grinstead
High Bullen	*Stafford* - Dudley
High Burnham	*Lincoln* - Gainsborough
Highburton	*York, W.R.* - Huddersfield
Highbury (part)	*London, N.5* - Clerkenwell
Highbury (part)	*London, N.5* - Shoreditch
Highbury	*Somerset* - Frome
Highbury Park	*London, N.5* - Clerkenwell
High Buston	*Northumberland* - Alnwick
High Butcher Race	*Durham* - Durham
High Callerton	*Northumberland* - Newcastle upon Tyne
High Catlowdy	*Cumberland* - Carlisle
High Catton	*York, E.R.* - York
High Cayton	*York W.R.* - Harrogate
High Church	*Northumberland* - Morpeth
Highclere	*Hants* - Newbury
Highcliff-on-Sea	*Hants* - Bournemouth
High Close	*Cumberland* - Workington
High Coley	*Stafford* - Stafford
High Coniscliffe	*Durham* - Darlington
High Corner	*Hants* - Salisbury
High Crompton	*Lancaster* - Oldham
High Crosby	*Cumberland* - Carlisle
High Cross	*Herts* - Hertford
High Cross	*Warwick* - Hinckley
High Cross	*Warwick* - Warwick
High Cummersdale	*Cumberland* - Carlisle
High Downs	*Durham* - Durham
High Easter	*Essex* - Braintree
High Ellington	*York, N.R.* - Harrogate
Higher Aisholt	*Somerset* - Bridgwater
Higher Alham	*Somerset* - Wells
Higher Batson	*Devon* - Kingsbridge
Higher Bebington	*Cheshire* - Birkenhead

Higher Broughton	*Lancaster* - Salford
Higher Burton	*Dorset* - Dorchester
High Ercall	*Salop* - Wellington (Salop)
Higher Coity	*Glamorgan* - Bridgend
Higher Coombe	*Wilts* - Shaftesbury
Higher Copthurst	*Lancs* - Chorley
Higher Coychurch	*Glamorgan* - Bridgend
Higher Crumpsall	*Lancaster* - Manchester
Higherford	*Lancs* - Nelson
Higher Green	*Lancs* - Leigh
Higher Hambleton	*Rutland* - Oakham
Higher Hurst	*Lancs* - Ashton-under-Lyne
Higher Ince	*Lancs* - Wigan
Higher Irlam	*Lancaster* - Salford
Higher Kingcombe	*Dorset* - Dorchester
Higher Kinnerton	*Flint* - Chester
Higher Lane	*Lancaster* - Bury
Higher Llangynwyd	*Glamorgan* - Bridgend
Higher Llansamlet	*Glamorgan* - Swansea
Higher Newcastle	*Glamorgan* - Bridgend
Higher Nyland	*Somerset* - Yeovil
Higher Openshaw	*Lancaster* - Manchester
Higher Quick	*York, W.R.* - Ashton-under-Lyne
Higher Ridge	*Salop* - Oswestry
Higher Sherford	*Devon* - Plymouth
Higher Spargo	*Cornwall* - Truro
Higher Strode	*Devon* - Plymouth
Higher Sutton	*Cheshire* - Macclesfield
Higher Tale	*Devon* - Exeter
Highertown	*Cornwall* - Bideford
Highertown	*Cornwall* - Truro
Higher Tranmere	*Cheshire* - Birkenhead
Higher Tythegstone	*Glamorgan* - Bridgend
Higher Walton	*Cheshire* - Warrington
Higher Walton	*Lancaster* - Preston
Higher Wheelton	*Lancaster* - Chorley
Higher Whitley	*Cheshire* - Warrington
Higher Wych	*Salop* - Whitchurch
High Felling	*Durham* - Gateshead
Highfield	*Durham* - Newcastle upon Tyne
Highfield	*Hants* - Southampton
Highfield	*Herts* - Hemel Hempstead
Highfield	*Hunts* - Biggleswade
Highfield	*Lancs* - Barrow-in-Furness
Highfield	*Lancaster* - Wigan
Highfields (Bilston)	*Stafford* - Wolverhampton
Highfields	*Stafford* - Stafford
Highfields	*York, W.R.* - Doncaster
Highfields	*York, W.R.* - Sheffield
High Flatt	*Cumberland* - Workington
High Flatts	*Durham* - Durham
High Flatts	*York, W.R.* - Huddersfield
High Fold	*York, W.R.* - Harrogate
High Forest	*Northumberland* - Hexham
High Fotherley	*Northumberland* - Hexham
High Foulshaw	*Westmorland* - Kendal
High Garrett	*Essex* - Braintree
Highgate	*Kent* - Cranbrook
Highgate (part)	*London, N.6* - Bloomsbury and Marylebone
Highgate (part)	*London, N.6* - Clerkenwell
Highgate	*Stafford* - Stourbridge
Highgate	*Warwick* - Birmingham
Highgate	*York, W.R.* - Doncaster
Highgate	*York, W.R.* - Sheffield
High Grange	*Durham* - Bishop Auckland
High Green	*Worcester* - Worcester
High Green	*York, W.R.* - Sheffield
High Halden	*Kent* - Cranbrook
High Hall	*Stafford* - Stafford
High Halstow	*Kent* - Rochester
High Ham	*Somerset* - Bridgwater
High Harrogate	*York, W.R.* - Harrogate
High Hatton	*Salop* - Market Drayton
High Heath	*Salop* - Market Drayton
High Heath	*Stafford* - Walsall
High Heath	*Worcester* - Birmingham
High Heighley	*Northumberland* - Morpeth
High Hesket	*Cumberland* - Penrith
High Hesleden	*Durham* - Hartlepool

High Highlaws	*Northumberland* - Morpeth
High Hold	*Durham* - Gateshead
High Hoyland	*York, W.R.* - Barnsley
High Hunsley	*York, E.R.* - Beverley
High Hurstwood	*Sussex* - Lewes
High Ireby	*Cumberland* - Carlisle
High Kelling	*Norfolk* - Norwich
High Knipe	*Westmorland* - Penrith
High Lane	*Cheshire* - Stockport
High Lane	*Stafford* - Stoke-on-Trent
High Lanes	*Cornwall* - Redruth
High Lanes	*Stafford* - Stafford
High Laver	*Essex* - Harlow
High Laws	*Cumberland* - Carlisle
Highlaws	*Northumberland* - Morpeth
Highlaws, High	*Northumberland* - Morpeth
Highlaws, Low	*Northumberland* - Morpeth
Highleadon	*Gloucester* - Gloucester
High Legh	*Cheshire* - Altrincham
Highleigh	*Sussex* - Chichester
High Leven	*York, N.R.* - Middlesbrough
Highley	*Salop* - Kidderminster
High Littleton	*Somerset* - Bristol
High Mellwood	*Lincoln* - Gainsborough
High Melton	*York, W.R.* - Doncaster
High Moor	*Cumberland* - Carlisle
High Moor	*Derby* - Chesterfield
High Moor	*Lancaster* - Wigan
Highmoor	*Oxford* - Reading
High Moor	*York, W.R.* - Oldham
Highmoor	*York, W.R.* - York
High Moorhouse	*Cumberland* - Carlisle
High Moorsley	*Durham* - Durham
Highmore	*Oxford* - Reading
Highmore Cross	*Oxford* - Reading
High Moresby	*Cumberland* - Whitehaven
Highnam	*Gloucester* - Gloucester
High Needham	*Derby* - Buxton
High Nibthwaite	*Lancaster* - Barrow-in-Furness
High Offley	*Stafford* - Stafford
High Onn	*Stafford* - Stafford
High Pittington	*Durham* - Durham
High Ridge	*Sussex* - Hastings
Highroad Well	*York, W.R.* - Halifax
High Roding	*Essex* - Chelmsford
High Rodingbury	*Essex* - Chelmsford
High Salvington	*Sussex* - Worthing
High Scathwaite	*Lancaster* - Barrow-in-Furness
High Sharpley	*Durham* - Sunderland
High Side	*Cumberland* - Workington
High Simonside	*Durham* - South Shields
High Skirlington	*York, E.R.* - Beverley
High Southwick	*Durham* - Sunderland
High Spen	*Durham* - Newcastle upon Tyne
High Stables	*Durham* - Consett
High Stanners	*Northumberland* - Morpeth
Highsted	*Kent* - Sittingbourne
High Stoop	*Durham* - Bishop Auckland
High Storrs	*York, W.R.* - Sheffield
High Street	*Cornwall* - St. Austell
Highters Heath	*Warwick* - Birmingham
Highthorne	*York, W.R.* - Rotherham
High Thornley	*Durham* - Newcastle upon Tyne
Hightown	*Denbigh* - Wrexham
Hightown	*Hants* - Bournemouth
Hightown	*Lancaster* - Liverpool
High Town	*Stafford* - Walsall
Hightown	*York, W.R.* - Dewsbury
Hightown Heights	*York, W.R.* - Dewsbury
High Toynton	*Lincoln* - Lincoln
High Trewhitt	*Northumberland* - Morpeth
High Utley	*York, W.R.* - Keighley
High Walton	*Salop* - Ludlow
High Ward	*Northumberland* - Morpeth
High Waupley	*York, N.R.* - Whitby
Highway (Lantesglos-by-Fowey)	*Cornwall* - Liskeard
Highway (St. Pinnock)	*Cornwall* - Liskeard
Highway (Illogan)	*Cornwall* - Redruth
Highway (Redruth)	*Cornwall* - Redruth

High Westwood	*Durham* - Consett
Highwood	*Dorset* - Swanage
Highwood	*Essex* - Chelmsford
Highwood	*Gloucester* - Bristol
High Wood	*Hants* - Salisbury
High Wood	*Lincoln* - Gainsborough
Highworth	*Wilts* - Swindon
High Wych	*Herts* - Bishop's Stortford
High Wycombe	*Bucks* - High Wycombe
Hilborough	*Norfolk* - King's Lynn
Hilbre Island	*Cheshire* - Birkenhead
Hilcot	*Stafford* - Stafford
Hilcot	*Wilts* - Devizes
Hilcote	*Derby* - Alreton
Hildenborough	*Kent* - Tonbridge
Hildenley	*York, N.R.* - Malton
Hildersham	*Cambridge* - Cambridge
Hildersley	*Hereford* - Monmouth
Hilderstone	*Stafford* - Stoke-on-Trent
Hilfield	*Dorset* - Dorchester
Hilgay	*Norfolk* - King's Lynn
Hill	*Cumberland* - Workington
Hill	*Gloucester* - Thornbury
Hill	*Warwick* - Birmingham
Hill	*Warwick* - Rugby
Hill	*Worcester* - Birmingham
Hillam	*York, W.R.* - Pontefract
Hill and Cakemore	*Worcester* - Stourbridge
Hill and Moor	*Worcester* - Evesham
Hillbeck	*Westmorland* - Penrith
Hillborough	*Kent* - Canterbury
Hillborough	*Warwick* - Stratford on Avon
Hill Brow	*Hants* - Petersfield
Hill Brow	*Sussex* - Petersfield
Hill Butts	*Dorset* - Wimborne Minster
Hill Chorlton	*Stafford* - Stoke-on-Trent
Hill Common	*Somerset* - Taunton
Hill Croome	*Worcester* - Worcester
Hill Deverill	*Wilts* - Warminster
Hill End	*Berks* - Oxford
Hill End	*Durham* - Bishop Auckland
Hill End	*Gloucester* - Cheltenham
Hill End	*Herts* - Hitchin
Hill End	*Herts* - St. Albans
Hillend Green	*Gloucester* - Gloucester
Hillersland	*Gloucester* - Monmouth
Hillesden	*Bucks* - Aylesbury
Hillesley	*Gloucester* - Bristol
Hillfarrance	*Somerset* - Taunton
Hill Furze	*Worcester* - Evesham
Hill Gate	*Hereford* - Hereford
Hillgrove	*Sussex* - Chichester
Hillhampton	*Worcester* - Worcester
Hill Head	*Hants* - Portsmouth
Hill Hook	*Warwick* - Birmingham
Hillhouse	*York, W.R.* - Huddersfield
Hillingdon	*Middlesex* - Uxbridge
Hillingdon, East	*Middlesex* - Uxbridge
Hillingdon Heath	*Middlesex* - Uxbridge
Hillingdon, West	*Middlesex* - Uxbridge
Hillington	*Norfolk* - King's Lynn
Hillington	*Norfolk* - Norwich
Hillmorton	*Warwick* - Rugby
Hillmorton Paddox	*Warwick* - Rugby
Hill Mountain	*Pembroke* - Haverfordwest
Hillock	*Lancaster* - Bury
Hill of Eaton	*Hereford* - Monmouth
Hill Pool	*Worcester* - Kidderminster
Hill Row	*Cambridge* - Ely
Hillsborough	*York, W.R.* - Sheffield
Hillstown	*Derby* - Chesterfield
Hill Top	*Durham* - Bishop Auckland
Hill Top (Backworth)	*Northumberland* - North Shields
Hill Top (Newthorpe)	*Notts* - Ilkeston
Hill Top (Much Wenlock)	*Salop* - Shrewsbury
Hill Top (Benthall)	*Salop* - Bridgnorth
Hill Top (Dawley Road)	*Salop* - Wellington (Salop)
Hill Top	*Stafford* - West Bromwich
Hill Top	*Worcester* - Bromsgrove

Hill Top (Webheath)	*Worcester* - Redditch
Hill Top (Warley)	*Worcester* - West Bromwich
Hill Top	*York, W.R.* - Rotherham
Hill Top	*York, W.R.* - Sheffield
Hill Wooton	*Warwick* - Warwick
Hilmarton	*Wilts* - Swindon
Hilperton	*Wilts* - Trowbridge
Hilperton Marsh	*Wilts* - Trowbridge
Hilsea	*Hants* - Portsmouth
Hilston	*York, E.R.* - Kingston-upon-Hull
Hilton	*Derby* - Burton-upon-Trent
Hilton	*Dorset* - Dorchester
Hilton	*Durham* - Bishop Auckland
Hilton	*Hunts* - Huntingdon
Hilton	*Rutland* - Stamford
Hilton	*Salop* - Bridgnorth
Hilton	*Stafford* - Lichfield
Hilton	*Stafford* - Wolverhampton
Hilton	*Westmorland* - Penrith
Hilton	*York, N.R.* - Middlesbrough
Hilton House	*Lancaster* - Bolton
Himbleton	*Worcester* - Worcester
Himley	*Stafford* - Wolverhampton
Hincaster	*Westmorland* - Kendal
Hincheslea	*Hants* - Lymington
Hinchley Wood	*Surrey* - Kingston-upon-Thames
Hinchliffe Mill	*York, W.R.* - Huddersfield
Hinckley	*Leicester* - Hinckley
Hincksford	*Stafford* - Wolverhampton
Hinckshay	*Salop* - Wellington (Salop)
Hinderclay	*Suffolk* - Bury St. Edmunds
Hinders Lane	*Gloucester* - Gloucester
Hinderton	*Cheshire* - Birkenhead
Hinderwell	*York, N.R.* - Whitby
Hindhead	*Surrey* - Guildford
Hindley	*Lancaster* - Wigan
Hindley Green	*Lancaster* - Wigan
Hindley Steele	*Northumberland* - Hexham
Hindlip	*Worcester* - Worcester
Hindlow	*Derby* - Buxton
Hindolveston	*Norfolk* - King's Lynn
Hindon	*Wilts* - Shaftesbury
Hindringham	*Norfolk* - King's Lynn
Hindsford	*Lancaster* - Leigh
Hines Heath	*Salop* - Shrewsbury
Hingham	*Norfolk* - Norwich
Hinksey Ferry	*Berks* - Oxford
Hinksey Hill	*Berks* - Oxford
Hinksey, New	*Oxford* - Oxford
Hinksey, North	*Berks* - Oxford
Hinksey, South	*Berks* - Oxford
Hinksford	*Stafford* - Stourbridge
Hinnington	*Salop* - Wellington (Salop)
Hinstock	*Salop* - Market Drayton
Hintlesham	*Suffolk* - Ipswich
Hinton	*Berks* - Reading
Hinton	*Gloucester* - Bristol
Hinton	*Gloucester* - Stroud
Hinton	*Hants* - Petersfield
Hinton	*Salop* - Shrewsbury
Hinton	*Salop* - Whitchurch
Hinton	*Suffolk* - Halesworth
Hinton Admiral	*Hants* - Bournemouth
Hinton Ampner	*Hants* - Winchester
Hinton Blewett	*Somerset* - Bristol
Hinton Charterhouse	*Somerset* - Bath
Hinton Friary	*Somerset* - Bath
Hinton, Great	*Wilts* - Trowbridge
Hinton-in-the-Hedges	*Northampton* - Banbury
Hinton, Little	*Wilts* - Swindon
Hinton Martell	*Dorset* - Wimborne Minster
Hinton-on-the-Green	*Gloucester* - Evesham
Hinton Parva	*Dorset* - Wimborne Minster
Hinton Parva	*Wilts* - Swindon
Hinton St. George	*Somerset* - Yeovil
Hinton St. Mary	*Dorset* - Shaftesbury
Hinton St. Mary	*Wilts* - Shaftesbury
Hinton Waldrist	*Berks* - Oxford
Hints	*Stafford* - Tamworth
Hinwick	*Beds* - Wellingborough

Hinxhill	*Kent* - Ashford
Hinxton	*Cambridge* - Cambridge
Hinxworth	*Herts* - Biggleswade
Hipley	*Hants* - Portsmouth
Hippenscombe	*Wilts* - Andover
Hipperholme	*York, W.R.* - Halifax
Hipswell	*York, N.R.* - Darlington
Hirael	*Caernarvon* - Bangor
Hirnant	*Montgomery* - Oswestry
Hirst	*Northumberland* - Morpeth
Hirst Courtney	*York, W.R.* - Pontefract
Hirwaun	*Brecon and Glamorgan* - Aberdare
Hisomley	*Wilts* - Trowbridge
Histfield	*Gloucester* - Stroud
Histon	*Cambridge* - Cambridge
Hitcham	*Bucks* - Slough
Hitcham	*Suffolk* - Stowmarket
Hitchin	*Herts* - Hitchin
Hitchins, New	*Somerset* - Frome
Hither Green	*London, S.E.13* - Bromley
Hittisleigh	*Devon* - Okehampton
Hixon	*Stafford* - Stafford
Hoaden	*Kent* - Deal
Hoarcross	*Stafford* - Lichfield
Hoarwithy	*Hereford* - Hereford
Hoath	*Kent* - Canterbury
Hoathly, East	*Sussex* - Lewes
Hoathly, West	*Sussex* - East Grinstead
Hobarris	*Salop* - Ludlow
Hobbergate	*Stafford* - Stafford
Hobbs Bottom	*Wilts* - Trowbridge
Hobbs Cross	*Essex* - Harlow
Hobhill	*Worcester* - Redditch
Hob Hole	*Lincoln* - Skegness
Hobson Colliery	*Durham* - Consett
Hoby	*Leicester* - Melton Mowbray
Hockenden	*Kent* - Bromley
Hockenhull	*Cheshire* - Chester
Hocker Edge	*Kent* - Cranbrook
Hockerill	*Herts* - Bishop's Stortford
Hockering	*Norfolk* - East Dereham
Hockerton	*Notts* - Newark
Hockham	*Norfolk* - Thetford
Hockley	*Essex* - Southend
Hockley	*Staffs* - Tamworth
Hockley	*Warwick* - Birmingham
Hockley Heath	*Warwick* - Birmingham
Hockley Hole	*Middlesex* - Uxbridge
Hockcliffe	*Beds* - Bletchley and Leighton Buzzard
Hockwold cum Wilton	*Norfolk* - Thetford
Hockworthy	*Devon* - Tiverton
Hoddesdon	*Herts* - Hertford
Hoddington	*Hants* - Basingstoke
Hoddlesden	*Lancaster* - Blackburn
Hodge Hill	*Warwick* - Birmingham
Hodge Hill Common	*Warwick* - Birmingham
Hodgeston	*Pembroke* - Haverfordwest
Hodley	*Montgomery* - Newtown
Hodnel, Lower	*Warwick* - Warwick
Hodnel, Upper	*Warwick* - Warwick
Hodnet	*Salop* - Market Drayton
Hodnet Heath	*Salop* - Market Drayton
Hodsock	*Notts* - Worksop
Hodsock Woodhouse	*Notts* - Worksop
Hodson	*Wilts* - Swindon
Hodthorpe	*Derby* - Worksop
Hoe	*Norfolk* - East Dereham
Hoe Benham	*Berks* - Newbury
Hoe, East (Hambledon)	*Hants* - Portsmouth
Hoff	*Westmorland* - Penrith
Hoggeston	*Bucks* - Aylesbury
Hoggrells End	*Warwick* - Birmingham
Hoghton (part)	*Lancaster* - Chorley
Hoghton (part)	*Lancaster* - Preston
Hoghton Bottoms	*Lancaster* - Chorley
Hognaston	*Derby* - Derby
Hogshaw	*Bucks* - Aylesbury
Hogs Norton	*Herts* - Hitchin
Hogsthorpe	*Lincoln* - Skegness

Hogstow, Lower	*Salop* - Shrewsbury
Hogstrough	*Kent* - Sevenoaks
Hog's Yeotham	*Herts* - St. Albans
Holback	*Bucks* - Bletchley and Leighton Buzzard
Holbeach	*Lincoln* - Spalding
Holbeach Bank	*Lincoln* - Spalding
Holbeach Clough	*Lincoln* - Spalding
Holbeach Crown Colony	*Lincoln* - Spalding
Holbeach Drove	*Lincoln* - Spalding
Holbeache	*Stafford* - Stourbridge
Holbeach Fen	*Lincoln* - Spalding
Holbeach Hurn	*Lincoln* - Spalding
Holbeach Marsh	*Lincoln* - Spalding
Holbeach St. Marks	*Lincoln* - Spalding
Holbeach St. Matthews	*Lincoln* - Spalding
Holbeck	*Lincoln* - Skegness
Holbeck	*Notts* - Worksop
Holbeck	*York, W.R.* - Leeds
Holbeck Woodhouse	*Notts* - Worksop
Holberrow Green	*Warwick* - Redditch
Holbeton	*Devon* - Plymouth
Holborn	*Durham* - Newcastle upon Tyne
Holborn (part)	*London, E.C.1* - Clerkenwell
Holborn (part)	*London, E.C.1* - Mayor's and City of London
Holborn (part)	*London, W.C.1* - Bloomsbury and Marylebone
Holborn (part)	*London, W.C.1* - Clerkenwell
Holborn (part)	*London, W.C.1* - Westminster
Holbrook	*Derby* - Derby
Holbrook	*Derby* - Sheffield
Holbrook	*Gloucester* - Bristol
Holbrook	*Salop* - Shrewsbury
Holbrook	*Suffolk* - Ipswich
Holbrooks	*Warwick* - Coventry
Holcombe	*Devon* - Newton Abbot
Holcombe	*Gloucester* - Stroud
Holcombe	*Lancaster* - Bury
Holcombe	*Oxford* - Didcot
Holcombe	*Somerset* - Wells
Holcombe Brook	*Lancaster* - Bury
Holcombe Burnell	*Devon* - Exeter
Holcombe, Great	*Oxford* - Didcot
Holcombe Rogus	*Devon* - Tiverton
Holcot	*Beds* - Bletchley and Leighton Buzzard
Holcot	*Northampton* - Northampton
Holden	*York, W.R.* - Blackburn
Holdenby	*Northampton* - Northampton
Holdenhurst	*Hants* - Bournemouth
Holdfast	*Worcester* - Cheltenham
Holdford	*Warwick* - Birmingham
Holdgate	*Salop* - Ludlow
Holdingham	*Lincoln* - Sleaford
Holditch	*Dorset* - Axminster and Chard
Holdshott	*Hants* - Basingstoke
Holdsworth	*York, W.R.* - Halifax
Holdsworth	*York, W.R.* - Sheffield
Holebiggerah	*Lancaster* - Barrow-in-Furness
Hole Haven	*Essex* - Southend
Hole-in-the-Wall	*Hereford* - Monmouth
Holeshole	*Devon* - Plymouth
Holestreet	*Sussex* - Worthing
Holford	*Somerset* - Minehead
Holker	*Lancaster* - Barrow-in-Furness
Holkham	*Norfolk* - King's Lynn
Holkham, New	*Norfolk* - King's Lynn
Hollacombe	*Devon* - Launceston
Holland	*Surrey* - Reigate
Holland Arms	*Anglesey* - Llangefni
Holland Fen, Dogdyke	*Lincoln* - Boston
Holland, New	*Lincoln* - Barton-on-Humber
Hollesley	*Suffolk* - Woodbridge
Holleth	*Lancaster* - Lancaster
Hollicott	*Salop* - Bridgnorth
Hollingbourne	*Kent* - Maidstone
Hollingbury	*Sussex* - Brighton
Hollingdean	*Sussex* - Brighton

HOL

Hollingdon	*Bucks* - Bletchley and Leighton Buzzard
Hollinghill	*Northumberland* - Morpeth
Hollingsclough	*Stafford* - Leek
Holling's Hill	*Worcester* - Great Malvern
Hollingthorpe	*York, W.R.* - Wakefield
Hollington	*Derby* - Derby
Hollington	*Stafford* - Uttoxeter
Hollington	*Sussex* - Hastings
Hollington Fields	*Stafford* - Uttoxeter
Hollingwood	*Derby* - Chesterfield
Hollingworth	*Cheshire* - Hyde
Hollingworth Lake	*Lancaster* - Rochdale
Hollinhurst	*York, W.R.* - Pontefract
Hollin Lane	*Cheshire* - Macclesfield
Hollin Root	*Cumberland* - Workington
Hollins	*Cheshire* - Ashton-under-Lyne
Hollins	*Lancaster* - Bury
Hollins	*Lancaster* - Oldham
Hollins End	*York, W.R.* - Sheffield
Hollins Green	*Lancaster* - Warrington
Hollins Grove	*Lancaster* - Blackburn
Hollins Lane	*Lancaster* - Lancaster
Hollinswood	*Salop* - Wellington (Salop)
Hollinwood	*Lancaster* - Oldham
Hollinwood	*Salop* - Whitchurch
Hollom Down	*Hants* - Andover
Holloway	*Derby* - Matlock
Holloway	*London, N.7* - Clerkenwell
Holloway	*Salop* - Ludlow
Holloway, Upper	*London, N.19* - Clerkenwell
Hollowell	*Northampton* - Northampton
Hollowfields	*Worcester* - Redditch
Hollow Meadows	*York, W.R.* - Sheffield
Hollows	*Cumberland* - Workington
Hollow Shore	*Kent* - Canterbury
Holly Bank	*Stafford* - Stoke-on-Trent
Holly Bank	*Stafford* - Wolverhampton
Hollybush	*Monmouth* - Blackwood
Holly Bush	*Stafford* - Wolverhampton
Holly Bush	*Worcester* - Great Malvern
Holly Estate	*Lancaster* - Oldham
Holly Green	*Worcester* - Cheltenham
Holly Hall	*Worcester* - Dudley
Holly Hill	*Hants* - Portsmouth
Hollyhurst	*Salop* - Whitchurch
Hollym	*York, E.R.* - Kingston-upon-Hull
Holly Park	*London, N.3* - Barnet
Hollywater	*Hants* - Aldershot and Farnham
Hollywater	*Hants* - Petersfield
Hollywell Moor	*Salop* - Shrewsbury
Hollywood	*Worcester* - Birmingham
Holmbridge	*York, W.R.* - Huddersfield
Holmbury St. Mary (part)	*Surrey* - Dorking
Holmbury St. Mary (part)	*Surrey* - Guildford
Holmbush	*Cornwall* - St. Austell
Holmby	*Northampton* - Northampton
Holme	*Hunts* - Peterborough
Holme	*Lancaster* - Burnley
Holme	*Lincoln* - Scunthorpe
Holme	*Notts* - Newark
Holme	*Westmorland* - Kendal
Holme	*York, W.R.* - Huddersfield
Holme Abbey	*Cumberland* - Carlisle
Holme Cultram	*Cumberland* - Carlisle
Holme East Waver	*Cumberland* - Carlisle
Holme Fen	*Hunts* - Peterborough
Holme Green	*Beds* - Biggleswade
Holme Green	*York, W.R.* - York
Holme Hale	*Norfolk* - King's Lynn
Holmehead	*Cumberland* - Carlisle
Holme Lacy	*Hereford* - Hereford
Holmelands Estate	*Durham* - Durham
Holme Marsh	*Hereford* - Hereford
Holme-next-the-Sea	*Norfolk* - King's Lynn
Holme-on-Spalding Moor	*York, E.R.* - York
Holme-on-the-Wolds	*York, E.R.* - Beverley
Holme Pierrepont	*Notts* - Nottingham
Holmer	*Hereford* - Hereford
Holmer Green	*Bucks* - Amersham

HOL

Holmer Green (Penn)	*Bucks* - High Wycombe
Holmes	*Lancaster* - Southport
Holmes	*York, W.R.* - Rotherham
Holme St. Cuthbert	*Cumberland* - Carlisle
Holmes Chapel	*Cheshire* - Congleton
Holmesfield	*Derby* - Chesterfield
Holmes Hill	*Herts* - Barnet
Holmes Marsh	*Hereford* - Kington
Holmeswood	*Lancaster* - Southport
Holmewood	*York, W.R.* - Bradford
Holmfield	*York, W.R.* - Halifax
Holmfirth	*York, W.R.* - Huddersfield
Holmgate	*Derby* - Chesterfield
Holmley Common	*Derby* - Chesterfield
Holmpton	*York, E.R.* - Kingston-upon-Hull
Holmrook	*Cumberland* - Whitehaven
Holmside	*Durham* - Durham
Holmsley, South	*Hants* - Lymington
Holmsley, North	*Hants* - Bournemouth
Holmwood	*Derby* - Chesterfield
Holmwood	*Surrey* - Dorking
Holne	*Devon* - Newton Abbot
Holnest	*Dorset* - Yeovil
Holnicote	*Somerset* - Minehead
Holsworthy	*Devon* - Bideford
Holt	*Denbigh* - Wrexham
Holt	*Dorset* - Wimborne Minster
Holt	*Hants* - Basingstoke
Holt	*Leicester* - Kettering
Holt	*Norfolk* - Norwich
Holt	*Wilts* - Trowbridge
Holt	*Worcester* - Worcester
Holtby	*York, N.R.* - York
Holt Common	*Wilts* - Trowbridge
Holt End	*Worcester* - Redditch
Holt Fleet	*Worcester* - Worcester
Holt Hill	*Lancaster* - Burnley
Holton	*Oxford* - Oxford
Holton	*Somerset* - Yeovil
Holton	*Suffolk* - Halesworth
Holton cum Beckering	*Lincoln* - Lincoln
Holton Heath	*Dorset* - Swanage
Holton-le-Clay	*Lincoln* - Great Grimsby
Holton-le-Moor	*Lincoln* - Scunthorpe
Holton St. Mary	*Suffolk* - Ipswich
Holt Preen	*Salop* - Shrewsbury
Holts	*Lancaster* - Oldham
Holtspur	*Bucks* - High Wycombe
Holt Wood	*Dorset* - Wimborne Minster
Holtye	*Sussex* - East Grinstead
Holverston	*Norfolk* - Norwich
Holway	*Flint* - Holywell
Holway	*Somerset* - Taunton
Holwell	*Beds* - Hitchin
Holwell	*Leicester* - Melton Mowbray
Holwell	*Oxford* - Witney
Holwell	*Somerset* - Frome
Holwell	*Somerset* - Yeovil
Holwell	*York, N.R.* - Bishop Auckland
Holybourne	*Hants* - Aldershot and Farnham
Holy Cross (Wallsend)	*Northumberland* - North Shields
Holy Cross	*Worcester* - Stourbridge
Holyhead	*Anglesey* - Llangefni
Holy Island	*Northumberland* - Berwick-upon-Tweed
Holymoorside	*Derby* - Chesterfield
Holyoakes	*Worcester* - Redditch
Holyport	*Berks* - Slough
Holystone	*Northumberland* - Morpeth
Holystone Estate	*Northumberland* - Newcastle-upon-Tyne
Holywell	*Cornwall* - Truro
Holywell	*Dorset* - Yeovil
Holywell	*Flint* - Holywell
Holywell	*Hunts* - Huntingdon
Holywell	*Lincoln* - Stamford
Holywell	*Northumberland* - North Shields
Holywell	*Warwick* - Warwick

HOL - HOP

Holywell Brook	*York, W.R.* - Halifax
Holywell, East	*Northumberland* - North Shields
Holywell Green	*York, W.R.* - Halifax
Holywell Lake	*Somerset* - Taunton
Holywell Row	*Suffolk* - Bury St. Edmunds
Holywell, West	*Northumberland* - North Shields
Homer	*Salop* - Bridgnorth
Homersfield	*Suffolk* - Halesworth
Homerton	*London, E.9* - Shoreditch
Homestall	*Kent* - Canterbury
Home, The	*Salop* - Shrewsbury
Hom Green	*Hereford* - Monmouth
Homington	*Wilts* - Salisbury
Honeyborough	*Pembroke* - Haverfordwest
Honeybourne	*Worcs* - Evesham
Honeycombe	*Cornwall* - Plymouth
Honeydon, Lower	*Beds* - Biggleswade
Honeydon, Upper	*Beds* - Biggleswade
Honeystreet	*Wilts* - Devizes
Honicknowle	*Devon* - Plymouth
Honiley	*Warwick* - Warwick
Honing	*Norfolk* - Norwich
Honingham	*Norfolk* - Norwich
Honington	*Lincoln* - Grantham
Honington	*Suffolk* - Thetford
Honington	*Warwick* - Stratford on Avon
Honiton	*Cornwall* - Launceston
Honiton	*Devon* - Exeter
Honiton, Clyst	*Devon* - Exeter
Honley	*York, W.R.* - Huddersfield
Honnington	*Salop* - Wellington (Salop)
Honor	*Somerset* - Bristol
Honor Oak (part)	*London, S.E.23* - Bromley
Honor Oak (part)	*London, S.E.23* - Lambeth
Hoo	*Kent* - Rochester
Hoo	*Salop* - Wellington (Salop)
Hoo	*Suffolk* - Woodbridge
Hoober	*York, W.R.* - Rotherham
Hood Green	*York, W.R.* - Barnsley
Hood Hill	*York, W.R.* - Rotherham
Hooe	*Devon* - Plymouth
Hooe	*Sussex* - Hastings
Hoo Green	*Cheshire* - Altrincham
Hook	*Cambridge* - March
Hook	*Dorset* - Dorchester
Hook	*Hants* - Basingstoke
Hook	*Pembroke* - Haverfordwest
Hook	*Surrey* - Kingston-upon-Thames
Hook	*Wilts* - Swindon
Hook	*York, W.R.* - Goole
Hook-a-Gate	*Salop* - Shrewsbury
Hook Common	*Worcester* - Great Malvern
Hookergate	*Durham* - Newcastle upon Tyne
Hook Gate	*Stafford* - Market Drayton
Hook Green	*Kent* - Dartford
Hook Green	*Kent* - Gravesend
Hook Green	*Kent* - Tunbridge Wells
Hook Moor	*York, W.R.* - Leeds
Hook Norton	*Oxford* - Banbury
Hooks Cross	*Herts* - Hertford
Hooks, The	*Salop* - Market Drayton
Hooksway	*Sussex* - Petersfield
Hookway	*Devon* - Exeter
Hook with Warsash	*Hants* - Portsmouth
Hookwood	*Surrey* - Reigate
Hoole	*Cheshire* - Chester
Hoole	*Lancaster* - Preston
Hoole, Little	*Lancaster* - Preston
Hoole, Much	*Lancaster* - Preston
Hoole Village	*Cheshire* - Chester
Hooley	*Surrey* - Croydon
Hooley Bridge	*Lancaster* - Bury
Hoon	*Derby* - Burton-upon-Trent
Hoo, The	*Gloucester* - Cheltenham
Hooton	*Cheshire* - Birkenhead
Hooton Levett	*York, W.R.* - Rotherham
Hooton Pagnell	*York, W.R.* - Doncaster
Hooton Roberts	*York, W.R.* - Rotherham
Hope	*Derby* - Buxton
Hope	*Devon* - Kingsbridge

HOP - HOR

Hope	*Flint* - Wrexham
Hope	*Montgomery* - Welshpool
Hope-all-Saints	*Kent* - Ashford
Hope Alone	*Northumberland* - Hexham
Hope Bagot	*Salop* - Ludlow
Hope Bowdler	*Salop* - Ludlow
Hope Cove	*Devon* - Kingsbridge
Hope Dale	*Stafford* - Leek
Hope, Lower	*Hereford* - Hereford
Hope Mansell	*Hereford* - Gloucester
Hope Mountain	*Flint* - Wrexham
Hopesay	*Salop* - Ludlow
Hope, The	*Salop* - Ludlow
Hopetown	*York, W.R.* - Harrogate
Hope under Dinmore	*Hereford* - Leominster
Hope Woodlands	*Derby* - Sheffield
Hopkinstown	*Carmarthen* - Ammanford
Hopley	*Salop* - Market Drayton
Hoppen	*Northumberland* - Berwick-upon-Tweed
Hopperton	*York, W.R.* - Harrogate
Hop Pole	*Lincoln* - Spalding
Hopshort	*Salop* - Market Drayton
Hopstone	*Salop* - Bridgnorth
Hopton	*Derby* - Matlock
Hopton	*Salop* - Market Drayton
Hopton	*Salop* - Shrewsbury
Hopton	*Stafford* - Stafford
Hopton	*Suffolk* - Thetford
Hopton Cangeford	*Salop* - Ludlow
Hopton Castle	*Salop* - Knighton
Hopton Heath	*Salop* - Ludlow
Hopton, Lower	*York, W.R.* - Dewsbury
Hopton-on-Sea	*Suffolk* - Great Yarmouth
Hopton, Upper	*York, W.R.* - Dewsbury
Hopton Wafers	*Salop* - Kidderminster
Hopwas Hayes	*Stafford* - Tamworth
Hopwell	*Derby* - Ilkeston
Hopwood	*Lancaster* - Bury
Hopwood	*Worcester* - Redditch
Horam	*Sussex* - Eastbourne
Horbling	*Lincoln* - Sleaford
Horbling Fen	*Lincoln* - Sleaford
Horbury	*York, W.R.* - Wakefield
Horbury Bridge	*York, W.R.* - Wakefield
Horbury Junction	*York, W.R.* - Wakefield
Horcott	*Gloucester* - Swindon
Horden	*Durham* - Hartlepool
Horden	*Kent* - Cranbrook
Horderley	*Salop* - Ludlow
Hordle	*Hants* - Lymington
Hordley	*Salop* - Oswestry
Horeb	*Cardigan* - Cardigan
Horeham Road	*Sussex* - Eastbourne
Horham	*Suffolk* - Norwich
Horkstow	*Lincoln* - Scunthorpe
Horkstow	*Lincoln* - Scunthorpe
Horley	*Oxford* - Banbury
Horley	*Surrey* - Reigate
Hormead, Great	*Herts* - Hitchin
Hormead, Little	*Herts* - Hitchin
Horn	*Rutland* - Melton Mowbray
Hornash	*Somerset* - Yeovil
Hornblottom	*Somerset* - Wells
Hornbrook Hill	*Sussex* - Horsham
Hornby	*Lancaster* - Lancaster
Horncastle	*Lincoln* - Lincoln
Hornchurch	*Essex* - Ilford
Hornchurch, South (part)	*Essex* - Grays Thurrock
Hornchurch, South (part)	*Essex* - Ilford
Horncliffe	*Northumberland* - Berwick-upon-Tweed
Horndean	*Hants* - Petersfield
Horndon, East	*Essex* - Brentwood
Horndon-on-the-Hill	*Essex* - Grays Thurrock
Horne	*Surrey* - Reigate
Horner	*Somerset* - Minehead
Horn Hill	*Bucks* - Amersham
Horning	*Norfolk* - Norwich
Horninghold	*Leicester* - Corby

Horninglow	*Stafford* - Burton-upon-Trent
Horningsea	*Cambridge* - Cambridge
Horningsham	*Wilts* - Warminster
Horningtoft	*Norfolk* - King's Lynn
Hornington	*York, W.R.* - York
Hornsby	*Cumberland* - Carlisle
Hornsbygate	*Cumberland* - Carlisle
Horns Cross	*Kent* - Dartford
Horns Cross	*Sussex* - Hastings
Hornsea	*York, E.R.* - Beverley
Hornsey (part)	*London, N.8* - Clerkenwell
Hornsey (part)	*London, N.8* - Edmonton
Hornsey Rise	*London, N.19* - Clerkenwell
Hornshill	*Sussex* - Horsham
Horns Lane	*Bucks* - High Wycombe
Hornsleazow	*Gloucester* - Cheltenham
Hornspike	*Salop* - Shrewsbury
Hornton	*Oxford* - Banbury
Horrabridge	*Devon* - Plymouth
Horringer	*Suffolk* - Bury St. Edmunds
Horrington, East	*Somerset* - Wells
Horrington, West	*Somerset* - Wells
Horsea Island	*Hants* - Portsmouth
Horse Bridge	*Cornwall* - Launceston
Horsebridge	*Devon* - Plymouth
Horsebridge	*Hants* - Winchester
Horsebridge	*Sussex* - Eastbourne
Horse Brook	*Stafford* - Wolverhampton
Horse Downs	*Cornwall* - Redruth
Horseferry Bridge	*Gloucester* - Cheltenham
Horsegate	*Lincoln* - Spalding
Horsehay	*Salop* - Wellington (Salop)
Horsehay Common	*Salop* - Wellington (Salop)
Horseheath	*Cambridge* - Cambridge
Horse Hill	*Stafford* - Wolverhampton
Horselees	*Kent* - Canterbury
Horseley Heath (part)	*Stafford* - Dudley
Horseley Heath (part)	*Staffs* - West Bromwich
Horsell	*Surrey* - Guildford
Horseman's Green	*Flint* - Whitchurch
Horsemoor Green	*Bucks* - Slough
Horsendon	*Bucks* - High Wycombe
Horsepool	*Cornwall* - Penzance
Horseshoes Village	*Herts* - St. Albans
Horsey	*Somerset* - Bridgwater
Horsey Island	*Essex* - Colchester
Horsey-next-Sea	*Norfolk* - Great Yarmouth
Horsford	*Norfolk* - Norwich
Horsforth	*York, W.R.* - Leeds
Horsham	*Sussex* - Horsham
Horsham	*Worcester* - Worcester
Horsham St. Faith	*Norfolk* - Norwich
Horsington	*Lincoln* - Lincoln
Horsington	*Somerset* - Yeovil
Horsington Marsh	*Somerset* - Yeovil
Horsley	*Derby* - Ilkeston
Horsley	*Gloucester* - Stroud
Horsley	*Northumberland* - Hexham
Horsley Cross	*Essex* - Harwich
Horsley, East	*Surrey* - Guildford
Horsley Hill	*Durham* - South Shields
Horsley, West	*Surrey* - Guildford
Horsley Woodhouse	*Derby* - Ilkeston
Horsmonden	*Kent* - Tunbridge Wells
Horspath	*Oxford* - Oxford
Horstead with Stanninghall	*Norfolk* - Norwich
Horsted Keynes	*Sussex* - East Grinstead
Hortham	*Gloucester* - Thornbury
Horton	*Bucks* - Bletchley and Leighton Buzzard
Horton	*Bucks* - Slough
Horton	*Dorset* - Wimborne Minster
Horton	*Glamorgan* - Swansea
Horton	*Gloucester* - Bristol
Horton	*Northampton* - Northampton
Horton	*Salop* - Shrewsbury
Horton	*Salop* - Wellington (Salop)
Horton	*Somerset* - Axminster and Chard

Horton	*Stafford* - Leek
Horton	*Surrey* - Epsom
Horton	*Wilts* - Devizes
Horton (Gisburn)	*York, W.R.* - Blackburn
Horton-by-Malpas	*Cheshire* - Whitchurch
Horton-cum-Peel	*Cheshire* - Chester
Horton cum Studley	*Oxford* - Oxford
Horton Grange	*Northumberland* - Morpeth
Horton, Great	*York, W.R.* - Bradford
Horton Hay	*Stafford* - Leek
Horton Heath	*Hants* - Southampton
Horton-in-Craven	*York, W.R.* - Skipton
Horton-in-Ribblesdale	*York, W.R.* Skipton
Horton Kirby	*Kent* - Dartford
Horton Wood	*Salop* - Wellington (Salop)
Horwich	*Lancaster* - Bolton
Horwich End	*Derby* - Buxton
Horwich Moor Bottoms	*Lancaster* - Bolton
Horwood	*Devon* - Bideford
Horwood, Great	*Bucks* - Bletchley and Leighton Buzzard
Horwood, Little	*Bucks* - Bletchley and Leighton Buzzard
Hoscar	*Lancaster* - Southport
Hose	*Leicester* - Melton Mowbray
Hosey Hill	*Kent* - Sevenoaks
Hosketh Hill	*Cumberland* - Carlisle
Hostler's Green	*Oxford* - High Wycombe
Hothersall	*Lancaster* - Preston
Hothfield	*Kent* - Ashford
Hothorpe	*Northampton* - Northampton
Hoton	*Leicester* - Loughborough
Houghall	*Durham* - Durham
Hougham	*Lincoln* - Grantham
Hougham Church	*Kent* - Dover
Hougham, West	*Kent* - Dover
Hougher Wall	*Stafford* - Stoke-on-Trent
Hough Green	*Lancaster* - St. Helens
Hough Hill	*Cheshire* - Ashton-under-Lyne
Hough-on-the-Hill	*Lincoln* - Grantham
Hough, The	*Cheshire* - Altrincham
Houghton	*Cumberland* - Carlisle
Houghton	*Hants* - Winchester
Houghton	*Hunts* - Huntingdon
Houghton	*Northumberland* - Newcastle upon Tyne
Houghton	*Pembroke* - Haverfordwest
Houghton	*Sussex* - Chichester
Houghton Conquest	*Beds* - Bedford
Houghton Gate	*Durham* - Durham
Houghton, Great	*Northampton* - Northampton
Houghton Green	*Lancaster* - Warrington
Houghton in the Brake	*Norfolk* - King's Lynn
Houghton in the Dale	*Norfolk* - King's Lynn
Houghton-le-Spring	*Durham* - Durham
Houghton, Little	*Northampton* - Northampton
Houghton, New	*Derby* - Mansfield
Houghton, New	*Norfolk* - King's Lynn
Houghton, North	*Hants* - Winchester
Houghton-on-the-Hill	*Leicester* - Leicester
Houghton-on-the-Hill	*Norfolk* - King's Lynn
Houghton Regis	*Beds* - Luton
Houghton St. Giles	*Norfolk* - King's Lynn
Houghton, Stoney	*Derby* - Mansfield
Hound	*Hants* - Southampton
Houndsmoor	*Somerset* - Taunton
Hounsdown	*Hants* - Southampton
Hounslow	*Middlesex* - Brentford
Housenrigg	*Cumberland* - Carlisle
Housham	*Lincoln* - Lincoln
Housham Tye	*Essex* - Harlow
Hove	*Sussex* - Brighton
Hoveringham	*Notts* - Newark
Hoveton St. John	*Norfolk* - Norwich
Hoveton St. Peter	*Norfolk* - Norwich
Hovingham	*York, N.R.* - Malton

Howarth, Great	*Lancaster* - Rochdale
Howburn (Alston)	*Cumberland* - Carlisle
Howburn	*Northumberland* - Hexham
Howburn	*Northumberland* - Carlisle
How Caple	*Hereford* - Hereford
Hondales	*Lincoln* - Louth
Howden	*York, E.R.* - Goole
Howden	*York, W.R.* - Skipton
Howden Clough	*York, W.R.* - Dewsbury
Howden-le-Wear	*Durham* - Bishop Auckland
Howdon	*Northumberland* - North Shields
Howdon-on-Tyne	*Northumberland* - North Shields
Howe	*Norfolk* - Norwich
Howe (Lyth)	*Westmorland* - Kendal
Howe Bridge	*Lancaster* - Leigh
Howe, East	*Hants* - Bournemouth
Howe Green	*Essex* - Chelmsford
Howe Green	*Herts* - Hertford
Howe Street	*Essex* - Chelmsford
Howe, West	*Hants* - Bournemouth
Howell	*Lincoln* - Sleaford
How End	*Cumberland* - Workington
Howey	*Radnor* - Builth
Howgate	*Cumberland* - Whitehaven
Howgill	*York, W.R.* - Kendal
Howgill Syke	*Cumberland* - Hexham
Howgrave	*York, W.R.* - Harrogate
How Green	*Essex* - Bishop's Stortford
How Green	*Kent* - Tonbridge
Howick	*Lancaster* - Preston
Howick	*Monmouth* - Chepstow
Howick	*Northumberland* - Alnwick
Howle	*Salop* - Market Drayton
Howle	*Salop* - Wellington (Salop)
Howle, East	*Durham* - Durham
Howle Hill	*Hereford* - Monmouth
Howleigh	*Somerset* - Taunton
Howlesyke	*York, N.R.* - Whitby
Howlett End	*Essex* - Bishop's Stortford
Howley Green	*Worcester* - Stourbridge
Howley Park	*York, W.R.* - Dewsbury
Howlish	*Durham* - Bishop Auckland
How Mill	*Cumberland* - Carlisle
Howsham	*Lincoln* - Scunthorpe
Howsham	*York, E.R.* - Malton
Howtel	*Northumberland* - Berwick-upon-Tweed
Howtown	*Westmorland* - Penrith
Hoxne	*Suffolk* - Norwich
Hoxton	*London, N.1* - Shoreditch
Hoylake	*Cheshire* - Birkenhead
Hoyland	*York, W.R.* - Barnsley
Hoyland Common	*York, W.R.* - Barnsley
Hoyland Swaine	*York, W.R.* - Barnsley
Hoyle	*Sussex* - Chichester
Hoyle Mill	*York, W.R.* - Barnsley
Hubberholme	*York, W.R.* - Skipton
Hubberston	*Pembroke* - Haverfordwest
Huby	*York, N.R.* - York
Huby	*York, W.R.* - Otley
Huccaby	*Devon* - Plymouth
Hucclecote	*Gloucester* - Gloucester
Hucking	*Kent* - Maidstone
Huckerby	*Lincoln* - Gainsborough
Hucklow, Great	*Derby* - Buxton
Hucklow, Little	*Derby* - Buxton
Hucknall	*Notts* - Nottingham
Huckworthy Bridge	*Devon* - Plymouth
Huddersfield	*York, W.R.* - Huddersfield
Huddington	*Worcester* - Worcester
Huddlesford	*Stafford* - Lichfield
Huddlestone	*Sussex* - Brighton
Hud Hey	*Lancaster* - Rawtenstall
Huggate	*York, E.R.* - York
Hugglescote	*Leicester* - Ashby-de-la-Zouch
Hughenden	*Bucks* - High Wycombe
Hughes Hill	*Sussex* - Chichester
Hughley	*Salop* - Shrewsbury
Huish	*Devon* - Bideford
Huish	*Dorset* - Blandford

Huish	*Wilts* - Swindon
Huish Champflower	*Somerset* - Taunton
Huish Episcopi	*Somerset* - Taunton
Huish, North	*Devon* - Plymouth
Huish, South	*Devon* - Kingsbridge
Hulam	*Durham* - Hartlepool
Hulcote	*Northampton* - Northampton
Hulcott	*Bucks* - Aylesbury
Hulland	*Derby* - Derby
Hulland Ward	*Derby* - Derby
Hulland Ward Intakes	*Derby* - Derby
Hullavington	*Wilts* - Malmesbury
Hullbridge	*Essex* - Southend
Hull Bridge	*York, E.R.* - Beverley
Hulme	*Lancaster* - Manchester
Hulme	*Stafford* - Stoke-on-Trent
Hulme End	*Stafford* - Leek
Hulme Walfield	*Cheshire* - Congleton
Hulton, Little	*Lancaster* - Salford
Hulton, Middle	*Lancaster* - Bolton
Hulton, Over	*Lancaster* - Bolton
Hulver	*Suffolk* - Lowestoft
Hulverstone	*I. of W.* - Newport (I.W.)
Humber	*Hereford* - Leominster
Humber, Little	*York, E.R.* - Kingston-upon-Hull
Humbers	*Salop* - Wellington
Humbershoe	*Beds* - Luton
Humberstone	*Leicester* - Leicester
Humberstone	*Lincoln* - Great Grimsby
Humbledon	*Durham* - Sunderland
Humbleton	*Northumberland* - Berwick-upon-Tweed
Humbleton	*York, E.R.* - Kingston-upon-Hull
Humburton	*York, N.R.* - Harrogate
Humby, Great	*Lincoln* - Grantham
Humby, Little	*Lincoln* - Grantham
Hummer	*Dorset* - Yeovil
Hummerbeck	*Durham* - Bishop Auckland
Hummersty	*York, N.R.* - Whitby
Humshaugh	*Northumberland* - Hexham
Huncoat	*Lancaster* - Accrington
Huncote	*Leicester* - Leicester
Hundall	*Derby* - Chesterfield
Hunderthwaite	*York, N.R.* - Bishop Auckland
Hunderton	*Hereford* - Hereford
Hundith Hill	*Cumberland* - Workington
Hundleby	*Lincoln* - Skegness
Hundleby Fen	*Lincoln* - Skegness
Hundle Houses	*Lincoln* - Boston
Hundleton	*Pembroke* - Haverfordwest
Hundon	*Suffolk* - Bury St. Edmunds
Hundred End	*Lancaster* - Southport
Hundred Fen	*Lincoln* - Spalding
Hundred House	*Salop* - Bridgnorth
Hungarton	*Leicester* - Leicester
Hungerford	*Berks* - Newbury
Hungerford	*Hants* - Salisbury
Hungerford	*Salop* - Ludlow
Hungerford	*Salop* - Shrewsbury
Hungerford, Little	*Berks* - Newbury
Hunger Hill Estate	*Lancaster* - Bolton
Hungersheath	*Stafford* - Market Drayton
Hungerton	*Lincoln* - Grantham
Hungry Bentley	*Derby* - Derby
Hungryhatton	*Salop* - Market Drayton
Hunkington	*Salop* - Shrewsbury
Hunmanby	*York, E.R.* - Bridlington
Hunningham	*Warwick* - Warwick
Hunnington	*Worcester* - Bromsgrove
Hunsdon	*Herts* - Hertford
Hunsingore	*York, W.R.* - Harrogate
Hunslet	*York, W.R.* - Leeds
Hunsley, High	*York, E.R.* - Beverley
Hunsley, Low	*York, E.R.* - Beverley
Hunsonby	*Cumberland* - Penrith
Hunstanton	*Norfolk* - King's Lynn
Hunstanton, Old	*Norfolk* - King's Lynn
Hunstanworth	*Durham* - Consett

HUN - HUS

Hunston	*Suffolk* - Bury St. Edmunds
Hunston	*Sussex* - Chichester
Hunstrete	*Somerset* - Bath
Hunsworth	*York, W.R.* - Dewsbury
Hunt End	*Worcester* - Redditch
Huntercombe	*Bucks* - Slough
Huntercombe	*Oxford* - Didcot
Huntercombe End	*Oxford* - Didcot
Hunters Bar	*York, W.R.* - Sheffield
Hunters Forstal	*Kent* - Canterbury
Huntilee	*Stafford* - Stoke-on-Trent
Huntingdon	*Hunts* - Huntingdon
Huntingdon Warren	*Devon* - Plymouth
Huntingfield	*Suffolk* - Halesworth
Huntingford	*Gloucester* - Stroud
Huntingford (Gillinham)	*Wilts* - Shaftesbury
Huntington	*Cheshire* - Chester
Huntington	*Hereford* - Hereford
Huntington	*Salop* - Wellington (Salop)
Huntington	*Stafford* - Walsall
Huntington	*York, W.R.* - York
Huntley	*Gloucester* - Gloucester
Huntley	*Gloucester* - Cheltenham
Huntley Brook	*Lancaster* - Bury
Hunton	*Hants* - Winchester
Hunton	*Kent* - Maidstone
Hunton	*York, N.R.* - Northallerton
Hunton Bridge	*Herts* - Watford
Hunt's Cross	*Lancaster* - Liverpool
Hunts Green	*Berks* - Newbury
Huntsham	*Devon* - Tiverton
Huntsham	*Hereford* - Monmouth
Huntshaw	*Devon* - Bideford
Huntspill, East	*Somerset* - Bridgwater
Huntspill, West	*Somerset* - Bridgwater
Huntwick	*York, W.R.* - Pontefract
Huntworth	*Somerset* - Bridgwater
Hunwick	*Durham* - Bishop Auckland
Hunwick Lane Ends	*Durham* - Bishop Auckland
Hunwick, New	*Durham* - Bishop Auckland
Hunworth	*Norfolk* - Norwich
Hurbuck Cottages	*Durham* - Durham
Hurcott Green	*Somerset* - Yeovil
Hurdcott	*Wilts* - Salisbury
Hurdley	*Montgomery* - Welshpool
Hurdlow	*Derby* - Buxton
Hurdsfield	*Cheshire* - Macclesfield
Hurleston	*Cheshire* - Crewe
Hurley	*Berks* - Reading
Hurley	*Warwick* - Tamworth
Hurlfield	*York, W.R.* - Sheffield
Hurn	*Hants* - Bournemouth
Hursley	*Hants* - Winchester
Hurst	*Berks* - Reading
Hurst	*Lancaster* - Ashton-under-Lyne
Hurst (Martock)	*Somerset* - Yeovil
Hurst	*Sussex* - Petersfield
Hurst	*York, N.R.* - Darlington
Hurstbourne Priors	*Hants* - Andover
Hurstbourne Tarrant	*Hants* - Andover
Hurst Castle	*Hants* - Lymington
Hurst Cross	*Lancaster* - Ashton-under-Lyne
Hurst Green	*Lancaster* - Blackburn
Hurst Green	*Stafford* - Stourbridge
Hurst Green	*Surrey* - Reigate
Hurst Green	*Sussex* - Tunbridge Wells
Hurst Green	*Worcester* - Dudley
Hurst Hill (part)	*Stafford* - Dudley
Hurst Hill (part)	*Stafford* - Wolverhampton
Hurst Hill	*Sussex* - Horsham
Hurston	*Sussex* - Worthing
Hurst Park	*Worcester* - Evesham
Hurstpierpoint	*Sussex* - Haywards Heath
Hurstwood	*Lancaster* - Burnley
Hurstwood	*Stafford* - Stafford
Hurstwood, High	*Sussex* - Lewes
Hurtmore	*Surrey* - Guildford
Hurworth	*Durham* - Darlington
Husbands Bosworth	*Leicester* - Rugby

HUS - IBW

Husborne Crawley	*Beds* - Bletchley and Leighton Buzzard
Husthwaite	*York, N.R.* - York
Huthwaite	*Notts* - Mansfield
Hutt Green	*York, W.R.* - Pontefract
Huttoft	*Lincoln* - Skegness
Hutton	*Cumberland* - Penrith
Hutton	*Essex* - Brentwood
Hutton	*Lancaster* - Preston
Hutton	*Somerset* - Weston Super Mare
Hutton Bank	*York, N.R.* - Harrogate
Hutton Buscel	*York, N.R.* - Scarborough
Hutton Conyers	*York, N.R.* - Harrogate
Hutton Cranswick	*York, E.R.* - Beverley
Hutton End	*Cumberland* - Penrith
Hutton Gate	*York, N.R.* - Middlesbrough
Hutton Henry	*Durham* - Hartlepool
Hutton-in-the-Forest	*Cumberland* - Penrith
Hutton John	*Cumberland* - Penrith
Hutton-le-Hole	*York, N.R.* - Malton
Hutton Lowcross	*York, N.R.* - Middlesbrough
Hutton Magna	*York, N.R.* - Darlington
Hutton Mulgrave	*York, N.R.* - Whitby
Hutton, New	*Westmorland* - Kendal
Hutton, Old	*Westmorland* - Kendal
Hutton Roof	*Cumberland* - Penrith
Hutton Roof	*Westmorland* - Kendal
Hutton Rudby	*York, N.R.* - Middlesbrough
Huttons Ambo	*York, N.R.* - Malton
Hutton Wandsley	*York, E.R.* - York
Huxham	*Devon* - Exeter
Huxley	*Cheshire* - Chester
Huyton	*Lancaster* - St. Helens
Huyton Quarry	*Lancaster* - St. Helens
Hyde	*Cheshire* - Hyde
Hyde	*Hants* - Salisbury
Hyde	*Dorset* - Swanage
Hyde	*Gloucester* - Stroud
Hyde	*Gloucester* - Cheltenham
Hyde Ash	*Hereford* - Leominster
Hyde, East	*Beds* - Luton
Hyde Heath	*Bucks* - Amersham
Hyde Lea	*Stafford* - Stafford
Hyde, North (part)	*Middlesex* - Uxbridge
Hyde Park (part)	*London, W.2* - West London
Hyde Park (part)	*London, W.2* - Westminster
Hyde Park	*York, W.R.* - Sheffield
Hyde, The (Hendon)	*London, N.W.9* - Willesden
Hyde, West	*Beds* - Luton
Hyde, West	*Herts* - Watford
Hyde's Pastures	*Warwick* - Nuneaton
Hykeham, North	*Lincoln* - Lincoln
Hykeham, South	*Lincoln* - Lincoln
Hylton Lane	*Durham* - Sunderland
Hylton, North (part)	*Durham* - Gateshead
Hylton, North (part)	*Durham* - Sunderland
Hylton, South	*Durham* - Sunderland
Hyssington	*Montgomery and Salop* - Welshpool
Hystfield	*Gloucester* - Stroud
Hythe	*Hants* - Southampton
Hythe	*Kent* - Folkestone
Hythe, New	*Kent* - Maidstone
Hythe, Small	*Kent* - Cranbrook
Hythe, West	*Kent* - Folkestone

I

Ibberton	*Dorset* - Dorchester
Ible	*Derby* - Matlock
Ibornden	*Kent* - Cranbrook
Ibsley	*Hants* - Salisbury
Ibstock	*Leicester* - Ashby-de-la-Zouch
Ibstone	*Bucks and Oxford* - High Wycombe
Iburndale	*York, N.R.* - Whitby
Ibworth	*Hants* - Newbury

Ickborough	*Norfolk* - King's Lynn
Ickburgh	*Norfolk* - King's Lynn
Ickenham	*Middlesex* - Uxbridge
Ickford	*Bucks* - Thame
Ickham	*Kent* - Canterbury
Ickleford	*Herts* - Hitchin
Ickles	*York, W.R.* - Rotherham
Icklesham	*Sussex* - Hastings
Ickleton	*Cambridge* - Cambridge
Icklingham	*Suffolk* - Bury St. Edmunds
Ickwell	*Beds* - Biggleswade
Ickworth	*Suffolk* - Bury St. Edmunds
Icomb	*Gloucester* - Cheltenham
Idbury	*Oxford* - Banbury
Iddesleigh	*Devon* - Okehampton
Iddinshall	*Cheshire* - Chester
Ide	*Devon* - Exeter
Ideford	*Devon* - Newton Abbott
Ide Hill	*Kent* - Sevenoaks
Idehurst	*Sussex* - Chichester
Iden	*Sussex* - Hastings
Iden Green (Benenden)	*Kent* - Cranbrook
Idle	*York, W.R.* - Bradford
Idless	*Cornwall* - Truro
Idlestop	*Lincoln* - Gainsborough
Idlicote	*Warwick* - Stratford on Avon
Idmiston	*Wilts* - Salisbury
Idridgehay	*Derby* - Matlock
Idsworth	*Hants* - Petersfield
Iffley	*Oxford* - Oxford
Ifield	*Kent* - Gravesend
Ifield	*Sussex* - Horsham
Iford	*Hants* - Bournemouth
Iford	*Somerset* - Bath
Iford	*Sussex* - Chichester
Iford	*Sussex* - Lewes
Iford	*Wilts* - Trowbridge
Ightenhill Park	*Lancaster* - Burnley
Ightfield	*Salop* - Whitchurch
Ightham	*Kent* - Sevenoaks
Ightham Common	*Kent* - Sevenoaks
Iken	*Suffolk* - Woodbridge
Ilam	*Stafford* - Leek
Ilam Tops	*Stafford* - Leek
Ilchester	*Somerset* - Yeovil
Ilderton	*Northumberland* - Alnwick
Ilford	*Essex* - Ilford
Ilford, Great	*Essex* - Ilford
Ilfracombe	*Devon* - Barnstaple
Ilkeston	*Derby* - Ilkeston
Ilkeston Junction	*Derby* - Ilkeston
Ilketshall St. Andrew	*Suffolk* - Lowestoft
Ilketshall St. John	*Suffolk* - Lowestoft
Ilketshall St. Lawrence	*Suffolk* - Lowestoft
Ilketshall St. Margaret	*Suffolk* - Halesworth
Ilkley	*York, W.R.* - Otley
Illey	*Worcester* - Stourbridge
Illington	*Norfolk* - Thetford
Illingworth	*York, W.R.* - Halifax
Illogan	*Cornwall* - Redruth
Illshaw Heath	*Warwick* - Birmingham
Illston-on-Hill	*Leicester* - Leicester
Ilmer	*Bucks* - High Wycombe
Ilmington	*Warwick* - Stratford on Avon
Ilminster	*Somerset* - Axminster and Chard
Ilsington	*Devon* - Newton Abbot
Ilsley, East	*Berks* - Didcot
Ilsley, West	*Berks* - Didcot
Ilston	*Glamorgan* - Swansea
Ilton	*Somerset* - Axminster and Chard
Ilton with Pott	*York, N.R.* - Harrogate
Immingham	*Lincoln* - Great Grimsby
Impington	*Cambridge* - Cambridge
Impney	*Worcester* - Bromsgrove
Ince	*Cheshire* - Ellesmere Port
Ince Blundell	*Lancaster* - Liverpool
Ince in Makerfield	*Lancaster* - Wigan
Inchbrook	*Gloucester* - Stroud
Inchmerry	*Hants* - Southampton
Incline	*Salop* - Wellington (Salop)

Indian Queens	*Cornwall* - Truro
Ingarsby	*Leicester* - Leicester
Ingatestone	*Essex* - Chelmsford
Ingbirchworth	*York, W.R.* - Barnsley
Ingerthorpe	*York, N.R.* - Harrogate
Ingestone	*Hereford* - Monmouth
Ingestre	*Stafford* - Stafford
Ingham	*Lincoln* - Lincoln
Ingham	*Norfolk* - Great Yarmouth
Ingham	*Suffolk* - Bury St. Edmunds
Ingleby	*Derby* - Derby
Ingleby	*Lincoln* - Lincoln
Ingleby Arncliffe	*York, N.R.* - Northallerton
Ingleby Barwick	*York, N.R.* - Stockton on Tees
Ingleby Cross	*York, N.R.* - Northallerton
Ingleby Greenhow	*York, N.R.* - Middlesbrough
Inglesham	*Wilts* - Swindon
Inglesham, Lower	*Wilts* - Swindon
Inglestone Common	*Gloucester* - Bristol
Ingleton	*Durham* - Darlington
Ingleton	*York, W.R.* - Lancaster
Ingleton Fells	*York, W.R.* - Lancaster
Ingleton, New	*York, W.R.* - Lancaster
Inglewhite	*Lancaster* - Preston
Ingmanthorpe	*York, W.R.* - Harrogate
Ingoe	*Northumberland* - Newcastle upon Tyne
Ingol	*Lancaster* - Preston
Ingoldisthorpe	*Norfolk* - King's Lynn
Ingoldmells	*Lincoln* - Skegness
Ingoldsby	*Lincoln* - Grantham
Ingram	*Northumberland* - Alnwick
Ingrave	*Essex* - Brentwood
Ingrow	*York, W.R.* - Keighley
Ings	*Westmorland* - Kendal
Ingst	*Gloucester* - Thornbury
Ingworth	*Norfolk* - Norwich
Inhurst	*Hants* - Basingstoke
Inkberrow	*Worcester* - Redditch
Inkerman Selston	*Notts* - Alfreton
Inkersall	*Derby* - Chesterfield
Inkford Brook	*Warwick* - Birmingham
Inkpen	*Berks* - Newbury
Innsworth	*Gloucester* - Gloucester
Inskip	*Lancaster* - Preston
Instow	*Devon* - Bideford
Intack (part)	*Lancaster* - Accrington
Intack (part)	*Lancaster* - Blackburn
Intake	*York, W.R.* - Doncaster
Intake	*York, W.R.* - Sheffield
Intwood	*Norfolk* - Norwich
Invention, New	*Salop* - Knighton
Inwardleigh	*Devon* - Okehampton
Inworth	*Essex* - Colchester
Ipersbridge	*Hants* - Southampton
Iping	*Sussex* - Petersfield
Ipley	*Hants* - Southampton
Ipplepen	*Devon* - Newton Abbot
Ippollitts	*Herts* - Hitchin
Ipsden	*Oxford* - Didcot
Ipsley	*Warwick* - Redditch
Ipstones	*Stafford* - Leek
Ipswich	*Suffolk* - Ipswich
Irby	*Cheshire* - Birkenhead
Irby	*Lincoln* - Great Grimsby
Irby in the Marsh	*Lincoln* - Skegness
Irchester	*Northampton* - Wellingborough
Irchester, Little	*Northampton* - Wellingborough
Ireby	*Lancaster* - Lancaster
Ireby, High	*Cumberland* - Carlisle
Ireby, Low	*Cumberland* - Carlisle
Ireland	*Beds* - Biggleswade
Ireland's Cross	*Salop* - Market Drayton
Ireleth	*Lancaster* - Barrow-in-Furness
Ireshopeburn	*Durham* - Bishop Auckland
Ireton Wood	*Derby* - Matlock

IRL - IXW

Irlam	*Lancaster* - Salford
Irlam, Higher	*Lancaster* - Salford
Irlams-o'-th'-Height	*Lancaster* - Salford
Irmingland	*Norfolk* - Norwich
Irnham	*Lincoln* - Grantham
Iron Acton	*Gloucester* - Bristol
Ironbridge	*Salop* - Wellington (Salop)
Ironville	*Notts* - Alfreton
Irstead	*Norfolk* - Norwich
Irthington	*Cumberland* - Carlisle
Irthlingborough	*Northampton* - Wellingborough
Irton	*Cumberland* - Whitehaven
Irton	*York, N.R.* - Scarborough
Irwell Vale (part)	*Lancaster* - Bury
Irwell Vale (part)	*Lancaster* - Rawtenstall
Iscoyd	*Flint* - Whitchurch
Isel	*Cumberland* - Workington
Isfield	*Sussex* - Lewes
Isham	*Northampton* - Wellingborough
Isington	*Hants* - Aldershot and Farnham
Island Pool	*Worcester* - Kidderminster
Islawrdref	*Merioneth* - Dolgellau
Isle Abbots	*Somerset* - Taunton
Isle Brewers	*Somerset* - Taunton
Isleham	*Cambridge* - Newmarket
Isle of Bardsey	*Caernarvon* - Portmadoc
Isle of Dogs	*London, E.14* - Bow
Isle of Oxney	*Kent* - Cranbrook
Isle, The	*Salop* - Shrewsbury
Isleworth	*Middlesex* - Brentford
Isley Walton	*Leicester* - Loughborough
Islington	*London, N.1* - Clerkenwell
Islington	*Norfolk* - King's Lynn
Islington	*Stafford* - Wellington (Salop)
Islington	*York, W.R.* - York
Islip	*Northampton* - Kettering
Islip	*Oxford* - Oxford
Isombridge	*Salop* - Wellington (Salop)
Istead Rise	*Kent* - Gravesend
Isycoed	*Denbigh* - Wrexham
Itchen	*Hants* - Southampton
Itchen Abbas	*Hants* - Winchester
Itchenor	*Sussex* - Chichester
Itchenor, West	*Sussex* - Chichester
Itchen Stoke	*Hants* - Winchester
Itchingfield	*Sussex* - Horsham
Itchingswell	*Hants* - Newbury
Itchington	*Gloucester* - Thornbury
Itchington, Long	*Warwick* - Warwick
Itewood	*Dorset* - Axminster and Chard
Itteringham	*Norfolk* - Norwich
Itton	*Monmouth* - Chepstow
Ivegill (part)	*Cumberland* - Carlisle
Ivegill (part)	*Cumberland* - Penrith
Iver	*Bucks* - Uxbridge
Iver Heath	*Bucks* - Uxbridge
Iverley (part)	*Worcester* - Kidderminster
Iverley (part)	*Worcester* - Stourbridge
Ives, North	*York, W.R.* - Keighley
Iveston	*Durham* - Consett
Ivetsey	*Stafford* - Stafford
Ivinghoe	*Bucks* - Bletchley and Leighton Buzzard
Ivinghoe Aston	*Bucks* - Bletchley and Leighton Buzzard
Ivington	*Hereford* - Leominster
Ivybridge	*Devon* - Plymouth
Ivy Chimneys	*Essex* - Harlow
Ivychurch	*Kent* - Ashford
Ivy Hatch	*Kent* - Sevenoaks
Iwade	*Kent* - Sittingbourne
Iwerne Courtney	*Dorset* - Shaftesbury
Iwerne Minster	*Dorset* - Shaftesbury
Ixworth	*Suffolk* - Bury St. Edmunds
Ixworth Thorpe	*Suffolk* - Bury St. Edmunds

J - KED

Jackfield	*Salop* - Wellington (Salop)
Jack-o'-Watton	*Warwick* - Birmingham
Jacksdale	*Notts* - Alfreton
Jacks Green	*Essex* - Bishop's Stortford
Jack's Hatch	*Essex* - Harlow
Jacks Hill	*Herts* - Hitchin
Jackson Bridge	*York, W.R.* - Huddersfield
Jacobstow	*Cornwall* - Launceston
Jacobstowe	*Devon* - Okehampton
Jagger Green	*York, W.R.* - Halifax
Jamage	*Stafford* - Stoke-on-Trent
James Bridge	*Stafford* - Walsall
Jammy Green	*York, W.R.* - Halifax
Jarrow	*Durham* - South Shields
Jarrow, East	*Durham* - South Shields
Jay	*Hereford* - Ludlow
Jaywick	*Essex* - Colchester
Jeffreyston	*Pembroke* - Haverfordwest
Jenningsbury	*Herts* - Hertford
Jericho	*Lancaster* - Bury
Jericho	*Pembroke* - Cardigan
Jersey Marine	*Glamorgan* - Neath
Jerusalem	*Lincoln* - Lincoln
Jesmond	*Northumberland* - Newcastle upon Tyne
Jesmond West	*Northumberland* - Newcastle upon Tyne
Jevington	*Sussex* - Eastbourne
Jingling Gate	*Durham* - Gateshead
Job's Cross	*Kent* - Cranbrook
Job's Hill	*Durham* - Bishop Auckland
Jobsons Bridge	*Lincoln* - Spalding
Jobson's Lane	*Sussex* - Chichester
Job's Water	*Cornwall* - Truro and Falmouth
Jock's Row (Bishop Auckland)	*Durham* - Bishop Auckland
Jodrell	*Cheshire* - Congleton
Jodrell Bank	*Cheshire* - Macclesfield
Johnby	*Cumberland* - Penrith
Johnson Fold	*Lancaster* - Bolton
Johnston	*Pembroke* - Haverfordwest
Johnstown	*Carmarthen* - Carmarthen
Johnstown	*Denbigh* - Wrexham
Joppa	*Cornwall* - Redruth
Jordanston	*Pembroke* - Haverfordwest
Jordans Village	*Bucks* - Amersham
Jordanthorpe	*York, W.R.* - Sheffield
Joss Bay	*Kent* - Margate
Joss Gap	*Kent* - Margate
Joyford	*Gloucester* - Monmouth
Joy's Green	*Gloucester* - Gloucester
Julian Park	*York, N.R.* - Whitby
Jump	*Devon* - Plymouth
Jump	*York, W.R.* - Barnsley
Jumpers	*Hants* - Bournemouth
Juniper Hill	*Oxford* - Banbury
Justice Town	*Cumberland* - Carlisle

K

Kaber	*Westmorland* - Penrith
Karslake	*Cornwall* - St. Austell
Kates Hill	*Stafford* - Dudley
Kea	*Cornwall* - Truro
Keadby	*Lincoln* - Scunthorpe
Keal Cotes	*Lincoln* - Skegness
Keal, East	*Lincoln* - Skegness
Keal, West	*Lincoln* - Skegness
Kearby-with-Netherby	*York, W.R.* - Harrogate
Kearsley	*Lancaster* - Bolton
Kearsley	*Northumberland* - Newcastle upon Tyne
Kearsley Mount	*Lancaster* - Bolton
Kearsney	*Kent* - Dover
Keasden	*York, W.R.* - Skipton
Keastwick	*Westmorland* - Kendal
Keaton	*Devon* - Kingsbridge
Keckwick	*Cheshire* - Runcorn
Keckwick	*Cheshire* - Warrington
Keddington	*Lincoln* - Louth

KED - KEN

Kedington	*Suffolk* - Sudbury
Kedleston	*Derby* - Derby
Keekle	*Cumberland* - Whitehaven
Keekle, Low	*Cumberland* - Whitehaven
Keelam	*York, W.R.* - Bradford
Keelby	*Lincoln* - Great Grimsby
Keele	*Stafford* - Stoke-on-Trent
Keenley	*Northumberland* - Hexham
Keeston	*Pembroke* - Haverfordwest
Keevil	*Wilts* - Trowbridge
Keevil Wick	*Wilts* - Trowbridge
Kegworth	*Leicester* - Loughborough
Kehelland	*Cornwall* - Redruth
Keighley	*York, W.R.* - Keighley
Keinton Mandeville	*Somerset* - Yeovil
Keisby	*Lincoln* - Grantham
Kelbrook	*York, W.R.* - Skipton
Kelby	*Lincoln* - Sleaford
Keld	*Westmorland* - Penrith
Keld	*York, N.R.* - Darlington
Keldholme	*York, N.R.* - Malton
Kelfield	*York, E.R.* - York
Kelfield, East	*Lincoln* - Gainsborough
Kelfield, West	*Lincoln* - Gainsborough
Kelham	*Notts* - Newark
Kelk	*York, E.R.* - Bridlington
Kellah	*Northumberland* - Hexham
Kellamergh	*Lancaster* - Preston
Kellaton	*Devon* - Kingsbridge
Kellaways	*Wilts* - Chippenham
Kelleth	*Westmorland* - Penrith
Kellet, Nether	*Lancaster* - Lancaster
Kellet, Over	*Lancaster* - Lancaster
Kelling	*Norfolk* - Norwich
Kelling, High	*Norfolk* - Norwich
Kellingley	*York, W.R.* - Pontefract
Kellington	*York, W.R.* - Pontefract
Kelloe	*Durham* - Durham
Kelly	*Devon* - Launceston
Kelly Bray	*Cornwall* - Liskeard
Kelmarsh	*Northampton* - Northampton
Kelmscott	*Oxford* - Witney
Kelsale	*Suffolk* - Woodbridge
Kelsall	*Cheshire* - Chester
Kelsey, North	*Lincoln* - Scunthorpe
Kelsey, South	*Lincoln* - Scunthorpe
Kelshall	*Herts* - Hitchin
Kelsick	*Cumberland* - Carlisle
Kelsick	*Cumberland* - Workington
Kelstedge	*Derby* - Chesterfield
Kelstern	*Lincoln* - Louth
Kelsterton	*Flint* - Holywell
Kelston	*Somerset* - Bath
Kelvedon	*Essex* - Braintree
Kelvedon Hatch	*Essex* - Brentwood
Kelvin	*York, W.R.* - Sheffield
Kelynack	*Cornwall* - Penzance
Kemberton	*Salop* - Wellington (Salop)
Kemble	*Gloucester* - Malmesbury
Kemble Wick	*Gloucester* - Malmesbury
Kemerton	*Worcs* - Evesham
Kemeys Commander	*Monmouth* - Pontypool and Abergavenny
Kemeys Inferior	*Monmouth* - Newport (Mon.)
Kempley	*Gloucester* - Gloucester
Kempley Green	*Gloucester* - Gloucester
Kemp's Corner	*Kent* - Ashford
Kempsey	*Worcester* - Worcester
Kempsford	*Gloucester* - Swindon
Kemp's Green	*Warwick* - Birmingham
Kempshott	*Hants* - Basingstoke
Kempston	*Beds* - Bedford
Kempstone	*Norfolk* - East Dereham
Kempston Hardwick	*Beds* - Bedford
Kempton	*Salop* - Ludlow
Kemp Town	*Sussex* - Brighton
Kemsing	*Kent* - Sevenoaks
Kemsley	*Kent* - Sittingbourne
Kenchester	*Hereford* - Hereford
Kencott	*Oxford* - Witney

KEN - KER

Kendal	*Westmorland* - Kendal
Kendall End	*Worcester* - Bromsgrove
Kenderchurch	*Hereford* - Hereford
Kendleshire	*Gloucester* - Bristol
Kendon	*Monmouth* - Blackwood
Kendray	*Warwick* - Barnsley
Kenfig Borough	*Glamorgan* - Bridgend
Kenfig Hill	*Glamorgan* - Bridgend
Kenilworth	*Warwick* - Warwick
Kenley	*Salop* - Shrewsbury
Kenley	*Surrey* - Croydon
Kenn	*Devon* - Exeter
Kenn	*Somerset* - Weston Super Mare
Kennall	*Cornwall* - Redruth
Kennardington	*Kent* - Cranbrook
Kenneggy	*Cornwall* - Penzance
Kennerleigh	*Devon* - Exeter
Kennesbourne Green	*Beds* - Luton
Kennett	*Cambridge* - Newmarket
Kennett, East	*Wilts* - Swindon
Kennett, West	*Wilts* - Swindon
Kennford	*Devon* - Exeter
Kenninghall	*Norfolk* - Thetford
Kennington	*Berks* - Oxford
Kennington	*Kent* - Ashford
Kennington	*London, S.E.11* - Lambeth
Kennington Lees	*Kent* - Ashford
Kenny Hill	*Suffolk* - Bury St. Edmunds
Kennythorpe	*York, E.R.* - Malton
Kensal Rise	*London, N.W.10* - Willesden
Kensal Town	*London, W.10* - Bloomsbury and Marylebone
Kensington	*Lancaster* - Liverpool
Kensington	*London, W.8* - West London
Kensington, North	*London, W.10* - Bloomsbury and Marylebone
Kensington, South	*London, S.W.7* - West London
Kensington, West	*London, W.14* - West London
Kenstone	*Salop* - Market Drayton
Kenswick	*Worcester* - Worcester
Kensworth	*Beds* - Luton
Kentchurch	*Hereford* - Hereford
Kentford	*Suffolk* - Newmarket
Kent Green	*Cheshire* - Congleton
Kent Hatch	*Kent* - Sevenoaks
Kentisbeare	*Devon* - Tiverton
Kentisbury	*Devon* - Barnstaple
Kentish Town	*London, N.W.5* - Bloomsbury and Marylebone
Kentmere	*Westmorland* - Kendal
Kenton	*Devon* - Exeter
Kenton	*Middlesex* - Willesden
Kenton	*Northumberland* - Newcastle upon Tyne
Kenton	*Suffolk* - Ipswich
Kenton Bank Foot	*Northumberland* - Newcastle upon Tyne
Kentonbar	*Northumberland* - Newcastle upon Tyne
Kenton North	*Northumberland* - Newcastle upon Tyne
Kenton, South	*Middlesex* - Willesden
Kents Bank	*Lancaster* - Barrow-in-Furness
Kents Green	*Gloucester* - Gloucester
Kenwick	*Salop* - Oswestry
Kenwyn	*Cornwall* - Truro
Kenyon	*Lancaster* - Leigh
Kepwick	*York, N.R.* - Northallerton
Kerdiston	*Norfolk* - Norwich
Keresley	*Warwick* - Coventry
Kergilliack	*Cornwall* - Truro
Kerley	*Cornwall* - Truro
Kermingham	*Cheshire* - Congleton
Kerne Bridge	*Hereford* - Monmouth
Kernwick	*Cornwall* - Truro
Kerridge	*Cheshire* - Macclesfield
Kerris	*Cornwall* - Penzance
Kerry	*Montgomery* - Newtown
Kerrys Gate	*Hereford* - Hereford

KER - KIL

Kersal	*Lancaster* - Salford
Kersall	*Notts* - Newark
Kersey	*Suffolk* - Ipswich
Kershope Foot	*Cumberland* - Carlisle
Kersoe	*Worcester* - Evesham
Kersworthy Gate	*Devon* - Launceston
Kersworthy Moor	*Devon* - Launceston
Kesgrave	*Suffolk* - Ipswich
Kessingland	*Suffolk* - Lowestoft
Kestle	*Cornwall* - St. Austell
Kestle Mill	*Cornwall* - Truro
Keston	*Kent* - Bromley
Keswick	*Cumberland* - Workington
Keswick	*Norfolk* - Norwich
Keswick, East	*York, W.R.* - Leeds
Ketchem's Inn	*Derby* - Matlock
Kete	*Pembroke* - Haverfordwest
Ketford	*Gloucester* - Gloucester
Ketley	*Salop* - Wellington (Salop)
Ketley Bank	*Salop* - Wellington (Salop)
Ketley Brook	*Salop* - Wellington (Salop)
Ketley Sands	*Salop* - Wellington (Salop)
Ketsby	*Lincoln* - Skegness
Kettering	*Northampton* - Kettering
Ketteringham	*Norfolk* - Norwich
Kettlebaston	*Suffolk* - Stowmarket
Kettlebrook	*Stafford* - Tamworth
Kettleburgh	*Suffolk* - Woodbridge
Kettleby	*Lincoln* - Scunthorpe
Kettlebythorpe	*Lincoln* - Scunthorpe
Kettle Green	*Herts* - Bishop's Stortford
Kettlehouse	*Stafford* - Birmingham
Kettleness	*York, N.R.* - Whitby
Kettleshulme	*Cheshire* - Buxton
Kettlesing	*York, W.R.* - Harrogate
Kettlestone	*Norfolk* - King's Lynn
Kettlethorpe	*Lincoln* - Gainsborough
Kettlethorpe	*York, W.R.* - Wakefield
Kettlewell	*York, W.R.* - Skipton
Ketton	*Rutland* - Stamford
Keverstone	*Durham* - Bishop Auckland
Kew	*Surrey* - Wandsworth
Kewstoke	*Somerset* - Weston Super Mare
Kexborough	*York, W.R.* - Barnsley
Kexby	*Lincoln* - Gainsborough
Kexby	*York, E.R.* - York
Key Green	*Cheshire* - Congleton
Keyham	*Leicester* - Leicester
Keyhaven	*Hants* - Lymington
Keyingham	*York, E.R.* - Kingston-upon-Hull
Keymer	*Sussex* - Haywards Heath
Keynsham	*Somerset* - Bristol
Keysoe	*Beds* - Bedford
Keyston	*Hunts* - Huntingdon
Key Street	*Kent* - Sittingbourne
Keyte Nest	*Worcester* - Evesham
Keyworth	*Notts* - Nottingham
Kibblesworth	*Durham* - Gateshead
Kibworth Beauchamp	*Leicester* - Leicester
Kibworth Harcourt	*Leicester* - Leicester
Kidbrooke	*London, S.E.3* - Woolwich
Kidderminster	*Worcester* - Kidderminster
Kiddermore Green	*Stafford* - Wolverhampton
Kiddington	*Oxford* - Oxford
Kiddington, Over	*Oxford* - Oxford
Kidgrave	*Warwick* - Birmingham
Kidland	*Northumberland* - Morpeth
Kidlandlee	*Northumberland* - Morpeth
Kidlington	*Oxford* - Oxford
Kidmore End	*Oxford* - Reading
Kidnall	*Cheshire* - Whitchurch
Kidsgrove	*Stafford* - Stoke-on-Trent
Kidwelly	*Carmarthen* - Llanelly
Kielder	*Northumberland* - Hexham
Kiffig	*Carmarthen* - Haverfordwest
Kighill	*Notts* - Mansfield
Kilburn	*Derby* - Ilkeston
Kilburn (part)	*London, N.W.6* - Bloomsbury and Marylebone
Kilburn (part)	*London, N.W.6* - Willesden

KIL - KIN

Kilburn	*York, N.R.* - Northallerton
Kilburn Park (part)	*London, N.W.6* - Bloomsbury and Marylebone
Kilburn Park (part)	*London, N.W.6* - Willesden
Kilby	*Leicester* - Leicester
Kilcot	*Gloucester* - Gloucester
Kilcott	*Gloucester* - Bristol
Kildale	*York, N.R.* - Middlesbrough
Kildwick	*York, W.R.* - Skipton
Kilgetty	*Pembroke* - Haverfordwest
Kilgwrrwg	*Monmouth* - Chepstow
Kilhallan	*Cornwall* - St. Austell
Kilham	*Northumberland* - Berwick-upon-Tweed
Kilham	*York, E.R.* - Bridlington
Kilkenny (Withington)	*Gloucester* - Cheltenham
Kilkenny (Bibury)	*Gloucester* - Cheltenham
Kilkhampton	*Cornwall* - Bideford
Killamarsh	*Derby* - Chesterfield
Killay	*Glamorgan* - Swansea
Killerby	*Durham* - Darlington
Killerby	*York, N.R.* - Darlington
Killhope	*Durham* - Bishop Auckland
Killinghall	*York, W.R.* - Harrogate
Killingholme Haven	*Lincoln* - Great Grimsby
Killingholme, North	*Lincoln* - Great Grimsby
Killingholme, South	*Lincoln* - Great Grimsby
Killington	*Westmorland* - Kendal
Killingworth	*Northumberland* - Newcastle upon Tyne
Killivose	*Cornwall* - Redruth
Kilmachallt	*Montgomery* - Newtown
Kilmersdon	*Somerset* - Frome
Kilmersdon Common	*Somerset* - Frome
Kilmington	*Devon* - Axminster and Chard
Kilmington	*Wilts* - Frome
Kilmiston	*Hants* - Winchester
Kilndown	*Kent* - Cranbrook
Kiln Green	*Berks* - Reading
Kiln Green	*Hereford* - Monmouth
Kilnhurst	*York, W.R.* - Rotherham
Kilnpit Hill	*Northumberland* - Consett
Kilnsea	*York, E.R.* - Kingston-upon-Hull
Kilnsey	*York, W.R.* - Skipton
Kilnwick	*York, E.R.* - Beverley
Kilnwick Percy	*York, E.R.* - York
Kilpeck	*Hereford* - Hereford
Kilpin	*York, E.R.* - Goole
Kilpin Hill	*York, W.R.* - Dewsbury
Kilreague	*Hereford* - Monmouth
Kilsby	*Northampton* - Rugby
Kilthorpe	*Northampton* - Stamford
Kilton	*Somerset* - Minehead
Kilton	*York, N.R.* - Middlesbrough
Kilve	*Somerset* - Minehead
Kilverstone	*Norfolk* - Thetford
Kilvington	*Notts* - Newark
Kilvington	*York, N.R.* - Northallerton
Kilworth, North	*Leicester* - Rugby
Kilworth, South	*Leicester* - Rugby
Kilworthy	*Devon* - Plymouth
Kimberley	*Norfolk* - Norwich
Kimberley	*Notts* - Nottingham
Kimberworth	*York, W.R.* - Rotherham
Kimble, Little	*Bucks* - Aylesbury
Kimblesworth	*Durham* - Durham
Kimblewick	*Bucks* - Aylesbury
Kimbolton	*Hereford* - Leominster
Kimbolton	*Hunts* - Huntingdon
Kimbridge	*Hants* - Southampton
Kimcote	*Leicester* - Rugby
Kimmeridge	*Dorset* - Swanage
Kimpton	*Hants* - Andover
Kimpton	*Herts* - Hitchin
Kinderton	*Cheshire* - Northwich
Kineton	*Gloucester* - Cheltenham
Kineton, Great	*Warwick* - Stratford on Avon
Kineton Green	*Warwick* - Birmingham
Kineton Hill	*Gloucester* - Cheltenham

Kineton, Little	*Warwick* - Stratford on Avon
Kingbeer	*Cornwall* - Launceston
Kingcombe, Higher	*Dorset* - Dorchester
Kingcombe, Lower	*Dorset* - Dorchester
King Cross	*York, W.R.* - Halifax
Kingdown	*Dorset* - Wimborne Minster
Kingebeston	*Somerset* - Yeovil
Kingerby	*Lincoln* - Lincoln
Kingham	*Oxford* - Banbury
King Harry	*Cornwall* - Truro
King Manor	*Wilts* - Salisbury
Kingmoor	*Cumberland* - Carlisle
King's Acre	*Hereford* - Hereford
Kingsand	*Cornwall* - Plymouth
King's Ash	*Bucks* - Aylesbury
Kingsbridge	*Devon* - Kingsbridge
Kingsbridge	*Glamorgan* - Swansea
King's Bromley	*Stafford* - Lichfield
King's Brompton	*Somerset* - Tiverton
Kings Broom	*Warwick* - Stratford on Avon
Kingsbury	*London, N.W.9* - Willesden
Kingsbury	*Stafford* - Tamworth
Kingsbury Episcopi	*Somerset* - Yeovil
Kingsbury Green	*London, N.W.9* - Willesden
King's Caple	*Hereford* - Hereford
Kingsclere	*Hants* - Newbury
King's Cliffe	*Northampton* - Peterborough
King's Cliff	*Northants* - Stamford
Kingscote	*Gloucester* - Stroud
Kingscourt	*Gloucester* - Stroud
King's Cross (part)	*London, N.1* - Bloomsbury and Marylebone
King's Cross (part)	*London, N.1* - Clerkenwell
Kingsdon	*Somerset* - Yeovil
Kingsdown	*Kent* - Deal
Kingsdown	*Kent* - Sittingbourne
Kingsdown	*Wilts* - Bath
King's Enham	*Hants* - Andover
Kingsey	*Bucks* - Thame
King's Ferry	*Kent* - Sittingbourne
Kingsfold (Warnham)	*Sussex* - Horsham
Kingsfold (Billingshurst)	*Sussex* - Horsham
Kingsford	*Worcester* - Kidderminster
Kingsgate	*Kent* - Margate
Kingsheanton	*Devon* - Barnstaple
King's Heath	*Warwick* - Birmingham
King's Hill	*Stafford* - Walsall
Kingshill, Great	*Bucks* - High Wycombe
Kingshill, Little	*Bucks* - Amersham
Kingsholm	*Gloucester* - Gloucester
King's Houghton	*Beds* - Luton
Kingshurst	*Warwick* - Birmingham
Kingside Hill	*Cumberland* - Carlisle
Kingskerswell	*Devon* - Newton Abbot
Kingsland	*Hereford* - Leominster
Kingsland	*London, E.8* - Shoreditch
Kings Langley (part)	*Herts* - Hemel Hempstead
Kings Langley (part)	*Middlesex* - Watford
Kingsley	*Cheshire* - Runcorn
Kingsley	*Hants* - Aldershot and Farnham
Kingsley	*Stafford* - Leek
Kingsley Green	*Sussex* - Petersfield
Kingsley Holt	*Stafford* - Leek
Kingsley Moor	*Stafford* - Leek
Kingsley Park	*Northampton* - Northampton
Kingslow	*Salop* - Bridgnorth
King's Lynn	*Norfolk* - King's Lynn
Kings Marsh	*Cheshire* - Chester
King's Meaburn	*Westmorland* - Penrith
Kingsmead	*York, W.R.* - Pontefract
King's Mills	*Leicester* - Loughborough
King's Newnham	*Warwick* - Rugby
King's Newton	*Derby* - Derby
King's Nordley	*Salop* - Bridgnorth
Kingsnorth	*Kent* - Ashford
King's Norton	*Leicester* - Leicester
King's Norton	*Warwick* - Birmingham
King's Nympton	*Devon* - Barnstaple
King's Pyon	*Hereford* - Hereford

Kings Ripton	*Hunts* - Huntingdon
King's Somborne	*Hants* - Winchester
King's Standing	*Stafford* - Burton-upon-Trent
King's Stanley	*Gloucester* - Stroud
King's Sutton	*Northampton* - Banbury
King Stag	*Dorset* - Shaftesbury
King's Tamerton	*Devon* - Plymouth
Kingstanding	*Warwick* - Birmingham
Kingsteignton	*Devon* - Newton Abbot
King Sterndale	*Derby* - Buxton
Kings Thorne	*Hereford* - Hereford
Kingsthorpe	*Northampton* - Northampton
Kingston	*Cambridge* - Cambridge
Kingston	*Devon* - Kingsbridge
Kingston	*Dorset* - Dorchester
Kingston	*Dorset* - Swanage
Kingston (Portsmouth)	*Hants* - Portsmouth
Kingston	*Kent* - Canterbury
Kingston	*Stafford* - Uttoxeter
Kingston (Ferring)	*Sussex* - Worthing
Kingston Bagpuize	*Berks* - Oxford
Kingston Blount	*Oxford* - Thame
Kingston-by-Sea	*Sussex* - Brighton
Kingston Deverill	*Wilts* - Warminster
Kingston Down	*Cornwall* - Plymouth
Kingstone	*Hereford* - Hereford
Kingstone (Ilminster)	*Somerset* - Yeovil
Kingston Gorse	*Sussex* - Worthing
Kingston Hill	*Surrey* - Kingston-upon-Thames
Kingston Lacey	*Dorset* - Wimborne Minster
Kingston Lisle	*Berks* - Didcot
Kingston, Lower	*Hants* - Bournemouth
Kingston near Lewes	*Sussex* - Lewes
Kingston Russelly	*Dorset* - Dorchester
Kingston St. Mary	*Somerset* - Taunton
Kingston Seymour	*Somerset* - Weston Super Mare
Kingston Stert	*Oxford* - Thame
Kingston-upon-Hull	*York, E.R.* - Kingston-upon-Hull
Kingston-upon-Soar	*Notts* - Loughborough
Kingston-upon-Thames	*Surrey* - Kingston-upon-Thames
Kingston, Upper	*Hants* - Bournemouth
Kingston Warren	*Berks* - Didcot
Kingstown	*Cumberland* - Carlisle
King's Walden	*Herts* - Hitchin
Kingswear	*Devon* - Torquay
King's Weston	*Gloucester* - Bristol
Kingswinford	*Stafford* - Stourbridge
Kingswood	*Bucks* - Aylesbury
Kingswood	*Cheshire* - Runcorn
Kingswood	*Gloucester* - Bristol
Kingswood (Wotton under Edge)	*Gloucester* - Stroud
Kingswood	*Herts* - Hitchin
Kingswood	*Herts* - Watford
Kingswood	*Stafford* - Wolverhampton
Kingswood	*Surrey* - Epsom
Kingswood	*Warwick* - Birmingham
Kingswood	*Warwick* - Warwick
Kingswood	*Worcester* - Worcester
Kingswood Common	*Hereford* - Hereford
Kingswood, Lower	*Surrey* - Reigate
King's Worthy	*Hants* - Winchester
Kingthorpe	*Lincoln* - Lincoln
Kington	*Gloucester* - Thornbury
Kington	*Hereford* - Hereford
Kington	*Worcester* - Redditch
Kington Langley	*Wilts* - Chippenham
Kington Magna	*Dorset* - Shaftesbury
Kington St. Michael	*Wilts* - Chippenham
Kingweston	*Somerset* - Yeovil
Kingwood	*Oxford* - Reading
Kinkry Hill	*Cumberland* - Carlisle
Kinlet	*Salop* - Kidderminster
Kinmel Bay	*Denbigh* - Rhyl
Kinnerley	*Salop* - Oswestry
Kinnersley	*Hereford* - Hereford
Kinnersley	*Salop* - Wellington (Salop)
Kinnersley	*Worcester* - Worcester
Kinnerton	*Radnor* - Knighton
Kinnerton	*Salop* - Shrewsbury

Kinnerton, Higher	*Flint* - Chester
Kinnerton, Lower	*Cheshire* - Chester
Kinninvie	*Durham* - Bishop Auckland
Kinniside	*Cumberland* - Whitehaven
Kinoulton	*Notts* - Nottingham
Kinsbourne Green	*Beds* - Luton
Kinsbourne Green	*Herts* - St. Albans
Kinsey Heath	*Salop* - Crewe
Kinsham	*Worcester* - Cheltenham
Kinsham, Lower	*Hereford* - Leominster
Kinsham, Upper	*Hereford* - Leominster
Kinsley	*York, W.R.* - Pontefract
Kinson	*Hants* - Bournemouth
Kintbury	*Berks* - Newbury
Kinton	*Hereford* - Ludlow
Kinton	*Salop* - Shrewsbury
Kinvaston	*Stafford* - Stafford
Kinver	*Stafford* - Stourbridge
Kinwalsey (part)	*Warwick* - Birmingham
Kinwarton	*Warwick* - Redditch
Kiplin	*York, N.R.* - Northallerton
Kiplingcotes	*York, E.R.* - Beverley
Kippax	*York, W.R.* - Pontefract
Kipings Cross	*Kent* - Tunbridge Wells
Kippington	*Kent* - Sevenoaks
Kirby Bedon	*Norfolk* - Norwich
Kirby Bellars	*Leicester* - Melton Mowbray
Kirby Cane	*Norfolk* - Norwich
Kirby Cross	*Essex* - Colchester
Kirby Grindalythe	*York, E.R.* - Malton
Kirby Hall	*York, W.R.* - Harrogate
Kirby Hill	*York, N.R.* - Harrogate
Kirby-in-Cleveland	*York, N.R.* - Middlesbrough
Kirby-le-Soken	*Essex* - Colchester
Kirby Misperton	*York, N.R.* - Malton
Kirby Muxloe	*Leicester* - Leicester
Kirby Sigston	*York, N.R.* - Northallerton
Kirby Underdale	*York, E.R.* - York
Kirby Wiske	*York, N.R.* - Northallerton
Kirdford	*Sussex* - Chichester
Kirkandrews Moat	*Cumberland* - Carlisle
Kirkandrews-upon-Eden	*Cumberland* - Carlisle
Kirkbampton	*Cumberland* - Carlisle
Kirkborough	*Cumberland* - Workington
Kirk Bramwith	*York, W.R.* - Doncaster
Kirkbride	*Cumberland* - Carlisle
Kirkburn	*York, E.R.* - Beverley
Kirkburton	*York, W.R.* - Huddersfield
Kirkby	*Lancaster* - Liverpool
Kirkby Beckside	*Lancaster* - Barrow-in-Furness
Kirkby cum Osgodby	*Lincoln* - Lincoln
Kirkby, East	*Lincoln* - Skegness
Kirkby Fleetham	*York, N.R.* - Northallerton
Kirkby Green	*Lincoln* - Sleaford
Kirkby in Ashfield	*Notts* - Mansfield
Kirkby Ireleth	*Lancaster* - Barrow-in-Furness
Kirkby la Thorpe	*Lincoln* - Sleaford
Kirkby Lonsdale	*Westmorland* - Kendal
Kirkby Malham	*York, W.R.* - Skipton
Kirkby Mallory	*Leicester* - Hinckley
Kirkby Malzeard	*York, W.R.* - Harrogate
Kirkby Mills	*York, N.R.* - Malton
Kirkby Moorside	*York, N.R.* - Malton
Kirkby on Bain	*Lincoln* - Lincoln
Kirkby Overblow	*York, W.R.* - Harrogate
Kirkby Sandside	*Lancaster* - Barrow-in-Furness
Kirkby Soutergate	*Lancaster* - Barrow-in-Furness
Kirkby, South	*York, W.R.* - Pontefract
Kirkby Stephen	*Westmorland* - Penrith
Kirkby Thore	*Westmorland* - Penrith
Kirkby Underwood	*Lincoln* - Spalding
Kirkby Wharfe	*York, W.R.* - York
Kirkcambeck	*Cumberland* - Carlisle
Kirkdale	*Lancaster* - Liverpool
Kirkdale	*York, N.R.* - Malton
Kirk Deighton	*York, W.R.* - Harrogate
Kirk Ella	*York, E.R.* - Kingston-upon-Hull
Kirk Hallam	*Derby* - Ilkeston
Kirkham	*Lancaster* - Preston
Kirkham	*York, N. & E.R.* - Malton

Kirkhamgate (part)	*York, W.R.* - Dewsbury
Kirkhamgate (part)	*York, W.R.* - Wakefield
Kirk Hammerton	*York, W.R.* - Harrogate
Kirkhams	*Lancaster* - Bury
Kirkharle	*Northumberland* - Hexham
Kirkhaugh	*Northumberland* - Carlisle
Kirkheaton	*Northumberland* - Newcastle upon Tyne
Kirkheaton	*York, W.R.* - Huddersfield
Kirkhouse	*Cumberland* - Carlisle
Kirkhouse Green	*York, W.R.* - Doncaster
Kirk Ireton	*Derby* - Matlock
Kirkland	*Cumberland* - Penrith
Kirkland	*Cumberland* - Whitehaven
Kirkland (Torpenhow)	*Cumberland* - Carlisle
Kirkland (Wigton)	*Cumberland* - Carlisle
Kirkland	*Lancaster* - Preston
Kirkland Guards	*Cumberland* - Carlisle
Kirk Langley	*Derby* - Derby
Kirkleatham	*York, N.R.* - Middlesbrough
Kirk Leavington	*York, N.R.* - Stockton on Tees
Kirkley	*Northumberland* - Newcastle upon Tyne
Kirklington	*Notts* - Newark
Kirklington with Upsland	*York, N.R.* - Harrogate
Kirk Merrington	*Durham* - Bishop Auckland
Kirknewton	*Northumberland* - Berwick-upon-Tweed
Kirkoswald	*Cumberland* - Penrith
Kirk Sandall	*York, W.R.* - Doncaster
Kirk Santon	*Cumberland* - Whitehaven
Kirk Smeaton	*York, W.R.* - Pontefract
Kirkstall	*York, W.R.* - Leeds
Kirkstead	*Lincoln* - Lincoln
Kirkthorpe	*York, W.R.* - Wakefield
Kirkwhelpington	*Northumberland* - Hexham
Kirmington	*Lincoln* - Scunthorpe
Kirmond-le-Mire	*Lincoln* - Louth
Kirstead	*Norfolk* - Norwich
Kirtling	*Cambridge* - Newmarket
Kirtlington	*Oxford* - Oxford
Kirton	*Lincoln* - Boston
Kirton	*Notts* - East Retford
Kirton	*Suffolk* - Ipswich
Kirton Drove	*Lincoln* - Boston
Kirton End	*Lincoln* - Boston
Kirton Fen	*Lincoln* - Boston
Kirton Holme	*Lincoln* - Boston
Kirton-in-Lindsey	*Lincoln* - Scunthorpe
Kirton Skeldyke	*Lincoln* - Boston
Kislingbury	*Northampton* - Northampton
Kitebrook	*Warwick* - Banbury
Kites Hardwick	*Warwick* - Rugby
Kitford	*Dorset* - Blandford
Kithill	*Cornwall* - Liskeard
Kitt Green	*Lancaster* - Wigan
Kittisford	*Somerset* - Taunton
Kittle	*Glamorgan* - Swansea
Kitts Green	*Warwick* - Birmingham
Kitty Brewster	*Northumberland* - Blyth
Kivernoll	*Hereford* - Hereford
Kiveton Park	*York, W.R.* - Worksop
Klondyke	*Northumberland* - North Shields
Knackersknowle	*Devon* - Plymouth
Knaith	*Lincoln* - Gainsborough
Knaith Park	*Lincoln* - Gainsborough
Knaphill	*Surrey* - Guildford
Knapp	*Somerset* - Taunton
Knapp, The	*Gloucester* - Thornbury
Knapthorpe	*Notts* - Newark
Knaptoft	*Leicester* - Rugby
Knapton	*Hereford* - Leominster
Knapton	*Norfolk* - Norwich
Knapton	*York, E.R.* - Malton
Knapton	*York, E.R.* - York
Knapwell	*Cambridge* - Cambridge
Knaresborough	*York, W.R.* - Harrogate
Knaresdale	*Northumberland* - Carlisle
Knarr Fen	*Cambridge* - Peterborough
Knaves Beech	*Bucks* - High Wycombe

Knayton	*York, N.R.* - Northallerton
Knebworth	*Herts* - Hitchin
Knebworth, Old	*Herts* - Hitchin
Knedlington	*York, E.R.* - Goole
Kneesall	*Notts* - Newark
Kneesworth	*Cambs* - Cambridge
Kneeton	*Notts* - Nottingham
Knells	*Cumberland* - Carlisle
Knelston	*Glamorgan* - Swansea
Knenhall	*Stafford* - Stafford
Knettishall	*Suffolk* - Thetford
Knightcote	*Warwick* - Banbury
Knightcott	*Somerset* - Weston Super Mare
Knightley	*Stafford* - Stoke-on-Trent
Knightley	*Stafford* - Stafford
Knighton	*Berks* - Swindon
Knighton	*Devon* - Plymouth
Knighton	*Dorset* - Dorchester
Knighton	*Dorset* - Wimborne Minster
Knighton (Sherborne)	*Dorset* - Yeovil
Knighton	*I. of W.* - Newport (I.W.)
Knighton	*Leicester* - Leicester
Knighton	*Radnor* - Knighton
Knighton	*Somerset* - Bridgwater
Knighton	*Stafford* - Market Drayton
Knighton, East	*Dorset* - Dorchester
Knighton-on-Teme	*Worcester* - Kidderminster
Knighton, South	*Leicester* - Leicester
Knighton, West	*Dorset* - Dorchester
Knightsbridge	*Gloucester* - Cheltenham
Knightsbridge	*Hants* - Newbury
Knight's Enham	*Hants* - Andover
Knights Green	*Gloucester* - Gloucester
Knight's Mill	*Cornwall* - Bideford
Knights Place	*Kent* - Gravesend
Knightwick	*Worcester* - Worcester
Knill	*Hereford* - Leominster
Knipe, High	*Westmorland* - Penrith
Knipe, Low	*Westmorland* - Penrith
Knipton	*Leicester* - Grantham
Knitsley	*Durham* - Consett
Kniveton	*Derby* - Derby
Knobs Crook	*Berks* - Slough
Knobs Crook	*Dorset* - Wimborne Minster
Knock	*Westmorland* - Penrith
Knockholt	*Kent* - Bromley
Knockin	*Salop* - Oswestry
Knodishall	*Suffolk* - Woodbridge
Knoll and Bassett House	*Leicester* - Leicester
Knollbeck	*York, W.R.* - Rotherham
Knolls Green	*Cheshire* - Altrincham
Knolton	*Flint* - Wrexham
Knolton Bryn	*Flint* - Wrexham
Knook	*Wilts* - Warminster
Knossington	*Leicester* - Melton Mowbray
Knostrop	*York, W.R.* - Leeds
Knotbury	*Stafford* - Buxton
Knott End-on-Sea	*Lancaster* - Blackpool
Knotting	*Beds* - Bedford
Knottingley	*York, W.R.* - Pontefract
Knotty Ash	*Lancaster* - Liverpool
Knowbury	*Salop* - Ludlow
Knowle	*Devon* - Barnstaple
Knowle	*Devon* - Exeter
Knowle	*Dorset* - Dorchester
Knowle	*Hants* - Portsmouth
Knowle	*Salop* - Ludlow
Knowle	*Somerset* - Bridgwater
Knowle	*Warwick* - Birmingham
Knowle	*York, W.R.* - Dewsbury
Knowle, East	*Devon* - Exeter
Knowle End	*Stafford* - Stoke-on-Trent
Knowle Green	*Lancaster* - Preston
Knowle Hill	*Hants* - Winchester
Knowle, The	*Staffs* - Dudley
Knowler Hill	*York, W.R.* - Dewsbury
Knowle St. Giles	*Somerset* - Axminster and Chard
Knowle Sands	*Salop* - Brigdnorth
Knowl Hill	*Berks* - Reading
Knowlton	*Dorset* - Wimborne Minster

Knowlton	*Kent* - Deal
Knowl Wall	*Stafford* - Stoke-on-Trent
Knowsley	*Lancaster* - St. Helens
Knowstone	*Devon* - Tiverton
Knoyle, East	*Wilts* - Shaftesbury
Knoyle Green	*Dorset* - Shaftesbury
Knoyle, West	*Wilts* - Shaftesbury
Knuck	*Salop* - Ludlow
Knucklas	*Radnor* - Knighton
Knutsford	*Cheshire* - Altrincham
Knutton	*Stafford* - Stoke-on-Trent
Knuzden	*Lancaster* - Blackburn
Knypersley	*Stafford* - Congleton
Kuggar	*Cornwall* - Penzance
Kyme Fen, North	*Lincoln* - Sleaford
Kyme Fen, South	*Lincoln* - Sleaford
Kyme, North	*Lincoln* - Sleaford
Kyme, South	*Lincoln* - Sleaford
Kynance	*Cornwall* - Penzance
Kynaston	*Hereford* - Hereford
Kynaston	*Salop* - Oswestry
Kynnersley	*Salop* - Wellington (Salop)
Kyo, East	*Durham* - Consett
Kyo, New	*Durham* - Consett
Kyo, West	*Durham* - Consett
Kyre	*Worcester* - Leominster
Kyre Magna	*Worcester* - Leominster
Kyre Parva	*Worcester* - Leominster
Kyre Wood	*Worcester* - Ludlow

L

Laceby	*Lincoln* - Great Grimsby
Lacey Green	*Bucks* - High Wycombe
Lacey Green	*Cheshire* - Macclesfield
Lach Dennis	*Cheshire* - Northwich
Lache	*Cheshire* - Chester
Lackenby	*York, N.R.* - Middlesbrough
Lackford	*Suffolk* - Bury St. Edmunds
Lacock	*Wilts* - Chippenham
Lacon	*Salop* - Shrewsbury
Ladbroke	*Warwick* - Warwick
Ladderedge	*Stafford* - Leek
Laddingford	*Kent* - Maidstone
Laddus Drove	*Cambridge* - Wisbech
Ladmanlow	*Derby* - Buxton
Ladock	*Cornwall* - Truro
Ladwell	*Hants* - Winchester
Lady Cross	*Hants* - Lymington
Lady Down	*Wilts* - Trowbridge
Lady Halton	*Salop* - Ludlow
Ladymoor	*Stafford* - Wolverhampton
Ladyridge	*Hereford* - Hereford
Ladyshore	*Lancaster* - Bolton
Lady Wath	*Cumberland* - Workington
Ladywell	*London, S.E.13* - Bromley
Ladywood	*Warwick* - Birmingham
Lagness	*Sussex* - Chichester
Laindon	*Essex* - Brentwood
Lainston	*Hants* - Winchester
Laira	*Devon* - Plymouth
Laisterdyke	*York, W.R.* - Bradford
Laithes Low	*York, W.R.* - Harrogate
Laithes	*Cumberland* - Penrith
Laithwaite	*Cumberland* - Workington
Laity	*Cornwall* - Helston
Laity Moors	*Cornwall* - Truro
Lake	*I. of W.* - Newport (Mon.)
Lake	*Wilts* - Salisbury
Lake End	*Bucks* - Slough
Lakenheath	*Suffolk* - Bury St. Edmunds
Lakes End	*Cambridge* - Wisbech
Lake Vyrnwy	*Montgomery* - Oswestry
Laleham-on-Thames	*Middlesex* - Slough
Laleston	*Glamorgan* - Bridgend
Lamack	*Lancaster* - Blackburn
Lamanvar Cross	*Cornwall* - Truro
Lamarsh	*Essex* - Sudbury
Lamcroft	*Lincoln* - Louth
Lamberhead Green	*Lancaster* - Wigan
Lamberhurst	*Kent and Sussex* - Tunbridge Wells

Lambeth (part)	*London, S.E.1* - Lambeth
Lambeth (part)	*London, S.E.1* - Southwark
Lambeth, South (part)	*London, S.W.8* - Lambeth
Lambeth, South (part)	*London, S.W.8* - Wandsworth
Lambfoot	*Cumberland* - Workington
Lamb Hill	*York, W.R.* - Sheffield
Lambley	*Northumberland* - Carlisle
Lambley	*Notts* - Nottingham
Lambourn	*Berks* - Newbury
Lambourne	*Essex* - Ilford
Lambourne End	*Essex* - Ilford
Lambourn, Upper	*Berks* - Newbury
Lambourn Woodlands	*Berks* - Newbury
Lambrigg	*Westmorland* - Kendal
Lambrook	*Somerset* - Taunton
Lambrook	*Somerset* - Yeovil
Lambrook, East	*Somerset* - Yeovil
Lambrook, Middle	*Somerset* - Yeovil
Lambrook, West	*Somerset* - Yeovil
Lambs Green	*Dorset* - Wimborne Minster
Lambs Green	*Sussex* - Horsham
Lambston	*Pembroke* - Haverfordwest
Lambton, Low	*Durham* - Durham
Lambton, New	*Durham* - Durham
Lambton Staiths	*Durham* - Durham
Lamcote	*Notts* - Nottingham
Lamerton	*Devon* - Plymouth
Lamesley	*Durham* - Gateshead
Lammacraft	*Devon* - Kingsbridge
Lammas	*Norfolk* - Norwich
Lamonby	*Cumberland* - Penrith
Lamorna	*Cornwall* - Penzance
Lamorran	*Cornwall* - Truro
Lampeter	*Cardigan* - Lampeter
Lampeter Velfrey	*Pembroke* - Haverfordwest
Lampha	*Glamorgan* - Bridgend
Lamphey	*Pembroke* - Haverfordwest
Lamplugh	*Cumberland* - Whitehaven
Lamport	*Northampton* - Northampton
Lampsons Clough	*Lincoln* - Spalding
Lamyatt	*Somerset* - Wells
Lancaster	*Lancaster* - Lancaster
Lancaut	*Gloucester* - Chepstow
Lanchester	*Durham* - Durham
Lancing, North	*Sussex* - Worthing
Lancing, South	*Sussex* - Worthing
Landbeach	*Cambridge* - Cambridge
Lancross	*Devon* - Bideford
Landewednack	*Cornwall* - Penzance
Landford	*Wilts* - Salisbury
Landgate	*Lancaster* - Wigan
Landican	*Cheshire* - Birkenhead
Landkey	*Devon* - Barnstaple
Landore	*Glamorgan* - Swansea
Landport	*Hants* - Portsmouth
Landrake	*Cornwall* - Plymouth
Lands Colliery	*Durham* - Bishop Auckland
Landscove	*Devon* - Newton Abbot
Lands End	*Cornwall* - Penzance
Landshipping	*Pembroke* - Haverfordwest
Landulph	*Cornwall* - Plymouth
Landywood	*Stafford* - Walsall
Lane	*Cornwall* - Truro
Laneast	*Cornwall* - Launceston
Lane End	*Bucks* - High Wycombe
Lane End	*Hants* - Winchester
Lane Ends	*Lancaster* - Bolton
Lane Green	*Stafford* - Wolverhampton
Laneham	*Notts* - East Retford
Lanehead	*Durham* - Bishop Auckland
Lane Head	*Lancaster* - Burnley
Lanehead	*Lancaster* - Rochdale
Lanehead	*Northumberland* - Hexham
Lanehead	*Northumberland* - Hexham
Lane Head	*Stafford* - Walsall
Lanehead	*York, N.R.* - Darlington
Lanelay	*Glamorgan* - Bridgend
Lanercost	*Cumberland* - Carlisle
Lanescot	*Cornwall* - St. Austell
Lanes End	*Kent* - Dartford

Lanesfield	*Stafford* - Wolverhampton
Laneshaw Bridge	*Lancaster* - Nelson
Langar cum Barnstone	*Notts* - Nottingham
Langbar	*York, W.R.* - Otley
Langcliffe	*York, W.R.* - Skipton
Langdale End	*York, N.R.* - Scarborough
Langdale, Great	*Westmorland* - Kendal
Langdale, Little	*Westmorland* - Kendal
Langdon	*Cornwall* - Launceston
Langdon	*Devon* - Launceston
Langdon Beck	*Durham* - Bishop Auckland
Langdon, East	*Kent* - Dover
Langdon Hills	*Essex* - Grays Thurrock
Langdon, West	*Kent* - Dover
Langenhoe	*Essex* - Colchester
Langford	*Beds* - Biggleswade
Langford	*Dorset* - Dorchester
Langford	*Essex* - Maldon
Langford	*Norfolk* - Swaffham
Langford	*Notts* - Newark
Langford	*Oxford* - Witney
Langford	*Somerset* - Taunton
Langford	*Somerset* - Weston Super Mare
Langford Budville	*Somerset* - Taunton
Langford Green	*Devon* - Tiverton
Langford, Little	*Wilts* - Salisbury
Langham	*Dorset* - Shaftesbury
Langham	*Essex* - Colchester
Langham	*Lincoln* - Skegness
Langham	*Norfolk* - Norwich
Langham	*Rutland* - Melton Mowbray
Langham	*Suffolk* - Bury St. Edmunds
Langho	*Lancaster* - Blackburn
Langholme	*Lincoln* - Gainsborough
Langland Bay	*Glamorgan* - Swansea
Langleeford	*Northumberland* - Alnwick
Langleeford Hope	*Northumberland* - Alnwick
Langley	*Bucks* - Slough
Langley	*Cheshire* - Macclesfield
Langley	*Derby* - Ilkeston
Langley	*Durham* - Durham
Langley	*Essex* - Bishop's Stortford
Langley	*Gloucester* - Cheltenham
Langley	*Hants* - Petersfield
Langley	*Hants* - Southampton
Langley	*Herts* - Hitchin
Langley	*Kent* - Maidstone
Langley	*Northumberland* - Hexham
Langley	*Oxford* - Oxford
Langley	*Salop* - Shrewsbury
Langley	*Warwick* - Warwick
Langley	*Worcester* - West Bromwich
Langley Broom	*Bucks* - Slough
Langley Burrell	*Wilts* - Chippenham
Langleybury	*Herts* - Watford
Langleydale with Shotton	*Durham* - Bishop Auckland
Langley Field	*Salop* - Wellington (Salop)
Langley Green	*Worcester* - West Bromwich
Langley Heath	*Warwick* - Birmingham
Langley Lane	*Lancaster* - Oldham
Langley Lawn	*Stafford* - Wolverhampton
Langley Marish	*Bucks* - Slough
Langley Marsh	*Somerset* - Taunton
Langley Mill	*Derby* - Ilkeston
Langley Mill	*Warwick* - Birmingham
Langley Moor	*Durham* - Durham
Langley Park Colliery	*Durham* - Durham
Langley Prior	*Leicester* - Loughborough
Langley with Hardley	*Norfolk* - Norwich
Langmere	*Norfolk* - Norwich
Langney	*Sussex* - Eastbourne
Langold	*Notts* - Worksop
Langore	*Cornwall* - Launceston
Langport	*Somerset* - Taunton
Langrick	*Lincoln* - Boston
Langridge	*Somerset* - Bath
Langrigg	*Cumberland* - Carlisle
Langrish	*Hants* - Petersfield
Langriville	*Lincoln* - Boston
Langsett	*York, W.R.* - Barnsley

Langston	*Devon* - Kingsbridge
Langstone	*Hants* - Portsmouth
Langstone	*Monmouth* - Newport (Mon.)
Langthorpe	*York, N.R.* - Harrogate
Langthwaite	*York, N.R.* - Darlington
Langtoft	*Lincoln* - Spalding
Langtoft	*York, E.R.* - Beverley
Langtoft Common	*Lincoln* - Spalding
Langtoft Fen	*Lincoln* - Spalding
Langton	*Kent* - Tunbridge Wells
Langton	*Lincoln* - Skegness
Langton	*York, E.R.* - Malton
Langton by Horncastle	*Lincoln* - Lincoln
Langton by Wragby	*Lincoln* - Lincoln
Langton, East	*Leicester* - Market Harborough
Langton Herring	*Dorset* - Weymouth
Langton Long	*Dorset* - Blandford
Langton Maltravers	*Dorset* - Swanage
Langton, West	*Leicester* - Leicester
Langtree	*Devon* - Bideford
Langwathby	*Cumberland* - Penrith
Langwith	*Derby* - Chesterfield
Langwith	*York, E.R.* - York
Langwith Junction	*Notts* - Mansfield
Langwith, Nether	*Notts* - Worksop
Langwith, Upper	*Derby* - Chesterfield
Langwm	*Pembroke* - Haverfordwest
Langworth	*Lincoln* - Lincoln
Lanham	*Hants* - Winchester
Lanherne	*Cornwall* - Truro
Lanhydrock	*Cornwall* - Bodmin
Lanivet	*Cornwall* - Bodmin
Lanjeth	*Cornwall* - St. Austell
Lankelly	*Cornwall* - St. Austell
Lanlivery	*Cornwall* - Bodmin
Lannacombe	*Devon* - Kingsbridge
Lannarth	*Cornwall* - Redruth
Lanner	*Cornwall* - Redruth
Lanreath	*Cornwall* - Liskeard
Lansallos	*Cornwall* - Liskeard
Lansdown	*Cornwall* - Truro
Lansdown	*Somerset* - Bath
Lanteglos	*Cornwall* - Bideford
Lanteglos-by-Fowey	*Cornwall* - Liskeard
Lanthwaite Green	*Cumberland* - Workington
Lapal	*Worcester* - Stourbridge
Lapford	*Devon* - Exeter
Lapley	*Stafford* - Wolverhampton
Lapworth	*Warwick* - Warwick
Larbreck	*Lancaster* - Blackpool
Larch Farm	*Notts* - Mansfield
Larkfield	*Kent* - Maidstone
Larkhill	*Wilts* - Salisbury
Larklands	*Derby* - Ilkeston
Lark Lane	*York, W.R.* - Harrogate
Larkton	*Cheshire* - Whitchurch
Larling	*Norfolk* - Thetford
Larrick	*Cornwall* - Launceston
Lartington	*York, N.R.* - Bishop Auckland
Larton	*Cheshire* - Birkenhead
Lasham	*Hants* - Basingstoke
Lashenden	*Kent* - Cranbrook
Lask Edge	*Stafford* - Congleton
Lassington	*Gloucester* - Gloucester
Lastingham	*York, N.R.* - Malton
Latchen	*Gloucester* - Gloucester
Latchford	*Oxford* - Thame
Latchford Green	*Herts* - Hertford
Latchingdon	*Essex* - Maldon
Latchley	*Cornwall* - Plymouth
Latchmore	*Hants* - Lymington
Latchmore Bank	*Essex* - Bishop's Stortford
Latchmore Green	*Hants* - Basingstoke
Late Brook	*Stafford* - Stoke-on-Trent
Lathbury	*Bucks* - Bletchley and Leighton Buzzard
Latherbrush	*Durham* - Bishop Auckland
Lathkill Dale	*Derby* - Matlock
Lathom	*Lancaster* - Wigan
Latimer	*Bucks* - Amersham

Latteridge	*Gloucester* - Bristol
Lattiford	*Somerset* - Yeovil
Latton	*Wilts* - Swindon
Laugharne	*Carmarthen* - Carmarthen
Laughterton	*Lincoln* - Gainsborough
Laughton	*Leicester* - Leicester
Laughton	*Lincoln* - Sleaford
Laughton	*Lincoln* - Gainsborough
Laughton	*Sussex* - Lewes
Laughton Common (part)	*York, W.R.* - Rotherham
Laughton Common (part)	*York, W.R.* - Worksop
Laughton-en-le-Morthen	*York, W.R.* - Rotherham
Launcells	*Cornwall* - Bideford
Launceston	*Cornwall* - Launceston
Laund Booth, Old	*Lancaster* - Nelson
Launde	*Leicester* - Leicester
Launton	*Oxford* - Oxford
Laurie Park	*Kent* - Bromley
Lavant	*Sussex* - Chichester
Lavant, East	*Sussex* - Chichester
Lavant, Mid	*Sussex* - Chichester
Lavendon	*Bucks* - Northampton
Lavenham	*Suffolk* - Sudbury
Laver, Little	*Essex* - Harlow
Lavernock	*Glamorgan* - Barry
Laversdale	*Cumberland* - Carlisle
Laverstock	*Wilts* - Salisbury
Laverstoke	*Hants* - Andover
Laverton	*Gloucester* - Cheltenham
Laverton	*Somerset* - Frome
Laverton	*York, W.R.* - Harrogate
Lavington, East	*Sussex* - Chichester
Lavington, East	*Wilts* - Devizes
Lavington Park	*Sussex* - Chichester
Lavington, West	*Sussex* - Chichester
Lavington, West	*Wilts* - Devizes
Lavister	*Denbigh* - Wrexham
Lawford	*Essex* - Colchester
Lawhitton	*Cornwall* - Launceston
Lawkland	*York, W.R.* - Skipton
Lawley	*Salop* - Shrewsbury
Lawley	*Salop* - Wellington (Salop)
Lawley Bank	*Salop* - Wellington (Salop)
Lawn Head	*Stafford* - Stafford
Lawn, South	*Oxford* - Witney
Lawnswood	*York, W.R.* - Leeds
Lawnt	*Salop* - Oswestry
Lawn, The	*Worcester* - Cheltenham
Lawrence Weston	*Gloucester* - Bristol
Lawrenny	*Pembroke* - Haverfordwest
Lawshall	*Suffolk* - Bury St. Edmunds
Lawton	*Salop* - Ludlow
Lawton Heath	*Cheshire* - Congleton
Laxfield	*Suffolk* - Halesworth
Laxton	*Northampton* - Peterborough
Laxton	*Northants* - Stamford
Laxton	*Notts* - Newark
Laxton	*York, N.R.* - Goole
Laycock	*York, W.R.* - Keighley
Layer Breton	*Essex* - Colchester
Layer-de-la-Haye	*Essex* - Colchester
Layer Marney	*Essex* - Colchester
Layham	*Suffolk* - Ipswich
Laymore	*Dorset* - Axminster and Chard
Laymore	*Dorset* - Yeovil
Layston	*Herts* - Hitchin
Layters Green	*Bucks* - Amersham
Laytham	*York, E.R.* - York
Laythes	*Cumberland* - Carlisle
Layton, East	*York, N.R.* - Darlington
Lazenby	*York, N.R.* - Middlesbrough
Lazenby	*York, N.R.* - Northallerton
Lazencroft	*York, W.R.* - Leeds
Lazonby	*Cumberland* - Penrith
Lea	*Derby* - Matlock
Lea	*Hereford* - Gloucester
Lea	*Lancaster* - Preston
Lea	*Lincoln* - Gainsborough
Lea	*Salop* - Shrewsbury
Lea	*Wilts* - Malmesbury

LEA - LED

Lea Bailey	*Gloucester* - Ross
Lea Bridge	*London, E.5* - Shoreditch
Lea Brook	*Stafford* - Dudley
Leabrooks	*Derby* - Alfreton
Lea-by-Backford	*Cheshire* - Chester
Lea Cross	*Salop* - Shrewsbury
Leacroft	*Stafford* - Walsall
Lead	*York, W.R.* - Leeds
Leadbeater Fold	*Lancaster* - Bolton
Leadenham	*Lincoln* - Sleaford
Leadenham Heath	*Lincoln* - Sleaford
Leadenham Low Fields	*Lincoln* - Sleaford
Leaden Roding	*Essex* - Chelmsford
Leadgate	*Cumberland* - Carlisle
Leadgate	*Durham* - Consett
Leadon	*Hereford* - Worcester
Lea End	*Worcester* - Redditch
Leafield	*Oxford* - Oxford
Leafield Assarts	*Oxford* - Oxford
Lea Ford	*Warwick* - Birmingham
Leagram	*Lancaster* - Preston
Leagrave	*Beds* - Luton
Lea Green	*Lancaster* - St. Helens
Lea Hall	*Derby* - Matlock
Lea Hall	*Warwick* - Birmingham
Lea Heath	*Stafford* - Stafford
Lea Hill	*Warwick* - Birmingham
Leake, East	*Notts* - Loughborough
Leake, New	*Lincoln* - Boston
Leake, Old	*Lincoln* - Boston
Leake, West	*Notts* - Loughborough
Lealholme	*York, N.R.* - Whitby
Lea Marston	*Warwick* - Birmingham
Leamington	*Warwick* - Warwick
Leamington Hastings	*Warwick* - Rugby
Leamore	*Stafford* - Walsall
Leamside	*Durham* - Durham
Leam, The	*Durham* - Gateshead
Lew Newbold	*Cheshire* - Chester
Learchild	*Northumberland* - Alnwick
Lease Rigg	*York, N.R.* - Whitby
Leasgill	*Westmorland* - Kendal
Leasingham	*Lincoln* - Sleaford
Leasingthorne	*Durham* - Bishop Auckland
Leasowe	*Cheshire* - Birkenhead
Leasowes	*Salop* - Ludlow
Leasows	*Salop* - Shrewsbury
Leasty	*Salop* - Shrewsbury
Leatherhead	*Surrey* - Epsom
Leathes, Low	*Cumberland* - Workington
Leathley	*York, W.R.* - Otley
Leaton	*Salop* - Shrewsbury
Leaton	*Salop* - Wellington (Salop)
Leaveland	*Kent* - Canterbury
Leavenheath	*Suffolk* - Sudbury
Leavening	*York, E.R.* - Malton
Leavesden	*Herts* - Watford
Leavesden Green	*Herts* - Watford
Leaves Green	*Kent* - Bromley
Lea Village	*Warwick* - Birmingham
Leazes	*Durham* - Consett
Leazes	*Northumberland* - Hexham
Lebberston	*York, N.R.* - Scarborough
Lechlade	*Gloucester* - Swindon
Leck	*Lancaster* - Lancaster
Leckbarrow	*Lancaster* - Barrow-in-Furness
Leckby	*York, N.R.* - Harrogate
Leckford	*Hants* - Andover
Leckhampstead	*Berks* - Newbury
Leckhampstead	*Bucks* - Bletchley and Leighton Buzzard
Leckhampton	*Gloucester* - Cheltenham
Lecknor Uphill	*Bucks* - High Wycombe
Leckwith	*Glamorgan* - Cardiff
Leconfield	*York, E.R.* - Beverley
Ledburn	*Bucks* - Bletchley and Leighton Buzzard
Ledbury	*Hereford* - Hereford
Leddington	*Gloucester* - Gloucester

LED - LEI

Ledgemore	*Hereford* - Leominster
Ledsham	*Cheshire* - Chester
Ledsham	*York, W.R.* - Pontefract
Ledston	*York, W.R.* - Pontefract
Ledston Luck	*York, W.R.* - Pontefract
Ledwell	*Oxford* - Banbury
Ledwyche	*Salop* - Ludlow
Lee	*Devon* - Barnstaple
Lee (Romsey)	*Hants* - Southampton
Lee (part)	*London, S.E.12* - Bromley
Lee (part)	*London, S.E.12* - Woolwich
Lee	*Northumberland* - Morpeth
Lee	*Salop* - Shrewsbury
Leebotwood	*Salop* - Shrewsbury
Lee Bridge	*Salop* - Shrewsbury
Lee Brigg	*York, W.R.* - Wakefield
Lee Brockhurst	*Salop* - Shrewsbury
Leece	*Lancaster* - Barrow-in-Furness
Lee Chapel North	*Essex* - Brentwood
Lee Chapel South	*Essex* - Brentwood
Lee Common	*Bucks* - Amersham
Leedon	*Beds* - Bletchley and Leighton Buzzard
Leeds	*Kent* - Maidstone
Leeds	*York, W.R.* - Leeds
Leedstown	*Cornwall* - Redruth
Leegate	*Cumberland* - Carlisle
Leegomery	*Salop* - Wellington (Salop)
Lee Green (part)	*London, S.E.12* - Bromley
Lee Green (part)	*London, S.E.12* - Woolwich
Lee Green	*York, W.R.* - Dewsbury
Leeholme	*Durham* - Bishop Auckland
Leek	*Stafford* - Leek
Leek Brook	*Stafford* - Leek
Leek Frith	*Stafford* - Leek
Leek Wooton	*Warwick* - Warwick
Leemaling	*Northumberland* - Hexham
Lee Mill Bridge	*Devon* - Plymouth
Leeming	*York, N.R.* - Northallerton
Leeming	*York, W.R.* - Keighley
Leeming Lane	*York, N.R.* - Harrogate
Lee Moor	*Devon* - Plymouth
Lee Moor	*York, W.R.* - Wakefield
Leemore	*Salop* - Ludlow
Lee-on-the-Solent	*Hants* - Portsmouth
Lees	*Lancaster* - Oldham
Leese	*Cheshire* - Congleton
Lees Head	*York, N.R.* - Whitby
Lees, North	*York, W.R.* - Harrogate
Lees, The	*Salop* - Wellington (Salop)
Leesthorpe	*Leicester* - Melton Mowbray
Leeswood	*Flint* - Mold
Lee, The	*Bucks* - Amersham
Leftwich	*Cheshire* - Northwich
Legacy	*Denbigh* - Wrexham
Legar	*Brecon* - Pontypool and Abergavenny
Legbourne	*Lincoln* - Louth
Legburthwaite	*Cumberland* - Workington
Legh, High	*Cheshire* - Altrincham
Legsby	*Lincoln* - Louth
Legs Cross	*Durham* - Bishop Auckland
Leicester	*Leicester* - Leicester
Leicester Forest	*Leicester* - Leicester
Leicester Frith	*Leicester* - Leicester
Leigh	*Devon* - Kingsbridge
Leigh	*Dorset* - Dorchester
Leigh	*Dorset* - Wimborne Minster
Leigh	*Dorset* - Yeovil
Leigh	*Gloucester* - Cheltenham
Leigh	*Kent* - Tonbridge
Leigh	*Lancaster* - Leigh
Leigh	*Somerset* - Axminster and Chard
Leigh	*Stafford* - Uttoxeter
Leigh	*Surrey* - Reigate
Leigh	*Wilts* - Swindon
Leigh	*Worcester* - Great Malvern
Leigh Common	*Somerset* - Yeovil
Leigh Cross	*Somerset* - Bristol
Leigh Delamere	*Wilts* - Chippenham

Leigh, East	*Devon* - Kingsbridge
Leighfield	*Rutland* - Melton Mowbray
Leigh Green	*Kent* - Cranbrook
Leigh Green	*Wilts* - Trowbridge
Leigh Hill	*Wilts* - Swindon
Leigh, Little	*Cheshire* - Northwich
Leigh, North	*Oxford* - Witney
Leigh-on-Mendip	*Somerset* - Frome
Leigh-on-Sea	*Essex* - Southend
Leigh Park	*Hants* - Portsmouth
Leighs, Great	*Essex* - Braintree
Leigh Sinton	*Worcester* - Great Malvern
Leighs, Little	*Essex* - Braintree
Leigh, South	*Oxford* - Witney
Leighs Wood	*Stafford* - Walsall
Leighterton	*Gloucester* - Malmesbury
Leighton	*Cheshire* - Crewe
Leighton	*Hereford* - Hereford
Leighton	*Hunts* - Huntingdon
Leighton	*Montgomery* - Welshpool
Leighton	*Salop* - Shrewsbury
Leighton	*Somerset* - Frome
Leighton Beck	*Westmorland* - Kendal
Leighton Buzzard	*Beds* - Bletchley and Leighton Buzzard
Leighton, Low	*Derby* - Buxton
Leigh, West	*Devon* - Kingsbridge
Leigh, West	*Hants*- Portsmouth
Leigh, West	*Lancaster* - Leigh
Leigh West	*Somerset* - Taunton
Leinthall Earles	*Hereford* - Leominster
Leinthall Starkes	*Hereford* - Ludlow
Leintwardine	*Hereford* - Ludlow
Leire	*Leicester* - Hinckley
Leiston	*Suffolk* - Woodbridge
Lelant	*Cornwall* - Penzance
Lelant Downs	*Cornwall* - Penzance
Lelley	*York, E.R.* - Kingston-upon-Hull
Lemington, Lower	*Gloucester* - Evesham
Lemington-on-Tyne	*Northumberland* - Newcastle upon Tyne
Lemmington	*Northumberland* - Alnwick
Lemsford	*Herts* - St. Albans
Lenches	*Lancaster* - Nelson
Lenchwick	*Worcester* - Evesham
Lenham	*Kent* - Maidstone
Lennerton	*York, W.R.* - Leeds
Lent Green	*Bucks* - Slough
Lenton	*Lincoln* - Grantham
Lent Rise	*Bucks* - Slough
Lenwade	*Norfolk* - Norwich
Leomansley	*Stafford* - Lichfield
Leominster	*Hereford* - Leominster
Leonard Moor	*Devon* - Tiverton
Leonardslee	*Sussex* - Horsham
Leonard Stanley	*Gloucester* - Stroud
Leonardstone	*Pembroke* - Haverfordwest
Lepe	*Hants* - Southampton
Lepton	*York, W.R.* - Huddersfield
Lerryn (St. Veep)	*Cornwall* - Liskeard
Lerryn (St. Winnow)	*Cornwall* - Bodmin
Lesbury	*Northumberland* - Alnwick
Lesnewth	*Cornwall* - Launceston
Lessingham	*Norfolk* - Great Yarmouth
Lessness Heath	*London, S.E.2* - Dartford
Lessonhall	*Cumberland* - Carlisle
Letchmore Green	*Herts* - Hitchin
Letchmore Heath	*Herts* - Watford
Letchworth	*Herts* - Hitchin
Letcombe Bassett	*Berks* - Didcot
Letcombe Bowers	*Berks* - Didcot
Letcombe Regis	*Berks* - Didcot
Letheringham	*Suffolk* - Woodbridge
Letheringsett	*Norfolk* - Norwich
Letterston	*Pembroke* - Haverfordwest
Letton	*Hereford* - Hereford
Letton	*Hereford* - Knighton
Letton	*Norfolk* - East Dereham
Letts Green	*Kent* - Bromley

Letty Green	*Herts* - Hertford
Letwell	*York, W.R.* - Worksop
Levalsa	*Cornwall* - St. Austell
Levedale	*Stafford* - Stafford
Levels Green	*Essex* - Bishop's Stortford
Leven	*York, E.R.* - Beverley
Leven Bridge (part)	*York, N.R.* - Stockton on Tees
Leven Bridge (part)	*York, N.R.* - Middlesbrough
Leven, High	*York, N.R.* - Middlesbrough
Levens	*Westmorland* - Kendal
Leven's Green	*Herts* - Hertford
Levenshulme	*Lancaster* - Manchester
Lever, Great	*Lancaster* - Bolton
Leverington	*Cambridge* - Wisbech
Leverington Common	*Cambridge* - Wisbech
Lever, Little	*Lancaster* - Bolton
Leverstock Green	*Herts* - Hemel Hempstead
Leverton	*Berks* - Newbury
Leverton	*Lincoln* - Boston
Leverton Fen Allotments	*Lincoln* - Boston
Leverton Ings	*Lincoln* - Boston
Leverton Marshes	*Lincoln* - Boston
Leverton, North	*Notts* - East Retford
Leverton, South	*Notts* - East Retford
Levington	*Suffolk* - Ipswich
Levisham	*York, N.R.* - Malton
Lew	*Oxford* - Witney
Lewannick	*Cornwall* - Launceston
Lewdown	*Devon* - Plymouth
Lewell	*Dorset* - Dorchester
Lewes	*Sussex* - Lewes
Leweston	*Dorset* - Yeovil
Lewisham	*London, S.E.13* - Bromley
Lewistown	*Glamorgan* - Bridgend
Lewknor	*Oxford* - Thame
Lewtrenchard	*Devon* - Plymouth
Lexden	*Essex* - Colchester
Lexham, East	*Norfolk* - King's Lynn
Lexham, West	*Norfolk* - King's Lynn
Ley	*Cornwall* - Liskeard
Ley	*Gloucester* - Gloucester
Leybourne	*Kent* - Maidstone
Leyburn	*York, N.R.* - Northallerton
Leycett	*Stafford* - Stoke-on-Trent
Ley Green	*Herts* - Hitchin
Leyhill	*Gloucester* - Thornbury
Ley Hill	*Warwick* - Birmingham
Leyland	*Lancaster* - Preston
Leysdown	*Kent* - Sheerness
Leys Green	*Wilts* - Warminster
Leys Hill	*Hereford* - Monmouth
Leysters	*Hereford* - Leominster
Leys, The	*Glamorgan* - Bridgend
Leyton	*Durham* - Stockton on Tees
Leyton	*London, E.10* - Bow
Leytonstone	*London, E.11* - Bow
Leywood	*Kent* - Gravesend
Lezant	*Cornwall* - Launceston
Lezerea	*Cornwall* - Penzance
Leziate	*Norfolk* - King's Lynn
Libanus	*Brecon* - Brecknock
Libbery	*Worcester* - Worcester
Lichfield	*Stafford* - Lichfield
Lickey (part)	*Worcester* - Birmingham
Lickey End	*Worcester* - Bromsgrove
Lickey Hill	*Worcester* - Bromsgrove
Lickey Rock	*Worcester* - Bromsgrove
Lickfold	*Sussex* - Chichester
Liddeston	*Pembroke* - Haverfordwest
Liddington	*Wilts* - Swindon
Liddington	*Northampton* - Corby
Lidgate	*Suffolk* - Newmarket
Lidget	*Lancaster* - Nelson
Lidget	*York, W.R.* - Keighley
Lidget Green	*York, W.R.* - Bradford
Lidlington	*Beds* - Bedford
Lidsey	*Sussex* - Chichester
Lidsing	*Kent* - Rochester
Lidstone	*Devon* - Kingsbridge
Lidstone	*Oxford* - Banbury

LID - LIN

Lidwell	*Cornwall* - Launceston
Lifford	*Warwick* - Birmingham
Lifton	*Devon* - Launceston
Lifton Down	*Cornwall* - Launceston
Lightcliffe	*York, W.R.* - Halifax
Lighthorne	*Warwick* - Warwick
Lightmoor	*Salop* - Wellington (Salop)
Lightwater	*Surrey* - Aldershot and Farnham
Lightwater Brougham	*Westmorland* - Penrith
Lightwood	*Stafford* - Stoke-on-Trent
Lightwood Green	*Flint* - Wrexham
Light Woods	*Stafford* - West Bromwich
Lilbourne	*Northampton* - Rugby
Lilford	*Northampton* - Corby
Lilford-cum-Wigsthorpe	*Northampton* - Corby
Lillapit	*Devon* - Plymouth
Lillesdon	*Somerset* - Taunton
Lilleshall	*Salop* - Wellington (Salop)
Lilley	*Berks* - Didcot
Lilley	*Herts* - Hitchin
Lilley Clough	*York, W.R.* - Dewsbury
Lilley Green	*Warwick* - Redditch
Lilley Hoo	*Herts* - Hitchin
Lillings Ambo	*York, N.R.* - York
Lillingstone Dayrell	*Bucks* - Northampton
Lillingstone Lovell	*Bucks* - Northampton
Lillington	*Dorset* - Yeovil
Lillington	*Warwick* - Warwick
Lilly Hall	*Cumberland* - Workington
Lilly Hill	*Berks* - Slough
Lilstock	*Somerset* - Minehead
Lilswood	*Northumberland* - Hexham
Lily Hill	*Lancaster* - Bury
Lilyhurst	*Salop* - Wellington (Salop)
Limber, Great	*Lincoln* - Great Grimsby
Limber, Little	*Lincoln* - Great Grimsby
Limber Magna	*Lincoln* - Great Grimsby
Limber Parva	*Lincoln* - Great Grimsby
Limbury	*Beds* - Luton
Limefield	*Lancaster* - Bury
Limehead	*Cornwall* - Bideford
Limehouse	*London, E.14* - Bow
Limeslade	*Glamorgan* - Swansea
Limestone Brae	*Northumberland* - Hexham
Limington	*Somerset* - Yeovil
Limley	*York, W.R.* - Harrogate
Limpenhoe	*Norfolk* - Norwich
Limpley Stoke	*Wilts* - Trowbridge
Limpsfield	*Surrey* - Reigate
Linbridge	*Northumberland* - Morpeth
Linbrook	*Hants* - Salisbury
Linbrook	*Stafford* - Burton-on-Trent
Linby	*Notts* - Nottingham
Linch	*Sussex* - Petersfield
Linchmere	*Sussex* - Petersfield
Linciter	*Hereford* - Hereford
Lincoln	*Lincoln* - Lincoln
Lincoln Green	*Gloucester* - Cheltenham
Lincoln Hill	*Salop* - Wellington (Salop)
Lincolns Inn	*London, W.C.2* - Westminster
Lincomb	*Worcester* - Kidderminster
Lindal Cote	*Lancaster* - Barrow-in-Furness
Lindale-in-Cartmel	*Lancaster* - Barrow-in-Furness
Lindal-in-Furness	*Lancaster* - Barrow-in-Furness
Lindeth	*Westmorland* - Kendal
Lindeth in Silverdale	*Lancaster* - Lancaster
Lindfield	*Sussex* - Haywards Heath
Lindford	*Hants* - Aldershot and Farnham
Lindholme	*York, W.R.* - Thorne
Lindley	*Leicester* - Hinckley
Lindley	*Wilts* - Shaftesbury
Lindley	*York, W.R.* - Huddersfield
Lindley	*York, W.R.* - Otley
Lindley, Old	*York, W.R.* - Halifax
Lindow	*Cheshire* - Macclesfield
Lindrick	*York, W.R.* - Doncaster
Lindrick	*York, W.R.* - Harrogate
Lindridge	*Worcester* - Kidderminster
Lindsell	*Essex* - Braintree
Lindsey	*Suffolk* - Sudbury

LIN - LIT

Lineholt	*Worcester* - Worcester
Line Houses	*Stafford* - Stoke-on-Trent
Liney	*Somerset* - Bridgwater
Linfits	*York, W.R.* - Oldham
Linford	*Essex* - Grays Thurrock
Linford, Great	*Bucks* - Bletchley and Leighton Buzzard
Linford, Little	*Bucks* - Bletchley and Leighton Buzzard
Lingards	*York, W.R.* - Huddersfield
Lingdale	*York, N.R.* - Middlesbrough
Lingen	*Hereford* - Knighton
Lingerfield	*York, W.R.* - Harrogate
Lingfield	*Surrey* - East Grinstead
Lingwell Gate	*York, W.R.* - Wakefield
Lingwood	*Norfolk* - Norwich
Linhope	*Northumberland* - Alnwick
Linkend	*Worcester* - Cheltenham
Linkenholt	*Hants* - Andover
Linkinhorne	*Cornwall* - Liskeard
Links, The	*Salop* - Market Drayton
Linley	*Salop* - Shrewsbury
Linley	*Salop* - Bridgnorth
Linley Brook	*Salop* - Bridgnorth
Linley Green	*Hereford* - Worcester
Linleys	*Wilts* - Chippenham
Linsheeles	*Northumberland* - Morpeth
Linslade	*Bucks* - Bletchley and Leighton Buzzard
Linstead, Great	*Suffolk* - Halesworth
Linstead, Little	*Suffolk* - Halesworth
Linstead Magna	*Suffolk* - Halesworth
Linstead Parva	*Suffolk* - Halesworth
Linstock	*Cumberland* - Carlisle
Linthorpe	*York, N.R.* - Middlesbrough
Linthurst	*Worcester* - Bromsgrove
Linthwaite	*York, W.R.* - Huddersfield
Lintley	*Northumberland* - Carlisle
Linton	*Cambridge* - Cambridge
Linton	*Derby* - Burton-upon-Trent
Linton	*Hereford* - Gloucester
Linton	*Kent* - Maidstone
Linton	*York, W.R.* - Skipton
Linton	*York, W.R.* - Leeds
Linton Colliery	*Northumberland* - Morpeth
Linton, East	*York, E.R.* - Goole
Linton-upon-Ouse	*York, N.R.* - York
Linton, West	*York, E.R.* - Goole
Lintz Colliery	*Durham* - Consett
Lintz Ford	*Durham* - Consett
Lintz Green	*Durham* - Consett
Linwood	*Hants* - Salisbury
Linwood	*Lincoln* - Lincoln
Lion Common	*Surrey* - Guildford
Lion Green	*Surrey* - Guildford
Lions Hill	*Hants* - Salisbury
Liphook	*Hants* - Petersfield
Lipley	*Salop* - Market Drayton
Lipson	*Devon* - Plymouth
Liscard	*Cheshire* - Birkenhead
Liskeard	*Cornwall* - Liskeard
Liss, East	*Hants* - Petersfield
Lissett	*York, E.R.* - Bridlington
Liss Forest	*Hants* - Petersfield
Lissinglea	*Lincoln* - Lincoln
Lissington	*Lincoln* - Lincoln
Liss, West	*Hants* - Petersfield
Liston	*Essex* - Sudbury
Lisvane	*Glamorgan* - Cardiff
Lisworney	*Glamorgan* - Bridgend
Litcham	*Norfolk* - East Dereham
Litchborough	*Northampton* - Northampton
Litchfield, North	*Hants* - Newbury
Litchfield, South	*Hants* - Basingstoke
Litherland	*Lancaster* - Liverpool
Litlington	*Cambridge* - Hitchin
Litlington	*Sussex* - Eastbourne
Little Abington	*Cambridge* - Cambridge
Little Acton	*Denbigh* - Wrexham
Little Addington	*Northampton* - Wellingborough

Little Almshoe	*Herts* - Hitchin
Little Alne	*Warwick* - Stratford on Avon
Little Altcar	*Lancaster* - Southport
Little Amwell	*Herts* - Hertford
Little Ann	*Hants* - Andover
Little Appledore	*Kent* - Cranbrook
Little Asby	*Westmorland* - Penrith
Little Aston (part)	*Stafford* - Lichfield
Little Ayton	*York, N.R.* - Middlesbrough
Little Baddow	*Essex* - Chelmsford
Little Badminton	*Gloucester* - Bristol
Little Bampton	*Cumberland* - Carlisle
Little Bardfield	*Essex* - Braintree
Little Barford	*Beds* - Biggleswade
Little Barningham	*Norfolk* - Norwich
Little Barrington	*Gloucester* - Cheltenham
Little Barugh	*York, N.R.* - Malton
Little Basing	*Hants* - Basingstoke
Little Bavington	*Northumberland* - Hexham
Little Bayton	*Warwick* - Nuneaton
Little Bealings	*Suffolk* - Ipswich
Littlebeck	*York, N.R.* - Whitby
Little Bedwyn	*Wilts* - Swindon
Little Bentley	*Essex* - Colchester
Little Benton	*Northumberland* - Newcastle-upon-Tyne
Little Berkhamsted	*Herts* - Hertford
Little Billing	*Northampton* - Northampton
Little Billington	*Beds* - Bletchley and Leighton Buzzard
Little Birch	*Hereford* - Hereford
Little Blakenham	*Suffolk* - Ipswich
Little Blenheim	*Oxford* - Oxford
Little Bloxwich	*Stafford* - Walsall
Little Bognor	*Sussex* - Chichester
Little Bolas	*Salop* - Market Drayton
Little Bookham	*Surrey* - Epsom
Littleborough	*Lancaster* - Rochdale
Littleborough	*Notts* - East Retford
Littlebourne	*Kent* - Canterbury
Little Bourton	*Oxford* - Banbury
Little Bowden	*Northampton* - Market Harborough
Little Brampton	*Salop* - Ludlow
Little Braxted	*Essex* - Maldon
Little Bredy	*Dorset* - Dorchester
Little Bricett	*Suffolk* - Stowmarket
Little Brickhill	*Bucks* - Bletchley and Leighton Buzzard
Little Bridgford	*Stafford* - Stafford
Little Brington	*Northampton* - Northampton
Little Brockhampton	*Gloucester* - Cheltenham
Little Bromley	*Essex* - Colchester
Little Bromwich	*Warwick* - Birmingham
Little Broughton	*Cumberland* - Workington
Little Broughton	*York, N.R.* - Middlesbrough
Little Budworth	*Cheshire* - Northwich
Little Burn	*Durham* - Durham
Little Burstead	*Essex* - Brentwood
Littlebury	*Essex* - Bishop's Stortford
Littlebury Green	*Essex* - Bishop's Stortford
Little Busby	*York, N.R.* - Middlesbrough
Little Bytham	*Lincoln* - Stamford
Little Callerton	*Northumberland* - Newcastle-upon-Tyne
Little Canfield	*Essex* - Braintree
Little Carleton	*Lancaster* - Blackpool
Little Carlton	*Lincoln* - Louth
Little Casterton	*Rutland* - Stamford
Little Catworth	*Hunts* - Huntingdon
Little Cawthorpe	*Lincoln* - Louth
Little Chalfield	*Wilts* - Trowbridge
Little Chalfont	*Bucks* - Amersham
Little Chart	*Kent* - Ashford
Little Chatwell	*Stafford* - Stafford
Little Chell	*Stafford* - Stoke-on-Trent
Little Chester	*Derby* - Derby
Little Chesterford	*Essex* - Cambridge
Little Chesterton	*Oxford* - Oxford
Little Cheverell	*Wilts* - Devizes

Little Chilton	*Durham* - Durham
Little Chishill	*Essex* - Cambridge
Little Clacton	*Essex* - Colchester
Little Clifton	*Cumberland* - Workington
Little Coggeshall	*Essex* - Braintree
Little Comberton	*Worcester* - Evesham
Little Common	*Sussex* - Hastings
Little Compton	*Warwick* - Banbury
Little Corby	*Cumberland* - Carlisle
Little Cornard	*Suffolk* - Sudbury
Littlecote	*Bucks* - Bletchley and Leighton Buzzard
Littlecote	*Wilts* - Swindon
Littlecott	*Wilts* - Devizes
Little Cowarne	*Hereford* - Hereford
Little Cowden	*York, E.R.* - Kingston-upon-Hull
Little Coxwell	*Berks* - Swindon
Little Cressingham	*Norfolk* - King's Lynn
Little Crossthwaite	*Cumberland* - Workington
Little Dalby	*Leicester* - Melton Mowbray
Littledale	*Lancaster* - Lancaster
Little Dawley	*Salop* - Wellington (Salop)
Little Dean	*Gloucester* - Gloucester
Little Dewchurch	*Hereford* - Hereford
Little Digmoor	*Lancaster* - Wigan
Little Dilwyn	*Hereford* - Leominster
Little Dorsington	*Warwick* - Stratford on Avon
Little Downham	*Cambridge* - Ely
Little Downham Fen	*Cambridge* - Ely
Little Dowsby	*Lincoln* - Spalding
Little Driffield	*York, E.R.* - Beverley
Little Droylsden	*Lancaster* - Oldham
Little Dunham	*Norfolk* - King's Lynn
Little Dunmow	*Essex* - Braintree
Little Easby	*Cumberland* - Carlisle
Little Easton	*Essex* - Braintree
Little Eaton	*Derby* - Derby
Little Eccleston-with-Larbreck	*Lancaster* - Blackpool
Little Edstone	*York, N.R.* - Malton
Little Ellingham	*Norfolk* - Norwich
Little Elmsall	*York, W.R.* - Pontefract
Little Eppleton	*Durham* - Durham
Little Everdon	*Northampton* - Northampton
Little Eversden	*Cambridge* - Cambridge
Little Faringdon	*Oxford* - Witney
Little Farmcote	*Gloucester* - Cheltenham
Little Fenton	*York, W.R.* - York
Little Fields	*Worcester* - West Bromwich
Little Finborough	*Suffolk* - Stowmarket
Little Fransham	*Norfolk* - East Dereham
Little Fryup	*York, N.R.* - Whitby
Little Gaddesden	*Herts* - Hemel Hempstead
Little Gidding	*Hunts* - Huntingdon
Little Givendale	*York, E.R.* - York
Little Glemham	*Suffolk* - Woodbridge
Little Gomersal	*York, W.R.* - Dewsbury
Little Gransden	*Cambridge* - Biggleswade
Little Green	*Flint* - Whitchurch
Little Green	*Herts* - Watford
Little Green	*Sussex* - Chichester
Little Greencroft	*Durham* - Durham
Little Grimsby	*Lincoln* - Louth
Little Grimston	*York, W.R.* - York
Little Gringley	*Notts* - East Retford
Little Habton	*York, N.R.* - Malton
Little Hadham	*Herts* - Bishop's Stortford
Little Hale	*Kent* - Margate
Little Hale	*Lincoln* - Sleaford
Little Hale Fen	*Lincoln* - Sleaford
Littlehales	*Salop* - Wellington (Salop)
Little Hallam	*Derby* - Ilkeston
Little Hallingbury	*Essex* - Bishop's Stortford
Littleham	*Devon* - Bideford
Littleham	*Devon* - Exeter
Little Hampden	*Bucks* - High Wycombe
Little Hampton	*Worcester* - Evesham
Littlehampton	*Sussex* - Chichester
Little Harle	*Northumberland* - Hexham

Little Harrowden	*Northampton* - Wellingborough
Little Harwood	*Lancaster* - Blackburn
Little Haseley	*Oxford* - Thame
Little Hautbois	*Norfolk* - Norwich
Little Haven	*Pembroke* - Haverfordwest
Little Haven	*Sussex* - Horsham
Little Hay	*Stafford* - Lichfield
Little Haywood	*Stafford* - Stafford
Little Heath	*Essex* - Ilford
Little Heath	*Herts* - St. Albans
Little Heath	*Warwick* - Birmingham
Little Heaton	*Lancaster* - Salford
Little Hempston	*Devon* - Newton Abbot
Little Henny	*Essex* - Sudbury
Little Hereford	*Hereford* - Ludlow
Little Hinton	*Wilts* - Swindon
Little Hockham	*Norfolk* - Thetford
Little Holland	*Essex* - Colchester
Little Hoole	*Lancaster* - Preston
Little Horkesley	*Essex* - Colchester
Little Horwood	*Bucks* - Bletchley and Leighton Buzzard
Little Houghton	*Northampton* - Northampton
Littlehoughton	*Northumberland* - Alnwick
Little Houghton	*York, W.R.* - Barnsley
Little Hucklow	*Derby* - Buxton
Little Hulton	*Lancaster* - Salford
Little Humber	*York, E.R.* - Kingston-upon-Hull
Little Humby	*Lincoln* - Grantham
Little Hungerford	*Berks* - Newbury
Little Ickford	*Bucks* - Thame
Little Irchester	*Northampton* - Wellingborough
Little Kelk	*York, E.R.* - Bridlington
Little Keyford	*Somerset* - Frome
Little Kimble	*Bucks* - Aylesbury
Little Kineton	*Warwick* - Stratford on Avon
Little Kingshill	*Bucks* - Amersham
Little Kyre	*Worcester* - Leominster
Little Langdale	*Westmorland* - Kendal
Little Langford	*Wilts* - Salisbury
Little Laver	*Essex* - Harlow
Little Lawford	*Warwick* - Rugby
Little Leigh	*Cheshire* - Northwich
Little Leighs	*Essex* - Braintree
Little Lever	*Lancaster* - Bolton
Little Limber	*Lincoln* - Great Grimsby
Little Linford	*Bucks* - Bletchley and Leighton Buzzard
Little Linstead	*Suffolk* - Halesworth
Little Livermere	*Suffolk* - Bury St. Edmunds
Little Liverpool	*Derby* - Burton-upon-Trent
Little London	*Bucks* - Aylesbury
Little London	*Bucks* - Thame
Little London	*Cambridge* - Newmarket
Little London	*Essex* - Bishop's Stortford
Little London	*Gloucester* - Evesham
Little London	*Gloucester* - Gloucester
Little London	*Hants* - Andover
Little London	*Hants* - Basingstoke
Little London	*Hereford* - Hereford
Little London (Long Sutton)	*Lincoln* - Spalding
Little London (Spalding)	*Lincoln* - Spalding
Little London	*Salop* - Ludlow
Little London	*Sussex* - Eastbourne
Little Longstone	*Derby* - Buxton
Little Malvern	*Worcester* - Great Malvern
Little Manchester	*Stafford* - Market Drayton
Little Maplestead	*Essex* - Braintree
Little Marcle	*Hereford* - Hereford
Little Marlow	*Bucks* - High Wycombe
Little Marston	*Somerset* - Yeovil
Little Massingham	*Norfolk* - King's Lynn
Little Matlock	*York, W.R.* - Sheffield
Little Melton	*Norfolk* - Norwich
Little Mill	*Monmouth* - Pontypool and Abergavenny
Little Milton	*Oxford* - Thame
Little Missenden	*Bucks* - Amersham

Littlemoor	*Dorset* - Weymouth
Littlemoor	*York, W.R.* - Bradford
Little Moors	*Lincoln* - Boston
Littlemore	*Oxford* - Oxford
Littlemoss	*Lancaster* - Ashton-under-Lyne
Little Munden	*Herts* - Hertford
Little Musgrave	*Westmorland* - Penrith
Little Ness	*Salop* - Shrewsbury
Little Neston	*Cheshire* - Birkenhead
Little Newcastle	*Pembroke* - Haverfordwest
Little Newsham	*Durham* - Darlington
Little Norton	*Somerset* - Yeovil
Little Norton	*Stafford* - Walsall
Little Oakley	*Essex* - Harwich
Little Oakley	*Northampton* - Kettering
Little Oaks	*Lancaster* - Bolton
Little Onn	*Stafford* - Stafford
Little Ormesby	*Norfolk* - Great Yarmouth
Little Orton	*Cumberland* - Carlisle
Little Ouse	*Cambridge* - Ely
Little Ouseburn	*York, W.R.* - Harrogate
Littleover	*Derby* - Derby
Little Packington	*Warwick* - Coventry
Little Palgrave	*Norfolk* - King's Lynn
Little Paxton	*Hunts* - Huntingdon
Little Petherick	*Cornwall* - Bodmin
Little Plumstead	*Norfolk* - Norwich
Little Ponton	*Lincoln* - Grantham
Littleport	*Cambridge* - Ely
Little Postland	*Lincoln* - Spalding
Little Poulton	*Lancaster* - Blackpool
Little Preston	*Northampton* - Northampton
Little Preston	*York, W.R.* - Pontefract
Little Raveley	*Hunts* - Huntingdon
Little Raynham	*Norfolk* - King's Lynn
Little Ribston	*York, W.R.* - Harrogate
Little Rissington	*Gloucester* - Cheltenham
Little Rollright	*Oxford* - Banbury
Little Russia	*Warwick* - Birmingham
Little Ryburgh	*Norfolk* - Fakenham
Little Ryle	*Northumberland* - Alnwick
Little Salkeld	*Cumberland* - Penrith
Little Sampford	*Essex* - Bishop's Stortford
Little Saredon	*Stafford* - Wolverhampton
Little Saxham	*Suffolk* - Bury St. Edmunds
Little Shelford	*Cambridge* - Cambridge
Little Shurdington	*Gloucester* - Cheltenham
Little Singleton	*Lancaster* - Blackpool
Little Smeaton	*York, W.R.* - Pontefract
Little Snoring	*Norfolk* - King's Lynn
Little Sodbury	*Gloucester* - Bristol
Little Somborne	*Hants* - Winchester
Little Somerford	*Wilts* - Malmesbury
Little Stainton	*Durham* - Stockton-on-Tees
Little Stanney	*Cheshire* - Ellesmere Port
Little Staughton	*Beds* - Bedford
Little Steeping	*Lincoln* - Skegness
Little Stoke	*Gloucester* - Bristol
Little Stoke	*Gloucester* - Thornbury
Little Stoke	*Oxford* - Didcot
Little Stoke	*Stafford* - Stafford
Littlestone-on-Sea	*Kent* - Ashford
Little Stonham	*Suffolk* - Stowmarket
Little Stretton	*Leicester* - Leicester
Little Strickland	*Westmorland* - Penrith
Little Stukeley	*Hunts* - Huntingdon
Little Sugnall	*Stafford* - Stafford
Little Sutton	*Cheshire* - Ellesmere Port
Little Sutton	*Lincoln* - Spalding
Little Sutton	*Warwick* - Birmingham
Little Tew	*Oxford* - Banbury
Little Tey	*Essex* - Colchester
Little Thetford	*Cambridge* - Ely
Little Thorpe	*Durham* - Sunderland
Littlethorpe	*Leicester* - Leicester
Littlethorpe	*York, W.R.* - Harrogate
Little Thurrock	*Essex* - Grays Thurrock
Littleton	*Cheshire* - Chester
Littleton	*Dorset* - Blandford
Littleton	*Hants* - Andover

LIT - LIV

Littleton	*Hants* - Winchester
Littleton	*Middlesex* - Kingston-upon-Thames
Littleton	*Somerset* - Bristol
Littleton	*Surrey* - Guildford
Littleton	*Wilts* - Trowbridge
Littleton Drew	*Wilts* - Chippenham
Littleton, High	*Somerset* - Bristol
Littleton, Middle	*Worcester* - Evesham
Littleton, North	*Worcester* - Evesham
Littleton Panell	*Wilts* - Devizes
Littleton, South	*Worcester* - Evesham
Littleton-upon-Severn	*Gloucester* - Thornbury
Littleton, West	*Gloucester* - Bristol
Little Tosson	*Northumberland* - Morpeth
Little Totham	*Essex* - Maldon
Littletown	*Cumberland* - Workington
Littletown	*Durham* - Durham
Littletown	*York, W.R.* - Dewsbury
Little Tring	*Herts* - Aylesbury
Little Urswick	*Lancaster* - Barrow-in-Furness
Little Wadd	*Kent* - Maidstone
Little Wakering	*Essex* - Southend
Little Walden	*Essex* - Bishop's Stortford
Little Waldingfield	*Suffolk* - Sudbury
Little Walsingham	*Norfolk* - King's Lynn
Little Waltham	*Essex* - Chelmsford
Little Walton	*Warwick* - Rugby
Little Warford	*Cheshire* - Altrincham
Little Warley	*Essex* - Brentwood
Little Washbourne	*Gloucester* - Cheltenham
Little Weighton	*York, E.R.* - Beverley
Little Wells	*Norfolk* - King's Lynn
Little Welnetham	*Suffolk* - Bury St. Edmunds
Little Wenham	*Suffolk* - Ipswich
Little Wenlock	*Salop* - Wellington (Salop)
Little Whittington	*Northumberland* - Hexham
Littlewick (part)	*Berks* - Reading
Littlewick (part)	*Berks* - Slough
Little Wigborough	*Essex* - Colchester
Little Wilbraham	*Cambridge* - Cambridge
Little Witchingham	*Norfolk* - Norwich
Little Witcombe	*Gloucester* - Cheltenham
Little Witley	*Worcester* - Worcester
Little Wittenham	*Berks* - Didcot
Little Wolford	*Warwick* - Stratford on Avon
Little Woolstone	*Bucks* - Bletchley and Leighton Buzzard
Littleworth	*Bucks* - Aylesbury
Littleworth	*Bucks* - Bletchley and Leighton Buzzard
Littleworth	*Derby and Leicester* - Ashby-de-la-Zouch
Littleworth	*Gloucester* - Stroud
Littleworth	*Lincoln* - Spalding
Littleworth	*Northampton* - Northampton
Littleworth	*Oxford* - Oxford
Littleworth	*Stafford* - Stafford
Littleworth (High Offley)	*Stafford* - Stafford
Littleworth (Stafford)	
Littleworth (Cannock)	*Stafford* - Walsall
Littleworth	*Sussex* - Horsham
Littleworth	*Worcester* - Redditch
Littleworth	*Worcester* - Worcester
Littleworth Common	*Bucks* - High Wycombe
Littleworth Common	*Bucks* - Slough
Little Wratting	*Suffolk* - Sudbury
Little Wymondley	*Herts* - Hitchin
Little Wyrley	*Stafford* - Walsall
Little Wytheford	*Salop* - Shrewsbury
Little Yeldham	*Essex* - Sudbury
Littley Green	*Essex* - Chelmsford
Litton	*Derby* - Buxton
Litton	*Somerset* - Wells
Litton	*York, W.R.* - Skipton
Litton Cheney	*Dorset* - Dorchester
Litton Dale	*Derby* - Buxton
Littywood	*Stafford* - Stafford
Liverpool	*Lancaster* - Liverpool

LIV - LLA

Liversedge	*York, W.R.* - Dewsbury
Livers Ocle	*Hereford* - Hereford
Liverton	*Devon* - Newton Abbot
Liverton	*York, N.R.* - Whitby
Lixton	*Devon* - Kingsbridge
Lixwm	*Flint* - Holywell
Lizard	*Cornwall* - Penzance
Lizard	*Salop* - Wellington (Salop)
Llaithbwlch	*Montgomery* - Oswestry
Llaithdu	*Radnor* - Newtown
Llammarch	*Brecon* - Pontypool and Abergavenny
Llanaber	*Merioneth* - Dolgellau
Llanaberuwch	*Merioneth* - Dolgellau
Llanaelhaiarn	*Caernarvon* - Portmadoc
Llanafan	*Cardigan* - Aberystwyth
Llanafanfawr	*Brecon* - Builth
Llanallgo	*Anglesey* - Llangefni
Llananno	*Radnor* - Newtown
Llanarmon	*Caernarvon* - Portmadoc
Llanarmon Dyffryn Ceiriog	*Denbigh* - Oswestry
Llanarmonmynyddmawr	*Denbigh* - Oswestry
Llanarmonyn Ial	*Denbigh* - Mold
Llanarth	*Cardigan* - Aberystwyth
Llanarth	*Monmouth* - Pontypool and Abergavenny
Llanarthney	*Carmarthen* - Carmarthen
Llanasa Village	*Flint* - Holywell
Llanbabo	*Anglesey* - Llangefni
Llanbadarnfawr	*Cardigan* - Aberystwyth
Llanbadarnfawr	*Radnor* - Llandrindod Wells
Llanbadarnfynydd	*Radnor* - Newtown
Llanbadarnodwyn	*Cardigan* - Lampeter
Llanbadarn-y-Garreg	*Radnor* - Builth
Llanbadoc	*Monmouth* - Pontypool and Abergavenny
Llanbedr	*Brecon* - Pontypool and Abergavenny
Llanbedr	*Denbigh* - Dengigh
Llanbedr	*Merioneth* - Portmadoc
Llanbedrgoch	*Anglesey* - Llangefni
Llanbedrog	*Caernarvon* - Portmadoc
Llanbedr-y-Cennin	*Caernarvon* - Conway
Llanberis	*Caernarvon* - Caernarvon
Llanbethery	*Glamorgan* - Barry
Llanbister	*Radnor* - Llandrindod Wells
Llanblethian	*Glamorgan* - Bridgend
Llanboidy	*Carmarthen* - Haverfordwest
Llanbradach	*Glamorgan* - Caerphilly
Llanbrynmair	*Montgomery* - Machynlleth
Llancadle	*Glamorgan* - Barry
Llancarfan	*Glamorgan* - Barry
Llancayo	*Monmouth* - Pontypool and Abergavenny
Llancilloe	*Hereford* - Hereford
Llancloudy	*Hereford* - Monmouth
Llancynfelin	*Cardigan* - Aberystwyth
Llandaff	*Glamorgan* - Cardiff
Llandaff, North	*Glamorgan* - Cardiff
Llandanwg	*Merioneth* - Portmadoc
Llandarcy	*Glamorgan* - Neath
Llandavenny	*Monmouth* - Newport (Mon.)
Llandawke	*Carmarthen* - Carmarthen
Llanddaniel	*Anglesey* - Llangefni
Llanddarog	*Carmarthen* - Carmarthen
Llanddeiniolen	*Caernarvon* - Caernarvon
Llanddeinol	*Cardigan* - Aberystwyth
Llandderfel	*Merioneth* - Dolgellau
Llanddeusant	*Carmarthen* - Llandovery
Llanddeusant	*Anglesey* - Llangefni
Llanddewi	*Glamorgan* - Swansea
Llanddewi Brefi	*Cardigan* - Lampeter
Llanddewi Ystradenny	*Radnor* - Llandrindod Wells
Llanddoget	*Denbigh* - Conway
Llanddona	*Anglesey* - Llangefni
Llanddowror	*Carmarthen* - Carmarthen
Llanddulas	*Denbigh* - Rhyl
Llanddyfnan	*Anglesey* - Llangefni
Llandebie	*Carmarthen* - Ammanford

Llandecwyn	*Merioneth* - Portmadoc
Llandefailog-fach	*Brecon* - Brecknock
Llandefalle	*Brecon* - Brecknock
Llandefeilog	*Carmarthen* - Carmarthen
Llandegal	*Caernarvon* - Bangor
Llandegfan	*Anglesey* - Llangefni
Llandegla	*Denbigh* - Mold
Llandegley	*Radnor* - Llandrindod Wells
Llandegveth	*Monmouth* - Pontypool and Abergavenny
Llandegwning	*Caernarvon* - Portmadoc
Llandeilo	*Carmarthen* - Ammanford
Llandeilograban	*Radnor* - Builth
Llandeilo'r fane	*Brecon* - Brecknock
Llandeloy	*Pembroke* - Haverfordwest
Llandenny	*Monmouth* - Monmouth
Llandetty	*Brecon* - Brecknock
Llandevaud	*Monmouth* - Newport (Mon.)
Llandew	*Brecon* - Brecknock
Llandewivelfrey	*Pembroke* - Haverfordwest
Llandewy	*Radnor* - Llandrindod Wells
Llandewy Ystradenny	*Radnor* - Llandrindod Wells
Llandilo	*Pembroke* - Haverfordwest
Llandilo Abercowin	*Carmarthen* - Carmarthen
Llandimore	*Glamorgan* - Swansea
Llandinabo	*Hereford* - Hereford
Llandinam	*Montgomery* - Newtown
Llandisilio	*Montgomery* - Oswestry
Llandisiliogogo	*Cardigan* - Cardigan
Llandissilio East	*Carmarthen* - Haverfordwest
Llandissilio West	*Pembroke* - Haverfordwest
Llandogo	*Monmouth* - Monmouth
Llandough (Cowbridge)	*Glamorgan* - Bridgend
Llandough by Penarth	*Glamorgan* - Cardiff
Llandovery	*Carmarthen* - Llandovery
Llandow	*Glamorgan* - Bridgend
Llandre	*Cardigan* - Aberystwyth
Llandrillo	*Merioneth* - Wrexham
Llandrillo-yn-Rhos	*Denbigh* - Conway
Llandrindod Wells	*Radnor* - Llandrindod Wells
Llandrinio	*Montgomery* - Oswestry
Llandrygarn	*Anglesey* - Llangefni
Llandudno	*Caernarvon* - Conway
Llandudno Junction	*Caernarvon* - Conway
Llandudwen	*Caernarvon* - Portmadoc
Llandwrog	*Caernarvon* - Caernarvon
Llandwrog, Upper	*Caernarvon* - Caernarvon
Llandyfriog	*Cardigan* - Cardigan
Llandyfrydog	*Anglesey* - Llangefni
Llandygwydd	*Cardigan* - Cardigan
Llandyrnog	*Denbigh* - Denbigh
Llandysilio	*Anglesey* - Bangor
Llandysilio	*Montgomery* - Oswestry
Llandyssil	*Montomery* - Newtown
Llandyssul	*Cardigan* - Lampeter
Llanedeyrne	*Glamorgan* - Cardiff
Llanedwen	*Anglesey* - Llangefni
Llanedi (part)	*Carmarthen* - Ammanford
Llanedi (part)	*Carmarthen* - Llanelli
Llanefydd	*Denbigh* - Denbigh
Llanegryn	*Merioneth* - Dolgellau
Llanegwad	*Carmarthen* - Carmarthen
Llanelian	*Anglesey* - Llangefni
Llanelian	*Denbigh* - Conway
Llanelidan	*Denbigh* - Denbigh
Llanelieu	*Brecon* - Brecknock
Llanellen	*Monmouth* - Pontypool and Abergavenny
Llanelltyd	*Merioneth* - Dolgellau
Llanelli	*Brecon* - Pontypool and Abergavenny
Llanelli	*Carmarthen* - Llanelli
Llanelli Hill	*Brecon* - Pontypool and Abergavenny
Llanelwedd	*Radnor* - Builth
Llanenddwyn	*Merioneth* - Dolgellau
Llanengan	*Caernarvon* - Portmadoc
Llanerchemrys	*Montgomery* - Oswestry
Llanerchkeel	*Montgomery* - Oswestry
Llanerchymedd	*Anglesey* - Llangefni
Llanerchymor	*Flint* - Holywell
Llanerfyl	*Montgomery* - Welshpool
Llanfabon	*Glamorgan* - Caerphilly
Llanfach	*Monmouth* - Blackwood
Llanfachreth	*Anglesey* - Llangefni
Llanfachreth	*Merioneth* - Dolgellau
Llanfaelog	*Anglesey* - Llangefni
Llanfaes	*Anglesey* - Llangefni
Llanfaes	*Brecon* - Brecknock
Llanfaethlu	*Anglesey* - Llangefni
Llanfaelrhys	*Caernarvon* - Portmadoc
Llanfaglan	*Caernarvon* - Caernarvon
Llanfair	*Glamorgan* - Bridgend
Llanfair	*Merioneth* - Portmadoc
Llanfairarybryn	*Carmarthen* - Llandovery
Llanfair Caereinion	*Montgomery* - Welshpool
Llanfairclydogau	*Cardigan* - Lampeter
Llanfair Dyffryn Clwyd	*Denbigh* - Denbigh
Llanfairfechan	*Caernarvon* - Bangor
Llanfairisgaer	*Caernarvon* - Caernarvon
Llanfairmathafarneithaf	*Anglesey* - Llangefni
Llanfairnantgwyn	*Pembroke* - Cardigan
Llanfairnantygof	*Pembroke* - Haverfordwest
Llanfair Orllwyn	*Cardigan* - Cardigan
Llanfairpwllgwyngyll	*Anglesey* - Llangefni
Llanfairtalhaiarn	*Denbigh* - Denbigh
Llanfairwaterdine	*Salop* - Knighton
Llanfairynghornwy	*Anglesey* - Llangefni
Llanfairynneubwll	*Anglesey* - Llangefni
Llanfallteg East	*Carmarthen* - Haverfordwest
Llanfallteg West	*Pembroke* - Haverfordwest
Llanfaredd	*Radnor* - Builth
Llanfarian	*Cardigan* - Aberystwyth
Llanfawr	*Merioneth* - Dolgellau
Llanfechain	*Montgomery* - Oswestry
Llanfechell	*Anglesey* - Llangefni
Llanferres	*Denbigh* - Mold
Llanffinan	*Anglesey* - Llangefni
Llanfigan	*Brecon* - Brecknock
Llanfihangel	*Brecon* - Brecknock
Llanfihangel	*Montgomery* - Oswestry
Llanfihangel Aberbythich	*Carmarthen* - Ammanford
Llanfihangel Abercowin	*Carmarthen* - Carmarthen
Llanfihangel ar Arth	*Carmarthen* - Carmarthen
Llanfihangel bachellaeth	*Caernarvon* - Portmadoc
Llanfihangel brynpabuan	*Brecon* - Builth
Llanfihangel Cilfargen	*Carmarthen* - Carmarthen
Llanfihangelcwmdu	*Brecon* - Pontypool and Abergavenny
Llanfihangel Glynmyfyr	*Denbigh* - Denbigh
Llanfihangel Helygen	*Radnor* - Llandrindod Wells
Llanfihangel Nantbran, Lower	*Brecon* - Brecknock
Llanfihangel Nant Melan	*Radnor* - Builth Wells
Llanfihangel Penbedw	*Pembroke* - Cardigan
Llanfihangel Rhosycorn	*Carmarthen* - Lampeter
Llanfihangel Rhydithon	*Radnor* - Knighton
Llanfihangel Talyllyn	*Brecon* - Brecknock
Llanfihangel y Croyddin	*Cardigan* - Aberystwyth
Llanfihangelypennant	*Caernarvon* - Portmadoc
Llanfihangel y Pennant	*Merioneth* - Dolgellau
Llanfihangel Ystrad	*Cardigan* - Lampeter
Llanfihangelytraethau	*Merioneth* - Portmadoc
Llanfillo	*Brecon* - Brecknock
Llanfoist	*Monmouth* - Pontypool and Abergavenny
Llanfor	*Merioneth* - Dolgellau
Llanforda	*Salop* - Oswestry
Llanfrechfa	*Monmouth* - Newport (Mon.)
Llanfrothen	*Merioneth* - Portmadoc

Llanfrynach	*Brecon* - Brecknock
Llanfwrog	*Anglesey* - Llangefni
Llanfwrog	*Denbigh* - Denbigh
Llanfyllin	*Montgomery* - Oswestry
Llanfynydd	*Carmarthen* - Carmarthen
Llanfynydd	*Flint* - Wrexham
Llanfyrnach	*Pembroke* - Cardigan
Llangadfan	*Montgomery* - Welshpool
Llangadock	*Carmarthen* - Llandovery
Llangadwaladr	*Anglesey* - Llangefni
Llangadwaladr	*Denbigh* - Oswestry
Llangaffo	*Anglesey* - Llangefni
Llangain	*Carmarthen* - Carmarthen
Llangammarch Wells	*Brecon* - Builth
Llangan	*Glamorgan* - Bridgend
Llangan East	*Carmarthen* - Haverfordwest
Llangan West	*Pembroke* - Haverfordwest
Llangar	*Merioneth* - Wrexham
Llangarren	*Hereford* - Monmouth
Llangasty Talyllyn	*Brecon* - Brecknock
Llangathen	*Carmarthen* - Carmarthen
Llangattock	*Brecon* - Pontypool and Abergavenny
Llangattock	*Monmouth* - Newport (Mon.)
Llangattock Hillside	*Brecon* - Pontypool and Abergavenny
Llangattock Lingoed	*Monmouth* - Pontypool and Abergavenny
Llangattock nigh Usk	*Monmouth* - Pontypool and Abergavenny
Llangattock Vibon Avell	*Monmouth* - Monmouth
Llangedwyn	*Denbigh* - Oswestry
Llangefni	*Anglesey* - Llangefni
Llangeinor	*Glamorgan* - Bridgend
Llangeitho	*Cardigan* - Lampeter
Llangeler	*Carmarthen* - Carmarthen
Llangelynin	*Caernarvon* - Conway
Llangelynin	*Merioneth* - Dolgellau
Llangendeirne	*Carmarthen* - Carmarthen
Llangennech	*Carmarthen* - Llanelli
Llangennith	*Glamorgan* - Swansea
Llangenny	*Brecon* - Pontypool and Abergavenny
Llangernyw	*Denbigh* - Conway
Llangeview	*Monmouth* - Pontypool and Abergavenny
Llangewydd	*Glamorgan* - Bridgend
Llangian	*Caernarvon* - Portmadoc
Llangibby	*Monmouth* - Pontypool and Abergavenny
Llanginning	*Carmarthen* - Carmarthen
Llanglydwen	*Carmarthen* - Haverfordwest
Llangoed	*Anglesey* - Llangefni
Llangoedmor	*Cardigan* - Cardigan
Llangollen	*Denbigh* - Wrexham
Llangolman	*Pembroke* - Haverfordwest
Llangorse	*Brecon* - Brecknock
Llangorwen	*Cardigan* - Aberystwyth
Llangoven	*Monmouth* - Monmouth
Llangower	*Merioneth* - Dolgellau
Llangrangog	*Cardigan* - Cardigan
Llangristiolus	*Anglesey* - Llangefni
Llangrove	*Hereford* - Monmouth
Llangrwyney	*Brecon* - Pontypool and Abergavenny
Llangua	*Monmouth* - Pontypool and Abergavenny
Llangunllo	*Radnor* - Knighton
Llangunnock	*Carmarthen* - Carmarthen
Llangunnock	*Hereford* - Hereford
Llangunnor	*Carmarthen* - Carmarthen
Llangurig	*Montgomery* - Newtown
Llangwm	*Denbigh* - Denbigh
Llangwm-Icha	*Monmouth* - Chepstow
Llangwm-Ucha	*Monmouth* - Chepstow
Llangwnadl	*Caernarvon* - Portmadoc
Llangwstennin	*Caernarvon* - Conway
Llagnwyfan	*Anglesey* - Llangefni
Llangwyfan	*Denbigh* - Denbigh
Llangwyllog	*Anglesey* - Llangefni

LLA

Llangwyryfon	*Cardigan* - Aberystwyth
Llangybi	*Caernarvon* - Portmadoc
Llangybi	*Cardigan* - Lampeter
Llangyfelach	*Glamorgan* - Swansea
Llangynhafal	*Denbigh* - Denbigh
Llangynidr	*Brecon* - Pontypool and Abergavenny
Llangyniew	*Montgomery* - Welshpool
Llangynllo	*Cardigan* - Cardigan
Llangynog	*Brecon* - Builth
Llangynog	*Montgomery* - Oswestry
Llangynwyd, Higher	*Glamorgan* - Bridgend
Llangynwyd, Lower	*Glamorgan* - Bridgend
Llangynwyd, Middle	*Glamorgan* - Bridgend
Llanhamlach	*Brecon* - Brecknock
Llanharan	*Glamorgan* - Bridgend
Llanharry	*Glamorgan* - Bridgend
Llanhennock	*Monmouth* - Newport (Mon.)
Llanhilleth	*Monmouth* - Blackwood
Llanhowell	*Pembroke* - Haverfordwest
Llanidan	*Anglesey* - Llangefni
Llanidloes	*Montgomery* - Newtown
Llaniestyn	*Anglesey* - Llangefni
Llaniestyn	*Caernarvon* - Portmadoc
Llanifyny	*Montgomery* - Newtown
Llanigon	*Brecon* - Brecknock
Llanilar	*Cardigan* - Aberystwyth
Llanilid	*Glamorgan* - Bridgend
Llanilterne	*Glamorgan* - Cardiff
Llanina	*Cardigan* - Aberystwyth
Llanio	*Cardigan* - Lampeter
Llanishen	*Glamorgan* - Cardiff
Llanishen	*Monmouth* - Monmouth
Llaniwared	*Montgomery* - Newtown
Llanliggo	*Radnor* Knighton
Llanllawddog	*Carmarthen* - Carmarthen
Llanllawer	*Pembroke* - Haverfordwest
Llanllowell	*Monmouth* - Pontypool and Abergavenny
Llanllugan	*Montgomery* - Newtown
Llanllwchaiarn	*Montgomery* - Newtown
Llanllwni	*Carmarthen* - Lampeter
Llanllyfni	*Caernarvon* - Caernarvon
Llanmadoc	*Glamorgan* - Swansea
Llanmaes	*Glamorgan* - Bridgend
Llanmartin	*Monmouth* - Newport (Mon.)
Llanmerewig	*Montgomery* - Newtown
Llanmihangel	*Glamorgan* - Bridgend
Llanmorlais	*Glamorgan* - Swansea
Llannor	*Caernarvon* - Portmadoc
Llanon	*Cardigan* - Aberystwyth
Llanon	*Carmarthen* - Llanelli
Llanover	*Monmouth* - Pontypool and Abergavenny
Llanpumpsaint	*Carmarthen* - Carmarthen
Llanreath	*Pembroke* - Haverfordwest
Llanrhaiadr-ym-mochnant	*Denbigh and Montgomery* - Oswestry
Llanrhaiadr-ym-mochnant, North	*Denbigh* - Oswestry
Llanrhaiadr-ym-mochnant, South	*Montgomery* - Oswestry
Llanrhaiadr-yn-Cimmerch	*Denbigh* - Denbigh
Llanrhian	*Pembroke* - Haverfordwest
Llanrhidian	*Glamorgan* - Swansea
Llanrhos	*Caernarvon* - Conway
Llanrhychwyn	*Caernarvon* - Conway
Llanrhydd	*Denbigh* - Denbigh
Llanrhyddlad	*Anglesey* - Llangefni
Llanrhystyd	*Cardigan* - Aberystwyth
Llanrithan	*Pembroke* - Haverfordwest
Llanrothal	*Hereford* - Monmouth
Llanrug	*Caernarvon* - Caernarvon
Llanrwst	*Denbigh* - Conway
Llansadurnen	*Carmarthen* - Carmarthen
Llansadwrn	*Anglesey* - Llangefni
Llansadwrn	*Carmarthen* - Llandovery
Llansaint	*Carmarthen* - Carmarthen
Llansaintffraed Cwmdauddwr	*Radnor* - Llandrindod Wells

LLA

Llansaintffraid Deythur	*Montgomery* - Oswestry
Llansaintffraid Glyndyfrdwy	*Merioneth* - Wrexham
Llansaintffraid in Elvel	*Radnor* - Builth
Llansamlet, Higher	*Glamorgan* - Swansea
Llansamlet, Lower	*Glamorgan* - Swansea
Llansannan	*Denbigh* - Denbigh
Llansannor	*Glamorgan* - Bridgend
Llansantffraed	*Monmouth* - Pontypool and Abergavenny
Llansantffraid-Glynceiriog	*Denbigh* - Wrexham
Llansawel	*Carmarthen* - Ammanford
Llansilin	*Denbigh* - Oswestry
Llansoy	*Monmouth* - Chepstow
Llanspyddid	*Brecon* - Brecknock
Llanstadwell	*Pembroke* - Haverfordwest
Llanstephan	*Carmarthen* - Carmarthen
Llanstephan	*Radnor* - Builth
Llanstinan	*Pembroke* - Haverfordwest
Llantarnam	*Monmouth* - Newport (Mon.)
Llanthewy Rytherch	*Monmouth* - Pontypool and Abergavenny
Llanthewy skirrid	*Monmouth* - Pontypool and Abergavenny
Llanthewy vach	*Monmouth* - Pontypool and Abergavenny
Llanthony	*Monmouth* - Pontypool and Abergavenny
Llantilio crossenny	*Monmouth* - Monmouth
Llantillio Forest	*Monmouth* - Pontypool and Abergavenny
Llantillio Pantygelly	*Monmouth* - Pontypool and Abergavenny
Llantillio Pertholey	*Monmouth* - Pontypool and Abergavenny
Llantillio Pertholey-Bettws	*Monmouth* - Pontypool and Abergavenny
Llantood	*Pembroke* - Cardigan
Llantrisant	*Anglesey* - Llangefni
Llantrisant	*Glamorgan* - Pontypridd
Llantrissent	*Monmouth* - Pontypool and Abergavenny
Llantrithyd	*Glamorgan* - Barry
Llantwit	*Glamorgan* - Neath
Llantwit Fardre	*Glamorgan* - Pontypridd
Llantwit, Lower	*Glamorgan* - Neath
Llantwit Major	*Glamorgan* - Bridgend
Llantysilio	*Denbigh* - Wrexham
Llanuwchllyn	*Merioneth* - Dolgellau
Llanvaches	*Monmouth* - Newport (Mon.)
Llanvair Discoed	*Monmouth* - Chepstow
Llanvair Kilgeddin	*Monmouth* - Pontypool and Abergavenny
Llanvapley	*Monmouth* - Pontypool and Abergavenny
Llanvetherine	*Monmouth* - Pontypool and Abergavenny
Llanveyno	*Hereford* - Pontypool and Abergavenny
Llanvihangel Crucorney	*Monmouth* - Pontypool and Abergavenny
Llanvihangel Gobion	*Monmouth* - Pontypool and Abergavenny
Llanvihangel Penbiddle	*Monmouth* - Pontypool and Abergavenny
Llanvihangel Pontymoile	*Monmouth* - Pontypool and Abergavenny
Llanivhangel - Torymynydd	*Monmouth* - Chepstow
Llanvihangel ysternllewern	*Monmouth* - Monmouth
Llanvrechfa, Lower	*Monmouth* - Newport (Mon.)
Llanvrechfa, Upper	*Monmouth* - Newport (Mon.)
Llanwarne	*Hereford* - Hereford
Llanwddyn	*Montgomery* - Oswestry
Llanwenarth	*Monmouth* - Pontypool and Abergavenny
Llanwenarth Citra	*Monmouth* - Pontypool and Abergavenny

LLA - LLY

Llanwenarth Garndyriss	*Monmouth* - Pontypool and Abergavenny
Llanwenarth Govilon	*Monmouth* - Pontypool and Abergavenny
Llanwenarth Pwlldu	*Monmouth* - Pontypool and Abergavenny
Llanwenarth Ultra	*Monmouth* - Pontypool and Avergavenny
Llanwenog	*Cardigan* - Lampeter
Llanwern	*Monmouth* - Newport (Mon.)
Llanwinio	*Carmarthen* - Carmarthen
Llanwnda	*Caernarvon* - Caernarvon
Llanwnda	*Pembroke* - Haverfordwest
Llanwnen	*Cardigan* - Lampeter
Llanwnog	*Montgomery* - Newtown
Llanwonno	*Glamorgan* - Aberdare
Llanwrda	*Carmarthen* - Llandovery
Llanwrin	*Montgomery* - Maychnlleth
Llanwrthwl	*Brecon* - Llandrindod Wells
Llanwrtyd Wells	*Brecon* - Builth
Llanwyddelan	*Montgomery* - Newtown
Llanyblodwel	*Salop* - Oswestry
Llanybri	*Carmarthen* - Carmarthen
Llanybyther	*Carmarthen* - Lampeter
Llanycefn	*Pembroke* - Haverfordwest
Llanychaer	*Pembroke* - Haverfordwest
Llanychan	*Denbigh* - Denbigh
Llanychlwydog	*Pembroke* - Cardigan
Llanycil	*Merioneth* - Dolgellau
Llanycrwys	*Carmarthen* - Lampeter
Llanymawddwy	*Merioneth* - Dolgellau
Llanymynech	*Salop* - Oswestry
Llanynghenedl	*Anglesey* - Llangefni
Llanynys	*Brecon* - Builth
Llanynys	*Denbigh* - Denbigh
Llanypwll	*Denbigh* - Wrexham
Llanyre	*Radnor* - Llandrindod Wells
Llanystumdwy	*Caernarvon* - Portmadoc
Llanywern	*Brecon* - Brecknock
Llawhaden	*Pembroke* - Haverfordwest
Llawrybettws	*Merioneth* - Dolgellau
Llawryglyn	*Montgomery* - Newtown
Llay	*Denbigh* - Wrexham
Llechfaen	*Brecon* - Brecknock
Llechryd	*Cardigan* - Cardigan
Llechryd	*Glamorgan* - Blackwood
Llechryd	*Monmouth* - Blackwood
Llechwedd	*Caernarvon* - Conway
Lledrod	*Cardigan* - Aberystwyth
Lledrod	*Denbigh* - Oswestry
Lledrod	*Montgomery* - Oswestry
Lletty Brongu	*Glamorgan* - Bridgend
Llidiardau	*Merioneth* - Dolgellau
Lliswerry	*Monmouth* - Newport (Mon.)
Llithfaen	*Caernarvon* - Portmadoc
Lloc	*Flint* - Holywell
Lloiney	*Radnor* - Knighton
Llong	*Flint* - Mold
Lloran Isa	*Denbigh* - Oswestry
Lloran Ucha	*Denbigh* - Oswestry
Llowes	*Radnor* - Brecknock
Lloyds	*Salop* - Wellington (Salop)
Lloyd, The	*Stafford* - Market Drayton
Llwydcoed	*Glamorgan* - Aberdare
Llwydcoed (Nantyglo)	*Monmouth* - Blackwood
Llwydiarth (part)	*Montgomery* - Oswestry
Llwydiarth (part)	*Montgomery* - Welshpool
Llwyncelyn	*Cardigan* - Aberystwyth
Llwyndafydd	*Cardigan* - Cardigan
Llwyndrain	*Pembroke* - Cardigan
Llwyndu	*Monmouth* - Pontypool and Abergavenny
Llwyngwen	*Glamorgan* - Merthyr Tydfil
Llwyngwril	*Merioneth* - Dolgellau
Llwynhendy	*Carmarthen* - Llanelli
Llwynmawr	*Denbigh* - Wrexham
Llwynypia	*Glamorgan* - Pontypridd
Llynclys	*Salop* - Oswestry
Llynfaes	*Anglesey* - Llangefni
Llynfi Valley	*Glamorgan* - Bridgend

Llyn Helyg	*Flint* - Holywell
Llys	*Montgomery* - Oswestry
Llysdinam	*Brecon* - Builth
Llysfaen	*Denbigh* - Conway
Llyswen	*Brecon* - Brecknock
Llysyfran	*Pembroke* - Haverfordwest
Loadsdean	*Northumberland* - Morpeth
Lobb	*Oxford* - Thame
Lobhill	*Devon* - Plymouth
Lobley Hill	*Durham* - Gateshead
Lobscombe Corner	*Hants* - Salisbury
Lobthorpe	*Lincoln* - Grantham
Locco Brook	*Derby* - Chesterfield
Lockeridge	*Wilts* - Swindon
Lockerley	*Hants* - Salisbury
Locking	*Somerset* - Weston Super Mare
Lockinge, East	*Berks* - Didcot
Lockinge, West	*Berks* - Didcot
Lockington	*Leicester* - Loughborough
Lockington	*York, E.R.* - Beverley
Lockley Wood	*Salop* - Market Drayton
Locko	*Derby* - Derby
Locksbottom	*Kent* - Bromley
Lock's Heath	*Hants* - Portsmouth
Lockton	*York, N.R.* - Malton
Lockwood	*York, W.R.* - Huddersfield
Lockwood Beck	*York, N.R.* - Middlesbrough
Loddington	*Kent* - Maidstone
Loddington	*Leicester* - Leicester
Loddington	*Northampton* - Kettering
Loddiswell	*Devon* - Kingsbridge
Loddon	*Norfolk* - Norwich
Lode	*Cambridge* - Cambridge
Lode, Lower	*Gloucester* - Cheltenham
Lodelow Lane	*Gloucester* - Cheltenham
Loders	*Dorset* - Dorchester
Lodge	*Denbigh* - Wrexham
Lodge	*Salop* - Oswestry
Lodge Furnaces	*Salop* - Wellington (Salop)
Lodge Green	*Warwick* - Coventry
Lodge Moor	*York, W.R.* - Sheffield
Lodge on the Wolds	*Notts* - Nottingham
Lodge Park	*Worcester* - Redditch
Lodge Wood	*Salop* - Wellington (Salop)
Lodsworth	*Sussex* - Chichester
Lofthouse	*York, W.R.* - Harrogate
Lofthouse Gate	*York, W.R.* - Wakefield
Lofthouse with Carlton	*York, W.R.* - Leeds
Loftus	*York, N.R.* - Whitby
Logan Beck	*Cumberland* - Whitehaven
Logaston	*Hereford* - Hereford
Loggans	*Cornwall* - Redruth
Loggerheads	*Stafford* - Market Drayton
Loggerheads	*Denbigh* - Mold
Login	*Carmarthen* - Haverfordwest
Lois Weedon	*Northampton* - Northampton
Lolworth	*Cambridge* - Cambridge
Londesborough	*York, E.R.* - Beverley
London Apprentice	*Cornwall* - St. Austell
London Beach	*Kent* - Cranbrook
London Bridge	*London, E.C.4* - Mayor's and City of London
London Bridge	*London, S.E.1* - Southwark
London Colney (part)	*Herts* - Barnet
London Colney (part)	*Herts* - St. Albans
Londonderry	*Stafford* - West Bromwich
Londonderry	*York, N.R.* - Northallerton
London Fields	*London, E.8* - Shoreditch
London, Little	*Cambridge* - Newmarket
London, Little	*Gloucester* - Evesham
London, Little	*Hants* - Andover
London, Little	*Hants* - Basingstoke
London, Little	*Hereford* - Hereford
London, Little (Long Sutton)	*Lincoln* - Spalding
London, Little (Spalding)	*Lincoln* - Spalding
London, Little	*Salop* - Ludlow
London, Little	*Sussex* - Eastbourne
London, New	*York, N.R.* - Whitby
Londonthorpe	*Lincoln* - Grantham

Long Ashton	*Somerset* - Bristol
Long Bennington	*Lincoln* - Newark
Long Benton	*Northumberland* - Newcastle upon Tyne
Longborough	*Gloucester* - Cheltenham
Long Bredy	*Dorset* - Dorchester
Longbridge	*Devon* - Axminster and Chard
Longbridge	*Devon* - Plymouth
Longbridge	*Warwick* - Birmingham
Longbridge	*Warwick* - Warwick
Longbridge Deverill	*Wilts* - Warminster
Longbridge Hayes	*Stafford* - Stoke-on-Trent
Long Buckby	*Northampton* - Northampton
Longburgh	*Cumberland* - Carlisle
Long Burton	*Dorset* - Yeovil
Longbyre	*Northumberland* - Hexham
Long Chimney	*Devon* - Axminster and Chard
Long Clawson	*Leicester* - Melton Mowbray
Longcliffe	*Derby* - Matlock
Long Compton	*Stafford* - Stafford
Long Compton	*Warwick* - Stratford on Avon
Longcot	*Berks* - Swindon
Long Crendon	*Bucks* - Thame
Long Crichel	*Dorset* - Wimborne Minster
Longcroft	*Cumberland* - Carlisle
Longcross	*Surrey* - Slough
Longdales	*Cumberland* - Penrith
Longden	*Salop* - Shrewsbury
Longden Common	*Salop* - Shrewsbury
Long Ditton	*Surrey* - Kingston-upon-Thames
Longdon	*Stafford* - Lichfield
Longdon	*Warwick* - Stratford-on-Avon
Longdon	*Worcester* - Cheltenham
Longdon Heath	*Worcester* - Great Malvern
Longdon Marsh	*Worcester* - Cheltenham
Longdon-upon-Tern	*Salop* - Wellington (Salop)
Longdown	*Devon* - Exeter
Longdown	*Hants* - Southampton
Long Drax	*York, W.R.* - Goole
Long Eaton	*Derby* - Nottingham
Longfield	*Kent* - Dartford
Longfield	*Worcester* - Redditch
Longfield, New Barn (part)	*Kent* - Dartford
Longfleet	*Dorset* - Poole
Longford	*Derby* - Derby
Longford	*Gloucester* - Gloucester
Longford	*Kent* - Sevenoaks
Longford	*Lancaster* - Warrington
Longford	*Middlesex* - Uxbridge
Longford	*Salop* - Market Drayton
Longford	*Salop* - Wellington (Salop)
Longford	*Warwick* - Coventry
Longford Marsh	*Derby* - Derby
Longford Turning	*Salop* - Market Drayton
Longframlington	*Northumberland* - Morpeth
Long Green	*Worcester* - Cheltenham
Longham	*Dorset* - Wimborne Minster
Longham	*Norfolk* - East Dereham
Long Handborough	*Oxford* - Witney
Longhedge	*Wilts* - Warminster
Longhills	*Lincoln* - Lincoln
Longhirst	*Northumberland* - Morpeth
Longhope	*Gloucester* - Gloucester
Longhoughton	*Northumberland* - Alnwick
Long Itchington	*Warwick* - Warwick
Longlands	*Cornwall* - Plymouth
Longlands	*Norfolk* - King's Lynn
Longlands Heads	*Cumberland* - Carlisle
Longlands Moor	*Cumberland* - Carlisle
Long Lane	*Cheshire* - Stockport
Long Lane	*Derby* - Derby
Long Lane	*Salop* - Wellington (Salop)
Long Lawford	*Warwick* - Rugby
Longlevens	*Gloucester* - Gloucester
Longley (Hade Edge)	*York, W.R.* - Huddersfield
Longley	*York, W.R.* - Sheffield
Long Load	*Somerset* - Yeovil
Long Marston	*Warwick* - Stratford on Avon
Long Marston	*Herts* - Aylesbury

Long Marston	*York, W.R.* - York
Long Marton	*Westmorland* - Penrith
Long Meadow End	*Salop* - Ludlow
Long Melford	*Suffolk* - Sudbury
Longmoor	*Hants* - Aldershot and Farnham
Long Newnton	*Wilts* - Malmesbury
Long Newton	*Cumberland* - Carlisle
Longney	*Gloucester* - Gloucester
Longnor	*Salop* - Shrewsbury
Longnor	*Stafford* - Leek
Longnor	*Stafford* - Wolverhampton
Longparish	*Hants* - Andover
Longport	*Stafford* - Stoke-on-Trent
Long Preston	*York, W.R.* - Skipton
Longridge	*Lancaster* - Preston
Longridge	*Stafford* - Stafford
Long Riston	*York, E.R.* - Beverley
Long Rock	*Cornwall* - Penzance
Longrorsley	*Northumberland* - Morpeth
Longroyd Bridge	*York, W.R.* - Huddersfield
Long Sandall	*York, W.R.* - Doncaster
Longsdon	*Stafford* - Leek
Longshaw	*Lancaster* - Wigan
Longshaw	*York, W.R.* - Sheffield
Longshaws	*Northumberland* - Morpeth
Longsight	*Lancaster* - Bolton
Longsight	*Lancaster* - Manchester
Longsleddale	*Westmorland* - Kendal
Longslow	*Salop* - Market Drayton
Long Stanton	*Salop* - Bridgnorth
Long Stanton	*Cambridge* - Cambridge
Longstock	*Hants* - Andover
Longstone	*Cornwall* - Bodmin
Longstone	*Cornwall* - St. Austell
Longstone, Great	*Derby* - Buxton
Longstone, Little	*Derby* - Buxton
Long Stowe	*Cambridge* - Cambridge
Long Stratton	*Norfolk* - Norwich
Long Sutton	*Hants* - Aldershot and Farnham
Long Sutton	*Lincoln* - Spalding
Long Sutton	*Somerset* - Yeovil
Long Sutton Fen	*Lincoln* - Spalding
Long Sutton Marsh	*Lincoln* - Spalding
Longthorns	*Dorset* - Blandford
Longthorpe	*Northampton* - Peterborough
Longthwaite	*Cumberland* - Carlisle
Longton	*Lancaster* - Preston
Longton	*Stafford* - Stoke-on-Trent
Longton, New	*Lancaster* - Preston
Longtown	*Cumberland* - Carlisle
Longtown	*Hereford* - Pontypool and Abergavenny
Longview	*Lancaster* - St. Helens
Longville	*Salop* - Ludlow
Longwaste	*Salop* - Wellington (Salop)
Longway Bank	*Derby* - Matlock
Longwell Green	*Gloucester* - Bristol
Long Whatton	*Leicester* - Loughborough
Longwick	*Bucks* - High Wycombe
Long Wittenham	*Berks* - Didcot
Long Witton	*Northumberland* - Morpeth
Longwood	*Salop* - Shrewsbury
Longwood	*York, W.R.* - Huddersfield
Longwood Dene	*Hants* - Winchester
Longwood Warren	*Hants* - Winchester
Longworth	*Berks* - Oxford
Longworth	*Lancaster* - Bolton
Lonlas	*Glamorgan* - Swansea
Lonnen, Little	*Dorset* - Wimborne Minster
Lonsdale	*York, N.R.* - Middlesbrough
Looe, East	*Cornwall* - Liskeard
Looe, West	*Cornwall* - Liskeard
Loose	*Kent* - Maidstone
Looseley Row	*Bucks* - High Wycombe
Lopen	*Somerset* - Yeovil
Lopham, North	*Norfolk* - Norwich
Lopham, South	*Norfolk* - Norwich
Loppergarth	*Lancaster* - Barrow-in-Furness
Lopperwood	*Hants* - Southampton
Loppington	*Salop* - Shrewsbury

Lopwell	*Devon* - Plymouth
Lorbottle	*Northumberland* - Alnwick
Lordington	*Sussex* - Chichester
Lords Bridge	*Cambridge* - Cambridge
Lordsley	*Stafford* - Market Drayton
Lordswood	*Hants* - Southampton
Lorton	*Cumberland* - Workington
Loscoe	*Derby* - Ilkeston
Loscoe	*York, W.R.* - Pontefract
Lostford	*Salop* - Market Drayton
Lostock	*Lancaster* - Bolton
Lostock Gralam	*Cheshire* - Northwich
Lostock Hall	*Lancaster* - Preston
Lostwithiel	*Cornwall* - Bodmin
Lothersdale	*York, W.R.* - Skipton
Lotherton	*York, W.R.* - Leeds
Lots Bridge	*Cambridge* - Wisbech
Lottisham	*Somerset* - Wells
Loudwater	*Bucks* - High Wycombe
Loughborough	*Leicester* - Loughborough
Loughor, Upper	*Glamorgan* - Swansea
Loughrigg	*Westmorland* - Kendal
Loughton	*Bucks* - Bletchley and Leighton Buzzard
Loughton	*Essex* - Edmonton
Loughton	*Salop* - Ludlow
Lound	*Lincoln* - Spalding
Lound	*Notts* - East Retford
Lound	*Suffolk* - Lowestoft
Lound, East	*Lincoln* - Gainsborough
Loundside	*York, W.R.* - Sheffield
Loundsley	*Derby* - Chesterfield
Lount	*Derby* - Ashby-de-la-Zouch
Louth	*Lincoln* - Louth
Loveclough	*Lancaster* - Rawtenstall
Lovedean	*Hants* - Petersfield
Loversall	*York, W.R.* - Doncaster
Loveston	*Pembroke* - Haverfordwest
Lovington	*Somerset* - Yeovil
Low Angerton	*Northumberland* - Morpeth
Low Baildon	*York, W.R.* - Bradford
Lowbands	*Gloucester* - Gloucester
Low Barmston	*Durham* - Gateshead
Low Beechburn	*Durham* - Bishop Auckland
Low Belthorpe	*York, E.R.* - York
Low Bentham	*York, W.R.* - Lancaster
Low Bishopside	*York, W.R.* - Harrogate
Low Bonwick	*York, E.R.* - Beverley
Low Bradley	*York, W.R.* - Skipton
Low Braithwaite	*Cumberland* - Penrith
Low Brinkburn	*Northumberland* - Morpeth
Low Burnham	*Lincoln* - Gainsborough
Low Buston	*Northumberland* - Alnwick
Low Butcher Race	*Durham* - Durham
Lowca	*Cumberland* - Whitehaven
Low Catlowdy	*Cumberland* - Carlisle
Low Catton	*York, E.R.* - York
Low Crompton	*Lancaster* - Oldham
Low Crosby	*Cumberland* - Carlisle
Low Cummersdale	*Cumberland* - Carlisle
Lowdham	*Notts* - Nottingham
Low Downs	*Durham* - Durham
Lowe	*Salop* - Shrewsbury
Low Edges	*York, W.R.* - Sheffield
Lowe Hill	*Stafford* - Leek
Low Ellington	*York, N.R.* - Harrogate
Lower Aber Canaid	*Glamorgan* - Merthyr Tydfil
Lower Aisholt	*Somerset* - Bridgwater
Lower Almondsbury	*Gloucester* - Thornbury
Lower Allithwaite	*Lancaster* - Barrow-in-Furness
Lower Arncott	*Oxford* - Oxford
Lower Assenden	*Oxford* - Reading
Lower Bangley	*Stafford* - Tamworth
Lower Basildon	*Berks* - Reading
Lower Batson	*Devon* - Kingsbridge
Lower Baynton	*Wilts* - Trowbridge
Lower Bebington	*Cheshire* - Birkenhead
Lower Beeding	*Sussex* - Horsham
Lower Benefield	*Northampton* - Corby
Lower Bentley	*Worcester* - Redditch

Lower Boddington	*Northampton* - Banbury
Lower Bourne	*Surrey* - Aldershot and Farnham
Lower Bourton	*Berks* - Swindon
Lower Brailes	*Warwick* - Banbury
Lower Braishfield	*Hants* - Winchester
Lower Brockhill	*Worcester* - Redditch
Lower Brockhurst	*Stafford* - Stafford
Lower Broughton	*Lancaster* - Salford
Lower Bullingham	*Hereford* - Hereford
Lower Buncton	*Sussex* - Worthing
Lower Burton	*Dorset* - Dorchester
Lower Caldecote	*Beds* - Biggleswade
Lower Cam	*Gloucester* - Stroud
Lower Canterton	*Hants* - Southampton
Lower Carron	*Cardigan* - Lampeter
Lower Cartmel	*Lancaster* - Barrow-in-Furness
Lower Chapel	*Brecon* - Brecknock
Lower Chirk	*Denbigh* - Wrexham
Lower Clapton	*London, E.5* - Shoreditch
Lower Coity	*Glamorgan* - Bridgend
Lower Cokeham	*Sussex* - Worthing
Lower Colliers Row	*Glamorgan* - Merthyr Tydfil
Lower Coombe	*Wilts* - Shaftesbury
Lower Copthurst	*Lancaster* - Chorley
Lower Coscomb	*Gloucester* - Cheltenham
Lower Coychurch	*Glamorgan* - Bridgend
Lowercroft	*Lancaster* - Bury
Lower Crumpsall	*Lancaster* - Manchester
Lower Cumberworth	*York, W.R.* - Huddersfield
Lower Cwmbargoed	*Glamorgan* - Merthyr Tydfil
Lower Darwen	*Lancaster* - Blackburn
Lower Dean	*Beds* - Bedford
Lower Dicker	*Sussex* - Eastbourne
Lower Down	*Salop* - Shrewsbury
Lower Dunsforth	*York, W.R.* - Harrogate
Lower Earley	*Berks* - Reading
Lower Eastern Green	*Warwick* - Coventry
Lower Edmonton	*London, N.9* - Edmonton
Lower Eldon	*Hants* - Winchester
Lower Eythorne	*Kent* - Dover
Lower Farringdon	*Hants* - Aldershot and Farnham
Lower Forest	*Wilts* - Chippenham
Lower Froyle	*Hants* - Aldershot and Farnham
Lower Goldicote	*Warwick* - Stratford on Avon
Lower Gornal	*Stafford* - Dudley
Lower Gravenhurst	*Beds* - Hitchin
Lower Green	*Essex* - Chelmsford
Lower Green	*Lancaster* - Leigh
Lower Green (Langley)	*Essex* - Bishop's Stortford
Lower Grove Common	*Hereford* - Monmouth
Lower Guiting	*Gloucester* - Cheltenham
Lower Halling	*Kent* - Rochester
Lower Hambleton	*Rutland* - Melton Mowbray
Lower Hardres	*Kent* - Canterbury
Lower Harpton	*Hereford* - Leominster
Lower Hayton	*Salop* - Ludlow
Lower Hazelor	*Worcester* - Evesham
Lower Hazle	*Gloucester* - Thornbury
Lower Heath	*Salop* - Whitchurch
Lower Heeley	*York, W.R.* - Sheffield
Lower Hergest	*Hereford* - Hereford
Lower Heyford	*Northampton* - Northampton
Lower Heyford	*Oxford* - Banbury
Lower Higham	*Kent* - Rochester
Lower Hodnell	*Warwick* - Warwick
Lower Hogstow	*Salop* - Shrewsbury
Lower Honeydon	*Beds* - Biggleswade
Lower Hope	*Hereford* - Hereford
Lower Hopton	*York, W.R.* - Dewsbury
Lower Houses	*York, W.R.* - Huddersfield
Lower Ince	*Lancaster* - Wigan
Lower Inglesham	*Wilts* - Swindon
Lower Kingcombe	*Dorset* - Dorchester
Lower Kingston	*Hants* - Bournemouth
Lower Kingswood	*Surrey* - Reigate
Lower Kinnerton	*Cheshire* - Chester
Lower Kinsham	*Hereford* - Leominster
Lower Lemington	*Gloucester* - Evesham
Lower Llanbadarn y Croyddin	*Cardigan* - Aberystwyth

LOW

Lower Llanfihangel y Croyddin	*Cardigan* - Aberystwyth
Lower Llangynwyd	*Glamorgan* - Bridgend
Lower Llansamlet	*Glamorgan* - Swansea
Lower Llanvrechfa	*Monmouth* - Newport (Mon)
Lower Lode	*Gloucester* - Cheltenham
Lower Luddesdown	*Kent* - Gravesend
Lower Lydbrook	*Gloucester* - Gloucester
Lower Midway	*Derby* - Burton-upon-Trent
Lower Moor	*Worcester* - Evesham
Lower Morden	*Surrey* - Croydon
Lower Newcastle	*Glamorgan* - Bridgend
Lower Newton	*Lancaster* - Barrow-in-Furness
Lower Norton	*Warwick* - Warwick
Lower Nyland	*Somerset* - Yeovil
Lower Penarth	*Glamorgan* - Cardiff
Lower Penn	*Stafford* - Wolverhampton
Lower Peover	*Cheshire* - Northwich
Lower Pitts	*Radnor* - Knighton
Lower Quick	*York, W.R.* - Ashton-under-Lyne
Lower Quinton	*Warwick* - Stratford on Avon
Lower Radbourne	*Warwick* - Warwick
Lower Rainham	*Kent* - Rochester
Lower Redbrook	*Gloucester* - Monmouth
Lower Reule	*Stafford* - Stafford
Lower Ridge	*Salop* - Oswestry
Lower Rochford	*Worcester* - Ludlow
Lower Sapey	*Worcester* - Worcester
Lower Seagry	*Wilts* - Chippenham
Lower Severalls (Crewkerne)	*Somerset* - Yeovil
Lower Shelton	*Beds* - Bedford
Lower Sherford	*Devon* - Plymouth
Lower Shuckburgh	*Warwick* - Rugby
Lower Slaughter	*Gloucester* - Cheltenham
Lower Soudley	*Gloucester* - Gloucester
Lower Spargo	*Cornwall* - Truro
Lower Spen	*York, W.R.* - Dewsbury
Lower Sticker	*Cornwall* - St. Austell
Lower Stoke	*Kent* - Rochester
Lower Stondon	*Beds* - Hitchin
Lower Stone	*Gloucester* - Stroud
Lower Stratton	*Wilts* - Swindon
Lower Strensham	*Worcester* - Cheltenham
Lower Strode	*Devon* - Plymouth
Lower Studley	*Wilts* - Trowbridge
Lower Sundon	*Beds* - Luton
Lower Swainswick	*Somerset* - Bath
Lower Swell	*Gloucester* - Cheltenham
Lower Sydenham (part)	*London, S.E.26* - Bromley
Lower Sydenham (part)	*London, S.E.26* - Lambeth
Lower Tale	*Devon* - Exeter
Lower Tean	*Stafford* - Uttoxeter
Lower Tockington	*Gloucester* - Thornbury
Lower Town	*Worcester* - Worcester
Lower Tranmere	*Cheshire* - Birkenhead
Lower Tregantle	*Cornwall* - Plymouth
Lower Twinhoe	*Somerset* - Bath
Lower Tysoe Farm	*Warwick* - Banbury
Lower Tythegstone	*Glamorgan* - Bridgend
Lower Walton	*Cheshire* - Warrington
Lower Wanborough	*Wilts* - Swindon
Lower Wavensmere	*Warwick* - Stratford on Avon
Lower Weald	*Bucks* - Bletchley and Leighton Buzzard
Lower Weare	*Somerset* - Wells
Lower Weedon	*Northampton* - Northampton
Lower Welson	*Hereford* - Hereford
Lower Westwood	*Wilts* - Trowbridge
Lower Whitbourne	*Wilts* - Warminster
Lower Whitley	*Berks* - Reading
Lower Whitley	*Cheshire* - Warrington
Lower Whitley	*York, W.R.* - Dewsbury
Lower Wick	*Worcester* - Worcester
Lower Wield	*Hants* - Winchester
Lower Winchendon	*Bucks* - Aylesbury
Lower Wintringham	*Hunts* - Huntingdon
Lower Withington	*Cheshire* - Macclesfield
Lower Woodford	*Wilts* - Salisbury

Lower Wych	*Cheshire* - Whitchurch
Lowesby	*Leicester* - Leicester
Lowestoft	*Suffolk* - Lowestoft
Loweswater	*Cumberland* - Workington
Low Fell	*Durham* - Gateshead
Low Felling	*Durham* - Gateshead
Lowfield	*Cumberland* - Workington
Lowfield	*Lancaster* - Barrow-in-Furness
Lowfield Heath	*Surrey* - Reigate
Lowfields	*York, W.R.* - Sheffield
Low Fold	*York, W.R.* - Harrogate
Low Forest	*Northumberland* - Hexham
Low Foulshaw	*Westmorland* - Kendal
Low Fulney	*Lincoln* - Spalding
Low Gate	*Northumberland* - Hexham
Low Gelt Bridge	*Cumberland* - Carlisle
Low Gill	*Westmorland* - Kendal
Lowgil	*Lancs* - Lancaster
Low Green	*Lancaster* - Wigan
Low Haddenham	*Bucks* - Thame
Low Ham	*Somerset* - Bridgwater
Low Harrogate	*York, W.R.* - Harrogate
Low Haswell	*Durham* - Durham
Low Heighley	*Northumberland* - Morpeth
Low Hesket	*Cumberland* - Penrith
Low Highlaws	*Northumberland* - Morpeth
Low Hill	*Essex* - Harlow
Low Hill	*Stafford* - Wolverhampton
Low Hill	*Worcester* - Worcester
Low Hold	*Durham* - Durham
Low Houses	*Cumberland* - Carlisle
Low Hunsley	*York, E.R.* - Beverley
Lowick	*Northampton* - Kettering
Lowick	*Northumberland* - Berwick-upon-Tweed
Lowick Bridge	*Lancaster* - Barrow-in-Furness
Lowick Green	*Lancaster* - Barrow-in-Furness
Low Ireby	*Cumberland* - Carlisle
Low Keekle	*Cumberland* - Whitehaven
Low Knipe	*Westmorland* - Penrith
Low Laithes	*York, W.R.* - Harrogate
Low Lambton	*Durham* - Durham
Low Leighton	*Derby* - Buxton
Low Mellwood	*Lincoln* - Gainsborough
Lowmire	*Cumberland* - Workington
Low Moor	*Cumberland* - Carlisle
Low Moor	*York, W.R.* - Bradford
Low Moorhouse	*Cumberland* - Carlisle
Low Moorsley	*Durham* - Durham
Low Moresby	*Cumberland* - Whitehaven
Low Nibthwaite	*Lancaster* - Barrow-in-Furness
Low Pittington	*Durham* - Durham
Low Row	*Cumberland* - Carlisle
Low Row	*York, N.R.* - Darlington
Lowry Hill	*Cumberland* - Carlisle
Low Scathwaite	*Lancaster* - Barrow-in-Furness
Low Skirlington	*York, E.R.* - Beverley
Lowsonford	*Warwick* - Warwick
Low Sorbies	*Cumberland* - Carlisle
Low Spennymoor	*Durham* - Bishop Auckland
Low Stanners	*Northumberland* - Morpeth
Low Swainston	*Durham* - Stockton on Tees
Lowther	*Westmorland* - Penrith
Lowther Newtown	*Westmorland* - Penrith
Lowthorpe	*York, E.R.* - Bridlington
Lowthwaite	*Cumberland* - Carlisle
Lowton	*Lancaster* - Leigh
Lowton	*Somerset* - Taunton
Lowton St. Luke	*Lancaster* - Leigh
Lowton St. Mary's	*Lancaster* - Leigh
Low Town	*Worcester* - Dudley
Low Toynton	*Lincoln* - Lincoln
Low Trewhitt	*Northumberland* - Morpeth
Low Utley	*York, W.R.* - Keighley
Low Valley	*York, W.R.* - Barnsley
Low Westwood	*Durham* - Consett
Low Wood	*Westmorland* - Kendal
Low Worsall	*York, N.R.* - Stockton on Tees
Loxbeare	*Devon* - Tiverton
Loxley	*Stafford* - Uttoxeter

Loxley	*Warwick* - Stratford on Avon
Loxley	*York, W.R.* - Sheffield
Loxton	*Somerset* - Weston Super Mare
Loxwood	*Sussex* - Chichester
Loynton	*Stafford* - Stafford
Loyters Green	*Essex* - Bishop's Stortford
Loyters Green	*Essex* - Harlow
Lozells	*Warwick* - Birmingham
Lubbersdown Hill	*Oxford* - Thame
Lubbesthorpe	*Leicester* - Leicester
Lubenham	*Leicester* - Leicester
Luccombe	*I. of W.* - Newport (I.W.)
Luccombe	*Somerset* - Minehead
Lucker	*Northumberland* - Berwick-upon-Tweed
Luckett	*Cornwall* - Launceston
Luckington	*Somerset* - Frome
Luckington	*Wilts* - Malmesbury
Lucknam	*Wilts* - Bath
Lucknow	*Stafford* - Walsall
Lucton	*Hereford* - Leominster
Ludborough	*Lincoln* - Louth
Ludbrooke	*Devon* - Kingsbridge
Ludchurch	*Pembroke* - Haverfordwest
Luddenden	*York, W.R.* - Halifax
Luddenden Booth	*York, W.R.* - Halifax
Luddenden Dean	*York, W.R.* - Halifax
Luddenden Foot	*York, W.R.* - Halifax
Luddenham	*Kent* - Sittingbourne
Luddesdown, Lower	*Kent* - Gravesend
Luddesdown, Upper	*Kent* - Gravesend
Luddington	*Lincoln* - Goole
Luddington	*Northampton* - Huntingdon
Luddington	*Warwick* - Stratford on Avon
Luddington	*York, W.R.* - Thorne
Ludford	*Lincoln* - Louth
Ludford	*Salop* - Ludlow
Ludgershall	*Bucks* - Thame
Ludgershall	*Wilts* - Andover
Ludgvan	*Cornwall* - Penzance
Ludham	*Norfolk* - Great Yarmouth
Ludlow	*Salop* - Ludlow
Ludney	*Lincoln* - Louth
Ludney	*Somerset* - Yeovil
Ludstone	*Salop* - Bridgnorth
Ludwell	*Wilts* - Shaftesbury
Ludworth	*Cheshire* - Stockport
Ludworth	*Durham* - Durham
Ludworth Moor	*Cheshire* - Stockport
Luffenhall	*Herts* - Hitchin
Luffenham, North	*Rutland* - Stamford
Luffenham, South	*Rutland* - Stamford
Luffield Abbey	*Bucks* - Northampton
Lufton	*Somerset* - Yeovil
Lugwardine	*Hereford* - Hereford
Lullingstone	*Kent* - Dartford
Lullington	*Derby* - Burton-upon-Trent
Lullington	*Somerset* - Frome
Lullington	*Sussex* - Eastbourne
Lulsgate Bottom	*Somerset* - Bristol
Lulsley	*Worcester* - Worcester
Lulworth, East	*Dorset* - Swanage
Lulworth, West	*Dorset* - Swanage
Lumb (Edenfield)	*Lancaster* - Bury
Lumb	*Lancaster* - Rawtenstall
Lumb Brook	*York, W.R.* - Halifax
Lumburn	*Devon* - Plymouth
Lumbutts	*Lancaster* - Todmorden
Lumby	*York, W.R.* - Pontefract
Lumley	*Sussex* - Chichester
Lumley, Great	*Durham* - Durham
Lumley Thicks	*Durham* - Durham
Lumsdale	*Derby* - Matlock
Lund	*York, E.R.* - Beverley
Lund	*York, E.R.* - York
Lund Wood	*York, W.R.* - Barnsley
Lundy Island	*Devon* - Bideford
Lunedale	*York, N.R.* - Bishop Auckland
Lunnon	*Glamorgan* - Swansea
Lunt's Heath	*Lancaster* - St. Helens

Luppitt	*Devon* - Exeter
Lupset	*York, W.R.* - Wakefield
Lupton	*Westmorland* - Kendal
Lurgashall	*Sussex* - Chichester
Lurkenhope	*Salop* - Knighton
Lurley	*Devon* - Tiverton
Lusby	*Lincoln* - Skegness
Luscombe	*Devon* - Kingsbridge
Luscombe	*Warwick* - Stratford on Avon
Lustleigh	*Devon* - Newton Abbot
Luston	*Hereford* - Leominster
Lutherburn	*Lancaster* - Barrow-in-Furness
Lutley	*Worcester* - Stourbridge
Luton	*Beds* - Luton
Luton	*Devon* - Exeter
Luton	*Kent* - Rochester
Luton Hoo	*Beds* - Luton
Lutterworth	*Leicester* - Rugby
Lutton	*Devon* - Plymouth
Lutton	*Lincoln* - Spalding
Lutton	*Northampton* - Peterborough
Lutton, East	*York, E.R.* - Beverley
Lutton Garnsgate	*Lincoln* - Spalding
Lutton Marsh	*Lincoln* - Spalding
Lutton, West	*York, E.R.* - Beverley
Lutwyche	*Salop* - Shrewsbury
Luxborough	*Somerset* - Minehead
Luxted	*Kent* - Bromley
Luxulyan	*Cornwall* - Bodmin
Luzborough	*Hants* - Southampton
Luzley	*Lancaster* - Ashton-under-Lyne
Luzley	*Northumberland* - Carlisle
Lydbrook	*Gloucester* - Gloucester
Lydbrook Junction	*Gloucester* - Monmouth
Lydbrook, Lower	*Gloucester* - Gloucester
Lydbrook, Upper	*Gloucester* - Gloucester
Lydbury, North	*Salop* - Shrewsbury
Lydd	*Kent* - Ashford
Lydden	*Kent* - Dover
Lydden	*Kent* - Margate
Lyddington	*Rutland* - Corby
Lyde	*Hereford* - Hereford
Lydeard St. Lawrence	*Somerset* - Taunton
Lyde Green	*Gloucester* - Bristol
Lyde Green	*Hants* - Basingstoke
Lydeway	*Wilts* - Devizes
Lydford	*Devon* - Plymouth
Lydford	*Somerset* - Wells
Lydgate	*York, W.R.* - Huddersfield
Lydgate	*York, W.R.* - Oldham
Lydgate	*Lancaster* - Todmorden
Lydham	*Salop* - Shrewsbury
Lydiard Millicent	*Wilts* - Swindon
Lydiard Tregoze	*Wilts* - Swindon
Lydiate	*Lancaster* - Liverpool
Lydiate Ash	*Worcester* - Bromsgrove
Lydley Hayes	*Salop* - Shrewsbury
Lydlinch	*Dorset* - Shaftesbury
Lydney	*Gloucester* - Chepstow
Lydstep	*Pembroke* - Haverfordwest
Lye	*Worcester* - Stourbridge
Lye Green	*Warwick* - Warwick
Lye Heath	*Hants* - Portsmouth
Lye Hole	*Somerset* - Weston Super Mare
Lyford	*Berks* - Didcot
Lyham, North	*Northumberland* - Alnwick
Lyham, South	*Northumberland* - Alnwick
Lyme Green	*Cheshire* - Macclesfield
Lyme Handley	*Cheshire* - Macclesfield
Lyme Regis	*Dorset* - Axminster and Chard
Lyminge	*Kent* - Folkestone
Lymington	*Hants* - Lymington
Lymington Bottom	*Hants* - Winchester
Lyminster	*Sussex* - Chichester
Lymm	*Cheshire* - Altrincham
Lymore	*Hants* - Lymington
Lympne	*Kent* - Folkestone
Lympsham	*Somerset* - Weston Super Mare
Lympstone	*Devon* - Exeter
Lynch Gate	*Salop* - Ludlow

Lyndhurst	*Hants* - Southampton
Lyndon	*Rutland* - Stamford
Lyndon	*Stafford* - West Bromwich
Lyndon End	*Warwick* - Birmingham
Lyndon Green	*Warwick* - Birmingham
Lyne	*Surrey* - Slough
Lyneal	*Salop* - Oswestry
Lyne Bank	*Cumberland* - Carlisle
Lyneham	*Devon* - Plymouth
Lyneham	*Oxford* - Banbury
Lyneham	*Wilts* - Swindon
Lynesack	*Durham* - Bishop Auckland
Lynford	*Norfolk* - Thetford
Lyng	*Norfolk* - East Dereham
Lyng	*Stafford* - West Bromwich
Lyng, East	*Somerset* - Bridgwater
Lyngford	*Somerset* - Taunton
Lyng, West	*Somerset* - Bridgwater
Lynholmes	*Derby* - Matlock
Lynmouth	*Devon* - Barnstaple
Lynmouth	*Northumberland* - Morpeth
Lynn	*Salop* - Wellington (Salop)
Lynn	*Stafford* - Lichfield
Lynn Shield	*Northumberland* - Haltwhistle
Lynn, West	*Norfolk* - King's Lynn
Lynsted	*Kent* - Sittingbourne
Lynton	*Devon* - Barnstaple
Lyon's Gate	*Dorset* - Dorchester
Lyonshall	*Hereford* - Hereford
Lyoth Common	*Sussex* - Haywards Heath
Lypeat	*Somerset* - Frome
Lypiatt	*Gloucester* - Stroud
Lyston	*Hereford* - Hereford
Lytchett Matravers	*Dorset* - Poole
Lytchett Minster	*Dorset* - Poole
Lyth	*Salop* - Shrewsbury
Lyth	*Westmorland* - Kendal
Lytham St. Annes	*Lancaster* - Blackpool
Lythe	*Salop* - Oswestry
Lythe	*York, N.R.* - Whitby
Lyth, Great	*Salop* - Shrewsbury
Lythwood	*Salop* - Shrewsbury
Lyveden	*Northampton* - Peterborough
Lywood Common	*Sussex* - Haywards Heath

M

Mabe	*Cornwall* - Truro
Mablethorpe	*Lincoln* - Louth
Macclesfield	*Cheshire* - Macclesfield
Macclesfield Forest	*Cheshire* - Macclesfield
Macefen	*Cheshire* - Whitchurch
Machen Lower	*Monmouth* - Newport (Mon.)
Machen Upper	*Monmouth* - Newport (Mon.)
Machynis	*Carmarthen* - Llanelli
Machynlleth	*Montgomery* - Machynlleth
Mackadown	*Warwick* - Birmingham
Mackerels Plain	*Kent* - Sevenoaks
Mackworth	*Derby* - Derby
Madehurst	*Sussex* - Chichester
Madeley	*Salop* - Wellington (Salop)
Madeley	*Stafford* - Stoke-on-Trent
Madeley Wood	*Salop* - Wellington
Maders	*Cornwall* - Liskeard
Madingley	*Cambridge* - Cambridge
Madley	*Hereford* - Hereford
Madley Heath	*Worcester* - Bromsgrove
Madresfield	*Worcester* - Great Malvern
Madron	*Cornwall* - Penzance
Maenaddfwyn	*Anglesey* - Llangefni
Maenan	*Caernarvon* - Conway
Maenclochog	*Pembroke* - Haverfordwest
Maengwynedd	*Denbigh* - Oswestry
Maenporth	*Cornwall* - Truro
Maentwrog	*Merioneth* - Portmadoc
Maer	*Stafford* - Stoke-on-Trent
Maerdy	*Glamorgan* - Pontypridd

MAE - MAL

Maer Heath	*Stafford* - Stoke-on-Trent
Maer Way Lane	*Stafford* - Stoke-on-Trent
Maesbrook	*Salop* - Oswestry
Maesbury	*Salop* - Oswestry
Maesgeirchen	*Caernarvon* - Bangor
Maesgwartha	*Brecon* - Pontypool and Abergavenny
Maesllyn	*Cardigan* - Cardigan
Maesmawr	*Montgomery* - Welshpool
Maesmynan	*Denbigh* - Mold
Maesmynis	*Brecon* - Builth
Maesteg	*Glamorgan* - Bridgend
Maestrayloe	*Radnor* - Knighton
Maestrefgomer	*Montgomery* - Newtown
Maestryfan	*Caernarvon* - Bangor
Maesycrugiau	*Carmarthen* - Lampeter
Maesycwmmer	*Glamorgan and Monmouth* - Blackwood
Maesydre	*Denbigh* - Wrexham
Magdalen Laver	*Essex* - Harlow
Mageston	*Dorset* - Dorchester
Maggotts End	*Essex* - Bishop's Stortford
Magham Down	*Sussex* - Eastbourne
Maghull	*Lancaster* - Liverpool
Magor	*Monmouth* - Newport (Mon.)
Magpie Bottom	*Kent* - Sevenoaks
Maida Hill	*London, W.9* - Bloomsbury
Maida Vale	*London, W.9* - Marylebone
Maiden Bradley	*Somerset* - Frome
Maidencombe	*Devon* - Torquay
Maiden Down (part)	*Devon* - Taunton
Maiden Down (part)	*Devon* - Tiverton
Maidenhead	*Berks* - Slough
Maidenhead Thicket	*Berks* - Slough
Maiden Hill	*Cumberland* - Penrith
Maiden Law (part)	*Durham* - Consett
Maiden Law (part)	*Durham* - Durham
Maiden Newton	*Dorset* - Dorchester
Maiden's Crouch	*Herts* - St. Albans
Maidens Green	*Berks* - Slough
Maidensgrove	*Oxford* - Reading
Maiden Way	*Northumberland* - Haltwhistle
Maidenwell	*Lincoln* - Louth
Maiden Wells	*Pembroke* - Haverfordwest
Maidford	*Northampton* - Northampton
Maids Moreton	*Bucks* - Aylesbury
Maidstone	*Kent* - Maidstone
Maidwell	*Northampton* - Northampton
Main	*Montgomery* - Oswestry
Mainsforth	*Durham* - Durham
Mainstone	*Salop* - Ludlow
Maisemore	*Gloucester* - Gloucester
Makeney	*Derby* - Derby
Maker	*Cornwall* - Plymouth
Malborough	*Devon* - Kingsbridge
Malcalf	*Derby* - Buxton
Malden, New	*Surrey* - Kingston-upon-Thames
Malden, Old	*Surrey* - Kingston-upon-Thames
Maldon	*Essex* - Maldon
Malham	*Sussex* - Chichester
Malham	*York, W.R.* - Skipton
Malham Moor	*York, W.R.* - Skipton
Malinslee	*Salop* - Wellington (Salop)
Mallard Hurn	*Lincoln* - Spalding
Malldraeth	*Anglesey* - Llangefni
Mallerstang	*Westmorland* - Penrith
Malling, East	*Kent* - Maidstone
Malling, West	*Kent* - Maidstone
Mallows Green	*Essex* - Bishop's Stortford
Mallsgate	*Cumberland* - Carlisle
Mallwyd	*Merioneth* - Dolgellau
Malmesbury	*Wilts* - Malmesbury
Malpas	*Cheshire* - Whitchurch
Malpas	*Cornwall* - Truro
Malpas	*Monmouth* - Newport (Mon.)
Malswick	*Gloucester* - Gloucester
Maltby	*York, W.R.* - Rotherham
Maltby in Cleveland	*York, N.R.* - Middlesbrough
Maltby le Marsh	*Lincoln* - Louth
Malthouse Lane	*Kent* - Ashford
Malton	*York, N.R.* - Malton

MAL - MAP

Malton, Old	*York, N.R.* - Malton
Malvern	*Worcester* - Great Malvern
Malvern, Great	*Worcester* - Great Malvern
Malvern Link	*Worcester* - Great Malvern
Malvern, Little	*Worcester* - Great Malvern
Malvern Wells	*Worcester* - Great Malvern
Malvern, West	*Worcester* - Great Malvern
Malvin's Close	*Northumberland* - Blyth
Mamble	*Worcester* - Kidderminster
Mamhead	*Devon* - Exeter
Mamhilad	*Monmouth* - Pontypool and Abergavenny
Mammerton	*Derby* - Derby
Mana Butts	*Devon* - Plymouth
Manaccan	*Cornwall* - Penzance
Manafon	*Montgomery* - Newtown
Manaton	*Devon* - Newton Abbot
Manby	*Lincoln* - Louth
Mancetter	*Warwick* - Nuneaton
Manchester	*Lancaster* - Manchester
Manchester, Little	*Stafford* - Market Drayton
Mancot	*Flint* - Chester
Mancot Royal	*Flint* - Chester
Manea	*Cambridge* - March
Manea Fen	*Cambridge* - March
Maney	*Warwick* - Birmingham
Manfield	*York, N.R.* - Darlington
Mangeston	*Dorset* - Dorchester
Mangotsfield	*Gloucester* - Bristol
Mangrove Green	*Herts* - Hitchin
Manhay	*Cornwall* - Penzance
Manledd	*Montgomery* - Newtown
Manley	*Cheshire* - Runcorn
Manmoel	*Monmouth* - Blackwood
Mannamead	*Devon* - Plymouth
Mannerley Lane	*Salop* - Wellington (Salop)
Manningford Abbotts	*Wilts* - Swindon
Manningford Bohune	*Wilts* - Swindon
Manningford Bruce	*Wilts* - Swindon
Manningham	*York, W.R.* - Bradford
Mannings Heath	*Sussex* - Horsham
Mannington	*Dorset* - Wimborne Minster
Mannington	*Norfolk* - Norwich
Manningtree	*Essex* - Colchester
Manor	*York, W.R.* - Sheffield
Manorbier	*Pembroke* - Haverfordwest
Manordeifi	*Pembroke* - Cardigan
Manordilo	*Carmarthen* - Ammanford
Manorowen	*Pembroke* - Haverfordwest
Manor Park	*London, E.12* - Bow
Manor Park	*York, W.R.* - Sheffield
Mansditch	*Derby* - Burton-on-Trent
Mansell Gamage	*Hereford* - Hereford
Mansell Lacy	*Hereford* - Hereford
Manselton	*Glamorgan* - Swansea
Mansergh	*Westmorland* - Kendal
Mansfield	*Notts* - Mansfield
Mansfield Woodhouse	*Notts* - Mansfield
Manstey	*Stafford* - Stafford
Manston	*Dorset* - Shaftesbury
Manston	*Kent* - Ramsgate
Manston	*York, W.R.* - Leeds
Manswood	*Dorset* - Wimborne Minster
Manthorpe	*Lincoln* - Grantham
Manthorpe	*Lincoln* - Spalding
Manton	*Lincoln* - Scunthorpe
Manton	*Notts* - Worksop
Manton	*Rutland* - Melton Mowbray
Manton	*Wilts* - Swindon
Manuden	*Essex* - Bishop's Stortford
Maperton	*Somerset* - Yeovil
Maplebeck	*Notts* - Newark
Maple Cross	*Hertford* - Watford
Mapledurham	*Oxford* - Reading
Mapledurwell	*Hants* - Basingstoke
Maplehurst	*Sussex* - Horsham
Maplestead, Great	*Essex* - Braintree
Maplestead, Little	*Essex* - Braintree
Mapperley	*Derby* - Ilkeston
Mapperley Brook	*Derby* - Ilkeston

Mapperton (Almer)	*Dorset* - Blandford
Mapperton	*Dorset* - Dorchester
Mappleborough Green	*Warwick* - Redditch
Mappleton	*Derby* - Derby
Mappleton	*York, E.R.* - Kingston-upon-Hull
Mapplewell	*York, W.R.* - Barnsley
Mappowder	*Dorset* - Dorchester
Marazanvose	*Cornwall* - Truro
Marazion	*Cornwall* - Penzance
Marbury	*Cheshire* - Northwich
Marbury	*Cheshire* - Whitchurch
March	*Cambridge* - March
Marcham	*Berks* - Oxford
Marchamley	*Salop* - Market Drayton
Marchamley Wood	*Salop* - Market Drayton
March End	*Stafford* - Wolverhampton
March Fen	*Cambridge* - March
Marchington	*Stafford* - Uttoxeter
Marchington Woodlands	*Stafford* - Uttoxeter
Marchup	*York, W.R.* - Skipton
Marchwiel	*Denbigh* - Wrexham
Marchwood	*Hants* - Southampton
Marcle, Little	*Hereford* - Hereford
Marcle, Much	*Hereford* - Hereford
Marcross	*Glamorgan* - Bridgend
Marden	*Hereford* - Hereford
Marden	*Kent* - Maidstone
Marden	*Sussex* - Chichester
Marden	*Northumberland* - North Shields
Marden	*Wilts* - Devizes
Marden Ash	*Essex* - Brentford
Marden, East	*Sussex* - Chichester
Marden, North	*Sussex* - Chichester
Marden, West	*Sussex* - Chichester
Mardock	*Herts* - Hertford
Mardu	*Salop* - Ludlow
Mardu Bridge	*Montgomery* - Oswestry
Mardy	*Monmouth* - Pontypool and Abergavenny
Marefield	*Leicester* - Leicester
Mareham le Fen	*Lincoln* - Boston
Mareham on the Hill	*Lincoln* - Lincoln
Marehay	*Derby* - Alfreton
Marehay	*Salop* - Shrewsbury
Mare Hill	*Sussex* - Chichester
Maresfield	*Sussex* - Lewes
Marfield	*Worcester* - Redditch
Marfleet	*York, E.R.* - Kingston-upon-Hull
Marford	*Flint* - Wrexham
Marford	*Herts* - St. Albans
Margam	*Glamorgan* - Neath
Margaret Marsh	*Dorset* - Shaftesbury
Margaret Roding	*Essex* - Chelmsford
Margaretting	*Essex* - Chelmsford
Margaretting Tye	*Essex* - Chelmsford
Margate	*Kent* - Margate
Margrove Park	*York, N.R.* - Middlesbrough
Marham	*Norfolk* - King's Lynn
Marhamchurch	*Cornwall* - Launceston
Marholm	*Northampton* - Peterborough
Marian Glas	*Anglesey* - Llangefni
Mariansleigh	*Devon* - Barnstaple
Marishes	*York, N.R.* - Malton
Maristow	*Devon* - Plymouth
Mark	*Somerset* - Wells
Mark Beech	*Kent* - Tonbridge
Markby	*Lincoln* - Skegness
Mark Cross	*Sussex* - Tunbridge Wells
Markeaton	*Derby* - Derby
Markenfield Hall	*York, W.R.* - Harrogate
Market Bosworth	*Leicester* - Hinckley
Market Deeping	*Lincoln* - Spalding
Market Deeping Fen	*Lincoln* - Spalding
Market Drayton	*Salop* - Market Drayton
Market Harborough	*Leicester* - Kettering
Market Lavington	*Wilts* - Devizes
Market Overton	*Rutland* - Melton Mowbray
Market Rasen	*Lincoln* - Lincoln
Market Stainton	*Lincoln* - Louth

Market Weighton	*York, E.R.* - Beverley
Market Weston	*Suffolk* - Thetford
Markfield	*Leicester* - Leicester
Markham Clinton	*Notts* - East Retford
Markham, East	*Notts* - East Retford
Markham Village	*Monmouth* - Blackwood
Markham, West	*Notts* - East Retford
Markington	*York, W.R.* - Harrogate
Markland Hill	*Lancaster* - Bolton
Mark Moor	*Somerset* - Wells
Marksbury	*Somerset* - Bath
Marks Gate	*Essex* - Ilford
Markshall	*Essex* - Braintree
Markshall	*Norfolk* - Norwich
Marks Tey	*Essex* - Colchester
Markyate	*Herts* - Luton
Marlborough	*Lincoln* - Lincoln
Marlborough	*Wilts* - Swindon
Marlborough Camp	*Warwick* - Banbury
Marlbrook	*Worcester* - Bromsgrove
Marlcliff	*Warwick* - Stratford on Avon
Marlcliff Hill	*Warwick* - Stratford on Avon
Marldon	*Devon* - Torquay
Marle Hill	*Gloucester* - Cheltenham
Marlesford	*Suffolk* - Woodbridge
Marley Green	*Cheshire* - Whitchurch
Marley Hill	*Durham* - Gateshead
Marli	*Denbigh* - Rhyl
Marling Cross	*Kent* - Gravesend
Marlingford	*Norfolk* - Norwich
Marloes	*Pembroke* - Haverfordwest
Marlow	*Hereford* - Ludlow
Marlow	*York, W.R.* - Keighley
Marlow Common	*Bucks* - High Wycombe
Marlow, Great	*Bucks* - High Wycombe
Marlow, Little	*Bucks* - High Wycombe
Malrpit Hill	*Kent* - Tonbridge
Marlpool	*Derby* - Ilkeston
Marlston	*Berks* - Newbury
Marlston-cum-Lacne	*Cheshire* - Chester
Marnham	*Notts* - East Retford
Marnhull	*Dorset* - Shaftesbury
Marple	*Cheshire* - Stockport
Marple Bridge	*Derby* - Stockport
Marr	*York, W.R.* - Doncaster
Marriage Hill	*Warwick* - Stratford on Avon
Marros	*Carmarthen* - Haverfordwest
Marsden	*Durham* - South Shields
Marsden	*York, W.R.* - Huddersfield
Marsh	*Bucks* - Aylesbury
Marsh	*Devon* - Exeter
Marsh	*York, W.R.* - Dewsbury
Marsh	*York, W.R.* - Huddersfield
Marsh	*York, W.R.* - Keighley
Marshalls Cross	*Lancaster* - St. Helens
Marshalsea	*Dorset* - Axminster and Chard
Marsham	*Norfolk* - Norwich
Marsh Baldon	*Oxford* - Oxford
Marsh Benham	*Berks* - Newbury
Marshborough	*Kent* - Deal
Marsh Brook	*Lancaster* - Bolton
Marshbrook	*Salop* - Ludlow
Marsh Chapel	*Lincoln* - Louth
Marsh Common	*Gloucester* - Thornbury
Marshfield	*Gloucester* - Bath
Marshfield	*Monmouth* - Newport (Mon.)
Marshgate	*Cornwall* - Launceston
Marsh Gibbon	*Bucks* - Aylesbury
Marsh Green	*Bucks* - High Wycombe
Marsh Green	*Kent* - Tonbridge
Marsh Green	*Lancaster* - Wigan
Marsh Green	*Salop* - Wellington (Salop)
Marshland Smeeth	*Norfolk* - Wisbech
Marsh Lane	*Derby* - Chesterfield
Marsh Lane	*Wilts* - Chippenham
Marshwood	*Dorset* - Axminster and Chard
Marske	*York, N.R.* - Middlesbrough
Marske	*York, N.R.* - Darlington
Marstin Moor	*Derby* - Chesterfield
Marston	*Cheshire* - Northwich

MAR - MAS

Marston	*Hereford* - Leominster
Marston	*Lincoln* - Grantham
Marston	*Oxford* - Oxford
Marston	*Somerset* - Frome
Marston (Church Eaton)	*Stafford* - Stafford
Marston (St. Marys)	*Stafford* - Stafford
Marston	*Wilts* - Devizes
Marston Bigot	*Somerset* - Frome
Marstone Stannett	*Hereford* - Leominster
Marston Green	*Warwick* - Birmingham
Marston Jabbett	*Warwick* - Nuneaton
Marston, Little	*Somerset* - Yeovil
Marston, Long	*Warwick* - Stratford on Avon
Marston, Long	*York, W.R.* - York
Marston Magna	*Somerset* - Yeovil
Marston Meysey	*Wilts* - Swindon
Marston Montgomery	*Derby* - Uttoxeter
Marston Moor	*York, W.R.* - York
Marston Moretaine	*Beds* - Bedford
Marston, North	*Bucks* - Aylesbury
Marston St. Lawrence	*Northampton* - Banbury
Marston Sicca	*Warwick* - Stratford on Avon
Marston, South	*Wilts* - Swindon
Marston Trussell	*Northampton* - Northampton
Marston-upon-Dove	*Derby* - Burton-upon-Trent
Marstow	*Hereford* - Monmouth
Marsworth	*Bucks* - Aylesbury
Marten	*Wilts* - Swindon
Marthall	*Cheshire* - Altrincham
Martham	*Norfolk* - Great Yarmouth
Martin	*Kent* - Dover
Martin	*Lincoln* - Lincoln
Martin	*Lincoln* - Sleaford
Martin	*Hants* - Salisbury
Martindale	*Westmorland* - Penrith
Martin Dales	*Lincoln* - Sleaford
Martin Fen	*Lincoln* - Sleaford
Martinhoe	*Devon* - Barnstaple
Martin Hussingtree	*Worcester* - Worcester
Martin Moor	*Lincoln* - Lincoln
Martin Raynham	*Norfolk* - King's Lynn
Martinscroft	*Lancaster* - Warrington
Martinsthorpe	*Rutland* - Melton Mowbray
Martinstown	*Dorset* - Dorchester
Martlesham	*Suffolk* - Woodbiidge
Martletwy	*Pembroke* - Haverfordwest
Martley	*Worcester* - Worcester
Martock	*Somerset* - Yeovil
Marton	*Cheshire* - Congleton
Marton	*Lancaster* - Barrow-in-Furness
Marton	*Lincoln* - Gainsborough
Marton	*Montgomery* - Welshpool
Marton	*Salop* - Shrewsbury
Marton	*Warwick* - Rugby
Marton	*York, E.R.* - Bridlington
Marton	*York, E.R.* - Kingston-upon-Hull
Marton	*York, N.R.* - Malton
Marton	*York, N.R.* - Middlesbrough
Marton	*York, W.R.* - Harrogate
Marton, East	*York, W.R.* - Skipton
Marton-le-Moor	*York, N.R.* - Harrogate
Marton Moor	*York, N.R.* - Middlesbrough
Marton, West	*York, W.R.* - Skipton
Marton-with-Moxby	*York, N.R.* - York
Martyr Worthy	*Hants* - Winchester
Marwell	*Hants* - Winchester
Marwood	*Devon* - Barnstaple
Marwood	*Durham* - Bishop Auckland
Marwood, Middle	*Devon* - Barnstaple
Maryland Point	*London, E.15* - Bow
Marylebone	*Lancaster* - Wigan
Marylebone	*London, N.W.1* - Bloomsbury and Marylebone
Marylebone	*London, W.1* - Bloomsbury and Marylebone
Maryport	*Cumberland* - Workington
Mary Tavy	*Devon* - Plymouth
Masbrough	*York, W.R.* - Rotherham
Masham	*York, N.R.* - Harrogate
Mashbury	*Essex* - Chelmsford

MAS - MAY

Mason	*Northumberland* - Newcastle upon Tyne
Masongill	*York, W.R.* - Lancaster
Massingham, Great	*Norfolk* - King's Lynn
Massingham, Little	*Norfolk* - King's Lynn
Master's Close	*Northumberland* - Hexham
Mastle Bridge	*Pembroke* - Haverfordwest
Matchams	*Hants* - Bournemouth
Matchborough	*Worcester* - Redditch
Matching	*Essex* - Harlow
Matching Green	*Essex* - Harlow
Matching Tye	*Essex* - Harlow
Matfen, East	*Northumberland* - Newcastle upon Tyne
Matfen, West	*Northumberland* - Newcastle upon Tyne
Matfield Green	*Kent* - Tunbridge Wells
Mathern	*Monmouth* - Chepstow
Mathon	*Worcester* - Great Malvern
Mathry	*Pembroke* - Haverfordwest
Matlask	*Norfolk* - Norwich
Matley	*Cheshire* - Hyde
Matlock	*Derby* - Matlock
Matlock Bath	*Derby* - Matlock
Matlock, Green	*Derby* - Matlock
Matlock, Little	*York, W.R.* - Sheffield
Matson	*Gloucester* - Gloucester
Matterdale End	*Cumberland* - Penrith
Matterly	*Hants* - Winchester
Mattersey	*Notts* - East Retford
Mattersey Thorpe	*Notts* - East Retford
Matthewstown	*Glamorgan* - Aberdare
Matties Green	*Northumberland* - Haltwhistle
Mattingley	*Hants* - Basingstoke
Mattishall	*Norfolk* - East Dereham
Mattishall Burgh	*Norfolk* - East Dereham
Maudlam	*Glamorgan* - Bridgend
Maudlin	*Sussex* - Chichester
Mauds Elm	*Gloucester* - Cheltenham
Maugersbury	*Gloucester* - Cheltenham
Maulden	*Beds* - Bedford
Maulds Meaburn	*Westmorland* - Penrith
Maund Bryan	*Hereford* - Leominster
Maundown	*Somerset* - Taunton
Mautby	*Norfolk* - Great Yarmouth
Mavesyn Ridware	*Stafford* - Lichfield
Mavis Enderby	*Lincoln* - Skegness
Mavis Enderby Fen	*Lincoln* - Skegness
Mawbray, New	*Cumberland* - Carlisle
Mawbray, Old	*Cumberland* - Carlisle
Mawdesley	*Lancaster* - Chorley
Mawgan-in-Meneage	*Cornwall* - Penzance
Mawgan Porth	*Cornwall* - Truro
Mawnan	*Cornwall* - Truro
Mawnan Smith	*Cornwall* - Truro
Mawthorpe	*Lincoln* - Skegness
Maxey	*Northampton* - Peterborough
Max Mills	*Somerset* - Weston Super Mare
Maxstoke	*Warwick* - Birmingham
Maxton	*Kent* - Dover
Maxworthy	*Devon* - Launceston
May Bank	*Stafford* - Stoke-on-Trent
Maybecks	*York, N.R.* - Whitby
Maybury	*Surrey* - Guildford
Maybush	*Hants* - Southampton
Maydensole	*Kent* - Deal
Mayes Green	*Surrey* - Dorking
Mayfair	*London, W.1* - Westminster
Mayfield	*Sussex* - Tunbridge Wells
Mayfield Church	*Stafford* - Uttoxeter
Mayfield, Middle	*Stafford* - Uttoxeter
Mayfield, Upper	*Stafford* - Uttoxeter
Mayford	*Surrey* - Guildford
Mayhill	*Glamorgan* - Swansea
May Hill	*Gloucester* - Gloucester
Mayland	*Essex* - Maldon
Maylands	*Durham* - Bishop Auckland
Maynards Green	*Sussex* - Eastbourne
Maypole	*Worcester* - Birmingham
May's Green	*Oxford* - Reading

Mays Hill	*Gloucester* - Thornbury
Meadle	*Bucks* - High Wycombe
Meadow Bank	*Cheshire* - Northwich
Meadowfield	*Durham* - Durham
Meadow Green	*Hereford* - Bromyard
Meadow Hall	*York, W.R.* - Rotherham
Mead Vale	*Surrey* - Reigate
Meaford	*Stafford* - Stafford
Meal Bank	*Westmorland* - Kendal
Mealo	*Cumberland* - Carlisle
Mealrigg	*Cumberland* - Carlisle
Mealsgate	*Cumberland* - Carlisle
Meanwood	*York, W.R.* - Leeds
Mearbeck	*York, W.R.* - Skipton
Meare	*Somerset* - Wells
Mears Ashby	*Northampton* - Wellingborough
Measham	*Derby* - Ashby-de-la-Zouch
Meathop	*Westmorland* - Kendal
Meaux	*York, E.R.* - Beverley
Meavy	*Devon* - Plymouth
Medbourn	*Herts* - Watford
Medbourne	*Leicester* - Kettering
Medge Hall	*York, W.R.* - Thorne
Medlar-with-Wesham	*Lancaster* - Preston
Medley	*Oxford* - Oxford
Medley Park	*Salop* - Ludlow
Medlicott	*Salop* - Shrewsbury
Medmenham	*Bucks* - Reading
Medomsley	*Durham* - Consett
Medrose	*Cornwall* - Bideford
Medstead	*Hants* - Winchester
Meerbrook	*Stafford* - Leek
Meer End	*Warwick* - Coventry
Meersbrook	*York, W.R.* - Sheffield
Meesden	*Herts* - Bishop's Stortford
Meeson	*Salop* - Wellington (Salop)
Meeth	*Devon* - Okehampton
Meifod	*Montgomery* - Oswestry
Meillteyrn	*Caernarvon* - Portmadoc
Meinciau	*Carmarthen* - Carmarthen
Meir	*Stafford* - Stoke-on-Trent
Meir Heath	*Stafford* - Stoke-on-Trent
Melbourn	*Cambridge* - Cambridge
Melbourne	*Derby* - Derby
Melbourne	*York, E.R.* - York
Melbury Abbas	*Dorset* - Shaftesbury
Melbury Bubb	*Dorset* - Yeovil
Melbury, East	*Dorset* - Shaftesbury
Melbury Osmond	*Dorset* - Yeovil
Melbury Sampford	*Dorset* - Yeovil
Melbury, West	*Dorset* - Shaftesbury
Melchbourne	*Beds* - Wellingborough
Melchet	*Hants* - Southampton
Melcombe Bingham	*Dorset* - Dorchester
Melcombe Horsey	*Dorset* - Dorchester
Meldon	*Devon* - Okehampton
Meldon	*Northumberland* - Morpeth
Meldreth	*Cambridge* - Cambridge
Meledor	*Cornwall* - St. Austell
Meliden	*Flint* - Rhyl
Melinbyrhedyn	*Montgomery* - Machynlleth
Melincourt	*Glamorgan* - Neath
Melincrythan	*Glamorgan* - Neath
Meline	*Pembroke* - Cardigan
Melingaerig	*Montgomery* - Machynlleth
Melingriffith	*Glamorgan* - Cardiff
Melin y Coed	*Denbigh* - Conway
Melkinthorpe	*Westmorland* - Penrith
Melkridge	*Northumberland* - Haltwhistle
Melksham	*Wilts* - Chippingham
Melling	*Lancaster* - Lancaster
Melling	*Lancaster* - Liverpool
Mellingey	*Cornwall* - Truro
Mellington	*Montgomery* - Welshpool
Mellis	*Suffolk* - Norwich
Mellor	*Cheshire* - Stockport
Mellor	*Lancaster* - Blackburn
Mellor Brook	*Lancaster* - Blackburn
Mells	*Somerset* - Frome
Mells	*Suffolk* - Halesworth

Mellwood, High	*Lincoln* - Gainsborough
Mellwood, Low	*Lincoln* - Gainsborough
Melmerby	*Cumberland* - Penrith
Melmerby	*York, N.R.* - Northallerton
Melmerby	*York, N.R.* - Harrogate
Melplash	*Dorset* - Dorchester
Melsonby	*York, N.R.* - Darlington
Meltham	*York, W.R.* - Huddersfield
Melton	*Lancaster* - Barrow-in-Furness
Melton	*Suffolk* - Woodbridge
Melton	*York, E.R.* - Kingston-upon-Hull
Meltonbrand	*York, W.R.* - Doncaster
Meltonby	*York, E.R.* - York
Melton Constable	*Norfolk* - King's Lynn
Melton, Great	*Norfolk* - Norwich
Melton, High	*York, W.R.* - Doncaster
Melton, Little	*Norfolk* - Norwich
Melton Mowbray	*Leicester* - Melton Mowbray
Melton Ross	*Lincoln* - Scunthorpe
Melverley	*Salop* - Oswestry
Melyniogfawr	*Montgomery* - Oswestry
Membury	*Devon* - Axminster and Chard
Membury	*Wilts* - Swindon
Menabilly	*Cornwall* - St. Austell
Menacuddle	*Cornwall* - St. Austell
Menadarva Bridge	*Cornwall* - Redruth
Menagissey	*Cornwall* - Truro
Menai Bridge	*Anglesey* - Bangor
Menai Bridge	*Caernarvon* - Bangor
Mendham	*Norfolk and Suffolk* - Halesworth
Mendlesham	*Suffolk* - Stowmarket
Menethorpe	*York, E.R.* - Malton
Menheniot	*Cornwall* - Liskeard
Menherion	*Cornwall* - Penzance
Menith Wood	*Worcester* - Kidderminster
Menston	*York, W.R.* - Otley
Menthorpe	*York, E.R.* - York
Mentmore	*Bucks* - Bletchley and Leighton Buzzard
Menutton	*Salop* - Ludlow
Meole Brace	*Salop* - Shrewsbury
Meols	*Cheshire* - Birkenhead
Meon, East	*Hants* - Petersfield
Meon Hill	*Warwick* - Stratford on Avon
Meonstoke	*Hants* - Petersfield
Meopham	*Kent* - Gravesend
Mepal	*Cambridge* - Ely
Meppershall	*Beds* - Biggleswade
Mercaston	*Derby* - Derby
Mere	*Cheshire* - Altrincham
Mere	*Wilts* - Shaftesbury
Mere Brow	*Lancaster* - Southport
Mereclough	*Lancaster* - Burnley
Mere Down	*Wilts* - Shaftesbury
Mere Green	*Warwick* - Birmingham
Mere Green	*Worcester* - Bromsgrove
Meretown	*Stafford* - Wellington (Salop)
Merevale	*Leicester and Warwick* - Nuneaton
Mereworth	*Kent* - Maidstone
Meriden	*Warwick* - Coventry
Meriden Heath	*Warwick* - Coventry
Merle Common	*Surrey* - Reigate
Merlin's Bridge	*Pembroke* - Haverfordwest
Merridale	*Stafford* - Wolverhampton
Merridge	*Somerset* - Bridgwater
Merrington	*Durham* - Bishop Auckland
Merrington	*Salop* - Shrewsbury
Merrington Lane	*Durham* - Bishop Auckland
Merriott	*Somerset* - Yeovil
Merrivale Bridge	*Devon* - Plymouth
Merrow	*Surrey* - Guildford
Merry Hill	*Hereford* - Hereford
Merry Hill	*Stafford* - West Bromwich
Merry Hill	*Stafford* - Wolverhampton
Merryknowe	*Northumberland* - Carlisle
Merrymeet	*Cornwall* - Liskeard
Merryshields	*Northumberland* - Hexham
Mersham	*Kent* - Ashford
Merstham	*Surrey* - Reigate

MER - MID

Merstham (Northern)	*Surrey* - Croydon
Merstham, South	*Surrey* - Reigate
Merston	*I. of W.* - Newport (I.W.)
Merston	*Sussex* - Chichester
Merther	*Cornwall* - Truro
Merthyr	*Carmarthen* - Carmarthen
Merthyr Cynog	*Brecon* - Brecknock
Merthyr Dyfan	*Glamorgan* - Barry
Merthyr Mawr	*Glamorgan* - Bridgend
Merthyr Tydfil	*Glamorgan* - Merthyr Tydfil
Merthyr Vale	*Glamorgan* - Merthyr Tydfil
Merton	*Devon* - Bideford
Merton	*Norfolk* - King's Lynn
Merton	*Oxford* - Oxford
Merton (part)	*London, S.W.19* - Croydon
Merton (part)	*London, S.W.19* - Kingston-upon-Thames
Merton Abbey	*London, S.W.19* - Croydon
Merton Park	*London, S.W.19* - Croydon
Meshaw	*Devon* - Barnstaple
Messing	*Essex* - Colchester
Messingham	*Lincoln* - Scunthorpe
Mesty Croft	*Stafford* - Dudley
Metal Bridge	*Durham* - Durham
Metfield	*Suffolk* - Halesworth
Metham	*York, E.R.* - Goole
Metham Grange	*York, E.R.* - Goole
Metherell	*Cornwall* - Plymouth
Metheringham	*Lincoln* - Lincoln
Metheringham Barf	*Lincoln* - Lincoln
Metheringham Fen	*Lincoln* - Lincoln
Metheringham Heath	*Lincoln* - Lincoln
Metheringham Tan Vats	*Lincoln* - Lincoln
Methley	*York, W.R.* - Leeds
Methwold	*Norfolk* - Thetford
Mettingham	*Suffolk* - Lowestoft
Metton	*Norfolk* - Norwich
Mevagissey	*Cornwall* - St. Austell
Mexborough	*York, W.R.* - Rotherham
Meysey Hampton	*Gloucester* - Swindon
Michaelchurch	*Hereford* - Hereford
Michaelchurch-on-Arrow	*Radnor* - Builth Wells
Michaelchurch Escley	*Hereford* - Hereford
Michaelstone-le-Pit	*Glamorgan* - Cardiff
Michaelstone-super-Ely	*Glamorgan* - Cardiff
Michaelstone-y-vedw	*Glamorgan* - Cardiff
Michaelstone-y-vedw	*Monmouth* - Newport (Mon.)
Michaelstow	*Cornwall* - Bideford
Micheldever	*Hants* - Winchester
Michelgrove	*Sussex* - Worthing
Michelmersh	*Hants* - Winchester
Mickfield	*Suffolk* - Stowmarket
Micklebring	*York, W.R.* - Doncaster
Mickleby	*York, N.R.* - Whitby
Micklefield	*York, W.R.* - Pontefract
Micklefield Green	*Herts* - Watford
Mickleham	*Surrey* - Dorking
Micklehurst	*Cheshire* - Ashton-under-Lyne
Mickleover	*Derby* - Derby
Micklethwaite	*Cumberland* - Carlisle
Micklethwaite	*York, W.R.* - Keighley
Micklethwaite	*York, W.R.* - Harrogate
Mickleton	*Gloucester* - Evesham
Mickleton	*York, N.R.* - Bishop Auckland
Mickletown	*York, W.R.* - Leeds
Mickle Trafford	*Cheshire* - Chester
Mickley (Stretton)	*Derby* - Alfreton
Mickley	*Salop* - Market Drayton
Mickley	*Northumberland* - Hexham
Mickley	*York, N.R.* - Harrogate
Middle	*Salop* - Shrewsbury
Middle Assenden	*Oxford* - Reading
Middle Aston	*Oxford* - Banbury
Middle Barton	*Oxford* - Banbury
Middle Bickenhill	*Warwick* - Birmingham
Middle Chinnock	*Somerset* - Yeovil
Middle Claydon	*Bucks* - Aylesbury
Middlecliffe	*York, W.R.* - Barnsley
Middle Coombe	*Wilts* - Shaftesbury
Middle Drove	*Norfolk* - Wisbech

MID

Middle Engine	*Northumberland* - North Shields
Middle Fen	*Cambridge* - Ely
Middleforth Green	*Lancaster* - Preston
Middle Foulshaw	*Westmorland* - Kendal
Middle Green	*Bucks* - Uxbridge
Middleham	*York, N.R.* - Northallerton
Middle Hambleton	*Rutland* - Melton Mowbray
Middle Handley	*Derby* - Chesterfield
Middle Herrington	*Durham* - Sunderland
Middlehill	*Worcester* - Evesham
Middle Hills	*Stafford* - Leek
Middlehope	*Durham* - Bishop Auckland
Middlehope	*Salop* - Ludlow
Middle Hulton	*Lancaster* - Bolton
Middle Lambrook	*Somerset* - Yeovil
Middle Littleton	*Worcester* - Evesham
Middle Llangynwyd	*Glamorgan* - Bridgend
Middle Madeley	*Stafford* - Stoke-on-Trent
Middlemarsh	*Dorset* - Dorchester
Middle Mayfield	*Stafford* - Uttoxeter
Middlemead	*Essex* - Chelmsford
Middlemoor	*Devon* - Plymouth
Middle Pitts	*Radnor* - Knighton
Middleport	*Stafford* - Stoke-on-Trent
Middle Rainton	*Durham* - Durham
Middle Rasen	*Lincoln* - Lincoln
Middlesbrough	*York, N.R.* - Middlesbrough
Middlesceugh	*Cumberland* - Penrith
Middlesex	*Worcester* - Evesham
Middleshaw	*Westmorland* - Kendal
Middlesmoor	*York, W.R.* - Harrogate
Middlestone	*Durham* - Bishop Auckland
Middlestone Moor	*Durham* - Bishop Auckland
Middlestown	*York, W.R.* - Wakefield
Middlethorpe	*York, W.R.* - York
Middleton	*Essex* - Sudbury
Middleton	*Glamorgan* - Swansea
Middleton	*Hereford* - Ludlow
Middleton	*Lancaster* - Oldham
Middleton	*Norfolk* - King's Lynn
Middleton	*Northampton* - Corby
Middleton	*Salop* - Ludlow
Middleton	*Salop* - Oswestry
Middleton (Chirbury)	*Salop* - Welshpool
Middleton	*Suffolk* - Halesworth
Middleton	*Sussex* - Chichester
Middleton	*Warwick* - Tamworth
Middleton	*Westmorland* - Kendal
Middleton	*York, N.R.* - Malton
Middleton	*York, W.R.* - Leeds
Middleton	*York, W.R.* - Otley
Middleton by Wirksworth	*Derby* - Matlock
Middleton-by-Youlgreave	*Derby* - Matlock
Middleton Cheney	*Northampton* - Banbury
Middleton Green	*Stafford* - Uttoxeter
Middleton Hall	*Northumberland* - Alnwick
Middleton in Heysham	*Lancaster* - Lancaster
Middleton-in-Teesdale	*Durham* - Bishop Auckland
Middleton Junction	*Lancaster* - Oldham
Middleton Malzor	*Northampton* - Northampton
Middleton, North	*Northumberland* - Morpeth
Middleton-one-Row	*Durham* - Darlington
Middleton-on-Sea	*Sussex* - Chichester
Middleton-on-the-Hill	*Hereford* - Leominster
Middleton-on-the-Wolds	*York, E.R.* - Beverley
Middleton Place	*Cumberland* - Whitehaven
Middleton Priors	*Salop* - Bridgnorth
Middleton Quernhow	*York, N.R.* - Harrogate
Middleton St. George	*Durham* - Darlington
Middleton Scriven	*Salop* - Bridgnorth
Middleton, South	*Northumberland* - Morpeth
Middleton Stoney	*Oxford* - Oxford
Middleton Tyas	*York, N.R.* - Darlington
Middleton upon Leven	*York, N.R.* - Middlesbrough
Middletown	*Montgomery* - Welshpool
Middle Tysoe	*Warwick* - Banbury
Middle Wallop	*Hants* - Andover
Middle Weald	*Bucks* - Bletchley and Leighton Buzzard
Middlewich	*Cheshire* - Northwich

Middlewood (Poynton)	*Cheshire* - Macclesfield
Middlewood	*Cheshire* - Stockport
Middlewood	*Cornwall* - Launceston
Middlewood	*York, W.R.* - Sheffield
Middle Woodford	*Wilts* - Salisbury
Middleyard	*Gloucester* - Stroud
Middlezoy	*Somerset* - Bridgwater
Middridge	*Durham* - Darlington
Middridge Village	*Durham* - Bishop Auckland
Midford	*Somerset* - Bath
Midge Hall	*Lancaster* - Preston
Midgeholme	*Cumberland* - Carlisle
Midgham	*Berks* - Newbury
Midgham	*Hants* - Salisbury
Midgley	*York, W.R.* - Halifax
Midgley	*York, W.R.* - Wakefield
Midhope Bridge	*York, W.R.* - Sheffield
Midhope Stones	*York, W.R.* - Sheffield
Midhope, Upper	*York, W.R.* - Sheffield
Midhurst	*Sussex* - Chichester
Mid Lavant	*Sussex* - Chichester
Midley	*Kent* - Ashford
Midsomer Norton	*Somerset* - Frome
Midville	*Lincoln* - Boston
Midway, Lower	*Derby* - Burton-upon-Trent
Midway, Upper	*Derby* - Burton-upon-Trent
Milborne Port	*Somerset* - Yeovil
Milborne Stileham	*Dorset* - Dorchester
Milbourne	*Northumberland* - Newcastle upon Tyne
Milbourne	*Wilts* - Malmesbury
Milbourne Grange	*Northumberland* - Newcastle upon Tyne
Milbourne St. Andrew	*Dorset* - Dorchester
Milbourne Wick	*Somerset* - Yeovil
Milburn	*Westmorland* - Penrith
Milburn Grange	*Westmorland* - Penrith
Milbury Heath	*Gloucester* - Thornbury
Milby	*York, N.R.* - Harrogate
Milcombe	*Oxford* - Banbury
Milcote	*Warwick* - Stratford on Avon
Milden	*Suffolk* - Sudbury
Mildenhall	*Suffolk* - Bury St. Edmunds
Mildenhall	*Wilts* - Swindon
Mildenhall Drove	*Cambridge* - Ely
Mile End	*Essex* - Colchester
Mile End	*Cambridge* - Ely
Mileham	*Norfolk* - East Dereham
Mile Oak	*Stafford* - Tamworth
Miles Green	*Stafford* - Stoke-on-Trent
Miles Platting	*Lancaster* - Manchester
Milfield	*Northumberland* - Berwick-upon-Tweed
Milford	*Derby* - Derby
Milford	*Salop* - Shrewsbury
Milford	*Stafford* - Stafford
Milford	*Surrey* - Guildford
Milford Haven	*Pembroke* - Haverfordwest
Milford, North	*York, W.R.* - York
Milford-on-Sea	*Hants* - Lymington
Milford, South	*York, W.R.* - Pontefract
Milkwall	*Gloucester* - Monmouth
Milkwell Burn	*Northumberland* - Newcastle upon Tyne
Milland	*Sussex* - Petersfield
Mill Bank	*York, W.R.* - Halifax
Mill Beach	*Essex* - Maldon
Millbeck	*Cumberland* - Workington
Millbridge	*York, W.R.* - Dewsbury
Millbrook	*Beds* - Bedford
Millbrook	*Cheshire* - Ashton-under-Lyne
Millbrook	*Cornwall* - Plymouth
Millbrook	*Hants* - Southampton
Millcombe	*Devon* - Kingsbridge
Mill Dale	*Stafford* - Leek
Mill End	*Bucks* - Reading
Mill End	*Bucks* - High Wycombe
Mill End	*Herts* - Watford
Millend Reath	*Cornwall* - Liskeard
Millen Neath	*Salop* - Whitchurch

Miller's Dale	*Derby* - Buxton
Millers Green	*Derby* - Matlock
Millfield	*Durham* - Sunderland
Mill Green	*Salop* - Market Drayton
Mill Green	*Essex* - Chelmsford
Mill Green	*Herts* - St. Albans
Mill Green (Pinchbeck)	*Lincoln* - Spalding
Mill Green (Spalding)	*Lincoln* - Spalding
Millhill	*Cumberland* - Carlisle
Millhill	*Devon* - Plymouth
Mill Hill	*London, N.W.7* - Willesden
Mill Holme (New Hutton)	*Westmorland* - Kendal
Millhouse	*Cumberland* - Penrith
Millhouse Green	*York, W.R.* - Barnsley
Millhouses	*York, W.R.* - Barnsley
Millhouses	*York, W.R.* - Sheffield
Millichope	*Salop* - Ludlow
Millington	*Cheshire* - Altrincham
Millington	*York, E.R.* - York
Mill Meece	*Stafford* - Stafford
Millom	*Cumberland* - Whitehaven
Mill Pool Hill	*Warwick* - Birmingham
Mill Quarry	*Devon* - Plymouth
Millstone Hill	*York, W.R.* - Rotherham
Millthorpe	*Derby* - Chesterfield
Millthorpe	*Northampton* - Northampton
Millthrop	*York, W.R.* - Kendal
Milltown	*Cornwall* - Bodmin
Milltown	*Derby* - Chesterfield
Millwall	*London, E.14* - Bow
Millwood	*Lancaster* - Barrow-in-Furness
Milly Bridge	*Berks* - Slough
Milnhay	*Derby* - Ilkeston
Milnrow	*Lancaster* - Rochdale
Milnsbridge	*York, W.R.* - Huddersfield
Milnthorpe	*Westmorland* - Kendal
Milnthorpe	*York, W.R.* - Wakefield
Milson	*Salop* - Ludlow
Milstead	*Kent* - Sittingbourne
Milston	*Wilts* - Salisbury
Milthorpe	*Lincoln* - Sleaford
Milton	*Berks* - Didcot
Milton	*Cambridge* - Cambridge
Milton	*Cumberland* - Carlisle
Milton	*Derby* - Burton-upon-Trent
Milton (Portsmouth)	*Hants* - Portsmouth
Milton	*Notts* - East Retford
Milton	*Oxford* - Banbury
Milton	*Somerset* - Wells
Milton	*Somerset* - Weston Super Mare
Milton (Martock)	*Somerset* - Yeovil
Milton	*Stafford* - Stoke-on-Trent
Milton	*Wilts* - Shaftesbury
Milton Abbas	*Dorset* - Dorchester
Milton Abbott	*Devon* - Plymouth
Milton Bryant	*Beds* - Bletchley and Leighton Buzzard
Milton Clevedon	*Somerset* - Wells
Milton Common	*Oxford* - Thame
Milton Damerell	*Devon* - Bideford
Milton Ernest	*Beds* - Bedford
Milton Green	*Cheshire* - Chester
Milton Heights	*Berks* - Oxford
Milton Hill	*Berks* - Oxford
Milton Keynes	*Bucks* - Bletchley and Leighton Buzzard
Milton Lilbourne	*Wilts* - Swindon
Milton Halsor	*Northampton* - Northampton
Milton next Gravesend	*Kent* - Gravesend
Milton Regis	*Kent* - Sittingbourne
Milton, South	*Devon* - Kingsbridge
Milton Street	*Sussex* - Eastbourne
Milton-under-Wychwood	*Oxford* - Banbury
Milton, West	*Dorset* - Dorchester
Milverton	*Somerset* - Taunton
Milverton	*Warwick* - Warwick
Milverton, Old	*Warwick* - Warwick
Milwich	*Stafford* - Stafford
Milwich Heath	*Stafford* - Stafford

MIL - MOH

Milwr	*Flint* - Holywell
Mimms, North	*Herts* - St. Albans
Mimms, South	*Herts* - Barnet
Minchington	*Dorset* - Dorchester
Minchinhampton	*Gloucester* - Stroud
Mincingfield (Durley)	*Hants* - Southampton
Mindrum	*Northumberland* - Berwick-upon-Tweed
Minehead	*Somerset* - Minehead
Minera	*Denbigh* - Wrexham
Minety	*Wilts* - Malmesbury
Minfford	*Caernarvon* - Bangor
Minffordd	*Merioneth* - Portmadoc
Mingoose	*Cornwall* - Truro
Miningsby	*Lincoln* - Boston
Minions	*Cornwall* - Liskeard
Minninglow	*Derby* - Matlock
Minnis Bay	*Kent* - Margate
Minshull Vernon	*Cheshire* - Crewe
Minskip	*York, W.R.* - Harrogate
Minsmere	*Suffolk* - Halesworth
Minstead	*Hants* - Southampton
Minsted	*Sussex* - Petersfield
Minster	*Cornwall* - Launceston
Minster in Thanet	*Kent* - Ramsgate
Minsterley	*Salop* - Shrewsbury
Minster Lovell	*Oxford* - Witney
Minster	*Kent* - Sheerness
Minsterworth	*Gloucester* - Gloucester
Minterne Magna	*Dorset* - Dorchester
Minterne Parva	*Dorset* - Dorchester
Minting	*Lincoln* - Lincoln
Mintlyn	*Norfolk* - King's Lynn
Minwear	*Pembroke* - Haverfordwest
Minworth	*Warwick* - Birmingham
Mire Lake	*Salop* - Wellington (Salop)
Mirfield	*York, W.R.* - Dewsbury
Mirfield Moor	*York, W.R.* - Dewsbury
Mirkside	*York, N.R.* - Whitby
Misbrooks Green	*Surrey* - Dorking
Miserden	*Gloucester* - Stroud
Miskin	*Glamorgan* - Aberdare
Miskin (Llantrisant)	*Glamorgan* - Pontypridd
Mislingford	*Hants* - Portsmouth
Missenden, Great	*Bucks* - Amersham
Missenden, Little	*Bucks* - Amersham
Misson	*Notts and Lincoln* - Doncaster
Misterton	*Leicester* - Rugby
Misterton	*Notts* - Gainsborough
Misterton	*Somerset* - Yeovil
Mistley	*Essex* - Harwich
Mitcham	*Surrey* - Croydon
Mitcheldean	*Gloucester* - Gloucester
Mitchell	*Cornwall* - Truro
Mitchel Troy	*Monmouth* - Monmouth
Mitford	*Northumberland* - Morpeth
Mithian	*Cornwall* - Truro
Mitton	*Stafford* - Stafford
Mitton	*Worcester* - Cheltenham
Mixbury	*Oxford* - Banbury
Mixenden	*York, W.R.* - Halifax
Mixon	*Stafford* - Leek
Moat Farm Estate	*Stafford* - Dudley
Moat Lane	*Montgomery* - Newtown
Mobberley	*Cheshire* - Altrincham
Mobb's Hill	*Herts* - Hitchin
Moccas	*Hereford* - Hereford
Mochdre	*Denbigh* - Conway
Mochdre	*Montgomery* - Newtown
Mochras	*Merioneth* - Portmadoc
Mockbeggar	*Hants* - Salisbury
Mockerkin	*Cumberland* - Workington
Mocktree	*Hereford* - Ludlow
Modbury	*Devon* - Kingsbridge
Moddershall	*Stafford* - Stafford
Moelfre	*Anglesey* - Llangefni
Moelfre	*Denbigh* - Oswestry
Mogador (Part)	*Surrey* - Reigate
Moggerhanger	*Beds* - Biggleswade
Mohope	*Northumberland* - Hexham

MOI - MON

Moilgrove	*Pembroke* - Cardigan
Moira	*Leicester* - Ashby-de-la-Zouch
Molash	*Kent* - Ashford
Mold	*Flint* - Mold
Moldgreen	*York, W.R.* - Huddersfield
Molehill Green	*Essex* - Bishop's Stortford
Molescroft	*York, E.R.* - Beverley
Molesdon	*Northumberland* - Morpeth
Molesey, East	*Surrey* - Kingston-upon-Thames
Molesey, West	*Surrey* - Kingston-upon-Thames
Moleshaugh	*Northumberland* - Alnwick
Molesworth	*Hunts* - Huntingdon
Molinnis	*Cornwall* - St. Austell
Molland	*Devon* - Barnstaple
Mollandleas	*Kent* - Deal
Mollington	*Cheshire* - Chester
Mollington	*Oxford and Warwick* - Banbury
Molton, North	*Devon* - Barnstaple
Molton, South	*Devon* - Barnstaple
Monaughty	*Radnor* - Knighton
Monaughty Poeth	*Salop* - Knighton
Monewden	*Suffolk* - Woodbridge
Money Bridge	*Lincoln* - Spalding
Money Moor	*Stafford* - Lichfield
Mongeham	*Kent* - Deal
Mongewell	*Oxford* - Didcot
Mongleath	*Cornwall* - Truro
Monington	*Pembroke* - Cardigan
Monk Bretton	*York, W.R.* - Barnsley
Monken Hadley	*Herts* - Barnet
Monk Fryston	*York, W.R.* - Pontefract
Monk Hall	*Salop* - Bridgnorth
Monk Heslesden	*Durham* - Hartlepool
Monkhill	*Cumberland* - Carlisle
Monkhill	*York, W.R.* - Pontefract
Monkhopton	*Salop* - Bridgnorth
Monkland	*Hereford* - Leominster
Monkleigh	*Devon* - Bideford
Monknash	*Glamorgan* - Bridgend
Monkokehampton	*Devon* - Okehampton
Monkridge	*Northumberland* - Morpeth
Monks Common	*Sussex* - Horsham
Monkseaton	*Northumberland* - North Shields
Monks Eleigh	*Suffolk* - Sudbury
Monks Gate	*Sussex* - Horsham
Monks Green	*Herts* - Hertford
Monks Hardwick	*Hunts* - Huntingdon
Monks Heath	*Cheshire* - Macclesfield
Monk Sherborne	*Hants* - Basingstoke
Monk's Horton	*Kent* - Folkestone
Monkshouse	*Northumberland* - Alnwick
Monksilver	*Somerset* - Minehead
Monks Kirby	*Warwick* - Rugby
Monk Soham	*Suffolk* - Ipswich
Monkspath	*Warwick* - Birmingham
Monks Risborough	*Bucks* - High Wycombe
Monksthorpe	*Lincoln* - Skegness
Monkswood	*Herts* - Hitchin
Monkswood	*Monmouth* - Pontypool and Abergavenny
Monkton	*Devon* - Exeter
Monkton	*Dorset* - Dorchester
Monkton	*Durham* - South Shields
Monkton	*Kent* - Ramsgate
Monkton	*Pembroke* - Haverfordwest
Monkton Combe	*Somerset* - Bath
Monkton Deverill	*Somerset* - Warminster
Monkton Farleigh	*Wilts* - Bath
Monkton Heathfield	*Somerset* - Taunton
Monkton Mains	*York, N.R.* - Harrogate
Monkton-up-Wimborne	*Dorset* - Wimborne Minster
Monkton, West	*Somerset* - Taunton
Monkton Wyld	*Dorset* - Axminster and Chard
Monkwearmouth	*Durham* - Sunderland
Monkwood Green	*Worcester* - Worcester
Monkwood Hill	*Dorset* - Dorchester
Monmouth	*Monmouth* - Monmouth
Monmouth Cap	*Hereford* - Hereford
Monnington-upon-Wye	*Hereford* - Hereford
Monsall Dale	*Derby* - Buxton

Montacute	*Somerset* - Yeovil
Montford	*Salop* - Shrewsbury
Montgomery	*Montgomery* - Welshpool
Monton	*Lancaster* - Salford
Montserrat	*Lancaster* - Bolton
Monxton	*Hants* - Andover
Monyash	*Derby* - Buxton
Moons Green	*Kent* - Cranbrook
Moon's Mill	*Lancaster* - Preston
Moons Moat	*Worcester* - Redditch
Moor	*Salop* - Ludlow
Moor	*Worcester* - Evesham
Moorby	*Lincoln* - Boston
Moorby Fen Allotment	*Lincoln* - Boston
Moorclose	*Lancaster* - Oldham
Moor Court	*Hants* - Southampton
Moordown	*Hants* - Bournemouth
Moore	*Cheshire* - Warrington
Moor End	*Cumberland* - Carlisle
Moor End	*Cumberland* - Workington
Moor End	*Northampton* - Northampton
Moor End	*York, W.R.* - Halifax
Moorends	*York, W.R.* - Thorne
Moore's End	*Bucks* - High Wycombe
Moorfield	*Northumberland* - Hexham
Moorgate	*Cornwall* - Camelford
Moor Gorse	*Stafford* - Stafford
Moor Green	*Hants* - Southampton
Moor Green	*Herts* - Hitchin
Moor Green	*Notts* - Nottingham
Moor Green	*Warwick* - Birmingham
Moorhaigh	*Notts* - Mansfield
Moorhampton	*Hereford* - Hereford
Moorhead	*Sussex* - Horsham
Moor Head	*York, W.R.* - Dewsbury
Moor House	*Cumberland* - Workington
Moorhouse	*Durham* - Durham
Moorhouse	*Notts* - Newark
Moorhouse, High	*Cumberland* - Wigton
Moorhouse Low	*Cumberland* - Wigton
Moorhouses	*York, W.R.* - Harrogate
Moorland	*Somerset* - Bridgwater
Moorlinch	*Somerset* - Bridgwater
Moor, Lower	*Worcester* - Evesham
Moor Monkton	*York, E.R.* - York
Moor Park	*Herts* - Watford
Moor Row	*Cumberland* - Whitehaven
Moor Row	*Cumberland* - Carlisle
Moor's End	*Bucks* - Reading
Moorsholm	*York, N.R.* - Middlesbrough
Moorshop	*Devon* - Plymouth
Moorside	*Durham* - Consett
Moorside	*Lancaster* - Oldham
Moorside Hartford Bridge	*Northumberland* - Blyth
Moorslade	*Gloucester* - Thornbury
Moorsley, High	*Durham* - Durham
Moorsley, Low	*Durham* - Durham
Moors, Little	*Lincoln* - Boston
Moorswater	*Cornwall* - Liskeard
Moors, West	*Dorset* - Wimborne Minster
Moor, The	*Kent* - Cranbrook
Moorthorpe	*York, W.R.* - Pontefract
Moorthwaite	*Cumberland* - Carlisle
Moortown	*Devon* - Plymouth
Moortown	*Lincoln* - Scunthorpe
Moortown	*Salop* - Wellington (Salop)
Moor Town	*York, E.R.* - Beverley
Moortown	*York, W.R.* - Leeds
Moor, Upper	*Worcester* - Evesham
Moorwood Hall	*York, W.R.* - Sheffield
Moota	*Cumberland* - Workington
Morborne	*Hunts* - Peterborough
Morchard Bishop	*Devon* - Exeter
Morcombelake	*Dorset* - Axminster and Chard
Morcott	*Rutland* - Stamford
Morda	*Salop* - Oswestry
Morden	*Dorset* - Swanage
Morden	*Surrey* - Croydon
Morden, Lower	*Surrey* - Croydon

Mordiford	*Hereford* - Hereford
Mordon	*Durham* - Stockton on Tees
More	*Salop* - Shrewsbury
Morebath	*Devon* - Tiverton
Morecambe	*Lancaster* - Lancaster
Moredon	*Wilts* - Swindon
Morehall	*Kent* - Folkestone
Morehay Lawn	*Northampton* - Peterborough
Moreleigh	*Devon* - Kingsbridge
Moresby, High	*Cumberland* - Whitehaven
Moresby, Low	*Cumberland* - Whitehaven
Moresby Parks	*Cumberland* - Whitehaven
Morestead	*Hants* - Winchester
Moreton	*Cheshire* - Birkenhead
Moreton	*Cheshire* - Congleton
Moreton	*Dorset* - Dorchester
Moreton	*Essex* - Harlow
Moreton	*Hereford* - Leominster
Moreton	*Oxford* - Thame
Moreton	*Stafford* - Stafford
Moreton Corbet	*Salop* - Shrewsbury
Moreton Hampstead	*Devon* - Newton Abbot
Moreton-in-Marsh	*Gloucester* - Evesham
Moreton Jeffries	*Hereford* - Hereford
Moreton Morrell	*Warwick* - Stratford on Avon
Moreton North	*Berks* - Didcot
Moreton-on-Lugg	*Hereford* - Hereford
Moreton Pinkney	*Northampton* - Banbury
Moreton Say	*Salop* - Market Drayton
Moreton South	*Berks* - Didcot
Moreton Valence	*Gloucester* - Gloucester
Moreton Wood (part)	*Salop* - Market Drayton
Moreton Wood (part)	*Salop* - Whitchurch
Morewood Moor	*Derby* - Alfreton
Morfa Bychan	*Caernarvon* - Portmadoc
Morfa Nevin	*Caernarvon* - Portmadoc
Morfe	*Salop* - Bridgnorth
Morfodion	*Montgomery* - Newtown
Morgans Green	*Sussex* - Horsham
Morganstown	*Glamorgan* - Cardiff
Morgans Vale	*Wilts* - Salisbury
Moriah	*Cardigan* - Aberystwyth
Morice Town	*Devon* - Plymouth
Morland	*Westmorland* - Penrith
Morley	*Cheshire* - Macclesfield
Morley	*Derby* - Ilkeston
Morley	*Durham* - Bishop Auckland
Morley	*York, W.R.* - Dewsbury
Morley Green	*Cheshire* - Macclesfield
Morley Ponds	*Herts* - Hertford
Morley St. Botolph	*Norfolk* - Norwich
Morley St. Michael	*Norfolk* - Norwich
Morley St. Peter	*Norfolk* - Norwich
Mornick	*Cornwall* - Liskeard
Morningthorpe	*Norfolk* - Norwich
Morpeth	*Northumberland* - Morpeth
Morpeth Castle	*Northumberland* - Morpeth
Morrey	*Stafford* - Lichfield
Morrey, The	*Salop* - Market Drayton
Morrick	*York, W.R.* - Leeds
Morrillow Heath	*Stafford* - Uttoxeter
Morris Green	*Lancaster* - Bolton
Morriston	*Glamorgan* - Swansea
Morse Lane (part)	*Gloucester* - Gloucester
Morse Lane (part)	*Gloucester* - Ross
Morston	*Norfolk* - Norwich
Morte Hoe	*Devon* - Barnstaple
Mortgrove	*Herts* - Hitchin
Morthen	*York, W.R.* - Rotherham
Mortimer	*Berks* - Reading
Mortimer Common	*Berks* - Reading
Mortimer's Cross	*Hereford* - Leominster
Mortimer West End	*Hants* - Basingstoke
Mortlake	*London, S.W.14* - Wandsworth
Mortomley	*York, W.R.* - Sheffield
Morton	*Cumberland* - Carlisle
Morton	*Derby* - Alfreton
Morton	*Gloucester* - Thornbury
Morton	*Lincoln* - Spalding
Morton	*Lincoln* - Gainsborough

MOR - MOU

Morton	*Notts* - East Retford
Morton	*Notts* - Newark
Morton	*Salop* - Oswestry
Morton Baggot	*Warwick* - Redditch
Morton Carr	*York, N.R.* - Middlesbrough
Morton, East	*York, W.R.* - Keighley
Morton Fen	*Lincoln* - Spalding
Morton Grange	*Durham* - Durham
Morton on the Hill	*Norfolk* - Norwich
Morton Palms	*Durham* - Darlington
Morton Rinmouth	*Durham* - Bishop Auckland
Morton-under-Hill	*Worcester* - Redditch
Morton-upon-Swale	*York, N.R.* - Northallerton
Morton, West	*York, W.R.* - Keighley
Morvah	*Cornwall* - Penzance
Morval	*Cornwall* - Liskeard
Morvil	*Pembroke* - Haverfordwest
Morville	*Salop* - Bridgnorth
Morville Heath	*Salop* - Bridgnorth
Morwelham	*Devon* - Plymouth
Morwenstow	*Cornwall* - Bideford
Morwick	*Northumberland* - Alnwick
Mosborough	*Derby* - Sheffield
Moscow (Alston)	*Cumberland* - Carlisle
Mose	*Salop* - Bridgnorth
Mosedale	*Cumberland* - Penrith
Moseley	*Stafford* - Wolverhampton
Moseley	*Warwick* - Birmingham
Moseley Village	*Stafford* - Wolverhampton
Moseley Wake Green	*Warwick* - Birmingham
Moses Gate	*Lancaster* - Bolton
Mosley Common	*Lancaster* - Leigh
Mosley Well	*Salop* - Whitchurch
Moss	*York, W.R.* - Doncaster
Mossband	*Cumberland* - Carlisle
Moss Bank	*Lancaster* - St. Helens
Mosser	*Cumberland* - Workington
Mossey Green	*Salop* - Wellington (Salop)
Mosside	*Cumberland* - Carlisle
Mosside	*Stafford* - Leek
Moss Lea	*Stafford* - Leek
Mossley	*Cheshire* - Congleton
Mossley	*Lancaster* - Ashton-under-Lyne
Mossley	*Stafford* - Stafford
Mossley Hill	*Lancaster* - Liverpool
Moss Nook	*Lancaster* - Manchester
Moss Nook	*Lancaster* - St. Helens
Moss Pit	*Stafford* - Stafford
Moss Side	*Cheshire* - Warrington
Moss Side	*Lancaster* - Blackpool
Moss Side (Risley)	*Lancaster* - Leigh
Moss Side	*Lancaster* - Manchester
Mossy Lee	*Lancaster* - Wigan
Mossywalls	*Northumberland* - Haltwhistle
Mosterton	*Dorset* - Yeovil
Moston	*Cheshire* - Chester
Moston	*Cheshire* - Crewe
Moston	*Lancaster* - Manchester
Moston	*Salop* - Shrewsbury
Mostyn	*Flint* - Holywell
Motcombe	*Dorset* - Shaftesbury
Mothecombe	*Devon* - Kingsbridge
Motherby	*Cumberland* - Penrith
Mottingham (part)	*London, S.E.9* - Bromley
Mottingham (part)	*London, S.E.9* - Woolwich
Mottisfont	*Hants* - Southampton
Mottistone	*I. of W.* - Newport (I.W.)
Mottram in Longdendale	*Cheshire* - Hyde
Mottram St. Andrew	*Cheshire* - Macclesfield
Motts Green	*Essex* - Bishop's Stortford
Mouldsworth	*Cheshire* - Chester
Moulsecoomb	*Sussex* - Brighton
Moulsford	*Berks* - Didcot
Moulsoe	*Bucks* - Bletchley and .. Leighton Buzzard
Moulton	*Cambridge* - Newmarket
Moulton	*Cheshire* - Northwich
Moulton	*Glamorgan* - Barry
Moulton	*Lincoln* - Spalding
Moulton	*Norfolk* - Norwich

MOU - MUL

Moulton	*Northampton* - Northampton
Moulton	*York, N.R.* - Darlington
Moulton Austendyke	*Lincoln* - Spalding
Moulton Chapel	*Lincoln* - Spalding
Moulton Euagate	*Lincoln* - Spalding
Moulton Marsh	*Lincoln* - Spalding
Moulton Park	*Northampton* - Northampton
Moulton Saint Michael	*Norfolk* - Norwich
Moulton Seas End	*Lincoln* - Spalding
Moulton West Fen	*Lincoln* - Spalding
Mount	*Cardigan* - Cardigan
Mount	*Cornwall* -Bodmin
Mountain (part)	*York, W.R.* - Bradford
Mountain (part)	*York, W.R.* - Halifax
Mountain Ash	*Glamorgan* - Aberdare
Mountain Hare	*Glamorgan* - Merthyr Tydfil
Mount Ambrose	*Cornwall* - Redruth
Mount Batten	*Devon* - Plymouth
Mount Bures	*Essex* - Sudbury
Mount Charles	*Cornwall* - St. Austell
Mountfield	*Sussex* - Hastings
Mount Hawke	*Cornwall* - Turro
Mount Healey	*Northumberland* - Morpeth
Mount Hill	*Gloucester* - Bristol
Mountnessing	*Essex* - Brentwood
Mounton	*Pembroke* - Haverdordwest
Mount Pleasant	*Cornwall* - Plymouth
Mount Pleasant	*Derby* - Burton-upon-Trent
Mount Pleasant	*Durham* - Bishop Auckland
Mount Pleasant	*Glamorgan* - Merthyr Tydfil
Mount Pleasant	*Northumberland* - Hexham
Mount Pleasant	*York, W.R.* - Dewsbury
Mounts	*Devon* - Kingsbridge
Mountsett	*Durham* - Consett
Mountsorrel	*Leicester* - Loughborough
Mount Tabor	*York, W.R.* - Halifax
Mousehole	*Cornwall* - Penzance
Mouse Sweet	*Worcester* - Dudley
Mousley End	*Warwick* - Warwick
Mow Acre Hill	*Leicester* - Leicester
Mow Cop	*Cheshire* - Congleton
Mow Cop	*Stafford* - Stoke-on-Trent
Mowsley	*Leicester* - Leicester
Mowthorpe	*York, E.R.* - Malton
Moxby	*York, N.R.* - York
Moxhull	*Warwick* - Birmingham
Moxley	*Stafford* - Walsall
Moyles Court	*Hants* - Salisbury
Moylgrove	*Pembroke* - Cardigan
Mucclestone	*Stafford* - Market Drayton
Much Birch	*Hereford* - Hereford
Much Cowarne	*Hereford* - Hereford
Much Dewchurch	*Hereford* - Hereford
Muchelney	*Somerset* - Taunton
Much Fawley	*Hereford* - Ross
Much Hadham	*Herts* - Bishop's Stortford
Much Hoole	*Lancaster* - Preston
Much Marcle	*Heregotf* - Hereford
Much Wenlock	*Salop* - Bridgnorth
Much Woolton	*Lancaster* - Liverpool
Mucking	*Essex* - Grays Thurrock
Muckleford	*Dorset* - Dorchester
Muckleton	*Norfolk* - King's Lynn
Muckleton	*Salop* - Shrewsbury
Muckley Corner	*Stafford* - Lichfield
Muckley Cross	*Salop* - Bridgnorth
Muckram	*Derby* - Alfreton
Muckton	*Lincoln* - Louth
Muckwell	*Devon* - Kingsbridge
Muddiford	*Devon* - Barnstaple
Muddles Green	*Sussex* - Eastbourne
Muddles Wood	*Sussex* - Haywards Heath
Mudeford	*Hants* - Bournemouth
Mudford	*Somerset* - Yeovil
Mudgeley	*Somerset* - Wells
Muggington	*Derby* - Derby
Muggleswick	*Durham* - Consett
Muker	*York, N.R.* - Darlington
Mulbarton	*Norfolk* - Norwich
Mulfra	*Cornwall* - Penzance

Mullin's Pond	*Hants* - Andover
Mullion	*Cornwall* - Penzance
Mulwith	*York, W.R.* - Harrogate
Mumbles	*Glamorgan* - Swansea
Mumbleys	*Gloucester* - Thornbury
Mumby	*Lincoln* - Skegness
Mumps	*Lancaster* - Oldham
Mumps Hall	*Cumberland* - Carlisle
Muncaster	*Cumberland* - Whitehaven
Munden, Great	*Herts* - Hertford
Munden, Little	*Herts* - Hertford
Mundesley	*Norfolk* - Norwich
Mundford	*Norfolk* - Thetford
Mundham	*Norfolk* - Norwich
Mundham	*Sussex* - Chichester
Mundon	*Essex* - Maldon
Mundon Hill	*Essex* - Maldon
Mungrisedale	*Cumberland* - Penrith
Munsley	*Hereford* - Hereford
Munslow	*Salop* - Ludlow
Munslow Aston	*Salop* - Ludlow
Muntham	*Sussex* - Horsham
Murcott	*Northampton* - Northampton
Murcott	*Oxford* - Oxford
Murcott	*Worcester* - Evesham
Murhill	*Wilts* - Trowbridge
Murrah	*Cumberland* - Penrith
Murrell Green	*Hants* - Basingstoke
Murrells End	*Gloucester* - Gloucester
Murrow	*Cambridge* - Wisbech
Mursley	*Bucks* - Bletchley and Leighton Buzzard
Murton	*Durham* - Sunderland
Murton	*Glamorgan* - Swansea
Murton	*Westmorland* - Penrith
Murton	*York, W.R.* - York
Murton Colliery	*Durham* - Sunderland
Murton, East	*Durham* - Sunderland
Murton Grange	*Durham* - Durham
Murton Moor	*Durham* - Sunderland
Murton Row	*Northumberland* - North Shields
Murton Village	*Northumberland* - North Shields
Murtry	*Somerset* - Frome
Musbury (Axminster)	*Devon* - Axminster and Chard
Muscliffe	*Hants* - Bournemouth
Muscott	*Northampton* - Northampton
Mushroom Castle	*Berks* - Slough
Mushroom Green	*Stafford* - Dudley
Muskham, North	*Notts* - Newark
Muskham, South	*Notts* - Newark
Muston	*Dorset* - Dorchester
Muston	*Leicester* - Grantham
Muston	*York, E.R.* - Scarborough
Mustow Green	*Worcester* - Kidderminster
Muswell Hill (part)	*London, N.10* - Barnet
Muswell Hill (part)	*London, N.10* - Clerkenwell
Mutford	*Suffolk* - Lowestoft
Mutley	*Devon* - Plymouth
Mutterton	*Devon* - Tiverton
Muxton	*Salop* - Wellington (Salop)
Myddfai	*Carmarthen* - Llandovery
Myddle	*Shropshire* - Shrewsbury
Mydrim	*Carmarthen* - Carmarthen
Mydroilyn	*Cardigan* - Aberystwyth
Myerscough	*Lancaster* - Preston
Mylor	*Cornwall* - Truro
Mylor Bridge	*Cornwall* - Truro
Mylor Church Town	*Cornwall* - Truro
Mynachdy	*Glamorgan* - Cardiff
Mynachlogddu	*Pembroke* - Haverfordwest
Mynde	*Salop* - Knighton
Myndtown	*Salop* - Shrewsbury
Mynnydd Bodafon	*Anglesey* - Llangefni
Mynyddbach	*Monmouth* - Chepstow
Mynyddbach	*Glamorgan* - Swansea
Mynyddgarngoch	*Glamorgan* - Swansea
Mynyddgarnlwyd	*Glamorgan* - Swansea
Mynydd Isa	*Flint* - Mold
Mynyddislwyn (part)	*Monmouth* - Blackwood
Mynydd Nevin	*Caernarvon* - Portmadoc

Mynyddgarreg	*Carmarthen* - Llanelli
Mynydd Sylen	*Carmarthen* - Llanelli
Mynyddyruthin	*Glamorgan* - Bridgend
Mynytho	*Caernarvon* - Portmadoc
Myrtlegrove	*Sussex* - Worthing
Mytchett	*Surrey* - Aldershot and Farnham
Mythe	*Gloucester* - Cheltenham
Mythe Hook	*Gloucester* - Cheltenham
Mytholm	*York, W.R.* - Todmorden
Mytholmroyd	*York, W.R.* - Todmorden
Mythop	*Lancaster* - Blackpool
Myton	*Warwick* - Warwick
Myton-upon-Swale	*York, N.R.* - York
Mytton	*Salop* - Shrewsbury

N

Nabb	*Salop* - Wellington (Salop)
Nab's Head	*Lancaster* - Preston
Naburn	*York, E.R.* - York
Nackington	*Kent* - Canterbury
Nacton	*Suffolk* - Ipswich
Nadderwater	*Devon* - Exeter
Naddle	*Cumberland* - Workington
Nafferton	*Northumberland* - Hexham
Nafferton	*York, E.R.* - Bridlington
Nagden	*Kent* - Canterbury
Nailbridge	*Gloucester* - Gloucester
Nailsbourne	*Somerset* - Taunton
Nailsea	*Somerset* - Bristol
Nailstone	*Leicester* - Ashby-de-la-Zouch
Nailsworth	*Gloucester* - Stroud
Nailwell	*Somerset* - Bath
Nancegollan	*Cornwall* - Penzance
Nancekuke	*Cornwall* - Redruth
Nancledra	*Cornwall* - Penzance
Nangreaves	*Lancaster* - Bury
Nannerch	*Flint* - Holywell
Nanpantan	*Leicester* - Loughborough
Nanpean	*Cornwall* - St. Austell
Nansladron	*Cornwall* - St. Austell
Nanstallon	*Cornwall* - Bodmin
Nant Bersham	*Denbigh* - Wrexham
Nantbwich-Yrhaiarn	*Caernarvon* - Conway
Nantclwyd	*Denbigh* - Denbigh
Nantcwnlle	*Cardigan* - Lampeter
Nantgaredig	*Carmarthen* - Carmarthen
Nantgarw	*Glamorgan* - Caerphilly
Nantglyn	*Denbigh* - Denbigh
Nantgwrtheyrn	*Caernarvon* - Portmadoc
Nantgwynant	*Merioneth* - Portmadoc
Nantlle	*Caernarvon* - Caernarvon
Nantmel	*Radnor* - Llandrindod Wells
Nantmor	*Caernarvon* - Portmadoc
Nantwich	*Cheshire* - Crewe
Nantbwch	*Monmouth* - Blackwood
Nantycaws	*Carmarthen* - Carmarthen
Nantycymdy	*Montgomery* - Oswestry
Nantyderry	*Monmouth* - Pontypool and Abergavenny
Nantyffrith	*Flint* - Wrexham
Nantyffyllon	*Glamorgan* - Bridgend
Nantyfin	*Glamorgan* - Merthyr Tydfil
Nantyglo	*Monmouth* - Blackwood
Nantygroes	*Radnor* - Knighton
Nantygwreiddyn	*Brecon* - Brecknock
Nantymeichiaid	*Montgomery* - Oswestry
Nantymoel	*Glamorgan* - Bridgend
Nantyr	*Denbigh* - Oswestry
Nant yrhiw	*Denbigh* - Conway
Naphill Common	*Bucks* - High Wycombe
Napley	*Stafford* - Market Drayton
Nappa	*York, W.R.* - Skipton
Napsbury	*Herts* - St. Albans
Napton	*Warwick* - Warwick
Narberth	*Pembroke* - Haverfordwest
Narberth, North	*Pembroke* - Haverfordwest

Narberth, South	*Pembroke* - Haverfordwest
Narborough	*Leicester* - Leicester
Narborough	*Norfolk* - King's Lynn
Narford	*Norfolk* - King's Lynn
Narrowdale	*Stafford* - Buxton
Narth, The	*Monmouth* - Monmouth
Naseby	*Northampton* - Northampton
Nash	*Bucks* - Bletchley and Leighton Buzzard
Nash	*Glamorgan* - Bridgend
Nash	*Hereford* - Leominster
Nash	*Kent* - Deal
Nash	*Monmouth* - Newport (Mon.)
Nash	*Pembroke* - Haverfordwest
Nash	*Salop* - Ludlow
Nashdon	*Bucks* - Slough
Nash End	*Worcester* - Kidderminster
Nash Lee	*Bucks* - Aylesbury
Nashmills	*Herts* - Watford
Nassington	*Northampton* - Peterborough
Nastend	*Gloucester* - Stroud
Nast Hyde	*Herts* - St. Albans
Nasty	*Herts* - Hertford
Nateby	*Lancaster* - Preston
Nateby	*Westmorland* - Penrith
Nately Scures	*Hants* - Basingstoke
Natland	*Westmorland* - Kendal
Natton	*Gloucester* - Cheltenham
Nattrass	*Cumberland* - Carlisle
Naughton	*Suffolk* - Stowmarket
Naunton	*Gloucester* - Cheltenham
Naunton	*Worcester* - Cheltenham
Naunton Beauchamp	*Worcester* - Evesham
Navenby	*Lincoln* - Lincoln
Navestock	*Essex* - Brentwood
Navestock Heath	*Essex* - Brentwood
Naworth	*Cumberland* - Carlisle
Naworth Castle	*Cumberland* - Carlisle
Nawton	*York, N.R.* - Malton
Nayland	*Suffolk* - Colchester
Nazareth	*Caernarvon* - Caernarvon
Nazeing	*Essex* - Harlow
Nazeing Bury	*Essex* - Harlow
Nazeing Gate	*Essex* - Harlow
Nea	*Hants* - Salisbury
Neach Hill	*Salop* - Wolverhampton
Neachills	*Stafford* - Wolverhampton
Neachley	*Salop* - Wolverhampton
Neacroft	*Hants* - Bournemouth
Neal House	*Cumberland* - Carlisle
Near Coton	*Leicester* - Hinckley
Neasden	*London, N.W.10* - Willesden
Neasham	*Durham* - Darlington
Neath	*Glamorgan* - Neath
Neath Abbey	*Glamorgan* - Neath
Neatishead	*Norfolk* - Norwich
Nebo	*Cardigan* - Aberystwyth
Nebo	*Denbigh* - Conway
Nebo Llanllyfni	*Caernarvon* - Caernarvon
Nechells	*Warwick* - Birmingham
Necton	*Norfolk* - King's Lynn
Nedderton	*Northumberland* - Morpeth
Nedderton Village	*Northumberland* - Blyth
Nedging	*Suffolk* - Stowmarket
Needham	*Norfolk* - Norwich
Needham, High	*Derby* - Buxton
Needham Market	*Suffolk* - Stowmarket
Needham Street	*Suffolk* - Newmarket
Neddingworth	*Hunts* - Huntingdon
Needwood	*Stafford* - Burton-upon-Trent
Neen Savage	*Salop* - Kidderminster
Neen Sollars	*Salop* - Kidderminster
Neenton	*Salop* - Bridgnorth
Neepsend	*York, W.R.* - Sheffield
Neighbour Moor	*Durham* - Bishop Auckland
Nelson	*Glamorgan* - Caerphilly
Nelson	*Lancaster* - Nelson
Nelson Green	*Gloucester* - Gloucester
Nempnett Thrubwell	*Somerset* - Bristol
Nenthall	*Cumberland* - Carlisle

Nenthead	*Cumberland* - Carlisle
Nentsbury	*Cumberland* - Carlisle
Nepgill	*Cumberland* - Workington
Nerquis	*Flint* - Mold
Nesbitt	*Northumberland* - Newcastle upon Tyne
Nesfield-with-Langbar	*York, W.R.* - Otley
Neslam Bridge	*Lincoln* - Spalding
Ness	*Cheshire* - Birkenhead
Nesscliffe	*Salop* - Shrewsbury
Ness, Great	*Salop* - Shrewsbury
Ness, Little	*Salop* - Shrewsbury
Neston	*Cheshire* - Birkenhead
Neston, Little	*Cheshire* - Birkenhead
Neswick	*York, E.R.* - Beverley
Netchwood	*Salop* - Bridgnorth
Nether Alderley	*Cheshire* - Macclesfield
Netheravon	*Wilts* - Salisbury
Nether Broughton	*Leicester* - Melton Mowbray
Nether Burrows	*Derby* - Derby
Netherbury	*Dorset* - Dorchester
Netherby	*Cumberland* - Carlisle
Netherby	*York, W.R.* - Harrogate
Nether Cerne	*Dorset* - Dorchester
Nether Compton	*Dorset* - Yeovil
Nethercote	*Northampton* - Banbury
Nethercote	*Warwick* - Rugby
Nethercote	*Warwick* - Stratford-on-Avon
Nethercott	*Oxford* - Oxford
Nethercott	*Oxford* - Thame
Nether Edge	*York, W.R.* - Sheffield
Netherend	*Worcester* - Stourbridge
Netherexe	*Devon* - Exeter
Nether Felling	*Durham* - Gateshead
Netherfield	*Notts* - Nottingham
Netherfield	*Sussex* - Hastings
Nethergate	*Lincoln* - Gainsborough
Nether Green	*Derby* - Chesterfield
Nether Green	*York, W.R.* - Sheffield
Nether Hallam	*York, W.R.* - Sheffield
Netherhampton	*Wilts* - Salisbury
Nether Handley	*Derby* - Chesterfield
Nether Heage	*Derby* - Alfreton
Nether Heyford	*Northampton* - Northampton
Nether Kellet	*Lancaster* - Lancaster
Netherland Green	*Stafford* - Uttoxeter
Nether Langwith	*Notts* - Worksop
Netherley (part)	*Lancaster* - St. Helens
Nethermore	*Wilts* - Chippenham
Netheroyd Hill	*York, W.R.* - Huddersfield
Nether Padley	*Derby* - Chesterfield
Nether Peover	*Chester* - Northwich
Nether Poppleton	*York, W.R.* - York
Nether Quarter Hartington	*Derby* - Buxton
Nether Row	*Cumberland* - Carlisle
Netheroyd Hill	*York, W.R.* - Huddersfield
Netherscales	*Cumberland* - Workington
Netherseal	*Derby* - Ashby-de-la-Zouch
Nether Stowey	*Somerset* - Bridgwater
Nether Street	*Herts* - Hertford
Netherstreet	*Wilts* - Devizes
Netherthong	*York, W.R.* - Huddersfield
Netherthorpe	*Derby* - Chesterfield
Netherthorpe	*York, W.R.* - Worksop
Nether Thurvaston	*Derby* - Derby
Netherton	*Berks* - Oxford
Netherton	*Cheshire* - Runcorn
Netherton	*Cumberland* - Workington
Netherton	*Hants* - Andover
Netherton	*Hereford* - Hereford
Netherton	*Lancaster* - Liverpool
Netherton	*Somerset* - Yeovil
Netherton	*Worcester* - Dudley
Netherton (Elmley Castle)	*Worcester* - Evesham
Netherton	*York, W.R.* - Huddersfield
Netherton	*York, W.R.* - Wakefield
Netherton Colliery	*Northumberland* - Blyth
Netherton North Side	*Northumberland* - Morpeth

Netherton South Side	*Northumberland* - Morpeth
Nethertown	*Cumberland* - Whitehaven
Nethertown	*Stafford* - Lichfield
Nether Wallop	*Hants* - Andover
Nether Wasdale	*Cumberland* - Whitehaven
Nether Welton	*Cumberland* - Carlisle
Nether Whitacre	*Warwick* - Birmingham
Nether Winchendon	*Bucks* - Aylesbury
Netherwitton	*Northumberland* - Morpeth
Nether Worton	*Oxford* - Banbury
Nether Wyresdale	*Lancaster* - Lancaster
Netley	*Hants* - Southampton
Netley	*Salop* - Shrewsbury
Netley Marsh	*Hants* - Southampton
Nettlebed	*Oxford* - Reading
Nettlebridge	*Somerset* - Wells
Nettlecombe	*Somerset* - Minehead
Nettleden with Potten End	*Herts* - Hemel Hempstead
Nettledon	*Herts* - Hemel Hempstead
Nettleham	*Lincoln* - Lincoln
Nettlestead	*Kent* - Maidstone
Nettlestead	*Suffolk* - Ipswich
Nettlestone	*I. of W.* - Newport (I.W.)
Nettlesworth	*Durham* - Durham
Nettleton	*Gloucester* - Cheltenham
Nettleton	*Lincoln* - Scunthorpe
Nettleton	*Wilts* - Chippenham
Nettleworth	*Notts* - Mansfield
Netton	*Wilts* - Salisbury
Nevern	*Pembroke* - Cardigan
Neville's Cross	*Durham* - Durham
Nevill Holt	*Leicester* - Kettering
Nevin	*Caernarvon* - Portmadoc
New Addington	*Surrey* - Croydon
Newall with Clifton	*York, W.R.* - Otley
New Alresford	*Hants* - Winchester
New Annesley	*Notts* - Mansfield
New Apley	*Lincoln* - Lincoln
Newark	*Notts* - Newark
New Arley	*Warwick* - Nuneaton
New Ash Green	*Kent* - Dartford
Newball	*Lincoln* - Lincoln
New Bampton	*Cumberland* - Carlisle
New Barnet	*Herts* - Barnet
Newbarn, Longfield (part)	*Kent* - Dartford
New Beckenham	*Kent* - Bromley
Newberry Side	*Cumberland* - Haltwhistle
New Bewick	*Northumberland* - Alnwick
Newbigg	*Lincoln* - Gainsborough
Newbiggin	*Cumberland* - Carlisle
Newbiggin (Croglin)	*Cumberland* - Penrith
Newbiggin (Dacre)	*Cumberland* - Penrith
Newbiggin	*Durham* - Bishop Auckland
Newbiggin	*Durham* - Durham
Newbiggin	*Lancaster* - Barrow-in-Furness
Newbiggin	*Northumberland* - Berwick-upon-Tweed
Newbiggin (Castle Ward)	*Northumberland* - Newcastle upon Tyne
Newbiggin (Ravenstonedale)	*Westmorland* - Penrith
Newbiggin (Temple Sowerby)	*Westmorland* - Penrith
Newbiggin	*Westmorland* - Kendal
Newbiggin	*York, N.R.* - Whitby
Newbiggin-by-the-Sea	*Northumberland* - Morpeth
Newbiggin Hall	*Northumberland* - Newcastle upon Tyne
New Bilsthorpe	*Notts* - Mansfield
New Bilton	*Warwick* - Rugby
Newbold	*Derby* - Chesterfield
Newbold	*Lancaster* - Rochdale
Newbold	*Leicester* - Ashby-de-la-Zouch
Newbold	*Lincoln* - Lincoln
Newbold Astbury	*Cheshire* - Congleton
Newbold Grounds	*Northampton* - Rugby
Newbold Moor	*Derby* - Chesterfield
Newbold on Stour	*Warwick* - Stratford on Avon
Newbold Pacey	*Warwick* - Stratford on Avon

Newbold Revel	*Warwick* - Rugby
Newbold Saucery	*Leicester* - Melton Mowbray
Newbold-upon-Avon	*Warwick* - Rugby
Newbold Verdon	*Leicester* - Leicester
New Bolingbroke	*Lincoln* - Boston
Newborough	*Anglesey* - Llangefni
Newborough	*Northampton* - Peterborough
Newborough	*Stafford* - Uttoxeter
Newbottle	*Durham* - Durham
Newbottle	*Northants* - Banbury
Newbottle Lane	*Durham* - Durham
Newbourne	*Suffolk* - Ipswich
New Bradwell	*Bucks* - Bletchley and Leighton Buzzard
New Brancepeth	*Durham* - Durham
Newbridge	*Berks* - Oxford
Newbridge	*Berks* - Witney
Newbridge	*Cornwall* - Penzance
Newbridge	*Denbigh* - Wrexham
Newbridge	*Hants* - Southampton
Newbridge	*I. of W.* - Newport (I.W.)
Newbridge	*Monmouth* - Blackwood
Newbridge	*Stafford* - Wolverhampton
Newbridge	*Sussex* - Horsham
New Bridge Cowick	*York, W.R.* - Goole
New Bridge Estate	*Warwick* - Birmingham
Newbridge-on-Wye	*Radnor* - Llandrindod Wells
New Brighton	*Cheshire* - Birkenhead
New Brighton	*Flint* - Mold
New Brighton	*Hants* - Portsmouth
New Brighton	*York, W.R.* - Bradford
New Brimington	*Derby* - Chesterfield
New Brookend	*Gloucester* - Stroud
Newbrough	*Northumberland* - Hexham
New Broughton	*Denbigh* - Wrexham
New Brumby	*Lincoln* - Scunthorpe
New Buckenham	*Norfolk* - Norwich
New Buildings (Sandford)	*Devon* - Exeter
New Buildings	*Sussex* - Horsham
Newburgh	*Lancaster* - Wigan
Newburgh	*York, N.R.* - York
Newburgh Colliery	*Northumberland* - Alnwick
Newburn	*Northumberland* - Newcastle upon Tyne
Newbury	*Berks* - Newbury
New Bury	*Lancaster* - Bolton
Newbury	*Somerset* - Frome
Newbury Park	*Essex* - Ilford
Newby	*Cumberland* - Carlisle
Newby	*Westmorland* - Penrith
Newby	*York, N.R.* - Scarborough
Newby	*York, N.R.* - Middlesbrough
Newby	*York, W.R.* - Skipton
Newby Bridge	*Lancaster* - Barrow in Furness
Newby Buildings	*Cumberland* - Workington
Newby Cote	*York, W.R.* - Skipton
Newby Cross	*Cumberland* - Carlisle
Newby, West	*Cumberland* - Carlisle
Newby Wiske	*York, N.R.* - Northallerton
Newby with Mulwith	*York, W.R.* - Harrogate
New Cassop	*Durham* - Durham
Newcastle	*Monmouth* - Monmouth
Newcastle	*Salop* - Ludlow
Newcastle Emlyn	*Carmarthen* - Cardigan
Newcastle, Higher	*Glamorgan* - Bridgend
Newcastle, Little	*Pembroke* - Haverfordwest
Newcastle, Lower	*Glamorgan* - Bridgend
Newcastle under Lyme	*Stafford* - Stoke-on-Trent
Newcastle upon Tyne	*Northumberland* - Newcastle upon Tyne
New Catton	*Norfolk* - Norwich
Newchapel	*Pembroke* - Cardigan
Newchapel	*Stafford* - Stoke-on-Trent
Newchapel	*Surrey* - Reigate
Newchurch	*Carmarthen* - Carmarthen
Newchurch	*I. of W.* - Newport (I.W.)
Newchurch	*Kent* - Ashford
Newchurch	*Lancaster* - Leigh

Place	County - Post Town
Newchurch	*Radnor* - Builth Wells
Newchurch, East	*Monmouth* - Chepstow
New Church Farm	*Lancaster* - Wigan
Newchurch-in-Pendle	*Lancaster* - Nelson
Newchurch-in-Rossendale	*Lancaster* - Rawtenstall
Newchurch, West	*Monmouth* - Chepstow
New Cooper	*Cumberland* - Carlisle
New Cornforth	*Durham* - Durham
New Coundon	*Durham* - Bishop Auckland
New Crofton	*York, W.R.* - Wakefield
New Cross	*Cardigan* - Aberystwyth
New Cross (part)	*London, S.E.14* - Lambeth
New Cross (part)	*London, S.E.14* - Southwark
New Dale	*Salop* : Wellington (Salop)
New Delaval	*Northumberland* - Blyth
Newdigate	*Surrey* - Dorking
New Durham	*Durham* - Durham
New Duston	*Northampton* - Northampton
New Earswick	*York, N.R.* - York
Newells	*Sussex* - Horsham
New Eltham (part)	*London, S.E.9* - Bromley
New Eltham (part)	*London, S.E.9* - Woolwich
New End	*Worcester* - Redditch
Newenden (part)	*Kent* - Cranbrook
Newent	*Gloucester* - Gloucester
New Ferry	*Cheshire* - Birkenhead
Newfield (Pelton)	*Durham* - Durham
Newfield Colliery	*Durham* - Bishop Auckland
Newfield Green	*York, W.R.* - Sheffield
Newfound	*Hants* - Basingstoke
Newfoundout	*Sussex* - Horsham
Newgale	*Pembroke* - Haverfordwest
Newgate Street	*Herts* - St. Albans
New Hadley	*Salop* - Wellington (Salop)
New Hall	*Salop* - Shrewsbury
Newhall	*Cheshire* - Crewe
Newhall	*Cheshire* - Northwich
Newhall	*Derby* - Burton-upon-Trent
Newhall	*Gloucester* - Cheltenham
Newhall	*Lancaster* - Leigh
New Hall	*Salop* - Shrewsbury
Newhall Green	*Lancaster* - Manchester
Newham	*Northumberland* - Alnwick
Newhampton	*Hereford* - Leominster
Newhaven	*Derby* - Buxton
Newhaven	*Sussex* - Lewes
New Haw	*Surrey* - Kingston-upon-Thames
New Headington	*Oxford* - Oxford
New Hedges	*Pembroke* - Haverfordwest
New Hesledon	*Durham* - Sunderland
Newhey	*Lancaster* - Rochdale
Newhill	*York, W.R.* - Rotherham
New Hinksey	*Oxford* - Oxford
New Holkham	*Norfolk* - King's Lynn
New Holland	*Lincoln* - Scunthorpe
Newholme-with-Dunsley	*York, N.R.* - Whitby
New Houghton	*Derby* - Mansfield
New Houghton	*Norfolk* - King's Lynn
Newhouse	*Devon* - Exeter
Newhouse	*Stafford* - Stafford
New Houses	*Lancaster* - Barrow-in-Furness
New Hunwick	*Durham* - Bishop Auckland
New Hutton	*Westmorland* - Kendal
New Hythe	*Kent* - Maidstone
Newick	*Sussex* - Lewes
New Ingleton	*York, W.R.* - Lancaster
Newingreen	*Kent* - Folkestone
Newington	*Kent* - Folkestone
Newington	*Kent* - Sittingbourne
Newington	*Oxford* - Didcot
Newington	*York, W.R.* - Doncaster
Newington Bagpath	*Gloucester* - Stroud
Newington, North	*Oxford* - Banbury
Newington	*Kent* - Ramsgate
Newington, South	*Oxford* - Banbury
New Inn	*Carmarthen* - Carmarthen
New Inn	*Monmouth* - Pontypool and Abergavenny

NEW

Place	County - Post Town
New Inn Bank	*Stafford* - Market Drayton
New Inns	*Derby* - Matlock
New Invention	*Salop* - Knighton
New Invention	*Stafford* - Walsall
New Kyo	*Durham* - Consett
Newlaithes	*York, W.R.* - Leeds
New Lambton	*Durham* - Durham
Newland	*Dorset* - Dorchester
Newland	*Gloucester* - Monmouth
Newland	*Lancaster* - Barrow-in-Furness
Newland	*Worcester* - Great Malvern
Newland	*York, E.R.* - Goole
Newland	*York, W.R.* - Goole
Newland Common	*Worcester* - Worcester
Newlands	*Cumberland* - Carlisle
Newlands	*Cumberland* - Workington
Newlands	*Lincoln* - Spalding
Newlands	*Northumberland* - Consett
Newlands	*Notts* - Mansfield
Newlands	*Stafford* - Stafford
Newlandside	*Durham* - Bishop Auckland
Newlands Park	*Kent* - Bromley
Newland with Woodhouse Moor	*York, W.R.* - Wakefield
New Lane	*Lancaster* - Southport
New Laund Booth	*Lancaster* - Burnley
Newlay	*York, W.R.* - Leeds
Newlay Wood	*York, W.R.* - Leeds
New Leake	*Lincoln* - Boston
New Lenton	*Nottingham* - Nottingham
New Lodge	*Salop* - Wellington (Salop)
New Lodge	*York, W.R.* - Barnsley
New London	*York, N.R.* - Whitby
New Longton	*Lancaster* - Preston
Newlyn	*Cornwall* - Penzance
New Malden	*Surrey* - Kingston-upon-Thames
Newman's End	*Essex* - Harlow
Newmarket	*Suffolk* - Newmarket
Newmarket	*Gloucester* - Stroud
Newmarket	*York, W.R.* - Leeds
New Mawbray	*Cumberland* - Carlisle
New Mill	*Cornwall* - Penzance
New Mill	*York, W.R.* - Huddersfield
New Mill Crossing	*Glamorgan* - Bridgend
New Mill End	*Beds* - Luton
New Miller Dam	*York, W.R.* - Wakefield
New Mills	*Cornwall* - St. Austell
New Mills (Kenwyn)	*Cornwall* - Truro
New Mills (Ladock)	*Cornwall* - Truro
New Mills	*Derby* - Buxton
New Mills	*Devon* - Launceston
New Mills	*Montgomery* - Newtown
New Milton	*Hants* - Lymington
Newminster Abbey	*Northumberland* - Morpeth
New Moat	*Pembroke* - Haverfordwest
New Moston	*Lancaster* - Manchester
Newney Green	*Essex* - Chelmsford
Newnham	*Gloucester* - Gloucester
Newnham	*Hants* - Basingstoke
Newnham	*Herts* - Hitchin
Newnham	*Kent* - Sittingbourne
Newnham	*Northampton* - Northampton
Newnham	*Northumberland* - Newcastle upon Tyne
Newnham	*Salop* - Shrewsbury
Newnham	*Warwick* - Stratford on Avon
Newnham Bridge	*Worcester* - Kidderminster
Newnham Paddox	*Warwick* - Rugby
Newnham Regis	*Warwick* - Rugby
Newnton, Long	*Wilts* - Malmesbury
Newnton, North	*Wilts* - Devizes
New Ollerton	*Notts* - Mansfield
New Orpington	*Kent* - Bromley
New Oscott	*Warwick* - Birmingham
New Oxted	*Surrey* - Reigate
New Park	*York, W.R.* - Harrogate
New Parks	*Leicester* - Leicester
New Passage	*Gloucester* - Thornbury
New Penshaw	*Durham* - Durham
New Pittington	*Durham* - Durham

NEW

Newport	*Essex* - Bishop's Stortford
Newport	*Gloucester* - Stroud
Newport	*I. of W.* - Newport (I.W.)
Newport	*Monmouth* - Newport (Mon.)
Newport	*Pembroke* - Cardigan
Newport	*Salop* - Wellington (Salop)
Newport	*York, E.R.* - Goole
Newport Pagnell	*Bucks* - Bletchley and Leighton Buzzard
New Pound	*Sussex* - Chichester
New Quay	*Cardigan* - Aberystwyth
Newquay	*Cornwall* - Truro
New Quay	*Devon* - Plymouth
New Radnor	*Radnor* - Knighton
New Rent	*Cumberland* - Penrith
New Rhosrobin	*Denbigh* - Wrexham
New Romney	*Kent* - Ashford
Newsam Green	*York, W.R.* - Leeds
New Scarborough (Wakefield)	*York, W.R.* - Wakefield
New Scarborough (Tingley)	*York, W.R.* - Dewsbury
New Seaham	*Durham* - Sunderland
New Selston	*Notts* - Alfreton
Newsham	*Durham* - Stockton on Tees
Newsham	*Lancaster* - Preston
Newsham	*Northumberland* - Blyth
Newsham	*York, N.R.* - Darlington
New Shildon	*Durham* - Bishop Auckland
New Shipton	*Warwick* - Birmingham
Newsholme	*York, E.R.* - Goole
Newsholme	*York, W.R.* - Blackburn
Newsholme Dean	*York, W.R.* - Keighley
New Smithy	*Derby* - Buxton
Newsome	*York, W.R.* - Huddersfield
New Southgate (part)	*London, N.11* - Barnet
New Southgate (part)	*London, N.11* - Edmonton
New Springs	*Lancaster* - Wigan
New Stanton	*Derby* - Ilkeston
Newstead	*Lincoln* - Scunthorpe
Newstead	*Notts* - Mansfield
Newstead	*Stafford* - Stoke-on-Trent
Newstead Abbey	*Notts* - Mansfield
Newstead Colliery Village	*Notts* - Mansfield
New Street Lane	*Salop* - Market Drayton
New Sunniside	*Durham* - Bishop Auckland
Newthorpe	*Notts* - Nottingham
Newthorpe (South)	*York, W.R.* - Leeds
Newthorpe	*York, W.R.* - Pontefract
Newthorpe Common	*Derby* - Ilkeston
Newtimber	*Sussex* - Brighton
Newton	*Cambridge* - Cambridge
Newton	*Cambridge* - Wisbech
Newton	*Cheshire* - Hyde
Newton (Prestbury)	*Cheshire* - Macclesfield
Newton	*Cheshire* - Birkenhead
Newton	*Cheshire* - Runcorn
Newton	*Cheshire* - Whitchurch
Newton	*Derby* - Alfreton
Newton	*Dorset* - Blandford
Newton	*Glamorgan* - Bridgend
Newton (Mumbles)	*Glamorgan* - Swansea
Newton	*Gloucester* - Cheltenham
Newton	*Gloucester* - Thornbury
Newton	*Hereford* - Hereford
Newton	*Hereford* - Leominster
Newton	*Lancaster* - Barrow-in-Furness
Newton	*Lancaster* - Lancaster
Newton	*Lincoln* - Sleaford
Newton	*Northampton* - Kettering
Newton	*Northumberland* - Hexham
Newton	*Northumberland* - Morpeth
Newton	*Notts* - Nottingham
Newton	*Pembroke* - Haverfordwest
Newton (Clun)	*Salop* - Ludlow
Newton (Stokesay)	*Salop* - Ludlow
Newton	*Salop* - Oswestry
Newton	*Salop* - Shrewsbury
Newton	*Stafford* - Uttoxeter

NEW

Newton	*Suffolk* - Sudbury
Newton	*Warwick* - Rugby
Newton	*York, N.R.* - Malton
Newton	*York, W.R.* - Pontefract
Newton Abbot	*Devon* - Newton Abbot
Newton Arlosh	*Cumberland* - Carlisle
Newton Aycliffe	*Durham* - Darlington
Newton Bewley	*Durham* - Stockton on Tees
Newton Blossomville	*Bucks* - Northampton
Newton Bromswold	*Northampton* - Wellingborough
Newton Burgoland	*Leicester* - Ashby-de-la-Zouch
Newton by Castleacre	*Norfolk* - King's Lynn
Newton-by-Chester	*Cheshire* - Chester
Newton-by-Daresbury	*Cheshire* - Warrington
Newton-by-Tattenhall	*Cheshire* - Chester
Newton-by-the-Sea	*Northumberland* - Alnwick
Newton-by-Toft	*Lincoln* - Lincoln
Newton Cap	*Durham* - Bishop Auckland
Newton Cloddock	*Hereford* - Hereford
Newton, East	*York, N.R.* - Malton
Newton, East	*York, E.R.* - Kingston-upon-Hull
Newton Ferrers	*Devon* - Plymouth
Newton Flotman	*Norfolk* - Norwich
Newton Grange	*Derby* - Matlock
Newton Hall	*Northumberland* - Hexham
Newton Harcourt	*Leicester* - Leicester
Newton Heath	*Lancaster* - Manchester
Newton House	*York, N.R.* - Whitby
Newton-in-Cartmel	*Lancaster* - Barrow-in-Furness
Newton Kyme	*York, W.R.* - York
Newton-le-Willows	*Lancaster* - Warrington
Newton-le-Willows	*York, N.R.* - Northallerton
Newton, Long	*Cumberland* - Carlisle
Newton, Long	*Durham* - Stockton on Tees
Newton Longville	*Bucks* - Bletchley and Leighton Buzzard
Newton, Lower	*Lancaster* - Barrow-in-Furness
Newton Morrell	*York, N.R.* - Darlington
Newton Mulgrave	*York, N.R.* - Whitby
Newton Nethercote	*Leicester* - Ashby-de-la-Zouch
Newton, North	*Somerset* - Bridgwater
Newton Nottage	*Glamorgan* - Bridgend
Newton, Old	*Suffolk* - Stowmarket
Newton-on-the-Hill	*Salop* - Shrewsbury
Newton-on-the-Moor	*Northumberland* - Alnwick
Newton on Trent	*Lincoln* - Gainsborough
Newton Park	*Northumberland* - Morpeth
Newton Poppleford	*Devon* - Exeter
Newton Purcell	*Oxford* - Banbury
Newton Regis	*Warwick* - Tamworth
Newton Reigny	*Cumberland* - Penrith
Newton Road	*Stafford* - West Bromwich
Newton St. Cyres	*Devon* - Exeter
Newton St. Faith	*Norfolk* - Norwich
Newton St. Loe	*Somerset* - Bath
Newton St. Petrock	*Devon* - Bideford
Newton Solney	*Derby* - Burton-upon-Trent
Newton, South	*Wilts* - Salisbury
Newton Stacey	*Hants* - Andover
Newton Toney	*Wilts* - Salisbury
Newton Tracey	*Devon* - Barnstaple
Newton under Roseberry	*York, N.R.* - Middlesbrough
Newton Underwood	*Northumberland* - Morpeth
Newton-upon-Derwent	*York, E.R.* - York
Newton-upon-Ouse	*York, N.R.* - York
Newton Valence	*Hants* - Aldershot and Farnham
Newton, West	*Norfolk* - King's Lynn
Newton, West	*Somerset* - Bridgwater
Newton, West	*York, E.R.* - Kingston-upon-Hull
Newton-with-Scales	*Lancaster* - Preston
Newtown	*Berks* - Newbury
Newtown	*Berks* - Didcot
Newtown (Germoe)	*Cornwall* - Penzance
Newtown (St. Martin)	*Cornwall* - Penzance
Newtown (Ludgvan)	*Cornwall* - Penzance
Newtown (St. Buryan)	*Cornwall* - Penzance
Newtown (Fowey)	*Cornwall* - St. Austell
Newtown	*Cumberland* - Carlisle
Newtown (Aspatria)	*Cumberland* - Carlisle
Newtown (Silloth)	*Cumberland* - Carlisle

NEW - NOB

Newtown	*Dorset* - Salisbury
Newtown	*Dorset* - Poole
Newtown	*Glamorgan* - Aberdare
Newtown (Toddington)	*Gloucester* - Cheltenham
Newtown (Sharpness)	*Gloucester* - Stroud
Newtown (Ashchurch)	*Gloucester* - Cheltenham
Newtown	*Gloucester* - Gloucester
Newtown (Soberton)	*Hants* - Portsmouth
Newtown (Kingsclere)	*Hants* - Newbury
Newtown	*Hereford* - Hereford
Newtown	*I. of W.* - Newport (I.W.)
Newtown	*Lancaster* - Wigan
Newtown (Ebbw Vale)	*Monmouth* - Blackwood
Newtown	*Montgomery* - Newtown
Newtown	*Northumberland* - Alnwick
Newtown	*Northumberland* - Morpeth
Newtown	*Salop* - Shrewsbury
Newtown (Newport)	*Salop* - Wellington (Salop)
Newtown (Dawley)	*Salop* - Wellington (Salop)
Newtown (Milborne Port)	*Somerset* - Yeovil
Newtown (Longnor)	*Stafford* - Leek
Newtown (Bloxwich)	*Stafford* - Walsall
Newtown (Wednesbury)	*Stafford* - Dudley
Newtown (Tisbury)	*Wilts* - Shaftesbury
Newtown	*Warwick* - Birmingham
Newtown	*Worcester* - Worcester
Newtown	*York, W.R.* - Pontefract
Newtown Linford	*Leicester* - Leicester
Newtown Unthank	*Leicester* - Leicester
New Tredegar	*Monmouth* - Blackwood
New Tupton	*Derby* - Chesterfield
New Waltham	*Lincoln* - Great Grimsby
New Washington	*Durham* - Gateshead
New Wells	*Montgomery* - Newtown
New Westwood	*Notts* - Alfreton
New Whittington	*Derby* - Chesterfield
New Windlestone	*Durham* - Durham
New Works	*Salop* - Wellington (Salop)
New Wortley	*York, W.R.* - Leeds
New Yard	*Salop* - Wellington (Salop)
New Yatt	*Oxford* - Witney
New York	*Durham* - Gateshead
New York	*Lancaster* - Bolton
New York	*Lincoln* - Boston
New York	*Northumberland* - North Shields
New York	*York, W.R.* - Harrogate
New Zealand	*Wilts* - Chippenham
New Zealand	*Wilts* - Swindon
Nextend	*Hereford* - Hereford
Neyland	*Pembroke* - Haverfordwest
Nibley	*Gloucester* - Bristol
Nibley	*Gloucester* - Gloucester
Nibley Hill	*Gloucester* - Bristol
Nibley, North	*Gloucester* - Stroud
Nibthwaite, High	*Lancaster* - Barrow-in-Furness
Nibthwaite, Low	*Lancaster* - Barrow-in-Furness
Nicholashayne	*Devon* - Taunton
Nicholston	*Glamorgan* - Swansea
Nidd	*York, W.R.* - Harrogate
Ninant	*Carmarthen* - Lampeter
Nine Banks	*Northumberland* - Hexham
Nine Elms (part)	*London, S.W.8* - Lambeth
Nine Elms (part)	*London, S.W.8* - Wandsworth
Nine Mile Point	*Monmouth* - Blackwood
Nine Springs	*Herts* - Hitchin
Nine Stones	*Cornwall* - St. Austell
Ninevah	*Kent* - Cranbrook
Ninfield	*Sussex* - Hastings
Ningwood	*I. of W.* - Newport (I.W.)
Ninnis	*Cornwall* - Redruth
Nithen End	*Derby* - Buxton
Niton	*I. of W.* - Newport (I.W.)
Nizell's Hoath	*Kent* - Tonbridge
Noah's Ark	*Kent* - Sevenoaks
Noah's Green	*Worcester* - Redditch
Noake	*Dorset* - Dorchester
Noak Hill	*Essex* - Ilford
Nob End	*Lancaster* - Bolton
Nobland Green	*Herts* - Hertford
Nobold	*Salop* - Shrewsbury

NOB - NOR

Nobottle	*Northampton* - Northampton
Nobridge	*Salop* - Market Drayton
Nobut	*Stafford* - Uttoxeter
Nocton	*Lincoln* - Lincoln
Nocton Fen	*Lincoln* - Lincoln
Nocton Heath	*Lincoln* - Lincoln
Noctorum	*Cheshire* - Birkenhead
Noke	*Oxford* - Oxford
Nolton	*Pembroke* - Haverfordwest
Nomans Heath	*Cheshire* - Whitchurch
No Man's Heath	*Warwick* - Tamworth
No Man's Land	*Cornwall* - Bodmin
No Man's Land	*Cornwall* - Liskeard
No Man's Land	*Devon* - Tiverton
No Man's Land	*Herts* - St. Albans
No Man's Land	*Wilts* - Salisbury
Noneley	*Salop* - Shrewsbury
Nonington	*Kent* - Canterbury
Nook	*Northumberland* - Hexham
Nook	*Westmorland* - Kendal
Norbiton	*Surrey* - Kingston-upon-Thames
Norbriggs	*Derby* - Chesterfield
Norbury	*Cheshire* - Stockport
Norbury	*Cheshire* - Whitchurch
Norbury	*Derby* - Uttoxeter
Norbury	*London, S.W.16* - Croydon
Norbury	*Salop* - Ludlow
Norbury	*Stafford* - Stafford
Norbury Moor	*Cheshire* - Stockport
Nordelph	*Norfolk* - King's Lynn
Norden	*Dorset* - Swanage
Norden	*Lancaster* - Rochdale
Nordley	*Salop* - Bridgnorth
Nordley Hill	*Stafford* - Wolverhampton
Norfolk Park	*York, W.R.* - Sheffield
Norgrove	*Worcester* - Redditch
Norham	*Northumberland* - Berwick-upon-Tweed
Norland	*York, W.R.* - Halifax
Norley Hall	*Lancaster* - Wigan
Norley Wood	*Hants* - Lymington
Normacot	*Stafford* - Stoke-on-Trent
Normanby	*York, N.R.* - Malton
Normanby	*York, N.R.* - Middlesbrough
Normanby	*York, N.R.* - Whitby
Normanby-by-Spital	*Lincoln* - Lincoln
Normanby-by-Stow	*Lincoln* - Gainsborough
Normanby le Wold	*Lincoln* - Great Grimsby
Norman Cross	*Hunts* - Peterborough
Normandy	*Surrey* - Aldershot and Farnham
Norman's Bay	*Sussex* - Hastings
Norman Street	*Kent* - Sevenoaks
Normanton	*Derby* - Derby
Normanton	*Leicester* - Grantham
Normanton	*Lincoln* - Grantham
Normanton (Southwell)	*Notts* - Newark
Normanton	*Rutland* - Stamford
Normanton	*Wilts* - Salisbury
Normanton	*York, W.R.* - Wakefield
Normanton Hills	*Notts* - Loughborough
Normanton Inn	*Notts* - East Retford
Normanton-le-Heath	*Leicester* - Ashby-de-la-Zouch
Normanton-on-the-Wolds	*Notts* - Nottingham
Normanton-on-Trent	*Notts* - East Retford
Normanton, South	*Derby* - Alfreton
Normanton Springs	*York, W.R.* - Sheffield
Normanton Turville	*Leicester* - Leicester
Normanton upon Soar	*Notts* - Loughborough
Normoss	*Lancaster* - Blackpool
Nornea	*Cambridge* - Ely
Nornea Fen	*Cambridge* - Ely
Nornea Lane	*Cambridge* - Ely
Norrington	*Wilts* - Chippenham
Norris Green	*Cornwall* - Plymouth
Norris Green	*Lancaster* - Liverpool
Norris Hill	*Leicester* - Ashby-de-la-Zouch
Norristhorpe	*York, W.R.* - Dewsbury
Northall	*Bucks* - Bletchley and Leighton Buzzard

Northallerton	*York, N.R.* - Northallerton
Northall Green	*Norfolk* - East Dereham
Northam	*Devon* - Bideford
Northam	*Hants* - Southampton
North Ambersham	*Sussex* - Petersfield
Northampton	*Northampton* - Northampton
Northampton	*Worcester* - Worcester
North Anston	*York, W.R.* - Worksop
North Ashton	*Lancaster* - Wigan
North Aston	*Oxford* - Banbury
Northaw	*Herts* - Barnet
North Baddesley	*Hants* - Southampton
North Bailey	*Durham* - Durham
North Barrow	*Somerset* - Yeovil
North Barsham	*Norfolk* - King's Lynn
North Bedburn	*Durham* - Bishop Auckland
North Beechburn	*Durham* - Bishop Auckland
North Benfleet	*Essex* - Brentwood
North Bersted	*Sussex* - Chichester
North Biddick	*Durham* - Gateshead
North Bierley	*York, W.R.* - Bradford
North Bitchburn	*Durham* - Bishop Auckland
North Blyth	*Northumberland* - Blyth
North Boarhunt	*Hants* - Portsmouth
Northborough	*Northampton* - Peterborough
Northbourne	*Berks* - Didcot
Northbourne	*Hants* - Bournemouth
Northbourne	*Kent* - Deal
North Bovey	*Devon* - Newton Abbot
North Bradley	*Wilts* - Trowbridge
North Brewham	*Somerset* - Yeovil
North Brixton	*London, S.W.9* - Lambeth
Northbrook	*Hants* - Winchester
North Burlingham	*Norfolk* - Norwich
North Cadbury	*Somerset* - Yeovil
North Carlton	*Lincoln* - Lincoln
North Carlton	*Notts* - Worksop
North Cave	*York, E.R.* - Beverley
North Cerney	*Gloucester* - Cheltenham
North Chapel	*Sussex* - Chichester
North Charford	*Hants* - Salisbury
North Charlton	*Northumberland* - Alnwick
North Cheriton	*Somerset* - Yeovil
Northchurch	*Herts* - Hemel Hempstead
North Cleobury	*Salop* - Bridgnorth
North Cliffe	*York, E.R.* - Beverley
North Clifton	*Notts* - Newark
North Coates	*Lincoln* - Louth
North Cockerington	*Lincoln* - Louth
North Coker	*Somerset* - Yeovil
North Collingham	*Notts* - Newark
North Common	*Gloucester* - Bristol
North Cornelly	*Glamorgan* - Bridgend
Northcott	*Devon* - Launceston
North Country	*Cornwall* - Redruth
North Cove	*Suffolk* - Lowestoft
North Cowton	*York, N.R.* - Darlington
North Crawley	*Bucks* - Bletchley and Leighton Buzzard
North Cray	*Kent* - Bromley
North Creake	*Norfolk* - King's Lynn
North Curry	*Somerset* - Taunton
North Dalton	*York, E.R.* - Beverley
North Damerham	*Hants* - Salisbury
North Darley	*Derby* - Matlock
North Dean	*Bucks* - High Wycombe
North Dean	*York, W.R.* - Halifax
North Deighton	*York, W.R.* - Harrogate
North Dissington	*Northumberland* - Newcastle upon Tyne
Northdown, East	*Kent* - Margate
North Downs	*Cornwall* - Redruth
Northdown, West	*Kent* - Margate
North Drove	*Lincoln* - Spalding
North Duffield	*York, E.R.* - York
North Dulwich	*London, S.E.24* - Lambeth
Northease	*Sussex* - Lewes
North Elkington	*Lincoln* - Louth
North Elmsall	*York, W.R.* - Pontefract
North End	*Bucks* - High Wycombe

NOR

North End	*Essex* - Chelmsford
North End	*Hants* - Portsmouth
North End	*London, N.W.3* - Bloomsbury and Marylebone
North End	*London, N.W.11* - Bloomsbury and Marylebone
North End	*Sussex* - Worthing
Northend	*Warwick* - Banbury
Northenden	*Lancaster* - Manchester
Northern Moor	*Lancaster* - Manchester
Northern Wood	*Bucks* - High Wycombe
North Evington	*Leicester* - Leicester
Northey Island	*Essex* - Maldon
North Fambridge	*Essex* - Maldon
North Farmcote	*Gloucester* - Cheltenham
North Fawley	*Berks* - Didcot
North Featherstone	*York, W.R.* - Pontefract
North Fen	*Cambridge* - Ely
North Ferriby	*York, E.R.* - Kingston-upon-Hull
North Ferring	*Sussex* - Worthing
Northfield	*Gloucester* - Cheltenham
Northfield	*Warwick* - Birmingham
North Finchley	*London, N.12* - Barnet
Northfleet	*Kent* - Gravesend
North Follingsby	*Durham* - Gateshead
North Forest	*Devon and Somerset* - Minehead
North Fortyfoot Bank	*Lincoln* - Boston
North Frodingham	*York, E.R.* - Bridlington
North Gate (Pinchbeck)	*Lincoln* - Spalding
Northgate	*Northumberland* - Morpeth
North Gorley	*Hants* - Salisbury
North Gosforth	*Northumberland* - Newcastle upon Tyne
North Grimston	*York, E.R.* - Malton
North Ground	*Devon* - Plymouth
North Harrow (part)	*Middlesex* - Watford
North Harrow (part)	*Middlesex* - Willesden
North Hayling	*Hants* - Portsmouth
North Heath	*Sussex* - Chichester
North Hill	*Cornwall* - Launceston
North Hill	*Devon* - Axminster and Chard
North Hinksey	*Berks* - Oxford
North Houghton	*Hants* - Winchester
North Huish	*Devon* - Plymouth
North Hyde (part)	*Middlesex* - Uxbridge
North Hykeham	*Lincoln* - Lincoln
North Hylton (part)	*Durham* - Sunderland
North Hylton (part)	*Durham* - Gateshead
Northiam	*Sussex* - Hastings
Northill	*Beds* - Biggleswade
Northill	*Devon* - Launceston
Northington	*Hants* - Winchester
North Ives	*York, W.R.* - Keighley
North Kelsey	*Lincoln* - Scunthorpe
North Kensington	*London, W.10* - Bloomsbury and Marylebone
North Kilworth	*Leicester* - Rugby
North Killingholme	*Lincoln* - Great Grimsby
North Kyme	*Lincoln* - Sleaford
North Kyme Fen	*Lincoln* - Sleaford
North Lancing	*Sussex* - Worthing
Northlands	*Lincoln* - Boston
Northleach	*Gloucester* - Cheltenham
North Lee	*Bucks* - Hemel Hempstead
North Lees	*York, W.R.* - Harrogate
Northleigh	*Devon* - Axminster
North Leigh	*Oxford* - Witney
Northleigh Offwell	*Devon* - Axminster
North Leverton	*Notts* - East Retford
Northlew	*Devon* - Okehampton
North Litchfield	*Hants* - Newbury
North Littleton	*Worcester* - Evesham
North Lopham	*Norfolk* - Norwich
North Luffenham	*Rutland* - Stamford
North Lydbury	*Salop* - Shrewsbury
North Lyham	*Northumberland* - Alnwick
North Marden	*Sussex* - Chichester
North Marston	*Bucks* - Aylesbury
North Middleton	*Northumberland* - Alnwick

North Middleton	*Northumberland* - Morpeth
North Milford	*York, W.R.* - York
North Mimms	*Herts* - St. Albans
North Molton	*Devon* - Barnstaple
Northmoor	*Lancaster* - Oldham
Northmoor	*Oxford* - Witney
North Moor	*York, E.R.* - Kingston-upon-Hull
Northmoor Green	*Somerset* - Bridgwater
North Moreton	*Berks* - Didcot
North Muskham	*Notts* - Newark
North Newbald	*York, E.R.* - Beverley
North Newington	*Oxford* - Banbury
North Newnton	*Wilts* - Devizes
North Newton	*Somerset* - Bridgwater
Northney (Hayling)	*Hants* - Portsmouth
North Nibley	*Gloucester* - Stroud
North Oakley	*Hants* - Basingstoke
North Ockendon	*Essex* - Grays Thurrock
Northolme	*Lincoln* - Skegness
Northolt	*Middlesex* - Brentford
Northop	*Flint* - Mold
Northop Hall	*Flint* - Mold
North Ormesby	*York, N.R.* - Middlesbrough
North Ormsby	*Lincoln* - Louth
Northorpe	*Lincoln* - Gainsborough
Northorpe (Donington)	*Lincoln* - Spalding
Northorpe (Thurlby)	*Lincoln* - Spalding
Northorpe	*York, W.R.* - Dewsbury
Northover (Ilchester)	*Somerset* - Yeovil
North Owersby	*Lincoln* - Scunthorpe
Northowram	*York, W.R.* - Halifax
North Perrott	*Somerset* - Yeovil
North Petherton	*Somerset* - Bridgwater
North Petherwin	*Devon* - Launceston
North Pickenham	*Norfolk* - King's Lynn
North Piddle	*Worcester* - Worcester
North Pinner	*Middlesex* - Watford
North Poorton	*Dorset* - Dorchester
North Rauceby	*Lincoln* - Sleaford
Northrepps	*Norfolk* - Norwich
North Reston	*Lincoln* - Louth
North Rigton	*York, W.R.* - Harrogate
North Roddymoor	*Durham* - Bishop Auckland
North Rode	*Cheshire* - Macclesfield
North Runcton	*Norfolk* - King's Lynn
North Scale	*Lancaster* - Barrow-in-Furness
North Scarle	*Lincoln* - Newark
Northsceugh	*Cumberland* - Carlisle
North Seaton	*Northumberland* - Morpeth
North Sheen	*Surrey* - Wandsworth
North Shields	*Northumberland* - North Shields
North Shoebury	*Essex* - Southend
North Skelton	*York, N.R.* - Middlesbrough
North Skirlaugh	*York, E.R.* - Kingston-upon-Hull
North Somercotes	*Lincoln* - Louth
North Stainley	*York, W.R.* - Harrogate
North Stainmore	*Westmorland* - Penrith
North Stanmore	*Middlesex* - Watford
North Staveley	*York, W.R.* - Rotherham
North Stifford	*Essex* - Grays Thurrock
North Stoke	*Lincoln* - Grantham
North Stoke	*Oxford* - Didcot
North Stoke	*Somerset* - Bath
North Stoke	*Sussex* - Chichester
North Stoneham	*Hants* - Southampton
North Sunderland	*Northumberland* - Alnwick
North Tamerton	*Cornwall* - Launceston
North Tawton	*Devon* - Okehampton
North Thoresby	*Lincoln* - Louth
North Tidworth	*Wilts* - Andover
North Town	*Berks* - Slough
North Town	*Lancaster* - Burnley
North Tuddenham	*Norfolk* - East Dereham
Northumberland Bottom	*Kent* - Gravesend
Northumberland Heath	*Kent* - Dartford
North Wallbottle Colliery	*Northumberland* - Newcastle upon Tyne
North Walsham	*Norfolk* - Norwich
North Waltham	*Hants* - Basingstoke

NOR

North Warnborough	*Hants* - Basingstoke
Northway	*Gloucester* - Cheltenham
Northway	*Oxford* - Oxford
North Weald Bassett	*Essex* - Harlow
North Weston	*Oxford* - Thame
North Weston	*Somerset* - Bristol
North Wheatley	*Notts* - East Retford
Northwich	*Cheshire* - Northwich
Northwick	*Gloucester* - Thornbury
Northwick (Chew Magna)	*Somerset* - Bristol
Northwick	*Worcester* - Worcester
Northwick Park	*Middlesex* - Willesden
North Willingham	*Lincoln* - Louth
North Wingfield	*Derby* - Chesterfield
North Witham	*Lincoln* - Grantham
Northwold	*Norfolk* - Thetford
Northwood	*Derby* - Uttoxeter
Northwood	*Hants* - Winchester
Northwood	*I. of W.* - Newport (I.W.)
Northwood (part)	*Middlesex* - Uxbridge
Northwood (part)	*Middlesex* - Watford
Northwood (Ellesmere)	*Salop* - Oswestry
Northwood	*Salop* - Shrewsbury
Northwood Green	*Gloucester* - Gloucester
Northwoods	*Gloucester* - Bristol
North Woolwich	*London, E.16* - Bow
North Wootton	*Dorset* - Yeovil
North Wootton	*Norfolk* - King's Lynn
North Wootton	*Somerset* - Wells
North Wraxall	*Wilts* - Chippenham
North Wylam	*Northumberland* - Newcastle upon Tyne
North Yantlett Creek	*Kent* - Rochester
Nortoft	*Northampton* - Northampton
Norton	*Cheshire* - Runcorn
Norton	*Glamorgan* - Swansea
Norton	*Gloucester* - Gloucester
Norton	*Hereford* - Worcester
Norton	*Herts* - Hitchin
Norton	*Kent* - Sittingbourne
Norton	*Northampton* - Northampton
Norton	*Radnor* - Knighton
Norton (Shifnal)	*Salop* - Bridgnorth
Norton	*Salop* - Shrewsbury
Norton	*Somerset* - Weston Super Mare
Norton	*Somerset* - Yeovil
Norton	*Suffolk* - Bury St. Edmunds
Norton	*Sussex* - Chichester
Norton	*Wilts* - Malmesbury
Norton	*Worcester* - Bromsgrove
Norton	*Worcester* - Evesham
Norton (Stourbridge)	*Worcester* - Stourbridge
Norton	*Worcester* - Worcester
Norton	*York, E.R.* - Malton
Norton	*York, W.R.* - Doncaster
Norton	*York, W.R.* - Sheffield
Norton Bavant	*Wilts* - Warminster
Norton Beauchamp	*Somerset* - Weston Super Mare
Norton Bridge	*Stafford* - Stafford
Norton Canes	*Stafford* - Walsall
Norton Canon	*Hereford* - Hereford
Norton Conyers	*York, N.R.* - Harrogate
Norton Cuckney	*Notts* - Worksop
Norton Curlieu	*Warwick* - Warwick
Norton Disney	*Lincoln* - Newark
Norton, East	*Leicester* - Leicester
Norton Ferris	*Somerset* - Frome
Norton Fine	*Durham* - Bishop Auckland
Norton Fitzwarren	*Somerset* - Taunton
Norton Green	*Herts* - Hitchin
Norton Green	*Stafford* - Stoke-on-Trent
Norton Hawkfield	*Somerset* - Bristol
Norton Heath	*Essex* - Chelmsford
Norton Hill	*Somerset* - Bristol
Norton-in-Hales	*Salop* - Market Drayton
Norton-in-Stockton	*Salop* - Bridgnorth
Norton-in-the-Moors	*Stafford* - Stoke-on-Trent
Norton-juxta-Twycross	*Leicester* - Ashby-de-la-Zouch
Norton-le-Clay	*York, N.R.* - Harrogate
Norton Lees	*York, W.R.* - Sheffield

NOR - NUP

Norton Lindsey	*Warwick* - Warwick
Norton, Little	*Somerset* - Yeovil
Norton, Little	*Stafford* - Walsall
Norton, Lower	*Warwick* - Warwick
Norton Malreward	*Somerset* - Bristol
Norton Mandeville	*Essex* - Chelmsford
Norton-on-Tees	*Durham* - Stockton on Tees
Norton St. Philip	*Somerset* - Frome
Norton Subcourse	*Norfolk* - Great Yarmouth
Norton Tower	*York, W.R.* - Halifax
Nortons Wood	*Somerset* - Weston Super Mare
Norton Wood	*Salop* - Market Drayton
Norton Woodseats	*York, W.R.* - Sheffield
Norwell	*Notts* - Newark
Norwell Woodhouse	*Notts* - Newark
Norwich	*Norfolk* - Norwich
Norwood	*Durham* - Gateshead
Norwood (part)	*London, S.E.19* - Croydon
Norwood (part)	*London, S.E.19* - Lambeth
Norwood	*Notts* - Mansfield
Norwood	*Sussex* - Chichester
Norwood	*York, W.R.* - Otley
Norwood	*York, W.R.* - Sheffield
Norwood Colliery	*Durham* - Bishop Auckland
Norwood Green	*York, W.R.* - Halifax
Norwood Green	*Middlesex* - Uxbridge
Norwood Hill	*Surrey* - Reigate
Norwood, South	*London, S.E.25* - Croydon
Norwood, Upper (part)	*London, S.E.19* - Croydon
Norwood, Upper (part)	*London, S.E.19* - Lambeth
Norwood, Upper	*Sussex* - Chichester
Norwood, West	*London, S.E.27* - Lambeth
Noseley	*Leicester* - Leicester
Noss Mayo	*Devon* - Plymouth
Nostell	*York, W.R.* - Pontefract
Nosterfield	*York, N.R.* - Harrogate
Notcliffe	*Gloucester* - Cheltenham
Notgrove	*Gloucester* - Cheltenham
Notley	*Bucks* - Thame
Nottage	*Glamorgan* - Bridgend
Notter	*Cornwall* - Plymouth
Nottingham	*Notts* - Nottingham
Notting Hill (part)	*London, W.11* - Bloomsbury and Marylebone
Notting Hill (part)	*London, W.11* - West London
Nottington	*Dorset* - Weymouth
Notton	*Dorset* - Dorchester
Notton	*Wilts* - Chippenham
Notton	*York, W.R.* - Barnsley
Nottswood	*Gloucester* - Gloucester
Nounsley	*Essex* - Chelmsford
Nova Scotia	*Durham* - Gateshead
Noverton	*Gloucester* - Cheltenham
Nowton	*Suffolk* - Bury St. Edmunds
Noyadd Cross	*Cardigan* - Cardigan
Nuffield	*Oxford* - Didcot
Nun Appleton	*York, W.R.* - York
Nunburnholme	*York, E.R.* - York
Nuncargate	*Notts* - Mansfield
Nunclose	*Cumberland* - Penrith
Nuneaton	*Warwick* - Nuneaton
Nuneham Courtney	*Oxford* - Oxford
Nuney Green	*Oxford* - Reading
Nunhead	*London, S.E.15* - Lambeth
Nun Keeling	*York, E.R.* - Beverley
Nun Monkton	*York, W.R.* - Harrogate
Nunney	*Somerset* - Frome
Nunnington	*York, N.R.* - Malton
Nunnykirk	*Northumberland* - Morpeth
Nunriding	*Northumberland* - Morpeth
Nunstainton East	*Durham* - Bishop Auckland
Nunthorpe	*York, N.R.* - Middlesbrough
Nunthorpe Station	*York, N.R.* - Middlesbrough
Nunton	*Wilts* - Salisbury
Nunts Park	*Warwick* - Coventry
Nunwick-with-Howgrave	*York, W.R.* - Harrogate
Nupdown	*Gloucester* - Thornbury
Nupend	*Gloucester* - Stroud
Nup End	*Herts* - Hitchin

NUR - OAK

Nursling	*Hants* - Southampton
Nursted	*Hants* - Petersfield
Nurstead	*Kent* - Gravesend
Nursteed	*Wilts* - Devizes
Nurston	*Glamorgan* - Barry
Nurton	*Stafford* - Wolverhampton
Nutbourne	*Sussex* - Chichester
Nutfield	*Surrey* - Reigate
Nutfield, South	*Surrey* - Reigate
Nutford	*Dorset* - Wimborne Minster
Nutgrove	*Lancaster* - St. Helens
Nuthall	*Notts* - Nottingham
Nuthampstead	*Herts* - Hitchin
Nuthurst	*Sussex* - Horsham
Nuthurst	*Warwick* - Birmingham
Nutley	*Hants* - Basingstoke
Nutley	*Sussex* - Lewes
Nuttall	*Lancaster* - Bury
Nutt Head	*York, W.R.* - Keighley
Nutwell	*York, W.R.* - Doncaster
Nye	*Somerset* - Weston Super Mare
Nyetimber	*Sussex* - Chichester
Nyewood	*Sussex* - Petersfield
Nyland Higher	*Somerset* - Yeovil
Nyland Lower	*Somerset* - Yeovil
Nymet Rowland	*Devon* - Exeter
Nymet Tracey	*Devon* - Exeter
Nymphsfield	*Gloucester* - Stroud
Nympsfield	*Gloucester* - Stroud
Nynehead	*Somerset* - Taunton
Nynehead, East	*Somerset* - Taunton
Nythe	*Somerset* - Bridgewater
Nyton	*Sussex* - Chichester

O

Oadby	*Leicester* - Leicester
Oakamoor	*Stafford* - Leek
Oak Bank	*Westmorland* - Kendal
Oakdale	*Monmouth* - Blackwood
Oake	*Somerset* - Taunton
Oaken	*Stafford* - Wolverhampton
Oakenbottoms	*Lancaster* - Bolton
Oakenclough	*Lancaster* - Lancaster
Oakengates	*Salop* - Wellington (Salop)
Oaken Grove	*Bucks* - High Wycombe
Oakenholt	*Flint* - Holywell
Oaken Lawn	*Stafford* - Wolverhampton
Oakenshaw	*Durham* - Bishop Auckland
Oakenshaw (Spenborough)	*York, W.R.* - Dewsbury
Oakenshaw (Crofton)	*York, W.R.* - Wakefield
Oakerside	*Derby* - Matlock
Oakerthorpe	*Derby* - Alfreton
Oakes	*York, W.R.* - Huddersfield
Oakford	*Cardigan* - Aberystwyth
Oakford	*Devon* - Tiverton
Oak Grove	*Cheshire* - Macclesfield
Oakham	*Rutland* - Melton Mowbray
Oakham	*Stafford* - Dudley
Oakhampton	*Worcester* - Kidderminster
Oakhanger	*Hants* - Aldershot
Oakhill	*Somerset* - Wells
Oakhill	*Stafford* - Stoke-on-Trent
Oakhill	*Wilts* - Marlborough
Oakhurst	*Sussex* - Horsham
Oakington	*Cambridge* - Cambridge
Oaklands	*Herts* - Hertford
Oaklea	*Lancaster* - Barrow-in-Furness
Oakleigh Park	*London, N.20* - Barnet
Oakle Street	*Gloucester* - Gloucester
Oakley	*Beds* - Bedford
Oakley	*Bucks and Oxford* - Thame
Oakley	*Dorset* - Wimborne Minster
Oakley	*Stafford* - Market Drayton
Oakley	*Suffolk* - Norwich

Oakley	*Warwick* - Tamworth
Oakley	*Worcester* - Worcester
Oakley, East	*Hants* - Basingstoke
Oakley Folly	*Stafford* - Market Drayton
Oakley, Great	*Northampton* - Corby
Oakley Green	*Berks* - Slough
Oakley, Little	*Northampton* - Corby
Oakley, North	*Hants* - Basingstoke
Oakmere	*Cheshire* - Northwich
Oakridge	*Gloucester* - Stroud
Oaks Evenwood	*Durham* - Bishop Auckland
Oaksey	*Wilts* - Malmesbury
Oakshaw	*Cumberland* - Carlisle
Oakshott	*Hants* - Petersfield
Oaks in Charnwood	*Leicester* - Loughborough
Oaks Row	*Durham* - Bishop Auckland
Oaks, The	*Lancaster* - Bolton
Oakthorpe	*Leicester* - Ashby-de-la-Zouch
Oak Tree	*Durham* - Darlington
Oakwood	*York, W.R.* - Leeds
Oakwood Hill	*Surrey* - Dorking
Oakworth	*York, W.R.* - Keighley
Oare	*Berks* - Newbury
Oare	*Kent* - Canterbury
Oare	*Somerset* - Minehead
Oare	*Wilts* - Swindon
Oasby	*Lincoln* - Grantham
Oaten Hole	*Somerset* - Bristol
Oathill	*Somerset* - Yeovil
Oatlands Park	*Surrey* - Kingston-upon-Thames
Obley	*Salop* - Ludlow
Oborne	*Dorset* - Yeovil
Obthorpe	*Lincoln* - Spalding
Oby	*Norfolk* - Great Yarmouth
Occaney	*York, W.R.* - Harrogate
Occold	*Suffolk* - Norwich
Ochryfoel	*Flint* - Rhyl
Ockbrook	*Derby* - Derby
Ockendon, North	*Essex* - Grays Thurrock
Ockendon, South	*Essex* - Grays Thurrock
Ocker Hill	*Stafford* - Dudley
Ockeridge	*Worcester* - Worcester
Ockham	*Surrey* - Guildford
Ockley	*Surrey* - Dorking
Ocle Pychard	*Hereford* - Hereford
Octon	*York, E.R.* - Bridlington
Odcombe	*Somerset* - Yeovil
Odd Down	*Somerset* - Bath
Oddingley	*Worcester* - Worcester
Oddington	*Gloucester* - Cheltenham
Oddington	*Oxford* - Oxford
Odd Rode	*Cheshire* - Congleton
Odell	*Beds* - Bedford
Odiham	*Hants* - Basingstoke
Odsal	*York, W.R.* - Bradford
Odsey	*Herts* - Hitchin
Odstock	*Wilts* - Salisbury
Odstone	*Leicester* - Ashby-de-la-Zouch
Offchurch	*Warwick* - Warwick
Offcote and Underwood	*Derby* - Derby
Offenham	*Worcester* - Evesham
Offerton	*Cheshire* - Stockport
Offerton	*Durham* - Durham
Offham	*Kent* - Maidstone
Offham	*Sussex* - Chichester
Offington	*Sussex* - Worthing
Offley	*Herts* - Hitchin
Offley Brook	*Stafford* - Stafford
Offley Grove	*Stafford* - Stafford
Offley Hay	*Stafford* - Stafford
Offley, High	*Stafford* - Stafford
Offley Marsh	*Stafford* - Market Drayton
Offord Cluny	*Hunts* - Huntingdon
Offord Darcy	*Hunts* - Huntingdon
Offoxey	*Salop* - Wellington (Salop)
Offton	*Suffolk* - Ipswich
Offwell	*Devon* - Axminster
Ogbourne St. Andrew	*Wilts* - Swindon
Ogbourne St. George	*Wilts* - Swindon
Ogden	*Lancaster* - Rochdale

Ogden	*York, W.R.* - Halifax
Ogdens	*Hants* - Salisbury
Ogle	*Northumberland* - Morpeth
Oglet	*Lancaster* - St. Helens
Ogley Hay	*Stafford* - Walsall
Ogmore-by-Sea	*Glamorgan* - Bridgend
Ogmore Vale	*Glamorgan* - Bridgend
Ogmore Valley	*Glamorgan* - Bridgend
Ogwell	*Devon* - Newton Abbot
Ogwen	*Caernarvon* - Bangor
Okeford Fitzpaine	*Dorset* - Shaftesbury
Okehampton	*Devon* - Okehampton
Okeover	*Stafford* - Uttoxeter
Old	*Northampton* - Northampton
Old Alresford	*Hants* - Winchester
Old Arley	*Warwick* - Nuneaton
Old Barrow	*Lancaster* - Barrow-in-Furness
Old Basing	*Hants* - Basingstoke
Oldberrow	*Worcester* - Redditch
Old Bewick	*Northumberland* - Alnwick
Old Bilsthorpe	*Notts* - Mansfield
Old Bolingbroke	*Lincoln* - Skegness
Old Borough	*Warwick* - Stratford on Avon
Old Bradwell	*Bucks* - Bletchley and Leighton Buzzard
Old Brampton	*Derby* - Chesterfield
Old Brumby	*Lincoln* - Scunthorpe
Old Buckenham	*Norfolk* - Norwich
Old Burdon	*Durham* - Sunderland
Oldbury	*Kent* - Sevenoaks
Oldbury	*Salop* - Bridgnorth
Oldbury	*Warwick* - Nuneaton
Oldbury (part)	*Worcester* - Dudley
Oldbury (part)	*Worcester* - West Bromwich
Oldbury Naite	*Gloucester* - Thornbury
Oldbury-upon-Severn	*Gloucester* - Thornbury
Old Byland	*York, N.R.* - Malton
Old Carlisle	*Cumberland* - Carlisle
Old Cassop	*Durham* - Durham
Oldcastle	*Cheshire* - Whitchurch
Oldcastle	*Glamorgan* - Bridgend
Old Castle	*Monmouth* - Pontypool and Abergavenny
Old Catton	*Norfolk* - Norwich
Old Chapel	*Montgomery* - Newtown
Old Church Stoke	*Montgomery* - Welshpool
Old Cleeve	*Somerset* - Minehead
Old Colwyn	*Denbigh* - Conway
Old Cornforth	*Durham* - Durham
Oldcotes	*Notts* - Worksop
Old Coundon	*Durham* - Bishop Auckland
Oldcroft	*Gloucester* - Monmouth
Old Dalby	*Leicester* - Melton Mowbray
Old Down	*Gloucester* - Thornbury
Old Durham	*Durham* - Durham
Old Earswick	*York, N.R.* - York
Oldfallow	*Stafford* - Walsall
Old Felton	*Northumberland* - Alnwick
Old Felton	*Somerset* - Bristol
Oldfield	*Cheshire* - Altrincham
Oldfield	*Cumberland* - Workington
Oldfield	*Worcester* - Worcester
Oldfield	*York, W.R.* - Huddersfiled
Oldfield	*York, W.R.* - Keighley
Oldford	*Somerset* - Frome
Old Forge	*Hereford* - Monmouth
Old Furnace	*Monmouth* - Pontypool and Abergavenny
Old Gore	*Hereford* - Monmouth
Old Gaudaloupe	*Leicester* - Melton Mowbray
Old Hall	*Montgomery* - Newtown
Old Hall Green	*Herts* - Hertford
Oldham	*Lancaster* - Oldham
Oldham's Estate	*Lancaster* - Bolton
Old Heath, The	*Salop* - Shrewsbury
Old Heathfield	*Sussex* - Eastbourne
Old Hill	*Stafford* - Dudley
Old Hills	*Worcester* - Worcester
Old Hunstanton	*Norfolk* - King's Lynn
Oldhurst	*Hunts* - Huntingdon

OLD - OLV

Old Hutton	*Westmorland* - Kendal
Oldington	*Salop* - Bridgnorth
Old Knebworth	*Herts* - Hitchin
Old Lakenham	*Norfolk* - Norwich
Oldland	*Gloucester* - Bristol
Old Laund Booth	*Lancaster* - Nelson
Old Leake	*Lincoln* - Boston
Old Lindley	*York, W.R.* - Halifax
Old Malden	*Surrey* - Kingston-upon-Thames
Old Malton	*York, N.R.* - Malton
Old Maybray	*Cumberland* - Carlisle
Old Milton	*Hants* - Lymington
Old Milverton	*Warwick* - Warwick
Oldmixon	*Somerset* - Weston Super Mare
Old Moor	*Northumberland* - Morpeth
Oldner	*Oxford* - Banbury
Old Newton	*Suffolk* - Stowmarket
Old Ollerton	*Notts* - Mansfield
Old Oscott	*Warwick* - Birmingham
Old Park	*Durham* - Bishop Auckland
Old Park	*Kent* - Dover
Old Park	*Salop* - Wellington (Salop)
Old Passage	*Gloucester* - Thornbury
Old Penshaw	*Durham* - Durham
Old Pound	*Cornwall* - St. Austell
Old Quarrington	*Durham* - Durham
Old Radnor	*Radnor* - Knighton
Oldridge	*Devon* - Exeter
Old Roan	*Lancaster* - Liverpool
Old Romney	*Kent* - Ashford
Old Sarum	*Wilts* - Salisbury
Old Scale	*Cumberland* - Workington
Old Seaham	*Durham* - Sunderland
Old Shildon	*Durham* - Bishop Auckland
Old Sodbury	*Gloucester* - Bristol
Old Somerby	*Lincoln* - Grantham
Old Southgate (part)	*London, N.14* - Barnet
Old Southgate (part)	*London, N.14* - Edmonton
Old Springs	*Stafford* - Market Drayton
Oldstead	*York, N.R.* - Malton
Old Stratford	*Northampton* - Northampton
Old Sulehay	*Northampton* - Peterborough
Old Sunniside	*Durham* - Bishop Auckland
Old Swan	*Lancaster* - Liverpool
Old Swinford	*Worcester* - Stourbridge
Old Tame	*York, W.R.* - Oldham
Old Tebay	*Westmorland* - Penrith
Old Town	*Northumberland* - Hexham
Old Town	*Westmorland* - Kendal
Old Town	*York, W.R.* - Todmorden
Old Trafford	*Lancaster* - Salford
Old Trimdon	*Durham* - Durham
Old Tupton	*Derby* - Chesterfield
Old Wall	*Cumberland* - Carlisle
Old Warden	*Beds* - Biggleswade
Oldways End	*Devon* - Tiverton
Old Weston	*Hunts* - Huntingdon
Old Westwood	*Notts* - Alfreton
Old Wheatbottom	*Durham* - Bishop Auckland
Old Whittington	*Derby* - Chesterfield
Old Windsor	*Berks* - Slough
Old Wives Leas	*Kent* - Canterbury
Old Wood	*Worcester* - Ludlow
Old Woodhall	*Lincoln* - Lincoln
Old Woodhouse	*Leicester* - Loughborough
Old Woodifield	*Durham* - Bishop Auckland
Old Woods	*Salop* - Shrewsbury
Old Woodstock	*Oxford* - Oxford
Old Yarr	*Worcester* - Redditch
Oliver Ford	*Durham* - Durham
Ollerton	*Cheshire* - Altrincham
Ollerton	*Salop* - Market Drayton
Ollerton	*Notts* - Mansfield
Ollerton, New	*Notts* - Mansfield
Olney	*Bucks* - Northampton
Olney Park Farm	*Northampton* - Northampton
Olton	*Warwick* - Birmingham
Olveston	*Gloucester* - Thornbury
Olveston Common	*Gloucester* - Thornbury
Olveston Green	*Gloucester* - Thornbury

OMB - OSB

Ombersley	*Worcester* - Worcester
Ompton	*Notts* - Newark
Onecote	*Stafford* - Leek
One House	*Suffolk* - Stowmarket
One, Acres	*York, W.R.* - Sheffield
Ongar	*Essex* - Brentwood
Onibury	*Salop* - Ludlow
Onley	*Warwick* - Rugby
Onllwyn	*Glamorgan* - Neath
Onneley	*Stafford* - Stoke-on-Trent
Onn, High	*Stafford* - Stafford
Onn, Little	*Stafford* - Stafford
Onslow Village	*Surrey* - Guildford
Onston	*Cheshire* - Northwich
Oozewood	*Lancaster* - Oldham
Openshaw	*Lancaster* - Manchester
Openwood Gate	*Derby* - Derby
Orby	*Lincoln* - Skegness
Orchard, East	*Dorset* - Shaftesbury
Orchardleigh	*Somerset* - Frome
Orchard Portman	*Somerset* - Taunton
Orchard, West	*Dorset* - Shaftesbury
Orcheston St. George	*Wilts* - Salisbury
Orcheston St. Mary	*Wilts* - Salisbury
Orcop	*Hereford* - Hereford
Ord, East	*Northumberland* - Berwick-upon-Tweed
Ordsall	*Lancaster* - Salford
Ore	*Sussex* - Hastings
Oreston	*Devon* - Poymouth
Oreton	*Salop* - Ludlow
Orford	*Lancaster* - Warrington
Orford	*Lincoln* - Louth
Orford	*Suffolk* - Woodbridge
Organford	*Dorset* - Poole
Orgarswick	*Kent* - Ashford
Orgrave Hill	*Lancaster* - Barrow-in-Furness
Orgreave	*Stafford* - Lichfield
Orgreave	*York, W.R.* - Rotherham
Orielton	*Pembroke* - Haverfordwest
Orlestone	*Kent* - Ashford
Orleton	*Hereford* - Leominster
Orlingbury	*Northampton* - Wellingborough
Orllwynteifi	*Cardigan* - Cardigan
Ormathwaite	*Cumberland* - Workington
Ormesby	*York, N.R.* - Middlesbrough
Ormesby, Great (St. Margaret)	*Norfolk* - Great Yarmouth
Ormesby, Little (St. Michael)	*Norfolk* - Great Yarmouth
Ormesby, North	*York, N.R.* - Middlesbrough
Ormsby, North	*Lincoln* - Louth
Ormsby, South	*Lincoln* - Skegness
Ormsgill	*Lancaster* - Barrow-in-Furness
Ormside, Great	*Westmorland* - Penrith
Ormskirk	*Lancaster* - Southport
Orpington	*Kent* - Bromley
Orrell	*Lancaster* - Liverpool
Orrell	*Lancaster* - Wigan
Orrell Park	*Lancaster* - Liverpool
Orrell Post	*Lancaster* - Wigan
Orsett	*Essex* - Grays Thurrock
Orsett Heath	*Essex* - Grays Thurrock
Orslow	*Stafford* - Stafford
Orston	*Notts* - Nottingham
Orthwaite	*Cumberland* - Carlisle
Orton	*Northampton* - Kettering
Orton	*Stafford* - Wolverhampton
Orton	*Westmorland* - Penrith
Orton, Great	*Cumberland* - Carlisle
Orton, Little	*Cumberland* - Carlisle
Orton Longueville	*Hunts* - Peterborough
Orton-on-the-Hill	*Leicester* - Ashby-de-la-Zouch
Orton Rigg	*Cumberland* - Carlisle
Orton Waterville	*Hunts* - Peterborough
Orwell	*Cambridge* - Cambridge
Osbaldwick	*York, N.R.* - York
Osbaston	*Leicester* - Hinckley
Osbaston	*Salop* - Oswestry
Osbaston	*Salop* - Wellington (Salop)

OSB - OUS

Osberton	*Notts* - Worksop
Osbourn By	*Lincoln* - Sleaford
Oscott	*Warwick* - Birmingham
Oscott, New	*Warwick* - Birmingham
Oscott, Old	*Warwick* - Birmingham
Oscroft	*Cheshire* - Chester
Osea Island	*Essex* - Maldon
Osgathorpe	*Leicester* - Ashby-de-la-Zouch
Osgodby	*Lincoln* - Grantham
Osgodby	*Lincoln* - Lincoln
Osgodby	*York, E.R.* - York
Osgodby	*York, N.R.* - Scarborough
Osleston	*Derby* - Derby
Osmaston	*Derby* - Derby
Osmington	*Dorset* - Weymouth
Osmondthorpe	*York, W.R.* - Leeds
Osmotherley	*York, N.R.* - Northallerton
Ospringe	*Kent* - Canterbury
Ospringe Street	*Kent* - Canterbury
Ossemsley	*Hants* - Lymington
Ossett	*York, W.R.* - Dewsbury
Ossett, South	*York, W.R.* - Dewsbury
Ossett Spa	*York, W.R.* - Dewsbury
Ossett Street Side	*York, W.R.* - Dewsbury
Ossington	*Notts* - Newark
Ostend	*Essex* - Maldon
Osterley	*Middlesex* - Brentford
Oswaldkirk	*York, N.R.* - Malton
Oswaldtwistle	*Lancaster* - Accrington
Oswestry	*Salop* - Oswestry
Otby	*Lincoln* - Lincoln
Oteley	*Salop* - Oswestry
Otford	*Kent* - Sevenoaks
Otham	*Kent* - Maidstone
Otherton	*Stafford* - Stafford
Otherby	*Somerset* - Bridgwater
Otley	*Suffolk* - Woodbridge
Otley	*York, W.R.* - Otley
Otterbourne	*Hants* - Winchester
Otterburn	*Northumberland* - Hexham
Otterburn	*York, W.R.* - Skipton
Otterden	*Kent* - Sittingbourne
Otterford	*Somerset* - Taunton
Otterham	*Cornwall* - Launceston
Otterhampton	*Somerset* - Bridgwater
Otterham Quay	*Kent* - Sittingbourne
Otterington, North	*York, N.R.* - Northallerton
Otterington, South	*York, N.R.* - Northallerton
Ottershaw	*Surrey* - Kingston-upon-Thames
Otterton	*Devon* - Exeter
Ottery	*Devon* - Plymouth
Ottery St. Mary	*Devon* - Exeter
Ottinge	*Kent* - Folkestone
Ottringham	*York, E.R.* - Kingston-upon-Hull
Ottringham Marsh	*York, E.R.* - Kingston-upon-Hull
Oughterby	*Cumberland* - Carlisle
Oughtershaw	*York, W.R.* - Skipton
Oughterside	*Cumberland* - Workington
Oughtonhead	*Herts* - Hitchin
Oughtrington	*Cheshire* - Altrincham
Oughtybridge	*York, W.R.* - Sheffield
Oulston	*York, N.R.* - York
Oulton	*Cumberland* - Carlisle
Oulton	*Norfolk* - Norwich
Oulton	*Stafford* - Stafford
Oulton	*Suffolk* - Lowestoft
Oulton Broad	*Suffolk* - Lowestoft
Oulton Heath	*Stafford* - Stafford
Oulton Low	*Cheshire* - Northwich
Oulton-with-Woodlesford	*York, W.R.* - Leeds
Oundle	*Northampton* - Corby
Ounsdale	*Stafford* - Wolverhampton
Ousby	*Cumberland* - Penrith
Ousden	*Suffolk* - Newmarket
Ouseburn, Great	*York, W.R.* - Harrogate
Ouseburn, Little	*York, W.R.* - Harrogate
Ousefleet	*York, W.R.* - Goole
Ouse. Little	*Cambridge* - Ely
Ousethorpe	*York, E.R.* - York
Ouston	*Durham* - Gateshead

OUS - OVI

Ouston	*Northumberland* - Newcastle upon Tyne
Ouston	*York, W.R.* - York
Outhgill	*Westmorland* - Penrith
Outhill	*Warwick* - Redditch
Outlands	*Stafford* - Stafford
Outlane	*York, W.R.* - Huddersfield
Outlanes	*Stafford* - Stafford
Out Newton	*York, E.R.* - Kingston-upon-Hull
Out Rawcliffe	*Lancaster* - Blackpool
Outseats	*Derby* - Sheffield
Outwell	*Cambridge and Norfolk* - Wisbech
Outwood	*Surrey* - Reigate
Outwood	*Worcester* - Kidderminster
Outwood (part)	*York, W.R.* - Leeds
Outwood (part)	*York, W.R.* - Wakefield
Outwoods	*Stafford* - Stafford
Outwoods (Tutbury)	*Stafford* - Burton-upon-Trent
Ovenden	*York, W.R.* - Halifax
Ovenden Green	*Kent* - Sevenoaks
Over	*Cambridge* - Huntingdon
Over	*Cheshire* - Northwich
Over	*Gloucester* - Gloucester
Over	*Gloucester* - Thornbury
Over Alderley	*Cheshire* - Macclesfield
Overbury	*Worcester* - Evesham
Overbury Hill	*Worcester* - Evesham
Overchurch	*Cheshire* - Birkenhead
Over Compton	*Dorset* - Yeovil
Overdale	*Salop* - Wellington
Overend	*Cumberland* - Workington
Overend	*Stafford* - West Bromwich
Over Green	*Warwick* - Birmingham
Over Haddon	*Derby* - Matlock
Over Hulton	*Lancaster* - Bolton
Over Kellet	*Lancaster* - Lancaster
Over Kiddington	*Oxford* - Oxford
Overley	*Stafford* - Lichfield
Overley Hill	*Salop* - Wellington (Salop)
Over Norton	*Oxford* - Banbury
Over Peover	*Cheshire* - Northwich
Overpool	*Cheshire* - Ellesmere Port
Over-Ross	*Hereford* - Monmouth
Overseal	*Derby* - Ashby-de-la-Zouch
Oversland	*Kent* - Canterbury
Oversley	*Warwick* - Redditch
Overstone	*Northampton* - Northampton
Over Stowey	*Somerset* - Bridgwater
Overstrand	*Norfolk* - Norwich
Over Stratton	*Somerset* - Yeovil
Overthorpe	*Northampton* - Banbury
Overthorpe	*York, W.R.* - Dewsbury
Overton	*Cheshire* - Runcorn
Overton	*Cheshire* - Whitchurch
Overton	*Flint* - Wrexham
Overton	*Glamorgan* - Swansea
Overton	*Gloucester* - Gloucester
Overton	*Hants* - Basingstoke
Overton	*Hereford* - Leominster
Overton	*Lancaster* - Lancaster
Overton (Richard's Castle)	*Salop* - Ludlow
Overton	*Wilts* - Swindon
Overton	*York, N.R.* - York
Overton	*York, W.R.* - Wakefield
Overton-on-Dee	*Flint* - Wrexham
Overtown	*Lancaster* - Burnley
Overtown	*Wilts* - Swindon
Over Wallop	*Hants* - Andover
Over Whitacre	*Warwick* - Birmingham
Over Worton	*Oxford* - Banbury
Over Wyresdale	*Lancaster* - Lancaster
Oving	*Bucks* - Aylesbury
Oving	*Sussex* - Chichester
Ovingdean	*Sussex* - Brighton
Ovingham	*Northumberland* - Hexham
Ovington	*Essex* - Sudbury
Ovington	*Hants* - Winchester
Ovington	*Norfolk* - King's Lynn
Ovington	*Northumberland* - Hexham
Ovington	*York, N.R.* - Darlington

Ovington Down	*Hants* - Winchester
Owborough	*York, E.R.* - Kingston-upon-Hull
Ower	*Hants* - Southampton
Owermoigne	*Dorset* - Weymouth
Owersby Moor	*Lincoln* - Scunthorpe
Owersby, North	*Lincoln* - Scunthorpe
Owersby, South	*Lincoln* - Scunthorpe
Owlerton	*York, W.R.* - Sheffield
Owley Wood	*Cheshire* - Northwich
Owl Hill	*Worcester* - Worcester
Owlpen	*Gloucester* - Stroud
Owlsmoor	*Berks* - Reading
Owlswick	*Bucks* - High Wycombe
Owmby	*Lincoln* - Lincoln
Owmby Cliff	*Lincoln* - Lincoln
Owslebury	*Hants* - Winchester
Owsthorpe	*York, E.R.* - Goole
Owston	*Leicester* - Melton Mowbray
Owston	*York, W.R.* - Doncaster
Owston Ferry	*Lincoln* - Gainsborough
Owstwick	*York, E.R.* - Kingston-upon-Hull
Owthorne	*York, E.R.* - Kingston-upon-Hull
Owthorpe	*Notts* - Nottingham
Owton Manor	*Durham* - Hartlepool
Oxbarn	*Stafford* - Wolverhampton
Oxborough	*Norfolk* - King's Lynn
Oxcliffe	*Lancaster* - Lancaster
Oxclose	*Durham* - Gateshead
Oxcombe	*Lincoln* - Louth
Oxcroft	*Derby* - Chesterfield
Oxcroft Bank	*Lincoln* - Spalding
Oxenbourne	*Hants* - Petersfield
Oxendon, Great	*Northampton* - Market Harborough
Oxenhall	*Gloucester* - Gloucester
Oxenholme	*Westmorland* - Kendal
Oxenhope	*York, W.R.* - Keighley
Oxen Law	*Durham* - Durham
Oxen Leaze	*Wilts* - Trowbridge
Oxen Park	*Lancaster* - Barrow-in-Furness
Oxenton	*Gloucester* - Cheltenham
Oxenton Hill	*Gloucester* - Cheltenham
Oxenwood	*Berks* - Newbury
Oxford	*Oxford* - Oxford
Oxford	*Stafford* - Stoke-on-Trent
Oxgate	*London, N.W.2* - Willesden
Oxhey	*Herts* - Watford
Oxhill	*Warwick* - Stratford on Avon
Ox Leasows	*Stafford* - Stafford
Oxley	*Stafford* - Wolverhampton
Oxlynch	*Gloucester* - Gloucester
Oxlode	*Cambridge* - Ely
Oxmardike	*York, E.R.* - Goole
Oxnead	*Norfolk* - Norwich
Oxney	*Kent* - Dover
Oxney Green	*Essex* - Chelmsford
Oxon	*Salop* - Shrewsbury
Oxshott	*Surrey* - Kingston-upon-Thames
Oxspring	*York, W.R.* - Barnsley
Oxted	*Surrey* - Reigate
Oxted, New	*Surrey* - Reigate
Oxton	*Cheshire* - Birkenhead
Oxton	*Notts* - Nottingham
Oxton	*York, W.R.* - York
Oxwich	*Glamorgan* - Swansea
Oxwick	*Norfolk* - King's Lynn
Oystermouth	*Glamorgan* - Swansea
Ozendyke	*York, W.R.* - York
Ozleworth	*Gloucester* - Stroud

P

Pabo	*Caernarvon* - Conway
Packington	*Leicester* - Ashby-de-la-Zouch
Packington	*Stafford* - Lichfield
Packington, Great	*Warwick* - Coventry
Packington, Little	*Warwick* - Coventry
Packington Outwoods	*Warwick* - Coventry
Packmoor	*Stafford* - Stoke-on-Trent
Packwood	*Warwick* - Birmingham
Padbury	*Bucks* - Aylesbury
Paddington	*Lancaster* - Warrington

Paddington	*London, W.2* - Bloomsbury and Marylebone
Paddlesworth	*Kent* - Folkestone
Paddock	*York, W.R.* - Huddersfield
Paddock Hill	*Cheshire* - Altrincham
Paddock Wood	*Kent* - Tunbridge Wells
Paddol Green	*Salop* - Shrewsbury
Padeswood	*Flint* - Mold
Padfield	*Derby* - Hyde
Padgate	*Lancaster* - Warrington
Padhams Green	*Essex* - Brentwood
Padiham	*Lancaster* - Burnley
Padiham Green	*Lancaster* - Burnley
Padley, Nether	*Derby* - Chesterfield
Padnal	*Cambridge* - Ely
Padnall Estate	*Essex* - Ilford
Padney	*Cambridge* - Newmarket
Padside	*York, W.R.* - Harrogate
Padstow	*Cornwall* - Bodmin
Padworth	*Berks* - Reading
Paganhill	*Gloucester* - Stroud
Page Bank	*Durham* - Bishop Auckland
Page Fields	*Stafford* - Stafford
Page Moss	*Lancaster* - St. Helens
Page Street	*London, N.W.7* - Willesden
Pagham	*Sussex* - Chichester
Paglesham	*Essex* - Southend
Paignton	*Devon* - Torquay
Pailton	*Warwick* - Rugby
Painsbrook	*Salop* - Shrewsbury
Painsdale	*Northumberland* - Haltwhistle
Painsdown	*Devon* - Axminster and Chard
Painswick	*Gloucester* - Stroud
Painswin	*Norfolk* - King's Lynn
Painters Forstal	*Kent* - Canterbury
Painters Green	*Flint* - Whitchurch
Painters Green	*Herts* - Hertford
Painthorpe	*York, W.R.* - Wakefield
Pakefield	*Suffolk* - Lowestoft
Pakenham	*Suffolk* - Bury St. Edmunds
Palestine	*Hants* - Andover
Paley Street	*Berks* - Slough
Palgrave	*Suffolk* - Norwich
Palgrave, Great	*Norfolk* - King's Lynn
Palgrave, Little	*Norfolk* - King's Lynn
Pallingham Quay	*Sussex* - Chichester
Pallington	*Dorset* - Dorchester
Pallion	*Durham* - Sunderland
Palm Bay	*Kent* - Margate
Palmer's Ford	*Hants* - Bournemouth
Palmers Green	*London, N.13* - Edmonton
Palmer's Village	*Devon* - Tiverton
Palmersville	*Northumberland* - Newcastle upon Tyne
Palms Hill	*Salop* - Shrewsbury
Palterton	*Derby* - Chesterfield
Pamber	*Hants* - Basingstoke
Pamber End	*Hants* - Basingstoke
Pamber Green	*Hants* - Basingstoke
Pamber Heath	*Hants* - Basingstoke
Pamington	*Gloucester* - Cheltenham
Pamphill	*Dorset* - Wimborne Minster
Pampisford	*Cambridge* - Cambridge
Pandborough	*Somerset* - Wells
Pandy	*Denbigh* - Wrexham
Pandy	*Monmouth* - Pontypool and Abergavenny
Pandyrhiwsaeson	*Montgomery* - Machynlleth
Pandy Tudur	*Denbigh* - Conway
Panfield	*Essex* - Braintree
Pangbourne	*Berks* - Reading
Pannal	*York, W.R.* - Harrogate
Pannal Ash	*York, W.R.* - Harrogate
Panpunton	*Salop* - Knighton
Panson, East	*Devon* - Launceston
Panson, West	*Devon* - Launceston
Pant	*Denbigh* - Wrexham
Pant	*Glamorgan* - Merthyr Tydfil
Pant	*Salop* - Oswestry
Pant Asaph	*Flint* - Holywell

PAN - PAR

Panteg	*Monmouth* - Pontypool and Abergavenny
Pantglas	*Caernarvon* - Caernarvon
Panton	*Lincoln* - Lincoln
Pantperthog	*Merioneth* - Machynlleth
Pantrhosla	*Glamorgan* - Bridgend
Pantruthin	*Glamorgan* - Bridgend
Pantscallog	*Glamorgan* - Merthyr Tydfil
Pantydwr	*Radnor* - Llandrindod Wells
Pantyffynon	*Carmarthen* - Ammanford
Pantyfin	*Glamorgan* - Merthyr Tydfil
Pantygasseg	*Monmouth* - Pontypool and Abergavenny
Pantylladron	*Glamorgan* - Cardiff
Pantywaun	*Glamorgan* - Bargoed
Panxworth	*Norfolk* - Norwich
Papcastle	*Cumberland* - Workington
Paper Mills	*Salop* - Shrewsbury
Papley	*Northampton* - Peterborough
Papplewick	*Notts* - Nottingham
Papworth Everard	*Cambridge* - Huntingdon
Papworth St. Agnes	*Cambridge* - Huntingdon
Par	*Cornwall* - St. Austell
Paradise	*Gloucester* - Stroud
Paradise	*Lancaster* - Barrow-in-Furness
Paradise	*Stafford* - Wolverhampton
Paradise	*Warwick* - Coventry
Paramoor	*Cornwall* - St. Austell
Parbold	*Lancaster* - Wigan
Parbrook	*Somerset* - Wells
Parbrook	*Sussex* - Horsham
Parc	*Merioneth* - Dolgellau
Parc Gwyllt	*Glamorgan* - Bridgend
Parchey Bridge	*Somerset* - Bridgwater
Parchfields	*Stafford* - Stafford
Parcllyn	*Cardigan* - Cardigan
Pardshaw	*Cumberland* - Workington
Parham	*Suffolk* - Woodbridge
Parham	*Sussex* - Chichester
Paris	*York, W.R.* - Huddersfield
Park	*Northumberland* - Hexham
Park Attwood	*Worcester* - Kidderminster
Park Bottom	*Cornwall* - Redruth
Parkbridge	*Lancaster* - Ashton-under-Lyne
Park Broom	*Cumberland* - Carlisle
Park Corner	*Oxford* - Reading
Park Drain Station	*Lincoln* - Gainsborough
Parke Hall	*Worcester* - Kidderminster
Parkend (Lydney)	*Gloucester* - Monmouth
Park End	*Worcester* - Kidderminster
Parkes Hall	*Stafford* - Dudley
Parkeston	*Essex* - Harwich
Parkfield	*Gloucester* - Bristol
Parkfields	*Hereford* - Gloucester
Parkfields	*Stafford* - Wolverhampton
Parkgate	*Cheshire* - Birkenhead
Park Gate	*Dorset* - Dorchester
Park Gate	*Hants* - Portsmouth
Parkgate	*Surrey* - Dorking
Park Gate	*Worcester* - Bromsgrove
Park Gate	*Worcester* - Kidderminster
Park Gate	*York, W.R.* - Rotherham
Park Hall	*Salop* - Oswestry
Park Hall	*Stafford* - Stoke-on-Trent
Park Hall	*Stafford* - Stafford
Parkham	*Devon* - Bideford
Park Head	*Cumberland* - Carlisle
Park Head (Renwick)	*Cumberland* - Penrith
Park Head	*York, W.R.* - Sheffield
Park Heath	*Salop* - Market Drayton
Park Hill	*York, W.R.* - Sheffield
Parkhurst	*I. of W.* - Newport (I.W.)
Park Langley	*Kent* - Bromley
Parkley	*Flint* - Whitchurch
Parkmill	*Glamorgan* - Swansea
Park Mills	*Bucks* - High Wycombe
Park Nook	*Stafford* - Stafford
Park, Old	*Kent* - Dover
Park Royal (part)	*London, N.W.10* - Brentford
Park Royal (part)	*London, N.W.10* - Willesden

PAR - PAX

Parkstone	*Dorset* - Poole
Park Street	*Herts* - St. Albans
Park Village	*Northumberland* - Hexham
Park Village	*Stafford* - Wolverhampton
Parkway	*Hereford* - Hereford
Parley, East	*Hants* - Bournemouth
Parley Green	*Hants* - Bournemouth
Parley, West	*Dorset* - Wimborne Minster
Parlington	*York, W.R.* - Leeds
Parmoor	*Oxford* - Reading
Parr	*Lancaster* - St. Helens
Parracombe	*Devon* - Barnstaple
Parramoor	*Cornwall* - St. Austell
Parrog	*Pembroke* - Cardigan
Parrot's Grove	*Warwick* - Coventry
Parsley Hay	*Derby* - Buxton
Parsonage Green	*Essex* - Chelmsford
Parson Bridge	*Cumberland* - Carlisle
Parsonby	*Cumberland* - Workington
Parson Cross	*York, W.R.* - Sheffield
Parson Drove	*Cambridge* - Wisbech
Parsons Barn	*Salop* - Wellington (Salop)
Parson's Brake	*Stafford* - Burton-upon-Trent
Parsons Green	*London, S.W.6* - West London
Partington	*Cheshire* - Altrincham
Partney	*Lincoln* - Skegness
Parton	*Cumberland* - Whitehaven
Parton	*Cumberland* - Carlisle
Partridge Green	*Sussex* - Horsham
Parwich	*Derby* - Matlock
Passage, New	*Gloucester* - Thornbury
Passage, Old	*Gloucester* - Thornbury
Passeford	*Devon* - Exeter
Passenham	*Northampton* - Northampton
Passfield	*Hants* - Petersfield
Paston	*Norfolk* - Norwich
Paston	*Northumberland* - Berwick-upon-Tweed
Pasture Fields	*Stafford* - Stafford
Patcham	*Sussex* - Brighton
Patchetts Green	*Herts* - Watford
Patching	*Sussex* - Worthing
Patchway	*Gloucester* - Thornbury
Patchway Common	*Gloucester* - Thornbury
Patchway, Lower	*Gloucester* - Thornbury
Pateley Bridge	*York, W.R.* - Harrogate
Pathlow	*Warwick* - Stratford on Avon
Patient End	*Herts* - Bishop's Stortford
Patmore Heath	*Herts* - Bishop's Stortford
Patney	*Wilts* - Devizes
Patricio	*Brecon* - Pontypool and Abergavenny
Patrick Brompton	*York, N.R.* - Northallerton
Patricroft	*Lancaster* - Salford
Patrington	*York, E.R.* - Kingston-upon-Hull
Patrington Haven	*York, E.R.* - Kingston-upon-Hull
Patrishow	*Brecon* - Pontypool and Abergavenny
Patrixbourne	*Kent* - Canterbury
Patshull	*Stafford* - Wolverhampton
Patterdale	*Westmorland* - Penrith
Patterdown	*Wilts* - Chippenham
Pattingham	*Stafford* - Wolverhampton
Pattishall	*Northampton* - Northampton
Pattiswick	*Essex* - Braintree
Patton	*Salop* - Bridgnorth
Patton	*Westmorland* - Kendal
Patton Bridge	*Westmorland* - Kendal
Paul	*Cornwall* - Penzance
Paulerspury	*Northampton* - Northampton
Paull	*York, E.R.* - Kingston-upon-Hull
Paulsgrove	*Hants* - Portsmouth
Paulton	*Somerset* - Bristol
Paultons	*Hants* - Southampton
Pauntley	*Gloucester* - Gloucester
Pauperhaugh	*Northumberland* - Morpeth
Pave Lane	*Salop* - Wellington (Salop)
Pavenham	*Beds* - Bedford
Pawlett	*Somerset* - Bridgwater
Paxcroft	*Wilts* - Trowbridge

PAX - PEL

Paxford	*Gloucester* - Evesham
Paxton, Great	*Hunts* - Huntingdon
Paxton, Little	*Hunts* - Huntingdon
Payford	*Glos* - Gloucester
Payhembury	*Devon* - Exeter
Paynters Lane End	*Cornwall* - Redruth
Paythorne	*York, W.R.* - Blackburn
Paytoe	*Hereford* - Ludlow
Peace (Carnkie, Redruth)	*Cornwall* - Redruth
Peacehaven	*Sussex* - Brighton
Peacock Gap	*Northumberland* - Morpeth
Pea Flatts	*Durham* - Durham
Peak Dale	*Derby* - Buxton
Peak Forest	*Derby* - Buxton
Peakhill	*Lincoln* - Spalding
Peakirk	*Northampton* - Peterborough
Pean	*Kent* - Folkestone
Peartree Green	*Hereford* - Hereford
Peasedown St. John	*Somerset* - Bath
Peasely Cross	*Lancaster* - St. Helens
Peasemeadows	*Northumberland* - Hexham
Peasemore	*Berks* - Newbury
Peasenhall	*Suffolk* - Woodbridge
Peaslake	*Surrey* - Guildford
Peasmarsh	*Sussex* - Hastings
Peas Pottage	*Sussex* - Haywards Heath
Peat Carr Estate	*Durham* - Durham
Peatcott	*Devon* - Plymouth
Peat Howe	*Cumberland* - Workington
Peatling Magna	*Leicester* - Leicester
Peatling Parva	*Leicester* - Leicester
Peaton	*Salop* - Ludlow
Peatswood	*Salop* - Market Drayton
Pebble Combe	*Surrey* - Dorking
Pebmarsh	*Essex* - Braintree
Pebworth	*Gloucester* - Evesham
Peckers Hill	*Lancaster* - St. Helens
Peckett Well	*York, W.R.* - Todmorden
Peckfield	*York, W.R.* - Pontefract
Peckforton	*Cheshire* - Crewe
Peckham (part)	*London, S.E.15* - Lambeth
Peckham (part)	*London, S.E. 15*- Southwark
Peckham, East	*Kent* - Maidstone
Peckham Rye	*London, S.E.15* - Lambeth
Peckham Rye	*London, S.E.22* - Lambeth
Peckham, West	*Kent* - Maidstone
Peckleton	*Leicester* - Hinckley
Pecklewell	*Cumberland* - Workington
Pedairffordd	*Montgomery* - Oswestry
Pedington	*Gloucester* - Stroud
Pedlar's Rest	*Salop* - Ludlow
Pedlinge	*Kent* - Folkestone
Pedmore	*Worcester* - Stourbridge
Pednor	*Bucks* - Amersham
Pedwell	*Somerset* - Bridgwater
Peel	*Lancaster* - Blackpool
Peelcauseway	*Cheshire* - Altrincham
Peel Green	*Lancaster* - Salford
Peel Hall	*Lancaster* - Manchester
Peels	*Northumberland* - Morpeth
Peening Quarter	*Kent* - Cranbrook
Pegglesworth	*Gloucester* - Cheltenham
Pegg's Green	*Leicester* - Ashby-de-la-Zouch
Pegsdon	*Herts* - Hitchin
Pegswood	*Northumberland* - Morpeth
Pelaw	*Durham* - Gateshead
Pelaw Colliery	*Durham* - Durham
Pelaw Grange	*Durham* - Gateshead
Pelaw Main	*Durham* - Gateshead
Pelaw, South	*Durham* - Durham
Pelcomb	*Pembroke* - Haverfordwest
Peldon	*Essex* - Colchester
Pelf-in-Tax	*Lincoln* - Gainsborough
Pelham's Lands	*Lincoln* - Boston
Pellon	*York, W.R.* - Halifax
Pell Wall	*Salop* - Market Drayton
Pelsall	*Stafford* - Walsall
Pelsall Wood	*Stafford* - Walsall
Pelton	*Durham* - Durham
Pelton Flatts	*Durham* - Durham

PEL - PEN

Pelton, West	*Durham* - Durham
Pelutho	*Cumberland* - Carlisle
Pelynt	*Cornwall* - Liskeard
Pemberton	*Carmarthen* - Llanelli
Pemberton	*Lancaster* - Wigan
Pembrey	*Carmarthen* - Llanelli
Pembridge	*Hereford* - Leominster
Pembroke	*Pembroke* - Haverfordwest
Pembroke Dock	*Pembroke* - Haverfordwest
Pembroke Ferry	*Pembroke* - Haverfordwest
Pembury	*Kent* - Tunbridge Wells
Penally	*Pembroke* - Haverfordwest
Penalt	*Hereford* - Hereford
Penalt	*Monmouth* - Monmouth
Penant	*Cardigan* - Aberystwyth
Penarth	*Glamorgan* - Cardiff
Penarth, Lower	*Glamorgan* - Cardiff
Penbedw	*Flint* - Mold
Penberth	*Cornwall* - Penzance
Penboyr	*Carmarthen* - Carmarthen
Penbryn	*Cardigan* - Cardigan
Pencader	*Carmarthen* - Carmarthen
Pencaenewydd	*Caernarvon* - Portmadoc
Pencarnisiog	*Anglesey* - Llangefni
Pencarreg	*Carmarthen* - Lampeter
Pencarrow	*Cornwall* - Bideford
Penceilogi	*Carmarthen* - Llanelli
Penclawdd	*Glamorgan* - Swansea
Penclose	*Berks* - Newbury
Pencoed	*Glamorgan* - Bridgend
Pencombe	*Hereford* - Hereford
Pencoyd	*Hereford* - Hereford
Pencoys	*Cornwall* - Redruth
Pencraig	*Hereford* - Monmouth
Pencricket Estate	*Stafford* - Dudley
Pendarren	*Glamorgan* - Merthyr Tydfil
Pendean	*Sussex* - Chichester
Pendeen	*Cornwall* - Penzance
Pendeford	*Stafford* - Wolverhampton
Penderyn	*Brecon* - Aberdare
Pendine	*Carmarthen* - Haverfordwest
Pendlebury	*Lancaster* - Salford
Pendleton	*Lancaster* - Salford
Pendleton Village	*Lancaster* - Blackburn
Pendock	*Worcester* - Cheltenham
Pendoggett	*Cornwall* - Bideford
Pendomer	*Somerset* - Yeovil
Pendower	*Cornwall* - Truro
Pendoylan	*Glamorgan* - Cardiff
Pendre	*Glamorgan* - Bridgend
Penegoes	*Montgomery* - Machynlleth
Penelewey	*Cornwall* - Truro
Pengam	*Glamorgan* - Bargoed
Pengam	*Monmouth* - Blackwood
Pengarnddu	*Glamorgan* - Merthyr Tydfil
Penge (part)	*London, S.E.20* - Bromley
Penge (part)	*London, S.E.20* - Croydon
Pengegon	*Cornwall* - Redruth
Pengelly	*Cornwall* - Bodmin
Pengover Green	*Cornwall* - Liskeard
Pengwern	*Montgomery* - Oswestry
Penhale	*Cornwall* - Penzance
Penhale	*Cornwall* - St. Austell
Penhallow	*Cornwall* - Truro
Penhalurick	*Cornwall* - Redruth
Penhalvean	*Cornwall* - Redruth
Penhalveor	*Cornwall* - Redruth
Penhellick	*Cornwall* - Redruth
Penherber	*Carmarthen* - Cardigan
Penhow	*Monmouth* - Newport (Mon.)
Penshurst	*Sussex* - Hastings
Peniarth	*Montgomery* - Oswestry
Peniel	*Denbigh* - Denbigh
Penisarwaen	*Caernarvon* - Caernarvon
Penistone	*York, W.R.* - Barnsley
Penkelly	*Brecon* - Brecknock
Penketh	*Lancaster* - Warrington
Penkhull	*Stafford* - Stoke-on-Trent
Penkridge	*Stafford* - Stafford
Penkridge Bank	*Stafford* - Stafford

PEN	
Penkuke	*Cornwall* - Launceston
Penlan	*Glamorgan* - Swansea
Penleigh	*Wilts* - Trowbridge
Penley	*Flint* - Wrexham
Penleys	*Oxford* - High Wycombe
Penllech	*Caernarvon* - Portmadoc
Penllergaer	*Glamorgan* - Swansea
Penllwyn	*Cardigan* - Aberystwyth
Penllwyn	*Monmouth* - Blackwood
Penllyn (Llanystumdwy)	*Caernarvon* - Portmadoc
Penllyn	*Glamorgan* - Bridgend
Penlocks	*Glamorgan* - Merthyr Tydfil
Penmachno	*Caernarvon* - Conway
Penmaen	*Glamorgan* - Swansea
Penmaen	*Monmouth* - Blackwood
Penmaenan	*Caernarvon* - Conway
Penmaen Head	*Denbigh* - Conway
Penmaenmawr	*Caernarvon* - Conway
Penman's Green	*Herts* - Watford
Penmark	*Glamorgan* - Barry
Penmark	*Monmouth* - Blackwood
Penmere	*Cornwall* - Truro
Penmon	*Anglesey* - Llangefni
Penmorfa	*Caernarvon* - Portmadoc
Penmyarth	*Brecon* - Pontypool and Abergavenny
Penmynydd	*Anglesey* - Llangefni
Penmynydd	*Caernarvon* - Conway
Penn	*Bucks* - High Wycombe
Pennal	*Merioneth* - Machynlleth
Pennance Mill	*Cornwall* - Truro
Pennant	*Cardigan* - Aberystwyth
Pennant	*Montgomery* - Oswestry
Pennant	*Montgomery* - Machynlleth
Pennantilliw	*Merioneth* - Denbigh
Pennar	*Pembroke* - Haverfordwest
Pennard	*Glamorgan* - Swansea
Pennard, East	*Somerset* - Wells
Pennard, West	*Somerset* - Wells
Pennerley	*Salop* - Shrewsbury
Penn Fields	*Stafford* - Wolverhampton
Pennington	*Hants* - Lymington
Pennington	*Lancaster* - Barrow-in-Furness
Pennington	*Lancaster* - Leigh
Pennington Green	*Lancaster* - Wigan
Penn, Lower	*Stafford* - Wolverhampton
Penns	*Warwick* - Birmingham
Penn Street	*Bucks* - Amersham
Penn Street	*Bucks* - High Wycombe
Penn, Upper	*Stafford* - Wolverhampton
Pennybridge	*Lancaster* - Barrow-in-Furness
Pennycomequick	*Devon* - Plymouth
Pennycross	*Devon* - Plymouth
Penny Hill	*Lincoln* - Spalding
Pennylands	*Lancaster* - Wigan
Pennymoor	*Devon* - Tiverton
Penparcau	*Cardigan* - Aberystwyth
Penpark	*Cardigan* - Cardigan
Penperlleni	*Monmouth* - Pontypool and Abergavenny
Penpeugh	*Northumberland* - Hexham
Penpillick	*Cornwall* - St. Austell
Penpoll	*Cornwall* - Liskeard
Penpoll	*Cornwall* - Truro
Penponds	*Cornwall* - Redruth
Penpont	*Brecon* - Brecknock
Penprisk	*Glamorgan* - Bridgend
Penquit	*Devon* - Kingsbridge
Penquite	*Cornwall* - Bideford
Penrhiewtyn	*Glamorgan* - Neath
Penrhiewfer	*Glamorgan* - Pontypridd
Penrhiewgoch	*Carmarthen* - Ammanford
Penrhiewllan	*Cardigan* - Cardigan
Penrhiw	*Monmouth* - Newport (Mon.)
Penrhiwceiber	*Glamorgan* - Aberdare
Penrhos	*Brecon* - Neath
Penrhos (Pwllheli)	*Caernarvon* - Portmadoc
Penrhos	*Denbigh* - Wrexham
Penrhos	*Monmouth* - Monmouth
Penrhosgarnedd	*Caernarvon* - Bangor

PEN	
Penrhoslligwy	*Anglesey* - Llangefni
Penrhyn Bay	*Caernarvon* - Conway
Penrhyncoch	*Cardigan* - Aberystwyth
Penrhyndeudraeth	*Merioneth* - Portmadoc
Penrhynfawr	*Montgomery* - Oswestry
Penrhynfechan	*Montgomery* - Oswestry
Penrhys	*Glamorgan* - Pontypridd
Penrice	*Cornwall* - St. Austell
Penrice	*Glamorgan* - Swansea
Penrith	*Cumberland* - Penrith
Penrose (Luxulyan)	*Cornwall* - Bodmin
Penrose (St. Ervan)	*Cornwall* - Truro
Penrose (St. Dennis)	*Cornwall* - St. Austell
Penruddock	*Cumberland* - Penrith
Penrydd	*Pembroke* - Cardigan
Penryn	*Cornwall* - Truro
Pensarn	*Anglesey* - Llangefni
Pensarn	*Carmarthen* - Carmarthen
Pensarn	*Denbigh* - Rhyl
Pensax	*Worcester* - Kidderminster
Pensby	*Cheshire* - Birkenhead
Penselwood	*Somerset* - Yeovil
Pensford	*Somerset* - Bristol
Pensham	*Worcester* - Evesham
Penshaw, New	*Durham* - Durham
Penshaw, Old	*Durham* - Durham
Penshaw Staiths	*Durham* - Durham
Penshurst	*Kent* - Tonbridge
Pensilva	*Cornwall* - Liskeard
Pensnett	*Stafford* - Stourbridge
Pensthorpe	*Norfolk* - King's Lynn
Penstone	*Devon* - Exeter
Penstraze	*Cornwall* - Truro
Penstrowed	*Montgomery* - Newtown
Pensylvania	*Somerset* - Bath
Penteg Cross	*Cardigan* - Cardigan
Pentewan	*Cornwall* - St. Austell
Pentillie	*Cornwall* - Plymouth
Pentir	*Caernarvon* - Bangor
Pentire, West	*Cornwall* - Truro
Pentlow	*Essex* - Sudbury
Pentney	*Norfolk* - King's Lynn
Penton	*Cumberland* - Carlisle
Penton	*Hants* - Andover
Penton Grafton	*Hants* - Andover
Penton Mewsey	*Hants* - Andover
Pentonville	*London, N.1* - Clerkenwell
Pentraeth	*Anglesey* - Llangefni
Pentre	*Denbigh* - Wrexham
Pentre (Hawarden)	*Flint* - Chester
Pentre	*Glamorgan* - Pontypridd
Pentre	*Montgomery* - Welshpool
Pentre	*Salop* - Knighton
Pentrebach	*Brecon* - Brecknock
Pentrebach	*Glamorgan* - Merthyr Tydfil
Pentre Bychan	*Denbigh* - Wrexham
Pentrecagal	*Carmarthen* - Carmarthen
Pentrecelyn	*Denbigh* - Denbigh
Pentreclawdd	*Salop* - Oswestry
Pentreclwyda	*Glamorgan* - Neath
Pentrecoed	*Salop* - Oswestry
Pentrecwrt	*Carmarthen* - Carmarthen
Pentredwr	*Denbigh* - Wrexham
Pentre Estyll	*Glamorgan* - Swansea
Pentre Felin	*Anglesey* - Llangefni
Pentrefelin	*Brecon* - Brecknock
Pentrefelin	*Caernarvon* - Portmadoc
Pentrefelin	*Denbigh* - Wrexham
Pentrefelin	*Denbigh* - Oswestry
Pentrefeolas	*Denbigh* - Conway
Pentreffynnon	*Flint* - Holywell
Pentregaer	*Salop* - Oswestry
Pentregwenlais	*Carmarthen* - Ammanford
Pentre Halkyn	*Flint* - Holywell
Pentre Llanrhaiadr	*Denbigh* - Denbigh
Pentrellyncymer	*Denbigh* - Denbigh
Pentrenant	*Montgomery* - Welshpool
Pentre Nesscliffe	*Salop* - Oswestry
Pentrepiod	*Monmouth* - Pontypool and Abergavenny

Pentre Treuddyn	*Flint* - Mold
Pentreuchaf	*Caernarvon* - Portmadoc
Pentrewilly	*Montgomery* - Welshpool
Pentrich	*Derby* - Alfreton
Pentridge	*Dorset* - Salisbury
Pentrobin	*Flint* - Chester
Pentwyn	*Glamorgan* - Bargoed
Pentwyn	*Monmouth* - Pontypool and Abergavenny
Pentyrch	*Glamorgan* - Cardiff
Pentywynmawr	*Glamorgan* - Blackwood
Penucharmynydd, Sydrydyn	*Flint* - Mold
Penuwch	*Cardigan* - Lampeter
Penventinue	*Cornwall* - St. Austell
Penwarne	*Cornwall* - Truro
Penwerris	*Cornwall* - Truro
Penwethers	*Cornwall* - Truro
Penwithick	*Cornwall* - St. Austell
Pen Wood	*Hants* - Newbury
Penwortham	*Lancaster* - Preston
Penwyllt	*Brecon* - Brecknock
Penwyllt	*Brecon* - Neath
Penyard	*Glamorgan* - Merthyr Tydfil
Penybank (Ammanford)	*Carmarthen* - Ammanford
Penybank (Llandilo)	*Carmarthen* - Ammanford
Penybont	*Carmarthen* - Carmarthen
Penybont	*Denbigh* - Oswestry
Penybont	*Radnor* - Llandrindod Wells
Penybontfawr	*Montgomery* - Oswestry
Penybryn	*Glamorgan* - Bargoed
Penycae	*Brecon* - Neath
Penycae	*Denbigh* - Wrexham
Penycae	*Glamorgan* - Bridgend
Penycefn	*Flint* - Holywell
Penychain	*Caernarvon* - Portmadoc
Penyclawdd	*Monmouth* - Monmouth
Penycoedcae	*Glamorgan* - Pontypridd
Penycwm	*Pembroke* - Haverfordwest
Penycwm	*Salop* - Welshpool
Penydarren	*Glamorgan* - Merthyr Tydfil
Penydre	*Pembroke* - Cardigan
Penyfai	*Glamorgan* - Bridgend
Penyffordd	*Flint* - Wrexham
Penygarn	*Cardigan* - Aberystwyth
Penygarn	*Glamorgan* - Cardiff
Penygarn	*Monmouth* - Pontypool and Abergavenny
Penygarnedd	*Montgomery* - Oswestry
Penygawsi	*Glamorgan* - Pontypridd
Penygelli	*Denbigh* - Wrexham
Penygloddfa	*Montgomery* - Newtown
Penygraig	*Glamorgan* - Pontypridd
Penygroes	*Caernarvon* - Caernarvon
Penygroes (Llanystumdwy)	*Caernarvon* - Portmadoc
Penygroes	*Carmarthen* - Ammanford
Penylan	*Denbigh* - Wrexham
Penylan	*Glamorgan* - Bridgend
Penylan (Cardiff)	*Glamorgan* - Cardiff
Penymynydd	*Flint* - Wrexham
Penymynydd	*Glamorgan* - Bridgend
Penymynydd	*Montgomery* - Oswestry
Penyparc	*Hereford* - Hereford
Penyrheol	*Glamorgan* - Caerphilly
Penyrheol	*Monmouth* - Pontypool and Abergavenny
Penywaun	*Glamorgan* - Aberdare
Penywaunfawr	*Glamorgan* - Merthyr Tydfil
Penywern	*Glamorgan* - Merthyr Tydfil
Penzance	*Cornwall* - Penzance
Peopleton	*Worcester* - Worcester
Peover Inferior	*Cheshire* - Northwich
Peover, Lower	*Cheshire* - Northwich
Peover, Nether	*Cheshire* - Northwich
Peover, Over	*Cheshire* - Northwich
Peover Superior	*Cheshire* - Northwich
Peplow	*Salop* - Market Drayton
Peppard	*Oxford* - Reading
Pepperstock	*Herts* - Luton

Pepper Street	*Salop* - Shrewsbury
Percombe	*Somerset* - Yeovil
Percuil	*Cornwall* - Truro
Percy Main	*Northumberland* - North Shields
Perham Down	*Wilts* - Andover
Perivale	*Middlesex* - Brentford
Perkins Beach	*Salop* - Shrewsbury
Perkinsville	*Durham* - Durham
Perlethorpe	*Notts* - Worksop
Perranarworthal	*Cornwall* - Truro
Perrancoombe	*Cornwall* - Truro
Perran Downs	*Cornwall* - Penzance
Perranporth	*Cornwall* - Truro
Perranuthhoe	*Cornwall* - Penzance
Perranwell (Perranporth)	*Cornwall* - Truro
Perranwell (Perranarworthal)	*Cornwall* - Truro
Perranzabuloe	*Cornwall* - Truro
Perrott, North	*Somerset* - Yeovil
Perrotts Brook	*Gloucester* - Cheltenham
Perrott, South	*Dorset* - Yeovil
Perry	*Stafford* - Birmingham
Perry Barr	*Warwick* - Birmingham
Perry Common	*Warwick* - Birmingham
Perry Green	*Herts* - Bishop's Stortford
Perry Hall	*Stafford* - Birmingham
Perrystone	*Hereford* - Monmouth
Perry Street	*Kent* - Gravesend
Perry Street	*Somerset* - Axminster and Chard
Perry, West	*Hunts* - Huntingdon
Perry Wood	*Kent* - Canterbury
Pershall	*Stafford* - Stafford
Pershore	*Worcester* - Evesham
Pershore Lane	*Worcester* - Worcester
Pertenhall	*Beds* - Bedford
Perthi	*Salop* - Oswestry
Perthygleision	*Glamorgan* - Merthyr Tydfil
Perton	*Stafford* - Wolverhampton
Pertwood	*Wilts* - Shaftesbury
Pesspool	*Durham* - Durham
Peterborough	*Northampton* - Peterborough
Peterchurch	*Hereford* - Hereford
Peterlee	*Durham* - Hartlepool
Peters	*Somerset* - Bristol
Petersfield	*Hants* - Petersfield
Peter's Green	*Herts* - Hitchin
Petersham	*Surrey* - Wandsworth
Peters Marland	*Devon* - Bideford
Peterstone	*Monmouth* - Newport (Mon.)
Peterstone	*Norfolk* - King's Lynn
Peterstone-super-Ely	*Glamorgan* - Cardiff
Peterston super Montem	*Glamorgan* - Bridgend
Peterstow	*Hereford* - Monmouth
Petertavy	*Devon* - Plymouth
Peterville	*Cornwall* - Truro
Petham	*Kent* - Canterbury
Petherick, Little	*Cornwall* - Bodmin
Petherton, North	*Somerset* - Bridgwater
Petherton, South	*Somerset* - Yeovil
Petherwin, North	*Devon* - Launceston
Petherwin, South	*Cornwall* - Launceston
Petrockstow	*Devon* - Bideford
Petsoe End	*Bucks* - Northampton
Petsoe Manor	*Bucks* - Northampton
Pett	*Sussex* - Hastings
Pettaugh	*Suffolk* - Ipswich
Petterill Green	*Cumberland* - Penrith
Pettistree	*Suffolk* - Woodbridge
Petton	*Devon* - Tiverton
Petton	*Salop* - Shrewsbury
Petts Wood	*Kent* - Bromley
Petworth	*Sussex* - Chichester
Pevensey	*Sussex* - Eastbourne
Pevensey Bay	*Sussex* - Eastbourne
Pewet Island	*Essex* - Maldon
Pewfall	*Lancaster* - Wigan
Pewsey	*Wilts* - Swindon
Pewsham	*Wilts* - Chippenham
Pex Hill	*Lancaster* - St. Helens

PHE - PIL

Pheasants Hill	*Bucks* - Reading
Phepson	*Worcester* - Worcester
Philadelphia	*Durham* - Durham
Phillack	*Cornwall* - Redruth
Philleigh	*Cornwall* - Truro
Phillips Town	*Monmouth* - Blackwood
Phocle Green	*Hereford* - Gloucester
Phoenix Green	*Hants* - Basingstoke
Phoenix Row	*Durham* - Bishop Auckland
Pica	*Cumberland* - Whitehaven
Piccadilly	*Warwick* - Tamworth
Piccadilly	*York, W.R.* - Rotherham
Piccotts' End	*Herts* - Hemel Hempstead
Pickenham, North	*Norfolk* - King's Lynn
Pickenham, South	*Norfolk* - King's Lynn
Pickering	*York, N.R.* - Malton
Pickering Nook	*Durham* - Consett
Picket Post	*Hants* - Bournemouth
Pickford Brook	*Warwick* - Coventry
Pickfords Hill	*Herts* - Luton
Pickhill	*Denbigh* - Wrexham
Pickhill	*York, N.R.* - Northallerton
Picklebatch	*Salop* - Bridgnorth
Picklecombe	*Cornwall* - Plymouth
Picklescott	*Salop* - Shrewsbury
Pickmere	*Cheshire* - Northwich
Pickstock	*Salop* - Wellington (Salop)
Picktree	*Durham* - Gateshead
Pickwell	*Leicester* - Melton Mowbray
Pickwick	*Wilts* - Chippenham
Pickworth	*Lincoln* - Grantham
Pickworth	*Rutland* - Stamford
Picton	*Cheshire* - Chester
Picton	*York, N.R.* - Stockton on Tees
Picts Cross	*Hereford* - Monmouth
Picts Hill	*Sussex* - Horsham
Piddinghoe	*Sussex* - Lewes
Piddington	*Bucks* - Aylesbury
Piddington	*Bucks* - High Wycombe
Piddington	*Northampton* - Northampton
Piddington	*Oxford* - Thame
Piddlehinton	*Dorset* - Dorchester
Piddle, North	*Worcester* - Worcester
Piddletrenthide	*Dorset* - Dorchester
Pidley	*Hunts* - Huntingdon
Piel	*Lancaster* - Barrow-in-Furness
Pied Heath	*Middlesex* - Uxbridge
Pielwyke	*Cumberland* - Workington
Piercebridge	*Durham* - Darlington
Piffs Elm	*Gloucester* - Cheltenham
Pigburn	*York, W.R.* - Doncaster
Pigdon	*Northumberland* - Morpeth
Pigeon's Wick	*Herts* - Hitchin
Piggotts Common	*Bucks* - High Wycombe
Pike Hall	*Derby* - Matlock
Pilgrims Hatch	*Essex* - Brentwood
Pilham	*Lincoln* - Gainsborough
Pilhough	*Derby* - Matlock
Pilkington	*Lancaster* - Bury
Pill	*Cornwall* - Truro
Pill	*Somerset* - Bristol
Pillaton	*Cornwall* - Plymouth
Pillaton	*Stafford* - Stafford
Pill Heath	*Hants* - Andover
Pillerton	*Warwick* - Stratford on Avon
Pillerton Prior	*Warwick* - Stratford on Avon
Pilleth	*Radnor* - Knighton
Pilley	*Hants* - Lymington
Pilley	*York, W.R.* - Barnsley
Pillowell	*Gloucester* - Monmouth
Pilning	*Gloucester* - Thornbury
Pilsbury	*Derby* - Buxton
Pilsdon	*Dorset* - Axminster and Chard
Pilsey Island	*Sussex* - Chichester
Pilsgate	*Huntingdon and Peterborough* - Stamford
Pilsley	*Derby* - Alfreton
Pilsley	*Derby* - Matlock
Pilsworth	*Lancaster* - Bury
Piltdown	*Sussex* - Lewes

PIL - PIZ

Pilton	*Devon* - Barnstaple
Pilton	*Northampton* - Kettering
Pilton	*Rutland* - Oakham
Pilton	*Somerset* - Wells
Pilton Green	*Glamorgan* - Swansea
Pimhole	*Lancaster* - Bury
Pimlico	*Herts* - Watford
Pimlico (part)	*London, S.W.1* - West London
Pimlico (part)	*London, S.W.1* - Westminster
Pimperne	*Dorset* - Wimborne Minster
Pinchbeck	*Lincoln* - Spalding
Pinchbeck Bars	*Lincoln* - Spalding
Pinchbeck Marsh	*Lincoln* - Spalding
Pinchbeck, West	*Lincoln* - Spadling
Pinchingthorpe	*York, N.R.* - Middlesbrough
Pine Apple Estate	*Warwick* - Birmingham
Pinged	*Carmarthen* - Llanelli
Pin Green	*Herts* - Hitchin
Pinhoe	*Devon* - Exeter
Pink Green	*Worcester* - Redditch
Pinkney	*Wilts* - Malmesbury
Pinkney's Green (Cookham)	*Berks* - Slough
Pinley	*Warwick* - Warwick
Pinner	*Middlesex* - Watford
Pinner Green	*Middlesex* - Watford
Pinner Hill	*Middlesex* - Watford
Pinner, North	*Middlesex* - Watford
Pinner, South	*Middlesex* - Watford
Pinnock	*Gloucester* - Cheltenham
Pinnock	*Kent* - Ashford
Pinsley Green	*Cheshire* - Crewe
Pinvin	*Worcester* - Evesham
Pinwall	*Leicester* - Nuneaton
Pinxton	*Derby* - Alfreton
Pipe and Lyde	*Hereford* - Hereford
Pipe Gate	*Salop* - Market Drayton
Pipe Hill	*Stafford* - Lichfield
Pipe House	*Somerset* - Bath
Pipe Ridware	*Stafford* - Lichfield
Pipers Ash	*Cheshire* - Chester
Pipers Corner	*Bucks* - High Wycombe
Pipers Hill	*Cambridge* - Ely
Pipewell (Rushton)	*Northampton* - Kettering
Pirbright	*Surrey* - Guildford
Pirton	*Herts* - Hitchin
Pirton	*Worcester* - Worcester
Pisford	*Northampton* - Northampton
Pisgah	*Cardigan* - Cardigan
Pishill	*Oxford* - Reading
Pistyll	*Caernarvon* - Portmadoc
Pitchcombe	*Gloucester* - Stroud
Pitchcott	*Bucks* - Aylesbury
Pitchford	*Salop* - Shrewsbury
Pitcombe	*Somerset* - Yeovil
Pit Green	*Durham* - Bishop Auckland
Pit House Lane	*Durham* - Durham
Pitminster	*Somerset* - Taunton
Pitney	*Somerset* - Yeovil
Pitsea	*Essex* - Brentwood
Pitses	*Lancaster* - Oldham
Pitsford	*Northampton* - Northampton
Pitsmoor	*York, W.R.* - Sheffield
Pitstone	*Bucks* - Aylesbury
Pitt	*Hants* - Winchester
Pittington	*Durham* - Durham
Pittington, High	*Durham* - Durham
Pittington, Low	*Durham* - Durham
Pittington, New	*Durham* - Durham
Pittleworth	*Hants* - Winchester
Pitton	*Wilts* - Salisbury
Pittshill	*Stafford* - Stoke-on-Trent
Pity Me	*Durham* - Durham
Pixey Green	*Suffolk* - Halesworth
Pixham	*Surrey* - Dorking
Pixham Ferry	*Worcester* - Worcester
Pixley	*Hereford* - Hereford
Pixley	*Salop* - Market Drayton
Pixley Hills	*Durham* - Bishop Auckland
Pizwell	*Devon* - Plymouth

Plainsfield	*Somerset* - Bridgwater
Plaish	*Salop* - Shrewsbury
Plaistow	*London, E.13* - Bow
Plaistow	*Sussex* - Chichester
Plaistow Green	*Derby* - Alfreton
Plaistow Green	*Hants* - Newbury
Plaitford	*Hants* - Southampton
Plank Lane	*Lancaster* - Leigh
Plank Lane	*Lancaster* - Wigan
Plardiwick	*Stafford* - Stafford
Plasmarl	*Glamorgan* - Swansea
Plasycoed	*Glamorgan* - Swansea
Platt	*Kent* - Sevenoaks
Platt Bridge	*Lancaster* - Wigan
Platt Hill Estate	*Lancaster* - Bolton
Platt Mill	*Salop* - Shrewsbury
Platts Common	*York, W.R.* - Barnsley
Plawsworth	*Durham* - Durham
Plaxtol	*Kent* - Sevenoaks
Playden	*Sussex* - Hastings
Playford	*Suffolk* - Ipswich
Play Hatch	*Berks* - Reading
Playing Place	*Cornwall* - Truro
Playley Green	*Gloucester* - Gloucester
Plealey	*Salop* - Shrewsbury
Pleamore Cross	*Somerset* - Taunton
Pleasington	*Lancaster* - Blackburn
Pleasley	*Derby* - Mansfield
Pleasley Hill	*Notts* - Mansfield
Pleasley, Upper	*Derby* - Mansfield
Pleasley Vale	*Derby* - Mansfield
Pleck	*Dorset* - Shaftesbury
Pleck	*Stafford* - Walsall
Pleckgate	*Lancaster* - Blackburn
Pledgdon	*Essex* - Bishop's Stortford
Pledgdon Green	*Essex* - Bishop's Stortford
Plemstall	*Cheshire* - Chester
Plenmeller	*Northumberland* - Hexham
Pleshey	*Essex* - Chelmsford
Plesseychecks	*Northumberland* - North Shields
Plessey Hall	*Northumberland* - North Shields
Plex, The	*Salop* - Shrewsbury
Plompton	*York, W.R.* - Harrogate
Plowden	*Salop* - Ludlow
Plox Green	*Salop* - Shrewsbury
Pluckley	*Kent* - Ashford
Pluckley Thorne	*Kent* - Ashford
Pludds, The	*Gloucester* - Gloucester
Plumbland	*Cumberland* - Workington
Plumgarths	*Westmorland* - Kendal
Plumley	*Cheshire* - Northwich
Plummers Plain	*Sussex* - Horsham
Plump Hill	*Gloucester* - Gloucester
Plumpton	*Cumberland* - Penrith
Plumpton	*Northampton* - Northampton
Plumpton	*Sussex* - Lewes
Plumpton Foot	*Cumberland* - Penrith
Plumpton Head	*Cumberland* - Penrith
Plumpton Wall	*Cumberland* - Penrith
Plum Pudding Island	*Kent* - Margate
Plumstead	*London, S.E.18* - Woolwich
Plumstead	*Norfolk* - Norwich
Plumstead, Great	*Norfolk* - Norwich
Plumstead, Little	*Norfolk* - Norwich
Plumtree	*Notts* - Nottingham
Plungar	*Leicester* - Melton Mowbray
Plurenden	*Kent* - Cranbrook
Plush	*Dorset* - Dorchester
Plwmp	*Pembroke* - Cardigan
Plymouth	*Devon* - Plymouth
Plympton St. Maurice	*Devon* - Plymouth
Plympton St. Mary	*Devon* - Plymouth
Plymstock	*Devon* - Plymouth
Plymtree	*Devon* - Exeter
Poaka Beck	*Lancaster* - Barrow-in-Furness
Pochin	*Monmouth* - Blackwood
Pocket Nook	*Lancaster* - St. Helens
Pockley	*York, N.R.* - Malton
Pocklington	*York, E.R.* - York
Pockthorpe	*York, E.R.* - Bridlington

Poddington	*Beds* - Wellingborough
Pode Hole	*Lincoln* - Spalding
Podimore	*Somerset* - Yeovil
Podmore	*Stafford* - Stafford
Podmore	*Worcester* - Kidderminster
Pogmoor	*York, W.R.* - Barnsley
Point	*Cornwall* - Truro
Point Clear	*Essex* - Colchester
Pointon	*Lincoln* - Sleaford
Pointon Fen	*Lincoln* - Sleaford
Pokesdown	*Hants* - Bournemouth
Polbathic (part)	*Cornwall* - Liskeard
Polbathic (part)	*Cornwall* - Plymouth
Polburder	*Cornwall* - Liskeard
Polebrook	*Northampton* - Peterborough
Polecats	*Sussex* - Chichester
Polegate	*Sussex* - Eastbourne
Polemere	*Salop* - Shrewsbury
Pole Moor	*York, W.R.* - Huddersfield
Poles	*Herts* - Hertford
Poleshole	*Wilts* - Trowbridge
Polesworth	*Warwick* - Tamworth
Polgooth	*Cornwall* - St. Austell
Polhampton	*Hants* - Basingstoke
Polhill	*Kent* - Sevenoaks
Poling	*Sussex* - Chichester
Polkerris	*Cornwall* - St. Austell
Polkyth	*Cornwall* - St. Austell
Pollards Hill	*Sussex* - Horsham
Pollards Moor	*Hants* - Southampton
Pollington	*York, W.R.* - Goole
Polmassick	*Cornwall* - St. Austell
Polmear	*Cornwall* - St. Austell
Polperro	*Cornwall* - Liskeard
Polruan	*Cornwall* - Liskeard
Polsham	*Somerset* - Wells
Polstead	*Suffolk* - Sudbury
Polstrong	*Cornwall* - Redruth
Poltair	*Cornwall* - St. Austell
Poltimore	*Devon* - Exeter
Polzeath	*Cornwall* - Bodmin
Pomphlete	*Devon* - Plymouth
Ponciau	*Denbigh* - Wrexham
Ponders End	*Middlesex* - Edmonton
Pond Farm	*Bucks* - High Wycombe
Ponsanooth (part)	*Cornwall* - Redruth
Ponsanooth (part)	*Cornwall* - Truro
Ponsbourne Park	*Herts* - St. Albans
Ponsharden	*Cornwall* - Truro
Ponsonby	*Cumberland* - Whitehaven
Pont	*Cornwall* - Liskeard
Pontantwn	*Carmarthen* - Carmarthen
Pontardawe	*Glamorgan* - Neath
Pontardulais (Hendy)	*Carmarthen* - Llanelli
Pontardulais	*Glamorgan* - Swansea
Pontblyddyn	*Flint* - Mold
Pontcych	*Carmarthen* - Cardigan
Pontcysyllte	*Denbigh* - Wrexham
Pontefract	*York, W.R.* - Pontefract
Ponteland	*Northumberland* - Newcastle upon Tyne
Ponterwyd	*Cardigan* - Aberystwyth
Pontesbury	*Salop* - Shrewsbury
Pontesbury Hill	*Salop* - Shrewsbury
Pontesford	*Salop* - Shrewsbury
Pontfadog	*Denbigh* - Wrexham
Pontfaen	*Pembroke* - Haverfordwest
Pontgarreg	*Cardigan* - Cardigan
Ponthenry	*Carmarthen* - Llanelli
Ponthir	*Monmouth* - Newport (Mon.)
Ponthirwen	*Cardigan* - Cardigan
Pontlasse	*Glamorgan* - Swansea
Pont Lawrence	*Monmouth* - Blackwood
Pontllanfraith	*Monmouth* - Blackwood
Pontllanio	*Cardigan* - Lampeter
Pont Lliw	*Glamorgan* - Swansea
Pont Llogel (part)	*Montgomery* - Oswestry
Pont Llogel (part)	*Montgomery* - Welshpool
Pontllolwyn	*Cardigan* - Aberystwyth

PON - POO

Pontlottyn	*Glamorgan* - Bargoed
Ponthorlais	*Glamorgan* - Merthyr Tydfil
Pontneathvaughan	*Glamorgan* - Neath
Pontneddfychan	*Glamorgan* - Neath
Pontnewydd	*Monmouth* - Newport (Mon.)
Pontnewynydd	*Monmouth* - Newport (Mon.)
Ponton, Great	*Lincoln* - Grantham
Ponton, Little	*Lincoln* - Grantham
Pontop Pike	*Durham* - Consett
Pontralltgoch	*Denbigh* - Denbigh
Pontrallt Goch	*Denbigh* - Rhyl
Pontrhydbont	*Anglesey* - Llangefni
Pontrhydfendigaid	*Cardigan* - Aberystwyth
Pontrhydycyff	*Glamorgan* - Bridgend
Pontrhydyfen	*Glamorgan* - Neath
Pontrhydygroes	*Cardigan* - Aberystwyth
Pontrhydyrun	*Monmouth* - Newport (Mon.)
Pontrhythallt	*Caernarvon* - Caernarvon
Pontrilas	*Hereford* - Hereford
Pont Robert ap Oliver (part)	*Montgomery* - Oswestry
Pont Robert ap Oliver (part)	*Montgomery* - Welshpool
Pont Rug	*Caernarvon* - Caernarvon
Pontsarn	*Brecon* - Merthyr Tydfil
Pontseli	*Pembroke* - Cardigan
Ponts Green	*Sussex* - Hastings
Pontshaen	*Cardigan* - Lampeter
Pontshill	*Hereford* - Gloucester
Pontsticill	*Brecon* - Merthyr Tydfil
Pontwalby (part)	*Glamorgan* - Aberdare
Pontwalby (part)	*Glamorgan* - Neath
Pontwelly	*Carmarthen* - Carmarthen
Pontyates (part)	*Carmarthen* - Carmarthen
Pontyates (part)	*Carmarthen* - Llanelli
Pontyberem	*Carmarthen* - Llanelli
Pontybodkin	*Denbigh* - Wrexham
Pontyclun (part)	*Glamorgan* - Bridgend
Pontyclun (part)	*Glamorgan* - Pontypridd
Pontycymmer	*Glamorgan* - Bridgend
Pontygwaith (Merthyr Vale)	*Glamorgan* - Merthyr Tydfil
Pontygwaith	*Glamorgan* - Pontypridd
Pontygwaithyrhaiarn	*Monmouth* - Blackwood
Pontygwyddel	*Denbigh* - Denbigh
Pontymister	*Monmouth* - Newport (Mon.)
Pontynyswen	*Carmarthen* - Carmarthen
Pont-y-Pant	*Caernarvon* - Conway
Pontypool	*Monmouth* - Pontypool
Pontypridd	*Glamorgan* - Pontypridd
Pontyrhyl	*Glamorgan* - Bridgend
Pontysaison	*Monmouth* - Chepstow
Pontywain	*Monmouth* - Newport (Mon.)
Pooks Green	*Hants* - Southampton
Pookwell	*Kent* - Cranbrook
Pool	*Cornwall* - Redruth
Pool	*York, W.R.* - Otley
Pool Brook	*Worcester* - Great Malvern
Poole	*Cheshire* - Crewe
Poole	*Dorset* - Poole
Poole	*Somerset* - Taunton
Poole	*York, W.R.* - Pontefract
Poole Keynes	*Gloucester* - Malmesbury
Pool End	*Stafford* - Leek
Pooley	*Warwick* - Tamworth
Pooley Bridge	*Westmorland* - Penrith
Poolham	*Lincoln* - Lincoln
Pool Hayes	*Stafford* - Walsall
Pool Head	*Salop* - Shrewsbury
Pool Hill	*Gloucester* - Gloucester
Pool Hill	*Salop* - Wellington (Salop)
Pool Mill	*Hereford* - Monmouth
Poolmouth	*Denbigh* - Wrexham
Pool Quay	*Montgomery* - Welshpool
Poolsbrook	*Derby* - Chesterfield
Pool, South	*Devon* - Kingsbridge
Poolstock	*Lancaster* - Wigan
Pool Village	*Derby* - Burton-upon-Trent
Poorstock	*Dorset* - Dorchester

POO - POR

Poorton, North	*Dorset* - Dorchester
Pootings	*Kent* - Sevenoaks
Pope Hill	*Pembroke* - Haverfordwest
Pope's Hill	*Gloucester* - Gloucester
Poham	*Hants* - Basingstoke
Poplar	*London, E.14* - Bow
Poppleton, Nether	*York, W.R.* - York
Poppleton, Upper	*York, W.R.* - York
Porchfield	*I. of W.* - Newport (I.W.)
Poringland	*Norfolk* - Norwich
Porkellis	*Cornwall* - Penzance
Porlock	*Somerset* - Minehead
Portbury	*Somerset* - Bristol
Port Carlisle	*Cumberland* - Carlisle
Portchester	*Hants* - Portsmouth
Port Clarence	*Durham* - Stockton on Tees
Portdinllaen	*Caernarvon* - Portmadoc
Port Dinorwic (part)	*Caernarvon* - Bangor
Port Dinorwic (part)	*Caernarvon* - Caernarvon
Portesham	*Dorset* - Weymouth
Port Eynon	*Glamorgan* - Swansea
Portfield	*Sussex* - Chichester
Portfield Gate	*Pembroke* - Haverfordwest
Portgate	*Northumberland* - Hexham
Port Gaverne	*Cornwall* - Bideford
Porth	*Cornwall* - Truro
Porth	*Glamorgan* - Pontypridd
Porthallow	*Cornwall* - Penzance
Porthallow	*Cornwall* - Liskeard
Porthcawl	*Glamorgan* - Bridgend
Porthcurno	*Cornwall* - Penzance
Porthgain	*Pembroke* - Haverfordwest
Porthgwarra	*Cornwall* - Penzance
Porthill	*Stafford* - Stoke-on-Trent
Porthkea	*Cornwall* - Truro
Porthkerry	*Glamorgan* - Barry
Porthleven	*Cornwall* - Penzance
Porth Mellin	*Cornwall* - Penzance
Porth Navas	*Cornwall* - Truro & Falmouth
Port Holland, West	*Cornwall* - Truro
Porthoustock	*Cornwall* - Penzance
Porthpean	*Cornwall* - St Austell
Porthtowan	*Cornwall* - Truro
Porthyrhyd	*Carmarthen* - Llandovery
Porthyryd	*Carmarthen* - Carmarthen
Portico	*Lancaster* - St. Helens
Portington	*York, E.R.* - Goole
Portinscale	*Cumberland* - Workington
Port Isaac	*Cornwall* - Bodmin
Portishead	*Somerset* - Bristol
Portland	*Dorset* - Weymouth
Portlemouth, East	*Devon* - Kingsbridge
Portley	*Salop* - Wellington (Salop)
Portloe	*Cornwall* - Truro
Portlooe	*Cornwall* - Liskeard
Portmadoc	*Caernarvon* - Portmadoc
Portmead	*Glamorgan* - Swansea
Portmellon	*Cornwall* - St. Austell
Portmore	*Hants* - Lymington
Port Mulgrave	*York, N.R.* - Whitby
Portnant	*Caernarvon* - Portmadoc
Portobello	*Durham* - Gateshead
Portobello	*Northumberland* - Hexham
Portobello	*Stafford* - Wolverhampton
Porto-bello	*York, W.R.* - Wakefield
Porton	*Wilts* - Salisbury
Port Quin	*Cornwall* - Bideford
Portreath	*Cornwall* - Redruth
Portscatho	*Cornwall* - Truro
Portsdown	*Hants* - Portsmouth
Portsea	*Hants* - Portsmouth
Portskewett	*Monmouth* - Chepstow
Portslade	*Sussex* - Brighton
Portsmouth	*Hants* - Portsmouth
Portsmouth	*York, W.R.* - Todmorden
Portsmouth Arms	*Devon* - Barnstaple
Port Sunlight	*Cheshire* - Birkenhead
Portswood	*Hants* - Southampton
Port Talbot	*Glamorgan* - Neath
Port Tennant	*Glamorgan* - Swansea

Port Victoria	*Kent* - Rochester
Portway	*Hereford* - Hereford
Portway	*Stafford* - Dudley
Portway	*Warwick* - Birmingham
Portway (part)	*Worcester* - Redditch
Portway (part)	*Worcester* - Dudley
Portway (part)	*Worcester* - West Bromwich
Portways	*Oxford* - Thame
Portwood	*Cheshire* - Stockport
Portwrinkle	*Cornwall* - Liskeard
Portwrinkle	*Cornwall* - Plymouth
Posbury	*Devon* - Exeter
Posenhall	*Salop* - Bridgnorth
Poslingford	*Suffolk* - Sudbury
Postbach	*Cardigan* - Cardigan
Postbridge	*Devon* - Plymouth
Postcoch Nevern	*Pembroke* - Cardigan
Postcombe	*Oxford* - Thame
Postland	*Lincoln* - Spalding
Postland, Little	*Lincoln* - Spalding
Postling	*Kent* - Folkestone
Postlip	*Gloucester* - Cheltenham
Postons	*Salop* - Ludlow
Postwick	*Norfolk* - Norwich
Poswick	*Hereford* - Worcester
Pot Common	*Sussex* - Horsham
Potcote	*Northampton* - Northampton
Potford	*Salop* - Market Drayton
Pot Hill	*Sussex* - Horsham
Potman's Heath	*Kent* - Cranbrook
Pots Gill	*Cumberland* - Carlisle
Potsgrove	*Beds* - Bletchley and Leighton Buzzard
Pott	*York, N.R.* - Harrogate
Pottal Pool	*Stafford* - Stafford
Potten End	*Herts* - Hemel Hempstead
Potter Brompton	*York, N.R.* - Scarborough
Potter Hanworth	*Lincoln* - Lincoln
Potter Heigham	*Norfolk* - Great Yarmouth
Potter Hill	*York, W.R.* - Sheffield
Potterne	*Wilts* - Devizes
Potters Bar	*Herts* - Barnet
Potters Cross	*Stafford* - Stourbridge
Potter's Crouch	*Herts* - St. Albans
Potters Green	*Herts* - Hertford
Potters Green	*Warwick* - Coventry
Potters Heath	*Herts* - Hertford
Potters Hill	*Somerset* - Bristol
Potters Marston	*Leicester* - Leicester
Potterspury	*Northampton* - Northampton
Potterton	*York, W.R.* - Leeds
Potton	*Beds* - Biggleswade
Pott Shrigley	*Cheshire* - Macclesfield
Pouces	*Kent* - Ramsgate
Pouchen End	*Herts* - Hemel Hempstead
Poughill	*Cornwall* - Bideford
Poughill	*Devon* - Tiverton
Pouk Hill	*Stafford* - Walsall
Poulner	*Hants* - Bournemouth
Poulshot	*Wilts* - Devizes
Poultney	*Leicester* - Rugby
Poulton	*Cheshire* - Chester
Poulton	*Gloucester* - Swindon
Poulton	*Salop* - Shrewsbury
Poulton-le-Fylde	*Lancaster* - Blackpool
Poulton, Little	*Lancaster* - Blackpool
Poulton-with-Fearnhead	*Lancaster* - Warrington
Poulton with Spital	*Cheshire* - Birkenhead
Poulton Wallasey	*Cheshire* - Birkenhead
Pound	*Devon* - Plymouth
Pound Bank	*Worcester* - Great Malvern
Poundgate	*Kent* - Gravesend
Pound Green	*Berks* - Reading
Pound Green	*Sussex* - Lewes
Pound Green	*Worcester* - Kidderminster
Pound Hill	*Sussex* - Horsham
Pound, New	*Sussex* - Chichester
Pound, Old	*Cornwall* - St. Austell
Poundon	*Bucks* - Aylesbury
Pounds Bridge	*Kent* - Tonbridge

Poundsgate	*Devon* - Newton Abbot
Poundstock	*Cornwall* - Launceston
Powburn	*Northumberland* - Alnwick
Powderham	*Devon* - Exeter
Powder Mills	*Devon* - Plymouth
Powder Mills	*Kent* - Tonbridge
Powerstock	*Dorset* - Dorchester
Pow Hill	*Cumberland* - Carlisle
Powick	*Worcester* - Worcester
Pownall Park	*Cheshire* - Macclesfield
Poxwell	*Dorset* - Weymouth
Poyle	*Bucks* - Slough
Poyle	*Oxford* - Oxford
Poynders End	*Herts* - Hitchin
Poynings	*Sussex* - Brighton
Poytington	*Dorset* - Yeovil
Poynton	*Cheshire* - Macclesfield
Poynton	*Salop* - Wellington (Salop)
Poynton-with-Worth	*Cheshire* - Macclesfield
Prah Sands	*Cornwall* - Penzance
Pratt Hall	*Derby* - Chesterfield
Pratt's Bottom	*Kent* - Bromley
Prawle, East	*Devon* - Kingsbridge
Praze	*Cornwall* - Penzance
Praze-an-Beeble	*Cornwall* - Redruth
Prees	*Salop* - Whitchurch
Preesall	*Lancaster* - Blackpool
Preesall-with-Hackinsall	*Lancaster* - Blackpool
Preesgweene	*Salop* - Oswestry
Prees Heath	*Salop* - Whitchurch
Prendergast	*Pembroke* - Haverfordwest
Prendwick	*Northumberland* - Alnwick
Prenteg	*Caernarvon* - Portmadoc
Prenton	*Cheshire* - Birkenhead
Prescot	*Lancaster* - St. Helens
Prescott	*Devon* - Taunton
Prescott	*Gloucester* - Cheltenham
Prescott	*Salop* - Shrewsbury
Preshaw	*Hants* - Winchester
Preshute	*Wilts* - Swindon
Press	*Derby* - Chesterfield
Prestatyn	*Flint* - Rhyl
Prestbury	*Cheshire* - Macclesfield
Prestbury	*Gloucester* - Cheltenham
Presteigne	*Radnor* - Knighton
Presthope	*Salop* - Bridgnorth
Prestolee	*Lancaster* - Bolton
Preston (Paignton)	*Devon* - Torquay
Preston	*Dorset* - Blandford
Preston	*Dorset* - Weymouth
Preston	*Gloucester* - Swindon
Preston	*Herts* - Hitchin
Preston	*Lancaster* - Preston
Preston	*Middlesex* - Willesden
Preston	*Northumberland* - Alnwick
Preston	*Rutland* - Melton Mowbray
Preston	*Suffolk* - Sudbury
Preston	*Wilts* - Swindon
Preston	*York, E.R.* - Kingston-upon-Hull
Preston Bagot	*Warwick* - Warwick
Preston Boats	*Salop* - Shrewsbury
Preston Bowyer	*Somerset* - Taunton
Preston Brook	*Cheshire* - Runcorn
Preston-by-Wingham	*Kent* - Canterbury
Preston Candover	*Hants* - Basingstoke
Preston Capes	*Northampton* - Northampton
Preston Coombe	*Devon* - Kingsbridge
Preston Crowmarsh	*Oxford* - Didcot
Preston Deanery	*Northampton* - Northampton
Preston, East	*Sussex* - Worthing
Preston, Great	*York, W.R.* - Pontefract
Preston Green	*Warwick* - Warwick
Preston Gubballs	*Salop* - Shrewsbury
Preston, Little	*Northampton* - Northampton
Preston, Little	*York, W.R.* - Pontefract
Preston Moors	*Salop* - Shrewsbury
Preston next Faversham	*Kent* - Canterbury
Preston on Severn	*Salop* - Shrewsbury

PRE - PRO

Preston-on-Stour	*Warwick* - Stratford-on-Avon
Preston-on-the-Hill	*Cheshire* - Runcorn
Preston Patrick	*Westmorland* - Kendal
Preston Plucknett (Yeovil)	*Somerset* - Yeovil
Preston Richard	*Westmorland* - Kendal
Preston-upon-the-Weald Moors	*Salop* - Wellington (Salop)
Preston-upon-Wye	*Hereford* - Hereford
Preston Vale	*Stafford* - Stafford
Preston Village	*Northumberland* - North Shields
Preston Wynne	*Hereford* - Hereford
Prestwich	*Lancaster* - Salford
Prestwick	*Northumberland* - Newcastle upon Tyne
Prestwold	*Leicester* - Loughborough
Prestwood	*Bucks* - Amersham
Prestwood (Hughenden)	*Bucks* - High Wycombe
Prestwood	*Stafford* - Uttoxeter
Prestwood	*Stafford* - Uttoxeter
Prestwood	*Stafford* - Stourbridge
Pricetown	*Glamorgan* - Bridgend
Prickshaw	*Lancaster* - Rochdale
Prickwillow	*Cambridge* - Ely
Priddbwll	*Denbigh* - Oswestry
Priddy	*Somerset* - Wells
Priddy's Hard	*Hants* - Portsmouth
Priding	*Gloucester* - Gloucester
Priestcliff	*Derby* - Buxton
Priestcroft	*Cumberland* - Carlisle
Priest End	*Oxford* - Thame
Priestfields	*Stafford* - Wolverhampton
Priest Hutton	*Lancaster* - Lancaster
Priestley Green	*York, W.R.* - Halifax
Priestweston	*Salop* - Welshpool
Priestwood	*Kent* - Gravesend
Primethorpe	*Leicester* - Hinckley
Primrose	*Durham* - South Shields
Primrose Hill	*Durham* - Bishop Auckland
Primrose Hill	*Durham* - Durham
Primrose Hill	*Lancaster* - Bury
Primrose Hill	*London, N.W.1.* - Bloomsbury and Marylebone
Primrose Hill	*Worcester* - Dudley
Primrose Valley	*York, E.R.* - Bridlington
Prince Hall	*Devon* - Plymouth
Princes End	*Stafford* - Dudley
Princes Park	*Lancaster* - Liverpool
Princes Risborough	*Bucks* - High Wycombe
Princethorpe	*Warwick* - Rugby
Princetown	*Devon* - Plymouth
Princetown	*Monmouth* - Blackwood
Prinknash	*Gloucester* - Gloucester
Prinsted	*Sussex* - Chichester
Prion	*Denbigh* - Denbigh
Priorsdean	*Hants* - Petersfield
Priors Halton	*Salop* - Ludlow
Priors Hardwicke	*Warwick* - Rugby
Prior's Heath	*Kent* - Cranbrook
Priors Heys	*Cheshire* - Chester
Priorslee	*Salop* - Wellington (Salop)
Priors Marston	*Warwick* - Rugby
Prior's Park	*Gloucester* - Cheltenham
Priory	*Pembroke* - Haverfordwest
Priory Wood	*Hereford* - Hereford
Prisk	*Glamorgan* - Cardiff
Priston	*Somerset* - Bath
Pritchard Sapey	*Worcester* - Worcester
Privett	*Hants* - Petersfield
Privett (Gosport)	*Hants* - Portsmouth
Prixford	*Devon* - Barnstaple
Probus	*Cornwall* - Truro
Prolley Moor	*Salop* - Shrewsbury
Prospect (Oughterside) (part)	*Cumberland* - Carlisle
Prospect (Isel)	*Cumberland* - Workington
Prospect (Oughterside) (part)	*Cumberland* - Workington
Prospect Hill	*Northumberland* - North Shields

PRO - PWL

Prospidnick	*Cornwall* - Penzance
Providence	*Cornwall* - St. Austell
Prudhoe	*Northumberland* - Hexham
Prussia Cove	*Cornwall* - Penzance
Publow	*Somerset* - Bristol
Puckeridge	*Herts* - Hertford
Puckington	*Somerset* - Axminster and Chard
Pucklechurch	*Gloucester* - Bristol
Puckshipton	*Wilts* - Devizes
Pudding Norton	*Norfolk* - King's Lynn
Puddington	*Cheshire* - Chester
Puddington	*Devon* - Tiverton
Puddle Hill	*Beds* - Luton
Puddletown (Haselbury Bucknett)	*Somerset* - Yeovil
Pudleston	*Hereford* - Leominster
Pudlicote	*Oxford* - Banbury
Pudsey	*York, W.R.* - Bradford
Pudsey Low Town (part)	*York, W.R.* - Bradford
Pudsey Low Town (part)	*York, W.R.* - Leeds
Pulborough	*Sussex* - Chichester
Puleston	*Salop* - Wellington (Salop)
Pulford	*Cheshire* - Chester
Pulham Green	*Dorset* - Dorchester
Pulham St. Mary Magdalene	*Norfolk* - Norwich
Pulham St. Mary the Virgin	*Norfolk* - Norwich
Pulla Cross	*Cornwall* - Redruth
Pulley	*Salop* - Shrewsbury
Pulley Common	*Salop* - Shrewsbury
Pulloxhill	*Beds* - Bedford
Pulverbatch	*Salop* - Shrewsbury
Pumpsaint	*Carmarthen* - Llandovery
Puncheston	*Pembroke* - Haverfordwest
Puncknowle	*Dorset* - Dorchester
Punnetts Town	*Sussex* - Eastbourne
Purbrook	*Hants* - Portsmouth
Purfleet	*Essex* - Grays Thurrock
Puriton	*Somerset* - Bridgwater
Purlbridge	*Devon* - Axminster and Chard
Purleigh	*Essex* - Maldon
Purley	*Berks* - Reading
Purley	*Surrey* - Croydon
Purlieu, The	*Gloucester* - Gloucester
Purlpit	*Wilts* - Chippenham
Purls Bridge	*Cambridge* - March
Purns Mill (Gillingham)	*Dorset* - Shaftesbury
Purse Caundle	*Dorset* - Yeovil
Purslow	*Salop* - Ludlow
Purston	*Northampton* - Banbury
Purston	*York, W.R.* - Pontefract
Purtington	*Somerset* - Axminster and Chard
Purton	*Gloucester* - Stroud
Purton	*Wilts* - Swindon
Purton Stoke	*Wilts* - Swindon
Pusey	*Berks* - Didcot
Putford, East	*Devon* - Bideford
Putford, West	*Devon* - Bideford
Putley	*Hereford* - Hereford
Putney	*London, S.W.15* - Wandsworth
Putney, East	*London, S.W.15* - Wandsworth
Putsham	*Somerset* - Minehead
Putson	*Hereford* - Hereford
Puttenham	*Herts* - Aylesbury
Puttenham	*Surrey* - Aldershot and Farnham
Putteridge Bury	*Herts* - Hitchin
Puxley	*Northampton* - Northampton
Puxton	*Somerset* - Weston Super Mare
Pwll	*Carmarthen* - Llanelli
Pwllandras	*Glamorgan* - Bridgend
Pwllcrochan	*Pembroke* - Haverfordwest
Pwlldu	*Glamorgan* - Swansea
Pwllglas	*Denbigh* - Denbigh
Pwllheli	*Caernarvon* - Portmadoc
Pwlltrap	*Carmarthen* - Carmarthen
Pwllyglaw	*Glamorgan* - Neath

Pwllypant	*Glamorgan* - Caerphilly
Pwllywhiad	*Glamorgan* - Merthyr Tydfil
Pydew	*Caernarvon* - Conway
Pye Bridge	*Derby* - Alfreton
Pyecombe	*Sussex* - Brighton
Pye Corner	*Hereford* - Worcester
Pye Corner	*Herts* - Hertford
Pye Green	*Stafford* - Walsall
Pye Hill	*Notts* - Alfreton
Pyle	*Glamorgan* - Bridgend
Pyleigh	*Somerset* - Taunton
Pylewell	*Hants* - Lymington
Pylle	*Somerset* - Wells
Pymore	*Cambridge* - Ely
Pymore Common	*Cambridge* - Ely
Pype Hayes	*Warwick* - Birmingham
Pyrford	*Surrey* - Guildford
Pyrton	*Bucks* - Thame
Pyrton Heath	*Oxford* - Thame
Pytchley	*Northampton* - Kettering
Pythingdean	*Sussex* - Chichester
Pyworthy	*Devon* - Launceston

Q

Quabbs, The	*Salop* - Knighton
Quadring	*Lincoln* - Spalding
Quadring Bank	*Lincoln* - Spalding
Quadring Eaudyke	*Lincoln* - Spalding
Quadring Fen	*Lincoln* - Spalding
Quadring Hundred Drove	*Lincoln* - Spalding
Quainton	*Bucks* - Aylesbury
Quaker's Bridge	*Lancaster* - Burnley
Quaker's Yard	*Glamorgan* - Merthyr Tydfil
Quaking Houses	*Durham* - Consett
Quanea	*Cambridge* - Ely
Quantoxhead, East	*Somerset* - Minehead
Quantoxhead, West	*Somerset* - Minehead
Quarles	*Norfolk* - King's Lynn
Quarley	*Hants* - Andover
Quarlton	*Lancaster* - Bolton
Quarmby	*York, W.R.* - Huddersfield
Quarndon	*Derby* - Derby
Quarnford	*Stafford* - Buxton
Quarr	*I. of W.* - Newport (I.W.)
Quarrel	*Cardigan* - Cardigan
Quarrendon	*Bucks* - Aylesbury
Quarrington	*Durham* - Durham
Quarrington	*Lincoln* - Sleaford
Quarrington Hill	*Durham* - Durham
Quarrington, Old	*Durham* - Durham
Quarry Bank	*Stafford* - Stourbridge
Quarry Brow	*Durham* - Bishop Auckland
Quarry Gap	*York, W.R.* - Bradford
Quarry Hill	*Stafford* - Tamworth
Quarry Moor	*York, N.R.* - Harrogate
Quarter, The (Biddenden)	*Kent* - Cranbrook
Quatford	*Salop* - Bridgnorth
Quatt	*Salop* - Bridgnorth
Quebb	*Hereford* - Hereford
Quebec	*Durham* - Durham
Quedgeley	*Gloucester* - Gloucester
Queen Adelaide	*Cambridge* - Ely
Queenborough	*Kent* - Sheerness
Queen Camel	*Somerset* - Yeovil
Queen Charlton	*Somerset* - Bristol
Queenhill	*Worcester* - Cheltenham
Queens Bank	*Lincoln* - Spalding
Queensbury	*Middlesex* - Willesden
Queensbury	*York, W.R.* - Halifax
Queensferry	*Flint* - Chester
Queens Head	*Salop* - Oswestry
Queen's Nympton	*Devon* - Barnstaple
Queens Park	*Denbigh* - Wrexham

Queens Park (part)	*London, N.W.6* - Bloomsbury and Marylebone
Queens Park (part)	*London, N.W.6* - Willesden
Queens Park (part)	*London, W.10* - Bloomsbury and Marylebone
Queens Park (part)	*London, W.10* - Willesden
Quell, The	*Sussex* - Chichester
Quemerford	*Wilts* - Chippenham
Quenby	*Leicester* - Leicester
Quendon	*Essex* - Bishop's Stortford
Queniborough	*Leicester* - Leicester
Quenington	*Gloucester* - Cheltenham
Quermore	*Lancaster* - Lancaster
Queslett (part)	*Stafford* - Birmingham
Queslett (part)	*Stafford* - Walsall
Quethiock	*Cornwall* - Liskeard
Quex	*Kent* - Margate
Quick Edge	*York, W.R.* - Ashton-under-Lyne
Quick, Higher	*York, W.R.* - Ashton-under-Lyne
Quick, Lower	*York, W.R.* - Ashton-under-Lyne
Quidenham	*Norfolk* - Norwich
Quidhampton	*Hants* - Basingstoke
Quidhampton	*Wilts* - Salisbury
Quina Brook	*Salop* - Shrewsbury
Quinton	*Northampton* - Northampton
Quinton (part)	*Warwick* - Birmingham
Quinton (part)	*Warwick* - Stratford on Avon
Quinton (part)	*Worcester* - Stourbridge
Quinton (part)	*Worcester* - West Bromwich
Quinton, Lower	*Warwick* - Stratford on Avon
Quinton, Upper	*Warwick* - Stratford on Avon
Quintrell Downs	*Cornwall* - Truro
Quither	*Devon* - Plymouth
Quixhill	*Stafford* - Uttoxeter
Quoisley	*Cheshire* - Whitchurch
Quorn	*Leicester* - Loughborough
Quy	*Cambridge* - Cambridge

R

Rabley	*Herts* - Barnet
Rabley Heath	*Herts* - Hitchin
Raby	*Cheshire* - Birkenhead
Raby	*Cumberland* - Carlisle
Raby with Keverstone	*Durham* - Bishop Auckland
Race, The	*Monmouth* - Pontypool and Abergavenny
Rachub	*Caernarvon* - Bangor
Rackenford	*Devon* - Tiverton
Rack Fen	*Cambridge* - Ely
Rackham	*Sussex* - Chichester
Rackheath	*Norfolk* - Norwich
Racton	*Sussex* - Chichester
Radbourne	*Derby* - Derby
Radbourne, Lower	*Warwick* - Warwick
Radbourne, Upper	*Warwick* - Warwick
Radbrook	*Salop* - Shrewsbury
Radcliffe	*Lancaster* - Bury
Radcliffe Colliery	*Northumberland* - Alnwick
Radcliffe-on-Trent	*Notts* - Nottingham
Radclive	*Bucks* - Aylesbury
Radcot	*Oxford* - Witney
Raddington	*Somerset* - Taunton
Radford	*Notts* - Nottingham
Radford	*Oxford* - Banbury
Radford	*Somerset* - Bristol
Radford	*Warwick* - Coventry
Radford	*Worcester* - Evesham
Radford (Alvechurch)	*Worcester* - Redditch
Radford Semele	*Warwick* - Warwick
Radford Woodhouse	*Notts* - Nottingham
Radipole Village	*Dorset* - Weymouth
Radlett	*Herts* - Watford
Radley	*Berks* - Oxford
Radley Green	*Essex* - Chelmsford
Radmanthwaite	*Notts* - Mansfield
Radmore Lane	*Stafford* - Wellington (Salop)
Radnage	*Bucks* - High Wycombe
Radnor	*Cheshire* - Congleton
Radnor, New	*Radnor* - Knighton

RAD - RAN

Radnor, Old	*Radnor* - Knighton
Radstock	*Somerset* - Frome
Radstone	*Northampton* - Banbury
Radway	*Warwick* - Banbury
Radway Green	*Cheshire* - Crewe
Radwell	*Beds* - Bedford
Radwell	*Herts* - Hitchin
Radwinter	*Essex* - Bishop's Stortford
Radyr	*Glamorgan* - Cardiff
Raffin Green	*Herts* - Hertford
Raffles	*Cumberland* - Carlisle
Ragdale	*Leicester* - Melton Mowbray
Ragdon	*Salop* - Shrewsbury
Raglan	*Monmouth* - Monmouth
Ragleth	*Salop* - Shrewsbury
Ragleth Hill	*Salop* - Shrewsbury
Ragnall	*Notts* - East Retford
Raikes	*Lancaster* - Bolton
Rainford	*Lancaster* - St. Helens
Rainford Junction	*Lancaster* - St. Helens
Rainham (part)	*Essex* - Grays Thurrock
Rainham (part)	*Essex* - Ilford
Rainham	*Kent* - Rochester
Rainham, Lower	*Kent* - Rochester
Rainham Mark	*Kent* - Rochester
Rainhill	*Lancaster* - St. Helens
Rainhill Stoops	*Lancaster* - St. Helens
Rainow	*Cheshire* - Macclesfield
Rainsbury	*Somerset* - Tiverton
Rainsough	*Lancaster* - Salford
Rainton, East	*Durham* - Durham
Rainton Gate	*Durham* - Durham
Rainton, Middle	*Durham* - Durham
Rainton, West	*Durham* - Durham
Rainton-with-Newby	*York, N.R.* - Harrogate
Rainworth	*Notts* - Mansfield
Raisbeck	*Westmorland* - Penrith
Raisthorpe	*York, E.R.* - Malton
Raithby	*Lincoln* - Skegness
Raithby	*Lincoln* - Louth
Raithby Fen	*Lincoln* - Skegness
Rake	*Hants* - Petersfield
Rake	*Sussex* - Petersfield
Rake Foot	*Cumberland* - Workington
Ralphs Ride	*Berks* - Reading
Rame	*Cornwall* - Penzance
Rame	*Cornwall* - Plymouth
Ramerick	*Herts* - Hitchin
Rampisham	*Dorset* - Dorchester
Rampside	*Lancaster* - Barrow-in-Furness
Rampton	*Cambridge* - Cambridge
Rampton	*Notts* - East Retford
Ramridge End	*Beds* - Luton
Ramsbottom	*Lancaster* - Bury
Ramsbury	*Wilts* - Swindon
Ramsdean	*Hants* - Petersfield
Ramsdell	*Hants* - Basingstoke
Ramsden	*Oxford* - Witney
Ramsden Bellhouse	*Essex* - Brentwood
Ramsden Crays	*Essex* - Brentwood
Ramsden Heath	*Essex* - Brentwood
Ramsey	*Essex* - Harwich
Ramsey	*Hunts* - Huntingdon
Ramsey End	*Hunts* - Huntingdon
Ramsey Forty Foot	*Hunts* - Huntingdon
Ramsey Heights	*Hunts* - Huntingdon
Ramsey Hollow	*Hunts* - Huntingdon
Ramsey Island	*Essex* - Maldon
Ramsey Mereside	*Hunts* - Huntingdon
Ramsey St. Mary's	*Hunts* - Huntingdon
Ramsey Wick	*Essex* - Maldon
Ramsgate	*Cornwall* - Redruth
Ramsgate	*Kent* - Ramsgate
Ramsgill	*York, W.R.* - Harrogate
Ramsgreave	*Lancaster* - Blackburn
Ramsholt	*Suffolk* - Woodbridge
Ramshope	*Northumberland* - Hexham
Ramshorn	*Stafford* - Uttoxeter
Ranby	*Lincoln* - Louth
Ranby	*Notts* - East Retford

RAN - RAW

Rand	*Lincoln* - Lincoln
Randal Holme	*Cumberland* - Carlisle
Randwick	*Gloucester* - Stroud
Randwyck	*Sussex* - Chichester
Rangemore	*Stafford* - Burton-upon-Trent
Rangeworthy	*Gloucester* - Thornbury
Ranmoor	*York, W.R.* - Sheffield
Ranmore Common	*Surrey* - Dorking
Ranskill	*Notts* - East Retford
Ranston	*Dorset* - Wimborne Minster
Ranton	*Stafford* - Stafford
Ranvilles	*Hants* - Southampton
Ranworth	*Norfolk* - Norwich
Rasen, Middle	*Lincoln* - Lincoln
Rasen, West	*Lincoln* - Lincoln
Raskelf	*York, N.R.* - York
Rassau	*Monmouth* - Blackwood
Rastrick	*York, W.R.* - Halifax
Ratby	*Leicester* - Leicester
Ratcliffe	*London, E.1* - Shoreditch
Ratcliffe Culey	*Leicester* - Nuneaton
Ratcliffe-on-Soar	*Notts* - Loughborough
Ratcliffe-on-Wreake	*Leicester* - Leicester
Rathmell	*York, W.R.* - Skipton
Ratlake	*Hants* - Winchester
Ratley	*Warwick* - Banbury
Ratlinghope	*Salop* - Shrewsbury
Ratten Row	*Cumberland* - Carlisle
Rattery	*Devon* - Torquay
Rattlesden	*Suffolk* - Stowmarket
Rauceby Heath	*Lincoln* - Sleaford
Rauceby, North	*Lincoln* - Sleaford
Rauceby, South	*Lincoln* - Sleaford
Raughton	*Cumberland* - Carlisle
Raughtonhead	*Cumberland* - Carlisle
Raunds	*Northampton* - Wellingborough
Raveley, Great	*Hunts* - Huntingdon
Raveley, Little	*Hunts* - Huntingdon
Ravendale, East	*Lincoln* - Great Grimsby
Ravendale, West	*Lincoln* - Great Grimsby
Ravenfield	*York, W.R.* - Rotherham
Ravenglass	*Cumberland* - Whitehaven
Ravenhead	*Lancaster* - St. Helens
Ravenhill	*Glamorgan* - Swansea
Ravenhill	*Stafford* - Stafford
Raveningham	*Norfolk* - Norwich
Ravenscar	*York, N.R.* - Scarborough
Ravenscliffe	*Stafford* - Stoke-on-Trent
Ravensdale	*Stafford* - Stoke-on-Trent
Ravensdale Park	*Derby* - Derby
Ravensden	*Beds* - Bedford
Ravensfleet	*Lincoln* - Gainsborough
Ravenshead	*Notts* - Mansfield
Ravenside	*Northumberland* - Hexham
Ravens Lane	*Stafford* - Stoke-on-Trent
Ravenslodge	*York, W.R.* - Dewsbury
Ravensmoor	*Cheshire* - Crewe
Ravensthorpe	*Northampton* - Northampton
Ravensthorpe	*York, W.R.* - Dewsbury
Ravenstone	*Bucks* - Northampton
Ravenstone	*Leicester* - Ashby-de-la-Zouch
Ravenstonedale	*Westmorland* - Penrith
Ravenstown	*Lancaster* - Barrow-in-Furness
Ravensworth	*Durham* - Gateshead
Ravensworth	*York, N.R.* - Darlington
Raw	*Northumberland* - Morpeth
Raw (Lyth)	*Westmorland* - Kendal
Raw	*York, N.R.* - Whitby
Rawcliffe	*York, N.R.* - York
Rawcliffe	*York, W.R.* - Goole
Rawcliffe Bridge	*York, W.R.* - Goole
Rawcliffe, Out	*Lancaster* - Blackpool
Rawcliffe, Upper	*Lancaster* - Preston
Rawdon	*York, W.R.* - Otley
Rawdon Hill	*York, W.R.* - Otley
Rawfolds	*York, W.R.* - Dewsbury
Rawmarsh	*York, W.R.* - Rotherham
Rawnsley	*Stafford* - Walsall
Rawnsley Hills	*Stafford* - Stafford
Rawreth	*Essex* - Southend

Rawridge	*Devon* - Exeter
Rawtenstall	*Lancaster* - Rawtenstall
Raydon	*Suffolk* - Ipswich
Rayleigh	*Essex* - Southend
Raymonds Hill, Axminster	*Devon* - Axminster and Chard
Rayne	*Essex* - Braintree
Rayner's Lane (part)	*Middlesex* - Watford
Rayner's Lane (part)	*Middlesex* - Willesden
Raynes Park (Merton)	*Surrey* - Croydon
Raynes Park (Wimbledon)	*Surrey* - Kingston-upon-Thames
Raynham, East	*Norfolk* - King's Lynn
Raynham, Great	*Norfolk* - King's Lynn
Raynham, Little	*Norfolk* - King's Lynn
Raynham Martin	*Norfolk* - King's Lynn
Raynham, South	*Norfolk* - King's Lynn
Raynham, West	*Norfolk* - King's Lynn
Raywell	*York, E.R.* - Kingston-upon-Hull
Reach	*Beds* - Bletchley and Leighton Buzzard
Reach	*Cambridge* - Newmarket
Reach Court	*Kent* - Dover
Read	*Lancaster* - Burnley
Reading	*Berks* - Reading
Reading Street	*Kent* - Cranbrook
Reagill	*Westmorland* - Penrith
Reaps Moor	*Stafford* - Leek
Rearsby	*Leicester* - Leicester
Reasby	*Lincoln* - Lincoln
Reaveley	*Northumberland* - Alnwick
Reawla	*Cornwall* - Redruth
Reculver	*Kent* - Canterbury
Red Ball (part)	*Devon* - Taunton
Red Ball (part)	*Devon* - Tiverton
Redberth	*Pembroke* - Haverfordwest
Redbourn	*Herts* - St. Albans
Redbourne	*Lincoln* - Scunthorpe
Redbridge	*Essex* - Ilford
Redbridge	*Hants* - Southampton
Redbridge	*Lancaster* - Bury
Redbrook	*Flint* - Whitchurch
Redbrook	*Gloucester and Monmouth* - Monmouth
Redbrook, Lower	*Gloucester* - Monmouth
Redbrook Street	*Kent* - Cranbrook
Red Bull	*Cheshire* - Congleton
Redbull	*Stafford* - Market Drayton
Redburn	*Northumberland* - Hexham
Redcar	*York, N.R.* - Middlesbrough
Redcliffe Bay	*Somerset* - Weston Super Mare
Redcoats Green	*Herts* - Hitchin
Red Cow Drove	*Lincoln* - Spalding
Red Cross	*Worcester* - Kidderminster
Reddall Hill	*Stafford* - Dudley
Red Dial	*Cumberland* - Carlisle
Reddicap Heath	*Warwick* - Birmingham
Reddings, The	*Gloucester* - Cheltenham
Reddish	*Lancaster* - Stockport
Redditch	*Worcester* - Redditch
Red Dyke	*Sussex* - Eastbourne
Rede	*Suffolk* - Bury St. Edmunds
Redenhall	*Norfolk* - Norwich
Redenham	*Hants* - Andover
Redford	*Sussex* - Petersfield
Red Furlongs	*Salop* - Ludlow
Redgate	*Cornwall* - Liskeard
Redgate	*Lancaster* - St. Helens
Red Gate	*York, N.R.* - Whitby
Redgrave	*Suffolk* - Norwich
Redhall	*Stafford* - Dudley
Redhill	*Glamorgan* - Bridgend
Redhill	*Hants* - Bournemouth
Redhill	*Hants* - Petersfield
Redhill	*Middlesex* - Willesden
Redhill	*Notts* - Nottingham
Redhill	*Salop* - Wellington (Salop)
Redhill	*Somerset* - Weston Super Mare
Redhill	*Stafford* - Stafford
Redhill	*Surrey* - Reigate
Redhill	*Warwick* - Birmingham

Redhill	*Worcester* - Birmingham
Redhouses	*Cumberland* - Workington
Red Houses	*Durham* - Durham
Redisham	*Suffolk* - Lowestoft
Redlake	*Salop* - Wellington (Salop)
Red Lees	*Salop* - Wellington
Redlingfield	*Suffolk* - Norwich
Redlish	*York, W.R.* - Harrogate
Red Lumb	*Lancaster* - Rochdale
Redlynch	*Wilts* - Salisbury
Redmain	*Cumberland* - Workington
Redmarchall	*Durham* - Stockton on Tees
Redmarley	*Gloucester* - Gloucester
Redmarley D'Abitot	*Gloucester* - Gloucester
Redmere	*Cambridge* - Ely
Redmile	*Leicester* - Melton Mowbray
Redmires	*York, W.R.* - Sheffield
Redmoor	*Cornwall* - Bodmin
Rednal	*Salop* - Oswestry
Rednal (part)	*Warwick* - Birmingham
Rednal (part)	*Worcester* - Bromsgrove
Redpath	*Northumberland* - Hexham
Red Rice	*Hants* - Andover
Red Rock	*Lancaster* - Wigan
Red Roses	*Carmarthen* - Haverfordwest
Redruth	*Cornwall* - Redruth
Redruth Highway	*Cornwall* - Redruth
Redstocks	*Wilts* - Chippenham
Red Street	*Stafford* - Stoke-on-Trent
Red Water	*Kent* - Cranbrook
Red Wharf Bay	*Anglesey* - Llangefni
Redwick	*Gloucester* - Thornbury
Redwick	*Monmouth* - Newport (Mon.)
Redworth	*Durham* - Darlington
Reed	*Herts* - Hitchin
Reedham	*Lincoln* - Boston
Reedham	*Norfolk* - Great Yarmouth
Reedley Hallows	*Lancaster* - Burnley
Reedness	*York, W.R.* - Goole
Reedsdale	*Northumberland* - Hexham
Reeds Holme	*Lancaster* - Rawtenstall
Reedsmouth	*Northumberland* - Hexham
Reeds Wood	*Stafford* - Walsall
Reen	*Cornwall* - Truro
Reepham	*Lincoln* - Lincoln
Reepham	*Norfolk* - Norwich
Reepham with Kerdiston	*Norfolk* - Norwich
Reeth	*York, N.R.* - Darlington
Reeves Green	*Warwick* - Coventry
Refel	*Montgomery* - Newtown
Regent's Park	*London, N.W.1* - Bloomsbury and Marylebone
Regent's Park	*London, N.W.8* - Bloomsbury and Marylebone
Reigate	*Surrey* - Reigate
Reighton	*York, E.R.* - Bridlington
Rejerrah	*Cornwall* - Truro
Releath	*Cornwall* - Redruth
Relubbus	*Cornwall* - Penzance
Remenham	*Berks* - Reading
Rempstone	*Dorset* - Swanage
Rempstone	*Notts* - Loughborough
Rendcombe	*Gloucester* - Cheltenham
Rendham	*Suffolk* - Woodbridge
Rendlesham	*Suffolk* - Woodbridge
Renhold	*Beds* - Bedford
Renishaw	*Derby* - Chesterfield
Rennington	*Northumberland* - Alnwick
Rent, New	*Cumberland* - Penrith
Renwick	*Cumberland* - Penrith
Repps	*Norfolk* - Great Yarmouth
Repton	*Derby* - Burton-upon-Trent
Repton Hayes	*Derby* - Burton-upon-Trent
Rescorla	*Cornwall* - St. Austell
Reskadinnick	*Cornwall* - Redruth
Reskivers	*Cornwall* - Truro
Resolven	*Glamorgan* - Neath
Resparveth	*Cornwall* - Truro
Respryn	*Cornwall* - Bodmin
Reston, North	*Lincoln* - Louth

RES - RHO

Reston, South	*Lincoln* - Louth
Restronguet	*Cornwall* - Truro
Resugga	*Cornwall* - St. Austell
Retallack	*Cornwall* - Helston
Retford, East	*Notts* - East Retford
Retford, West	*Notts* - East Retford
Rettendon	*Essex* - Chelmsford
Reule, Lower	*Stafford* - Stafford
Reule, Upper	*Stafford* - Stafford
Revel End	*Herts* - St. Albans
Revels	*Dorset* - Dorchester
Revelstoke	*Devon* - Plymouth
Revesby	*Lincoln* - Boston
Revesby Fen Allotment	*Lincoln* - Boston
Rew	*Devon* - Kingsbridge
Rew	*Dorset* - Dorchester
Rewe	*Devon* - Exeter
Reydon	*Suffolk* - Halesworth
Reymerstone	*Norfolk* - East Dereham
Reynoldston	*Glamorgan* - Swansea
Reynoldston	*Pembroke* - Haverfordwest
Rezare	*Cornwall* - Launceston
Rhanberfedd	*Flint* - Wrexham
Rhandirmwyn	*Carmarthen* - Llandovery
Rhantregynwen	*Montgomery* - Oswestry
Rhayader	*Radnor* - Llandrindod Wells
Rheola	*Glamorgan* - Neath
Rhesycae	*Flint* - Holywell
Rhewl	*Denbigh* - Denbigh
Rhewl Fawr	*Flint* - Holywell
Rhewl Llantysilio	*Denbigh* - Wrexham
Rhewl Mostyn	*Flint* - Holywell
Rhigos	*Glamorgan* - Aberdare
Rhiston	*Salop* - Welshpool
Rhiw	*Caernarvon* - Portmadoc
Rhiwargor	*Montgomery* - Oswestry
Rhiwarth	*Montgomery* - Oswestry
Rhiwbina	*Glamorgan* - Cardiff
Rhiwderyn	*Monmouth* - Newport (Mon.)
Rhiwfawr (part)	*Glamorgan* - Ammanford
Rhiwlas	*Caernarvon* - Caernarvon
Rhiwlas	*Denbigh* - Oswestry
Rhiwlas	*Montgomery* - Oswestry
Rhiwsaeson	*Montgomery* - Machynlleth
Rhode	*Somerset* - Bridgwater
Rhode Common	*Kent* - Canterbury
Rhodes	*Lancaster* - Oldham
Rhodesia	*Notts* - Worksop
Rhodes Minnis	*Kent* - Folkestone
Rhodogeidio	*Anglesey* - Llangefni
Rhoidiad	*Pembroke* - Haverfordwest
Rhondda	*Glamorgan* - Pontypridd
Rhoose	*Glamorgan* - Barry
Rhos	*Glamorgan* - Neath
Rhos	*Pembroke* - Haverfordwest
Rhosamman	*Carmarthen* - Ammanford
Rhoscefnhir	*Anglesey* - Llangefni
Rhoscolyn	*Anglesey* - Llangefni
Rhoscrowther	*Pembroke* - Haverfordwest
Rhosddu	*Denbigh* - Wrexham
Rhosesmor	*Flint* - Mold
Rhosfawr	*Caernarvon* - Portmadoc
Rhosgadfan	*Caernarvon* - Caernarvon
Rhosgoch	*Anglesey* - Llangefni
Rhosgoch	*Montgomery* - Welshpool
Rhos Hill	*Pembroke* - Cardigan
Rhosilli	*Glamorgan* - Swansea
Rhoslan (Criccieth)	*Caernarvon* - Portmadoc
Rhoslan Tydwediog	*Caernarvon* - Portmadoc
Rhosllanerchrugog	*Denbigh* - Wrexham
Rhosmaen	*Carmarthen* - Ammanford
Rhosmeirch	*Anglesey* - Llangefni
Rhosneigr	*Anglesey* - Llangefni
Rhosnensnei	*Denbigh* - Wrexham
Rhos-on-Sea	*Denbigh* - Conway
Rhosrobin	*Denbigh* - Wrexham
Rhosrobin, New	*Denbigh* - Wrexham
Rhos, The	*Radnor* - Knighton
Rhostrehwfa	*Anglesey* - Llangefni
Rhostryfan	*Caernarvon* - Caernarvon

RHO - RID

Rhostyllen	*Denbigh* - Wrexham
Rhosybol	*Anglesey* - Llangefni
Rhosygadfa	*Salop* - Oswestry
Rhosygell	*Cardigan* - Aberystwyth
Rhosygwaliau	*Merioneth* - Dolgellau
Rhosymedre	*Denbigh* - Wrexham
Rhosywaen	*Denbigh* - Wrexham
Rhuallt	*Flint* - Rhyl
Rhuddlan	*Flint* - Rhyl
Rhulen	*Radnor* - Builth
Rhyd	*Merioneth* - Portmadoc
Rhydargaeau	*Carmarthen* - Carmarthen
Rhydcwmere	*Carmarthen* - Lampeter
Rhyd-ddu	*Caernarvon* - Caernarvon
Rhydd, The	*Worcester* - Great Malvern
Rhydgaled	*Denbigh* - Denbigh
Rhydlanfair	*Denbigh* - Conway
Rhydlewis	*Cardigan* - Cardigan
Rhydlios	*Caernarvon* - Portmadoc
Rhyd Owen	*Carmarthen* - Haverfordwest
Rhyducha	*Merioneth* - Dolgellau
Rhydwyn	*Anglesey* - Llangefni
Rhydyblew (Beaufort)	*Monmouth* - Blackwood
Rhydyclafdy	*Caernarvon* - Portmadoc
Rhydyfelin	*Cardigan* - Aberystwyth
Rhydyfelin	*Glamorgan* - Pontypridd
Rhydyfen	*Merioneth* - Dolgellau
Rhydyfoel	*Denbigh* - Rhyl
Rhydyfro	*Glamorgan* - Neath
Rhydygolan	*Flint* - Mold
Rhydymain	*Merioneth* - Dolgellau
Rhydymwyn	*Flint* - Mold
Rhydypandy	*Cardigan* - Aberystwyth
Rhydypennau	*Cardigan* - Aberystwyth
Rhydyronen	*Merioneth* - Machynlleth
Rhydysarn	*Merioneth* - Portmadoc
Rhydytalog	*Flint* - Mold
Rhyl	*Flint* - Rhyl
Rhymney	*Monmouth* - Blackwood
Rhymney Bridge	*Monmouth* - Blackwood
Rhysnant	*Montgomery* - Oswestry
Ribblehead	*York, W.R.* - Lancaster
Ribbleton	*Lancaster* - Preston
Ribby-with-Wrea	*Lancaster* - Preston
Ribchester	*Lancaster* - Preston
Riber	*Derby* - Matlock
Ribston Bridge	*York, W.R.* - Harrogate
Ribston, Great	*York, W.R.* - Harrogate
Ribston, Little	*York, W.R.* - Harrogate
Ribton	*Cumberland* - Workington
Riby	*Lincoln* - Great Grimsby
Riccall	*York, E.R.* - York
Richard's Castle	*Hereford and Salop* - Ludlow
Richborough	*Kent* - Deal
Richings Park	*Bucks* - Uxbridge
Richmond	*Surrey* - Wandsworth
Richmond	*York, N.R.* - Darlington
Richmond	*York, W.R.* - Sheffield
Rich's Wolford	*Somerset* - Taunton
Rickelton	*Durham* - Gateshead
Rickerby	*Cumberland* - Carlisle
Rickerscote	*Stafford* - Stafford
Rickford	*Somerset* - Weston Super Mare
Rickham	*Devon* - Kingsbridge
Rickinghall Inferior	*Suffolk* - Bury St. Edmunds
Rickinghall Superior	*Suffolk* - Norwich
Rickling	*Essex* - Bishop's Stortford
Rickling Green	*Essex* - Bishop's Stortford
Rickmansworth	*Herts* - Watford
Riddell's Quarter	*Northumberland* - Morpeth
Riddings	*Derby* - Alfreton
Riddings Junction	*Cumberland* - Carlisle
Riddlecombe	*Devon* - Barnstaple
Riddlesden	*York, W.R.* - Keighley
Riddlesworth	*Norfolk* - Thetford
Ridgacre	*Stafford* - Birmingham
Ridge	*Dorset* - Swanage
Ridge	*Hants* - Southampton
Ridge	*Herts* - Barnet
Ridge (Chilmark)	*Wilts* - Shaftesbury

RID - RIP

Ridge	*York, W.R.* - Todmorden
Ridgebourne	*Hereford* - Hereford
Ridge Hill	*Hereford* - Hereford
Ridge Hill	*Lancaster* - Ashton-under-Lyne
Ridgehill	*Somerset* - Bristol
Ridge Lane	*Warwick* - Nuneaton
Ridgeway	*Derby* - Alfreton
Ridgeway	*Derby* - Chesterfield
Ridgeway	*Devon* - Plymouth
Ridgeway	*Dorset* - Weymouth
Ridgeway	*Hants* - Andover
Ridgeway	*Salop* - Ludlow
Ridgeway	*Somerset* - Frome
Ridgeway	*Stafford* - Stoke-on-Trent
Ridgeway	*Warwick* - Redditch
Ridgewell	*Essex* - Sudbury
Ridgmont	*Beds* - Bedford
Ridgwardine	*Salop* - Market Drayton
Ridgway Cross	*Hereford* - Worcester
Ridham Dock	*Kent* - Sittingbourne
Riding Mill	*Northumberland* - Hexham
Ridley	*Kent* - Dartford
Ridley	*Northumberland* - Hexham
Ridley Wood	*Denbigh* - Wrexham
Ridlington	*Norfolk* - Norwich
Ridlongton	*Rutland* - Melton Mowbray
Ridsdale	*Northumberland* - Hexham
Rievaulx	*York, N.R.* - Malton
Riffa	*York, W.R.* - Otley
Rigg	*York, N.R.* - Whitby
Rigg Head	*Cumberland* - Workington
Rigghouse	*Cumberland* - Workington
Riggs	*Cumberland* - Workington
Rigmaden Park	*Westmorland* - Kendal
Rigsby with Ailby	*Lincoln* - Skegness
Rigsby-with-Well	*Lincoln* - Skegness
Rigton, North	*York, W.R.* - Harrogate
Riley Green	*Lancaster* - Chorley
Riley Hill	*Stafford* - Lichfield
Rilla Mill	*Cornwall* - Liskeard
Rillaton	*Cornwall* - Liskeard
Rillington	*York, E.R.* - Malton
Rimmington	*York, W.R.* - Blackburn
Rimpton	*Somerset* - Yeovil
Rimswell	*York, E.R.* - Kingston-upon-Hull
Rindleford	*Salop* - Bridgnorth
Ringing Low	*York, W.R.* - Sheffield
Ringland	*Norfolk* - Norwich
Ringles Cross	*Sussex* - Lewes
Ringley Bridge	*Lancaster* - Bolton
Ringley Fold	*Lancaster* - Bolton
Ringmer	*Sussex* - Lewes
Ringmore	*Devon* - Kingsbridge
Ring's End	*Cambridge* - Wisbech
Ringsfield	*Suffolk* - Lowestoft
Ringshall	*Herts* - Hemel Hempstead
Ringshall	*Suffolk* - Stowmarket
Ringstead	*Dorset* - Weymouth
Ringstead	*Norfolk* - King's Lynn
Ringstead	*Northampton* - Wellingborough
Ringway (part)	*Cheshire* - Manchester
Ringway (part)	*Cheshire* - Altrincham
Ringwood	*Hants* - Bournemouth
Ringwould	*Kent* - Deal
Rinsey	*Cornwall* - Penzance
Ripe	*Sussex* - Lewes
Ripley	*Derby* - Alfreton
Ripley	*Hants* - Bournemouth
Ripley	*Surrey* - Guildford
Ripley	*York, W.R.* - Harrogate
Ripleyville	*York, W.R.* - Bradford
Riplingham	*York, E.R.* - Beverley
Riplington	*Hants* - Petersfield
Riplington	*Northumberland* - Morpeth
Ripon	*York, W.R.* - Harrogate
Rippingale	*Lincoln* - Spalding
Rippingale Fen	*Lincoln* - Spalding
Ripple	*Kent* - Deal
Ripple	*Worcester* - Cheltenham
Ripponden	*York, W.R.* - Halifax

RIS - ROC

Risbury	*Hereford* - Leominster
Risby	*Lincoln* - Lincoln
Risby	*Lincoln* - Scunthorpe
Risby	*Suffolk* - Bury St. Edmunds
Risby	*York, E.R.* - Beverley
Risca	*Monmouth* - Newport (Mon.)
Rise	*York, E.R.* - Beverley
Risebridge	*Kent* - Cranbrook
Riseburn	*Durham* - Bishop Auckland
Riseden	*Kent* - Cranbrook
Riseholme	*Lincoln* - Lincoln
Riseley	*Beds* - Bedford
Risely Common	*Wilts* - Reading
Rise Park	*Essex* - Ilford
Rishangles	*Suffolk* - Norwich
Rishton	*Lancaster* - Blackburn
Rishworth	*York, W.R.* - Halifax
Rising Bridge	*Lancaster* - Rawtenstall
Rising Brook	*Stafford* - Stafford
Rising Sun	*Cornwall* - Plymouth
Risley	*Derby* - Ilkeston
Risley	*Lancaster* - Warrington
Risley (Culcheth)	*Lancaster* - Leigh
Rispey	*Durham* - Bishop Auckland
Risplith	*York, N.R.* - Harrogate
Rissington, Great	*Gloucester* - Cheltenham
Rissington, Little	*Gloucester* - Cheltenham
Riston, Long	*York, E.R.* - Beverley
Ritton Castle	*Salop* - Shrewsbury
Ritton Colt Park	*Northumberland* - Morpeth
Ritton White House	*Northumberland* - Morpeth
Rivelin Bridge	*York, W.R.* - Sheffield
Rivenhall	*Essex* - Braintree
River	*Sussex* - Chichester
Riverdale	*Northumberland* - Hexham
Rivergreen	*Northumberland* - Morpeth
Riverhead	*Kent* - Sevenoaks
Riversbridge	*Devon* - Kingsbridge
Rivington	*Lancaster* - Chorley
Rixton	*Lancaster* - Warrington
Roach Bridge	*Lancaster* - Preston
Roachill	*Devon* - Tiverton
Roade	*Northampton* - Northampton
Roadwater	*Somerset* - Minehead
Roa Island	*Lancaster* - Barrow-in-Furness
Roall	*York, W.R.* - Pontefract
Roanhead	*Lancaster* - Barrow-in-Furness
Roan, Old	*Lancaster* - Liverpool
Roans Green	*Cumberland* - Carlisle
Robberby	*Cumberland* - Penrith
Robertsbridge	*Sussex* - Hastings
Robertstown	*Glamorgan* - Aberdare
Robert Town	*York, W.R.* - Dewsbury
Robeston Wathen	*Pembroke* - Haverfordwest
Robeston West	*Pembroke* - Haverfordwest
Robin Hood	*Cumberland* - Workington
Robin Hood	*Derby* - Alfreton
Robin Hood	*Warwick* - Birmingham
Robin Hood	*York, W.R.* - Leeds
Robin Hood's Bay	*York, N.R.* - Whitby
Roblaw	*Cumberland* - Carlisle
Roborough	*Devon* - Plymouth
Roborough	*Devon* - Barnstaple
Roby	*Lancaster* - St. Helens
Roby Mill	*Lancaster* - Wigan
Rocester	*Stafford* - Uttoxeter
Roch	*Pembroke* - Haverfordwest
Rochdale	*Lancaster* - Rochdale
Roche	*Cornwall* - St. Austell
Roche Abbey	*York, W.R.* - Rotherham
Rochester	*Kent* - Rochester
Rochester Ward	*Northumberland* - Hexham
Rochford	*Essex* - Southend
Rochford, Lower	*Worcester* - Ludlow
Rochford, Upper	*Worcester* - Ludlow
Rock	*Cornwall* - Bodmin
Rock	*Northumberland* - Alnwick
Rock	*Salop* - Ludlow
Rock	*Salop* - Wellington (Salop)
Rock	*Worcester* - Kidderminster

ROC - ROL

Rockbeare	*Devon* - Exeter
Rockbourne	*Hants* - Salisbury
Rockcliffe	*Cumberland* - Carlisle
Rock Ferry	*Cheshire* - Birkenhead
Rockfield	*Monmouth* - Monmouth
Rockford	*Hants* - Salisbury
Rockhampton	*Gloucester* - Thornbury
Rockhead	*Cornwall* - Bideford
Rock Hill	*Salop* - Ludlow
Rock Hill	*Worcester* - Bromsgrove
Rock House	*Northumberland* - Haltwhistle
Rockingham	*Northampton* - Corby
Rockland All Saints	*Norfolk* - Norwich
Rocklands	*Hereford* - Monmouth
Rockland St. Andrew	*Norfolk* - Norwich
Rockland St. Mary	*Norfolk* - Norwich
Rockland St. Peter	*Norfolk* - Norwich
Rockley	*Notts* - East Retford
Rockley	*Wilts* - Swindon
Rocks Green	*Salop* - Ludlow
Rockwell End	*Bucks* - Reading
Rockwell Green	*Somerset* - Taunton
Rodbaston	*Stafford* - Stafford
Rodborough	*Gloucester* - Stroud
Rodbourne	*Wilts* - Malmesbury
Rodd	*Hereford* - Leominster
Roddam	*Northumberland* - Alnwick
Rodden	*Dorset* - Weymouth
Rodden	*Somerset* - Frome
Rodderupside	*Cumberland* - Haltwhistle
Roddymoor, West	*Durham* - Bishop Auckland
Roddymoor, North	*Durham* - Bishop Auckland
Roddymoor, West	*Durham* - Bishop Auckland
Rode	*Somerset* - Frome
Rode Common	*Somerset* - Frome
Rode Heath	*Cheshire* - Congleton
Roden	*Salop* - Wellington (Salop)
Rodenhurst Hall	*Salop* - Wellington (Salop)
Rodford	*Gloucester* - Bristol
Rodhuish	*Somerset* - Minehead
Roding High	*Essex* - Chelmsford
Rodington	*Salop* - Wellington (Salop)
Rodington Heath	*Salop* - Wellington (Salop)
Rodley	*Gloucester* - Gloucester
Rodley (part)	*York, W.R.* - Bradford
Rodley (part)	*York, W.R.* - Leeds
Rodmarton	*Gloucester* - Stroud
Rodmel	*Sussex* - Lewes
Rodmersham	*Kent* - Sittingbourne
Rodney Stoke	*Somerset* - Wells
Rodridge	*Durham* - Hartlepool
Rodsley	*Derby* - Derby
Roebuck	*Lancaster* - Preston
Roeburndale	*Lancaster* - Lancaster
Roecliffe	*York, W.R.* - Harrogate
Roecombe Bottom	*Devon* - Axminster and Chard
Roedean	*Sussex* - Brighton
Roe Down	*Hants* - Aldershot and Farnham
Roe Green	*Herts* - St. Albans
Roe Green	*London, N.W.9* - Willesden
Roehampton	*London, S.W.15* - Wandsworth
Roe Hyde	*Herts* - St. Albans
Roel	*Gloucester* - Cheltenham
Roeshot Park, Highcliffe	*Hants* - Bournemouth
Roe Stock	*Herts* - St. Albans
Roffey	*Sussex* - Horsham
Rofford	*Oxford* - Thame
Rogate	*Sussex* - Petersfield
Rogerscale	*Cumberland* - Workington
Rogerstone	*Monmouth* - Newport (Mon.)
Roggerham	*Lancaster* - Burnley
Roggiett	*Monmouth* - Chepstow
Roke	*Dorset* - Swanage
Roke	*Hants* - Southampton
Roke	*Oxford* - Didcot
Rokeby	*York, N.R.* - Bishop Auckland
Roke Marsh	*Oxford* - Didcot
Roker	*Durham* - Sunderland
Rollesby	*Norfolk* - Great Yarmouth
Rolleston	*Notts* - Newark

ROL - ROS

Rolleston	*Stafford* - Burton-upon-Trent
Rollestone	*Leicester* - Leicester
Rollright, Great	*Oxford* - Banbury
Rollright, Little	*Oxford* - Banbury
Rolston	*York, E.R.* - Beverley
Rolstone	*Somerset* - Weston Super Mare
Rolvenden	*Kent* - Cranbrook
Rolvenden Hill	*Kent* - Cranbrook
Rolvenden Layne	*Kent* - Cranbrook
Romald Kirk	*York, N.R.* - Bishop Auckland
Roman Bridge	*Caernarvon* - Conway
Romanby	*York, N.R.* - Northallerton
Romansleigh	*Devon* - Barnstaple
Romansleigh Beacon	*Devon* - Barnstaple
Romansleigh Valley	*Devon* - Barnstaple
Romden Smarden	*Kent* - Ashford
Romford	*Essex* - Ilford
Romiley	*Cheshire* - Stockport
Romney, New	*Kent* - Ashford
Romney, Old	*Kent* - Ashford
Romney Street	*Kent* - Sevenoaks
Romsey	*Hants* - Southampton
Romsley	*Salop* - Bridgnorth
Romsley	*Worcester* - Bromsgrove
Rood Ashton	*Wilts* - Trowbridge
Rood End	*Stafford* - West Bromwich
Rookery	*Herts* - St. Albans
Rookery	*Stafford* - Stoke-on-Trent
Rookhope	*Durham* - Bishop Auckland
Rookley	*I. of W.* - Newport (I.W.)
Rooksbridge	*Somerset* - Weston Super Mare
Rooks Nest	*Herts* - Hitchin
Rookwith	*York, N.R.* - Northallerton
Rooley Moor	*Lancaster* - Bury
Roos	*York, E.R.* - Kingston-upon-Hull
Roose	*Lancaster* - Barrow-in-Furness
Roosebeck	*Lancaster* - Barrow-in-Furness
Roosecote	*Lancaster* - Barrow-in-Furness
Roosegate Estate	*Lancaster* - Barrow-in-Furness
Ropehaugh	*Northumberland* - Hexham
Ropley	*Hants* - Winchester
Ropsley	*Lincoln* - Grantham
Rorrington (Chirbury)	*Salop* - Welshpool
Roscare	*Cornwall* - Launceston
Roscarrack	*Cornwall* - Truro
Roscorla	*Cornwall* - St. Austell
Roscroggan	*Cornwall* - Redruth
Rose	*Cornwall* - Truro
Roseacre	*Lancaster* - Preston
Rose Ash	*Devon* - Barnstaple
Rosedale, East	*York, N.R.* - Malton
Roseden	*Northumberland* - Alnwick
Rose Green	*Sussex* - Chichester
Rose Grove	*Lancaster* - Burnley
Rose Hill	*Cheshire* - Stockport
Rose Hill	*Northumberland* - North Shields
Rose Hill	*Oxford* - Oxford
Rose Hill	*Salop* - Market Drayton
Rosehill	*York, W.R.* - Rotherham
Roseland	*Cornwall* - Liskeard
Rosemarket	*Pembroke* - Haverfordwest
Rosemaund	*Hereford* - Hereford
Rosemore	*Hereford* - Hereford
Rosevean	*Cornwall* - St. Austell
Rosevear	*Cornwall* - Penzance
Roseville	*Stafford* - Dudley
Rosevine	*Cornwall* - Truro
Rosewain	*Cumberland* - Carlisle
Rosewarne	*Cornwall* - Redruth
Roseworthy	*Cornwall* - Redruth
Rosgill	*Westmorland* - Penrith
Rosherville	*Kent* - Gravesend
Roskear	*Cornwall* - Redruth
Roskerwell	*Cornwall* - Penzance
Rosley	*Cumberland* - Carlisle
Rosliston	*Derby* - Burton-upon-Trent
Rossall	*Salop* - Shrewsbury
Rossett	*Denbigh* - Wrexham
Rossett Green	*York, W.R.* - Harrogate
Rosshead	*Lancaster* - Barrow-in-Furness

ROS - ROW

Rossington	*York, W.R.* - Doncaster
Rossmore	*Dorset* - Poole
Ross-on-Wye	*Hereford* - Monmouth
Rostherne	*Cheshire* - Altrincham
Rosthwaite	*Cumberland* - Workington
Rosthwaite	*Lancaster* - Barrow-in-Furness
Roston	*Stafford* - Uttoxeter
Roston Common	*Stafford* - Uttoxeter
Rosudgeon	*Cornwall* - Penzance
Rothbury	*Northumberland* - Morpeth
Rotherby	*Leicester* - Melton Mowbray
Rotherfield	*Hants* - Aldershot and Farnham
Rotherfield	*Sussex* - Tunbridge Wells
Rotherfield Greys	*Oxford* - Reading
Rotherfield Peppard	*Oxford* - Reading
Rotherham	*York, W.R.* - Rotherham
Rotherhithe	*London, S.E.16* - Southwark
Rotherhopeside	*Cumberland* - Carlisle
Rothersthorpe	*Northampton* - Northampton
Rotherwick	*Hants* - Basingstoke
Rothley	*Leicester* - Leicester
Rothley	*Northumberland* - Morpeth
Rothwell	*Lincoln* - Great Grimsby
Rothwell	*Northampton* - Kettering
Rothwell	*York, W.R.* - Leeds
Rothwell Haigh	*York, W.R.* - Leeds
Rotsea	*York, E.R.* - Beverley
Rottingdean	*Sussex* - Brighton
Rottington	*Cumberland* - Whitehaven
Rotton Park	*Warwick* - Birmingham
Roud	*I. of W.* - Newport (I.W.)
Roudham	*Norfolk* - Thetford
Rougham	*Norfolk* - King's Lynn
Rougham	*Suffolk* - Bury St. Edmunds
Rough Close	*Stafford* - Stoke-on-Trent
Rough Common	*Kent* - Canterbury
Roughcote	*Stafford* - Stoke-on-Trent
Roughdown	*Hants* - Southampton
Roughdown	*Herts* - Hemel Hempstead
Rough Hill	*Cheshire* - Chester
Rough Hills	*Stafford* - Wolverhampton
Roughlea Colliery	*Durham* - Bishop Auckland
Roughlee Booth	*Lancaster* - Nelson
Roughley	*Warwick* - Birmingham
Roughton	*Lincoln* - Lincoln
Roughton	*Norfolk* - Norwich
Roughton	*Salop* - Bridgnorth
Roughtown	*York, W.R.* - Ashton-under-Lyne
Roughway	*Kent* - Sevenoaks
Round Chimneys	*Dorset* - Dorchester
Round Green	*Beds* - Luton
Round Green	*York, W.R.* - Barnsley
Roundham (Crewkerne)	*Somerset* - Yeovil
Roundhay	*York, W.R.* - Leeds
Roundhurst	*Sussex* - Chichester
Round Oak	*Salop* - Ludlow
Round Oak	*Stafford* - Stourbridge
Roundpond	*Wilts* - Chippenham
Rounds Green	*Kent* - Cranbrook
Rounds Green	*Worcester* - Dudley
Rounds Hill	*Stafford* - Dudley
Round Street	*Sussex* - Chichester
Roundthorn	*Lancaster* - Oldham
Roundway	*Wilts* - Devizes
Roundwood	*York, W.R.* - Dewsbury
Rounton, East	*York, N.R.* - Northallerton
Rounton, West	*York, N.R.* - Northallerton
Rousdon	*Devon* - Axminster and Chard
Rouse Lench	*Worcester* - Evesham
Rousham	*Oxford* - Banbury
Routenbeck	*Cumberland* - Workington
Routh	*York, E.R.* - Beverley
Routs Green	*Bucks* - High Wycombe
Row	*Westmorland* - Appleby
Rowarth	*Derby* - Buxton
Rowbarton	*Somerset* - Taunton
Rowberrow	*Somerset* - Weston Super Mare
Rowde	*Wilts* - Devizes
Rowden	*Hereford* - Leominster
Rowe	*Cornwall* - Bideford

ROW - RUD

Rowe	*Salop* - Oswestry
Rowell	*Westmorland* - Kendal
Roweltown	*Cumberland* - Carlisle
Rowen	*Caernarvon* - Conway
Rowfant	*Sussex* - East Grinstead
Rowfoot	*Northumberland* - Hexham
Rowford	*Somerset* - Taunton
Row Hedge	*Essex* - Colchester
Rowhook	*Sussex* - Horsham
Rowington	*Warwick* - Warwick
Rowington Green	*Warwick* - Warwick
Rowland	*Derby* - Buxton
Rowland's Castle	*Hants* - Petersfield
Rowlands Gill	*Durham* - Newcastle upon Tyne
Rowledge	*Hants and Surrey* - Aldershot and Farnham
Rowlestone	*Hereford* - Hereford
Rowley	*Durham* - Consett
Rowley	*Salop* - Bridgnorth
Rowley	*Salop* - Shrewsbury
Rowley	*York, E.R.* - Beverley
Rowley Green	*Herts* - Barnet
Rowley Regis	*Stafford* - Dudley
Rowley's Green	*Warwick* - Coventry
Rownall	*Stafford* - Leek
Rowner	*Hants* - Portsmouth
Rowney Green	*Worcester* - Redditch
Rownhams	*Hants* - Southampton
Row of Trees	*Cheshire* - Macclesfield
Rowrah	*Cumberland* - Whitehaven
Rowsham	*Bucks* - Aylesbury
Rowsley	*Derby* - Matlock
Rowstock	*Berks* - Didcot
Rowston	*Lincoln* - Sleaford
Rowthorne	*Derby* - Chesterfield
Rowton	*Cheshire* - Chester
Rowton (Stokesay)	*Salop* - Ludlow
Rowton (Alberbury)	*Salop* - Shrewsbury
Rowton (Telford)	*Salop* - Wellington (Salop)
Roxby	*York, W.R.* - Whitby
Roxby cum Risby	*Lincoln* - Scunthorpe
Roxeth	*Middlesex* - Willesden
Roxford	*Herts* - Hertford
Roxham	*Norfolk* - King's Lynn
Roxholme	*Lincoln* - Sleaford
Roxpole	*Hereford* - Leominster
Roxton	*Beds* - Bedford
Roxton	*Lincoln* - Great Grimsby
Roxwell	*Essex* - Chelmsford
Royal George	*York, W.R.* - Oldham
Royal Hill	*Gloucester* - Cheltenham
Royal Oak	*Durham* - Bishop Auckland
Royal's Green	*Cheshire* - Whitchurch
Roydhouse	*York, W.R.* - Huddersfield
Royd Moor	*York, W.R.* - Pontefract
Roydon	*Essex* - Harlow
Roydon	*Norfolk* - Norwich
Roydon	*Norfolk* - King's Lynn
Roydon Hamlet	*Essex* - Harlow
Royds Green (part)	*York, W.R.* - Leeds
Royley	*Lancaster* - Oldham
Royston	*Cambridge and Herts* - Hitchin
Royston	*York, W.R.* - Barnsley
Royston Grange	*Derby* - Matlock
Royton	*Lancaster* - Oldham
Ruabon	*Denbigh* - Wrexham
Ruan Highlanes	*Cornwall* - Truro
Ruan Lanihorne	*Cornwall* - Truro
Ruan Minor	*Cornwall* - Penzance
Ruardean	*Gloucester* - Gloucester
Ruardean Hill	*Gloucester* - Gloucester
Ruardean Woodside	*Gloucester* - Gloucester
Rubery (part)	*Warwick* - Birmingham
Rubery (part)	*Worcester* - Bromsgrove
Ruckinge	*Kent* - Ashford
Ruckland	*Lincoln* - Louth
Ruckley (Acton Burnell)	*Salop* - Shrewsbury
Ruckley (Tong)	*Salop* - Wellington (Salop)
Ruckroft	*Cumberland* - Penrith
Rudbaxton	*Pembroke* - Haverfordwest

RUD - RUS

Rudby	*York, N.R.* - Middlesbrough
Rudchester	*Northumberland* - Newcastle upon Tyne
Rudding Park	*York, W.R.* - Harrogate
Ruddings	*Cumberland* - Workington
Ruddington	*Notts* - Nottingham
Ruddle	*Gloucester* - Gloucester
Ruddlemoor	*Cornwall* - St. Austell
Rudford	*Gloucester* - Gloucester
Rudge	*Somerset* - Frome
Rudge	*Stafford* - Stafford
Rudge	*Wilts* - Swindon
Rudge Heath	*Salop* - Bridgnorth
Rudgeway	*Gloucester* - Thornbury
Rudgwick	*Sussex* - Horsham
Rudham, East	*Norfolk* - King's Lynn
Rudham, Great	*Norfolk* - King's Lynn
Rudham, West	*Norfolk* - King's Lynn
Rudheath	*Cheshire* - Northwich
Rudhill	*Hereford* - Gloucester
Rudloe	*Wilts* - Bath
Rudloe	*Wilts* - Chippenham
Rudry	*Glamorgan* - Caerphilly
Rudston	*York, E.R.* - Bridlington
Rudyard	*Stafford* - Leek
Rue Barn	*Stafford* - Stafford
Rue Wood	*Salop* - Shrewsbury
Ruffit, The	*Gloucester* - Gloucester
Rufford	*Lancaster* - Southport
Rufford	*Notts* - Mansfield
Rufforth	*York, W.R.* - York
Rugby	*Warwick* - Rugby
Rugeley	*Stafford* - Stafford
Rugley	*Northumberland* - Alnwick
Ruins	*Lancaster* - Bolton
Ruishton	*Somerset* - Taunton
Ruislip	*Middlesex* - Uxbridge
Ruislip Common	*Middlesex* - Uxbridge
Ruislip Manor	*Middlesex* - Uxbridge
Ruiton	*Stafford* - Dudley
Ruleholme	*Cumberland* - Carlisle
Ruloe	*Cheshire* - Northwich
Rumboldswhyke	*Sussex* - Chichester
Rumburgh	*Suffolk* - Halesworth
Rumby Hill	*Durham* - Bishop Auckland
Rumer Hill	*Stafford* - Walsall
Rumney	*Monmouth* - Cardiff
Rumwell	*Somerset* - Taunton
Rumworth	*Lancaster* - Bolton
Runcorn	*Cheshire* - Runcorn
Runcton	*Sussex* - Chichester
Runcton Holme	*Norfolk* - King's Lynn
Runcton, North	*Norfolk* - King's Lynn
Runcton, South	*Norfolk* - King's Lynn
Rundlestone	*Devon* - Plymouth
Runfold	*Surrey* - Aldershot and Farnham
Runhall	*Norfolk* - Norwich
Runham	*Norfolk* - Great Yarmouth
Runnerfoot	*Northumberland* - Hexham
Runninghill	*York, W.R.* - Oldham
Runnington	*Somerset* - Taunton
Running Waters	*Durham* - Durham
Runsell Green	*Essex* - Chelmsford
Runswick	*York, N.R.* - Whitby
Runton, East	*Norfolk* - Norwich
Runton, West	*Norfolk* - Norwich
Runwell	*Essex* - Southend
Ruperra	*Glamorgan* - Cardiff
Ruscombe	*Berks* - Reading
Ruscombe	*Gloucester* - Stroud
Rushall	*Hereford* - Hereford
Rushall	*Norfolk* - Norwich
Rushall	*Stafford* - Walsall
Rushall	*Wilts* - Devizes
Rushbrooke	*Suffolk* - Bury St. Edmunds
Rushbury	*Salop* - Ludlow
Rushcroft	*Lancaster* - Oldham
Rushden	*Herts* - Hitchin
Rushden	*Northampton* - Wellingborough
Rushey Flanders	*Warwick* - Tamworth

RUS - RYE

Rushey Green	*London, S.E.6* - Bromley
Rushford	*Norfolk* - Thetford
Rushford	*Worcester* - Redditch
Rush Green	*Essex* - Ilford
Rush Green	*Herts* - Hertford
Rush Green	*Herts* - Hitchin
Rushington	*Hants* - Southampton
Rushlake Green	*Sussex* - Eastbourne
Rushmere	*Suffolk* - Ipswich
Rushmere	*Suffolk* - Lowestoft
Rush Mills	*Northampton* - Northampton
Rushmoor	*Salop* - Wellington (Salop)
Rushmore	*Wilts* - Shaftesbury
Rushock	*Hereford* - Leominster
Rushock	*Worcester* - Kidderminster
Rusholme	*Lancaster* - Manchester
Rushton	*Cheshire* - Crewe
Rushton	*Northampton* - Kettering
Rushton	*Salop* - Shrewsbury
Rushton James	*Stafford* - Leek
Rushton Marsh	*Stafford* - Leek
Rushton Spencer	*Stafford* - Leek
Rushwick	*Worcester* - Worcester
Rushyford	*Durham* - Bishop Auckland
Ruskington	*Lincoln* - Sleaford
Ruskington Fen	*Lincoln* - Sleaford
Rusland	*Lancaster* - Barrow-in-Furness
Rusper	*Sussex* - Horsham
Ruspidge	*Gloucester* - Gloucester
Russells Green	*Sussex* - Hastings
Russell's Water	*Oxford* - Reading
Russia, Little	*Warwick* - Birmingham
Russley	*Wilts* - Swindon
Rustington	*Sussex* - Chichester
Ruston	*York, N.R.* - Scarborough
Ruston, East	*Norfolk* - Norwich
Ruston Parva	*York, N.R.* - Bridlington
Ruston, South	*Norfolk* - Norwich
Rustrall	*Kent* - Tunbridge Wells
Ruswarp	*York, N.R.* - Whitby
Ruthern	*Cornwall* - Bodmin
Ruthin	*Denbigh* - Denbigh
Ruthvoes	*Cornwall* - Truro
Ruthwaite	*Cumberland* - Carlisle
Ruxley	*Kent* - Bromley
Ruxley	*Surrey* - Epsom
Ruxton	*Hereford* - Hereford
Ruxton Green	*Hereford* - Monmouth
Ruyton of the Eleven Towns	*Salop* - Oswestry
Ryal	*Northumberland* - Newcastle upon Tyne
Ryall Grove	*Worcester* - Cheltenham
Ryarsh	*Kent* - Maidstone
Ryburgh, Great	*Norfolk* - King's Lynn
Ryburgh, Little	*Norfolk* - King's Lynn
Rycote	*Oxford* - Thame
Rydal	*Westmorland* - Kendal
Ryde	*I. of W.* - Newport (I.W.)
Ryder's Green	*Stafford* - West Bromwich
Rye	*Sussex* - Hastings
Rye Bank	*Salop* - Shrewsbury
Rye Common	*Hants* - Basingstoke
Ryecroft	*Lancaster* - Ashton-under-Lyne
Ryecroft	*Stafford* - Walsall
Ryecroft	*York, W.R.* - Keighley
Ryecroft	*York, W.R.* - Rotherham
Ryeford	*Gloucester* - Stroud
Ryeford	*Hereford* - Ross
Rye Foreign	*Sussex* - Hastings
Rye Harbour	*Sussex* - Hastings
Rye Hill	*Essex* - Harlow
Rye Hill	*Northumberland* - Hexham
Ryehill	*Northumberland* - Morpeth
Rye Hill	*York, E.R.* - Kingston-upon-Hull
Rye House	*Herts* - Hertford
Ryeish Green	*Berks* - Reading
Rye Lane	*Kent* - Sevenoaks
Rye Park	*Herts* - Hertford
Ryeworth	*Gloucester* - Cheltenham

Ryhall	*Rutland* - Stamford
Ryhill	*York, W.R.* - Barnsley
Ryhope	*Durham* - Sunderland
Ryhope Colliery	*Durham* - Sunderland
Ryland	*Lincoln* - Lincoln
Rylstone	*York, W.R.* - Skipton
Ryme Intrinsica	*Dorset* - Yeovil
Ryston	*Norfolk* - King's Lynn
Ryther	*York, W.R.* - York
Ryton	*Durham* - Newcastle upon Tyne
Ryton	*Gloucester* - Gloucester
Ryton	*Salop* - Bridgnorth
Ryton	*Salop* - Shrewsbury
Ryton	*Warwick* - Nuneaton
Ryton-upon-Dunsmore	*Warwick* - Coventry
Ryton Woodside	*Durham* - Newcastle upon Tyne

S

Sabden	*Lancaster* - Burnley
Sacombe	*Herts* - Hertford
Sacombe Green	*Herts* - Hertford
Sacriston	*Durham* - Durham
Sadberge	*Durham* - Darlington
Saddington	*Leicester* - Leicester
Saddlebow	*Norfolk* - King's Lynn
Saddlescombe	*Sussex* - Brighton
Saddlewood	*Gloucester* - Bristol
Saddleworth	*York, W.R.* - Oldham
Sadgeston	*Pembroke* - Haverfordwest
Sadgill	*Westmorland* - Kendal
Saffron Walden	*Essex* - Bishop's Stortford
Sageston	*Pembroke* - Haverfordwest
Saham Toney	*Norfolk* - King's Lynn
Saighton	*Cheshire* - Chester
Saint Agnes	*Cornwall* - Truro
Saint Agnes	*Scilly Isles* - Penzance
Saint Albans	*Herts* - St. Albans
Saint Aldhelms	*Dorset* - Swanage
Saint Allen	*Cornwall* - Truro
Saint Andrew's Major	*Glamorgan* - Barry
Saint Andrew's Minor	*Glamorgan* - Bridgend
Saint Annes-on-Sea	*Lancaster* - Blackpool
Saint Anns	*Caernarvon* - Bangor
Saint Ann's Chapel	*Cornwall* - Plymouth
Saint Ann's Chapel	*Devon* - Kingsbridge
Saint Anthony	*Cornwall* - Truro
Saint Anthony-in-Meneage	*Cornwall* - Penzance
Saint Arvans	*Monmouth* - Chepstow
Saint Asaph	*Flint* - Rhyl
Saint Athans	*Glamorgan* - Bridgend
Saint Austell	*Cornwall* - St. Austell
Saint Bees	*Cumberland* - Whitehaven
Saint Blazey	*Cornwall* - St. Austell
Saint Blazey Gate	*Cornwall* - St. Austell
Saint Botolphs	*Pembroke* - Haverfordwest
Saint Breock	*Cornwall* - Bodmin
Saint Breward	*Cornwall* - Bideford
Saint Briavels	*Gloucester* - Chepstow
Saint Briavels Common	*Gloucester* - Gloucester
Saint Brides	*Pembroke* - Haverfordwest
Saint Bride's Major	*Glamorgan* - Bridgend
Saint Bride's Minor	*Glamorgan* - Bridgend
Saint Bride's Netherwent	*Monmouth* - Chepstow
Saint Bride's-super-Ely	*Glamorgan* - Cardiff
Saint Bride's Wentlloog	*Monmouth* - Newport (Mon.)
Saint Budeaux	*Devon* - Plymouth
Saintbury	*Gloucester* - Evesham
Saint Buryan	*Cornwall* - Penzance
Saint Catherine's	*Somerset* - Bath
Saint Catherine's Hill	*Hants* - Bournemouth
Saint Chloe	*Gloucester* - Stroud
Saint Clears	*Carmarthen* - Carmarthen
Saint Cleer	*Cornwall* - Liskeard
Saint Clement	*Cornwall* - Truro
Saint Clether	*Cornwall* - Launceston
Saint Columb Major	*Cornwall* - Truro
Saint Columb Minor	*Cornwall* - Truro

Saint Columb Road	*Cornwall* - Truro
Saint Cross	*Hants* - Winchester
Saint David's	*Pembroke* - Haverfordwest
Saint Day	*Cornwall* - Redruth
Saint Decuman's	*Somerset* - Minehead
Saint Dennis	*Cornwall* - St. Austell
Saint Denys	*Hants* - Southampton
Saint Devereux	*Hereford* - Hereford
Saint Dogmells	*Pembroke* - Cardigan
Saint Dogwells	*Pembroke* - Haverfordwest
Saint Dominick	*Cornwall* - Liskeard
Saint Donat's	*Glamorgan* - Bridgend
Saint Edrens	*Pembroke* - Haverfordwest
Saint Elvis	*Pembroke* - Haverfordwest
Saint Endellion	*Cornwall* - Bideford
Saint Enoder	*Cornwall* - Truro
Saint Erme	*Cornwall* - Truro
Saint Erney	*Cornwall* - Plymouth
Saint Erth	*Cornwall* - Penzance
Saint Erth Praze	*Cornwall* - Penzance
Saint Ervan	*Cornwall* - Truro
Saint Eval	*Cornwall* - Truro
Saint Ewe	*Cornwall* - St. Austell
Saint Fagans	*Glamorgan* - Cardiff
Saint Freock	*Cornwall* - Truro
Saint Florence	*Pembroke* - Haverfordwest
Saint Gennys	*Cornwall* - Launceston
Saint George	*Denbigh* - Rhyl
Saint George-in-the East	*London, E.1* - Shoreditch
Saint George's	*Salop* - Wellington (Salop)
Saint George's	*Somerset* - Weston Super Mare
Saint Georges-super-Ely	*Glamorgan* - Cardiff
Saint Germans	*Cornwall* - Liskeard
Saint Giles (Houghton)	*Norfolk* - King's Lynn
Saint Giles in the Wood	*Devon* - Bideford
Saint Giles on the Heath	*Devon* - Launceston
Saint Gluvias	*Cornwall* - Truro
Saint Harmon	*Radnor* - Llandrindod Wells
Saint Helena	*Warwick* - Tamworth
Saint Helens	*I. of W.* - Newport (I.W.)
Saint Helens	*Lancaster* - St. Helens
Saint Helens, Hastings	*Sussex* - Hastings
Saint Helen Without	*Berks* - Oxford
Saint Helier's Estate	*Surrey* - Croydon
Saint Hilary	*Cornwall* - Penzance
Saint Hilary	*Glamorgan* - Bridgend
Saint Ippollitts	*Herts* - Hitchin
Saint Ishmael	*Carmarthen* - Carmarthen
Saint Ishmael's	*Pembroke* - Haverfordwest
Saint Issells	*Pembroke* - Haverfordwest
Saint Issey	*Cornwall* - Bodmin
Saint Ive	*Cornwall* - Liskeard
Saint Ives	*Cornwall* - Penzance
Saint Ives	*Hants* - Bournemouth
Saint Ives	*Hunts* - Huntingdon
Saint Ives	*York, W.R.* - Keighley
Saint James End	*Northampton* - Northampton
Saint James's	*London, S.W.1* - Westminster
Saint John	*Durham* - Bishop Auckland
Saint John's	*Cornwall* - Penzance
Saint Johns	*Cornwall* - Plymouth
Saint John's Chapel	*Durham* - Bishop Auckland
Saint John's Common	*Sussex* - Haywards Heath
Saint Johns Wood	*London, N.W.8* - Bloomsbury & Marylebone
Saint Juliot	*Cornwall* - Launceston
Saint Just (in Penwith)	*Cornwall* - Penzance
Saint Just in Roseland	*Cornwall* - Truro
Saint Keverne	*Cornwall* - Penzance
Saint Kew	*Cornwall* - Bideford
Saint Keyne	*Cornwall* - Liskeard
Saint Lawrence	*Cornwall* - Bodmin
Saint Lawrence	*Essex* - Maldon
Saint Lawrence	*I. of W.* - Newport (I.W.)
Saint Lawrence	*Pembroke* - Haverfordwest
Saint Leonards	*Bucks* - Amersham
Saint Leonards	*Hants* - Bournemouth
Saint Leonards	*Sussex* - Hastings
Saint Levan	*Cornwall* - Penzance
Saint Luke's (part)	*London, E.C.1* - Clerkenwell

Saint Luke's (part)	*London, E.C.1* - Shoreditch
Saint Lythan's	*Glamorgan* - Barry
Saint Lythan's Downs	*Glamorgan* - Cardiff
Saint Mabyn	*Cornwall* - Bodmin
Saint Margaret's	*Hereford* - Hereford
Saint Margarets	*Herts* - Hemel Hempstead
Saint Margarets	*Herts* - Hertford
Saint Margaret's at Cliffe	*Kent* - Dover
Saint Margaret's Bay	*Kent* - Dover
Saint Martha	*Surrey* - Guildford
Saint Martin	*Cornwall* - Liskeard
Saint Martin-in-Meneage	*Cornwall* - Penzance
Saint Martin's	*Kent* - Ashford
Saint Martins	*Salop* - Oswestry
Saint Martin's	*Scilly Isles* - Penzance
Saint Martins Without	*Huntingdon and Peterborough* - Stamford
Saint Mary	*Pembroke* - Haverfordwest
Saint Mary Bourne	*Hants* - Andover
Saint Marychurch	*Devon* - Torquay
Saint Mary Church	*Glamorgan* - Bridgend
Saint Mary Church	*Glamorgan* - Barry
Saint Mary Cray	*Kent* - Bromley
Saint Mary Hill	*Glamorgan* - Bridgend
Saint Mary Hoo	*Kent* - Rochester
Saint Mary in the Marsh	*Kent* - Ashford
Saint Mary Platt	*Kent* - Sevenoaks
Saint Mary's Bay	*Kent* - Ashford
Saint Mary's	*Scilly Isles* - Penzance
Saint Marys	*Lancaster* - Oldham
Saint Mary's Field	*Northumberland* - Morpeth
Saint Maughans	*Monmouth* - Monmouth
Saint Mawes	*Cornwall* - Truro
Saint Mawgan	*Cornwall* - Truro
Saint Mellion	*Cornwall* - Liskeard
Saint Mellons	*Monmouth* - Cardiff
Saint Merryn	*Cornwall* - Bodmin
Saint Mewan	*Cornwall* - St. Austell
Saint Michael	*Pembroke* - Haverfordwest
Saint Michael Caerhayes	*Cornwall* - St. Austell
Saint Michael Church	*Somerset* - Bridgwater
Saint Michael Penkevil	*Cornwall* - Truro
Saint Michael's	*Kent* - Cranbrook
Saint Michaels	*Lancaster* - Preston
Saint Michaels	*Worcester* - Ludlow
Saint Michaels Mount	*Cornwall* - Penzance
Saint Minver Highlands	*Cornwall* - Bodmin
Saint Minver Lowlands	*Cornwall* - Bodmin
Saint Neot	*Cornwall* - Liskeard
Saint Neots	*Hunts* - Huntingdon
Saint Newlyn East	*Cornwall* - Truro
Saint Nicholas	*Glamorgan* - Barry
Saint Nicholas	*Pembroke* - Haverfordwest
Saint Nicholas at Wade	*Kent* - Margate
Saint Olaves	*Suffolk* - Lowestoft
Saint Osyth	*Essex* - Colchester
Saint Owens Cross	*Hereford* - Hereford
Saint Paul's Cray	*Kent* - Bromley
Saint Paul's Walden	*Herts* - Hitchin
Saint Peter	*Dorset* - Dorchester
Saint Peter's	*Kent* - Margate
Saint Petrox	*Devon* - Torquay
Saint Petrox	*Pembroke* - Haverfordwest
Saint Pierre	*Monmouth* - Chepstow
Saint Pinnock	*Cornwall* - Liskeard
Saint Quintin	*Dorset* - Dorchester
Saint Sampson	*Cornwall* - St. Austell
Saint Saviour	*Devon* - Torquay
Saint Stephen	*Kent* - Canterbury
Saint Stephens	*Cornwall* - Launceston
Saint Stephens	*Cornwall* - Plymouth
Saint Stephens (Coombe)	*Cornwall* - St. Austell
Saint Stephens in Brannel	*Cornwall* - St. Austell
Saint Teath	*Cornwall* - Bideford
Saint Thomas	*Glamorgan* - Swansea
Saint Thomas	*Pembroke* - Haverfordwest
Saint Thomas the Apostle	*Cornwall* - Launceston
Saint Thomas Cross	*Warwick* - Rugby
Saint Tudy	*Cornwall* - Bideford
Saint Twynnells	*Pembroke* - Haverfordwest
Saint Veep	*Cornwall* - Liskeard
Saint Wenn	*Cornwall* - Bodmin
Saint Weonards	*Hereford* - Hereford
Saint Winnow	*Cornwall* - Bodmin
Salcey Lodge	*Northampton* - Northampton
Salcombe	*Devon* - Kingsbridge
Salcombe Regis	*Devon* - Exeter
Salcot	*Essex* - Colchester
Salden	*Bucks* - Bletchley and Leighton Buzzard
Sale	*Cheshire* - Altrincham
Saleby	*Lincoln* - Louth
Sale Green	*Worcester* - Worcester
Salehurst	*Sussex* - Hastings
Salem	*Caernarvon* - Caernarvon
Salem	*Cardigan* - Aberystwyth
Salem	*Carmarthen* - Ammanford
Salem	*Cornwall* - Truro
Salem	*Lancaster* - Oldham
Salendine Nook	*York, W.R.* - Huddersfield
Salesbury	*Lancaster* - Blackburn
Saleway	*Worcester* - Worcester
Salford	*Beds* - Bletchley and Leighton Buzzard
Salford	*Lancaster* - Salford
Salford	*Oxford* - Banbury
Salford Bridge	*Warwick* - Stratford on Avon
Salford Priors	*Warwick* - Redditch
Salfords	*Surrey* - Reigate
Salhouse	*Norfolk* - Norwich
Saling, Great	*Essex* - Braintree
Salisbury	*Wilts* - Salisbury
Salkeld Dykes	*Cumberland* - Penrith
Salkend, Great	*Cumberland* - Penrith
Salkend, Little	*Cumberland* - Penrith
Sall	*Norfolk* - Norwich
Salmony	*Lincoln* - Skegness
Salperton	*Gloucester* - Cheltenham
Salph End	*Beds* - Bedford
Salt	*Stafford* - Stafford
Saltaire	*York, W.R.* - Bradford
Saltash	*Cornwall* - Plymouth
Saltash Passage	*Devon* - Plymouth
Salt Boxes	*Worcester* - Evesham
Saltburn-by-Sea	*York, N.R.* - Middlesbrough
Saltby	*Leicester* - Melton Mowbray
Saltcoats	*Cumberland* - Carlisle
Saltdean	*Sussex* - Brighton
Salterbeck	*Cumberland* - Workington
Salterforth	*York, W.R.* - Skipton
Salterhebble	*York, W.R.* - Halifax
Salterley	*Gloucester* - Cheltenham
Salterley Grange	*Gloucester* - Cheltenham
Saltersbrook	*Derby* - Sheffield
Salters Gate (part)	*Durham* - Bishop Auckland
Salters Gate (part)	*Durham* - Durham
Salters Heath	*Kent* - Sevenoaks
Saltersley Common	*Cheshire* - Altrincham
Salters Lode	*Norfolk* - King's Lynn
Saltfleet	*Lincoln* - Louth
Saltfleetby All Saints	*Lincoln* - Louth
Saltfleetby St. Clement	*Lincoln* - Louth
Saltfleetby St. Peter	*Lincoln* - Louth
Saltford	*Somerset* - Bristol
Salt Hill	*Bucks* - Slough
Salthill	*Sussex* - Chichester
Salthouse	*Cumberland* - Whitehaven
Salthouse	*Lancaster* - Barrow-in-Furness
Salthouse	*Norfolk* - Norwich
Saltley	*Warwick* - Birmingham
Saltmarshe	*Hereford* - Worcester
Saltmarshe	*York, E.R.* - Goole
Saltney	*Cheshire* - Chester
Saltney, East	*Flint* - Chester
Saltney Ferry	*Flint* - Chester
Saltney, West	*Flint* - Chester
Salton	*York, N.R.* - Malton
Saltwells (part)	*Stafford* - Dudley

SAL - SAN

Saltwood	*Kent* - Folkestone
Salvington	*Sussex* - Worthing
Salvington, High	*Sussex* - Wortling
Salwarpe	*Worcester* - Worcester
Salwayash	*Dorset* - Dorchester
Salwick	*Lancaster* - Preston
Sambourne	*Warwick* - Redditch
Sambrook	*Salop* - Market Drayton
Sambrook	*Salop* - Wellington (Salop)
Samlesbury	*Lancaster* - Preston
Sampford Arundel	*Somerset* - Taunton
Sampford Brett	*Somerset* - Minehead
Sampford Courteney	*Devon* - Okehampton
Sampford, Great	*Essex* - Bishop's Stortford
Sampford, Little	*Essex* - Bishop's Stortford
Sampford Moor	*Somerset* - Taunton
Sampford Peverell	*Devon* - Tiverton
Sampford Spiney	*Devon* - Plymouth
Sancreed	*Cornwall* - Penzance
Sancton and Houghton	*York, E.R.* - Beverley
Sancton Dale	*York, E.R.* - Beverley
Sancton Wold	*York, E.R.* - Beverley
Sand	*Somerset* - Weston Super Mare
Sand	*Somerset* - Wells
Sandal	*York, W.R.* - Wakefield
Sandale	*Cumberland* - Carlisle
Sandall, Long	*York, W.R.* - Doncaster
Sandbach	*Cheshire* - Crewe
Sandbanks	*Dorset* - Poole
Sand Bay	*Somerset* - Weston Super Mare
Sandbeck	*York, W.R.* - Rotherham
Sand Beds	*Stafford* - Walsall
Sanderstead	*Surrey* - Croydon
Sandfield	*Worcester* - Evesham
Sandford	*Cheshire* - Whitchurch
Sandford	*Devon* - Exeter
Sandford	*Dorset* - Swanage
Sandford	*Hants* - Bournemouth
Sandford	*I. of W.* - Newport (I.W.)
Sandford	*Salop* - Bridgnorth
Sandford	*Salop* - Oswestry
Sandford	*Somerset* - Weston Super Mare
Sandford	*Westmorland* - Penrith
Sandford	*Worcester* - Worcester
Sandford Hill	*Stafford* - Stoke-on-Trent
Sandford-on-Thames	*Oxford* - Oxford
Sandford Orcas	*Dorset* - Yeovil
Sandford St. Martin	*Oxford* - Banbury
Sandgate	*Kent* - Folkestone
Sandgate	*Lancaster* - Barrow-in-Furness
Sandhall	*Lancaster* - Barrow-in-Furness
Sand Hall House	*York, E.R.* - Goole
Sandhayes	*Wiltshire* - Warminster
Sandhill	*York, W.R.* - Rotherham
Sandhill Park	*Somerset* - Taunton
Sandhoe	*Northumberland* - Hexham
Sandholme	*York, E.R.* - Goole
Sandholme Landing	*York, E.R.* - Goole
Sand House	*Beds* - Bletchley and Leighton Buzzard
Sandhurst	*Berks* - Reading
Sandhurst	*Gloucester* - Gloucester
Sandhurst	*Kent* - Cranbrook
Sand Hutton	*York, N.R.* - Northallerton
Sand Hutton	*York, N.R.* - York
Sandiacre	*Derby* - Ilkeston
Sandiway	*Cheshire* - Northwich
Sandleford	*Berks* - Newbury
Sandleheath	*Hants* - Salisbury
Sandlemere	*York, E.R.* - Kingston-upon-Hull
Sandlin	*Worcester* - Great Malvern
Sandling	*Kent* - Maidstone
Sandon	*Essex* - Chelmsford
Sandon	*Herts* - Hitchin
Sandon	*Stafford* - Stafford
Sandon Bank	*Stafford* - Stafford
Sandon Wood	*Stafford* - Stafford
Sandown	*I. of W.* - Newport (I.W.)
Sandplace	*Cornwall* - Liskeard
Sandraw	*Cumberland* - Carlisle

SAN - SAT

Sandridge	*Herts* - St. Albans
Sandridge	*Wilts* - Chippenham
Sandridge Common	*Wilts* - Chippenham
Sandringham	*Norfolk* - King's Lynn
Sands	*Bucks* - High Wycombe
Sandscale	*Lancaster* - Barrow-in-Furness
Sandsend	*York, N.R.* - Whitby
Sandside	*Lancaster* - Barrow-in-Furness
Sandside	*Westmorland* - Kendal
Sandtoft	*Lincoln* - Thorne
Sandway	*Kent* - Maidstone
Sandwell Park	*Stafford* - West Bromwich
Sandwich	*Kent* - Deal
Sandwick	*Westmorland* - Penrith
Sandy	*Beds* - Biggleswade
Sandy Bank	*Lincoln* - Boston
Sandy Bottom	*Cornwall* - St. Austell
Sandy Brook	*Derby* - Derby
Sandybury	*Salop* - Bridgnorth
Sandycroft	*Flint* - Chester
Sandy Cross	*Hereford* - Worcester
Sandy Down	*Hants* - Lymington
Sandy Down	*Hants* - Andover
Sandyfields (part)	*Stafford* - Dudley
Sandyfields (part)	*Stafford* - Wolverhampton
Sandyford	*Salop* - Market Drayton
Sandyford	*Stafford* - Stoke-on-Trent
Sandygate	*York, W.R.* - Sheffield
Sandy Lane	*Wilts* - Chippenham
Sandy Lane	*York, W.R.* - Bradford
Sandy Park	*Devon* - Okehampton
Sandysyke	*Cumberland* - Carlisle
Sandy Way	*Hereford* - Hereford
Sanham Green	*Berks* - Newbury
Sankey, Great	*Lancaster* - Warrington
Sansaw	*Salop* - Shrewsbury
Sansaw Heath	*Salop* - Shrewsbury
Santon Bridge	*Cumberland* - Whitehaven
Santon Downham	*Suffolk* - Thetford
Santon	*Lincoln* - Scunthorpe
Sapcote	*Leicester* - Hinckley
Sapey Bridge	*Hereford* - Worcester
Sapey Common	*Hereford* - Worcester
Sapey Court	*Worcester* - Worcester
Sapey, Lower	*Worcester* - Worcester
Sapey, Upper	*Hereford* - Worcester
Sapiston	*Suffolk* - Thetford
Sapley	*Hunts* - Huntingdon
Sapperton	*Derby* - Burton-upon-Trent
Sapperton	*Gloucester* - Stroud
Sapperton	*Lincoln* - Grantham
Sardis	*Pembroke* - Haverfordwest
Saredon, Great	*Stafford* - Wolverhampton
Saredon, Little	*Stafford* - Wolverhampton
Sarisbury Green	*Hants* - Portsmouth
Sarn	*Caernarvon* - Portmadoc
Sarn	*Flint* - Holywell
Sarn	*Glamorgan* - Bridgend
Sarn	*Montgomery* - Newtown
Sarn	*Salop* - Oswestry
Sarnau	*Brecon* - Brecknock
Sarnau	*Cardigan* - Cardigan
Sarnau	*Merioneth* - Dolgellau
Sarnau	*Montgomery* - Oswestry
Sarn Bach	*Caernarvon* - Portmadoc
Sarn Bridge	*Flint* - Wrexham
Sarnesfield	*Hereford* - Hereford
Saron	*Carmarthen* - Ammanford
Saron	*Carmarthen* - Carmarthen
Saron	*Denbigh* - Denbigh
Sarratt	*Herts* - Watford
Sarratt Bottom	*Herts* - Watford
Sarratt Green	*Herts* - Watford
Sarre	*Kent* - Ramsgate
Sarsden	*Oxford* - Banbury
Sarson	*Hants* - Andover
Sarum, Old	*Wilts* - Salisbury
Sascott	*Salop* - Shrewsbury
Satley	*Durham* - Durham
Satterleigh	*Devon* - Barnstaple

SAT - SCA

Satterthwaite	*Lancaster* - Kendal
Satwell	*Oxford* - Reading
Saughall	*Cheshire* - Chester
Saughall, Little	*Cheshire* - Chester
Saughall Massie	*Cheshire* - Birkenhead
Saul	*Gloucester* - Gloucester
Saundby	*Lincoln* - Gainsborough
Saundersfoot	*Pembroke* - Haverfordwest
Saunderton	*Bucks* - High Wycombe
Saunderton Lee	*Bucks* - High Wycombe
Saunton	*Devon* - Barnstaple
Sausthorpe	*Lincoln* - Skegness
Saverley Green	*Stafford* - Stoke-on-Trent
Savernake	*Wilts* - Swindon
Savile Town	*York, W.R.* - Dewsbury
Sawbridge	*Warwick* - Rugby
Sawbridgeworth	*Herts* - Bishop's Stortford
Sawdon	*York, N.R.* - Scarborough
Sawley	*Derby* - Nottingham
Sawley	*York, W.R.* - Blackburn
Sawley	*York, W.R.* - Harrogate
Sawrey	*Lancaster* - Kendal
Sawston	*Cambridge* - Cambridge
Sawtry	*Hunts* - Huntingdon
Saxby	*Leicester* - Melton Mowbray
Saxby	*Lincoln* - Lincoln
Saxby All Saints	*Lincoln* - Barton-on-Humber
Saxelby	*Leicester* - Melton Mowbray
Saxilby	*Lincoln* - Lincoln
Saxilby Syke	*Lincoln* - Lincoln
Saxley	*Hants* - Andover
Saxlingham	*Norfolk* - Norwich
Saxlingham Nethergate	*Norfolk* - Norwich
Saxlingham Thorpe	*Norfolk* - Norwich
Saxmundham	*Suffolk* - Woodbridge
Saxondale	*Notts* - Nottingham
Saxon Street	*Suffolk* - Newmarket
Saxon's Lode	*Worcester* - Cheltenham
Saxtead	*Suffolk* - Woodbridge
Saxthorpe	*Norfolk* - Norwich
Saxton	*York, W.R.* - Leeds
Sayers Common	*Sussex* - Haywards Heath
Scackleton	*York, N.R.* - Malton
Scaftworth	*Notts* - East Retford
Scagglethorpe	*York, E.R.* - Malton
Scalby	*York, E.R.* - Goole
Scalby	*York, N.R.* - Scarborough
Scalby Nabs	*York, N.R.* - Scarborough
Scaldwell	*Northampton* - Northampton
Scale Bank	*Lancaster* - Barrow-in-Furness
Scaleby	*Cumberland* - Carlisle
Scaleby Hill	*Cumberland* - Carlisle
Scalegill Place	*Cumberland* - Whitehaven
Scalehill	*Cumberland* - Workington
Scalehouses	*Cumberland* - Penrith
Scale, North	*Lancaster* - Barrow-in-Furness
Scale, Old	*Cumberland* - Workington
Scales (Kirkoswald)	*Cumberland* - Penrith
Scales	*Cumberland* - Carlisle
Scales	*Cumberland* - Workington
Scales	*Lancaster* - Barrow-in-Furness
Scales	*Lancaster* - Preston
Scalford	*Leicester* - Melton Mowbray
Scaling	*York, N.R.* - Whitby
Scamblesby	*Lincoln* - Louth
Scammonden	*York, W.R.* - Huddersfield
Scampston	*York, E.R.* - Malton
Scampton	*Lincoln* - Lincoln
Scant Row	*Lancaster* - Bolton
Scarborough	*Worcester* - Cheltenham
Scarborough	*York, N.R.* - Scarborough
Scarborough, New (Tingley)	*York, W.R.* - Dewsbury
Scarborough, New (Wakefield)	*York, W.R.* - Wakefield
Scarcewater	*Cornwall* - Truro
Scarcliffe	*Derby* - Chesterfield
Scarcroft	*York, W.R.* - Leeds
Scarisbrick	*Lancaster* - Southport
Scarle, North	*Lincoln* - Newark

SCA - SCR

Scarle, South	*Notts* - Newark
Scarning	*Norfolk* - East Dereham
Scarrington	*Notts* - Nottingham
Scarrowmanwick	*Cumberland* - Penrith
Scarthingwell	*York, W.R.* - Leeds
Scar Village	*York, W.R.* - Harrogate
Scawby	*Lincoln* - Scunthorpe
Scawsby	*York, W.R.* - Doncaster
Scawthorpe	*York, W.R.* - Doncaster
Scawton	*York, N.R.* - Malton
Scaynes Hill	*Sussex* - Haywards Heath
Scethrog	*Brecon* - Brecknock
Scholar Green	*Cheshire* - Congleton
Scholes	*Lancaster* - Wigan
Scholes (Cleckheaton)	*York, W.R.* - Dewsbury
Scholes	*York, W.R.* - Huddersfield
Scholes	*York, W.R.* - Rotherham
Scholes	*York, W.R.* - Leeds
Scholes, West (Thornton)	*York, W.R.* - Bradford
School Aycliffe	*Durham* - Darlington
Schoolgreen	*Berks* - Reading
School Hill	*Lancaster* - Bolton
School House	*Dorset* - Axminster and Chard
Scilly Isles	*Cornwall* - Penzance
Scissett	*York, W.R.* - Huddersfield
Scleddau	*Pembroke* - Haverfordwest
Scofton	*Notts* - Worksop
Scole	*Norfolk* - Norwich
Scopwick	*Lincoln* - Sleaford
Scorborough	*York, E.R.* - Beverley
Scoreby	*York, E.R.* - York
Scorrier (part)	*Cornwall* - Redruth
Scorrier (part)	*Cornwall* - Truro
Scorriton	*Devon* - Newton Abbot
Scorton	*Lancaster* - Lancaster
Scorton	*York, N.R.* - Darlington
Sco' Ruston	*Norfolk* - Norwich
Scosthrop	*York, W.R.* - Skipton
Scotby	*Cumberland* - Carlisle
Scotch Corner	*York, N.R.* - Darlington
Scotforth	*Lancaster* - Lancaster
Scotgrove	*Bucks* - Thame
Scot Hay	*Stafford* - Stoke-on-Trent
Scothern	*Lincoln* - Lincoln
Scotland Farm	*Lincoln* - Gainsborough
Scotland Gate	*Northumberland* - Blyth
Scotland Green	*Warwick* - Birmingham
Scotlands	*Stafford* - Wolverhampton
Scotscoulthard	*Northumberland* - Hexham
Scots Gap	*Northumberland* - Morpeth
Scotswood	*Northumberland* - Newcastle upon Tyne
Scotter	*Lincoln* - Gainsborough
Scotterthorpe	*Lincoln* - Gainsborough
Scotterwood	*Lincoln* - Gainsborough
Scottlethorpe	*Lincoln* - Spalding
Scotton	*Lincoln* - Gainsborough
Scotton	*York, N.R.* - Darlington
Scotton	*York, W.R.* - Harrogate
Scottow	*Norfolk* - Norwich
Scott's Green	*Worcester* - Dudley
Scott Willoughby	*Lincoln* - Sleaford
Scoulton	*Norfolk* - Norwich
Scounslow Green	*Stafford* - Uttoxeter
Scoveston	*Pembroke* - Haverfordwest
Scrafield	*Lincoln* - Lincoln
Scrafton	*York, N.R.* - Northallerton
Scrag Hill	*Hants* - Southampton
Scrainwood	*Northumberland* - Alnwick
Scraptoft	*Leicester* - Leicester
Scrapton	*Somerset* - Axminster and Chard
Scratby	*Norfolk* - Great Yarmouth
Scrathe House	*York, W.R.* - Sheffield
Scrayingham	*York, E.R.* - Malton
Scredda	*Cornwall* - St. Austell
Scredington	*Lincoln* - Sleaford
Scremby	*Lincoln* - Skegness
Scremerston	*Northumberland* - Berwick-upon-Tweed

SCR - SEB

Screveton	*Notts* - Nottingham
Scrivelsby	*Lincoln* - Boston
Scriven	*York, W.R.* - Harrogate
Scrooby	*Notts* - East Retford
Scropton	*Derby* - Burton-upon-Trent
Scrub Hill	*Lincoln* - Boston
Scrubwood	*Bucks* - Aylesbury
Scruton	*York, N.R.* - Northallerton
Scrwgan	*Denbigh* - Oswestry
Sculls Gate	*Kent* - Cranbrook
Sculthorpe	*Norfolk* - King's Lynn
Scunthorpe	*Lincoln* - Scunthorpe
Scupholme	*Lincoln* - Louth
Scwrfa	*Monmouth* - Blackwood
Seaborough	*Dorset* - Yeovil
Seabridge	*Stafford* - Stoke-on-Trent
Seabrook	*Bucks* - Bletchley and Leighton Buzzard
Seabrook	*Kent* - Folkestone
Seaburn	*Durham* - Sunderland
Seacombe	*Cheshire* - Birkenhead
Seacourt	*Berks* - Oxford
Seacroft	*York, W.R.* - Leeds
Seadyke	*Lincoln* - Boston
Seaford	*Sussex* - Lewes
Seaforth	*Lancaster* - Liverpool
Seagrave	*Leicester* - Loughborough
Seagry	*Wilts* - Chippenham
Seagry Heath	*Wilts* - Malmesbury
Seaham	*Durham* - Sunderland
Seaham Colliery	*Durham* - Sunderland
Seaham Grange	*Durham* - Sunderland
Seaham Harbour	*Durham* - Sunderland
Seaham, New	*Durham* - Sunderland
Seaham, Old	*Durham* - Sunderland
Sea Houses	*Northumberland* - Alnwick
Seal	*Kent* - Sevenoaks
Sealand	*Cheshire* - Chester
Sealand	*Flint* - Chester
Sealand Garden City	*Flint* - Chester
Seal Chart	*Kent* - Sevenoaks
Seale	*Surrey* - Aldershot and Farnham
Sealwood	*Derby* - Burton-upon-Trent
Seamer	*York, N.R.* - Scarborough
Seamer-in-Cleveland	*York, N.R.* - Middlesbrough
Sea Palling	*Norfolk* - Great Yarmouth
Searby cum Owmby	*Lincoln* - Scunthorpe
Seasalter	*Kent* - Canterbury
Seascale	*Cumberland* - Whitehaven
Seathwaite	*Cumberland* - Workington
Seathwaite	*Lancaster* - Barrow-in-Furness
Seatle	*Lancaster* - Barrow-in-Furness
Seatoller	*Cumberland* - Workington
Seaton	*Cornwall* - Liskeard
Seaton	*Cumberland* - Workington
Seaton	*Devon* - Axminster and Chard
Seaton	*Durham* - Sunderland
Seaton	*Kent* - Canterbury
Seaton	*Northumberland* - Blyth
Seaton	*Rutland* - Corby
Seaton	*York, E.R.* - Beverley
Seaton Burn	*Northumberland* - Newcastle upon Tyne
Seaton Carew	*Durham* - Hartlepool
Seaton Delaval	*Northumberland* - North Shields
Seaton Delaval Hall	*Northumberland* - Blyth
Seaton Lane	*Durham* - Sunderland
Seaton Moor	*Durham* - Sunderland
Seaton, North	*Northumberland* - Morpeth
Seaton Ross	*York, E.R.* - York
Seaton Sluice	*Northumberland* - North Shields
Seaton Terrace	*Northumberland* - North Shields
Sea View	*I. of W.* - Newport (I.W.)
Seavington Abbotts	*Somerset* - Yeovil
Seavington St. Mary	*Somerset* - Yeovil
Seavington St. Michael	*Somerset* - Yeovil
Sebastopol	*Cambridge* - Ely
Sebastopol	*Monmouth* - Pontypool and Abergavenny
Sebergham	*Cumberland* - Carlisle

SEC - SEV

Seckington	*Warwick* - Tamworth
Sector (Axminster)	*Devon* - Axminster and Chard
Sedbergh	*York, W.R.* - Kendal
Sedbury	*Gloucester* - Chepstow
Seddington	*Beds* - Biggleswade
Sedgeberrow	*Worcester* - Evesham
Sedgebrook	*Lincoln* - Grantham
Sedgefield	*Durham* - Stockton on Tees
Sedgeford	*Norfolk* - King's Lynn
Sedgeletch	*Durham* - Durham
Sedghill	*Wilts* - Shaftesbury
Sedgley	*Stafford* - Dudley
Sedgwick	*Westmorland* - Kendal
Sedlescombe	*Sussex* - Hastings
Sedling	*Durham* - Bishop Auckland
Sedrup	*Bucks* - Aylesbury
Sedsall	*Derby* - Uttoxeter
Seedley	*Lancaster* - Salford
Seend	*Wilts* - Devizes
Seend Cleeve	*Wilts* - Devizes
Seer Green	*Bucks* - High Wycombe
Seething	*Norfolk* - Norwich
Sefton	*Lancaster* - Liverpool
Sefton Park	*Lancaster* - Liverpool
Segensworth	*Hants* - Portsmouth
Seghill	*Northumberland* - North Shields
Seghill Colliery	*Northumberland* - North Shields
Seifton	*Salop* - Ludlow
Seighford	*Stafford* - Stafford
Seisdon	*Stafford* - Wolverhampton
Selattyn	*Salop* - Oswestry
Selborne	Hants - Aldershot and Farnham
Selby	*York, W.R.* - Selby
Seldom Seen	*Durham* - Bishop Auckland
Selham	*Sussex* - Chichester
Selhurst	*Surrey* - Croydon
Selhurst	*Sussex* - Chichester
Sellack	*Hereford* - Monmouth
Sellafield	*Cumberland* - Whitehaven
Selling	*Kent* - Canterbury
Sellinge	*Kent* - Folkestone
Sells Green	*Wilts* - Devizes
Selly Hill	*Warwick* - Birmingham
Selly Oak	*Warwick* - Birmingham
Selly Park	*Warwick* - Birmingham
Selmeston	*Sussex* - Lewes
Selsdon	*Surrey* - Croydon
Selsey	*Sussex* - Chichester
Selside	*Westmorland* - Kendal
Selside (Horton-in-Ribblesdale)	*York, W.R.* - Skipton
Selsley	*Gloucester* - Stroud
Selsted	*Kent* - Folkestone
Selston	*Notts* - Alfreton
Selston, New	*Notts* - Alfreton
Selworthy	*Somerset* - Minehead
Semer	*Suffolk* - Ipswich
Semington	*Wilts* - Trowbridge
Semley	*Wilts* - Shaftesbury
Sempringham	*Lincoln* - Sleaford
Sempringham Fen	*Lincoln* - Sleaford
Send	*Surrey* - Guildford
Senghenydd	*Glamorgan* - Caerphilly
Sennen	*Cornwall* - Penzance
Sennen Cove	*Cornwall* - Penzance
Sennowe Hall	*Norfolk* - King's Lynn
Senny Bridge	*Brecon* - Brecknock
Serlby	*Notts* - East Retford
Sesswick	*Denbigh* - Wrexham
Setch	*Norfolk* - King's Lynn
Setchey	*Norfolk* - King's Lynn
Setley	*Hants* - Lymington
Setmabanning	*Cumberland* - Workington
Setmurthy	*Cumberland* - Workington
Setthorns	*Hants* - Lymington
Settle	*York, W.R.* - Skipton
Settrington	*York, E.R.* - Malton
Seven Ash	*Somerset* - Taunton
Seven Barrows	*Berks* - Newbury

Sevenhampton	*Gloucester* - Cheltenham
Sevenhampton	*Wilts* - Swindon
Seven Kings	*Essex* - Ilford
Seven Oaks	*Cheshire* - Northwich
Sevenoaks	*Kent* - Sevenoaks
Sevenoaks Common	*Kent* - Sevenoaks
Sevenoaks Weald	*Kent* - Sevenoaks
Seven Score	*Kent* - Ramsgate
Seven Sisters	*Glamorgan* - Neath
Seven Springs	*Gloucester* - Cheltenham
Seven Springs	*Stafford* - Stafford
Seven Waters	*Gloucester* - Stroud
Seveock	*Cornwall* - Truro
Severalls, Lower (Crewkerne)	*Somerset* - Yeovil
Severn Beach	*Gloucester* - Thornbury
Severn Stoke	*Worcester* - Worcester
Sevington	*Kent* - Ashford
Sevington	*Wilts* - Chippenham
Sevorgan	*Cornwall* - Truro and Falmouth
Sewards End	Essex - Bishop's Stortford
Sewardstone	*Essex* - Edmonton
Sewell	*Beds* - Luton
Sewell Houses	*Cumberland* - Penrith
Sewerby	*York, E.R.* - Bridlington
Sewstern	*Leicester* - Melton Mowbray
Sexhow	*York, N.R.* - Middlesbrough
Sexton's Lode	*Worcester* - Cheltenham
Seymour	*Derby* - Chesterfield
Seywell Grounds	*Northampton* - Northampton
Sezincote	*Gloucester* - Evesham
Shabbington	*Bucks* - Thame
Shackerstone	*Leicester* - Ashby-de-la-Zouch
Shackleford	*Surrey* - Guildford
Shacklewell	*London, E.8* - Shoreditch
Shadfen	*Northumberland* - Morpeth
Shadforth	*Durham* - Durham
Shadingfield	*Suffolk* - Lowestoft
Shadoxhurst	*Kent* - Ashford
Shadwell	*London, E.1* - Shoreditch
Shadwell	*Norfolk* - Thetford
Shadwell	*Salop* - Ludlow
Shadwell	*York, W.R.* - Leeds
Shadycombe	*Devon* - Kingsbridge
Shadymoor	*Salop* - Shrewsbury
Shaftesbury	*Dorset* - Shaftesbury
Shaft Hill (Coanwood)	*Northumberland* - Hexham
Shaftoe, East	*Northumberland* - Newcastle upon Tyne
Shaftoe Moor	*Northumberland* - Newcastle upon Tyne
Shaftoe, West	*Northumberland* - Newcastle upon Tyne
Shafton	*York, W.R.* - Barnsley
Shakerley	*Lancaster* - Leigh
Shakespeares Crab	*Warwick* - Stratford on Avon
Shalbourne	*Wilts* - Newbury
Shalden	*Hants* - Aldershot and Farnham
Shaldon	*Devon* - Newton Abbot
Shalfleet	*I. of W.* - Newport (I.W.)
Shalford	*Essex* - Braintree
Shalford	*Surrey* - Guildford
Shallowford	*Devon* - Barnstaple
Shallowford	*Stafford* - Stafford
Shalmsford Street	*Kent* - Canterbury
Shalstone	*Bucks* - Banbury
Shamley Green	*Surrey* - Guildford
Shammer	*Norfolk* - King's Lynn
Shangton	*Leicester* - Leicester
Shankfoot	*Northumberland* - Hexham
Shankhouse	*Northumberland* - North Shields
Shanklin	*I. of W.* - Newport (I.W.)
Shanters	*Northumberland* - Hexham
Shap	*Westmorland* - Penrith
Shapwick	*Dorset* - Wimborne Minster
Shapwick	*Somerset* - Bridgwater
Sharcot	*Wilts* - Swindon
Shard End	*Warwick* - Birmingham
Shardlow	*Derby* - Derby

Shareshill	*Stafford* - Wolverhampton
Sharlston	*York, W.R.* - Wakefield
Sharmans Cross	*Warwick* - Birmingham
Sharnal Green	*Dorset* - Dorchester
Sharnbrook	*Beds* - Bedford
Sharnford	*Leicester* - Hinckley
Sharow	*York, W.R.* - Harrogate
Sharpenhoe	*Beds* - Luton
Sharperton	*Northumberland* - Morpeth
Sharpes Green	*Kent* - Rochester
Sharples	*Lancaster* - Bolton
Sharpley Heath	*Stafford* - Stoke-on-Trent
Sharpley, High	*Durham* - Sunderland
Sharpness	*Gloucester* - Stroud
Sharpthorne	*Sussex* - East Grinstead
Sharrington	*Hereford* - Kidderminster
Sharrington	*Norfolk* - King's Lynn
Sharrow Vale	*York, W.R.* - Sheffield
Sharsted	*Kent* - Rochester
Sharsted	*Kent* - Sittingbourne
Sharston (part)	*Cheshire* - Manchester
Shatterford	*Worcester* - Kidderminster
Shatterwell	*Somerset* - Yeovil
Shatton	*Cumberland* - Workington
Shatton	*Derby* - Buxton
Shaugh	*Devon* - Plymouth
Shavington	*Salop* - Market Drayton
Shavington cum Gresty	*Cheshire* - Crewe
Shaw	*Berks* - Newbury
Shaw	*Lancaster* - Oldham
Shaw	*Wilts* - Chippenham
Shaw	*Wilts* - Swindon
Shawbirch	*Salop* - Wellington (Salop)
Shaw Brook	*Worcester* - Birmingham
Shawbury	*Salop* - Shrewsbury
Shawbury Heath	*Salop* - Shrewsbury
Shawclough	*Lancashire* - Rochdale
Shaw Cross	*York, W.R.* - Dewsbury
Shawdon	*Northumberland* - Alnwick
Shawell	*Leicester* - Rugby
Shawford	*Hants* - Winchester
Shawforth	*Lancaster* - Rochdale
Shaw Green	*Lancaster* - Chorley
Shaw Hill	*Wilts* - Chippenham
Shaw Hill	*York, W.R.* - Halifax
Shaw Mills	*York, W.R.* - Harrogate
Shaws Cottages	*Northumberland* - Haltwhistle
Shearsby	*Leicester* - Leicester
Shearston	*Somerset* - Bridgwater
Shearwater Ash	*Kent* - Deal
Shebbear	*Devon* - Bideford
Shebdon	*Stafford* - Stafford
Shedfield	*Hants* - Portsmouth
Sheen	*Stafford* - Leek
Sheen, East	*London, S.W.14* - Wandsworth
Sheen, North	*Surrey* - Wandsworth
Sheepbridge	*Derby* - Chesterfield
Sheep Lane	*Beds* - Bletchley and Leighton Buzzard
Sheepridge	*Bucks* - High Wycombe
Sheepridge	*Yorks, W.R.* - Huddersfield
Sheepscombe	*Gloucester* - Stroud
Steepstor	*Devon* - Plymouth
Sheepwalks	*Durham* - Durham
Sheepwash	*Devon* - Bideford
Sheepwash	*Northumberland* - Blyth
Sheepwash	*Stafford* - Stoke-on-Trent
Sheepwash	*Stafford* - Stafford
Sheepway	*Somerset* - Bristol
Sheepy Magna	*Leicester* - Nuneaton
Sheepy Parva	*Leicester* - Nuneaton
Sheering	*Essex* - Harlow
Sheerness	*Kent* - Sheerness
Sheerwater	*Surrey* - Guildford
Sheet	*Hants* - Petersfield
Sheffield	*Cornwall* - Penzance
Sheffield	*York, W.R.* - Sheffield
Sheffield Park	*Sussex* - Lewes
Shefford	*Beds* - Biggleswade
Shefford, East	*Berks* - Newbury

SHE

Shefford, Great	*Berks* - Newbury
Shefford Hardwicke	*Beds* - Biggleswade
Shefford, West	*Berks* - Newbury
Shefford Woodlands	*Berks* - Newbury
Sheinton	*Salop* - Shrewsbury
Sheinwood	*Salop* - Shrewsbury
Shelbrook	*Leicester* - Ashby-de-la-Zouch
Shelderslow	*York, W.R.* - Oldham
Sheldon	*Derby* - Buxton
Sheldon	*Devon* - Exeter
Sheldon	*Warwick* - Birmingham
Sheldon Heath	*Warwick* - Birmingham
Sheldwich	*Kent* - Canterbury
Shelf	*York, W.R.* - Halifax
Shelfanger	*Norfolk* - Norwich
Shelfield	*Stafford* - Walsall
Shelfield	*Warwick* - Stratford on Avon
Shelford	*Notts* - Nottingham
Shelford, Great	*Cambridge* - Cambridge
Shelford, Little	*Cambridge* - Cambridge
Shell	*Worcester* - Worcester
Shelland	*Suffolk* - Stowmarket
Shelley	*Essex* - Brentwood
Shelley	*Suffolk* - Ipswich
Shelley	*York, W.R.* - Huddersfield
Shell Haven	*Essex* - Grays Thurrock
Shellingford	*Berks* - Didcot
Shellness	*Kent* - Sheerness
Shellow Bowels	*Essex* - Chelmsford
Shellow Cross	*Essex* - Chelmsford
Shelsley Beauchamp	*Worcester* - Worcester
Shelsley Kings	*Worcester* - Worcester
Shelsley Walsh	*Worcester* - Worcester
Shelspit	*Bucks* - Bletchley and Leighton Buzzard
Shelton	*Norfolk* - Norwich
Shelton	*Notts* - Newark
Shelton	*Salop* - Shrewsbury
Shelton	*Stafford* - Stoke-on-Trent
Shelton (Dean)	*Beds* - Bedford
Shelton Lock	*Derby* - Derby
Shelton, Lower	*Beds* - Bedford
Shelton, Nether	*Beds* - Bedford
Shelton under Harley	*Stafford* - Stoke-on-Trent
Shelton, Upper	*Beds* - Bedford
Shelve	*Salop* - Shrewsbury
Shelven	*Kent* - Dover
Shelvock	*Salop* - Oswestry
Shelwick	*Hereford* - Hereford
Shenfield	*Essex* - Brentwood
Shenington	*Oxford* - Banbury
Shenley	*Herts* - Barnet
Shenley Brook End	*Bucks* - Bletchley and Leighton Buzzard
Shenley Church End	*Bucks* - Bletchley and Leighton Buzzard
Shenley Fields	*Warwick* - Birmingham
Shenley Hill	*Herts* - Barnet
Shenmore	*Hereford* - Hereford
Shenstone	*Stafford* - Lichfield
Shenstone	*Worcester* - Kidderminster
Shenstone Wood End	*Stafford* - Lichfield
Shenton	*Leicester* - Hinckley
Shepeau Stowe	*Lincoln* - Spalding
Shephall	*Herts* - Hitchin
Shepherds	*Cornwall* - Truro
Shepherd's Bush (part)	*London, W.12* - Brentford
Shepherd's Bush (part)	*London, W.12* - West London
Shepherd's Bush (part)	*London, W.12* - Willesden
Shepherds Green	*Oxford* - Reading
Shepherds Green	*Warwick* - Birmingham
Shepherdswell	*Kent* - Dover
Shepley	*Cheshire* - Ashton-under-Lyne
Shepley	*York, W.R.* - Huddersfield
Shepperdine	*Gloucester* - Thornbury
Shepperton	*Middlesex* - Kingston-upon-Thames
Shepreth	*Cambridge* - Cambridge
Shepshed	*Leicester* - Loughborough
Shepton Beauchamp	*Somerset* - Yeovil
Shepton Mallet	*Somerset* - Wells

SHE - SHI

Shepton Montague	*Somerset* - Yeovil
Sheraton	*Durham* - Hartlepool
Sherborne	*Dorset* - Yeovil
Sherborne	*Gloucester* - Cheltenham
Sherborne St. John	*Hants* - Basingstoke
Sherborne West End	*Hants* - Basingstoke
Sherbourne	*Warwick* - Warwick
Sherburn	*Durham* - Durham
Sherburn	*York, E.R.* - Scarborough
Sherburn Hill	*Durham* - Durham
Sherburn-in-Elmet	*York, W.R.* - Leeds
Sherburn Lenarton	*Durham* - Durham
Sherburn Village	*Durham* - Durham
Sherburn, West	*Durham* - Durham
Shere	*Surrey* - Guildford
Shereford	*Norfolk* - King's Lynn
Sherfield English	*Hants* - Southampton
Sherfield on Loddon	*Hants* - Basingstoke
Sherford	*Devon* - Kingsbridge
Sherford	*Somerset* - Taunton
Sherford, Higher	*Devon* - Plymouth
Sherford, Lower	*Devon* - Plymouth
Sheriff Hales	*Salop* - Wellington (Salop)
Sheriff Hill	*Durham* - Gateshead
Sheriff Hutton	*York, N.R.* - Malton
Sheringham	*Norfolk* - Norwich
Sherington	*Bucks* - Bletchley and Leighton Buzzard
Shermanbury	*Sussex* - Brighton
Shernall Green	*Worcester* - Worcester
Shernborne	*Norfolk* - King's Lynn
Sherrards Green	*Worcester* - Great Malvern
Sherridge	*Worcester* - Great Malvern
Sherrington	*Wilts* - Warminster
Sherston	*Wilts* - Malmesbury
Sherwill	*Devon* - Barnstaple
Sherwood	*Notts* - Nottingham
Sherwood Hall	*Notts* - Mansfield
Shevington	*Lancaster* - Wigan
Sheviock	*Cornwall* - Plymouth
Shibden	*York, W.R.* - Halifax
Shibdon	*Durham* - Newcastle upon Tyne
Shidlaw	*Northumberland* - Berwick-upon-Tweed
Shield Hill (Alston)	*Cumberland* - Carlisle
Shield Hill (Haltwhistle)	*Northumberland* - Hexham
Shield Hill, East	*Northumberland* - Morpeth
Shield Hill, West	*Northumberland* - Morpeth
Shield Row	*Durham* - Consett
Shields, South	*Durham* - South Shields
Shifford	*Oxford* - Witney
Shifnal	*Salop* - Wellington (Salop)
Shilbottle	*Northumberland* - Alnwick
Shilbottle Grange Colliery	*Northumberland* - Alnwick
Shildon	*Durham* - Bishop Auckland
Shildon, New	*Durham* - Bishop Auckland
Shildon, Old	*Durham* - Bishop Auckland
Shillingford	*Devon* - Tiverton
Shillingford	*Oxford* - Didcot
Shillingford Abbot	*Devon* - Exeter
Shillingford St. George	*Devon* - Exeter
Shillinglee	*Sussex* - Chichester
Shillingstone	*Dorset* - Shaftesbury
Shillington	*Beds* - Hitchin
Shilton	*Berks* - Witney
Shilton	*Warwick* - Coventry
Shilvinghampton	*Dorset* - Weymouth
Shilvington	*Dorset* - Weymouth
Shilvington	*Northumberland* - Morpeth
Shimpling	*Norfolk* - Norwich
Shimpling	*Suffolk* - Sudbury
Shincliffe	*Durham* - Durham
Shincliffe Bank Top	*Durham* - Durham
Shiney Row	*Durham* - Durham
Shinfield	*Berks* - Reading
Shingay	*Cambridge* - Cambridge
Shingham	*Norfolk* - King's Lynn
Shingle End	*Kent* - Deal

SHI - SHO

Shingle Street	*Suffolk* - Woodbridge
Shingrigtirphil	*Glamorgan* - Bargoed
Shipbourne	*Kent* - Sevenoaks
Shipdham	*Norfolk* - East Dereham
Shipham	*Somerset* - Weston Super Mare
Shiphay	*Devon* - Torquay
Shiplake	*Oxford* - Reading
Shiplake Bottom	*Oxford* - Reading
Shiplate	*Somerset* - Weston Super Mare
Shipley	*Derby* - Ilkeston
Shipley	*Durham* - Bishop Auckland
Shipley	*Northumberland* - Alnwick
Shipley	*Salop* - Bridgnorth
Shipley	*Sussex* - Horsham
Shipley	*York, W.R.* - Bradford
Shipley Bridge	*Surrey* - Reigate
Shipley Gate	*Derby* - Ilkeston
Shipley Glen	*York, W.R.* - Bradford
Shipley High Moor	*York, W.R.* - Bradford
Shipmeadow	*Suffolk* - Lowestoft
Shippea Hill Station	*Cambridge* - Ely
Shippon	*Berks* - Oxford
Shipston on Stour	*Warwick* - Stratford on Avon
Shipstow	*Dorset* - Swanage
Shipton	*Salop* - Bridgnorth
Shipton	*York, N.R.* - York
Shipton Bellinger	*Hants* - Andover
Shipton Gorge	*Dorset* - Dorchester
Shipton Lee	*Bucks* - Aylesbury
Shipton Moyne	*Gloucester* - Malmesbury
Shipton, New	*Warwick* - Birmingham
Shipton Oliffe	*Gloucester* - Cheltenham
Shipton-on-Cherwell	*Oxford* - Oxford
Shipton Sollars	*Gloucester* - Cheltenham
Shiptonthorpe	*York, E.R.* - York
Shipton-under-Wychwood	*Oxford* - Banbury
Shirburn	*Oxford* - Thame
Shirdley Hill	*Lancaster* - Southport
Shirebrook	*Derby* - Mansfield
Shirecliffe	*York, W.R.* - Sheffield
Shire Green	*York, W.R.* - Sheffield
Shirehampton	*Gloucester* - Bristol
Shire Moor	*Northumberland* - North Shields
Shirenewton	*Monmouth* - Chepstow
Shire Oak	*Stafford* - Walsall
Shireoaks	*Notts* - Worksop
Shirk Oak	*Kent* - Cranbrook
Shirland	*Derby* - Alfreton
Shirlett	*Salop* - Bridgnorth
Shirley	*Derby* - Derby
Shirley (Sopley)	*Hants* - Bournemouth
Shirley	*Hants* - Southampton
Shirley	*Surrey* - Croydon
Shirley	*Warwick* - Birmingham
Shirley Holmes	*Hants* - Lymington
Shirley Warren	*Hants* - Southampton
Shirleywich	*Stafford* - Stafford
Shirlheath	*Hereford* - Leominster
Shirlowe	*Salop* - Wellington
Shirnock	*Worcester* - Redditch
Shirrell Heath	*Hants* - Portsmouth
Shitlington	*Northumberland* - Hexham
Shitterton	*Dorset* - Swanage
Shittlehopeburn	*Durham* - Bishop Auckland
Shobdon	*Hereford* - Leominster
Shobrooke	*Devon* - Exeter
Shoby	*Leicester* - Melton Mowbray
Shockerwick	*Wilts* - Bath
Shocklach	*Cheshire* - Whitchurch
Shoddesdon	*Hants* - Andover
Shoeburyness	*Essex* - Southend
Sholden	*Kent* - Deal
Sholebrook	*Northampton* - Northampton
Sholing	*Hants* - Southampton
Sholver	*Lancaster* - Oldham
Shootash	*Hants* - Southampton
Shooters Hill	*Salop* - Shrewsbury
Shooters Hill	*Stafford* - Stoke-on-Trent
Shop	*Devon* - Launceston

SHO - SHR

Shopham	*Sussex* - Chichester
Shopland	*Essex* - Southend
Shopwhyke	*Sussex* - Chichester
Shordley	*Flint* - Wrexham
Shore	*Lancaster* - Rochdale
Shore	*Lancaster* - Todmorden
Shoreditch	*London, E.1* - Shoreditch
Shoreditch	*London, E.2* - Shoreditch
Shoreditch	*London, E.C.2* - Shoreditch
Shoreditch	*Somerset* - Taunton
Shore Edge	*Lancaster - Oldham*
Shoreham	*Kent* - Sevenoaks
Shoreham by Sea	*Sussex* - Brighton
Shoreston	*Northumberland* - Alnwick
Shoreswood	*Northumberland* - Berwick-upon-Tweed
Shorncliffe	*Kent* - Folkestone
Shorncote	*Gloucester* - Malmesbury
Shorne	*Kent* - Gravesend
Shorne Mead Fort	*Kent* - Gravesend
Shorne Ridgeway	*Kent* - Gravesend
Shorta Cross	*Cornwall* - Liskeard
Short Ferry	*Lincoln* - Lincoln
Shortflatt	*Northumberland* - Newcastle upon Tyne
Shortgate	*Sussex* - Lewes
Shorthampton	*Oxford* - Banbury
Short Heath	*Derby* - Ashby-de-la-Zouch
Short Heath	*Stafford* - Walsall
Short Heath	*Warwick* - Birmingham
Shortlands	*Kent* - Bromley
Shortlanesend	*Cornwall* - Truro
Shortstown	*Beds* - Bedford
Shortwood	*Gloucester* - Bristol
Shortwood	*Gloucester* - Stroud
Shorwell	*I. of W.* - Newport (I.W.)
Shoscombe	*Somerset* - Bath
Shotatton	*Salop* - Oswestry
Shotesham	*Norfolk* - Norwich
Shotesham All Saints	*Norfolk* - Norwich
Shotesham St. Mary	*Norfolk* - Norwich
Shotgate	*Essex* - Brentwood
Shotley	*Suffolk* - Ipswich
Shotley Bridge	*Durham* - Consett
Shotley Field	*Northumberland* - Consett
Shotover	*Oxford* - Oxford
Shottendane	*Kent* - Margate
Shottenden	*Kent* - Canterbury
Shottermill	*Surrey* - Guildford
Shotter Mill	*Sussex* - Petersfield
Shottery	*Warwick* - Stratford on Avon
Shottesbrook	*Berks* - Slough
Shotteswell	*Warwick* - Banbury
Shottisham	*Suffolk* - Woodbridge
Shottle	*Derby* - Derby
Shottle Gate	*Derby* - Derby
Shotton	*Durham* - Bishop Auckland
Shotton	*Durham* - Stockton on Tees
Shotton	*Durham* - Hartlepool
Shotton	*Flint* - Chester
Shotton	*Salop* - Shrewsbury
Shotton Edge	*Northumberland* - Morpeth
Shotwick	*Cheshire* - Chester
Shotwick Park	*Cheshire* - Chester
Shouldham	*Norfolk* - King's Lynn
Shouldham Thorpe	*Norfolk* - King's Lynn
Shoulton	*Worcester* - Worcester
Showborough	*Gloucester* - Cheltenham
Showell Grange	*Salop* - Wellington (Salop)
Showell Green	*Warwick* - Birmingham
Showsley	*Northampton* - Northampton
Shraley Brook	*Stafford* - Stoke-on-Trent
Shrawardine	*Salop* - Shrewsbury
Shrawley	*Worcester* - Worcester
Shray Hill	*Salop* - Wellington (Salop)
Shredding Green	*Bucks* - Uxbridge
Shredicote	*Stafford* - Stafford
Shrewley	*Warwick* - Warwick
Shrewly Common	*Warwick* - Warwick
Shrewsbury	*Salop* - Shrewsbury

SHR - SIL

Shrewton	*Wilts* - Salisbury
Shripney	*Sussex* - Chichester
Shrivenham	*Berks* - Swindon
Shropham	*Norfolk* - Norwich
Shroton	*Dorset* - Shaftesbury
Shrubcote	*Kent* - Cranbrook
Shrubs End	*Essex* - Colchester
Shrubland	*Suffolk* - Ipswich
Shuart	*Kent* - Margate
Shuckburgh, Lower	*Warwick* - Rubgy
Shuckburgh, Upper	*Warwick* - Rugby
Shudy Camps	*Cambridge* - Cambridge
Shugborough	*Stafford* - Stafford
Shurdington, Great	*Gloucester* - Cheltenham
Shurdington, Little	*Gloucester* - Cheltenham
Shurlock Row	*Berks* - Slough
Shurnhold	*Wilts* - Chippenham
Shurton	*Somerset* - Bridgwater
Shustoke	*Warwick* - Birmingham
Shute	*Devon* - Axminster and Chard
Shutford	*Oxford* - Banbury
Shut Heath	*Stafford* - Stafford
Shuthonger	*Gloucester* - Cheltenham
Shutlane Head	*Stafford* - Stoke-on-Trent
Shutlanger	*Northampton* - Northampton
Shuttington	*Stafford* - Tamworth
Shuttlewood	*Derby* - Chesterfield
Shuttleworth	*Lancaster* - Bury
Shutt Mill	*Worcester* - Bromsgrove
Shwt	*Glamorgan* - Bridgend
Sibberscott	*Salop* - Shrewsbury
Sibbertoft	*Northampton* - Northampton
Sibdon	*Salop* - Ludlow
Sibdon Carwood	*Salop* - Ludlow
Sibertswold	*Kent* - Dover
Sibford Ferris	*Oxford* - Banbury
Sibford Gower	*Oxford* - Banbury
Sibland	*Gloucester* - Thornbury
Sible Hedingham	*Essex* - Braintree
Sibsey	*Lincoln* - Boston
Sibsey Fen Side	*Lincoln* - Boston
Sibsey Northlands	*Lincoln* - Boston
Sibson	*Hunts* - Peterborough
Sibson	*Leicester* - Nuneaton
Sibthorpe	*Notts* - Newark
Sibton	*Suffolk* - Woodbridge
Sicklesmere	*Suffolk* - Bury St. Edmunds
Sicklinghall	*York, W.R.* - Harrogate
Sidbury	*Devon* - Exeter
Sidbury	*Salop* - Bridgnorth
Sidcot	*Somerset* - Weston Super Mare
Sidcup (part)	*Kent* - Bromley
Sidcup (part)	*Kent* - Dartford
Siddal	*York, W.R.* - Halifax
Siddick	*Cumberland* - Workington
Siddington	*Cheshire* - Macclesfield
Siddington	*Gloucester* - Swindon
Sidemoor	*Worcester* - Bromsgrove
Sidestrand	*Norfolk* - Norwich
Sidford	*Devon* - Exeter
Sidlesham	*Sussex* - Chichester
Sidley	*Sussex* - Hastings
Sidlow	*Surrey* - Reigate
Sidmouth	*Devon* - Exeter
Sidney	*Salop* - Wellington (Salop)
Sigginstone	*Glamorgan* - Bridgend
Sigglesthorne	*York, E.R.* - Beverley
Signal Hayes	*Warwick* - Birmingham
Signet	*Oxford* - Witney
Silchester	*Hants* - Basingstoke
Sileby	*Leicester* - Loughborough
Silecroft	*Cumberland* - Whitehaven
Silfield	*Norfolk* - Norwich
Silian	*Cardigan* - Lampeter
Silksted	*Hants* - Winchester
Silkstone	*York, W.R.* - Barnsley
Silkstone Common	*York, W.R.* - Barnsley
Silksworth	*Durham* - Sunderland
Silk Willoughby	*Lincoln* - Sleaford
Silloth	*Cumberland* - Carlisle

SIL - SKE

Silloth, West	*Cumberland* - Carlisle
Silpho	*York, N.R.* - Scarborough
Silsden	*York, W.R.* - Skipton
Silsden Moor	*York, W.R,* - Skipton
Silsoe	*Beds* - Bedford
Silton	*Dorset* - Shaftesbury
Silton, Nether	*York, N.R.* - Northallerton
Silton, Over	*York, W.R.* - Northallerton
Silverdale	*Lancaster* - Lancaster
Silverdale	*Stafford* - Stoke-on-Trent
Silver End	*Essex* - Braintree
Silverlake (Sherborne)	*Dorset* - Yeovil
Silverstone	*Northampton* - Northampton
Silverton	*Devon* - Tiverton
Silvertown	*London, E.16* - Bow
Silverwell	*Cornwall* - Truro
Silverwood	*York, W.R.* - Rotherham
Silvington	*Salop* - Ludlow
Simondley	*Derby* - Hyde
Simms Cross	*Lancaster* - St. Helens
Simms Lane End	*Lancaster* - Wigan
Simonburn	*Northumberland* - Hexham
Simonsbath	*Somerset* - Barnstaple
Simonside	*Durham* - South Shields
Simonside, High	*Durham* - South Shields
Simonstone	*Lancaster* - Burnley
Simonswood	*Lancaster* - Liverpool
Simon Weir (Kirton Holme)	*Lincoln* - Boston
Simpson	*Bucks* - Bletchley and Leighton Buzzard
Sinderby	*York, N.R.* - Northallerton
Sinderhope	*Northumberland* - Hexham
Sinderland	*Cheshire* - Altrincham
Sindlesham	*Berks* - Reading
Sinfin	*Derby* - Derby
Singleborough	*Bucks* - Bletchley and Leighton Buzzard
Single Hill	*Somerset* - Bath
Single Street	*Kent* - Bromley
Singleton	*Lancaster* - Blackpool
Singleton	*Sussex* - Chichester
Singleton, Great	*Lancaster* - Blackpool
Singleton, Little	*Lancaster* - Blackpool
Singlewell	*Kent* - Gravesend
Sinnington	*York, N.R.* - Malton
Sinope	*Leicester* - Ashby-de-la-Zouch
Sinton	*Worcester* - Worcester
Sinton Green	*Worcester* - Worcester
Sipson	*Middlesex* - Uxbridge
Sipton	*Northumberland* - Hexham
Sireford	*Gloucester* - Cheltenham
Sirhowy	*Monmouth* - Blackwood
Sisland	*Norfolk* - Norwich
Sissinghurst	*Kent* - Cranbrook
Siston	*Gloucester* - Bristol
Sithney	*Cornwall* - Penzance
Sithney Green	*Cornwall* - Penzance
Sithington	*York, W.R.* - Wakefield
Sittingbourne	*Kent* - Sittingbourne
Six Ashes	*Salop* - Bridgnorth
Six Ashes	*Stafford* - Stourbridge
Six Bells	*Monmouth* - Blackwood
Six Hills	*Leicester* - Loughborough
Sixhills	*Lincoln* - Louth
Sixhouses Bank	*Lincoln* - Spalding
Six Mile Bottom	*Cambs* - Newmarket
Sixpenny Handly	*Dorset* - Salisbury
Six Turnings	*Cornwall* - Truro
Sizergh	*Westmorland* - Kendal
Sizewell	*Suffolk* - Woodbridge
Skeeby	*York, N.R.* - Darlington
Skeethill	*Kent* - Bromley
Skeffington	*Leicester* - Leicester
Skeffling	*York, E.R.* - Kingston-upon-Hull
Skegby	*Notts* - Mansfield
Skegness	*Lincoln* - Skegness
Skelbrooke	*York, W.R.* - Pontefract
Skelding	*York, W.R.* - Harrogate

SKE - SLA

Skeldon Moor	*Lancaster* - Barrow-in-Furness
Skeldyke (Kirton)	*Lincoln* - Boston
Skelgill	*Cumberland* - Carlisle
Skelgill	*Cumberland* - Workington
Skellingthorpe	*Lincoln* - Lincoln
Skellow	*York, W.R.* - Doncaster
Skelmanthorpe	*York, W.R.* - Huddersfield
Skelmersdale	*Lancaster* - Wigan
Skelsmergh	*Westmorland* - Kendal
Skelton	*Cumberland* - Penrith
Skelton	*York, E.R.* - Goole
Skelton	*York, N.R.* - Middlesbrough
Skelton	*York, N.R.* - York
Skelton	*York, W.R.* - Harrogate
Skelton	*York, W.R.* - Leeds
Skelton Green	*York, N.R.* - Middlesbrough
Skelton-in-Cleveland	*York, N.R.* - Middlesbrough
Skelton, North	*York, N.R.* - Middlesbrough
Skelton Pasture	*Cumberland* - Penrith
Skelton Wood End	*Cumberland* - Penrith
Skelwith	*Lancaster* - Kendal
Skendleby	*Lincoln* - Skegness
Skenfrith	*Monmouth* - Monmouth
Sker	*Glamorgan* - Bridgend
Skerne	*York, E.R.* - Beverley
Skerton	*Lancaster* - Lancaster
Sketchley	*Leicester* - Hinckley
Sketty	*Glamorgan* - Swansea
Skewen	*Glamorgan* - Neath
Skewsby	*York, N.R.* - York
Skeyton	*Norfolk* - Norwich
Skibeden	*York, W.R.* - Skipton
Skidbrook	*Lincoln* - Louth
Skidby	*York, E.R.* - Kingston-upon-Hull
Skidby Ings	*York, E.R.* - Kingston-upon-Hull
Skilgate	*Somerset* - Tiverton
Skillington	*Lincoln* - Grantham
Skinburness	*Cumberland* - Carlisle
Skinnand	*Lincoln* - Lincoln
Skinners Bottom	*Cornwall* - Truro
Skinningrove	*York, N.R.* - Whitby
Skiplam	*York, N.R.* - Malton
Skippet	*Dorset* - Dorchester
Skippool	*Lancaster* - Blackpool
Skipsea	*York, E.R.* - Bridlington
Skipsea Brough	*York, E.R.* - Bridlington
Skipton	*York, W.R.* - Skipton
Skipton-on-Swale	*York, N.R.* - Northallerton
Skipwith	*York, E.R.* - York
Skirbeck	*Lincoln* - Boston
Skirbeck Quarter	*Lincoln* - Boston
Skircoat Green	*York, W.R.* - Halifax
Skirlaugh,	*York, E.R.* - Kingston-upon-Hull
Skirlington, High	*York, E.R.* - Beverley
Skirlington, Low	*York, E.R.* - Beverley
Skirmett	*Bucks* - Reading
Skirpenbeck	*York, E.R.* - York
Skirwith	*Cumberland* - Penrith
Skutterskelfe	*York, N.R.* - Middlesbrough
Skyborrah	*Salop* - Knighton
Skydes	*Cumberland* - Carlisle
Slackhead	*Westmorland* - Kendal
Slacksted	*Hants* - Winchester
Slad	*Gloucester* - Stroud
Slade End	*Berks* - Didcot
Slade Heath	*Stafford* - Wolverhampton
Slade Hooton	*York, W.R.* - Rotherham
Sladen Bridge	*York, W.R.* - Keighley
Slades	*Cornwall* - St. Austell
Sladesbridge	*Cornwall* - Bodmin
Slades Brook	*Wilts* - Trowbridge
Slades Green	*Kent* - Dartford
Slaggyford	*Northumberland* - Carlisle
Slaidburn	*York, W.R.* - Blackburn
Slaithwaite	*York, W.R.* - Huddersfield
Slaley	*Derby* - Matlock
Slaley	*Northumberland* - Hexham
Slapton	*Bucks* - Bletchley and Leighton Buzzard
Slapton	*Devon* - Kingsbridge

SLA - SMI

Slapton	*Northampton* - Northampton
Slateyford	*Northumberland* - Newcastle upon Tyne
Slattocks	*Lancaster* - Oldham
Slaugham (part)	*Sussex* - Haywards Heath
Slaugham (part)	*Sussex* - Horsham
Slaughter Bridge	*Cornwall* - Launceston
Slaughterford	*Wilts* - Chippenham
Slaughter, Lower	*Gloucester* - Cheltenham
Slaughter, Upper	*Gloucester* - Cheltenham
Slawston	*Leicester* - Kettering
Sleaford	*Hants* - Aldershot and Farnham
Sleaford	*Lincoln* - Sleaford
Sleagill	*Westmorland* - Penrith
Sleap	*Salop* - Shrewsbury
Sleap	*Salop* - Wellington (Salop)
Sleap Hall	*Salop* - Shrewsbury
Sleap's Hyde	*Herts* - St. Albans
Slebech	*Pembroke* - Haverfordwest
Sleddale	*York, N.R.* - Middlesbrough
Sledmere	*York, E.R.* - Beverley
Sleetburn	*Durham* - Durham
Sleightholme	*Cumberland* - Carlisle
Sleights	*York, N.R.* - Whitby
Sleningford	*York, W.R.* - Harrogate
Slimbridge	*Gloucester* - Stroud
Slindon	*Stafford* - Stafford
Slindon	*Sussex* - Chichester
Slinfold	*Sussex* - Horsham
Slingsby	*York, N.R.* - Malton
Slip End	*Beds* - Luton
Slipperyford	*York, W.R.* - Keighley
Slipton	*Northampton* - Kettering
Slitting Mill	*Stafford* - Stafford
Sloley	*Norfolk* - Norwich
Sloothby	*Lincoln* - Skegness
Slopshole	*Gloucester* - Cheltenham
Slough	*Bucks* - Slough
Slough	*Hereford* - Knighton
Slough Green	*Sussex* - Haywards Heath
Slyne with Hest	*Lancaster* - Lancaster
Smalesmouth	*Northumberland* - Hexham
Smallburgh	*Norfolk* - Norwich
Smallburn	*Northumberland* - Hexham
Small Dale	*Derby* - Buxton
Small Dole	*Sussex* - Brighton
Smalley	*Derby* - Ilkeston
Smalley Common	*Derby* - Ilkeston
Smallfields	*Surrey* - Reigate
Smallford	*Herts* - St. Albans
Small Heath	*Warwick* - Birmingham
Small Hythe	*Kent* - Cranbrook
Smallrise	*Stafford* - Stafford
Smallshaw	*Lancaster* - Ashton-under-Lyne
Smallthorne	*Stafford* - Stoke-on-Trent
Smallwood	*Cheshire* - Congleton
Smallwood	*Stafford* - Uttoxeter
Smallridge	*Devon* - Axminster & Chard
Smannell	*Hants* - Andover
Smarden	*Kent* - Ashford
Smarden Bell	*Kent* - Ashford
Smart's Hill	*Kent* - Tonbridge
Smeatharp	*Devon* - Exeter
Smeaton	*York, W.R.* - Pontefract
Smeaton, Little	*York, W.R.* - Pontefract
Smeeth	*Kent* - Ashford
Smeeth Road	*Norfolk* - Wisbech
Smeeton Westerby	*Leicester* - Leicester
Smelhouses	*York, W.R.* - Harrogate
Smestow	*Stafford* - Wolverhampton
Smethcott	*Salop* - Shrewsbury
Smethwick	*Stafford* - West Bromwich
Smethwick, West	*Stafford* - West Bromwich
Smisby	*Derby* - Ashby-de-la-Zouch
Smithend Green	*Worcester* - Great Malvern
Smithers Cross	*Gloucester* - Gloucester
Smithfield	*Cumberland* - Carlisle
Smithies	*Salop* - Bridgnorth
Smithies	*York, W.R.* - Barnsley
Smithies	*York, W.R.* - Dewsbury

Smithills	*Lancaster* - Bolton
Smith's Green	*Essex* - Bishop's Stortford
Smithy Bridge	*Lancaster* - Rochdale
Smithy Carr	*York, W.R.* - Sheffield
Smithy Moor	*Derby* - Alfreton
Smockington	*Leicester and Warwick* - Hinckley
Smythemoor	*Salop* - Market Drayton
Snailbeach	*Salop* - Shrewsbury
Snailswell	*Herts* - Hitchin
Snailwell	*Cambridge* - Newmarket
Snainton	*York, N.R.* - Scarborough
Snainton Dale	*York, N.R.* - Scarborough
Snaith	*York, W.R.* - Goole
Snakeholme	*Lincoln* - Lincoln
Snake Row	*Durham* - Durham
Snape	*Suffolk* - Woodbridge
Snape	*York, N.R.* - Harrogate
Snapethorpe	*York, W.R.* - Wakefield
Snappergill	*Cumberland* - Carlisle
Snarehill	*Norfolk* - Thetford
Snaresbrook	*London, E.11* - Bow
Snarestone	*Leicester* - Ashby-de-la-Zouch
Snarford	*Lincoln* - Lincoln
Snargate	*Kent* - Ashford
Snarlton Lane	*Wilts* - Chippenham
Snave	*Kent* - Ashford
Sneachill	*Worcester* - Worcester
Snead	*Montgomery* - Welshpool
Sneads Green	*Worcester* - Kidderminster
Sneaton	*York, N.R.* - Whitby
Sneaton Thorpe	*York, N.R.* - Whitby
Sneck Yeat	*Cumberland* - Workington
Snedshill	*Salop* - Wellington (Salop)
Snelland	*Lincoln* - Lincoln
Snelsmore	*Berks* - Newbury
Snelson	*Cheshire* - Macclesfield
Snelston	*Derby* - Derby
Snetterton	*Norfolk* - Norwich
Snettisham	*Norfolk* - King's Lynn
Sneyd Green	*Stafford* - Stoke-on-Trent
Snibston	*Leicester* - Ashby-de-la-Zouch
Snigsend	*Gloucester* - Gloucester
Snilesworth	*York, N.R.* - Malton
Snitter	*Northumberland* - Morpeth
Snitterby	*Lincoln* - Scunthorpe
Snitterfield	*Warwick* - Stratford on Avon
Snitterton	*Derby* - Matlock
Snitton	*Salop* - Ludlow
Snodland	*Kent* - Maidstone
Snoggygate	*Northumberland* - Hexham
Snoreham	*Essex* - Maldon
Snoring, Great	*Norfolk* - King's Lynn
Snoring, Little	*Norfolk* - King's Lynn
Snowden	*York, W.R.* - Otley
Snowdown	*Kent* - Canterbury
Snowford	*Warwick* - Warwick
Snow Hill Estate	*Lancaster* - Bolton
Snowshill	*Gloucester* - Cheltenham
Snydale	*York, W.R.* - Pontefract
Soar	*Anglesey* - Llangefni
Soberton	*Hants* - Portsmouth
Sockbridge	*Westmorland* - Penrith
Sodbury, Little	*Gloucester* - Bristol
Sodbury, Old	*Gloucester* - Bristol
Sodom	*Denbigh* - Denbigh
Sodom	*Stafford* - Burton-upon-Trent
Softley	*Durham* - Bishop Auckland
Soham	*Cambridge* - Ely
Soham Fen	*Cambridge* - Ely
Soho	*London, W.1* - Westminster
Soho	*Warwick* - Birmingham
Soho Foundry	*Stafford* - West Bromwich
Soldridge	*Hants* - Winchester
Sole Street	*Kent* - Gravesend
Soley	*Wilts* - Swindon
Solihull	*Warwick* - Birmingham
Solihull Lodge	*Warwick* - Birmingham
Sollars Dilwyn	*Hereford* - Leominster
Sollers Hope	*Hereford* - Hereford
Sollom	*Lancaster* - Southport

Solton	*Kent* - Dover
Solva	*Pembroke* - Haverfordwest
Somborne, Little	*Hants* - Winchester
Somborne, Upper	*Hants* - Winchester
Somerby	*Leicester* - Melton Mowbray
Somerby (Gainsborough)	*Lincoln* - Gainsborough
Somerby	*Lincoln* - Scunthorpe
Somerby, Old	*Lincoln* - Grantham
Somercotes	*Derby* - Alfreton
Somercotes, North	*Lincoln* - Louth
Somercotes, South	*Lincoln* - Louth
Somerford	*Cheshire* - Congleton
Somerford	*Hants* - Bournemouth
Somerford	*Stafford* - Walsall
Somerford Booths	*Cheshire* - Congleton
Somerford, Great	*Wilts* - Malmesbury
Somerford Keynes	*Gloucester* - Malmesbury
Somerford, Little	*Wilts* - Malmesbury
Somerley	*Hants* - Salisbury
Somerleyton	*Suffolk* - Lowestoft
Somersall Herbert	*Derby* - Uttoxeter
Somersby	*Lincoln* - Skegness
Somerset Bridge	*Somerset* - Bridgwater
Somersham	*Hunts* - Huntingdon
Somersham	*Suffolk* - Ipswich
Somersham Fen	*Hunts* - Huntingdon
Somers Town	*London, N.W.1* - Bloomsbury and Marylebone
Somerton	*Oxford* - Banbury
Somerton	*Somerset* - Yeovil
Somerton	*Suffolk* - Sudbury
Somerton, East	*Norfolk* - Great Yarmouth
Somerton, West	*Norfolk* - Great Yarmouth
Somerwood	*Salop* - Shrewsbury
Somer Wood	*Salop* - Wellington (Salop)
Sompting	*Sussex* - Worthing
Sonning	*Berks* - Reading
Sonning Common	*Oxford* - Reading
Sonning Eye	*Oxford* - Reading
Sontley	*Denbigh* - Wrexham
Sook Hill	*Northumberland* - Hexham
Sookholme	*Notts* - Mansfield
Soolbank	*York, W.R.* - Kendal
Soothill	*York, W.R.* - Dewsbury
Sopley	*Hants* - Bournemouth
Sopworth	*Wilts* - Malmesbury
Sotby	*Lincoln* - Lincoln
Sothall	*Derby* - Sheffield
Sotherton	*Suffolk* - Halesworth
Sotterley	*Suffolk* - Lowestoft
Soudley	*Gloucester* - Gloucester
Soudley	*Salop* - Ludlow
Soudley, Lower	*Gloucester* - Gloucester
Soughton	*Flint* - Mold
Soulbury	*Bucks* - Bletchley and Leighton Buzzard
Soulby	*Cumberland* - Penrith
Soulby	*Westmorland* - Penrith
Souldern	*Oxford* - Banbury
Soulton	*Salop* - Shrewsbury
Sound	*Cheshire* - Crewe
Soundborough	*Gloucester* - Cheltenham
Souracre	*Lancaster* - Ashton-under-Lyne
Sourhall	*Lancaster* - Todmorden
Sourton	*Devon* - Okehampton
Souter	*York, W.R.* - Harrogate
Souterfell	*Cumberland* - Workington
Soutergate	*Lancaster* - Barrow-in-Furness
Southacre	*Norfolk* - King's Lynn
Southall	*Salop* - Wellington
Southall	*Middlesex* - Uxbridge
Southall Green	*Middlesex* - Uxbridge
South Allington	*Devon* - Kingsbridge
Southam	*Gloucester* - Cheltenham
Southam	*Warwick* - Warwick
South Ambersham	*Sussex* - Chichester
Southampton	*Hants* - Southampton
South Anston	*York, W.R.* - Worksop
South Baddesley	*Hants* - Lymington
South Bailey	*Durham* - Durham

South Bank	*York, N.R.* - Middlesbrough
South Barrow	*Somerset* - Yeovil
South Bedburn	*Durham* - Bishop Auckland
South Benfleet	*Essex* - Southend
South Bersted	*Sussex* - Chichester
South Biddick	*Durham* - Durham
South Boldon	*Durham* - South Shields
Southborough	*Kent* - Tunbridge Wells
Southbourne	*Hants* - Bournemouth
Southbourne	*Sussex* - Chichester
Southbourne, West	*Hants* - Bournemouth
South Bradon	*Somerset* - Axminster and Chard
South Bramwith	*York, W.R.* - Thorne
South Brent	*Devon* - Torquay
South Brent	*Somerset* - Weston Super Mare
South Brewham	*Somerset* - Yeovil
South Brinkburn	*Northumberland* - Morpeth
Southburgh	*Norfolk* - East Dereham
South Burlingham	*Norfolk* - Norwich
Southburn	*York, E.R.* - Beverley
South Cadbury	*Somerset* - Yeovil
South Carlton	*Lincoln* - Lincoln
South Carlton	*Notts* - Worksop
South Cave	*York, E.R.* - Beverley
South Cerney	*Gloucester* - Malmesbury
Southchard	*Somerset* - Axminster and Chard
South Charford	*Hants* - Salisbury
South Charlton	*Northumberland* - Alnwick
South Cheriton	*Somerset* - Yeovil
South Church	*Durham* - Bishop Auckland
Southchurch	*Essex* - Southend
South Cleatham	*Durham* - Darlington
South Cliffe	*York, E.R.* - Beverley
South Clifton	*Notts* - Newark
South Cockerington	*Lincoln* - Louth
South Collingham	*Notts* - Newark
Southcomb	*Oxford* - Banbury
South Combe	*Devon* - Axminster and Chard
South Common	*Devon* - Axminster and Chard
South Coombe	*Somerset* - Yeovil
South Cornelly	*Glamorgan* - Bridgend
Southcott	*Cornwall* - Launceston
Southcourt (Aylesbury)	*Bucks* - Aylesbury
Southcourt	*Bucks* - Bletchley and Leighton Buzzard
South Cove	*Suffolk* - Lowestoft
South Cramlington	*Northumberland* - North Shields
South Creake	*Norfolk* - King's Lynn
Southcrest	*Worcester* - Redditch
South Crosland	*York, W.R.* - Huddersfield
South Croxton	*Leicester* - Leicester
South Dalton	*York, E.R.* - Beverley
South Damerham	*Hants* - Salisbury
South Darenth	*Kent* - Dartford
South Darley	*Derby* - Matlock
South Dissington	*Northumberland* - Newcastle upon Tyne
Southdown	*Wilts* - Bath
South Downs	*Cornwall* - Redruth
South Drove	*Lincoln* - Spalding
South Duffield	*York, E.R.* - York
Southea	*Cambridge* - Wisbech
Southease	*Sussex* - Lewes
South Eden Park	*Kent* - Bromley
South Elkington	*Lincoln* - Louth
South Elmham All Saints	*Suffolk* - Halesworth
South Elmham St. Cross	*Suffolk* - Halesworth
South Elmham St. James	*Suffolk* - Halesworth
South Elmham St. Margaret	*Suffolk* - Halesworth
South Elmham St. Mary	*Suffolk* - Halesworth
South Elmham St. Michael	*Suffolk* - Halesworth
South Elmham St. Nicholas	*Suffolk* - Halesworth
South Elmham St. Peter	*Suffolk* - Halesworth
South Elmsall	*York, W.R.* - Pontefract

SOU

South End	*Bucks* - High Wycombe
Southend	*Essex* - Southend
Southend	*London, S.E.6* - Bromley
Southerfield	*Cumberland* - Carlisle
Southernby	*Cumberland* - Penrith
Southerndown	*Glamorgan* - Bridgend
Southerndown Road	*Glamorgan* - Bridgend
Southery	*Norfolk* - King's Lynn
Southey	*York, W.R.* - Sheffield
South Fambridge	*Essex* - Southend
South Fawley	*Berks* - Didcot
South Ferriby	*Lincoln* - Scunthorpe
South Ferris	*Sussex* - Worthing
Southfield	*Lancaster* - Nelson
Southfield House	*Durham* - Bishop Auckland
South Fields	*Lincoln* - Spalding
Southfields	*London, S.W.18* - Wandsworth
Southfleet	*Kent* - Dartford
South Follingsby	*Durham* - Gateshead
Southgate (part)	*London, N.14* - Barnet
Southgate (part)	*London, N.14* - Edmonton
Southgate, New (part)	*London, N.11* - Barnet
Southgate, New (part)	*London, N.11* - Edmonton
Southgate, Old (part)	*London, N.14* - Barnet
Southgate, Old (part)	*London, N.14* - Edmonton
South Godstone	*Surrey* - Redhill
South Gorley	*Hants* - Salisbury
South Gosforth	*Northumberland* - Newcastle upon Tyne
South Green	*Norfolk* - East Dereham
South Hackney	*London, E.9* - Shoreditch
South Hanningfield	*Essex* - Brentwood
South Harp	*Somerset* - Yeovil
South Harrow	*Middlesex* - Willesden
South Harting	*Sussex* - Petersfield
South Hay	*Hants* - Aldershot and Farnham
South Hayling	*Hants* - Portsmouth
South Heighton	*Sussex* - Lewes
South Hetton	*Durham* - Durham
South Hiendley	*York, W.R.* - Barnsley
South Hill	*Cornwall* - Liskeard
South Hinksey	*Berks* - Oxford
South Hornchurch (part)	*Essex* - Ilford
South Hornchurch (part)	*Essex* - Grays Thurrock
South Huish	*Devon* - Kingsbridge
South Hykeham	*Lincoln* - Lincoln
South Hylton	*Durham* - Sunderland
Southill	*Beds* - Biggleswade
Southington	*Hants* - Basingstoke
South Kelsey	*Lincoln* - Scunthorpe
South Kensington	*London, S.W.7* - West London
South Kenton	*Middlesex* - Willesden
South Killingholme	*Lincoln* - Great Grimsby
South Kilworth	*Leicester* - Rugby
South Kirkby	*York, W.R.* - Pontefract
South Kyme	*Lincoln* - Sleaford
South Kyme Fen	*Lincoln* - Sleaford
South Lambeth (part)	*London, S.W.8* - Lambeth
South Lambeth (part)	*London, S.W.8* - Wandsworth
South Lancing	*Sussex* - Worthing
South Lawn	*Oxford* - Witney
Southleigh	*Devon* - Axminster
South Leigh	*Oxford* - Witney
South Leverton	*Notts* - East Retford
South Litchfield	*Hants* - Basingstoke
South Littleton	*Worcester* - Evesham
South Lopham	*Norfolk* - Norwich
Southlow	*Stafford* - Leek
South Luffenham	*Rutland* - Stamford
South Lyham	*Northumberland* - Alnwick
South Marston	*Wilts* - Swindon
South Merstham	*Surrey* - Reigate
South Middleton	*Northumberland* - Alnwick
South Middleton	*Northumberland* - Morpeth
South Milford	*York, W.R.* - Pontefract
South Milton	*Devon* - Kingsbridge
South Mimms	*Herts* - Barnet
Southminster	*Essex* - Maldon
South Molton	*Devon* - Barnstaple
Southmoor	*Berks* - Oxford

South Moor	*Durham* - Consett
South Moreton	*Berks* - Didcot
South Muskham	*Notts* - Newark
South Newington	*Oxford* - Banbury
South Newsham	*Northumberland* - Blyth
South Newton	*Wilts* - Salisbury
South Normanton	*Derby* - Alfreton
South Norwood	*London, S.E.25* - Croydon
South Nutfield	*Surrey* - Reigate
South Ockendon	*Essex* - Grays Thurrock
Southoe	*Hunts* - Huntingdon
Southolt	*Suffolk* - Halesworth
South Ormsby	*Lincoln* - Skegness
Southorpe	*Lincoln* - Gainsborough
Southorpe	*Huntingdon and Peterborough* - Stamford
South Ossett	*York, W.R.* - Dewsbury
Southover	*Dorset* - Dorchester
South Owersby	*Lincoln* - Scunthorpe
Southowram	*York, W.R.* - Halifax
South Park	*Surrey* - Reigate
South Pelaw	*Durham* - Durham
South Perrott	*Dorset* - Yeovil
South Petherton	*Somerset* - Yeovil
South Petherwin	*Cornwall* - Launceston
South Pickenham	*Norfolk* - King's Lynn
South Pinner	*Herts* - Watford
South Pool	*Devon* - Kingsbridge
Southport	*Lancaster* - Southport
South Rauceby	*Lincoln* - Sleaford
South Raynham	*Norfolk* - King's Lynn
Southrepps	*Norfolk* - Norwich
South Reston	*Lincoln* - Louth
Southrey	*Lincoln* - Lincoln
Southridge	*Berks* - Didcot
Southrop	*Gloucester* - Cheltenham
Southrope	*Hants* - Basingstoke
South Runcton	*Norfolk* - King's Lynn
South Ruston	*Norfolk* - Norwich
South Scarle	*Notts* - Newark
Southsea	*Denbigh* - Wrexham
Southsea	*Hants* - Portsmouth
South Shields	*Durham* - South Shields
Southside Butterknowle	*Durham* - Bishop Auckland
South Somercotes	*Lincoln* - Louth
South Stainley with Cayton	*York, W.R.* - Harrogate
South Stainmore	*Westmorland* - Penrith
South Stannington	*Northumberland* - Morpeth
South Stifford	*Essex* - Grays Thurrock
South Stoke	*Lincoln* - Grantham
South Stoke	*Oxford* - Didcot
South Stoke	*Somerset* - Bath
South Stoke	*Sussex* - Chichester
South Stoneham	*Hants* - Southampton
South Streatham (part)	*London, S.W.16* - Lambeth
South Street	*Kent* - Canterbury
South Tarring	*Sussex* - Worthing
South Tawton	*Devon* - Okehampton
South Thoresby	*Lincoln* - Louth
South Tidworth	*Hants* - Andover
South Tottenham	*London, N.15* - Edmonton
Southwaite	*Cumberland* - Penrith
South Walsham	*Norfolk* - Norwich
Southwark (part)	*London, S.E.1* - Lambeth
Southwark (part)	*London, S.E.1* - Southwark
South Warnborough	*Hants* - Basingstoke
Southwater	*Sussex* - Horsham
Southway	*Devon* - Plymouth
South Weald	*Essex* - Brentwood
Southwell	*Notts* - Newark
South Weston	*Oxford* - Thame
South Wheatley	*Notts* - East Retford
Southwick	*Gloucester* - Cheltenham
Southwick	*Hants* - Portsmouth
Southwick	*Northampton* - Corby
Southwick	*Sussex* - Brighton
Southwick	*Wilts* - Trowbridge
Southwick, High	*Durham* - Sunderland
Southwick-on-Wear	*Durham* - Sunderland

South Wigston	*Leicester* - Leicester
South Willingham	*Lincoln* - Louth
South Wimbledon (part)	*London, S.W.19* - Croydon
South Wingate	*Durham* - Durham
South Wingfield	*Derby* - Alfreton
South Witham	*Lincoln* - Grantham
Southwold	*Suffolk* - Halesworth
Southwood	*Norfolk* - Norwich
South Woodford	*London, E.18* - Bow
South Woodham	*Essex* - Maldon
South Wootton	*Norfolk* - King's Lynn
South Wraxall	*Wilts* - Trowbridge
South Yardley	*Warwick* - Birmingham
South Zeal	*Devon* - Okehampton
Sowbatch	*Salop* - Shrewsbury
Sowdley	*Salop* - Market Drayton
Sowe	*Warwick* - Coventry
Sowe Common	*Warwick* - Coventry
Sowerbutts	*Lancaster* - Preston
Sowerbutts Green	*Lancaster* - Preston
Sowerby	*Lancaster* - Barrow-in-Furness
Sowerby	*Lancaster* - Preston
Sowerby	*York, N.R.* - Northallerton
Sowerby	*York, W.R.* - Halifax
Sowerby Bridge	*York, W.R.* - Halifax
Sowerby Row	*Cumberland* - Penrith
Sowerby-under-Cotcliffe	*York, N.R.* - Northallerton
Sowgar	*Cornwall* - Truro
Sowley Pond	*Hants* - Southampton
Sowood	*York, W.R.* - Halifax
Sowton	*Devon* - Exeter
Soyland	*York, W.R.* - Halifax
Spacey Houses	*York, W.R.* - Harrogate
Spadeadam	*Cumberland* - Carlisle
Spade Oak Ferry	*Berks* - Slough
Spalding	*Lincoln* - Spalding
Spalding Common	*Lincoln* - Spalding
Spalding Marsh	*Lincoln* - Spalding
Spaldington	*York, E.R.* - Goole
Spaldwick	*Hunts* - Huntingdon
Spalford	*Notts* - Newark
Spanby	*Lincoln* - Sleaford
Spargo Bridge	*Cornwall* - Truro
Sparham	*Norfolk* - East Dereham
Sparkbridge	*Lancaster* - Barrow-in-Furness
Sparkbrook	*Warwick* - Birmingham
Sparket	*Cumberland* - Penrith
Sparkford	*Somerset* - Yeovil
Sparkhill	*Warwick* - Birmingham
Sparkwell Near Plympton	*Devon* - Plymouth
Sparnon	*Cornwall* - Penzance
Sparnon Gate	*Cornwall* - Redruth
Sparrow Pit	*Derby* - Buxton
Sparsholt	*Berks* - Didcot
Sparsholt	*Hants* - Winchester
Sparty Lea	*Northumberland* - Hexham
Spath	*Stafford* - Uttoxeter
Spaunton	*York, N.R.* - Malton
Spaxton	*Somerset* - Bridgwater
Speech House	*Gloucester* - Gloucester
Speen	*Berks* - Newbury
Speen	*Bucks* - High Wycombe
Speenhamland	*Berks* - Newbury
Speeton	*York, E.R.* - Bridlington
Speke	*Lancaster* - Liverpool
Spelbrook	*Herts* - Bishop's Stortford
Speldhurst	*Kent* - Tunbridge Wells
Spelsbury	*Oxford* - Banbury
Spelter Works	*Cumberland* - Carlisle
Spen	*Durham* - Newcastle upon Tyne
Spencers Wood	*Berks* - Reading
Spen, High	*Durham* - Newcastle upon Tyne
Spen, Lower	*York, W.R.* - Dewsbury
Spennithorne	*York, N.R.* - Northallerton
Spennymoor	*Durham* - Bishop Auckland
Spennymoor, Low	*Durham* - Bishop Auckland
Spen, Upper	*York, W.R.* - Dewsbury
Spernall	*Warwick* - Redditch
Spetchley	*Worcester* - Worcester
Spetisbury	*Dorset* - Wimborne Minster

SPE - STA

Spexhall	*Suffolk* - Halesworth
Spilsby	*Lincoln* - Skegness
Spinkhill	*Derby* - Chesterfield
Spinner's End	*Stafford* - Dudley
Spion Kop	*Notts* - Mansfield
Spirthill	*Wilts* - Chippenham
Spital	*Berks* - Slough
Spital	*Cheshire* - Birkenhead
Spital	*Derby* - Chesterfield
Spital	*York, N.R.* - Bishop Auckland
Spitalfields	*London, E.1* - Shoreditch
Spitalgate	*Lincoln* - Grantham
Spital Hill	*Northumberland* - Morpeth
Spital in the Street	*Lincoln* - Lincoln
Spital Tongues	*Northumberland* - Wigan
Spithead	*Hants* - Portsmouth
Spithurst	*Sussex* - Lewes
Spittal	*Cumberland* - Carlisle
Spittal	*Northumberland* - Berwick-upon-Tweed
Spittal	*Northumberland* - Hexham
Spittal	*Pembroke* - Haverfordwest
Spittal	*Westmorland* - Kendal
Spittle	*Northumberland* - Hexham
Spixworth	*Norfolk* - Norwich
Splayne's Green	*Sussex* - Lewes
Spofforth	*York, W.R.* - Harrogate
Spon Croft	*Stafford* - West Bromwich
Spondon	*Derby* - Derby
Spooner Row	*Norfolk* - Norwich
Spoonley	*Salop* - Market Drayton
Sporle-with-Palgrave	*Norfolk* - King's Lynn
Spotacre	*Stafford* - Stafford
Spout Lane	*Salop* - Shrewsbury
Spratton	*Northampton* - Northampton
Spreyton	*Devon* - Okehampton
Spriddlescombe	*Devon* - Kingsbridge
Spriddlestone	*Devon* - Plymouth
Spridlington	*Lincoln* - Lincoln
Spriggs Alley	*Oxford* - Thame
Spring Bank	*Lancaster* - Wigan
Springbourne	*Hants* - Bournemouth
Springfield	*Essex* - Chelmsford
Springfield	*Monmouth* - Blackwood
Springfield	*Stafford* - Dudley
Springfields	*Stafford* - Wolverhampton
Spring Gardens	*Durham* - Bishop Auckland
Springhead	*Kent* - Gravesend
Spring Head	*Stafford* - Dudley
Springhead	*York, W.R.* - Oldham
Springhill	*Northumberland* - Morpeth
Spring Hill	*Stafford* - Lichfield
Spring Hill	*Worcester* - Redditch
Springkell	*Cumberland* - Carlisle
Springside	*Lancaster* - Bury
Spring Slade	*Stafford* - Stafford
Springs, The	*Salop* - Shrewsbury
Springthorpe	*Lincoln* - Gainsborough
Spring Vale	*York, W.R.* - Barnsley
Spring View	*Lancaster* - Wigan
Springwell (Village)	*Durham* - Gateshead
Springwell Colliery	*Durham* - Gateshead
Springwell Newhouses	*Durham* - Gateshead
Spring Wood	*Stafford* - Stoke-on-Trent
Sproatley	*York, E.R.* - Kingston-upon-Hull
Sproston	*Cheshire* - Northwich
Sprotborough	*York, W.R.* - Doncaster
Sproughton	*Suffolk* - Ipswich
Sprowston	*Norfolk* - Norwich
Sproxton	*Leicester* - Melton Mowbray
Sproxton	*York, N.R.* - Malton
Sprytown	*Devon* - Plymouth
Spunhill	*Salop* - Oswestry
Spurley Brook	*Stafford* - Stafford
Spurn	*York, E.R.* - Kingston-upon-Hull
Spursholt	*Hants* - Southampton
Spurstow	*Cheshire* - Crewe
Squirrels Heath	*Essex* - Ilford
Stableford	*Salop* - Bridgnorth
Stableford	*Stafford* - Stoke-on-Trent

STA

Stable Hobba	*Cornwall* - Penzance
Stables, High	*Durham* - Consett
Stackhouse	*York, W.R.* - Skipton
Stackpole Elidor	*Pembroke* - Haverfordwest
Stacksteads	*Lancaster* - Rawtenstall
Staddiscombe	*Devon* - Plymouth
Staddlethorpe	*York, E.R.* - Goole
Staddon	*Devon* - Plymouth
Stadhampton	*Oxford* - Oxford
Staffhurst Wood	*Surrey* - Reigate
Staffield	*Cumberland* - Penrith
Stafford	*Dorset* - Dorchester
Stafford	*Stafford* - Stafford
Stafford's Green	*Somerset* - Yeovil
Stag and Pheasant	*Carmarthen* - Carmarthen
Stagenhoe	*Herts* - Hitchin
Stagenhoe Bottom	*Herts* - Hitchin
Stagsbatch	*Hereford* - Leominster
Stagsden	*Beds* - Bedford
Stagshaw	*Northumberland* - Hexham
Stag's Head	*Devon* - Barnstaple
Stag's Holt	*Cambridge* - Wisbech
Stain	*Lincoln* - Louth
Stainbrough	*York, W.R.* - Barnsley
Stainburn	*York, W.R.* - Otley
Stainby	*Lincoln* - Grantham
Staincliffe	*York, W.R.* - Dewsbury
Staincross	*York, W.R.* - Barnsley
Staindrop	*Durham* - Bishop Auckland
Staines	*Middlesex* - Slough
Staines Green	*Herts* - Hertford
Stainfield	*Lincoln* - Spalding
Stainfield	*Lincoln* - Lincoln
Stainforth	*York, W.R.* - Skipton
Stainforth	*York, W.R.* - Thorne
Staining	*Lancaster* - Blackpool
Stainland	*York, W.R.* - Halifax
Stainley, North	*York, W.R.* - Harrogate
Stainley, South	*York, W.R.* - Harrogate
Stainmore, North	*Westmorland* - Penrith
Stainmore, South	*Westmorland* - Penrith
Stainsacre	*York, N.R.* - Whitby
Stainsby	*Derby* - Chesterfield
Stainsby	*Lincoln* - Skegness
Stainton	*Cumberland* - Carlisle
Stainton	*Cumberland* - Penrith
Stainton	*Durham* - Bishop Auckland
Stainton	*Lancaster* - Barrow-in-Furness
Stainton	*Lincoln* - Lincoln
Stainton	*Westmorland* - Kendal
Stainton	*York, W.R.* - Doncaster
Stainton, Great	*Durham* - Stockton on Tees
Stainton Grove	*Durham* - Bishop Auckland
Stainton-in-Cleveland	*York, N.R.* - Middlesbrough
Stainton le Vale	*Lincoln* - Louth
Stair	*Cumberland* - Workington
Stairfoot	*Somerset* - Taunton
Stairfoot	*York, W.R.* - Barnsley
Staithes	*York, N.R.* - Whitby
Stakeford	*Northumberland* - Blyth
Stakehill	*Lancaster* - Oldham
Stakenbridge	*Worcester* - Kidderminster
Stalbridge	*Dorset* - Shaftesbury
Stalbridge Weston	*Dorset* - Shaftesbury
Stalham	*Norfolk* - Great Yarmouth
Stalisfield	*Kent* - Sittingbourne
Stallingborough	*Lincoln* - Great Grimsby
Stallington	*Stafford* - Stoke-on-Trent
Stallions Green	*Kent* - Tonbridge
Stalmine with Staynall	*Lancaster* - Blackpool
Stalybridge	*Cheshire* - Ashton-under-Lyne
Stambermill	*Worcester* - Stourbridge
Stambourne	*Essex* - Braintree
Stambridge, Great	*Essex* - Southend
Stamford (St. Martins Without)	*Huntingdon and Peterborough* - Stamford
Stamford	*Lincoln* - Stamford
Stamford	*Northumberland* - Alnwick
Stamford Bridge	*Cheshire* - Chester

Stamford Bridge	*York, E.R.* - York
Stamfordham	*Northumberland* - Newcastle upon Tyne
Stamford Hill	*London, N.16* - Shoreditch
Stammerham (Christ's Hospital)	*Sussex* - Horsham
Stammerham (Rusper)	*Sussex* - Horsham
Stamshaw	*Hants* - Portsmouth
Stanage	*Radnor* - Knighton
Stanborough	*Herts* - St. Albans
Stanbridge	*Bucks* - Bletchley and Leighton Buzzard
Stanbridge	*Dorset* - Wimborne Minster
Stanbury	*York, W.R.* - Keighley
Stand	*Lancaster* - Bury
Standard Hill	*Leicester* - Ashby-de-la-Zouch
Standean	*Sussex* - Brighton
Standedge	*York, W.R.* - Oldham
Standeford	*Stafford* - Wolverhampton
Standen	*Kent* - Cranbrook
Standen	*Kent* - Dover
Standen Street	*Kent* - Cranbrook
Standerwick	*Somerset* - Frome
Standford	*Hants* - Aldershot and Farnham
Standford Bridge	*Salop* - Wellington (Salop)
Standhill	*Oxford* - Thame
Standingstone	*Cumberland* - Carlisle
Standish	*Gloucester* - Gloucester
Standish	*Lancaster* - Wigan
Standish Cote	*Lancaster* - Barrow-in-Furness
Standish Lower Ground	*Lancaster* - Wigan
Standlake	*Oxford* - Witney
Standlynch	*Wilts* - Salisbury
Standon	*Devon* - Plymouth
Standon	*Hants* - Winchester
Standon	*Herts* - Hertford
Standon	*Stafford* - Stoke-on-Trent
Standon Friars	*Herts* - Hertford
Standon Green End	*Herts* - Hertford
Standon Lordships	*Herts* - Hertford
Stane Street	*Surrey* - Dorking
Stanfield	*Norfolk* - East Dereham
Stanfield	*Norfolk* - Norwich
Stanfield	*Stafford* - Stoke-on-Trent
Stanford	*Beds* - Biggleswade
Stanford	*Kent* - Folkestone
Stanford	*Notts* - Loughborough
Stanford	*Warwick* - Rugby
Stanford	*Worcester* - Kidderminster
Stanford Bishop	*Hereford* - Worcester
Stanford Bridge	*Worcester* - Kidderminster
Standford Dingley	*Berks* - Newbury
Stanford Hills	*Notts* - Loughborough
Stanford in the Vale	*Berks* - Didcot
Stanford-le-Hope	*Essex* - Grays Thurrock
Stanford on Avon	*Warwick* - Rugby
Stanford Rivers	*Essex* - Brentwood
Stanfree	*Derby* - Chesterfield
Stanghow	*York, N.R.* - Middlesbrough
Stanhoe	*Norfolk* - King's Lynn
Stanhope	*Durham* - Bishop Auckland
Stanion	*Northampton* - Corby
Stank	*Lancaster* - Barrow-in-Furness
Stanks	*York, W.R.* - Leeds
Stanley	*Derby* - Ilkeston
Stanley	*Notts* - Mansfield
Stanley (part)	*Stafford* - Stoke-on-Trent
Stanley (part)	*Stafford* - Leek
Stanley	*Wilts* - Chippenham
Stanley	*York, W.R.* - Wakefield
Stanley Common	*Derby* - Ilkeston
Stanley Downton	*Gloucester* - Stroud
Stanley	*Durham* - Consett
Stanley Houses	*Durham* - Bishop Auckland
Stanley Moor	*Stafford* - Stoke-on-Trent
Stanley Pit	*Durham* - Bishop Auckland
Stanley Pontlarge	*Gloucester* - Cheltenham
Stanley P.O. Crook	*Durham* - Bishop Auckland
Stanleytown	*Glamorgan* - Pontypridd
Stanlow	*Cheshire* - Ellesmere Port
Stanlow	*Salop* - Bridgnorth
Stanlow Point	*Cheshire* - Ellesmere Port
Stanmer	*Sussex* - Brighton
Stanmore	*Berks* - Newbury
Stanmore	*Hants* - Winchester
Stanmore (part)	*Middlesex* - Watford
Stanmore (part)	*Middlesex* - Willesden
Stanmore	*Salop* - Bridgnorth
Stanmore, Great	*Middlesex* - Watford
Stanmore, North	*Middlesex* - Watford
Stannersburn	*Northumberland* - Hexham
Stanners, High	*Northumberland* - Morpeth
Stanners, Low	*Northumberland* - Morpeth
Stanney, Great	*Cheshire* - Ellesmere Port
Stanney, Little	*Cheshire* - Ellesmere Port
Stanningfield	*Suffolk* - Bury St. Edmunds
Stanninghall	*Norfolk* - Norwich
Stanningley (part)	*York, W.R.* - Bradford
Stanningley (part)	*York, W.R.* - Leeds
Stannington	*Northumberland* - Morpeth
Stannington, East	*Northumberland* - Morpeth
Stannington, East	*York, W.R.* - Sheffield
Stannington, South	*Northumberland* - Morpeth
Stannington, West	*York, W.R.* - Sheffield
Stanpit	*Hants* - Bournemouth
Stansbatch	*Hereford* - Leominster
Stansfield	*Suffolk* - Bury St. Edmunds
Stansgate Abbey	*Essex* - Maldon
Stanshope	*Stafford* - Buxton
Stansill	*York, W.R.* - Doncaster
Stansley	*Northumberland* - Hexham
Stanstead	*Kent* - Sevenoaks
Stanstead	*Suffolk* - Sudbury
Stanstead	*Sussex* - Chichester
Stanstead Abbots	*Herts* - Hertford
Stanstead Park	*Sussex* - Chichester
Stansted	*Essex* - Bishop's Stortford
Stantsted Mountfichet	*Essex* - Bishop's Stortford
Stansty	*Denbigh* - Wrexham
Stanthorne	*Cheshire* - Northwich
Stanton	*Derby* - Burton-upon-Trent
Stanton	*Gloucester* - Cheltenham
Stanton	*Northumberland* - Morpeth
Stanton	*Salop* - Shrewsbury
Stanton	*Stafford* - Uttoxeter
Stanton	*Suffolk* - Bury St. Edmunds
Stanton and Pilhough	*Derby* - Matlock
Stantonbury	*Bucks* - Bletchley and Leighton Buzzard
Stanton-by-Bridge	*Derby* - Derby
Stanton by Dale	*Derby* - Ilkeston
Stanton Drew	*Somerset* - Bristol
Stanton Fitzwarren	*Wilts* - Swindon
Stanton Gate	*Derby* - Ilkeston
Stanton Harcourt	*Oxford* - Witney
Stanton Hill	*Notts* - Mansfield
Stanton Lacey	*Salop* - Ludlow
Stanton Lees	*Derby* - Matlock
Stanton Lodge	*Derby* - Matlock
Stanton Long	*Salop* - Bridgnorth
Stanton on the Wolds	*Notts* - Nottingham
Stanton Prior	*Somerset* - Bath
Stanton St. Bernard	*Wilts* - Devizes
Stanton St. Gabriels	*Dorset* - Axminster and Chard
Stanton St. John	*Oxford* - Oxford
Stanton St. Quintin	*Wilts* - Chippenham
Stanton-under-Bardon	*Leicester* - Leicester
Stanton upon Hine Heath	*Salop* - Shrewsbury
Stanton Wick	*Somerset* - Bristol
Stantway Lane	*Gloucester* - Gloucester
Stanwardine in the Fields	*Salop* - Shrewsbury
Stanwardine in the Wood	*Salop* - Shrewsbury
Stanway	*Essex* - Colchester
Stanway	*Gloucester* - Cheltenham
Stanway	*Salop* - Ludlow
Stanwell	*Middlesex* - Slough

Stanwell Moor	*Middlesex* - Slough
Stanwick	*Northampton* - Wellingborough
Stanwix	*Cumberland* - Carlisle
Stape	*York, N.R.* - Malton
Stapehill	*Dorset* - Wimborne Minster
Stapeley	*Salop* - Welshpool
Stapely	*Hants* - Basingstoke
Staple	*Kent* - Deal
Staplecross	*Sussex* - Hastings
Staplefield	*Sussex* - Haywards Heath
Staple Fitzpaine	*Somerset* - Taunton
Stapleford	*Cambridge* - Cambridge
Stapleford	*Herts* - Hertford
Stapleford	*Leicester* - Melton Mowbray
Stapleford	*Lincoln* - Newark
Stapleford	*Notts* - Nottingham
Stapleford	*Wilts* - Salisbury
Stapleford Abbots	*Essex* - Ilford
Stapleford Tawney	*Essex* - Harlow
Staplegrove	*Somerset* - Taunton
Staplehay	*Somerset* - Taunton
Staple Hill	*Worcester* - Bromsgrove
Staplehurst	*Kent* - Maidstone
Staple Street	*Kent* - Canterbury
Stapleton	*Cumberland* - Carlisle
Stapleton	*Hereford* - Leominster
Stapleton	*Leicester* - Hinckley
Stapleton	*Salop* - Shrewsbury
Stapleton (Martock)	*Somerset* - Yeovil
Stapleton	*York, N.R.* - Darlington
Stapleton	*York, W.R.* - Pontefract
Stapleton Hill	*Hereford* - Leominster
Stapley	*Somerset* - Taunton
Staploe	*Beds* - Biggleswade
Staplow	*Hereford* - Hereford
Star	*Pembroke* - Cardigan
Star	*Somerset* - Weston Super Mare
Starbeck	*York, W.R.* - Harrogate
Starbotton	*York, W.R.* - Skipton
Star Carr	*Lincoln* - Gainsborough
Starcross	*Devon* - Exeter
Stareton	*Warwick* - Coventry
Stargate	*Durham* - Newcastle upon Tyne
Starkholmes	*Derby* - Matlock
Starling	*Lancaster* - Bury
Starlings Green	*Essex* - Bishop's Stortford
Starmore	*Leicester* - Rugby
Starrick Moor	*Cornwall* - St. Austell
Starston	*Norfolk* - Norwich
Start	*Devon* - Kingsbridge
Startforth	*York, N.R.* - Bishop Auckland
Startforth Park	*York, N.R.* - Bishop Auckland
Start Hill	*Essex* - Bishop's Stortford
Startley	*Wilts* - Malmesbury
Starve All	*Gloucester* - Bristol
Starveall	*Gloucester* - Cheltenham
Starve Crow	*Kent* - Tonbridge
Statfold	*Stafford* - Tamworth
Statham	*Cheshire* - Altrincham
Stathe	*Somerset* - Taunton
Stathern	*Leicester* - Melton Mowbray
Station Hill	*Cumberland* - Carlisle
Station Town	*Durham* - Hartlepool
Staughton, Great	*Hunts* - Huntingdon
Staughton, Little	*Beds* - Bedford
Staughton Moor	*Hunts* - Huntingdon
Staunton	*Devon* - Kingsbridge
Staunton	*Gloucester* - Monmouth
Staunton	*Gloucester* - Gloucester
Staunton	*Notts* - Newark
Staunton Harrold	*Leicester* - Ashby-de-la-Zouch
Staunton-on-Arrow	*Hereford* - Leominster
Staunton-upon-Wye	*Hereford* - Hereford
Staveley	*Derby* - Chesterfield
Staveley	*Lancaster* - Barrow-in-Furness
Staveley	*Westmorland* - Kendal
Staveley	*York, W.R.* - Harrogate
Staverton	*Devon* - Newton Abbot
Staverton	*Gloucester* - Cheltenham
Staverton	*Northampton* - Northampton

Staverton	*Wilts* - Trowbridge
Stawell	*Somerset* - Bridgwater
Stawley	*Somerset* - Taunton
Staxton	*York, E.R.* - Scarborough
Staxton Wold	*York, E.R.* - Scarborough
Stayley	*Cheshire* - Ashton-under-Lyne
Staylittle	*Montgomery* - Newtown
Staythorpe	*Notts* - Newark
Steam Mills	*Gloucester* - Gloucester
Stean	*York, W.R.* - Harrogate
Steane	*Northampton* - Banbury
Stearsby	*York, N.R.* - York
Steart	*Somerset* - Bridgwater
Steart (West Camel)	*Somerset* - Yeovil
Stebbing	*Essex* - Braintree
Stechford	*Warwick* - Birmingham
Stedham	*Sussex* - Petersfield
Steed Quarter	*Kent* - Cranbrook
Steel Cross	*Sussex* - Tunbridge Wells
Steele	*Salop* - Whitchurch
Steele Heath	*Salop* - Whitchurch
Steel End	*Cumberland* - Workington
Steens Bridge	*Hereford* - Leominster
Steep	*Hants* - Petersfield
Steeping, Great	*Lincoln* - Skegness
Steeping, Little	*Lincoln* - Skegness
Steeple	*Dorset* - Swanage
Steeple	*Essex* - Maldon
Steeple Ashton	*Wilts* - Trowbridge
Steeple Aston	*Oxford* - Banbury
Steeple Barton	*Oxford* - Banbury
Steeple Bumpstead	*Essex* - Cambridge
Steeple Claydon	*Bucks* - Aylesbury
Steeple Gidding	*Hunts* - Huntingdon
Steeple Grange	*Derby* - Matlock
Steeple Langford	*Wilts* - Salisbury
Steeple Morden	*Cambridge* - Hitchin
Steepleton	*Dorset* - Dorchester
Steepleton Iwerne	*Dorset* - Shaftesbury
Steepmarsh	*Hants* - Petersfield
Steeraway	*Salop* - Wellington (Salop)
Steetley	*Derby* - Worksop
Steetley	*Durham* - Durham
Steeton	*York, W.R.* - Keighley
Stella	*Durham* - Newcastle upon Tyne
Stelling	*Kent* - Folkestone
Stelling	*Northumberland* - Hexham
Stelling Minnis	*Kent* - Folkestone
Stembridge (Martock)	*Somerset* - Yeovil
Stenalees	*Cornwall* - St. Austell
Stenders, The	*Gloucester* - Gloucester
Stenigot	*Lincoln* - Louth
Stennack (St. Ives)	*Cornwall* - Penzance
Stennack (Camborne)	*Cornwall* - Redruth
Stents	*Cornwall* - St. Austell
Stenwith	*Lincoln* - Grantham
Stepaside	*Montgomery* - Newtown
Stepaside	*Pembroke* - Haverfordwest
Stephens Hall	*Durham* - Newcastle upon Tyne
Stephen's Hill	*Stafford* - Uttoxeter
Stepney	*London, E.1* - Shoreditch
Stepney Green	*London, E.1* - Shoreditch
Steppingley	*Beds* - Bedford
Sterndale Moor	*Derby* - Buxton
Sternfield	*Suffolk* - Woodbridge
Stert	*Wilts* - Devizes
Stetchworth	*Cambridge* - Newmarket
Stevenage	*Herts* - Hitchin
Steventon	*Berks* - Didcot
Steventon	*Hants* - Basingstoke
Steventon	*Salop* - Ludlow
Stevington	*Beds* - Bedford
Stewartby	*Beds* - Bedford
Stewkley	*Bucks* - Bletchley and Leighton Buzzard
Stewner	*Lancaster* - Barrow-in-Furness
Stewponey	*Stafford* - Stourbridge
Stewton	*Lincoln* - Louth
Steyning	*Sussex* - Brighton
Steynton	*Pembroke* - Haverfordwest

STI - STO

Stiants Bottom	*Kent*	Sevenoaks
Stibbard	*Norfolk*	King's Lynn
Stibbington	*Hunts*	Peterborough
Stichings Hill	*Worcester*	Great Malvern
Sticken Bridge	*Cornwall*	Truro
Sticker	*Cornwall*	St. Austell
Sticker, Lower	*Cornwall*	St. Austell
Stickford	*Lincoln*	Boston
Sticklepath	*Devon*	Okehampton
Sticklers Corner	*Cornwall*	Truro
Stickling Green	*Essex*	Bishop's Stortford
Stickney	*Lincoln*	Boston
Stidcot	*Gloucester*	Thornbury
Stidstone	*Devon*	Torquay
Stiffkey	*Norfolk*	King's Lynn
Stifford, North	*Essex*	Grays Thurrock
Stifford's Bridge	*Hereford*	Worcester
Stifford, South	*Essex*	Grays Thurrock
Stillingfleet	*York, E. and W.R.*	York
Stillington	*Durham*	Stockton on Tees
Stillington	*York, N.R.*	York
Stilton	*Hunts*	Peterborough
Stinchcombe	*Gloucester*	Stroud
Stinsford	*Dorset*	Dorchester
Stirchley	*Salop*	Wellington (Salop)
Stirchley	*Warwick*	Birmingham
Stirtloe	*Hunts*	Huntingdon
Stirton-with Thorlby	*York, W.R.*	Skipton
Stisted	*Essex*	Braintree
Stithians (part)	*Cornwall*	Redruth
Stitt	*Salop*	Shrewsbury
Stittenham	*York, N.R.*	Malton
Stivichall	*Warwick*	Coventry
Stixwould	*Lincoln*	Lincoln
Stoak	*Chester*	Chester
Stoat's Nest	*Surrey*	Croydon
Stobhill	*Northumberland*	Morpeth
Stoborough	*Dorset*	Swanage
Stobswood Colliery	*Northumberland*	Morpeth
Stock	*Essex*	Chelmsford
Stock	*Somerset*	Weston Super Mare
Stockbridge	*Hants*	Andover
Stockbrook	*Lancaster*	Oldham
Stockbury	*Kent*	Sittingbourne
Stockcross	*Berks*	Newbury
Stockeld	*York, W.R.*	Harrogate
Stocken	*Rutland*	Melton Mowbray
Stockens Green	*Herts*	Hitchin
Stockerston	*Leicester*	Corby
Stockett	*Salop*	Oswestry
Stock Gaylard	*Dorset*	Shaftesbury
Stock Green	*Worcester*	Redditch
Stockgrove	*Bucks*	Bletchley and Leighton Buzzard
Stockheath	*Hants*	Portsmouth
Stockingfield	*Hereford*	Leominster
Stockingford	*Warwick*	Nuneaton
Stocking Green	*Essex*	Bishop's Stortford
Stocking Pelham	*Herts*	Bishop's Stortford
Stockland	*Devon*	Axminster and Chard
Stockland Bristol	*Somerset*	Bridgwater
Stockland Green	*Warwick*	Birmingham
Stockledalewath	*Cumberland*	Carlisle
Stockleigh English	*Devon*	Tiverton
Stockleigh Pomeroy	*Devon*	Tiverton
Stockley	*Middlesex*	Uxbridge
Stockley	*Wilts*	Chippenham
Stockley Farm	*Durham*	Bishop Auckland
Stocklinch Magdalen	*Somerset*	Yeovil
Stocklinch Ottersey	*Somerset*	Yeovil
Stockmoor	*Cumberland*	Workington
Stockport	*Cheshire*	Stockport
Stocks	*Kent*	Cranbrook
Stocks	*Salop*	Oswestry
Stocksbridge	*York, W.R.*	Sheffield
Stocksfield	*Northumberland*	Hexham
Stocks Green	*Kent*	Tonbridge
Stocksmoor (Thurstonland)	*York, W.R.*	Huddersfield
Stockton	*Cheshire*	Whitchurch

STO

Stockton	*Hereford*	Leominster
Stockton	*Norfolk*	Lowestoft
Stockton	*Salop*	Bridgnorth
Stockton	*Salop*	Wellington (Salop)
Stockton	*Warwick*	Warwick
Stockton	*Wilts*	Warminster
Stockton	*Worcester*	Kidderminster
Stockton Brook (part)	*Stafford*	Stoke-on-Trent
Stockton Brook (part)	*Stafford*	Leek
Stockton Heath	*Cheshire*	Warrington
Stockton on Tees	*Durham*	Stockton on Tees
Stockton on the Forest	*York, N.R.*	York
Stockwell (part)	*London, S.W.9*	Lambeth
Stockwell (part)	*London, S.W.9*	Wandsworth
Stockwell Heath	*Stafford*	Stafford
Stockwith, East	*Lincoln*	Gainsborough
Stockwith, West	*Notts*	Gainsborough
Stockwood	*Dorset*	Yeovil
Stockwood and Bradley	*Worcester*	Redditch
Stodday	*Lancaster*	Lancaster
Stodmarsh	*Kent*	Canterbury
Stody	*Norfolk*	Norwich
Stoford	*Dorset*	Yeovil
Stoford	*Wilts*	Salisbury
Stogumber	*Somerset*	Minehead
Stogursey	*Somerset*	Bridgwater
Stoke	*Devon*	Bideford
Stoke	*Devon*	Plymouth
Stoke	*Hants*	Andover
Stoke (Hayling)	*Hants*	Portsmouth
Stoke	*Salop*	Ludlow
Stoke	*Surrey*	Guildford
Stoke	*Warwick*	Coventry
Stoke Abbott	*Dorset*	Yeovil
Stoke Albany	*Northampton*	Corby
Stoke Aldermoor	*Warwick*	Coventry
Stoke Ash	*Suffolk*	Norwich
Stoke Bardolph	*Notts*	Nottingham
Stoke Beach	*Devon*	Plymouth
Stoke Bliss	*Worcester*	Leominster
Stoke Bottom	*Somerset*	Frome
Stoke Bruerne	*Northampton*	Northampton
Stoke by Clare	*Suffolk*	Sudbury
Stoke by Nayland	*Suffolk*	Sudbury
Stoke Canon	*Devon*	Exeter
Stoke Charity	*Hants*	Winchester
Stoke Climsland	*Cornwall*	Launceston
Stoke Common	*Bucks*	Slough
Stoke Cross	*Worcester*	Bromsgrove
Stoke D'Abernon	*Surrey*	Kingston-upon-Thames
Stoke Damerel	*Devon*	Plymouth
Stoke Doyle	*Northampton*	Corby
Stoke Dry	*Rutland*	Corby
Stoke, East	*Dorset*	Swanage
Stoke, East	*Notts*	Newark
Stoke Edith	*Hereford*	Hereford
Stoke End	*Warwick*	Tamworth
Stoke Farthing	*Wilts*	Salisbury
Stoke Ferry	*Norfolk*	King's Lynn
Stokefield	*Oxford*	Thame
Stokefleming	*Devon*	Kingsbridge
Stoke Gabriel	*Devon*	Torquay
Stoke Gifford	*Gloucester*	Bristol
Stoke Golding	*Leicester*	Hinckley
Stoke Goldington	*Bucks*	Northampton
Stoke Grange	*Oxford*	Thame
Stoke Grange	*Salop*	Market Drayton
Stoke Green	*Warwick*	Coventry
Stokeham	*Notts*	East Retford
Stoke Hammond	*Bucks*	Bletchley and Leighton Buzzard
Stoke Heath	*Salop*	Market Drayton
Stoke Heath	*Warwick*	Coventry
Stoke Heath	*Worcester*	Bromsgrove
Stoke Holy Cross	*Norfolk*	Norwich
Stokeinteignhead	*Devon*	Torquay
Stoke Knapps	*Dorset*	Yeovil
Stoke Lacy	*Hereford*	Hereford
Stoke Lane	*Somerset*	Frome

Stoke, Little	*Gloucester* - Bristol
Stoke, Little	*Gloucester* - Thornbury
Stoke, Little	*Oxford* - Didcot
Stoke, Little	*Stafford* - Stafford
Stoke, Lower	*Kent* - Rochester
Stoke Lyne	*Oxford* - Banbury
Stoke Mandeville	*Bucks* - Aylesbury
Stokenchurch	*Bucks* - High Wycombe
Stoke Newington	*London, N.16* - Shoreditch
Stokenham	*Devon* - Kingsbridge
Stoke, North	*Lincoln* - Grantham
Stoke, North	*Oxford* - Didcot
Stoke, North	*Somerset* - Bath
Stoke, North	*Sussex* - Chichester
Stoke Orchard	*Gloucester* - Cheltenham
Stoke Park	*Gloucester* - Cheltenham
Stoke Park	*Salop* - Market Drayton
Stoke Pero	*Somerset* - Minehead
Stoke Poges	*Bucks* - Slough
Stoke Pound	*Worcester* - Bromsgrove
Stoke Prior	*Hereford* - Leominster
Stoke Prior	*Worcester* - Bromsgrove
Stoke Rivers	*Devon* - Barnstaple
Stoke Rochford	*Lincoln* - Grantham
Stoke Row	*Oxford* - Didcot
Stoke St. Gregory	*Somerset* - Taunton
Stoke St. Michael	*Somerset* - Frome
Stoke St. Mary	*Somerset* - Taunton
Stoke St. Milborough	*Salop* - Ludlow
Stokesay	*Salop* - Ludlow
Stokes Bay	*Hants* - Portsmouth
Stokesby with Herringby	*Norfolk* - Great Yarmouth
Stokes Cross	*Hereford* - Hereford
Stokes Hill	*Hereford* - Hereford
Stokesley	*York, N.R.* - Middlesbrough
Stoke South	*Lincoln* - Grantham
Stoke, South	*Oxford* - Didcot
Stoke, South	*Somerset* - Bath
Stoke, South	*Sussex* - Chichester
Stoke-sub-Hamden	*Somerset* - Yeovil
Stoke Talmage	*Oxford* - Thame
Stoke Trister	*Somerset* - Yeovil
Stoke-upon-Tern	*Salop* - Market Drayton
Stoke-upon-Trent	*Stafford* - Stoke-on-Trent
Stoke, Upper	*Kent* - Rochester
Stoke Wake	*Dorset* - Blandford
Stoke, West	*Sussex* - Chichester
Stolford	*Somerset* - Bridgwater
Stonar	*Kent* - Deal
Stondon, Lower	*Beds* - Hitchin
Stondon Massey	*Essex* - Brentwood
Stondon, Upper	*Beds* - Biggleswade
Stone	*Bucks* - Aylesbury
Stone	*Essex* - Maldon
Stone	*Gloucester* - Stroud
Stone	*Hants* - Southampton
Stone	*Kent* - Cranbrook
Stone	*Kent* - Dartford
Stone	*Kent* - Sittingbourne
Stone	*Stafford* - Stafford
Stone	*Worcester* - Kidderminster
Stone	*York, W.R.* - Rotherham
Stonea	*Cambridge* - March
Stone Acton	*Salop* - Shrewsbury
Stone Allerton	*Somerset* - Wells
Ston Easton	*Somerset* - Wells
Stonebeck Down	*York, W.R.* - Harrogate
Stonebeck Upper	*York, W.R.* - Harrogate
Stonebench	*Gloucester* - Gloucester
Stonebow	*Worcester* - Evesham
Stonebridge	*Surrey* - Dorking
Stonebridge Green	*Kent* - Ashford
Stonebridge Park	*London, N.W.10* - Willesden
Stonebroom	*Derby* - Alfreton
Stone Chair	*York, W.R.* - Halifax
Stoneclough	*Lancaster* - Bolton
Stone Creek	*York, E.R.* - Kingston-upon-Hull
Stone Cross	*Stafford* - West Bromwich
Stone Cross	*Sussex* - Eastbourne

Stonedge	*Derby* - Chesterfield
Stonefall	*York, W.R.* - Harrogate
Stone Ferry	*York, E.R.* - Kingston-upon-Hull
Stonegate	*Sussex* - Tunbridge Wells
Stonegate	*York, N.R.* - Whitby
Stonehall	*Kent* - Dover
Stonehall Common	*Worcester* - Worcester
Stoneham, North	*Hants* - Southampton
Stoneham, South	*Hants* - Southampton
Stonehanger	*Hants* - Andover
Stone Hill (Egerton)	*Kent* - Ashford
Stonehouse	*Gloucester* - Stroud
Stonehouse, East	*Devon* - Plymouth
Stoneleigh	*Surrey* - Epsom
Stoneleigh	*Warwick* - Coventry
Stoneley	*Hunts* - Huntingdon
Stoneley	*Worcester* - Redditch
Stone, Lower	*Gloucester* - Stroud
Stone Pound	*Sussex* - Haywards Heath
Stoneraise	*Cumberland* - Carlisle
Stonesby	*Leicester* - Melton Mowbray
Stonesfield	*Oxford* - Oxford
Stones Green	*Essex* - Harwich
Stone Street	*Kent* - Sevenoaks
Stonethwaite	*Cumberland* - Workington
Stoneton	*Warwick* - Banbury
Stonewall Hill	*Hereford and Radnor* - Knighton
Stoney Corner	*Kent* - Gravesend
Stoneycroft	*Lancaster* - Liverpool
Stoney Cross	*Hants* - Southampton
Stoney Delph	*Stafford* - Tamworth
Stoneyford	*Derby* - Ilkeston
Stoneyford	*Stafford* - Lichfield
Stoney Gutter	*Wilts* - Trowbridge
Stoney Hall	*Herts* - Hitchin
Stoney Heap	*Durham* - Consett
Stoney Hill (Telford)	*Salop* - Wellington
Stoney Hill	*Worcester* - Bromsgrove
Stoneyhills	*Essex* - Maldon
Stoney Hills	*Herts* - Hertford
Stoney Houghton	*Notts* - Mansfield
Stoney Knapps	*Dorset* - Yeovil
Stoney Littleton	*Somerset* - Bath
Stoney Middleton	*Derby* - Buxton
Stoney Ridge	*York, W.R.* - Bradford
Stoney Stanton	*Leicester* - Hinckley
Stoney Stoke	*Somerset* - Yeovil
Stoney Stratton	*Somerset* - Wells
Stoney Stretton	*Salop* - Shrewsbury
Stoney Thorpe	*Warwick* - Warwick
Stoneywell	*Stafford* - Lichfield
Stonham Aspall	*Suffolk* - Stowmarket
Stonham Earl	*Suffolk* - Stowmarket
Stonham, Little	*Suffolk* - Stowmarket
Stonham, Parva	*Suffolk* - Stowmarket
Stonnall	*Stafford* - Lichfield
Stonor	*Oxford* - Reading
Stonton Wyville	*Leicester* - Leicester
Stony Heath	*Hants* - Basingstoke
Stonyhills	*Essex* - Maldon
Stonyhurst	*Lancaster* - Blackburn
Stony Pound	*Salop* - Knighton
Stony Stratford	*Bucks* - Bletchley and Leighton Buzzard
Stoodleigh	*Devon* - Tiverton
Stoodley	*Lancaster* - Todmorden
Stopes	*Lancaster* - Bolton
Stopham	*Sussex* - Chichester
Stopsley	*Beds* - Luton
Storefield	*Northants* - Kettering
Storeton	*Cheshire* - Birkenhead
Storiths	*York, W.R.* - Skipton
Stormore	*Wilts* - Trowbridge
Stormy	*Glamorgan* - Bridgend
Storridge	*Hereford* - Worcester
Storridge	*Wilts* - Trowbridge
Storrington	*Sussex* - Worthing
Storrs	*Westmorland* - Kendal
Storth	*Westmorland* - Kendal
Storwood	*York, E.R.* - York

Stotfold	*Beds* - Biggleswade
Stotsfield Burn	*Durham* - Bishop Auckland
Stottesdon	*Salop* - Bridgnorth
Stott Park	*Lancaster* - Barrow-in-Furness
Stoughton	*Leicester* - Leicester
Stoughton	*Somerset* - Wells
Stoughton	*Surrey* - Guildford
Stoughton	*Sussex* - Chichester
Stoulton	*Worcester* - Worcester
Stourbridge	*Worcester* - Stourbridge
Stour, East	*Dorset* - Shaftesbury
Stourfield	*Hants* - Bournemouth
Stourmouth	*Kent* - Canterbury
Stourpaine	*Dorset* - Shaftesbury
Stourport	*Worcester* - Kidderminster
Stour Provost	*Dorset* - Shaftesbury
Stour Row	*Dorset* - Shaftesbury
Stourton	*Stafford* - Stourbridge
Stourton	*Warwick* - Stratford on Avon Shipston on Stour
Stourton	*York, W.R.* - Leeds
Stourton Caundle	*Dorset* - Shaftesbury
Stourton Park	*Wilts* - Shaftesbury
Stourton with Gasper	*Wilts* - Shaftesbury
Stour, West	*Dorset* - Shaftesbury
Stourwood	*Hants* - Bournemouth
Stoven	*Suffolk* - Halesworth
Stow	*Lincoln* - Gainsborough
Stow Bardolph	*Norfolk* - King's Lynn
Stow Bedon	*Norfolk* - Thetford
Stow Bridge	*Norfolk* - King's Lynn
Stow Brow	*York, N.R.* - Whitby
Stow cum Quy	*Cambridge* - Cambridge
Stowe	*Lincoln* - Stamford
Stowe	*Salop* - Knighton
Stowe	*Stafford* - Stafford
Stowe Hill Wharf	*Northampton* - Northampton
Stowell	*Gloucester* - Cheltenham
Stowell	*Somerset* - Yeovil
Stowell, West	*Wilts* - Swindon
Stowe Nine Churches	*Northampton* - Northampton
Stowey	*Somerset* - Bristol
Stowey, Nether	*Somerset* - Bridgwater
Stowey, Over	*Somerset* - Bridgwater
Stow Fen	*Norfolk* - King's Lynn
Stowford	*Devon* - Plymouth
Stowford	*Wilts* - Trowbridge
Stowlangtoft	*Suffolk* - Bury St. Edmunds
Stow Longa	*Hunts* - Huntingdon
Stow Maries	*Essex* - Maldon
Stowmarket	*Suffolk* - Stowmarket
Stow on the Wold	*Gloucester* - Cheltenham
Stowood	*Oxford* - Oxford
Stow Park	*Lincoln* - Gainsborough
Stow Saint Mary's	*Essex* - Maldon
Stowting	*Kent* - Folkestone
Stowupland	*Suffolk* - Stowmarket
Stradbroke	*Suffolk* - Halesworth
Stradbroke	*York, W.R.* - Sheffield
Stradishall	*Suffolk* - Newmarket
Stradsett	*Norfolk* - King's Lynn
Stragglethorpe	*Lincoln* - Newark
Stragglethorpe	*Notts* - Nottingham
Straits Green	*Stafford* - Dudley
Straits, The (part)	*Stafford* - Dudley
Straits, The (part)	*Stafford* - Wolverhampton
Stramshall	*Stafford* - Uttoxeter
Strand-on-the-Green	*London, W.4* - Brentford
Strands	*Cumberland* - Whitehaven
Strangeways	*Lancaster* - Manchester
Strangford	*Hereford* - Monmouth
Strata Florida	*Cardigan* - Lampeter
Stratfield Mortimer	*Berks* - Reading
Stratfieldsaye	*Hants* - Basingstoke
Stratfield Turgis	*Hants* - Basingstoke
Stratford	*Beds* - Biggleswade
Stratford	*London, E.15* - Bow
Stratford Bridge	*Worcester* - Cheltenham
Stratford, Old	*Northampton* - Northampton
Stratford on Avon	*Warwick* - Stratford on Avon
Stratford St. Andrew	*Suffolk* - Woodbridge
Stratford St. Mary	*Suffolk* - Ipswich
Stratford-sub-Castle	*Wilts* - Salisbury
Stratford Toney	*Wilts* - Salisbury
Stratton	*Cornwall* - Bideford
Stratton	*Dorset* - Dorchester
Stratton	*Gloucester* - Swindon
Stratton Audley	*Oxford* - Oxford
Stratton, East	*Hants* - Winchester
Stratton, Long	*Norfolk* - Norwich
Stratton, Lower	*Wilts* - Swindon
Stratton-on-the-Fosse	*Somerset* - Wells
Stratton St. Margaret	*Wilts* - Swindon
Stratton St. Mary	*Norfolk* - Norwich
Stratton St. Michael	*Norfolk* - Norwich
Stratton Strawless	*Norfolk* - Norwich
Stratton, Upper	*Wilts* - Swindon
Stratton, West	*Hants* - Winchester
Strawberry Hill	*Middlesex* - Brentford
Strawberry Vale	*Middlesex* - Brentford
Streat	*Sussex* - Lewes
Streatham (part)	*London, S.W.16* - Lambeth
Streatham (part)	*London, S.W.16* - Wandsworth
Streatham Common (part)	*London, S.W.16* - Lambeth
Streatham Common (part)	*London, S.W.16* - Wandsworth
Streatham, South (part)	*London, S.W.16* - Lambeth
Streatlam and Stainton	*Durham* - Bishop Auckland
Streatlam Camp	*Durham* - Bishop Auckland
Streatley	*Beds* - Luton
Streatley	*Berks* - Didcot
Street	*Somerset* - Wells
Street	*York, W.R.* - Rotherham
Street and Leigh	*Somerset* - Axminster and Chard
Street Ashton	*Warwick* - Rugby
Street End	*Kent* - Canterbury
Streetfield	*Hereford* - Leominster
Streetgate	*Durham* - Gateshead
Streethay	*Stafford* - Lichfield
Street House	*Cumberland* - Carlisle
Streethouse	*York, W.R.* - Pontefract
Street Houses	*York, N.R.* - Whitby
Streetley End	*Cambridge* - Cambridge
Streetly (part)	*Stafford* - Lichfield
Streetly (part)	*Stafford* - Walsall
Strefford	*Salop* - Ludlow
Strelley	*Notts* - Nottingham
Strensall	*York, N.R.* - York
Strensham, Lower	*Worcester* - Cheltenham
Strensham, Upper	*Worcester* - Cheltenham
Stretcholt	*Somerset* - Bridgwater
Strete	*Devon* - Kingsbridge
Stretford	*Hereford* - Leominster
Stretford	*Lancaster* - Salford
Strethall	*Essex* - Bishop's Stortford
Stretham	*Cambridge* - Ely
Stretham Ferry	*Cambridge* - Ely
Strettington	*Sussex* - Chichester
Stretton	*Cheshire* - Chester
Stretton	*Cheshire* - Warrington
Stretton	*Derby* - Alfreton
Stretton	*Rutland* - Melton Mowbray
Stretton	*Stafford* - Burton-upon-Trent
Stretton	*Stafford* - Wolverhampton
Stretton Baskerville	*Warwick* - Nuneaton
Stretton-en-le-Field	*Leicester* - Ashby-de-la-Zouch
Stretton Grandison	*Hereford* - Hereford
Stretton, Great	*Leicester* - Leicester
Stretton, Little	*Leicester* - Leicester
Stretton, Little	*Salop* - Ludlow
Stretton-on-the-Fosse	*Warwick* - Stratford on Avon
Stretton Sugwas	*Hereford* - Hereford
Stretton-under-Fosse	*Warwick* - Rugby
Stretton-upon-Dunsmore	*Warwick* - Rugby
Strickland, Great	*Westmorland* - Penrith
Strickland, Little	*Westmorland* - Penrith
Strines	*Cheshire* - Stockport
Strinesdale	*Lancaster* - Oldham
Stringston	*Somerset* - Minehead
Stroat	*Gloucester* - Chepstow

Strode	*Somerset* - Bristol
Strode, Higher	*Devon* - Plymouth
Strode, Lower	*Devon* - Plymouth
Strongford	*Stafford* - Stoke-on-Trent
Strongstry	*Lancaster* - Bury
Strood	*Kent* - Rochester
Strood Green	*Surrey* - Dorking
Strood Green	*Sussex* - Chichester
Stroud	*Gloucester* - Stroud
Stroud	*Hants* - Petersfield
Strouden	*Hants* - Bournemouth
Stroude	*Surrey* - Slough
Strouden Park	*Hants* - Bournemouth
Stroud Green	*London, N.4* - Clerkenwell
Stroudwood (Upham)	*Hants* - Winchester
Stroxton	*Lincoln* - Grantham
Strubby	*Lincoln* - Lincoln
Strubby	*Lincoln* - Louth
Strumpshaw	*Norfolk* - Norwich
Stubber's Green	*Stafford* - Walsall
Stubbin	*York, W.R.* - Rotherham
Stubbings	*Berks* - High Wycombe
Stubbington	*Hants* - Portsmouth
Stubbins	*Lancaster* - Bury
Stubbs Cross	*Kent* - Ashford
Stubhampton	*Dorset* - Wimborne Minster
Stubshaw Cross	*Lancaster* - Wigan
Stubton	*Lincoln* - Newark
Stubwood	*Stafford* - Uttoxeter
Stuckton	*Hants* - Bournemouth
Studdle	*Kent* - Deal
Studdon	*Northumberland* - Hexham
Studfold	*York, W.R.* - Skipton
Studham	*Beds* - Luton
Studholme	*Cumberland* - Carlisle
Studland	*Dorset* - Swanage
Studley	*Bucks* - Oxford
Studley	*Warwick* - Redditch
Studley	*Wilts* - Chippenham
Studley, Lower	*Wilts* - Trowbridge
Studley Roger	*York, W.R.* - Harrogate
Studley Royal	*York, W.R.* - Harrogate
Studley, Upper	*Wilts* - Trowbridge
Stuffynwood	*Derby* - Mansfield
Stukeley, Great	*Hunts* - Huntingdon
Stukeley, Little	*Hunts* - Huntingdon
Stump Cross (Morley)	*York, W.R.* - Dewsbury
Stump Cross	*York, W.R.* - Halifax
Stuntney	*Cambridge* - Ely
Stunt's Green	*Sussex* - Eastbourne
Sturbridge	*Stafford* - Stafford
Sturgate	*Lincoln* - Gainsborough
Sturmer	*Suffolk* - Sudbury
Sturminster Marshall	*Dorset* - Wimborne Minster
Sturminster Newton	*Dorset* - Shaftesbury
Sturry	*Kent* - Canterbury
Sturston	*Derby* - Derby
Sturt Green	*Berks* - Slough
Sturton by Scawby	*Lincoln* - Scunthorpe
Sturton-by-Stow	*Lincoln* - Gainsborough
Sturton Grange	*Northumberland* - Alnwick
Sturton Grange	*York, W.R.* - Leeds
Sturton, Great	*Lincoln* - Lincoln
Sturton-le-Steeple	*Notts* - East Retford
Stuston	*Suffolk* - Norwich
Stutton	*Suffolk* - Ipswich
Stutton	*York, W.R.* - Leeds
Stutton Grove	*York, W.R.* - Leeds
Styal	*Cheshire* - Macclesfield
Stychbrook	*Stafford* - Lichfield
Styche	*Salop* - Market Drayton
Stydd	*Derby* - Derby
Styford	*Northumberland* - Hexham
Styrrup	*Notts* - Worksop
Styvechale	*Warwick* - Coventry
Subberthwaite	*Lancaster* - Barrow-in-Furness
Success	*Durham* - Durham
Success Row	*Durham* - Durham
Suckley	*Worcester* - Worcester
Sudborough	*Northampton* - Kettering

Sudbourne	*Suffolk* - Woodbridge
Sudbrook	*Monmouth* - Chepstow
Sudbrooke	*Lincoln* - Grantham
Sudbrooke	*Lincoln* - Lincoln
Sudbury	*Derby* - Uttoxeter
Sudbury	*Middlesex* - Willesden
Sudbury	*Suffolk* - Sudbury
Sudbury Heights	*Middlesex* - Willesden
Sudbury Hill	*Middlesex* - Willesden
Sudden	*Lancaster* - Rochdale
Sudehill	*York, W.R.* - Huddersfield
Sudeley	*Gloucester* - Cheltenham
Sudgrove	*Gloucester* - Stroud
Suffield	*Norfolk* - Norwich
Suffield	*York, N.R.* - Scarborough
Suffield cum Everley	*York, N.R.* - Scarborough
Suffield Hatch	*Essex* - Harlow
Sugdon	*Salop* - Wellington (Salop)
Sugley	*Northumberland* - Newcastle upon Tyne
Sugnall, Great	*Stafford* - Stafford
Sugnall, Little	*Stafford* - Stafford
Sugnall Magna	*Stafford* - Stafford
Sugnall Parva	*Stafford* - Stafford
Sulby	*Northampton* - Northampton
Sulehay, Old	*Northampton* - Peterborough
Sulgrave	*Northampton* - Banbury
Sulham	*Berks* - Reading
Sulhampstead Abbots	*Berks* - Reading
Sulhampstead Bannister	*Berks* - Reading
Sullington	*Sussex* - Worthing
Sully	*Glamorgan* - Barry
Summerbridge	*York, W.R.* - Harrogate
Summercourt	*Cornwall* - Truro
Summerfield	*Norfolk* - King's Lynn
Summerfield	*Worcester* - Kidderminster
Summerhill	*Denbigh* - Wrexham
Summer Hill	*Stafford* - Dudley
Summer Hill	*Warwick* - Stratford on Avon
Summerhouse	*Durham* - Darlington
Summers	*Sussex* - Horsham
Summersdale	*Sussex* - Chichester
Summerseat	*Lancaster* - Bury
Summerstown	*London, S.W.17* - Wandsworth
Sun Bank	*Denbigh* - Wrexham
Sunbury	*Middlesex* - Kingston-upon-Thames
Sunday's Hill	*Gloucester* - Thornbury
Sunderland	*Cumberland* - Workington
Sunderland	*Durham* - Sunderland
Sunderland	*Norfolk* - King's Lynn
Sunderland Bridge	*Durham* - Durham
Sunderland Point	*Lancaster* - Lancaster
Sunderlandwick	*York, E.R.* - Beverley
Sundon, Lower	*Beds* - Luton
Sundon, Upper	*Beds* - Luton
Sundridge	*Kent* - Sevenoaks
Sunk Island	*York, E.R.* - Kingston-upon-Hull
Sunningdale	*Berks* - Slough
Sunninghill	*Berks* - Slough
Sunningwell	*Berks* - Oxford
Sunniside	*Durham* - Durham
Sunniside	*Durham* - Gateshead
Sunniside, New	*Durham* - Bishop Auckland
Sunniside, Old	*Durham* - Bishop Auckland
Sunny Bank	*Lancaster* - Barrow-in-Furness
Sunny Brow	*Durham* - Bishop Auckland
Sunnyside	*York, W.R.* - Rotherham
Surbiton	*Surrey* - Kingston-upon-Thames
Surfeit Hill	*Stafford* - Dudley
Surfleet	*Lincoln* - Spalding
Surfleet Marsh	*Lincoln* - Spalding
Surlingham	*Norfolk* - Norwich
Susan's Hill	*Kent* - Cranbrook
Suspension Bridge	*Cambridge* - Ely
Sustead	*Norfolk* - Norwich
Susworth	*Lincoln* - Gainsborough
Sutcombe	*Devon* - Bideford
Suton	*Norfolk* - Norwich
Sutterby	*Lincoln* - Skegness

SUT

Sutterton	*Lincoln* - Boston
Sutterton Dowdyke	*Lincoln* - Boston
Sutterton Fen	*Lincoln* - Boston
Sutterton Roman Bank	*Lincoln* - Boston
Sutton	*Beds* - Biggleswade
Sutton	*Bucks* - Uxbridge
Sutton	*Cambridge* - Ely
Sutton	*Cheshire* - Macclesfield
Sutton	*Essex* - Southend
Sutton	*Hereford* - Hereford
Sutton	*Kent* - Deal
Sutton	*Lancaster* - St. Helens
Sutton	*Norfolk* - Great Yarmouth
Sutton	*Northampton* - Peterborough
Sutton (Granby)	*Notts* - Nottingham
Sutton	*Oxford* - Witney
Sutton	*Pembroke* - Haverfordwest
Sutton	*Salop* - Bridgnorth
Sutton	*Salop* - Shrewsbury
Sutton	*Somerset* - Wells
Sutton	*Stafford* - Wellington (Salop)
Sutton	*Suffolk* - Woodbridge
Sutton	*Surrey* - Epsom
Sutton	*Sussex* - Chichester
Sutton	*Warwick* - Stratford on Avon
Sutton	*Worcester* - Ludlow
Sutton	*York, E.R.* - Kingston-upon-Hull
Sutton	*York, E.R.* - York
Sutton (Masham)	*York, N.R.* - Harrogate
Sutton	*York, W.R.* - Doncaster
Sutton	*York, W.R.* - Keighley
Sutton	*York, W.R.* - Pontefract
Sutton America	*Cambridge* - Ely
Sutton-at-Hone	*Kent* - Dartford
Sutton Bassett	*Northampton* - Corby
Sutton Benger	*Wilts* - Chippenham
Sutton Bingham	*Somerset* - Yeovil
Sutton Bonington	*Notts* - Loughborough
Sutton Bridge	*Lincoln* - Spalding
Sutton Cheney	*Leicester* - Hinckley
Sutton Coldfield	*Warwick* - Birmingham
Sutton Courtney	*Berks* - Didcot
Sutton Crosses	*Lincoln* - Spalding
Sutton-cum-Duckmanton	*Derby* - Chesterfield
Sutton-cum-Lound	*Notts* - East Retford
Sutton, East	*Kent* - Maidstone
Sutton, Fen, Long	*Lincoln* - Spalding
Sutton Gault	*Cambridge* - Ely
Sutton Grange	*York, W.R.* - Harrogate
Sutton, Great	*Cheshire* - Ellesmere Port
Sutton Green (Woking)	*Surrey* - Guildford
Sutton, Heath	*Lancaster* - St. Helens
Sutton, Higher	*Cheshire* - Macclesfield
Sutton Hill	*Salop* - Wellington (Salop)
Sutton Howgrave	*York, W.R.* - Harrogate
Sutton-in-Ashfield	*Notts* - Mansfield
Sutton in the Elms	*Leicester* - Hinckley
Sutton Junction	*Notts* - Mansfield
Sutton Leach	*Lancaster* - St. Helens
Sutton, Little	*Cheshire* - Ellesmere Port
Sutton, Little	*Lincoln* - Spalding
Sutton, Little	*Warwick* - Birmingham
Sutton, Long	*Hants* - Aldershot and Farnham
Sutton, Long	*Lincoln* - Spalding
Sutton, Long	*Somerset* - Yeovil
Sutton Maddock	*Salop* - Bridgnorth
Sutton Mallet	*Somerset* - Bridgwater
Sutton Mandeville	*Wilts* - Shaftesbury
Sutton Manor	*Lancaster* - St. Helens
Sutton Marsh, Long	*Lincoln* - Spalding
Sutton Medlands	*Cambridge* - Ely
Sutton Montis	*Somerset* - Yeovil
Sutton Oak	*Lancaster* - St. Helens
Sutton-on-Sea	*Lincoln* - Louth
Sutton-on-the-Forest	*York, N.R.* - York
Sutton-on-the Hill	*Derby* - Derby
Sutton Poyntz	*Dorset* - Weymouth
Sutton St. Edmunds	*Lincoln* - Spalding
Sutton St. James	*Lincoln* - Spalding

SUT - SWE

Sutton St. Mary	*Lincoln* - Spalding
Sutton St. Michael	*Hereford* - Hereford
Sutton St. Nicholas	*Hereford* - Hereford
Sutton Scarsdale	*Derby* - Chesterfield
Sutton Scotney	*Hants* - Winchester
Sutton Spring Woods	*Derby* - Chesterfield
Sutton under Brailes	*Warwick* - Banbury
Sutton-under-Whitestone Cliffe	*York, N.R.* - Northallerton
Sutton-upon-Derwent	*York, E.R.* - York
Sutton upon Tern	*Salop* - Market Drayton
Sutton-upon-Trent	*Notts* - Newark
Sutton Valence	*Kent* - Maidstone
Sutton Veney	*Wilts* - Warminster
Sutton Waldron	*Dorset* - Shaftesbury
Sutton Weaver	*Cheshire* - Runcorn
Sutton Wick	*Berks* - Oxford
Swaby	*Lincoln* - Louth
Swadlincote	*Derby* - Burton-upon-Trent
Swaffham	*Norfolk* - King's Lynn
Swaffham Bulbeck	*Cambridge* - Newmarket
Swaffham Prior	*Cambridge* - Newmarket
Swafield	*Norfolk* - Norwich
Swainby	*York, N.R.* - Northallerton
Swainshill	*Hereford* - Hereford
Swainsley	*Derby* - Derby
Swainsthorpe	*Norfolk* - Norwich
Swainswick, Lower	*Somerset* - Bath
Swainswick, Upper	*Somerset* - Bath
Swaithe	*York, W.R.* - Barnsley
Swalcliffe	*Oxford* - Banbury
Swalecliffe	*Kent* - Canterbury
Swallow	*Lincoln* - Great Grimsby
Swallowcliffe	*Wilts* - Shaftesbury
Swallowfield	*Berks* - Reading
Swallownest	*York, W.R.* - Rotherham
Swallows Cross	*Essex* - Brentwood
Swalwell	*Durham* - Gateshead
Swanage	*Dorset* - Swanage
Swan Bottom	*Bucks* - Aylesbury
Swanbourne	*Bucks* - Aylesbury
Swanbridge	*Glamorgan* - Barry
Swancote	*Salop* - Bridgnorth
Swanland	*York, E.R.* - Kingston-upon-Hull
Swanley	*Kent* - Dartford
Swanley Village	*Kent* - Dartford
Swanmoor	*Gloucester* - Thornbury
Swanmore	*Hants* - Winchester
Swannaton	*Devon* - Kingsbridge
Swannington	*Leicester* - Ashby-de-la-Zouch
Swannington	*Norfolk* - Norwich
Swan, Old	*Lancaster* - Liverpool
Swanpool	*Cornwall* - Truro
Swanscombe	*Kent* - Gravesend
Swansea	*Glamorgan* - Swansea
Swansmoor	*Stafford* - Stafford
Swanton Abbott	*Norfolk* - Norwich
Swanton Morley	*Norfolk* - East Dereham
Swanton Novers	*Norfolk* - King's Lynn
Swanvale	*Cornwall* - Truro
Swan Village	*Stafford* - West Bromwich
Swan Village	*Warwick* - Tamworth
Swanwick	*Derby* - Alfreton
Swanwick	*Hants* - Portsmouth
Swarby	*Lincoln* - Sleaford
Swardeston	*Norfolk* - Norwich
Swarkestone	*Derby* - Derby
Swarland	*Northumberland* - Alnwick
Swarraton	*Hants* - Winchester
Swartha	*York, W.R.* - Skipton
Swarthmoor	*Lancaster* - Barrow-in-Furness
Swathwick	*Derby* - Dartford
Swaton	*Lincoln* - Sleaford
Swaton Fen	*Lincoln* - Sleaford
Swavesey	*Cambridge* - Huntingdon
Sway	*Hants* - Lymington
Swayfield	*Lincs* - Grantham
Swaythling	*Hants* - Southampton
Swaythorpe	*York, E.R.* - Beverley
Sweeney	*Salop* - Oswestry

Sweet Apple Tree	*Salop* - Market Drayton
Sweet Hill	*Sussex* - Brighton
Sweethope	*Northumberland* - Hexham
Sweets House	*Cornwall* - Bodmin
Swefling	*Suffolk* - Woodbridge
Swell	*Somerset* - Taunton
Swelling Hill	*Hants* - Winchester
Swell, Lower	*Gloucester* - Cheltenham
Swell, Upper	*Gloucester* - Cheltenham
Swepstone	*Leicester* - Ashby-de-la-Zouch
Swerford	*Oxford* - Banbury
Swettenham	*Cheshire* - Congleton
Swift's Green	*Kent* - Ashford
Swilland	*Suffolk* - Ipswich
Swillett, The	*Herts* - Watford
Swillington	*York, W.R.* - Leeds
Swillington Common	*York, W.R.* - Leeds
Swimbridge	*Devon* - Barnstaple
Swinbrook	*Oxford* - Witney
Swinburne, Great	*Northumberland* - Hexham
Swincliffe	*York, W.R.* - Harrogate
Swindale	*Westmorland* - Penrith
Swinden	*York, W.R.* - Skipton
Swinderby	*Lincoln* - Newark
Swindon	*Stafford* - Wolverhampton
Swindon	*Wilts* - Swindon
Swindon Village	*Gloucester* - Cheltenham
Swine	*York, E.R.* - Kingston-upon-Hull
Swinefleet	*York, W.R.* - Goole
Swineford	*Gloucester* - Bath
Swineshead	*Beds* - Beford
Swineshead	*Lincoln* - Boston
Swineshead	*Worcester* - Worcester
Swineshead Chapel Hill	*Lincoln* - Boston
Swineshead Fen	*Lincoln* - Boston
Swinethorpe	*Lincoln* - Lincoln
Swinfen	*Stafford* - Lichfield
Swinford	*Berks* - Oxford
Swingate	*Kent* - Dover
Swingfield	*Kent* - Folkestone
Swinhoe	*Northumberland* - Alnwick
Swinhope	*Lincoln* - Louth
Swinhope	*Northumberland* - Hexham
Swinley	*Lancaster* - Wigan
Swinley Green	*Gloucester* - Cheltenham
Swinley Woods	*Berks* - Slough
Swinmore	*Hereford* - Hereford
Swinnow Moor	*York, W.R.* - Leeds
Swinscoe	*Stafford* - Leek
Swinscoe Common	*Stafford* - Uttoxeter
Swinsford	*Gloucester* - Bath
Swinside	*Cumberland* - Workington
Swinstead	*Lincoln* - Grantham
Swinsty	*Cumberland* - Carlisle
Swinsty	*York, W.R.* - Otley
Swinthorpe	*Lincoln* - Lincoln
Swinton	*Lancaster* - Salford
Swinton	*York, W.R.* - Rotherham
Swinton-with-Wathermarske	*York, N.R.* - Harrogate
Swiss Cottage	*London, N.W.3* - Bloomsbury and Marylebone
Swithland	*Leicester* - Leicester
Swyddffynnon	*Cardigan* - Lampeter
Swyncombe	*Oxford* - Reading
Swynnerton	*Stafford* - Stoke-on-Trent
Swyre	*Dorset* - Dorchester
Swythamley	*Stafford* - Leek
Sycharth	*Denbigh* - Oswestry
Sychtyn	*Salop* - Oswestry
Syde	*Gloucester* - Cheltenham
Sydenham (part)	*London, S.E.26* - Bromley
Sydenham (part)	*London, S.E.26* - Lambeth
Sydenham	*Oxford* - Thame
Sydenham Damerell	*Devon* - Plymouth
Sydenham, Lower (part)	*London, S.E.26* - Bromley
Sydenham, Lower (part)	*London, S.E.26* - Lambeth
Sydenham, Upper	*London, S.E.26* - Lambeth
Syderstone	*Norfolk* - King's Lynn
Sydling St. Nicholas	*Dorset* - Dorchester

Sydmonton	*Hants* - Newbury
Sydnal, The	*Salop* - Market Drayton
Sydnope	*Derby* - Matlock
Syerscote	*Stafford* - Tamworth
Syerston	*Notts* - Newark
Syke	*Lancaster* - Rochdale
Sykehouse	*Lancaster* - Barrow-in-Furness
Sykehouse	*York, W.R.* - Thorne
Syleham	*Suffolk* - Halesworth
Symondsbury	*Dorset* - Dorchester
Symonds Green	*Herts* - Hitchin
Symonds Yat	*Hereford* - Monmouth
Synod Inn	*Cardigan* - Aberystwyth
Synwell	*Gloucester* - Stroud
Syresham	*Northampton* - Banbury
Sysonby	*Leicester* - Melton Mowbray
Syston	*Leicester* - Leicester
Syston	*Lincoln* - Grantham
Sytchampton	*Worcester* - Worcester
Sytch Lane	*Salop* - Wellington (Salop)
Sytch, The	*Salop* - Shrewsbury
Sywell	*Northampton* - Wellingborough

T

Tabley Inferior	*Cheshire* - Northwich
Tabley Superior	*Cheshire* - Altrincham
Tachbrook Mallory	*Warwick* - Warwick
Tackley	*Oxford* - Oxford
Tacolnestone	*Norfolk* - Norwich
Tadcaster	*York, W.R.* - York
Taddington	*Derby* - Buxton
Tadhill	*Somerset* - Frome
Tadley	*Hants* - Basingstoke
Tadlow	*Cambridge* - Biggleswade
Tadmarton	*Oxford* - Banbury
Tadwick	*Somerset* - Bath
Tadworth	*Surrey* - Dorking
Taff's Well	*Glamorgan* - Caerphilly
Tafolog	*Montgomery* - Machynlleth
Tagdale	*Stafford* - Market Drayton
Taibach (Pentrebach)	*Glamorgan* - Merthyr Tydfil
Taibach	*Glamorgan* - Neath
Tairgwaith	*Glamorgan* - Ammanford
Takeley Street	*Essex* - Bishop's Stortford
Talachddu	*Brecon* - Brecknock
Talacre	*Flint* - Holywell
Talaton	*Devon* - Exeter
Talbenny	*Pembroke* - Haverfordwest
Talbot Green	*Glamorgan* - Pontypridd
Talbot Village	*Hants* - Bournemouth
Tale, Higher	*Devon* - Exeter
Tale, Lower	*Devon* - Exeter
Talerddig	*Montgomery* - Machynlleth
Talewater	*Devon* - Exeter
Talgarreg	*Cardigan* - Cardigan
Talgarth	*Brecon* - Brecknock
Talgarth (Cynghordy)	*Carmarthen* - Llandovery
Talgarth Hall	*Merioneth* - Machynlleth
Taliaris	*Carmarthen* - Ammanford
Taliesin	*Cardigan* - Aberystwyth
Talke	*Stafford* - Stoke-on-Trent
Talke Pitts	*Stafford* - Stoke-on-Trent
Talkin	*Cumberland* - Carlisle
Talkin Head	*Cumberland* - Carlisle
Talland	*Cornwall* - Liskeard
Tallarn Green	*Flint* - Whitchurch
Tallentire	*Cumberland* - Workington
Talley	*Carmarthen* - Ammanford
Tallington	*Lincoln* - Stamford
Tally Ho	*Gloucester* - Cheltenham
Talog	*Carmarthen* - Carmarthen
Talsarn	*Cardigan* - Lampeter
Talsarnau	*Merioneth* - Portmadoc

TAL - TAR

Talton	*Warwick* - Stratford on Avon
Talwrn	*Anglesey* - Llangefni
Talybont	*Cardigan* - Aberystwyth
Talybont	*Caernarvon* - Bangor
Talybont-Dolgarrog	*Caernarvon* - Conway
Talybont-on-Usk	*Brecon* - Brecknock
Taly-cafn	*Caernarvon* - Conway
Talycafn	*Denbigh* - Conway
Talyllyn	*Merioneth* - Dolgellau
Talysarn	*Caernarvon* - Caernarvon
Talywain	*Monmouth* - Pontypool and Abergavenny
Talywern	*Montgomery* - Machynlleth
Tame Bridge	*Stafford* - West Bromwich
Tame, Old	*York, W.R.* - Oldham
Tamerton Folliott	*Devon* - Plymouth
Tamerton, North	*Cornwall* - Launceston
Tamworth	*Stafford* - Tamworth
Tandridge	*Surrey* - Reigate
Tanerdy	*Carmarthen* - Carmarthen
Tanfield	*Durham* - Consett
Tanfield, East	*York, N.R.* - Harrogate
Tanfield Lea	*Durham* - Consett
Tanfield, West	*York, N.R.* - Harrogate
Tangier	*Hants* - Basingstoke
Tangiers	*Pembroke* - Haverfordwest
Tangley	*Hants* - Andover
Tangmere	*Sussex* - Chichester
Tan Hills	*Durham* - Durham
Tanhouse	*Lancaster* - Wigan
Tankersley	*York, W.R.* - Barnsley
Tankerton	*Kent* - Canterbury
Tan Lan	*Flint* - Holywell
Tanner's Green	*Worcester* - Birmingham
Tannington	*Suffolk* - Halesworth
Tansey Green	*Stafford* - Stourbridge
Tanshelf	*York, W.R.* - Pontefract
Tansley	*Derby* - Matlock
Tansley Moor	*Derby* - Matlock
Tansor	*Northampton* - Peterborough
Tansterne	*York, E.R.* - Kingston-upon-Hull
Tantany Estate	*Stafford* - West Bromwich
Tantobie	*Durham* - Consett
Tanwood	*Worcester* - Kidderminster
Tanworth in Arden	*Warwick* - Birmingham
Tan-y-Bwlch	*Merioneth* - Portmadoc
Tanyfron	*Denbigh* - Wrexham
Tanygrisian	*Merioneth* - Portmadoc
Tanygroes	*Cardigan* - Cardigan
Tanymaes	*Caernarvon* - Caernarvon
Taphouse, East	*Cornwall* - Liskeard
Taphouse, West	*Cornwall* - Liskeard
Taplow	*Bucks* - Slough
Taplow Common	*Bucks* - Slough
Tapton	*Derby* - Chesterfield
Tarbock	*Lancaster* - St. Helens
Tardebigg	*Worcester* - Redditch
Tardy Gate	*Lancaster* - Preston
Tarleton	*Lancaster* - Southport
Tarlton	*Gloucester* - Stroud
Tarnacre	*Lancaster* - Preston
Tarn Flat	*Lancaster* - Barrow-in-Furness
Tarnock	*Somerset* - Weston Super Mare
Tarnrigg Moor	*Cumberland* - Carlisle
Tarns	*Cumberland* - Carlisle
Tarporley	*Cheshire* - Crewe
Tarraby	*Cumberland* - Carlisle
Tarrant Crawford	*Dorset* - Wimborne Minster
Tarrant Gunville	*Dorset* - Wimborne Minster
Tarrant Hinton	*Dorset* - Wimborne Minster
Tarrant Keynstone	*Dorset* - Wimborne Minster
Tarrant Launceston	*Dorset* - Wimborne Minster
Tarrant Monkton	*Dorset* - Wimborne Minster
Tarrant Rawston	*Dorset* - Wimborne Minster
Tarrant Rushton	*Dorset* - Wimborne Minster
Tarretburn	*Northumberland* - Hexham
Tarrington	*Hereford* - Hereford
Tarring, West	*Sussex* - Worthing
Tarset	*Northumberland* - Hexham
Tarvin	*Cheshire* - Chester

TAS - TEM

Tasburgh	*Norfolk* - Norwich
Tasley	*Salop* - Bridgnorth
Taston	*Oxford* - Banbury
Tat Bank	*Stafford* - West Bromwich
Tatchbury	*Hants* - Southampton
Tatenhill	*Stafford* - Burton-upon-Trent
Tatham	*Lancaster* - Lancaster
Tathwell	*Lincoln* - Louth
Tatsfield	*Kent* - Bromley
Tatsfield	*Surrey* - Reigate
Tattenhall	*Cheshire* - Chester
Tattenhoe	*Bucks* - Bletchley and Leighton Buzzard
Tatterford	*Norfolk* - King's Lynn
Tattersett	*Norfolk* - King's Lynn
Tattershall	*Lincoln* - Boston
Tattershall Bridge	*Lincoln* - Sleaford
Tattershall Thorpe	*Lincoln* - Boston
Tattingstone	*Suffolk* - Ipswich
Tatton	*Cheshire* - Altrincham
Tatworth	*Somerset* - Axminster and Chard
Taunton	*Lancaster* - Ashton-under-Lyne
Taunton	*Somerset* - Taunton
Tavarnaubach	*Monmouth* - Blackwood
Tavaton	*Devon* - Tavistock
Taverham	*Norfolk* - Norwich
Tavernspite	*Pembroke* - Haverfordwest
Tavistock	*Devon* - Plymouth
Tawd Bridge	*Lancaster* - Wigan
Tawney Common	*Essex* - Harlow
Tawstock	*Devon* - Barnstaple
Tawton, North	*Devon* - Okehampton
Tawton, South	*Devon* - Okehampton
Taxal	*Derby* - Buxton
Taylor Burn	*Northumberland* - Hexham
Taynton	*Oxford* - Witney
Tea Green	*Herts* - Hitchin
Teagues Bridge	*Salop* - Wellington (Salop)
Tealby	*Lincoln* - Lincoln
Tealby Thorpe	*Lincoln* - Lincoln
Team Colliery	*Durham* - Gateshead
Tean	*Stafford* - Uttoxeter
Teanford (part)	*Stafford* - Stoke-on-Trent
Teanford (part)	*Stafford* - Uttoxeter
Tean, Lower	*Stafford* - Uttoxeter
Tearnside	*Westmorland* - Kendal
Tebay	*Westmorland* - Penrith
Tebay, Old	*Westmorland* - Penrith
Tebworth	*Beds* - Luton
Tedburn St. Mary	*Devon* - Exeter
Teddesley	*Stafford* - Stafford
Teddesley Hay	*Stafford* - Stafford
Teddington	*Middlesex* - Kingston-upon-Thames
Teddington	*Worcester* - Cheltenham
Tedfold	*Sussex* - Horsham
Tedham Green	*Northumberland* - Hexham
Tedney	*Hereford* - Worcester
Tedsmore	*Salop* - Oswestry
Tedstone Delamere	*Hereford* - Worcester
Tedstone Wafer	*Hereford* - Worcester
Tees Port	*York, N.R.* - Middlesbrough
Teeton	*Northampton* - Northampton
Teffont Evias	*Wilts* - Shaftesbury
Teffont Magna	*Wilts* - Shaftesbury
Teffont, West	*Wilts* - Shaftesbury
Tegryn	*Pembroke* - Cardigan
Tehidy	*Cornwall* - Redruth
Teigh	*Rutland* - Melton Mowbray
Teignmouth	*Devon* - Newton Abbot
Teirtref	*Montgomery* - Oswestry
Telford	*Salop* - Wellington (Salop)
Tellisford	*Somerset* - Frome
Telscombe	*Sussex* - Lewes
Telscombe Cliffs	*Sussex* - Brighton
Templand	*Lancaster* - Barrow-in-Furness
Temple	*Cornwall* - Bodmin
Temple	*Wilts* - Swindon
Temple Balsall	*Warwick* - Coventry
Temple Bar	*Cardigan* - Lampeter

TEM - THA

Temple Bar	*Sussex* - Chichester
Templeborough	*York, W.R.* - Rotherham
Temple Bruer	*Lincoln* - Sleaford
Temple Cloud	*Somerset* - Bristol
Templecombe	*Somerset* - Yeovil
Temple Ewell	*Kent* - Dover
Temple Fortune	*London, N.W.11* - Willesden
Temple Grange	*Lincoln* - Sleaford
Temple Grafton	*Warwick* - Stratford on Avon
Temple Guiting	*Gloucester* - Cheltenham
Temple Hall	*Leicester* - Hinckley
Temple High Grange	*Lincoln* - Sleaford
Temple Hirst	*York, W.R.* - Pontefract
Temple Newsam	*York, W.R.* - Leeds
Temple Normanton	*Derby* - Chesterfield
Temple Sowerby	*Westmorland* - Penrith
Temple, The (part)	*London, W.C.2* - Westminster
Templeton	*Devon* - Tiverton
Templeton	*Pembroke* - Haverfordwest
Templetown	*Durham* - Consett
Tempsford	*Beds* - Biggleswade
Ten Acres	*Warwick* - Birmingham
Tenbury	*Worcester* - Ludlow
Tenby	*Pembroke* - Haverfordwest
Tenby St. Mary in Liberty	*Pembroke* - Haverfordwest
Tenby St. Mary out Liberty	*Pembroke* - Haverfordwest
Tencrofts	*Bucks* - High Wycombe
Tendring	*Essex* - Harwich
Tendring Green	*Essex* - Harwich
Tendring Heath	*Essex* - Harwich
Ten Mile Bank (Hilgay)	*Norfolk* - King's Lynn
Tenterden	*Kent* - Cranbrook
Terling	*Essex* - Chelmsford
Tern	*Salop* - Wellington (Salop)
Ternhill	*Salop* - Market Drayton
Terras	*Cornwall* - St. Austell
Terrick	*Bucks* - Aylesbury
Terriers	*Bucks* - High Wycombe
Terrington	*York, N.R.* - Malton
Terrington St. Clement	*Norfolk* - King's Lynn
Terrington St. John	*Norfolk* - King's Lynn
Terry Lug	*York, W.R.* - Leeds
Terwick	*Sussex* - Petersfield
Testcombe Bridge	*Hants* - Andover
Testerton	*Norfolk* - Fakenham
Teston	*Kent* - Maidstone
Testwood	*Hants* - Southampton
Tetbury	*Gloucester* - Malmesbury
Tetbury Upton	*Gloucester* - Malmesbury
Tetchill	*Salop* - Oswestry
Tetcott	*Devon* - Launceston
Tetford	*Lincoln* - Skegness
Tetney	*Lincoln* - Great Grimsby
Tetney Lock	*Lincoln* - Great Grimsby
Tetsworth	*Oxford* - Thame
Tettenhall	*Stafford* - Wolverhampton
Tettenhall Wood	*Stafford* - Wolverhampton
Tetton	*Cheshire* - Crewe
Tetworth	*Hunts* - Biggleswade
Teversal	*Notts* - Mansfield
Teversham	*Cambridge* - Cambridge
Tew, Great	*Oxford* - Banbury
Tewin	*Herts* - Hertford
Tewkesbury	*Gloucester* - Cheltenham
Tewkesbury Park	*Gloucester* - Cheltenham
Tew, Little	*Oxford* - Banbury
Teynham	*Kent* - Sittingbourne
Thackley	*York, W.R.* - Bradford
Thackthwaite	*Cumberland* - Penrith
Thackthwaite	*Cumberland* - Workington
Thakeham	*Sussex* - Chichester
Thame	*Oxford* - Thame
Thame Park	*Oxford* - Thame
Thames Ditton	*Surrey* - Kingston-upon-Thames
Thames Haven	*Essex* - Grays Thurrock
Thanington	*Kent* - Canterbury
Tharston	*Norfolk* - Norwich
Thatcham	*Berks* - Newbury

THA - THE

Thatto Heath	*Lancaster* - St. Helens
Thaxted	*Essex* - Braintree
Thealby	*Lincoln* - Scunthorpe
Theale	*Berks* - Reading
Theale	*Somerset* - Wells
Thearne	*York, E.R.* - Beverley
The Asps	*Warwick* - Warwick
The Bache	*Salop* - Ludlow
Theberton	*Suffolk* - Woodbridge
The Blabbs	*Warwick* - Birmingham
The Bog	*Salop* - Shrewsbury
The Brand	*Salop* - Market Drayton
The Crippetts	*Gloucester* - Cheltenham
The Crooks	*Northumberland* - Hexham
Thedden	*Hants* - Aldershot and Farnham
Theddingworth	*Leicester* - Rugby
Theddlethorpe All Saints	*Lincoln* - Louth
Theddlethorpe St. Helen	*Lincoln* - Louth
The Down	*Salop* - Bridgnorth
The Draethen	*Monmouth* - Newport (Mon.)
Theescombe	*Gloucester* - Stroud
The Freight	*Kent* - Cranbrook
The Gore	*Kent* - Cranbrook
The Grange	*Kent* - Cranbrook
The Green	*Cumberland* - Whitehaven
The Green, St. Martin-in-Meneage	*Cornwall* - Penzance
The Grove	*Durham* - Bishop Auckland
The Grove	*Durham* - Consett
The Grove	*Worcester* - Cheltenham
The Hackett	*Gloucester* - Thornbury
The Hale	*London, N.W.7* - Willesden
The Haven	*Sussex* - Horsham
The Haw	*Gloucester* - Cheltenham
The Haye	*Salop* - Shrewsbury
The Heath	*Gloucester* - Gloucester
The Holt	*Salop* - Bridgnorth
The Home	*Salop* - Shrewsbury
The Hoo	*Gloucester* - Cheltenham
The Hooks	*Salop* - Market Drayton
The Hope	*Salop* - Ludlow
The Hyde (Hendon)	*London, N.W.9* - Willesden
The Isle	*Salop* - Shrewsbury
The Knapp	*Gloucester* - Thornbury
The Kymin	*Monmouth* - Monmouth
The Lawn	*Worcester* - Cheltenham
Thelbridge	*Devon* - Tiverton
The Leam	*Durham* - Gateshead
The Lees	*Salop* - Wellington (Salop)
The Leigh	*Gloucester* - Cheltenham
The Leys	*Glamorgan* - Bridgend
The Links	*Salop* - Market Drayton
The Lloyd	*Stafford* - Market Drayton
Thelnetham	*Suffolk* - Thetford
Thelveton	*Norfolk* - Norwich
Thelwall	*Cheshire* - Warrington
Themelthorpe	*Norfolk* - King's Lynn
The Moor	*Kent* - Cranbrook
The Morrey	*Salop* - Market Drayton
The Narth	*Monmouth* - Monmouth
Thenford	*Northampton* - Banbury
The Oak	*Salop* - Knighton
The Oaks	*Lancaster* - Bolton
Theobald's Green	*Wilts* - Chippenham
The Old Heath	*Salop* - Shrewsbury
The Plex	*Salop* - Shrewsbury
The Pludds	*Gloucester* - Ross
The Purlieu	*Gloucester* - Gloucester
The Quarter	*Kent* - Cranbrook
The Quell	*Sussex* - Chichester
The Reddings	*Gloucester* - Cheltenham
Therfield	*Herts* - Hitchin
The Race	*Monmouth* - Pontypool and Abergavenny
The Rowe	*Stafford* - Stoke-on-Trent
The Ruffitt	*Gloucester* - Gloucester
The Speech House	*Gloucester* - Monmouth
The Springs	*Salop* - Shrewsbury
The Stenders	*Gloucester* - Gloucester

The Swillett	*Herts* - Watford
The Sydnal	*Salop* - Market Drayton
The Sytch	*Salop* - Shrewsbury
The Tack	*Worcester* - Redditch
Thetford	*Norfolk* - Thetford
Thetford, Little	*Cambridge* - Ely
The Warren	*Salop* - Market Drayton
The Wash	*Herts* - Bishop's Stortford
The Wham	*Durham* - Bishop Auckland
The Wrekin	*Salop* - Wellington (Salop)
Theydon Bois	*Essex* - Harlow
Theydon Garnon	*Essex* - Harlow
Theydon Mount	*Essex* - Harlow
The Yeld	*Cheshire* - Northwich
Thickbroom	*Stafford* - Lichfield
Thickley	*Durham* - Bishop Auckland
Thickley, East	*Durham* - Bishop Auckland
Thickley, West	*Durham* - Bishop Auckland
Thickthorn	*Warwick* - Warwick
Thickwood	*Wilts* - Bath
Thimbleby	*Lincoln* - Lincoln
Thimbleby	*York, N.R.* - Northallerton
Thimbleby Moor	*Lincoln* - Lincoln
Thimble End	*Warwick* - Birmingham
Thinford	*Durham* - Durham
Thingley	*Wilts* - Chippenham
Thingwall	*Cheshire* - Birkenhead
Thirkleby	*York, E.R.* - Malton
Thirkleby	*York, N.R.* - Northallerton
Thirlby	*York, N.R.* - Northallerton
Thirn	*York, N.R.* - Northallerton
Thirsk	*York, N.R.* - Northallerton
Thirston, East	*Northumberland* - Morpeth
Thirston, West	*Northumberland* - Morpeth
Thirston with Shothaugh	*Northumberland* - Morpeth
Thirtleby	*York, E.R.* - Kingston-upon-Hull
Thistleflat Colliery	*Durham* - Bishop Auckland
Thistleton	*Lancaster* - Preston
Thistleton	*Rutland* - Melton Mowbray
Thistlewood	*Cumberland* - Carlisle
Thixendale	*York, E.R.* - Malton
Thockrington	*Northumberland* - Hexham
Tholthorpe	*York, N.R.* - York
Thomas Close	*Cumberland* - Penrith
Thomastown	*Glamorgan* - Pontypridd
Thomley	*Bucks* - Thame
Thompson	*Norfolk* - Thetford
Thompson Hill	*York, W.R.* - Sheffield
Thong	*Kent* - Gravesend
Thonglands	*Salop* - Ludlow
Thongsbridge	*York, W.R.* - Huddersfield
Thong, Upper	*York, W.R.* - Huddersfield
Thonock	*Lincoln* - Gainsborough
Thoralby	*York, N.R.* - Northallerton
Thoresby	*Notts* - Worksop
Thoresby	*York, N.R.* - Northallerton
Thoresby Bridge	*Lincoln* - Louth
Thoresby, North	*Lincoln* - Louth
Thoresby, South	*Lincoln* - Louth
Thoresthorpe	*Lincoln* - Louth
Thoresway	*Lincoln* - Great Grimsby
Thorganby	*Lincoln* - Great Grimsby
Thorganby	*York, E.R.* - York
Thorington	*Essex* - Colchester
Thorington	*Suffolk* - Halesworth
Thorlby	*York, W.R.* - Skipton
Thorley	*Herts* - Bishop's Stortford
Thorley	*I. of W.* - Newport (I.W.)
Thormanby	*York, N.R.* - York
Thorn	*Beds* - Luton
Thornaby on Tees	*York, N.R.* - Stockton on Tees
Thornage	*Norfolk* - Norwich
Thornbank	*Lancaster* - Bolton
Thornborough	*Bucks* - Bletchley and Leighton Buzzard
Thornborough	*Leicester* - Ashby-de-la-Zouch
Thornborough	*York, N.R.* - Harrogate
Thornbrough	*Northumberland* - Hexham
Thornbury	*Devon* - Bideford
Thornbury	*Gloucester* - Thornbury
Thornbury	*Hereford* - Leominster
Thornbury	*York, W.R.* - Bradford
Thornby	*Cumberland* - Carlisle
Thornby	*Northampton* - Northampton
Thorncliffe	*York, W.R.* - Sheffield
Thorn Coffin (Yeovil)	*Somerset* - Yeovil
Thorn Combe	*Dorset* - Axminster and Chard
Thorncombe	*Surrey* - Guildford
Thorncote	*Beds* - Biggleswade
Thorndon	*Suffolk* - Norwich
Thorne	*Kent* - Ramsgate
Thorne	*York, W.R.* - Thorne
Thorner	*York, W.R.* - Leeds
Thornes	*York, W.R.* - Wakefield
Thorness	*I. of W.* - Newport (I.W.)
Thorne St. Margaret	*Somerset* - Taunton
Thorney	*Bucks* - Uxbridge
Thorney	*Cambridge* - Peterborough
Thorney	*Nottingham* - Lincoln
Thorneyburn	*Northumberland* - Hexham
Thorney Close	*Durham* - Sunderland
Thorney Dyke	*Cambridge* - Peterborough
Thorney, East	*Sussex* - Chichester
Thorney Fen	*Cambridge* - Peterborough
Thorney Hill	*Hants* - Bournemouth
Thorney Island	*Sussex* - Chichester
Thorney Pits	*Salop* - Market Drayton
Thorneythwaite	*Cumberland* - Workington
Thorney Toll	*Cambridge* - Wisbech
Thorney, West	*Sussex* - Chichester
Thorn Falcon	*Somerset* - Taunton
Thornford	*Dorset* - Yeovil
Thorngrove	*Somerset* - Bridgwater
Thorngumbald	*York, E.R.* - Kingston-upon-Hull
Thorngumbald Marsh	*York, E.R.* - Kingston-upon-Hull
Thornham (part)	*Lancaster* - Oldham
Thornham (part)	*Lancaster* - Rochdale
Thornham	*Norfolk* - King's Lynn
Thornham Magna	*Suffolk* - Norwich
Thornham Parva	*Suffolk* - Norwich
Thornhaugh	*Huntingdon and Peterborough* - Stamford
Thornhill	*Cumberland* - Whitehaven
Thornhill	*Derby* - Buxton
Thornhill	*Glamorgan* - Cardiff
Thornhill	*Wilts* - Swindon
Thornhill	*York, W.R.* - Dewsbury
Thornhill	*York, W.R.* - Rotherham
Thornhill Edge	*York, W.R.* - Dewsbury
Thornhill Lees	*York, W.R.* - Dewsbury
Thornholme	*York, E.R.* - Bridlington
Thornhope	*Northumberland* - Carlisle
Thornicombe	*Dorset* - Wimborne Minster
Thornley	*Durham* - Durham
Thornley Gate	*Durham* - Bishop Auckland
Thornley Gate	*Northumberland* - Hexham
Thornley, High	*Durham* - Newcastle upon Tyne
Thornley Junction Station	*Durham* - Hartlepool
Thornley, Little (Towlaw)	*Durham* - Bishop Auckland
Thornley-with-Wheatley	*Lancaster* - Preston
Thorn, Little	*Radnor* - Knighton
Thornsett	*Derby* - Buxton
Thornthwaite	*Cumberland* - Workington
Thornthwaite with Padside	*York, W.R.* - Harrogate
Thornton	*Bucks* - Bletchley and Leighton Buzzard
Thornton	*Lancaster* - Blackpool
Thornton, Liverpool 23	*Lancaster* - Liverpool
Thornton	*Leicester* - Ashby-de-la-Zouch
Thornton	*Lincoln* - Lincoln
Thornton	*Pembroke* - Haverfordwest
Thornton	*York, E.R.* - York
Thornton	*York, N.R.* - Malton
Thornton	*York, W.R.* - Bradford
Thornton Bridge	*York, N.R.* - Harrogate
Thornton Cleveleys	*Lancaster* - Blackpool
Thornton Curtis	*Lincoln* - Great Grimsby

Thornton Dale	*York, N.R.* - Malton
Thornton, East	*Northumberland* - Morpeth
Thornton Heath	*Surrey* - Croydon
Thornton Hough	*Cheshire* - Birkenhead
Thornton in Cleveland	*York, N.R.* - Middlesbrough
Thornton-in-Craven	*York, W.R.* - Skipton
Thornton-in-Lonsdale	*York, W.R.* - Lancaster
Thornton-le-Beans	*York, N.R.* - Northallerton
Thornton-le-Clay	*York, N.R.* - Malton
Thornton-le-Fen	*Lincoln* - Boston
Thornton-le-Fylde	*Lancaster* - Blackpool
Thornton-le-Moor	*Lincoln* - Scunthorpe
Thornton-le-Moor	*York, N.R.* - Northallerton
Thornton-le-Moors	*Cheshire* - Chester
Thornton-le-Rust	*York, N.R.* - Northallerton
Thornton-le-Street	*York, N.R.* - Northallerton
Thornton Moor	*Lincoln* - Lincoln
Thornton Steward	*York, N.R.* - Northallerton
Thornton Watlass	*York, N.R.* - Northallerton
Thornton, West	*Northumberland* - Morpeth
Thornville	*York, W.R.* - Harrogate
Thornwood	*Essex* - Harlow
Thoroton	*Notts* - Nottingham
Thorp Arch	*York, W.R.* - Harrogate
Thorp Audlin	*York, W.R.* - Pontefract
Thorp Clough	*Lancaster* - Oldham
Thorpe	*Derby* - Derby
Thorpe	*Lincoln* - Lincoln
Thorpe	*Notts* - Newark
Thorpe	*Surrey* - Slough
Thorpe Constantine	*Warwick* - Tamworth
Thorpe	*York, E.R.* - Goole
Thorpe	*York, N.R.* - Darlington
Thorpe	*York, N.R.* - Whitby
Thorpe	*York, W.R.* - Leeds
Thorpe	*York, W.R.* - Harrogate
Thorpe	*York, W.R.* - Skipton
Thorpe Abbotts	*Norfolk* - Norwich
Thorpe Achurch	*Northampton* - Kettering
Thorpeacre	*Leicester* - Loughborough
Thorpe Arnold	*Leicester* - Melton Mowbray
Thorpe Bassett	*York, E.R.* - Malton
Thorpe Bay	*Essex* - Southend
Thorpe by Water	*Rutland* - Corby
Thorpe Common	*York, W.R.* - Rotherham
Thorpe Dales	*Lincoln* - Sleaford
Thorpe, East	*Lincoln* - Lincoln
Thorpe Hamlet	*Norfolk* - Norwich
Thorpe Hesley (part)	*York, W.R.* - Rotherham
Thorpe Hesley (part)	*York, W.R.* - Sheffield
Thorpe-in-Balne	*York, W.R.* - Doncaster
Thorpe in the Fallows	*Lincoln* - Lincoln
Thorpe in the Glebe	*Notts* - Loughborough
Thorpe Langton	*Leicester* - Leicester
Thorpe Latimer	*Lincoln* - Sleaford
Thorpe le Soken	*Essex* - Colchester
Thorpe-le-Street	*York, E.R.* - York
Thorpe-le-Vale	*Lincoln* - Louth
Thorpe, Little	*Durham* - Sunderland
Thorpe Lubenham	*Leicester* - Leicester
Thorpe Malsor	*Northampton* - Kettering
Thorpe Mandeville	*Northampton* - Banbury
Thorpe Market	*Norfolk* - Norwich
Thorpe Morieux	*Suffolk* - Bury St. Edmunds
Thorpeness	*Suffolk* - Woodbridge
Thorpe next Haddiscoe	*Norfolk* - Great Yarmouth
Thorpe-next-Norwich	*Norfolk* - Norwich
Thorpe-on-the-Hill	*Lincoln* - Lincoln
Thorpe Parva	*Norfolk* - Norwich
Thorpe St. Andrew	*Norfolk* - Norwich
Thorpe St. Peters	*Lincoln* - Skegness
Thorpe Salvin	*York, W.R.* - Worksop
Thorpe Satchville	*Leicester* - Melton Mowbray
Thorpe Stapleton	*York, W.R.* - Leeds
Thorpe Thewles	*Durham* - Stockton on Tees
Thorpe Tilney	*Lincoln* - Sleaford
Thorpe Tilney Dales	*Lincoln* - Sleaford
Thorpe Underwoods	*York, W.R.* - Harrogate
Thorpe Waterville	*Northampton* - Peterborough

Thorpe Willoughby	*York, W.R.* - York
Thorrington	*Essex* - Colchester
Thoverton	*Devon* - Tiverton
Thrandeston	*Suffolk* - Norwich
Thrapston	*Northampton* - Kettering
Threapland	*Cumberland* - Workington
Threapwood	*Cheshire* - Whitchurch
Three Ashes	*Hereford* - Monmouth
Three Bridges	*Lancaster* - Barrow-in-Furness
Three Bridges	*Sussex* - Horsham
Three Chimneys	*Kent* - Cranbrook
Three Cocks	*Brecon* - Brecknock
Three Counties	*Beds* - Biggleswade
Three Crosses	*Glamorgan* - Swansea
Three Cups	*Sussex* - Eastbourne
Three Elm Lane	*Kent* - Tonbridge
Three Gates	*Salop* - Ludlow
Three Hammers	*Cornwall* - Launceston
Three Hammers	*Devon* - Tiverton
Three Holes	*Cambridge* - Wisbech
Threekingham	*Lincoln* - Sleaford
Three Legged Cross	*Dorset* - Wimborne Minster
Three Mile Cross	*Berks* - Reading
Three Mile Stone	*Cornwall* - Truro
Threlkeld	*Cumberland* - Workington
Threshfield	*York, W.R.* - Skipton
Threxton	*Norfolk* - King's Lynn
Thrigby	*Norfolk* - Great Yarmouth
Thrimby	*Westmorland* - Penrith
Thringstone	*Leicester* - Ashby-de-la-Zouch
Thrintoft	*York, N.R.* - Northallerton
Thriplow	*Cambridge* - Cambridge
Thrislington Colliery	*Durham* - Durham
Throapham	*York, W.R.* - Worksop
Throapham Common	*York, W.R.* - Worksop
Throckenholt (part)	*Lincoln* - Spalding
Throcking	*Herts* - Hitchin
Throckley	*Northumberland* - Newcastle upon Tyne
Throckmorton	*Worcester* - Evesham
Throne Estate	*Stafford* - Dudley
Throop	*Dorset* - Dorchester
Throop	*Hants* - Bournemouth
Throphill	*Northumberland* - Morpeth
Thropton	*Northumberland* - Morpeth
Througham	*Gloucester* - Stroud
Throwleigh	*Devon* - Okehampton
Throwley	*Kent* - Sittingbourne
Throwley	*Stafford* - Leek
Throxenby	*York, N.R.* - Scarborough
Thrumpton	*Notts* - Nottingham
Thrunton Farm	*Northumberland* - Morpeth
Thrupp	*Berks* - Didcot
Thrupp	*Gloucester* - Stroud
Thrupp	*Northampton* - Northampton
Thrupp	*Oxford* - Oxford
Thruscross	*York, W.R.* - Harrogate
Thrushelton	*Devon* - Plymouth
Thrushesbush	*Essex* - Harlow
Thrussington	*Leicester* - Leicester
Thruxton	*Hants* - Andover
Thruxton	*Hereford* - Hereford
Thrybergh	*York, W.R.* - Rotherham
Thulston	*Derby* - Derby
Thunder Bridge	*York, W.R.* - Huddersfield
Thundersley	*Essex* - Southend
Thundridge	*Herts* - Hertford
Thurcaston	*Leicester* - Leicester
Thurcroft	*York, W.R.* - Rotherham
Thurgarton	*Norfolk* - Norwich
Thurgarton	*Notts* - Newark
Thurgoland	*York, W.R.* - Barnsley
Thurlaston	*Leicester* - Leicester
Thurlaston	*Warwick* - Rugby
Thurlbear	*Somerset* - Taunton
Thurlby	*Lincoln* - Spalding
Thurlby	*Lincoln* - Newark
Thurlby	*Lincoln* - Skegness
Thurlby Fen	*Lincoln* - Spalding
Thurlby Wood	*Lincoln* - Gainsborough

Thurleigh	*Beds* - Bedford
Thurleston	*Suffolk* - Ipswich
Thurlestone	*Devon* - Kingsbridge
Thurlow Booth	*Derby* - Alfreton
Thurlow, Great	*Suffolk* - Newmarket
Thurlow, Little	*Suffolk* - Newmarket
Thurloxton	*Somerset* - Bridgwater
Thurlstone	*York, W.R.* - Barnsley
Thurlton	*Norfolk* - Great Yarmouth
Thurmaston	*Leicester* - Leicester
Thurnby	*Leicester* - Leicester
Thurne	*Norfolk* - Great Yarmouth
Thurnham	*Kent* - Maidstone
Thurnham	*Lancaster* - Lancaster
Thurning	*Norfolk* - King's Lynn
Thurning	*Northampton* - Huntingdon
Thurnscoe	*York, W.R.* - Doncaster
Thurrock, Little	*Essex* - Grays Thurrock
Thurrock, West	*Essex* - Grays Thurrock
Thursby	*Cumberland* - Carlisle
Thursden Valley	*Lancaster* - Burnley
Thursford	*Norfolk* - King's Lynn
Thursley	*Surrey* - Guildford
Thurstaston	*Cheshire* - Birkenhead
Thurston	*Suffolk* - Bury St. Edmunds
Thurstonfield	*Cumberland* - Carlisle
Thurstonland	*York, W.R.* - Huddersfield
Thurstons	*York, W.R.* - Oldham
Thurton	*Norfolk* - Norwich
Thurvaston	*Derby* - Derby
Thurvaston, Nether	*Derby* - Derby
Thuxton	*Norfolk* - East Dereham
Thwaite	*Norfolk* - Norwich
Thwaite	*Suffolk* - Stowmarket
Thwaite	*York, N.R.* - Darlington
Thwaite Flat	*Lancaster* - Barrow-in-Furness
Thwaites	*Cumberland* - Whitehaven
Thwaites	*York, W.R.* - Keighley
Thwing	*York, E.R.* - Bridlington
Tibberton	*Gloucester* - Gloucester
Tibberton	*Salop* - Wellington (Salop)
Tibberton	*Worcester* - Worcester
Tibenham	*Norfolk* - Norwich
Tiberton	*Hereford* - Hereford
Tibshelf	*Derby* - Alfreton
Tibthorpe	*York, E.R.* - Beverley
Ticehurst	*Sussex* - Tunbridge Wells
Tichborne	*Hants* - Winchester
Tickencote	*Rutland* - Stamford
Tickenham	*Somerset* - Bristol
Tickham	*Kent* - Sittingbourne
Tickhill	*York, W.R.* - Doncaster
Ticklerton	*Salop* - Ludlow
Ticknall	*Derby* - Ashby-de-la-Zouch
Tickton	*York, E.R.* - Beverley
Tidcombe	*Wilts* - Andover
Tiddington	*Oxford* - Thame
Tiddington	*Warwick* - Stratford on Avon
Tiddycross	*Salop* - Wellington
Tideford	*Cornwall* - Liskeard
Tidenham	*Gloucester* - Chepstow
Tideswell	*Derby* - Buxton
Tidmarsh	*Berks* - Reading
Tidmington	*Warwick* - Stratford on Avon
Tidworth, North	*Wilts* - Andover
Tidworth, South	*Hants* - Andover
Tiers Cross	*Pembroke* - Haverfordwest
Tiffield	*Northampton* - Northampton
Tigers Island	*Warwick* - Birmingham
Tigfold	*Lancaster* - Bolton
Tilbrook	*Northampton* - Huntingdon
Tilbury	*Essex* - Grays Thurrock
Tilbury, East	*Essex* - Grays Thurrock
Tilbury Juxta Clare	*Essex* - Sudbury
Tilbury, West	*Essex* - Grays Thurrock
Tile Cross	*Warwick* - Birmingham
Tilegate Green	*Essex* - Harlow
Tile Hill	*Warwick* - Coventry
Tilehurst	*Berks* - Reading
Tilehurst Common	*Berks* - Reading

Tilekiln Green	*Essex* - Bishop's Stortford
Tiley	*Dorset* - Dorchester
Tilford	*Surrey* - Aldershot and Farnham
Tilgate	*Sussex* - Horsham
Tilla	*Brecon* - Pontypool and Abergavenny
Tillbridge	*Lincoln* - Lincoln
Tillers Green	*Gloucester* - Gloucester
Tilley	*Salop* - Shrewsbury
Tillingbourne Valley (part)	*Surrey* - Dorking
Tillingbourne Valley (part)	*Surrey* - Guildford
Tillingham	*Essex* - Malden
Tillington	*Hereford* - Hereford
Tillington	*Stafford* - Stafford
Tillington	*Sussex* - Chichester
Tillmouth	*Northumberland* - Berwick-upon-Tweed
Tilly Down	*Hants* - Andover
Tilmanstone	*Kent* - Deal
Tiln	*Notts* - East Retford
Tilney All Saints	*Norfolk* - King's Lynn
Tilney-cum-Islington	*Norfolk* - King's Lynn
Tilney St. Lawrence	*Norfolk* - King's Lynn
Tilshead	*Wilts* - Devizes
Tilsop	*Salop* - Ludlow
Tilstock	*Salop* - Whitchurch
Tilston	*Cheshire* - Whitchurch
Tilsworth	*Beds* - Bletchley and Leighton Buzzard
Tilton-on-the-Hill	*Leicester* - Leicester
Tiltups End	*Gloucester* - Stroud
Tilty	*Essex* - Braintree
Timberden	*Kent* - Sevenoaks
Timberhonger	*Worcester* - Bromsgrove
Timberland	*Lincoln* - Sleaford
Timberland Dales	*Lincoln* - Sleaford
Timberland Fen	*Lincoln* - Sleaford
Timbersbrook	*Cheshire* - Congleton
Timberscombe	*Somerset* - Minehead
Timble	*York, W.R.* - Otley
Timperley	*Cheshire* - Altrincham
Timsbury	*Hants* - Winchester
Timsbury	*Somerset* - Bristol
Timworth	*Suffolk* - Bury St. Edmunds
Tincleton	*Dorset* - Dorchester
Tindale	*Cumberland* - Carlisle
Tindale Crescent	*Durham* - Bishop Auckland
Tindale Bank	*Lincoln* - Gainsborough
Tindon End	*Essex* - Bishop's Stortford
Tingewick	*Bucks* - Aylesbury
Tingley	*York, W.R.* - Dewsbury
Tingley Common	*York, W.R.* - Dewsbury
Tingrith	*Beds* - Luton
Tinhead	*Wilts* - Trowbridge
Tinkerborough	*Stafford* - Stafford
Tinkers Hall	*Beds* - Luton
Tinkers Hill	*Salop* - Ludlow
Tinkersley	*Derby* - Matlock
Tinsley	*York, W.R.* - Sheffield
Tinsley Green (part)	*Surrey* - Horsham
Tinsley Green (part)	*Surrey* - Reigate
Tinsley Park	*York, W.R.* - Sheffield
Tintagel	*Cornwall* - Launceston
Tintern	*Monmouth* - Chepstow
Tintinhull	*Somerset* - Yeovil
Tintwhistle	*Cheshire* - Hyde
Tinwell	*Rutland* - Stamford
Tipnor	*Hants* - Portsmouth
Tip's End	*Cambridge* - Wisbech
Tip's End (Welney)	*Norfolk* - King's Lynn
Tiptoe	*Hants* - Lymington
Tipton	*Stafford* - Dudley
Tipton	*Hereford* - Knighton
Tipton St. Johns	*Devon* - Exeter
Tiptree	*Essex* - Maldon
Tiptree Heath	*Essex* - Maldon
Tirabad	*Brecon* - Builth

Tirley	*Gloucester* - Gloucester
Tirphil	*Glamorgan* - Bargoed
Tirril	*Westmorland* - Penrith
Tiryberth	*Glamorgan* - Bargoed
Tirydail	*Carmarthen* - Ammanford
Tisbury	*Wilts* - Shaftesbury
Tisbury, East	*Wilts* - Shaftesbury
Tisbury, West	*Wilts* - Shaftesbury
Tismans Common	*Sussex* - Horsham
Tissington	*Derby* - Matlock
Tissington Wood	*Derby* - Matlock
Tisted, East	*Hants* - Aldershot and Farnham
Tisted, West	*Hants* - Winchester
Titchfield	*Hants* - Portsmouth
Titchmarsh	*Northampton* - Kettering
Titchwell	*Norfolk* - King's Lynn
Titcombe	*Berks* - Newbury
Titford	*Worcester* - West Bromwich
Tithby	*Notts* - Nottingham
Tithe Barn	*Lancaster* - Barrow-in-Furness
Titley	*Hereford* - Leominster
Titlington	*Northumberland* - Alnwick
Titmore Green	*Herts* - Hitchin
Titsey	*Surrey* - Reigate
Tittenley	*Salop* - Market Drayton
Tittensor	*Stafford* - Stoke-on-Trent
Titterstone	*Salop* - Ludlow
Tittesworth	*Stafford* - Leek
Tittleshall	*Norfolk* - East Dereham
Titton	*Worcester* - Kidderminster
Tiverton	*Cheshire* - Crewe
Tiverton	*Devon* - Tiverton
Tiverton Junction	*Devon* - Tiverton
Tivetshall St. Margaret	*Norfolk* - Norwich
Tivetshall St. Mary	*Norfolk* - Norwich
Tividale	*Stafford* - Dudley
Tixall	*Stafford* - Stafford
Tixover	*Rutland* - Stamford
Toadsmoor	*Gloucester* - Stroud
Toat Hill (Slinfold)	*Sussex* - Horsham
Tockenham Wick	*Wilts* - Swindon
Tockholes	*Lancaster* - Blackburn
Tockington	*Gloucester* - Thornbury
Tockington, Lower	*Gloucester* - Thornbury
Tockwith	*York, W.R.* - York
Todber	*Dorset* - Shaftesbury
Todburn	*Northumberland* - Morpeth
Toddington	*Beds* - Luton
Toddington	*Gloucester* - Cheltenham
Toddington	*Sussex* - Chichester
Todd's Green	*Herts* - Hitchin
Todenham	*Gloucester* - Evesham
Todhills	*Cumberland* - Carlisle
Todhills	*Durham* - Bishop Auckland
Todleth	*Montgomery* - Welshpool
Todmorden	*Lancaster* - Todmorden
Todpool (part)	*Cornwall* - Redruth
Todpool (part)	*Cornwall* - Truro
Todridge	*Northumberland* - Morpeth
Todsworthy	*Devon* - Plymouth
Todwick	*York, W.R.* - Worksop
Todwick Common	*York, W.R.* - Worksop
Toft	*Cambridge* - Cambridge
Toft (part)	*Cheshire* - Altrincham
Toft (part)	*Cheshire* - Northwich
Toft	*Lincoln* - Spalding
Toft	*Warwick* - Rugby
Toft Hill	*Durham* - Bishop Auckland
Toft Monks	*Norfolk* - Great Yarmouth
Toft next Newton	*Lincoln* - Lincoln
Toftrees	*Norfolk* - King's Lynn
Toftshaw Bottom	*York, W.R.* - Dewsbury
Toftshaw Moor	*York, W.R.* - Dewsbury
Toftshaw Tanhouse	*York, W.R.* - Dewsbury
Toftwood Common	*Norfolk* - East Dereham
Toghill	*Gloucester* - Bath
Togston	*Northumberland* - Alnwick
Tokers Green	*Oxford* - Reading
Tolcarne (Camborne)	*Cornwall* - Redruth

Tolcarne (St. Day)	*Cornwall* - Redruth
Tolethorpe	*Rutland* - Stamford
Tolgarrack	*Cornwall* - Redruth
Tolgus	*Cornwall* - Redruth
Tolland	*Somerset* - Taunton
Tollard Common	*Wilts* - Shaftesbury
Tollard Green	*Wilts* - Shaftesbury
Tollard Royal	*Wilts* - Shaftesbury
Toll Bar	*Lancaster* - St. Helens
Tolldish	*Stafford* - Stafford
Toll Down	*Gloucester* - Bristol
Toll End (part)	*Stafford* - Dudley
Toll End (part)	*Stafford* - West Bromwich
Tollerford	*Dorset* - Dorchester
Toller Fratrum	*Dorset* - Dorchester
Toller Porcorum	*Dorset* - Dorchester
Tollerton	*Notts* - Nottingham
Tollerton	*York, N.R.* - York
Toller Whelme	*Dorset* - Yeovil
Tollesbury	*Essex* - Maldon
Tolleshunt D'Arcy	*Essex* - Maldon
Tolleshunt Knights	*Essex* - Maldon
Tolleshunt Major	*Essex* - Maldon
Toll Gate	*Kent* - Gravesend
Toll Hill	*York, W.R.* - Pontefract
Tollingham	*York, E.R.* - Goole
Tollington Park	*London, N.4* - Clerkenwell
Tolpuddle	*Dorset* - Dorchester
Tolworth	*Surrey* - Kingston-upon-Thames
Tomlow	*Warwick* - Warwick
Tompkin	*Stafford* - Stoke-on-Trent
Tonbridge	*Kent* - Tonbridge
Ton Brigam	*Glamorgan* - Bridgend
Tondu	*Glamorgan* - Bridgend
Tone	*Northumberland* - Hexham
Tone Vale	*Somerset* - Taunton
Tong	*Salop* - Wellington (Salop)
Tong	*York, W.R.* - Bradford
Tongdean	*Sussex* - Brighton
Tonge	*Kent* - Sittingbourne
Tonge	*Lancaster* - Bolton
Tonge	*Lancaster* - Oldham
Tonge	*Leicester* - Loughborough
Tonge Fold	*Lancaster* - Bolton
Tonge Moor	*Lancaster* - Bolton
Tonge with Haulgh	*Lancaster* - Bolton
Tongham	*Surrey* - Aldershot and Farnham
Tong Havannah	*Salop* - Wellington (Salop)
Tong Norton	*Salop* - Wellington (Salop)
Tong Park	*York, W.R.* - Bradford
Tongswood	*Kent* - Cranbrook
Tongue End	*Lincoln* - Spalding
Tongwell	*Bucks* - Bletchley and Leighton Buzzard
Tongwynlais	*Glamorgan* - Cardiff
Tonmawr	*Glamorgan* - Neath
Tonna	*Glamorgan* - Neath
Ton Pentre	*Glamorgan* - Pontypridd
Tonteg	*Glamorgan* - Pontypridd
Tontine	*Lancaster* - Wigan
Tonwell	*Herts* - Hertford
Tonypandy	*Glamorgan* - Pontypridd
Tonyrefail	*Glamorgan* - Pontypridd
Toot Baldon	*Oxford* - Oxford
Toot Hill	*Essex* - Brentwood
Toothill	*Hants* - Southampton
Toothill Bank	*York, W.R.* - Halifax
Tooting	*London, S.W.17* - Wandsworth
Tooting Bec	*London, S.W.16* - Wandsworth
Tooting Bec	*London, S.W.17* - Wandsworth
Tooting Junction (part)	*London, S.W.17* - Croydon
Tooting Junction (part)	*London, S.W.17* - Wandsworth
Tooting, Upper	*London, S.W.17* - Wandsworth
Topcliffe	*York, W.R.* - Northallerton
Topcliffe	*York, W.R.* - Dewsbury
Topcroft	*Norfolk* - Norwich
Tophilow	*York, E.R.* - Beverley
Top Lock	*Lancaster* - Wigan
Top o' th' Brow	*Lancaster* - Bolton
Top o' th' Lodge	*Lancaster* - Bolton

Top o' th' Moss	*Lancaster* - Bolton
Top o' th' Slack	*Lancaster* - Bolton
Toppesfield	*Essex* - Braintree
Topping's Estate	*Lancaster* - Bolton
Topsham Bridge	*Devon* - Kingsbridge
Torcross	*Devon* - Kingsbridge
Torkington	*Cheshire* - Stockport
Torksey	*Lincoln* - Gainsborough
Torksey Lock	*Lincoln* - Gainsborough
Tormarton	*Gloucester* - Bristol
Toronto	*Durham* - Bishop Auckland
Torpantau	*Brecon* - Brecknock
Torpenhow	*Cumberland* - Carlisle
Torpenhow	*Cumberland* - Workington
Torpoint	*Cornwall* - Plymouth
Torquay	*Devon* - Torquay
Torr	*Devon* - Plymouth
Torr (Kingston)	*Devon* - Kingsbridge
Torrington, East	*Lincoln* - Louth
Torrington, Great	*Devon* - Bideford
Torrington, Little	*Devon* - Bideford
Torrington Park	*London, N.12* - Barnet
Torrington, West	*Lincoln* - Lincoln
Torrisholme	*Lancaster* - Lancaster
Tor Royal	*Devon* - Plymouth
Tortington	*Sussex* - Chichester
Torton	*Worcester* - Kidderminster
Tortworth	*Gloucester* - Thornbury
Torver	*Lancaster* - Kendal
Torworth	*Notts* - East Retford
Toseland	*Hunts* - Huntingdon
Tosside	*York, W.R.* - Skipton
Tosson, Great	*Northumberland* - Morpeth
Tosson, Little	*Northumberland* - Morpeth
Tostock	*Suffolk* - Stowmarket
Totham, Great	*Essex* - Maldon
Totham Hill	*Essex* - Maldon
Totham, Little	*Essex* - Maldon
Tothby	*Lincoln* - Skegness
Tothill	*Lincoln* - Louth
Totland Bay	*I. of W.* - Newport (I.W.)
Totley	*York, W.R.* - Sheffield
Totnes	*Devon* - Torquay
Toton	*Notts* - Nottingham
Tottenham	*Durham* - Bishop Auckland
Tottenham	*London, N.17* - Edmonton
Tottenham, South	*London, N.15* - Edmonton
Tottenhill	*Norfolk* - King's Lynn
Totterdown	*Wilts* - Swindon
Totteridge	*Bucks* - High Wycombe
Totteridge	*London, N.20* - Barnet
Totternhoe	*Beds* - Luton
Totties	*York, W.R.* - Huddersfield
Tottington	*Lancaster* - Bury
Tottlebank	*Lancaster* - Barrow-in-Furness
Tottlebank Colton	*Lancaster* - Barrow-in-Furness
Totton	*Hants* - Southampton
Touchen End	*Berks* - Slough
Toulston	*York, W.R.* - York
Tovil	*Kent* - Maidstone
Towan Cross	*Cornwall* - Truro
Towborough	*Gloucester* - Cheltenham
Towcester	*Northampton* - Northampton
Towednack	*Cornwall* - Penzance
Tower Hill	*Stafford* - Birmingham
Tower Hill	*Sussex* - Horsham
Tower Hill	*Warwick* - Stratford on Avon
Towersey	*Bucks* - Thame
Tow House	*Northumberland* - Haltwhistle
Tow Law	*Durham* - Bishop Auckland
Towneley	*Lancaster* - Burnley
Towngate	*Lincoln* - Spalding
Town Green	*Lancaster* - Southport
Townhill	*Glamorgan* - Swansea
Townsend	*Stafford* - Stoke-on-Trent
Townsend Fold	*Lancaster* - Rawtenstall
Townshend	*Cornwall* - Redruth
Townstall	*Devon* - Torquay
Townville	*York, W.R.* - Pontefract
Tows Bank	*Northumberland* - Hexham

Tows, Great	*Linconl* - Louth
Towthorpe	*York, E.R.* - Beverley
Towthorpe	*York, N.R.* - York
Towton	*York, W.R.* - York
Towyn	*Denbigh* - Rhyl
Toynton All Saints	*Lincoln* - Skegness
Toynton, High	*Lincoln* - Lincoln
Toynton, Low	*Lincoln* - Lincoln
Toynton St. Peters	*Lincoln* - Skegness
Toynton St. Peters Fen	*Lincoln* - Skegness
Toys Hill	*Kent* - Sevenoaks
Toy Top	*Durham* - Bishop Auckland
Traboe	*Cornwall* - Penzance
Trafalgar	*Gloucester* - Gloucester
Trafalgar	*Gloucester* - Cheltenham
Trafford, Old	*Lancaster* - Salford
Trafford Park	*Lancaster* - Salford
Traianglas	*Brecon* - Brecknock
Trallong	*Brecon* - Brecknock
Trallwn	*Glamorgan* - Swansea
Tram Inn	*Hereford* - Hereford
Tranby	*York, E.R.* - Kingston-upon-Hull
Tranch	*Glamorgan* - Bridgend
Tranch	*Monmouth* - Pontypool and Abergavenny
Tranmere	*York, N.R.* - Whitby
Tranmere, Higher	*Cheshire* - Birkenhead
Tranmere, Lower	*Cheshire* - Birkenhead
Tranwell	*Northumberland* - Morpeth
Trapnell	*Salop* - Ludlow
Trapp	*Carmarthen* - Ammanford
Traps Green	*Warwick* - Birmingham
Trawden	*Lancaster* - Nelson
Trawscoed	*Cardigan* - Aberystwyth
Trawsfynydd	*Merioneth* - Portmadoc
Trealaw	*Glamorgan* - Pontypridd
Treales	*Lancaster* - Preston
Trearddur Bay	*Anglesey* - Llangefni
Trebanog	*Glamorgan* - Pontypridd
Trebanos	*Glamorgan* - Neath
Trebartha	*Cornwall* - Launceston
Trebarwith	*Cornwall* - Launceston
Trebeath	*Cornwall* - Launceston
Trebeddau	*Glamorgan* - Merthyr Tydfil
Trebles Holford	*Somerset* - Taunton
Treboeth	*Glamorgan* - Swansea
Treborough	*Somerset* - Minehead
Treborth	*Caernarvon* - Bangor
Trebray	*Cornwall* - Launceston
Trebryn	*Glamorgan* - Bridgend
Trebrys Fach	*Montgomery* - Oswestry
Trebrys Fawr	*Montgomery* - Oswestry
Trebudannan	*Cornwall* - Truro
Trebullett	*Cornwall* - Launceston
Treburtle	*Cornwall* - Launceston
Trecarrell Mill	*Cornwall* - Launceston
Trecastell	*Caernarvon* - Conway
Trecastle	*Brecon* - Brecknock
Trecatty	*Glamorgan* - Merthyr Tydfil
Trecrogo	*Cornwall* - Launceston
Trecwn	*Pembroke* - Haverfordwest
Trecynon	*Glamorgan* - Aberdare
Tredavoe	*Cornwall* - Penzance
Tredegar	*Monmouth* - Blackwood
Tredegar, New	*Monmouth* - Blackwood
Trederwen	*Montgomery* - Oswestry
Trederwen Fawr	*Montgomery* - Oswestry
Tredington	*Gloucester* - Cheltenham
Tredington	*Warwick* - Stratford on Avon
Tredinnick	*Cornwall* - Bodmin
Tredinnick	*Cornwall* - Liskeard
Tredodridge	*Glamorgan* - Cardiff
Tredogan	*Glamorgan* - Barry
Tredomen	*Glamorgan* - Caerphilly
Tredunnock	*Monmouth* - Newport (Mon.)
Tredworth	*Gloucester* - Gloucester
Treen	*Cornwall* - Penzance
Treeton	*York, W.R.* - Rotherham
Treeve	*Cornwall* - Redruth
Trefdraeth	*Anglesey* - Llangefni

Trefecca	*Brecon* - Brecknock
Trefechan	*Cardigan* - Aberystwyth
Trefedrid	*Montgomery* - Oswestry
Trefeglwys	*Montgomery* - Newtown
Trefeinon	*Brecon* - Brecknock
Trefeirig	*Cardigan* - Aberystwyth
Treffgarne	*Pembroke* - Haverfordwest
Trefgarne Owen	*Pembroke* - Haverfordwest
Trefilan	*Cardigan* - Lampeter
Treflach	*Salop* - Oswestry
Treflan	*Caernarvon* - Caernarvon
Treflyn	*Montgomery* - Newtown
Treflys	*Caernarvon* - Portmadoc
Trefnanney	*Montgomery* - Oswestry
Trefnant	*Denbigh* - Denbigh
Trefnant	*Salop* - Shrewsbury
Trefonen	*Salop* - Oswestry
Trefor	*Flint* - Holywell
Treforest	*Glamorgan* - Caerphilly
Trefriw	*Caernarvon* - Conway
Trefula	*Cornwall* - Redruth
Trefusis	*Cornwall* - Truro
Trefynant	*Denbigh* - Wrexham
Tregadillet	*Cornwall* - Launceston
Tregagorran	*Cornwall* - Redruth
Tregaian	*Anglesey* - Llangefni
Tregantle, Lower	*Cornwall* - Plymouth
Tregare	*Monmouth* - Monmouth
Tregarland	*Cornwall* - Liskeard
Tregaron	*Cardigan* - Lampeter
Tregarth	*Caernarvon* - Bangor
Tregarthen	*Cornwall* - Penzance
Tregavarah	*Cornwall* - Penzance
Tregavethan	*Cornwall* - Truro
Tregeare	*Cornwall* - Launceston
Tregeiriog	*Denbigh* - Oswestry
Tregele	*Anglesey* - Llangefni
Tregeseal	*Cornwall* - Penzance
Tregiskey	*Cornwall* - St. Austell
Tregonetha	*Cornwall* - Truro
Tregoney	*Cornwall* - Truro
Tregongeeves	*Cornwall* - St. Austell
Tregonhawke	*Cornwall* - Plymouth
Tregonissey	*Cornwall* - St. Austell
Tregoodwell	*Cornwall* - Bideford
Tregorrick	*Cornwall* - St. Austell
Tregoss	*Cornwall* - St. Austell
Tregowris	*Cornwall* - Penzance
Tregrehan	*Cornwall* - St. Austell
Tregroes	*Cardigan* - Lampeter
Tregullan	*Cornwall* - Bodmin
Tregurrian	*Cornwall* - Truro
Tregynon	*Montgomery* - Newtown
Trehafod	*Glamorgan* - Pontypridd
Trehale Fach	*Pembroke* - Haverfordwest
Treharne	*Cornwall* - Plymouth
Treharris	*Glamorgan* - Merthyr Tydfil
Treherbert	*Glamorgan* - Pontypridd
Trekelland Bridge	*Devon* - Launceston
Treknow	*Cornwall* - Launceston
Trelash	*Cornwall* - Launceston
Trelavour	*Cornwall* - St. Austell
Trelawnyd	*Flint* - Holywell
Trelech-ar-Bettws	*Carmarthen* - Carmarthen
Treleigh	*Cornwall* - Redruth
Treleiver	*Cornwall* - Truro
Trelewis	*Glamorgan* - Bargoed
Trelill	*Cornwall* - Redruth
Trelion	*Cornwall* - St. Austell
Trellan	*Montgomery* - Oswestry
Trellan Isa	*Montgomery* - Oswestry
Trellan Ucha	*Montgomery* - Oswestry
Trelleck	*Monmouth* - Monmouth
Trelleck Grange	*Monmouth* - Chepstow
Trelogan	*Flint* - Holywell
Treloquithack	*Cornwall* - Penzance
Treloweth	*Cornwall* - St. Austell
Trelusback	*Cornwall* - Redruth
Treluswell	*Cornwall* - Truro
Trelystan	*Montgomery* - Welshpool

Tremadoc	*Caernarvon* - Portmadoc
Tremail	*Cornwall* - Launceston
Tremain	*Cardigan* - Cardigan
Tremaine	*Cornwall* - Launceston
Tremar	*Cornwall* - Liskeard
Tremar Coombe	*Cornwall* - Liskeard
Trematon	*Cornwall* - Plymouth
Tremayne	*Cornwall* - Penzance
Trembath	*Cornwall* - Penzance
Tremerchion	*Flint* - Rhyl
Tremethick Cross	*Cornwall* - Penzance
Tremough	*Cornwall* - Truro
Trenance	*Cornwall* - St. Austell
Trenarren	*Cornwall* - St. Austell
Trench (Telford)	*Salop* - Wellington (Salop)
Trench and Tilley	*Salop* - Shrewsbury
Trench Lock	*Salop* - Wellington (Salop)
Trencreek	*Cornwall* - Truro
Trencrom	*Cornwall* - Penzance
Trenear	*Cornwall* - Penzance
Treneglos	*Cornwall* - Launceston
Trenewan	*Cornwall* - Liskeard
Trenholme Bar	*York, N.R.* - Middlesbrough
Trenhorne	*Cornwall* - Launceston
Treninnick	*Cornwall* - Truro
Trenoweth	*Cornwall* - Truro
Trent	*Derby* - Nottingham
Trent	*Dorset* - Yeovil
Trentham	*Stafford* - Stoke-on-Trent
Trentham Park	*Stafford* - Stoke-on-Trent
Trentishoe	*Devon* - Barnstaple
Trent Lock	*Derby* - Nottingham
Trent Vale	*Stafford* - Stoke-on-Trent
Treorchy	*Glamorgan* - Pontypridd
Treos	*Glamorgan* - Bridgend
Treovis	*Cornwall* - Liskeard
Treowen	*Monmouth* - Blackwood
Trepenal	*Salop* - Oswestry
Trerddol	*Cardigan* - Aberystwyth
Trerhingyll	*Glamorgan* - Bridgend
Trerice	*Cornwall* - St. Austell
Trerule Foot	*Cornwall* - Liskeard
Tresaith	*Cardigan* - Cardigan
Tresamble (Gwennap)	*Cornwall* - Redruth
Tresayes	*Cornwall* - St. Austell
Tresco	*Scilly Isles* - Penzance
Trescobeas	*Cornwall* - Truro
Trescott	*Stafford* - Wolverhampton
Trescott Grange	*Stafford* - Wolverhampton
Trescowe	*Cornwall* - Penzance
Tresham	*Gloucester* - Bristol
Tresillian	*Cornwall* - Truro
Tresinney	*Cornwall* - Bideford
Treskerby	*Cornwall* - Redruth
Treskillard	*Cornwall* - Redruth
Tresmere	*Cornwall* - Launceston
Tresowas	*Cornwall* - Penzance
Tresparrett	*Cornwall* - Launceston
Tresplatt	*Cornwall* - Launceston
Treswell	*Notts* - East Retford
Treswithiam	*Cornwall* - Redruth
Trethomas	*Monmouth* - Newport (Mon.)
Trethosa	*Cornwall* - St. Austell
Trethurgy	*Cornwall* - St. Austell
Tretire	*Hereford* - Hereford
Tretire with Michaelchurch	*Hereford* - Hereford
Tretower	*Brecon* - Pontypool and Abergavenny
Treuddyd	*Flint* - Mold
Trevadlock	*Cornwall* - Launceston
Trevalga	*Cornwall* - Launceston
Trevallet	*Cornwall* - Launceston
Trevarno	*Cornwall* - Penzance
Trevarren	*Cornwall* - Truro
Trevarrian	*Cornwall* - Truro
Trevarth	*Cornwall* - Redruth
Trevaughan	*Carmarthen* - Carmarthen
Trevaunance	*Cornwall* - Truro
Treveighan	*Cornwall* - Bideford

Trevellas	*Cornwall* - Truro
Trevelmond	*Cornwall* - Liskeard
Trevena	*Cornwall* - Bideford
Treverbyn	*Cornwall* - Liskeard
Treverbyn	*Cornwall* - St. Austell
Treverva	*Cornwall* - Truro
Trevescam	*Cornwall* - Penzance
Trevetham	*Cornwall* - Redruth
Trevia	*Cornwall* - Bideford
Trevil	*Brecon* - Blackwood
Trevigro	*Cornwall* - Liskeard
Treville	*Hereford* - Hereford
Trevine	*Pembroke* - Haverfordwest
Trevingey	*Cornwall* - Redruth
Treviscoe	*Cornwall* - St. Austell
Trevissome	*Cornwall* - Truro
Trevol	*Cornwall* - Plymouth
Trevone	*Cornwall* - Truro
Trevor	*Anglesey* - Llangefni
Trevor	*Caernarvon* - Portmadoc
Trevor	*Denbigh* - Wrexham
Trewalder	*Cornwall* - Bideford
Trewarmett	*Cornwall* - Launceston
Trewassa	*Cornwall* - Launceston
Trewedna	*Cornwall* - Truro
Trewellard	*Cornwall* - Penzance
Trewen	*Cornwall* - Launceston
Trewennack	*Cornwall* - Penzance
Trewern	*Montgomery* - Oswestry
Trewern	*Montgomery* - Welshpool
Trewern and Gwaithla	*Radnor* - Builth Wells
Trewhiddle	*Cornwall* - St. Austell
Trewhitt, High	*Northumberland* - Morpeth
Trewhitt, Low	*Northumberland* - Morpeth
Trewick	*Northumberland* - Newcastle upon Tyne
Trewidland	*Cornwall* - Liskeard
Trewint	*Cornwall* - Launceston
Trewithian	*Cornwall* - Truro
Trewoon	*Cornwall* - St. Austell
Trewylan	*Montgomery* - Oswestry
Treyford	*Sussex* - Petersfield
Triangle	*York, W.R.* - Halifax
Triangle Terrace	*Stafford* - Lichfield
Trigon	*Dorset* - Swanage
Trimdon	*Durham* - Durham
Trimdon Grange	*Durham* - Durham
Trimdon, Old	*Durham* - Durham
Trimmingham	*Norfolk* - Norwich
Trimley St. Martin	*Suffolk* - Ipswich
Trimley St. Mary	*Suffolk* - Ipswich
Trimpley	*Worcester* - Kidderminster
Trimsaran	*Carmarthen* - Llanelli
Trinant	*Monmouth* - Blackwood
Tring	*Herts* - Aylesbury
Tring, Little	*Herts* - Aylesbury
Tring Station	*Herts* - Hemel Hempstead
Trinkelt	*Lancaster* - Barrow-in-Furness
Tripp Hill	*Sussex* - Chichester
Trippleton	*Hereford* - Ludlow
Trisant	*Cardigan* - Aberystwyth
Triscombe	*Somerset* - Taunton
Triscombe	*Somerset* - Tiverton
Trispin	*Cornwall* - Truro
Tritlington	*Northumberland* - Morpeth
Troedrhiwfwch	*Glamorgan* - Bargoed
Troedrhiwgwair	*Monmouth* - Blackwood
Troedyraur	*Cardigan* - Cardigan
Troedyrhiewgarth	*Glamorgan* - Bridgend
Troedyrhiw	*Glamorgan* - Merthyr Tydfil
Trofarth	*Denbigh* - Rhyl
Trolvis	*Cornwall* - Redruth
Troon (Breage)	*Cornwall* - Penzance
Troon (Camborne)	*Cornwall* - Redruth
Troston	*Suffolk* - Bury St. Edmunds
Trostrey	*Monmouth* - Pontypool and Abergavenny
Trotterscliffe	*Kent* - Maidstone
Trotton	*Sussex* - Petersfield
Trotton Marsh	*Sussex* - Petersfield

Trough	*Cumberland* - Carlisle
Trough Bridge	*Cumberland* - Workington
Trough End	*Northumberland* - Hexham
Troutbeck	*Cumberland* - Penrith
Troutbeck	*Westmorland* - Kendal
Troutbeck Bridge	*Westmorland* - Kendal
Troutsdale	*York, N.R.* - Scarborough
Troway	*Derby* - Chesterfield
Trowbridge	*Wilts* - Trowbridge
Trowell	*Notts* - Nottingham
Trowell Forge	*Notts* - Ilkeston
Trowle Common	*Wilts* - Trowbridge
Trowley Bottom (Flamstead)	*Herts* - St. Albans
Trowley Bottom (Abbots Langley)	*Herts* - Watford
Trowse with Newton	*Norfolk* - Norwich
Troy Town	*Dorset* - Dorchester
Trudoxhill	*Somerset* - Frome
Trueman's Heath	*Warwick* - Birmingham
Truleigh Hill	*Sussex* - Brighton
Trull	*Somerset* - Taunton
Trumfleet	*York, W.R.* - Doncaster
Trumpet	*Hereford* - Hereford
Trumpington	*Cambridge* - Cambridge
Trumps Green	*Surrey* - Slough
Trunch	*Norfolk* - Norwich
Truro	*Cornwall* - Truro
Truscott	*Cornwall* - Launceston
Trusham	*Devon* - Newton Abbot
Trusley	*Derby* - Derby
Trusthorpe	*Lincoln* - Louth
Truthan	*Cornwall* - Truro
Trysull	*Stafford* - Wolverhampton
Tubney	*Berks* - Oxford
Tuckenhay	*Devon* - Torquay
Tuckermarsh	*Devon* - Plymouth
Tuck Hill	*Salop* - Bridgnorth
Tuckingmill	*Cornwall* - Redruth
Tucking Mill	*Somerset* - Bath
Tuckton	*Hants* - Bournemouth
Tuddenham	*Suffolk* - Bury St. Edmunds
Tuddenham	*Suffolk* - Ipswich
Tuddenham, East	*Norfolk* - East Dereham
Tuddenham, North	*Norfolk* - East Dereham
Tudely	*Kent* - Tonbridge
Tudhoe	*Durham* - Durham
Tudhoe Colliery	*Durham* - Bishop Auckland
Tudhoe Grange	*Durham* - Bishop Auckland
Tudorville	*Hereford* - Monmouth
Tudwick	*Essex* - Maldon
Tue Brook	*Lancaster* - Liverpool
Tuffley	*Gloucester* - Gloucester
Tufnell Park	*London, N.7* - Clerkenwell
Tufton	*Hants* - Andover
Tufton	*Pembroke* - Haverfordwest
Tugby	*Leicester* - Leicester
Tugford	*Salop* - Ludlow
Tughall	*Northumberland* - Alnwick
Tug Mutton	*Kent* - Bromley
Tulse Hill	*London, S.W.2* - Lambeth
Tumble	*Carmarthen* - Llanelli
Tumbledown Dick	*Berks* - Oxford
Tumble Hill	*Glamorgan* - Barry
Tumby	*Lincoln* - Boston
Tumby Woodside	*Lincoln* - Boston
Tunbridge Wells	*Kent* - Tunbridge Wells
Tunley	*Gloucester* - Stroud
Tunley	*Somerset* - Bath
Tunshill	*Lancaster* - Rochdale
Tunstall	*Durham* - Bishop Auckland
Tunstall (Sunderland)	*Durham* - Sunderland
Tunstall	*Kent* - Sittingbourne
Tunstall	*Lancaster* - Lancaster
Tunstall	*Norfolk* - Great Yarmouth
Tunstall	*Salop* - Market Drayton
Tunstall	*Stafford* - Stoke-on-Trent
Tunstall	*Stafford* - Market Drayton
Tunstall	*Suffolk* - Woodbridge
Tunstall	*York, E.R.* - Kingston-upon-Hull

TUN - TWO

Tunstall	*York, N.R.* - Darlington
Tunstead	*Derby* - Buxton
Tunstead	*Norfolk* - Norwich
Tunstead Milton	*Derby* - Buxton
Tunworth	*Hants* - Basingstoke
Tupholme	*Lincoln* - Lincoln
Tupsley	*Hereford* - Hereford
Tupton	*Derby* - Chesterfield
Tupton, New	*Derby* - Chesterfield
Tupton, Old	*Derby* - Chesterfield
Turf Lea	*Cheshire* - Stockport
Turkdean	*Gloucester* - Cheltenham
Tur Langton	*Leicester* - Leicester
Turleigh	*Wilts* - Trowbridge
Turley Green	*Salop* - Bridgnorth
Turn	*Lancaster* - Bury
Turnastone	*Hereford* - Hereford
Turnchapel	*Devon* - Plymouth
Turnditch	*Derby* - Derby
Turners Court	*Oxford* - Didcot
Turners Hill	*Stafford* - Dudley
Turner's Hill	*Sussex* - East Grinstead
Turner's Puddle	*Dorset* - Dorchester
Turners Tump	*Hereford* - Gloucester
Turnerwood	*York, W.R.* - Worksop
Turnford	*Herts* - Edmonton
Turnham Green	*London, W.4* - Brentford
Turnworth	*Dorset* - Dorchester
Turpin	*Lincoln* - Gainsborough
Turrells Hall	*Essex* - Chelmsford
Tursdale Colliery	*Durham* - Durham
Turton	*Lancaster* - Bolton
Turton Bottoms	*Lancaster* - Bolton
Turvelaws	*Northumberland* - Alnwick
Turves Green	*Warwick* - Birmingham
Turvey	*Beds* - Bedford
Turville	*Bucks* - High Wycombe
Turville Heath	*Bucks* - High Wycombe
Turweston	*Bucks* - Banbury
Turweston Lower	*Warwick* - Banbury
Turweston Middle	*Warwick* - Banbury
Turweston Upper	*Warwick* - Banbury
Tushingham	*Cheshire* - Whitchurch
Tusmore	*Oxford* - Banbury
Tutbury	*Stafford* - Burton-upon-Trent
Tutnall	*Worcester* - Redditch
Tutshill	*Gloucester* - Chepstow
Tuttington	*Norfolk* - Norwich
Tuxford	*Notts* - East Retford
Tweedale	*Salop* - Wellington (Salop)
Tweedmouth	*Northumberland* - Berwick-upon-Tweed
Twelveheads (part)	*Cornwall* - Redruth
Twelveheads (part)	*Cornwall* - Truro
Twemlow	*Cheshire* - Congleton
Twemlows	*Salop* - Whitchurch
Twenty	*Lincoln* - Spalding
Twentypence Bridge	*Cambridge* - Ely
Twerlow	*Stafford* - Stafford
Twerton-on-Avon	*Somerset* - Bath
Twice Brewed	*Northumberland* - Hexham
Twickenham	*Middlesex* - Brentford
Twigworth	*Gloucester* - Gloucester
Twineham	*Sussex* - Haywards Heath
Twinhoe, Lower	*Somerset* - Bath
Twinhoe, Upper	*Somerset* - Bath
Twinstead	*Essex* - Sudbury
Twiston	*Lancaster* - Blackburn
Twitchen	*Devon* - Barnstaple
Twitchen	*Salop* - Ludlow
Twitton	*Kent* - Sevenoaks
Twizell	*Durham* - Durham
Twizell	*Northumberland* - Morpeth
Two Bridges	*Devon* - Plymouth
Two Bridges	*Gloucester* - Gloucester
Two Dales	*Derby* - Matlock
Two Gates	*Warwick* - Tamworth
Two Mile Ash	*Sussex* - Horsham
Two Mills	*Cheshire* - Chester
Two Waters	*Herts* - Hemel Hempstead

TWY - TYT

Twycross	*Leicester* - Ashby-de-la-Zouch
Twyford	*Berks* - Reading
Twyford	*Bucks* - Aylesbury
Twyford	*Derby* - Derby
Twyford	*Dorset* - Shaftesbury
Twyford	*Hants* - Winchester
Twyford	*Herts* - Bishop's Stortford
Twyford	*Leicester* - Melton Mowbray
Twyford	*London, N.W.10* - Willesden
Twyford	*Norfolk* - King's Lynn
Twyford	*Notts* - East Retford
Twyford	*Oxford* - Banbury
Twyford	*Salop* - Oswestry
Twyford Abbey	*London, N.W.10* - Brentford
Twyford, West	*Middlesex* - Brentford
Twyning	*Gloucester* - Cheltenham
Twyning Green	*Gloucester* - Cheltenham
Twynllannan	*Carmarthen* - Llandovery
Twynwenallt	*Brecon* - Pontypool and Abergavenny
Twynyrodyn	*Glamorgan* - Barry
Twynyrodyn	*Glamorgan* - Merthyr Tydfil
Twywell	*Northampton* - Kettering
Tyberton	*Hereford* - Hereford
Tybroughton	*Flint* - Whitchurch
Tyburn	*Warwick* - Birmingham
Tycoch	*Glamorgan* - Swansea
Tycoch Bridge	*Monmouth* - Newport (Mon.)
Tycroes	*Anglesey* - Llangefni
Tycroes	*Carmarthen* - Ammanford
Tycrwyn	*Montgomery* - Oswestry
Tydd Gote	*Cambridge* - Wisbech
Tydd Gote	*Lincoln* - Spalding
Tydd St. Giles	*Cambridge* - Wisbech
Tydd St. Mary	*Lincoln* - Spalding
Tydweiliog	*Caernarvon* - Portmadoc
Tye Green (Elsenham)	*Essex* - Bishop's Stortford
Tye Green	*Essex* - Chelmsford
Tye Green (Wimbish)	*Essex* - Bishop's Stortford
Tyersal	*York, W.R.* - Bradford
Tyldesley	*Lancaster* - Leigh
Tyler's Causeway	*Herts* - St. Albans
Tylers Green	*Bucks* - High Wycombe
Tylers Green	*Surrey* - Reigate
Tyle-y-Garw	*Glamorgan* - Bridgend
Tylorstown	*Glamorgan* - Pontypridd
Tylwch	*Montgomery* - Newtown
Tynant	*Denbigh* - Denbigh and Ruthin
Tyne Docks	*Durham* - South Shields
Tyneham	*Dorset* - Swanage
Tynehead	*Northumberland* - Hexham
Tyneley	*Northumberland* - Alnwick
Tyne Main	*Durham* - Gateshead
Tynemouth	*Northumberland* - North Shields
Tynewydd	*Glamorgan* - Bridgend
Tyntesfield	*Somerset* - Bristol
Tynetown	*Glamorgan* - Aberdare
Tynycoed	*Salop* - Oswestry
Tynygarn	*Glamorgan* - Bridgend
Tynygongl	*Anglesey* - Llangefni
Tynygroes	*Caernarvon* - Conway
Tynymaes	*Caernarvon* - Bangor
Tyrdeunaw	*Glamorgan* - Swansea
Tyringham with Filgrave	*Bucks* - Bletchley and Leighton Buzzard
Tyrley	*Stafford* - Market Drayton
Tyseley	*Warwick* - Birmingham
Tysoe	*Warwick* - Banbury
Tythby	*Notts* - Nottingham
Tythegstone	*Glamorgan* - Bridgend
Tythegstone, Higher	*Glamorgan* - Bridgend
Tythegstone, Lower	*Glamorgan* - Bridgend
Tytherington	*Cheshire* - Macclesfield
Tytherington	*Gloucester* - Thornbury
Tytherington	*Somerset* - Frome
Tytherington	*Wilts* - Warminster
Tytherley, East	*Hants* - Salisbury
Tytherley, West	*Hants* - Salisbury
Tytherton Kellaways	*Wilts* - Chippenham
Tytherton Lucas	*Wilts* - Chippenham

Tythrop	*Oxford* - Thame
Tyttenhanger Green	*Herts* - St. Albans
Tytup	*Lancaster* - Barrow-in-Furness
Tywardreath	*Cornwall* - St. Austell
Tywardreath Highway	*Cornwall* - St. Austell
Tywith	*Glamorgan* - Bridgend
Tywyn	*Montgomery* - Machynlleth

U

Ubberley	*Stafford* - Stoke-on-Trent
Ubbeston	*Suffolk* - Halesworth
Ubley	*Somerset* - Wells
Uckfield	*Sussex* - Lewes
Uckinghall	*Worcester* - Cheltenham
Uckington	*Gloucester* - Cheltenham
Uckington	*Salop* - Shrewsbury
Udimore	*Sussex* - Hastings
Udlington	*Salop* - Shrewsbury
Uffcott	*Wilts* - Swindon
Uffculme	*Devon* - Tiverton
Uffington	*Berks* - Didcot
Uffington	*Lincoln* - Stamford
Uffington	*Salop* - Shrewsbury
Ufford	*Huntingdon and Peterborough* - Stamford
Ufford	*Suffolk* - Woodbridge
Ufton	*Berks* - Reading
Ufton	*Warwick* - Warwick
Ugborough	*Devon* - Plymouth
Uggeshall	*Suffolk* - Halesworth
Ugglebarnby	*York, N.R.* - Whitby
Ughill	*York, W.R.* - Sheffield
Ugley	*Essex* - Bishop's Stortford
Ugley Green	*Essex* - Bishop's Stortford
Ugthorpe	*York, N.R.* - Whitby
Ulcat Row	*Cumberland* - Penrith
Ulceby	*Lincoln* - Great Grimsby
Ulceby Cross	*Lincoln* - Skegness
Ulceby Skitter	*Lincoln* - Barton-on-Humber
Ulceby with Fordington	*Lincoln* - Skegness
Ulcombe	*Kent* - Maidstone
Uldale	*Cumberland* - Whitehaven
Uldale	*Cumberland* - Carlisle
Uley	*Gloucester* - Stroud
Ulgham	*Northumberland* - Morpeth
Ulgham Grange	*Northumberland* - Morpeth
Ullenhall	*Warwick* - Stratford on Avon
Ullenwood	*Gloucester* - Cheltenham
Ulleskelf	*York, W.R.* - York
Ullesthorpe	*Leicester* - Hinckley
Ulley	*York, W.R.* - Rotherham
Ullingswick	*Hereford* - Hereford
Ullington	*Gloucester* - Evesham
Ullock	*Cumberland* - Workington
Ulnes Walton	*Lancaster* - Chorley
Ulpha	*Cumberland* - Whitehaven
Ulpha	*Lancaster* - Barrow-in-Furness
Ulpha	*Westmorland* - Kendal
Ulpham	*Northumberland* - Carlisle
Ulrome	*York, E.R.* - Bridlington
Ulting	*Essex* - Maldon
Ulverscroft	*Leicester* - Leicester
Ulverston	*Lancaster* - Barrow-in-Furness
Ulwell	*Dorset* - Swanage
Umberleigh	*Devon* - Barnstaple
Umberslade	*Warwick* - Birmingham
Underbank	*York, W.R.* - Huddersfield
Underbarrow	*Westmorland* - Kendal
Undercliffe	*York, W.R.* - Bradford
Underdale	*Salop* - Shrewsbury
Underhill	*Cornwall* - Launceston
Underhill	*Kent* - Cranbrook
Underhill	*York, W.R.* - Huddersfield
Underley	*Hereford* - Leominster
Underriver	*Kent* - Sevenoaks
Underskiddaw	*Cumberland* - Workington
Underton	*Salop* - Bridgnorth
Underwood	*Devon* - Plymouth
Underwood	*Notts* - Alfreton

Undy	*Monmouth* - Chepstow
Unstone	*Derby* - Chesterfield
Unstone Green	*Derby* - Chesterfield
Unsworth	*Lancaster* - Bury
Unthank	*Cumberland* - Carlisle
Unthank (Gamblesby)	*Cumberland* - Penrith
Unthank (Skelton)	*Cumberland* - Penrith
Unthank	*Derby* - Chesterfield
Unthank	*Northumberland* - Alnwick
Unthank	*Northumberland* - Consett
Unthank	*Northumberland* - Hexham
Unthank End	*Cumberland* - Penrith
Upavon	*Wilts* - Devizes
Up Cerne	*Dorset* - Dorchester
Upchurch	*Kent* - Sittingbourne
Upcott	*Devon* - Launceston
Upcott	*Devon* - Barnstaple
Upend	*Cambridge* - Newmarket
Uphall	*Lincoln* - Louth
Upham	*Hants* - Winchester
Uphampton	*Hereford* - Leominster
Uphampton	*Worcester* - Worcester
Up Hatherley	*Gloucester* - Cheltenham
Uphill	*Somerset* - Weston Super Mare
Upholland	*Lancaster* - Wigan
Uplands	*Gloucester* - Stroud
Upleadon	*Gloucester* - Gloucester
Upleatham	*York, N.R.* - Middlesbrough
Uplees	*Kent* - Canterbury
Uplowman	*Devon* - Tiverton
Uplyme	*Devon* - Axminster and Chard
Up Marden	*Sussex* - Chichester
Upminster	*Essex* - Ilford
Up Nately	*Hants* - Basingstoke
Upney	*Essex* - Ilford
Upnor	*Kent* - Rochester
Upottery	*Devon* - Exeter
Upper Aber Canaid	*Glamorgan* - Merthyr Tydfil
Upper Allithwaite	*Lancaster* - Barrow-in-Furness
Upper Almondsbury	*Gloucester* - Thornbury
Upper Arley	*Worcester* - Kidderminster
Upper Arncott	*Oxford* - Oxford
Upper Assenden	*Oxford* - Reading
Upper Basildon	*Berks* - Reading
Upper Batley	*York, W.R.* - Dewsbury
Upper Baynton	*Wilts* - Trowbridge
Upper Beeding	*Sussex* - Brighton
Upper Benefield	*Northampton* - Corby
Upper Bentley	*Worcester* - Redditch
Upper Berrow	*Worcester* - Redditch
Upper Bittell	*Worcester* - Redditch
Upper Boat	*Glamorgan* - Pontypridd
Upper Boddington	*Northampton* - Banbury
Upper Bourne	*Surrey* - Aldershot and Farnham
Upper Brailes	*Warwick* - Banbury
Upper Brockhill	*Worcester* - Redditch
Upper Broughton	*Notts* - Melton Mowbray
Upper Bullingham	*Hereford* - Hereford
Upper Buncton	*Sussex* - Worthing
Upperby	*Cumberland* - Carlisle
Upper Caldecote	*Beds* - Biggleswade
Upper Cam	*Gloucester* - Stroud
Upper Canterton	*Hants* - Southampton
Upper Carron	*Cardigan* - Lampeter
Upper Cheddon	*Somerset* - Taunton
Upper Chirk	*Denbigh* - Wrexham
Upper Clapton	*London, E.5* - Shoreditch
Upper Clatford	*Hants* - Andover
Upper Cokeham	*Sussex* - Worthing
Upper Colliers Row	*Glamorgan* - Merthyr Tydfil
Upper Coscomb	*Gloucester* - Cheltenham
Upper Cumberworth	*York, W.R.* - Huddersfield
Upper Cwmbargoed	*Glamorgan* - Merthyr Tydfil
Upper Cwmbran	*Monmouth* - Newport (Mon.)
Upper Dean	*Beds* - Bedford
Upper Denham	*Bucks* - Uxbridge
Upper Denton	*Cumberland* - Carlisle
Upper Dicker	*Sussex* - Eastbourne
Upper Dunsford	*York, W.R.* - Harrogate
Upper Edmonton	*London, N.18* - Edmonton

Upper Eldon	*Hants* - Winchester
Upper Elkstone	*Stafford* - Leek
Upper Elmhurst	*York, W.R.* - Barnsley
Upper Ettingshall	*Stafford* - Dudley
Upper Exe	*Devon* - Tiverton
Upper Farringdon	*Hants* - Aldershot and Farnham
Upper Froyle	*Hants* - Aldershot and Farnham
Upper Garth	*Denbigh* - Wrexham
Upper Goldicote	*Warwick* - Stratford on Avon
Upper Gornal	*Stafford* - Dudley
Upper Gravenhurst	*Beds* - Hitchin
Upper Green (Langley)	*Essex* - Bishop's Stortford
Upper Green	*Herts* - Hertford
Upper Green	*York, W.R.* - Dewsbury
Upper Grove Common	*Hereford* - Monmouth
Upper Hackney	*Derby* - Matlock
Upper Hagg	*York, W.R.* - Huddersfield
Upper Hale	*Kent* - Margate
Upper Hale	*Surrey* - Aldershot and Farnham
Upper Hallam	*York, W.R.* - Sheffield
Upper Halling	*Kent* - Rochester
Upper Hardres	*Kent* - Canterbury
Upper Harpton	*Radnor* - Knighton
Upper Hartshay	*Derby* - Alfreton
Upper Hayton	*Salop* - Ludlow
Upper Hazelor	*Worcester* - Evesham
Upper Hazle	*Gloucester* - Thornbury
Upper Heage	*Derby* - Alfreton
Upper Helmsley	*York, N.R.* - York
Upper Hergest	*Hereford* - Hereford
Upper Heyford	*Northampton* - Northampton
Upper Heyford	*Oxford* - Banbury
Upper Higham	*Kent* - Rochester
Upper Hill	*Hereford* - Leominster
Upper Hodnell	*Warwick* - Warwick
Upper Holloway	*London, N.19* - Clerkenwell
Upper Honeydon	*Beds* - Biggleswade
Upper Hopton	*York, W.R.* - Dewsbury
Upperhouse	*York, W.R.* - Huddersfield
Upper Kingston	*Hants* - Bournemouth
Upper Kinsham	*Hereford* - Leominster
Upper Lambourn	*Berks* - Newbury
Upper Langwith	*Derby* - Chesterfield
Upper Llandwrog	*Caernarvon* - Caernarvon
Upper Llanvrecha	*Monmouth* - Newport (Mon.)
Upper Loughor	*Glamorgan* - Swansea
Upper Luddesdown	*Kent* - Gravesend
Upper Lydbrook	*Gloucester* - Gloucester
Upper Mayfield	*Stafford* - Uttoxeter
Upper Midhope	*York, W.R.* - Sheffield
Upper Midway	*Derby* - Burton-upon-Trent
Uppermill	*York, W.R.* - Oldham
Upper Moor	*Worcester* - Evesham
Upper Norwood (part)	*London, S.E.19* - Croydon
Upper Norwood (part)	*London, S.E.19* - Lambeth
Upper Norwood	*Sussex* - Chichester
Upper Penn	*Stafford* - Wolverhampton
Upper Pleasley	*Derby* - Mansfield
Upper Poppleton	*York, W.R.* - York
Upper Quinton	*Warwick* - Stratford on Avon
Upper Radbourne	*Warwick* - Warwick
Upper Rawcliffe	*Lancaster* - Preston
Upper Reule	*Stafford* - Stafford
Upper Rochford	*Worcester* - Ludlow
Upper Sapey	*Hereford* - Worcester
Upper Shelton	*Beds* - Bedford
Upper Shuckburgh	*Warwick* - Rugby
Upper Slaughter	*Gloucester* - Cheltenham
Upper Somborne	*Hants* - Winchester
Upper Spen	*York, W.R.* - Dewsbury
Upper Stoke	*Kent* - Rochester
Upper Stondon	*Beds* - Biggleswade
Upper Stonebeck	*York, W.R.* - Harrogate
Upper Strensham	*Worcester* - Cheltenham
Upper Studley	*Wilts* - Trowbridge
Upper Sundon	*Beds* - Luton
Upper Swainswick	*Somerset* - Bath
Upper Swell	*Gloucester* - Cheltenham
Upper Sydenham	*London, S.E.26* - Lambeth

Upper Thong	*York, W.R.* - Huddersfield
Upperthorpe	*Lincoln* - Gainsborough
Upperthorpe	*York, W.R.* - Sheffield
Upperton	*Sussex* - Chichester
Upper Tooting	*London, S.W.17* - Wandsworth
Uppertown	*Derby* - Chesterfield
Upper Town	*York, W.R.* - Keighley
Upper Twinhoe	*Somerset* - Bath
Upper Tysoe	*Warwick* - Banbury
Upper Wavensmere	*Warwick* - Stratford on Avon
Upper Weald	*Bucks* - Bletchley and Leighton Buzzard
Upper Weedon	*Northampton* - Northampton
Upper Welton	*Cumberland* - Carlisle
Upper Westwood	*Wilts* - Trowbridge
Upper Whitbourne	*Wilts* - Warminster
Upper Wick	*Worcester* - Worcester
Upper Wield	*Hants* - Winchester
Upper Winchendon	*Bucks* - Aylesbury
Upper Windrush	*Gloucester* - Cheltenham
Upper Wintringham	*Hunts* - Huntingdon
Upper Wood	*Derby* - Matlock
Upper Woodford	*Wilts* - Salisbury
Upper Wootton	*Hants* - Basingstoke
Upincott	*Devon* - Tiverton
Uppingham	*Rutland* - Corby
Uppington	*Montgomery* - Welshpool
Uppington	*Salop* - Wellington (Salop)
Upsall	*York, N.R.* - Middlesbrough
Upsall	*York, N.R.* - Northallerton
Upshire	*Essex* - Edmonton
Upsland	*York, N.R.* - Harrogate
Upstreet	*Kent* - Canterbury
Upton	*Berks* - Didcot
Upton	*Bucks* - Aylesbury
Upton	*Cheshire* - Macclesfield
Upton	*Devon* - Kingsbridge
Upton	*Devon* - Torquay
Upton	*Dorset* - Poole
Upton	*Dorset* - Weymouth
Upton	*Hants* - Andover
Upton	*Hereford* - Ludlow
Upton	*Hunts* - Huntingdon
Upton	*Lancaster* - St. Helens
Upton	*Leicester* - Nuneaton
Upton	*Lincoln* - Gainsborough
Upton	*Northampton* - Northampton
Upton	*Northampton* - Peterborough
Upton	*Notts* - East Retford
Upton	*Notts* - Newark
Upton	*Oxford* - Witney
Upton	*Pembroke* - Haverfordwest
Upton	*Somerset* - Tiverton
Upton (Long Sutton)	*Somerset* - Yeovil
Upton	*York, W.R.* - Pontefract
Upton Bishop	*Hereford* - Gloucester
Upton by Chester	*Cheshire* - Chester
Upton Cheyney	*Gloucester* - Bristol
Upton Cressett	*Salop* - Bridgnorth
Upton Crews	*Hereford* - Gloucester
Upton Cross	*Cornwall* - Liskeard
Upton End	*Beds* - Hitchin
Upton Grey	*Hants* - Basingstoke
Upton Hellions	*Devon* - Exeter
Upton Lea	*Bucks* - Slough
Upton Lovell	*Wilts* - Warminster
Upton Magna	*Salop* - Shrewsbury
Upton Noble	*Somerset* - Frome
Upton-on-Severn	*Worcester* - Great Malvern
Upton Park	*Bucks* - Slough
Upton Park	*London, E.6* - Bow
Upton Pyne	*Devon* - Exeter
Upton St. Leonards	*Gloucester* - Gloucester
Upton Scudamore	*Wilts* - Warminster
Upton Snodsbury	*Worcester* - Worcester
Upton Towans	*Cornwall* - Redruth
Upton Warren	*Worcester* - Bromsgrove
Upton, Wirral	*Cheshire* - Birkenhead
Upton with Fishley	*Norfolk* - Norwich
Upwaltham	*Sussex* - Chichester

Upware	*Cambridge* - Newmarket
Upwell	*Cambridge and Norfolk* - Wisbech
Upwey	*Dorset* - Weymouth
Upwick	*Herts* - Bishop's Stortford
Upwood	*Hunts* - Huntingdon
Urchfont	*Wilts* - Devizes
Uridge	*Wilts* - Bath
Urlay Nook	*Durham* - Stockton on Tees
Urmston	*Lancaster* - Salford
Urpeth	*Durham* - Gateshead
Urpeth Forge	*Durham* - Gateshead
Urpeth Lodge	*Durham* - Gateshead
Urpeth Mill	*Durham* - Gateshead
Urpeth Pits	*Durham* - Gateshead
Urswick, Great	*Lancaster* - Barrow-in-Furness
Urswick, Little	*Lancaster* - Barrow-in-Furness
Ushaw College	*Durham* - Durham
Ushaw Moor Colliery	*Durham* - Durham
Usk	*Monmouth* - Pontypool and Abergavenny
Usselby	*Lincoln* - Lincoln
Usworth	*Durham* - Gateshead
Usworth Colliery	*Durham* - Gateshead
Usworth, Great	*Durham* - Gateshead
Utkinton	*Cheshire* - Chester
Utley, High	*York, W.R.* - Keighley
Utley, Low	*York, W.R.* - Keighley
Uton	*Devon* - Exeter
Utterby	*Lincoln* - Louth
Uttoxeter	*Stafford* - Uttoxeter
Uwchygarreg	*Montgomery* - Machynlleth
Uxbridge	*Middlesex* - Uxbridge
Uxbridge Common	*Middlesex* - Uxbridge
Uxbridge Moor	*Middlesex* - Uxbridge
Uzmaston	*Pembroke* - Haverfordwest

V

Vagg (Yeovil Marsh)	*Somerset* - Yeovil
Valley	*Anglesey* - Llangefni
Valley End	*Surrey* - Guildford
Valley Terrace	*Durham* - Bishop Auckland
Van	*Montgomery* - Newtown
Vange	*Essex* - Brentwood
Van Terrace	*Glamorgan* - Caerphilly
Varteg	*Monmouth* - Pontypool and Abergavenny
Vauxhall	*London S.E.11* - Lambeth
Vauxhall	*Salop* - Wellington (Salop)
Vauxhall	*Warwick* - Birmingham
Vaynol	*Caernarvon* - Bangor
Vaynor	*Glamorgan* - Merthyr Tydfil
Velindre	*Brecon* - Pontypool and Abergavenny
Velindre	*Brecon* - Brecknock
Velindre	*Carmarthen* - Carmarthen
Velindre (part)	*Glamorgan* - Neath
Velindre (part)	*Glamorgan* - Swansea
Velindre	*Radnor* - Knighton
Velindre Farchog	*Pembroke* - Cardigan
Velvet Stone	*Hereford* - Leominster
Venn	*Devon* - Kingsbridge
Venn	*Pembroke* - Haverfordwest
Venn Cross	*Somerset* - Taunton
Vennington	*Salop* - Shrewsbury
Venn Ottery	*Devon* - Exeter
Vennyfach	*Brecon* - Brecknock
Venny Tedburn	*Devon* - Exeter
Venterden	*Cornwall* - Launceston
Ventnor	*I. of W.* - Newport (I.W.)
Venton	*Devon* - Plymouth
Ventongimps	*Cornwall* - Truro
Ventonleague	*Cornwall* - Redruth
Vernham	*Hants* - Andover
Vernolds Common	*Salop* - Ludlow
Verrington (Wincanton)	*Somerset* - Yeovil
Verwig	*Cardigan* - Cardigan

Verwood	*Dorset* - Wimborne Minster
Veryan	*Cornwall* - Truro
Vicarage Cottages	*Gloucester* - Cheltenham
Vickerstown-Walney	*Lancaster* - Barrow-in-Furness
Victoria	*Cornwall* - St. Austell
Victoria	*Durham* - Bishop Auckland
Victoria (part)	*London, S.W.1* - West London
Victoria (part)	*London, S.W.1* - Westminster
Victoria	*York, W.R.* - Huddersfield
Victoria Colliery	*Durham* - Bishop Auckland
Victoria Garesfield Colliery	*Durham* - Newcastle upon Tyne
Victoria Park	*London, E.2* - Shoreditch
Victoria Park (part)	*London, E.9* - Bow
Victoria Park (part)	*London, E.9* - Shoreditch
Victoria Town	*Monmouth* - Blackwood
Victoria Village	*Monmouth* - Pontypool and Abergavenny
Victory	*Lancaster* - Bolton
Vigo	*Durham* - Gateshead
Vigo	*Worcester* - Redditch
Villa Real	*Durham* - Consett
Vinegar Hill	*Beds* - Biggleswade
Vinehall	*Sussex* - Hastings
Viney Hill (West Dean)	*Gloucester* - Monmouth
Viney Hill (East Dean)	*Gloucester* - Gloucester
Vinnals	*Salop* - Shrewsbury
Virginia Water	*Berks and Surrey* - Slough
Virgin's End	*Stafford* - West Bromwich
Virginstow	*Devon* - Launceston
Virley	*Essex* - Colchester
Vobster	*Somerset* - Frome
Voel Gastell	*Carmarthen* - Carmarthen
Vogue St. Day	*Cornwall* - Redruth
Vorlan	*Pembroke* - Haverfordwest
Vowchurch	*Hereford* - Hereford
Vro	*Brecon* - Pontypool and Abergavenny
Vron	*Denbigh* - Wrexham
Vroncysyllte	*Denbigh* - Wrexham
Vrongate	*Salop* - Shrewsbury
Vulcan	*Lancaster* - Warrington

W

Waberthwaite	*Cumberland* - Whitehaven
Wackerfield	*Durham* - Bishop Auckland
Wacton	*Hereford* - Leominster
Wacton	*Norfolk* - Norwich
Wacton's Green	*Hereford* - Leominster
Wadborough	*Worcester* - Evesham
Waddesdon	*Bucks* - Aylesbury
Waddeton	*Devon* - Torquay
Wadd, Great	*Kent* - Maidstone
Waddingham	*Lincoln* - Scunthorpe
Waddington	*Lincoln* - Lincoln
Waddington	*York, W.R.* - Blackburn
Waddingworth	*Lincoln* - Lincoln
Wadd Little	*Kent* - Maidstone
Waddock	*Dorset* - Dorchester
Waddon	*Surrey* - Croydon
Wadebridge	*Cornwall* - Bodmin
Wadeford	*Somerset* - Axminster and Chard
Wadenhoe	*Northampton* - Kettering
Wadesmill	*Herts* - Hertford
Wadhurst	*Sussex* - Tunbridge Wells
Wadshelf	*Derby* - Chesterfield
Wadsley	*York, W.R.* - Sheffield
Wadsley Bridge	*York, W.R.* - Sheffield
Wadswick	*Wilts* - Bath
Wadworth	*York, W.R.* - Doncaster
Waen	*Denbigh* - Denbigh
Waen (St. Asaph)	*Flint* - Rhyl
Waen	*Flint* - Mold
Waenfawr	*Caernarvon* - Caernarvon

WAE - WAL

Place	County - Post Town
Waen Isa	*Flint* - Mold
Waenpentir	*Caernarvon* - Caernarvon
Waenwen	*Brecon* - Pontypool and Abergavenny
Wagbeach	*Salop* - Shrewsbury
Waggoners Wells	*Hants* - Petersfield
Wagtail	*Durham* - Durham
Wainfelin	*Monmouth* - Pontypool and Abergavenny
Wainfleet All Saints	*Lincoln* - Skegness
Wainfleet St. Marys	*Lincoln* - Skegness
Waingroves	*Derby* - Alfreton
Wainhouse Corner	*Cornwall* - Launceston
Wainscot	*Kent* - Rochester
Wainsford	*Hants* - Lymington
Wainstalls	*York, W.R.* - Halifax
Waitby	*Westmorland* - Penrith
Waithe	*Lincoln* - Great Grimsby
Wakefield	*York, W.R.* - Wakefield
Wakefield Lodge	*Northampton* - Northampton
Wakely	*Herts* - Hertford
Wakering, Great	*Essex* - Southend
Wakering, Little	*Essex* - Southend
Wakerley	*Northampton* - Stamford
Wakes Colne	*Essex* - Colchester
Walberswick	*Suffolk* - Halesworth
Walberton	*Sussex* - Chichester
Walby	*Cumberland* - Carlisle
Walcot	*Lincoln* - Scunthorpe
Walcot (Billinghay)	*Lincoln* - Sleaford
Walcot (Folkingham)	*Lincoln* - Sleaford
Walcot	*Norfolk* - Norwich
Walcot	*Salop* - Wellington (Salop)
Walcot	*Worcester* - Evesham
Walcot Dales	*Lincoln* - Sleaford
Walcote	*Leicester* - Rugby
Walcot Fen	*Lincoln* - Sleaford
Walcot Waste	*Salop* - Wellington (Salop)
Walden Stubbs	*York, W.R.* - Pontefract
Waldersea	*Cambridge* - Wisbech
Waldershare	*Kent* - Dover
Walderslade	*Kent* - Rochester
Walderton	*Sussex* - Chichester
Walditch	*Dorset* - Dorchester
Waldley	*Derby* - Uttoxeter
Waldridge	*Bucks* - Aylesbury
Waldridge	*Durham* - Durham
Waldringfield	*Suffolk* - Ipswich
Waldron	*Sussex* - Eastbourne
Wales	*York, W.R.* - Worksop
Wales Bar	*York, W.R.* - Worksop
Walesby	*Lincoln* - Lincoln
Walesby	*Notts* - East Retford
Walesby Moor	*Lincoln* - Lincoln
Waleswood	*York, W.R.* - Worksop
Walford	*Hereford* - Knighton
Walford	*Hereford* - Monmouth
Walford	*Salop* - Shrewsbury
Walford	*Stafford* - Stafford
Walford Cross	*Somerset* - Taunton
Walgrave	*Northampton* - Northampton
Walham Green	*London, S.W.6* - West London
Walhampton	*Hants* - Lymington
Walkden	*Lancaster* - Salford
Walker	*Northumberland* - Newcastle upon Tyne
Walker Barn	*Cheshire* - Macclesfield
Walker Gate	*Northumberland* - Newcastle upon Tyne
Walkeringham	*Notts* - Gainsborough
Walkerith	*Lincoln* - Gainsborough
Walkern	*Herts* - Hitchin
Walker's Heath	*Warwick* - Birmingham
Walkerville	*Northumberland* Newcastle upon Tyne
Walkerville	*York, N.R.* - Darlington
Walkford	*Hants* - Bournemouth
Walkhampton	*Devon* - Plymouth
Walkingham Hill with Occaney	*York, W.R.* - Harrogate

WAL

Place	County - Post Town
Walkington	*York, E.R.* - Beverley
Walkley	*York, W.R.* - Sheffield
Walk Mill	*Lancaster* - Burnley
Walk Mill	*Northumberland* - Alnwick
Walk Mill	*Salop* - Shrewsbury
Walk Mill	*Stafford* - Stafford
Walkwood	*Worcester* - Redditch
Wall	*Cornwall* - Redruth
Wall	*Northumberland* - Hexham
Wall	*Stafford* - Lichfield
Wallas	*Glamorgan* - Bridgend
Wallasea Island	*Essex* - Southend
Wallasey	*Cheshire* - Birkenhead
Wallbottle	*Northumberland* - Newcastle upon Tyne
Wallbottle Colliery, North	*Northumberland* - Newcastle upon Tyne
Wallbridge	*Gloucester* - Stroud
Wallbrook	*Stafford* - Dudley
Wall, East	*Salop* - Ludlow
Wallerthwaite	*York, W.R.* - Harrogate
Wall Grange	*Stafford* - Leek
Wallheath	*Stafford* - Stourbridge
Wall Hill	*Warwick* - Coventry
Wall Hill	*York, W.R.* - Oldham
Wallingford	*Berks* - Didcot
Wallington	*Hants* - Portsmouth
Wallington	*Herts* - Hitchin
Wallington	*Norfolk* - King's Lynn
Wallington	*Surrey* - Croydon
Wallington Demesne	*Northumberland* - Morpeth
Wallington Heath	*Stafford* - Walsall
Wallingwells	*York, W.R.* - Worksop
Wallisdown (High Road North Side)	*Hants* - Bournemouth
Wallisdown (High Road, South Side)	*Dorset* - Poole
Wallis Wood	*Surrey* - Dorking
Wallop	*Salop* - Shrewsbury
Wallop, Middle	*Hants* - Andover
Wallop, Nether	*Hants* - Andover
Wallop, Over	*Hants* - Andover
Wallow Green	*Gloucester* - Stroud
Wallridge	*Northumberland* - Newcastle upon Tyne
Wallsend	*Northumberland* - North Shields
Walls Green	*Essex* - Chelmsford
Wallshield	*Northumberland* - Hexham
Wall's Quarry	*Gloucester* - Stroud
Wallthwaite	*Cumberland* - Workington
Walltown	*Northumberland* - Hexham
Wall under Heywood	*Salop* - Ludlow
Walmer	*Kent* - Deal
Walmer Bridge	*Lancaster* - Preston
Walmersley	*Lancaster* - Bury
Walmley	*Warwick* - Birmingham
Walmley Ash	*Warwick* - Birmingham
Walmore Common	*Gloucester* - Gloucester
Walmsgate	*Lincoln* - Louth
Walmsley	*Lancaster* - Bolton
Walney Lighthouse	*Lancaster* - Barrow-in-Furness
Walpole	*Suffolk* - Halesworth
Walpole Cross Keys	*Norfolk* - Wisbech
Walpole Highway	*Norfolk* - Wisbech
Walpole Marsh	*Norfolk* - Wisbech
Walpole St. Andrew	*Norfolk* - Wisbech
Walpole St. Peter	*Norfolk* - Wisbech
Walsall	*Stafford* - Walsall
Walsall End	*Warwick* - Birmingham
Walsall Wood	*Stafford* - Walsall
Walsden	*Lancaster* - Todmorden
Walsgrave-on-Sowe	*Warwick* - Coventry
Walsham-le-Willows	*Suffolk* - Bury St. Edmunds
Walsham, North	*Norfolk* - Norwich
Walsham, South	*Norfolk* - Norwich
Walshaw	*Lancaster* - Bury
Walshaw	*York, W.R.* - Todmorden
Walshford	*York, W.R.* - Harrogate
Walsingham, Great	*Norfolk* - King's Lynn
Walsingham, Little	*Norfolk* - King's Lynn

Walsoken	*Cambridge* - Wisbech
Walstead Common	*Sussex* - Haywards Heath
Walsworth	*Herts* - Hitchin
Walters Ash	*Bucks* - High Wycombe
Walters Green	*Kent* - Tonbridge
Walterston	*Glamorgan* - Barry
Walterstone	*Hereford* - Pontypool and Abergavenny
Waltham	*Kent* - Canterbury
Waltham	*Lincoln* - Great Grimsby
Waltham Abbey	*Essex* - Edmonton
Waltham Chase	*Hants* - Portsmouth
Waltham Cross	*Herts* - Edmonton
Waltham Forest (part)	*Essex* - Edmonton
Waltham, Great	*Essex* - Chelmsford
Waltham, Little	*Essex* - Chelmsford
Waltham, New	*Lincoln* - Great Grimsby
Waltham, North	*Hants* - Basingstoke
Waltham-on-the-Wolds	*Leicester* - Melton Mowbray
Waltham St. Lawrence	*Berks* - Slough
Walthamstow	*London, E.17* - Bow
Walton	*Bucks* - Aylesbury
Walton	*Bucks* - Bletchley and Leighton Buzzard
Walton	*Cumberland* - Carlisle
Walton	*Derby* - Chesterfield
Walton	*Hereford* - Kington
Walton	*Leicester* - Rugby
Walton	*Radnor* - Knighton
Walton	*Salop* - Ludlow
Walton (Telford)	*Salop* - Wellington
Walton	*Somerset* - Wells
Walton	*Stafford* - Stafford
Walton	*Suffolk* - Ipswich
Walton	*Warwick* - Stratford on Avon
Walton	*York, W.R.* - Harrogate
Walton	*York, W.R.* - Wakefield
Walton Bay	*Somerset* - Weston Super Mare
Walton Cardiff	*Gloucester* - Cheltenham
Walton, East	*Norfolk* - King's Lynn
Walton, East	*Pembroke* - Haverfordwest
Walton Grounds	*Northampton* - Banbury
Walton Heath	*Stafford* - Stafford
Walton Heath	*Surrey* - Reigate
Walton, High	*Salop* - Ludlow
Walton, Higher	*Cheshire* - Warrington
Walton, Higher	*Lancaster* - Preston
Walton Highway	*Norfolk* - Wisbech
Walton Hill	*Gloucester* - Cheltenham
Walton Hills	*Worcester* - Stourbridge
Walton Hurst	*Stafford* - Stafford
Walton-in-Gordano	*Somerset* - Weston Super Mare
Walton-le-Dale	*Lancaster* - Preston
Walton, Little	*Warwick* - Rugby
Walton, Lower	*Cheshire* - Warrington
Walton-on-Thames	*Surrey* - Kingston-upon-Thames
Walton-on-the-Hill	*Stafford* - Stafford
Walton-on-the-Hill	*Surrey* - Epsom
Walton on the Naze	*Essex* - Colchester
Walton on the Wolds	*Leicester* - Loughborough
Walton-on-Trent	*Derby* - Burton-upon-Trent
Walton, West	*Norfolk* - Wisbech
Walton, West	*Pembroke* - Haverfordwest
Walves	*Lancaster* - Bury
Walwen Axton	*Flint* - Holywell
Walworth	*Durham* - Darlington
Walworth	*London, S.E.17* - Lambeth
Walwyns Castle	*Pembroke* - Haverfordwest
Wambrook	*Somerset* - Axminster and Chard
Wampool	*Cumberland* - Carlisle
Wanborough	*Surrey* - Guildford
Wanborough	*Wilts* - Swindon
Wanborough, Lower	*Wilts* - Swindon
Wandon	*Stafford* - Stafford
Wandon End	*Herts* - Hitchin
Wandsworth	*London, S.W.18* - Wandsworth
Wandsworth Common	*London, S.W.11* - Wandsworth
Wandsworth Common	*London, S.W.18* - Wandsworth
Wangford	*Suffolk* - Halesworth
Wangford	*Suffolk* - Thetford

Wanlip	*Leicester* - Leicester
Wannerton	*Worcester* - Kidderminster
Wannock	*Sussex* - Eastbourne
Wansford	*Huntingdon and Peterborough* - Stamford
Wansford	*York, E.R.* - Beverley
Wansley	*Notts* - Alfreton
Wanstead	*London, E.11* - Bow
Wanstone	*Kent* - Dover
Wanstrow	*Somerset* - Frome
Wanswell	*Gloucester* - Stroud
Wantage	*Berks* - Didcot
Wantisden	*Suffolk* - Woodbridge
Wapley	*Gloucester* - Bristol
Waplington	*York, E.R.* - York
Wappenbury	*Warwick* - Warwick
Wappenham	*Northampton* - Northampton
Wappenshall	*Salop* - Wellington (Salop)
Wapping	*London, E.1* - Shoreditch
Warble Bank	*Cumberland* - Carlisle
Warbleton	*Sussex* - Eastbourne
Warblington	*Hants* - Portsmouth
Warborough	*Oxford* - Didcot
Warboys	*Hunts* - Huntingdon
Warboys High Fen	*Hunts* - Huntingdon
Warboys Puddock Drove	*Hunts* - Huntingdon
Warbstow	*Cornwall* - Launceston
Warbstow Cross	*Cornwall* - Launceston
Warburton	*Cheshire* - Altrincham
Warburton	*York, W.R.* - Barnsley
Warcop	*Westmorland* - Penrith
Wardale	*Salop* - Market Drayton
Warden	*Beds* - Biggleswade
Warden	*Northumberland* - Hexham
Ward End	*Warwick* - Birmingham
Warden, Old	*Beds* - Biggleswade
Ward Gate	*Derby* - Derby
Ward Green	*York, W.R.* - Barnsley
Wardhedges	*Beds* - Bedford
Ward, High	*Northumberland* - Morpeth
Wardington	*Oxford* - Banbury
Wardle	*Cheshire* - Crewe
Wardle	*Lancaster* - Rochdale
Wardley	*Durham* - Gateshead
Wardley	*Rutland* - Corby
Wardley Marsh	*Sussex* - Petersfield
Wardleys	*Lancaster* - Blackpool
Wardlow	*Derby* - Buxton
Wardlow Mires	*Derby* - Buxton
Wardour	*Wilts* - Shaftesbury
Wards End	*Cheshire* - Macclesfield
Wardy Hill	*Cambridge* - Ely
Ware	*Herts* - Hertford
Ware	*Kent* - Deal
Wareham	*Dorset* - Swanage
Warehead	*Sussex* - Chichester
Warhorne	*Kent* - Ashford
Warenford	*Northumberland* - Berwick-upon-Tweed
Wareside	*Herts* - Hertford
Waresley	*Hunts* - Biggleswade
Waresley	*Worcester* - Kidderminster
Warfield	*Berks* - Reading
Warford, Great	*Cheshire* - Macclesfield
Wargate Bridge	*Lincoln* - Spalding
Wargrave	*Berks* - Reading
Warham	*Hereford* - Hereford
Warham St. Mary	*Norfolk* - King's Lynn
Warings Green	*Warwick* - Birmingham
Wark	*Northumberland* - Berwick-upon-Tweed
Wark	*Northumberland* - Hexham
Warkleigh	*Devon* - Barnstaple
Warksburn	*Northumberland* - Hexham
Warkton	*Northampton* - Kettering
Warkworth	*Northampton* - Banbury
Warkworth	*Northumberland* - Alnwick
Warlaby	*York, N.R.* - Northallerton
Warleggon	*Cornwall* - Bodmin

WAR - WAS

Warleigh	*Somerset* - Bath
Warley	*Worcester* - West Bromwich
Warley	*York, W.R.* - Halifax
Warley, Great	*Essex* - Brentwood
Warley, Little	*Essex* - Brentwood
Warlingham	*Surrey* - Croydon
Warlingham, Upper	*Surrey* - Croydon
Warmfield	*York, W.R.* - Wakefield
Warmingham	*Cheshire* - Crewe
Warminghurst	*Sussex* - Worthing
Warmington	*Northampton* - Peterborough
Warmington	*Warwick* - Banbury
Warminster	*Wilts* - Warminster
Warmley	*Gloucester* - Bristol
Warmsworth	*York, W.R.* - Doncaster
Warmwell	*Dorset* - Dorchester
Warnborough, North	*Hants* - Basingstoke
Warnborough, South	*Hants* - Basingstoke
Warnell	*Cumberland* - Carlisle
Warners End	*Herts* - Hemel Hempstead
Warnford	*Hants* - Petersfield
Warnham	*Sussex* - Horsham
Warningcamp	*Sussex* - Chichester
Warninglid	*Sussex* - Haywards Heath
Warpsgrove	*Oxford* - Thame
Warren	*Pembroke* - Haverfordwest
Warren	*York, W.R.* - Sheffield
Warrenby	*York, N.R.* - Middlesbrough
Warren Court	*Hants* - Andover
Warren Row	*Berks* - Reading
Warren's Green	*Herts* - Hitchin
Warren Street	*Kent* - Maidstone
Warren Street	*Kent* - Sittingbourne
Warren, The	*Salop* - Market Drayton
Warrington	*Lancaster* - Warrington
Warrington	*Northampton* - Northampton
Warsash	*Hants* - Portsmouth
Warsill	*York, W.R.* - Harrogate
Warslow	*Stafford* - Leek
Warsop	*Notts* - Mansfield
Warsop Church	*Notts* - Mansfield
Warsop Vale	*Notts* - Mansfield
Warstock	*Warwick* - Birmingham
Warstone Fields	*Stafford* - West Bromwich
Warstones	*Stafford* - Wolverhampton
Warter	*York, E.R.* - York
Warth	*Lancaster* - Bury
Warthill	*York, N.R.* - York
Warthole	*Cumberland* - Workington
Wartling	*Sussex* - Eastbourne
Wartnaby	*Leicester* - Melton Mowbray
Warton	*Lancaster* - Preston
Warton	*Northumberland* - Morpeth
Warton	*Stafford* - Wellington (Salop)
Warton	*Warwick* - Tamworth
Warton with Lindeth	*Lancaster* - Lancaster
Warwick	*Cumberland* - Carlisle
Warwick	*Warwick* - Warwick
Warwick Bridge	*Cumberland* - Carlisle
Warwicks	*Essex* - Harlow
Warwicks Wold	*Surrey* - Reigate
Wasdale	*Cumberland* - Whitehaven
Washaway	*Cornwall* - Bodmin
Washbourne	*Devon* - Torquay
Washbourne, Great	*Gloucester* - Cheltenham
Washbourne, Little	*Gloucester* - Cheltenham
Washbrook	*Lancaster* - Oldham
Washbrook	*Suffolk* - Ipswich
Washerwall	*Stafford* - Stoke-on-Trent
Washfield	*Devon* - Tiverton
Washford	*Somerset* - Minehead
Washford	*Worcester* - Redditch
Washford Pyne	*Devon* - Tiverton
Washingborough	*Lincoln* - Lincoln
Washingborough Fen	*Lincoln* - Lincoln
Washingley	*Hunts* - Peterborough
Washingpool	*Gloucester* - Thornbury
Washington	*Durham* - Gateshead
Washington	*Sussex* - Worthing
Washington, New	*Durham* - Gateshead

WAS - WAT

Washington Staiths	*Durham* - Gateshead
Washington Station	*Durham* - Gateshead
Washpool	*Gloucester* - Stroud
Wash, The	*Herts* - Bishop's Stortford
Washwood Heath	*Warwick* - Birmingham
Wasing	*Berks* - Newbury
Waskerley	*Durham* - Consett
Wasperton	*Warwick* - Warwick
Wass	*York, N.R.* - Malton
Wassand	*York, E.R.* - Beverley
Watchet	*Somerset* - Minehead
Watchfield	*Berks* - Swindon
Watchfield	*Somerset* - Weston Super Mare
Watch Hill	*Cumberland* - Carlisle
Watcombe	*Devon* - Torquay
Watendlath	*Cumberland* - Workington
Water	*Lancaster* - Rawtenstall
Waterbeach	*Cambridge* - Cambridge
Waterbeach	*Sussex* - Chichester
Watercombe	*Dorset* - Dorchester
Waterdales	*Kent* - Gravesend
Waterden	*Norfolk* - King's Lynn
Waterditch	*Hants* - Bournemouth
Water Eaton	*Bucks* - Bletchley and Leighton Buzzard
Water Eaton	*Oxford* - Oxford
Water Eaton	*Stafford* - Stafford
Water Eaton	*Wilts* - Swindon
Water End	*Herts* - Hemel Hempstead
Water End	*Oxford* - High Wycombe
Waterfall	*Stafford* - Leek
Waterfall Cross	*Stafford* - Leek
Waterfoot	*Lancaster* - Rawtenstall
Waterford	*Herts* - Hertford
Watergall	*Warwick* - Warwick
Watergate	*Cornwall* - Truro
Watergate	*Sussex* - Chichester
Watergate Colliery	*Durham* - Gateshead
Water Greens	*Cumberland* - Carlisle
Waterhall	*Sussex* - Brighton
Waterham	*Kent* - Canterbury
Waterhead	*Devon* - Kingsbridge
Waterhead	*Lancaster* - Oldham
Waterhouses	*Durham* - Durham
Waterhouses	*Stafford* - Leek
Wateringbury	*Kent* - Maidstone
Water Lane	*Gloucester* - Stroud
Waterloo	*Cumberland* - Workington
Waterloo	*Glamorgan* - Cardiff
Waterloo	*Lancaster* - Ashton-under-Lyne
Waterloo	*Lancaster* - Liverpool
Waterloo	*Lincoln* - Lincoln
Waterloo	*Northumberland* - Hexham
Waterloo	*Salop* - Whitchurch
Waterloo	*Warwick* - Stratford on Avon
Waterloo	*Worcester* - Cheltenham
Waterloo Cross	*Devon* - Tiverton
Waterlooville	*Hants* - Portsmouth
Watermillock	*Cumberland* - Penrith
Watermoor	*Gloucester* - Swindon
Water Newton	*Hunts* - Peterborough
Water Oakley	*Berks* - Slough
Water Orton	*Warwick* - Birmingham
Waterperry	*Oxford* - Thame
Waterperry Common	*Oxford* - Thame
Watersfield	*Sussex* - Chichester
Waters Green	*Kent* - Tonbridge
Watersheddings	*Lancaster* - Oldham
Waterside	*Cumberland* - Carlisle
Waterside	*Herts* - Hemel Hempstead
Waterside	*Somerset* - Frome
Waterstock	*Oxford* - Thame
Waterston	*Pembroke* - Haverfordwest
Water Stratford	*Bucks* - Banbury
Waters Upton	*Salop* - Wellington (Salop)
Waterton	*Glamorgan* - Bridgend
Water Yeat	*Lancaster* - Barrow-in-Furness
Watford	*Herts* - Watford
Watford	*Northampton* - Rugby
Watford Gap	*Stafford* - Lichfield

WAT - WED

Watford Gap	*Warwick* - Birmingham
Wath	*Cumberland* - Carlisle
Wath	*York, N.R.* - Harrogate
Wath	*York, W.R.* - Harrogate
Wathermarske	*York, N.R.* - Harrogate
Wath-upon-Dearne	*York, W.R.* - Rotherham
Watledge	*Gloucester* - Stroud
Watley's End	*Gloucester* - Bristol
Watlington	*Norfolk* - King's Lynn
Watlington	*Oxford* - Thame
Watnall	*Notts* - Nottingham
Wattisfield	*Suffolk* - Bury St. Edmonds
Wattisham	*Suffolk* - Stowmarket
Wattlefield	*Norfolk* - Norwich
Wattlesborough	*Salop* - Shrewsbury
Watton	*Norfolk* - King's Lynn
Watton	*York, E.R.* - Beverley
Watton-at-Stone	*Herts* - Hertford
Wattons Ford	*Hants* - Bournemouth
Wattstown	*Glamorgan* - Pontypridd
Wattsville	*Monmouth* - Blackwood
Wauldby	*York, E.R.* - Kingston-upon-Hull
Waunarlwydd	*Glamorgan* - Swansea
Waunfawr	*Cardigan* - Aberystwyth
Waunllwyd	*Monmouth* - Blackwood
Waunwen	*Glamorgan* - Swansea
Waupley	*York, N.R.* - Whitby
Waupley, High	*York, N.R.* - Whitby
Wavendon	*Bucks* - Bletchley and Leighton Buzzard
Wavensmere, Lower	*Warwick* - Stratford on Avon
Wavensmere, Upper	*Warwick* - Stratford on Avon
Waver Bridge	*Cumberland* - Carlisle
Waverley	*Surrey* - Aldershot and Farnham
Waverton	*Cheshire* - Chester
Waverton	*Cumberland* - Carlisle
Wavertree	*Lancaster* - Liverpool
Wawne	*York, E.R.* - Beverley
Waxham	*Norfolk* - Great Yarmouth
Waxholme	*York, E.R.* - Kingston-upon-Hull
Wayend Street	*Hereford* - Hereford
Wayford	*Somerset* - Yeovil
Waygill Hill	*Cumberland* - Carlisle
Wayhead	*Cambridge* - Ely
Waytown	*Dorset* - Dorchester
Weakey	*York, W.R.* - Oldham
Weald	*Hunts* - Huntingdon
Weald	*Kent* - Sevenoaks
Weald	*Oxford* - Witney
Weald Bassett, North	*Essex* - Harlow
Weald Gullett	*Essex* - Harlow
Weald, Lower	*Bucks* - Bletchley and Leighton Buzzard
Weald, Middle	*Bucks* - Bletchley and Leighton Buzzard
Wealdstone	*Middlesex* - Willesden
Weald, South	*Essex* - Brentwood
Weald, Upper	Bucks - Bletchley and Leighton Buzzard
Wearde	*Cornwall* - Plymouth
Weardley	*York, W.R.* - Otley
Weare	*Somerset* - Wells
Weare Gifford	*Devon* - Bideford
Weare, Lower	*Somerset* - Wells
Wearhead	*Durham* - Bishop Auckland
Wearne	*Somerset* - Taunton
Weasenham All Saints	*Norfolk* - King's Lynn
Weasenham St. Peter	*Norfolk* - King's Lynn
Weaste	*Lancaster* - Salford
Weatherhill	*Surrey* - Reigate
Weatheroak	*Worcester* - Redditch
Weaveley	*Oxford* - Oxford
Weaverham	*Cheshire* - Northwich
Weaverthorpe	*York, E.R.* - Beverley
Webbington	*Somerset* - Weston Super Mare
Webbs Heath	*Gloucester* - Bristol
Webheath	*Worcester* - Redditch
Weddington	*Kent* - Deal
Weddington	*Warwick* - Nuneaton
Wedges Mills	*Stafford* - Walsall

WED - WEL

Wedgnock Park	*Warwick* - Warwick
Wedgwood	*Stafford* - Stoke-on-Trent
Wedhampton	*Wilts* - Devizes
Wedholme Hill	*Cumberland* - Carlisle
Wedmore	*Somerset* - Wells
Wednesbury	*Stafford* - Dudley
Wednesbury Oak	*Stafford* - Dudley
Wednesfield	*Stafford* - Wolverhampton
Wednesfield Heath	*Stafford* - Wolverhampton
Weedland	*York, E.R.* - Beverley
Weedley	*York, E.R.* - Beverley
Weedon	*Bucks* - Aylesbury
Weedon Bec	*Northampton* - Northampton
Weedon Lois	*Northampton* - Northampton
Weedon, Lower	*Northampton* - Northampton
Weedon, Upper	*Northampton* - Northampton
Weeford	*Stafford* - Lichfield
Week	*Devon* - Torquay
Weeke	*Hants* - Winchester
Weekaborough	*Devon* - Newton Abbot
Weekley	*Northampton* - Kettering
Week St. Mary	*Cornwall* - Launceston
Week, West	*Cornwall* - Launceston
Weel	*York, E.R.* - Beverley
Weeley	*Essex* - Colchester
Weeping Cross	*Salop* - Shrewsbury
Weeping Cross	*Stafford* - Stafford
Weethley	*Warwick* - Redditch
Weeting	*Norfolk* - Thetford
Weeton	*York, E.R.* - Kingston-upon-Hull
Weeton	*York, W.R.* - Otley
Weeton-with-Prees	*Lancaster* - Blackpool
Weetslade	*Northumberland* - Newcastle upon Tyne
Weetwood	*Northumberland* - Alnwick
Weetwood	*York, W.R.* - Leeds
Weetwood Common	*Cheshire* - Chester
Weighton, Little	*York, E.R.* - Beverley
Weir	*Lancaster* - Rawtenstall
Weir Brook	*Salop* - Oswestry
Weirend	*Hereford* - Monmouth
Weirs	*Berks* - Oxford
Welbatch	*Salop* - Shrewsbury
Welbeck	*Notts* - Worksop
Welbeck Colliery Village	*Notts* - Mansfield
Welborne	*Norfolk* - Norwich
Welbourn	*Lincoln* - Sleaford
Welbourn Heath	*Lincoln* - Sleaford
Welbourn Low Fields	*Lincoln* - Sleaford
Welburn	*York, N.R.* - Malton
Welby	*Leicester* - Melton Mowbray
Welby	*Lincoln* - Grantham
Welches Dam	*Cambridge* - March
Welcombe	*Devon* - Bideford
Weldon	*Northampton* - Corby
Weldon Bridge	*Northumberland* - Morpeth
Welford	*Berks* - Newbury
Welford	*Northampton* - Northampton
Welford-on-Avon	*Warwick* - Stratford on Avon
Welham	*Leicester* - Kettering
Welham	*Notts* - East Retford
Welham Green	*Herts* - Hertford
Well	*Hants* - Aldershot and Farnham
Well	*Lincoln* - Skegness
Well	*York, N.R.* - Harrogate
Welland	*Worcester* - Great Malvern
Wellbury	*Herts* - Hitchin
Wellbury	*York, N.R.* - Northallerton
Well End	*Bucks* - High Wycombe
Well End	*Herts* - Barnet
Wellers Town	*Kent* - Tonbridge
Wellesbourne Hastings	*Warwick* - Stratford on Avon
Wellesbourne Mountford	*Warwick* - Stratford on Avon
Wellfield	*Northumberland* - North Shields
Well Fold (Liversedge)	*York, W.R.* - Dewsbury
Wellgill	*Cumberland* - Carlisle
Wellhaugh	*Northumberland* - Hexham

Well Head	*Bucks* - Bletchley and Leighton Buzzard
Well Hill (part)	*Kent* - Bromley
Well Hill (part)	*Kent* - Sevenoaks
Wellhope	*Durham* - Bishop Auckland
Wellhouse	*Berks* - Newbury
Welling	*Kent* - Dartford
Wellingborough	*Northampton* - Wellingborough
Wellingham	*Norfolk* - King's Lynn
Wellingley	*York, W.R.* - Doncaster
Wellingore	*Lincoln* - Sleaford
Wellingore Heath	*Lincoln* - Sleaford
Wellingore Low Fields	*Lincoln* - Sleaford
Wellington	*Hereford* - Hereford
Wellington	*Salop* - Wellington (Salop)
Wellington	*Somerset* - Taunton
Wellington College	*Berks* - Reading
Wellington Heath	*Hereford* - Hereford
Wellington Hill	*York, W.R.* - Leeds
Wellisford	*Somerset* - Taunton
Wellow	*I. of W.* - Newport (I.W.)
Wellow	*Notts* - Mansfield
Wellow	*Somerset* - Bath
Wellow, East	*Hants* - Southampton
Wellow, West	*Hants* - Southampton
Wellpond Green	*Herts* - Hertford
Wells	*Somerset* - Wells
Wellsborough	*Leicester* - Hinckley
Wells Green	*Warwick* - Birmingham
Wells, Little	*Norfolk* - King's Lynn
Wells-next-the-Sea	*Norfolk* - King's Lynn
Welney	*Norfolk* - King's Lynn
Welney, West	*Norfolk* - King's Lynn
Welshampton	*Salop* - Oswestry
Welsh Bicknor	*Hereford* - Monmouth
Welsh Frankton	*Salop* - Oswestry
Welsh Hook	*Pembroke* - Haverfordwest
Welsh Newton	*Hereford* - Monmouth
Welshpool	*Montgomery* - Welshpool
Welsh St. Donats	*Glamorgan* - Cardiff
Welson, Lower	*Hereford* - Hereford
Welton	*Lincoln* - Lincoln
Welton	*Northampton* - Northampton
Welton	*Northumberland* - Hexham
Welton	*York, E.R.* - Kingston-upon-Hull
Welton in the Marsh	*Lincoln* - Skegness
Welton-le-Wold	*Lincoln* - Louth
Welton, Nether	*Cumberland* - Carlisle
Welton, Upper	*Cumberland* - Carlisle
Welwick	*York, E.R.* - Kingston-upon-Hull
Welwyn	*Herts* - Hertford
Welwyn Garden City	*Herts* - Hertford
Wem	*Salop* - Shrewsbury
Wembdon	*Somerset* - Bridgwater
Wembley	*Middlesex* - Willesden
Wembley Hill	*Middlesex* - Willesden
Wembley Park	*Middlesex* - Willesden
Wembury	*Devon* - Plymouth
Wembworthy	*Devon* - Barnstaple
Wemmergill	*York, N.R.* - Bishop Auckland
Wenallt	*Glamorgan* - Cardiff
Wenden Lofts	*Essex* - Bishop's Stortford
Wendens Ambo	*Essex* - Bishop's Stortford
Wendlebury	*Oxford* - Oxford
Wendling	*Norfolk* - East Dereham
Wendover	*Bucks* - Aylesbury
Wendover Dean	*Bucks* - Aylesbury
Wendron	*Cornwall* - Penzance
Wendy	*Cambridge* - Cambridge
Wenford	*Cornwall* - Bideford
Wenham, Little	*Suffolk* - Ipswich
Wenham Magna	*Suffolk* - Ipswich
Wenhaston	*Suffolk* - Halesworth
Wenlock, Little	*Salop* - Wellington (Salop)
Wenlock, Much	*Salop* - Bridgnorth
Wennington	*Essex* - Grays Thurrock
Wennington	*Hunts* - Huntingdon
Wennington	*Lancaster* - Lancaster
Wensley	*Derby* - Matlock

Wensley	*York, N.R.* - Northallerton
Wentbridge	*York, W.R.* - Pontefract
Wentnor	*Salop* - Shrewsbury
Wentworth	*Cambridge* - Ely
Wentworth	*Surrey* - Slough
Wentworth	*York, W.R.* - Rotherham
Wenvoe	*Glamorgan* - Barry
Weobley	*Hereford* - Leominster
Weobley Marsh	*Hereford* - Leominster
Weoley Castle	*Warwick* - Birmingham
Wepham	*Sussex* - Chichester
Wephurst Park	*Sussex* - Chichester
Wepre	*Flint* - Holywell
Wereham	*Norfolk* - King's Lynn
Wergs	*Stafford* - Wolverhampton
Wern	*Montgomery* - Machynlleth
Werneth	*Lancaster* - Oldham
Werneth, Low	*Cheshire* - Hyde
Werrington	*Devon* - Launceston
Werrington	*Northampton* - Peterborough
Werrington	*Stafford* - Stoke-on-Trent
Wervin	*Cheshire* - Chester
Wescoe	*Cumberland* - Workington
Wesham	*Lancaster* - Preston
Wessington	*Derby* - Alfreton
West Aberthaw	*Glamorgan* - Bridgend
West Acomb	*Northumberland* - Hexham
Westacre	*Norfolk* - King's Lynn
West Adderbury	*Oxford* - Banbury
West Alkham	*Kent* - Dover
West Allen	*Northumberland* - Hexham
West Allotment	*Northumberland* - Newcastle upon Tyne
West Alvington	*Devon* - Kingsbridge
West Anstey	*Devon* - Tiverton
West Ardsley	*York, W.R.* - Dewsbury
West Ashby	*Lincoln* - Lincoln
West Ashling	*Sussex* - Chichester
West Ashton	*Wilts* - Trowbridge
West Auckland	*Durham* - Bishop Auckland
West Ayton	*York, N.R.* - Scarborough
West Bagborough	*Somerset* - Taunton
West Bank	*Lancaster* - St. Helens
West Barkwith	*Lincoln* - Lincoln
West Barsham	*Norfolk* - King's Lynn
West Bay	*Dorset* - Dorchester
West Beckham	*Norfolk* - Norwich
West Bedfont	*Middlesex* - Slough
Westbeech	*Stafford* - Wolverhampton
Westbere	*Kent* - Canterbury
West Bergholt	*Essex* - Colchester
West Bexington	*Dorset* - Dorchester
West Bilney	*Norfolk* - King's Lynn
West Black Dean	*Durham* - Bishop Auckland
West Blatchington	*Sussex* - Brighton
West Boldon	*Durham* - Southshields
Westborough	*Lincoln* - Newark
West Boston	*Lincoln* - Boston
Westbourne	*Hants* - Bournemouth
Westbourne	*Sussex* - Chichester
Westbourne Park	*London, W.9* - Bloomsbury and Marylebone
West Bourton	*Dorset* - Shaftesbury
West Bower	*Somerset* - Bridgwater
West Bowling	*York, W.R.* - Bradford
West Brabourne	*Kent* - Ashford
West Bradenham	*Norfolk* - East Dereham
West Bradford	*York, W.R.* - Blackburn
West Bradley	*Somerset* - Wells
West Brandon	*Durham* - Durham
West Bretton	*York, W.R.* - Wakefield
West Bridgford	*Notts* - Nottingham
West Brompton	*London, S.W.10* - West London
West Bromwich	*Stafford* - West Bromwich
Westbrook	*Berks* - Newbury
Westbrook	*Hereford* - Hereford
Westbrook	*Kent* - Margate
West Broughton	*Derby* - Uttoxeter
West Brunton	*Northumberland* - Newcastle upon Tyne

West Buckland	*Devon* - Kingsbridge
West Buckland	*Devon* - Barnstaple
West Buckland	*Somerset* - Taunton
West Burton	*Notts* - Gainsborough
West Burton	*Sussex* - Chichester
West Burton	*York, N.R.* - Northallerton
Westbury	*Bucks* - Banbury
Westbury	*Hants* - Petersfield
Westbury	*Salop* - Shrewsbury
Westbury	*Somerset* - Wells
Westbury	*Wilts* - Trowbridge
Westbury Leigh	*Wilts* - Trowbridge
Westbury-on-Severn	*Gloucester* - Gloucester
Westbury-on-Trym	*Gloucester* - Bristol
West Butsfield	*Durham* - Durham
West Butterwick	*Lincoln* - Scunthorpe
Westby	*Lincoln* - Grantham
Westby-with-Plumpton	*Lancaster* - Blackpool
West Camel	*Somerset* - Yeovil
West Chaldon	*Dorset* - Weymouth
West Challow	*Berks* - Didcot
West Charlton	*Northumberland* - Hexham
West Chelborough	*Dorset* - Yeovil
West Chevington	*Northumberland* - Morpeth
West Chiltington	*Sussex* - Chichester
West Chiltington Common (part)	*Sussex* - Worthing
West Chinnock	*Somerset* - Yeovil
West Chivingstone	*Northumberland* - Morpeth
West Cilrledyn	*Pembroke* - Cardigan
West Cliff	*Kent* - Dover
Westcliff on Sea	*Essex* - Southend
West Close Booth	*Lancaster* - Burnley
West Coker	*Somerset* - Yeovil
Westcombe	*Somerset* - Frome
Westcombe Park	*London, S.E.3* - Woolwich
West Compton	*Dorset* - Dorchester
West Compton	*Somerset* - Wells
West Cornforth	*Durham* - Durham
Westcote	*Gloucester* - Cheltenham
Westcott	*Berks* - Didcot
Westcott	*Bucks* - Aylesbury
Westcott	*Salop* - Shrewsbury
Westcott	*Surrey* - Dorking
Westcott Barton	*Oxford* - Banbury
West Cottingwith	*York, E.R.* - York
West Coulston	*Wilts* - Trowbridge
Westcourt	*Wilts* - Swindon
West Cowick	*York, W.R.* - Goole
West Cranmore	*Somerset* - Wells
West Crewkerne	*Somerset* - Yeovil
West Croft	*Stafford* - Wolverhampton
West Cross	*Glamorgan* - Swansea
West Curthwaite	*Cumberland* - Carlisle
West Dean	*Sussex* - Chichester
West Dean	*Sussex* - Eastbourne
West Dean	*Wilts* - Salisbury
West Deeping	*Lincoln* - Stamford
West Denton	*Northumberland* - Newcastle upon Tyne
West Derby	*Lancaster* - Liverpool
West Dereham	*Norfolk* - King's Lynn
West Didsbury	*Lancaster* - Manchester
West Dowlish	*Somerset* - Axminster and Chard
West Drayton	*Middlesex* - Uxbridge
West Drayton	*Notts* - East Retford
West Dulwich	*London, S.E.21* - Lambeth
West Dundry	*Somerset* - Bristol
West Ealing	*London, W.13* - Brentford
West Ella	*York, E.R.* - Kingston-upon-Hull
West End (Wickwar)	*Gloucester* - Bristol
Westend	*Gloucester* - Stroud
West End	*Hants* - Southampton
West End (Wormley)	*Herts* - Hertford
West End	*Lincoln* - Boston
West End (Harlington)	*Middlesex* - Uxbridge
West End (Northolt)	*Middlesex* - Uxbridge
West End (Haslemere)	*Surrey* - Guildford
West End (Woking)	*Surrey* - Guildford
West End	*York, W.R.* - Harrogate

Westenhanger	*Kent* - Folkestone
Westerdale	*York, N.R.* - Whitby
Westerfield	*Suffolk* - Ipswich
Westergate	*Sussex* - Chichester
Westerham	*Kent* - Sevenoaks
Westerham Hill (part)	*Kent* - Bromley
Westerhope	*Northumberland* - Newcastle upon Tyne
Wester Hope Fell	*Durham* - Bishop Auckland
Westerleigh	*Gloucester* - Bristol
Westerton	*Durham* - Bishop Auckland
Westerton	*Sussex* - Chichester
West Ewell	*Surrey* - Epsom
West Farleigh	*Kent* - Maidstone
West Farndon	*Northampton* - Banbury
West Felton	*Salop* - Oswestry
West Fen	*Lincoln* - Boston
Westfield	*Gloucester* - Cheltenham
Westfield	*Norfolk* - East Dereham
Westfield	*Sussex* - Hastings
Westfield (Crawley)	*Sussex* - Horsham
Westfields	*Berks* - Newbury
Westfields	*Hereford* - Hereford
West Finchley	*London, N.12* - Barnet
West Firsby	*Lincoln* - Lincoln
Westford	*Somerset* - Taunton
West Freshwater	*Pembroke* - Haverfordwest
Westgate Hill	*York, W.R.* - Bradford
Westgate-in-Weardale	*Durham* - Bishop Auckland
Westgate-on-Sea	*Kent* - Margate
West Gorton	*Lancaster* - Manchester
West Grafton	*Wilts* - Swindon
West Green	*Hants* - Basingstoke
West Green (Crawley)	*Sussex* - Horsham
West Grimstead	*Wilts* - Salisbury
West Grinstead	*Sussex* - Horsham
West Hackney	*London, E.8* - Shoreditch
West Haddlesey	*York, W.R.* - Pontefract
West Haddon	*Northampton* - Rugby
West Hagbourne	*Berks* - Didcot
West Hagley	*Worcester* - Stourbridge
Westhall	*Suffolk* - Halesworth
West Hallam	*Derby* - Ilkeston
West Halsham	*York, E.R.* - Kingston-upon-Hull
West Halton	*Lincoln* - Scunthorpe
West Ham	*London, E.15* - Bow
Westham	*Sussex* - Eastbourne
West Hampnett	*Sussex* - Chichester
West Handley	*Derby* - Chesterfield
West Hanney	*Berks* - Didcot
West Hanningfield	*Essex* - Chelmsford
West Hardwick	*York, W.R.* - Pontefract
West Harle	*Northumberland* - Hexham
West Harling	*Norfolk* - Thetford
West Harnham	*Wilts* - Salisbury
West Harptree	*Somerset* - Wells
West Harrow	*Middlesex* - Willesden
West Harting	*Sussex* - Petersfield
West Harton	*Durham* - South Shields
West Hatch	*Somerset* - Taunton
Westhay	*Somerset* - Wells
Westhead	*Lancaster* - Southport
West Head (Stow)	*Norfolk* - Kings Lynn
West Heath	*Hants* - Basingstoke
West Heath (part)	*Warwick* - Birmingham
West Heath (part)	*Worcester* - Redditch
West Heath Common	*Worcester* - Redditch
West Heddon	*Northumberland* - Newcastle upon Tyne
West Hendred	*Berks* - Didcot
West Herrington	*Durham* - Durham
West Heslerton	*York, E.R.* - Malton
Westhide	*Hereford* - Hereford
West Hill	*Devon* - Exeter
West Hill	*Hants* - Portsmouth
West Hill	*Stafford* - Walsall
West Hill	*York, E.R.* - Kingston-upon-Hull
West Hillingdon	*Middlesex* - Uxbridge
West Hoathly	*Sussex* - East Grinstead
Westhope	*Salop* - Ludlow

WES

West Horndon	*Essex* - Brentwood
Westhorpe (Gosberton)	*Lincoln* - Spalding
Westhorpe	*Suffolk* - Stowmarket
West Horrington	*Somerset* - Wells
West Hougham	*Kent* - Dover
Westhoughton	*Lancaster* - Bolton
Westhouse	*York, W.R.* - Lancaster
Westhouses	*Derby* - Alfreton
West Howe	*Hants* - Bournemouth
Westhumble	*Surrey* - Dorking
West Huntspill	*Somerset* - Bridgwater
West Hyde	*Beds* - Luton
West Hyde	*Herts* - Watford
West Hythe	*Kent* - Folkestone
West Ilsley	*Berks* - Didcot
Westington	*Gloucester* - Evesham
West Itchenor	*Sussex* - Chichester
West Keal	*Lincoln* - Skegness
West Kelfield	*Notts* - Gainsborough
West Kennet	*Wilts* - Swindon
West Kensington	*London, W.14* - West London
West Kingsdown	*Kent* - Dartford
West Kington	*Wilts* - Chippenham
West Kirby	*Cheshire* - Birkenhead
West Knighton	*Dorset* - Dorchester
West Knoye	*Wilts* - Shaftesbury
Westlaby	*Lincoln* - Lincoln
West Lambrook	*Somerset* - Yeovil
Westland Green	*Herts* - Bishop's Stortford
Westlands	*Stafford* - Newcastle-under-Lyme
Westlands	*Wilts* - Chippenham
West Langdon	*Kent* - Dover
West Langton	*Leicester* - Leicester
West Lavington	*Sussex* - Chichester
West Lavington	*Wilts* - Devizes
West Layton	*York, N.R.* - Richmond (York)
West Leake	*Notts* - Loughborough
Westleigh	*Devon* - Bideford
West Leigh	*Devon* - Kingsbridge
Westleigh	*Devon* - Tiverton
West Leigh	*Hants* - Portsmouth
West Leigh	*Lancaster* - Leigh
West Leigh	*Somerset* - Taunton
Westleton	*Suffolk* - Halesworth
West Lexham	*Norfolk* - King's Lynn
Westley	*Hants* - Winchester
Westley	*Salop* - Shrewsbury
Westley	*Suffolk* - Bury St. Edmunds
Westley Waterless	*Cambridge* - Newmarket
West Lilburn	*Northumberland* - Alnwick
Westlington	*Bucks* - Aylesbury
Westlinton	*Cumberland* - Carlisle
West Linton	*York, E.R.* - Goole
West Liss	*Hants* - Petersfield
West Littleton	*Gloucester* - Bristol
West Lockinge	*Berks* - Didcot
West Looe	*Cornwall* - Liskeard
West Lulworth	*Dorset* - Dorchester
West Lutton	*York, E.R.* - Beverley
West Lydford	*Somerset* - Wells
West Lyng	*Somerset* - Bridgwater
West Lynn	*Norfolk* - King's Lynn
West Malling	*Kent* - Maidstone
Westmancote	*Worcester* - Cheltenham
West Marden	*Sussex* - Chichester
West Markham	*Notts* - East Retford
Westmarsh Ash	*Kent* - Deal
West Marton	*York, W.R.* - Skipton
West Matfen	*Northumberland* - Newcastle upon Tyne
West Melbury	*Dorset* - Shaftesbury
West Melton	*York, W.R.* - Rotherham
Westmeon	*Hants* - Petersfield
West Mersea	*Essex* - Colchester
Westmeston	*Sussex* - Lewes
West Mill (Ware)	*Herts* - Hertford
Westmill	*Herts* - Hertford
West Milton	*Dorset* - Dorchester
Westminster (part)	*London, S.W.1* - West London
Westminster (part)	*London, S.W.1* - Westminster

WES

West Molesey	*Surrey* - Kingston-upon-Thames
West Monkton	*Somerset* - Taunton
Westmoor	*Cambridge* - Ely
Westmoor	*Northumberland* - Newcastle upon Tyne
West Moors	*Dorset* - Wimborne Minster
West Morton	*York, W.R.* - Keighley
West Murton	*Durham* - Stockton on Tees
West Newchurch	*Monmouth* - Chepstow
Westnewton	*Cumberland* - Carlisle
West Newton	*Norfolk* - King's Lynn
West Newton	*Somerset* - Bridgwater
West Newton	*York, E.R.* - Kingston-upon-Hull
West Norwood	*London, S.E.27* - Lambeth
Westoe	*Durham* - South Shields
Westoe Village	*Durham* - South Shields
Weston	*Berks* - Newbury
Weston	*Cheshire* - Crewe
Weston	*Cheshire* - Runcorn
Weston	*Devon* - Exeter
Weston	*Hants* - Petersfield
Weston	*Herts* - Hitchin
Weston	*Lincoln* - Spalding
Weston	*Norfolk* - Norwich
Weston	*Notts* - Newark
Weston	*Salop* - Bridgnorth
Weston	*Salop* - Knighton
Weston	*Salop* - Shrewsbury
Weston	*Salop* - Ludlow
Weston	*Salop* - Whitchurch
Weston	*Somerset* - Bath
Weston	*Stafford* - Stafford
Weston	*Suffolk* - Lowestoft
Weston	*York, W.R.* - Otley
Weston Bamfylde	*Somerset* - Yeovil
Weston Beggard	*Hereford* - Hereford
Westonbirt	*Gloucester* - Malmesbury
Weston-by-Weedon	*Northampton* - Northampton
Weston-by-Welland	*Northampton* - Corby
Weston Colley	*Hants* - Winchester
Weston Colville	*Cambridge* - Newmarket
Weston Corbett	*Hants* - Basingstoke
Weston Coyney	*Stafford* - Stoke-on-Trent
Weston Favell	*Northampton* - Northampton
Weston Fen	*Lincoln* - Spalding
Weston Heath	*Salop* - Wellington (Salop)
Weston Hills	*Lincoln* - Spalding
Weston in Arden	*Warwick* - Nuneaton
Westoning	*Beds* - Luton
Weston in Gordano	*Somerset* - Weston Super Mare
Weston Jones	*Stafford* - Stafford
Weston Longville	*Norfolk* - Norwich
Weston Lullingfields	*Salop* - Shrewsbury
Weston Marsh	*Lincoln* - Spalding
Weston, North	*Somerset* - Bristol
Weston, Old	*Hunts* - Huntingdon
Weston-on-Avon	*Warwick* - Stratford on Avon
Weston-on-the-Green	*Oxford* - Oxford
Weston Patrick	*Hants* - Basingstoke
Weston Point	*Cheshire* - Runcorn
Weston Rhyn	*Salop* - Oswestry
Weston-Subedge	*Gloucester* - Evesham
Weston Super Mare	*Somerset* - Weston Super Mare
Weston Town	*Somerset* - Frome
Weston Turville	*Bucks* - Aylesbury
Weston under Lizard	*Stafford* - Wellington (Salop)
Weston-under-Penyard	*Hereford* - Gloucester
Weston-under-Redcastle	*Salop* - Whitchurch
Weston under Weatherley	*Warwick* - Warwick
Weston Underwood	*Bucks* - Northampton
Weston-under-Wood	*Derby* - Derby
Weston-upon-Trent	*Derby* - Derby
Weston-upon-Trent	*Stafford* - Stafford
Westonzoyland	*Somerset* - Bridgwater
West Orchard	*Dorset* - Shaftesbury
Westover	*Hants* - Andover
Westow	*York, E.R.* - Malton
West Panson	*Devon* - Launceston
West Park	*Lancaster* - St. Helens
West Parley	*Dorset* - Wimborne Minster

West Peckham	*Kent* - Maidstone
West Pelton	*Durham* - Durham
West Pennard	*Somerset* - Wells
West Pentire	*Cornwall* - Truro
West Perry	*Hunts* - Huntingdon
West Pinchbeck	*Lincoln* - Spalding
West Pit	*Durham* - Bishop Auckland
West Pontnewydd	*Monmouth* - Newport (Mon)
Westport	*Somerset* - Taunton
West Port Holland	*Cornwall* - Truro
West Quantoxhead	*Somerset* - Minehead
West Rainton	*Durham* - Durham
West Rasen	*Lincoln* - Lincoln
West Ravendale	*Lincoln* - Great Grimsby
Westray	*Cumberland* - Workington
West Raynham	*Norfolk* - King's Lynn
West Retford	*Notts* - East Retford
Westridge	*Berks* - Didcot
Westrill and Starmore	*Leicester* - Rugby
Westrip	*Gloucester* - Stroud
West Roddymoor	*Durham* - Bishop Auckland
Westrop	*Wilts* - Swindon
West Row	*Suffolk* - Bury St. Edmunds
West Rudham	*Norfolk* - King's Lynn
West Runton	*Norfolk* - Norwich
West Saltney	*Flint* - Chester
West Scholes (Thornton)	*York, W.R.* - Bradford
West Shaftoe	*Northumberland* - Newcastle upon Tyne
West Shefford	*Berks* - Newbury
West Sherburn	*Durham* - Durham
West Shield Hill	*Northumberland* - Morpeth
West Silloth	*Cumberland* - Carlisle
West Sleekburn	*Northumberland* - Blyth
West Smethwick	*Stafford* - West Bromwich
West Somerton	*Norfolk* - Great Yarmouth
West Southbourne	*Hants* - Bournemouth
West Stafford	*Dorset* - Dorchester
West Stannington	*York, W.R.* - Sheffield
West Stockwith	*Notts* - Gainsborough
West Stoke	*Sussex* - Chichester
West Stour	*Dorset* - Shaftesbury
West Stow	*Suffolk* - Bury St. Edmunds
West Stowell	*Wilts* - Swindon
West Stratton	*Hants* - Winchester
West Tanfield	*York, N.R.* - Harrogate
West Taphouse	*Cornwall* - Liskeard
West Tarring	*Sussex* - Worthing
West Tarset	*Northumberland* - Hexham
West Teffont	*Wilts* - Shaftesbury
West Thickley	*Durham* - Bishop Auckland
West Thirston	*Northumberland* - Morpeth
West Thorney	*Sussex* - Chichester
West Thornton	*Northumberland* - Morpeth
West Thurrock	*Essex* - Grays Thurrock
West Tilbury	*Essex* - Grays Thurrock
West Tisbury	*Wilts* - Shaftesbury
West Tisted	*Hants* - Winchester
West Tofts	*Norfolk* - Thetford
West Torrington	*Lincoln* - Lincoln
West Town	*Somerset* - Bristol
West Town	*Sussex* - Haywards Heath
Westtown	*York, W.R.* - Dewsbury
West Twyford	*Middlesex* - Brentford
West Tytherley	*Hants* - Salisbury
West Vale	*York, W.R.* - Halifax
West Waddon	*Dorset* - Weymouth
West Walton	*Norfolk* - Wisbech
West Walton	*Pembroke* - Haverfordwest
Westward	*Cumberland* - Carlisle
Westward Ho	*Devon* - Bideford
West Week	*Cornwall* - Launceston
Westwell	*Kent* - Ashford
Westwell	*Oxford* - Witney
Westwell Leacon	*Kent* - Ashford
West Wellow	*Hants* - Southampton
Westwells	*Wilts* - Chippenham
West Welney	*Norfolk* - King's Lynn
West Whelpington	*Northumberland* - Hexham

West Whorlton	*Northumberland* - Newcastle upon Tyne
Westwick	*Cambridge* - Cambridge
Westwick	*Durham* - Darlington
Westwick	*Somerset* - Weston Super Mare
Westwick	*York, W.R.* - Harrogate
Westwick Row	*Herts* - St. Albans
West Wickham	*Cambridge* - Cambridge
West Wickham	*Kent* - Bromley
West Willoughby	*Lincoln* - Grantham
West Winch	*Norfolk* - King's Lynn
West Wittering	*Sussex* - Chichester
West Witton	*Durham* - Bishop Auckland
West Witton	*York, N.R.* - Northallerton
Westwood	*Gloucester* - Cheltenham
Westwood	*Kent* - Margate
Westwood	*Lancaster* - Wigan
Westwood	*Lancaster* - Oldham
Westwood	*Lancaster* - Bolton
Westwood	*Salop* - Bridgnorth
Westwood	*Worcester* - Worcester
Westwood	*York, W.R.* - Sheffield
Westwood	*York, W.R.* - Huddersfield
West Woodburn	*Northumberland* - Hexham
West Woodhay	*Berks* - Newbury
Westwood Heath	*Warwick* - Coventry
West Woodlands	*Somerset* - Frome
Westwood, Lower	*Wilts* - Trowbridge
Westwood, New	*Notts* - Alfreton
Westwood, Old	*Notts* - Alfreton
West Woodside	*Cumberland* - Carlisle
Westwoodside	*Lincoln* - Gainsborough
Westwood, Upper	*Wilts* - Trowbridge
West Woodyates	*Dorset* - Salisbury
West Worldham	*Hants* - Aldershot and Farnham
West Worlington	*Devon* - Tiverton
West Wratting	*Cambridge* - Newmarket
West Wretham	*Norfolk* - Thetford
West Wycombe	*Bucks* - High Wycombe
West Wylam	*Northumberland* - Hexham
Wetheral	*Cumberland* - Carlisle
Wetherby	*York, W.R.* - Harrogate
Wetherden	*Suffolk* - Stowmarket
Wetheringsett	*Suffolk* - Stowmarket
Wethersfield	*Essex* - Braintree
Whetley Moor	*Stafford* - Stoke-on-Trent
Whetley Rocks	*Stafford* - Leek
Wet Sandford	*Oxford* - Oxford
Wettenhall	*Cheshire* - Crewe
Wettleton	*Salop* - Ludlow
Wetton	*Stafford* - Leek
Wetwang	*York, E.R.* - Beverley
Wetwood	*Stafford* - Stafford
Wexham	*Bucks* - Uxbridge
Weybourne	*Norfolk* - Norwich
Weybourne	*Surrey* - Aldershot and Farnham
Weybread	*Suffolk* - Halesworth
Weybridge	*Surrey* - Kingston-upon-Thames
Weyhill	*Hants* - Andover
Weymouth	*Dorset* - Weymouth
Weymouth	*Stafford* - Market Drayton
Whaddon	*Bucks* - Bletchley and Leighton Buzzard
Whaddon	*Cambridge* - Cambridge
Whaddon	*Gloucester* - Gloucester
Whaddon	*Wilts* - Trowbridge
Whaddon	*Wilts* - Salisbury
Whaddon Chase	*Bucks* - Bletchley and Leighton Buzzard
Whale	*Westmorland* - Penrith
Whale Island	*Hants* - Portsmouth
Whaley	*Derby* - Chesterfield
Whaley Bridge	*Derby* - Buxton
Whaley Thorns	*Derby* - Chesterfield
Whalley	*Lancaster* - Blackburn
Whalley Range	*Lancaster* - Manchester
Whalton	*Northumberland* - Morpeth
Wham Grange	*Durham* - Bishop Auckland
Wham, The	*Durham* - Bishop Auckland
Whaplode	*Lincoln* - Spalding

WHA - WHE

Whaplode Drove	*Lincoln* - Spalding
Whaplode Fen	*Lincoln* - Spalding
Whaplode Marsh	*Lincoln* - Spalding
Whaplode	*Lincoln* - Spalding
St. Catherine's	
Wharles	*Lancaster* - Preston
Wharncliffeside	*York, W.R.* - Sheffield
Wharram-le-Street	*York, E.R.* - Malton
Wharram Percy	*York, E.R.* - Malton
Wharton	*Cheshire* - Northwich
Wharton	*Hereford* - Leominster
Wharton	*Lincoln* - Gainsborough
Whashton	*York, N.R.* - Darlington
Whassett	*Westmorland* - Kendal
Whatborough	*Leicester* - Melton Mowbray
Whatcombe	*Dorset* - Dorchester
Whatcote	*Warwick* - Stratford on Avon
Whatcroft	*Cheshire* - Northwich
Whateley Green	*Warwick* - Birmingham
Whatfield	*Suffolk* - Ipswich
Whatley	*Somerset* - Frome
Whatlington	*Sussex* - Hastings
Whatmore	*Salop* - Ludlow
Whatstandwell (part)	*Derby* - Alfreton
Whatstandwell (part)	*Derby* - Matlock
Whatton	*Notts* - Nottingham
Whatton, Long	*Leicester* - Loughborough
Wheal Alfred	*Cornwall* - Redruth
Wheal Frances	*Cornwall* - Truro
Wheal Kitty	*Cornwall* - Truro
Wheal Rose	*Cornwall* - Truro
Wheatacre	*Norfolk* - Lowestoft
Wheatall	*Salop* - Shrewsbury
Wheatbottom	*Durham* - Bishop Auckland
Wheatbottom, Old	*Durham* - Bishop Auckland
Wheat Common	*Salop* - Ludlow
Wheatcroft	*Derby* - Alfreton
Wheatcroft	*York, N.R.* - Scarborough
Wheatfield	*Oxford* - Thame
Wheatfield Gardens	*Durham* - Bishop Auckland
Wheathampstead	*Herts* - St. Albans
Wheathill	*Salop* - Ludlow
Wheathill	*Somerset* - Yeovil
Wheathold Green	*Hants* - Newbury
Wheatlesowes	*Salop* - Wellington
Wheatley	*Hants* - Aldershot and Farnham
Wheatley	*Lancaster* - Preston
Wheatley	*Oxford* - Oxford
Wheatley	*York, W.R.* - Doncaster
Wheatley	*York, W.R.* - Halifax
Wheatley Carr Booth	*Lancaster* - Nelson
Wheatley Hill	*Durham* - Durham
Wheatley Lane	*Lancaster* - Nelson
Wheatley, North	*Notts* - East Retford
Wheatley, South	*Notts* - East Retford
Wheaton Aston	*Stafford* - Wolverhampton
Wheatsheaf	*Cumberland* - Workington
Wheddon Cross	*Somerset* - Minehead
Wheel	*York, W.R.* - Sheffield
Wheelbarrow Town	*Kent* - Folkestone
Wheeldon Mill	*Derby* - Chesterfield
Wheeler End	*Bucks* - High Wycombe
Wheelock	*Cheshire* - Crewe
Wheelton	*Lancaster* - Chorley
Wheldrake	*York, E.R.* - York
Whelford	*Gloucester* - Cirencester
Whelley	*Lancaster* - Wigan
Whelpington, West	*Northumberland* - Hexham
Whelpo	*Cumberland* - Carlisle
Whempstead	*Herts* - Hertford
Whenby	*York, N.R.* - York
Whepstead	*Suffolk* - Bury St. Edmunds
Wherstead	*Suffolk* - Ipswich
Wherwell	*Hants* - Andover
Wheston	*Derby* - Buxton
Whetstone	*Leicester* - Leicester
Whetstone	*London, N.20* - Barnet
Whettall	*Salop* - Oswestry
Wheyrigg	*Cumberland* - Carlisle

WHI

Whicham	*Cumberland* - Whitehaven
Whichford	*Warwick* - Stratford on Avon
Whickham	*Durham* - Gateshead
Whilton	*Northampton* - Northampton
Whimple	*Devon* - Exeter
Whimpstone	*Warwick* - Stratford on Avon
Whimsey	*Gloucester* - Gloucester
Whinburgh	*Norfolk* - East Dereham
Whinclose	*Cumberland* - Carlisle
Whinfell	*Cumberland* - Workington
Whinfell	*Westmorland* - Kendal
Whinfell	*Westmorland* - Penrith
Whinmoor	*York, W.R.* - Leeds
Whinney Bank	*York, W.R.* - Huddersfield
Whinney Hill	*Northumberland* - Morpeth
Whinney Hill	*York, W.R.* - Rotherham
Whinnow	*Cumberland* - Carlisle
Whinnow	*Cumberland* - Workington
Whippingham	*I. of W.* - Newport (I.W.)
Whipsnade	*Beds* - Luton
Whirley	*Cheshire* - Macclesfield
Whirlow	*York, W.R.* - Sheffield
Whisby	*Lincoln* - Lincoln
Whissendine	*Rutland* - Melton Mowbray
Whissenthorpe	*Rutland* - Oakham
Whissonsett	*Norfolk* - King's Lynn
Whiston	*Lancaster* - St. Helens
Whiston	*Northampton* - Northampton
Whiston	*Stafford* - Leek
Whiston	*Stafford* - Stafford
Whiston	*York, W.R.* - Rotherham
Whiston Eaves	*Stafford* - Leek
Whiston's Cross	*Salop* - Wolverhampton
Whitacre, Nether	*Warwick* - Birmingham
Whitacre, Over	*Warwick* - Birmingham
Whitbach	*Salop* - Ludlow
Whitbeck	*Cumberland* - Whitehaven
Whitbourne	*Hereford* - Worcester
Whitburn	*Durham* - South Shields
Whitby	*Cheshire* - Ellesmere Port
Whitby	*York, N.R.* - Whitby
Whitby Heath	*Cheshire* - Ellesmere Port
Whitby Laithes	*York, N.R.* - Whitby
Whitchester	*Northumberland* - Hexham
Whitchester	*Northumberland* - Newcastle upon Tyne
Whitchurch	*Bucks* - Aylesbury
Whitchurch	*Devon* - Plymouth
Whitchurch	*Glamorgan* - Cardiff
Whitchurch	*Hants* - Andover
Whitchurch	*Hereford* - Monmouth
Whitchurch (part)	*Middlesex* - Watford
Whitchurch (part)	*Middlesex* - Willesden
Whitchurch	*Oxford* - Reading
Whitchurch	*Salop* - Whitchurch
Whitchurch	*Somerset* - Bristol
Whitchurch	*Warwick* - Stratford on Avon
Whitchurch Heath	*Salop* - Whitchurch
Whitchurch Hill End	*Oxford* - Reading
Whitcombe	*Dorset* - Dorchester
Whitcot	*Salop* - Shrewsbury
Whitcott Keysett	*Salop* - Ludlow
White Ball	*Somerset* - Taunton
Whiteborough	*Notts* - Mansfield
Whitebrook	*Monmouth* - Monmouth
Whitechapel	*Lancaster* - Preston
Whitechapel	*London, E.1.* - Shoreditch
Whitechurch	*Pembroke* - Cardigan
Whitechurch Canonicorum	*Dorset* - Axminster and Chard
Whitechurch in Duesland	*Pembroke* - Haverfordwest
White City	*Glamorgan* - Bargoed
White City	*Kent* - Canterbury
White Cliff	*Gloucester* - Monmouth
Whiteclose	*Cumberland* - Carlisle
Whiteclosegate	*Cumberland* - Carlisle
White Colne	*Essex* - Colchester
White Coppice	*Lancaster* - Chorley
Whitecroft	*Gloucester* - Monmouth

Whitecross	*Cornwall* - Bodmin
White Cross (Cury)	*Cornwall* - Penzance
White Cross	*Cornwall* - Penzance
White Cross	*Glamorgan* - Caerphilly
Whitedale	*York, E.R.* - Kingston-upon-Hull
Whitefield	*Dorset* - Dorchester
Whitefield	*Gloucester* - Cheltenham
Whitefield	*Lancaster* - Bury
Whitegate	*Cheshire* - Northwich
Whitegate	*Denbigh* - Wrexham
White Gritt	*Montgomery* - Welshpool
Whitehall	*Cumberland* - Carlisle
Whitehall	*Gloucester* - Cheltenham
Whitehall	*Herts* - Hertford
Whitehall	*Lancaster* - Barrow-in-Furness
Whitehaven	*Cumberland* - Whitehaven
Whitehawk	*Sussex* - Brighton
Whiteheath Gate	*Worcester* - Dudley
White Hill	*Dorset* - Dorchester
Whitehill	*Hants* - Aldershot and Farnham
Whitehill	*Kent* - Canterbury
Whitehill	*Oxford* - Oxford
Whitehill	*Stafford* - Stoke-on-Trent
Whitehill	*Warwick* - Birmingham
White Horse	*Lancaster* - Preston
Whitehough	*Derby* - Buxton
Whitehouse Colliery	*Durham* - Durham
Whitehouse Common	*Warwick* - Birmingham
Whitehouse Drive	*Cambridge* - Ely
Whitehurst	*Denbigh* - Wrexham
White Kirkley Houses	*Durham* - Bishop Auckland
White Lackington	*Dorset* - Dorchester
White Lackington	*Somerset* - Axminster and Chard
White Ladies	*Salop* - Wolverhampton
White Ladies Aston	*Worcester* - Worcester
White Lane	*Derby* - Sheffield
White Lea	*York, W.R.* - Dewsbury
White Lea Colliery	*Durham* - Bishop Auckland
Whiteleaf Cross	*Bucks* - High Wycombe
White Lees	*York, W.R.* - Sheffield
White-le-Head	*Durham* - Consett
Whiteley Green	*Cheshire* - Macclesfield
Whiteley Wood	*York, W.R.* - Sheffield
White Lund	*Lancaster* - Lancaster
White Lye	*Monmouth* - Monmouth
White Mill	*Carmarthen* - Carmarthen
Whitemoor	*Cheshire* - Congleton
Whitemoor	*Cornwall* - St. Austell
Whitemoor	*Warwick* - Warwick
Whitemoss	*Lancaster* - Oldham
White Notley	*Essex* - Braintree
White Oxmead	*Somerset* - Bath
Whiteparish	*Wilts* - Salisbury
White Roding	*Essex* - Harlow
Whitesheet	*Wilts* - Shaftesbury
Whiteshill	*Gloucester* - Stroud
Whitestake	*Lancaster* - Preston
White Staunton	*Somerset* - Axminster and Chard
White Stock	*Lancaster* - Barrow-in-Furness
Whitestone	*Devon* - Exeter
White Waltham	*Berks* - Slough
Whiteway Bottom	*Herts* - Hitchin
Whitewell	*Lancaster* - Preston
Whitewell Bottom	*Lancaster* - Rawtenstall
Whiteworks	*Devon* - Plymouth
Whitfield	*Gloucester* - Thornbury
Whitfield	*Hereford* - Monmouth
Whitfield	*Kent* - Dover
Whitfield	*Northampton* - Banbury
Whitfield	*Northumberland* - Hexham
Whitfield	*Stafford* - Stoke-on-Trent
Whitford	*Devon* - Axminster and Chard
Whitford	*Flint* - Holywell
Whitford	*Worcester* - Bromsgrove
Whitgift	*York, W.R.* - Goole
Whitgreave	*Stafford* - Stafford
Whitkirk	*York, W.R.* - Leeds
Whitland	*Carmarthen* - Haverfordwest
Whitledge	*Lancaster* - Wigan
Whitleigh	*Devon* - Plymouth
Whitley	*Berks* - Oxford
Whitley	*Berks* - Reading
Whitley	*Kent* - Sevenoaks
Whitley	*Lancaster* - Wigan
Whitley	*Salop* - Shrewsbury
Whitley	*Warwick* - Coventry
Whitley	*Wilts* - Chippenham
Whitley	*York, W.R.* - Pontefract
Whitley	*York, W.R.* - Sheffield
Whitley Bay	*Northumberland* - North Shields
Whitley Bridge	*York, W.R.* - Pontefract
Whitley Chapel	*Northumberland* - Hexham
Whitley Eaves	*Stafford* - Stafford
Whitley Ford	*Stafford* - Stafford
Whitley, Higher	*Cheshire* - Warrington
Whitley, Lower	*Berks* - Reading
Whitley, Lower	*Cheshire* - Warrington
Whitley, Lower	*York, W.R.* - Dewsbury
Whitley Row	*Kent* - Sevenoaks
Whitley Shield	*Northumberland* - Hexham
Whitley Wood	*Berks* - Reading
Whitlingham	*Norfolk* - Norwich
Whitlingham Little	*Norfolk* - Norwich
Whitlock End	*Warwick* - Birmingham
Whitminster	*Gloucester* - Gloucester
Whitmore	*Stafford* - Stoke-on-Trent
Whitmore Park	*Warwick* - Coventry
Whitmore Reans	*Stafford* - Wolverhampton
Whitnage	*Devon* - Tiverton
Whitnash	*Warwick* - Warwick
Whitney	*Hereford* - Hereford
Whitney Lane	*Cheshire* - Whitchurch
Whitridge	*Northumberland* - Morpeth
Whitrigg (Bowness)	*Cumberland* - Carlisle
Whitrigg (Torpenhow)	*Cumberland* - Carlisle
Whitrigglees	*Cumberland* - Carlisle
Whitsands	*Cornwall* - Plymouth
Whitsbury	*Hants* - Salisbury
Whitson	*Monmouth* - Newport (Mon.)
Whitstable	*Kent* - Canterbury
Whitstone	*Cornwall* - Launceston
Whitstones	*Worcester* - Worcester
Whittingham	*Lancaster* - Preston
Whittingham	*Northumberland* - Alnwick
Whittingslow	*Salop* - Ludlow
Whittington	*Gloucester* - Cheltenham
Whittington	*Lancaster* - Lancaster
Whittington	*Norfolk* - Thetford
Whittington	*Salop* - Oswestry
Whittington	*Stafford* - Stafford
Whittington	*Stafford* - Stourbridge
Whittington	*Warwick* - Tamworth
Whittington	*Worcester* - Worcester
Whittington, Great	*Northumberland* - Hexham
Whittington, Hurst	*Stafford* - Lichfield
Whittington, Little	*Northumberland* - Hexham
Whittington Moor	*Derby* - Chesterfield
Whittington, New	*Derby* - Chesterfield
Whittington, Old	*Derby* - Chesterfield
Whittle	*Northumberland* - Alnwick
Whittle	*Northumberland* - Hexham
Whittlebury	*Northampton* - Northampton
Whittle Farm	*Northumberland* - Morpeth
Whittle-le-Woods	*Lancaster* - Chorley
Whittlesey	*Cambridge* - Peterborough
Whittlesford	*Cambridge* - Cambridge
Whitton	*Durham* - Stockton on Tees
Whitton	*Hereford* - Ludlow
Whitton	*Lincoln* - Scunthorpe
Whitton	*Middlesex* - Brentford
Whitton	*Northumberland* - Morpeth
Whitton	*Radnor* - Knighton
Whitton	*Salop* - Shrewsbury
Whitton	*Salop* - Ludlow
Whitton	*Suffolk* - Ipswich

WHI - WID

Whittonditch	*Wilts* - Swindon
Whittonstall	*Northumberland* - Consett
Whitway	*Hants* - Newbury
Whitwell	*Derby* - Worksop
Whitwell	*Durham* - Durham
Whitwell	*Herts* - Hitchin
Whitwell	*I. of W.* - Newport (I.W.)
Whitwell	*Norfolk* - Norwich
Whitwell	*Rutland* - Stamford
Whitwell	*York, N.R.* - Malton
Whitwell	*York, W.R.* - Sheffield
Whitwell Common	*Derby* - Worksop
Whitwick	*Leicester* - Ashby-de-la-Zouch
Whitwood	*York, W.R.* - Pontefract
Whitwood Mere	*York, W.R.* - Pontefract
Whitworth	*Durham* - Bishop Auckland
Whitworth	*Lancaster* - Rochdale
Whixall	*Salop* - Whitchurch
Whixley	*York, W.R.* - Harrogate
Whoberley	*Warwick* - Coventry
Whomerley Wood	*Herts* - Hitchin
Whorlton	*Durham* - Darlington
Whorlton	*Northumberland* - Newcastle upon Tyne
Whorlton, East	*Northumberland* - Newcastle upon Tyne
Whorlton, West	*Northumberland* - Newcastle upon Tyne
Whydown	*Sussex* - Hastings
Whyke	*Sussex* - Chichester
Whyol	*Somerset* - Bristol
Whyteleafe	*Surrey* - Croydon
Wibsey	*York, W.R.* - Bradford
Wibtoft	*Warwick* - Hinckley
Wichenford	*Worcester* - Worcester
Wick	*Glamorgan* - Bridgend
Wick (Berkeley)	*Gloucester* - Stroud
Wick	*Hants* - Bournemouth
Wick	*Somerset* - Bridgwater
Wick	*Somerset* - Wells
Wick	*Sussex* - Chichester
Wick	*Worcester* - Evesham
Wick and Abson	*Gloucester* - Bristol
Wick, East	*Wilts* - Swindon
Wicken	*Cambridge* - Newmarket
Wicken	*Northampton* - Northampton
Wicken Bonhunt	*Essex* - Bishop's Stortford
Wickenby	*Lincoln* - Lincoln
Wickersley	*York, W.R.* - Rotherham
Wick Fifteen Acres	*Gloucester* - Bristol
Wickford	*Essex* - Brentwood
Wickham	*Berks* - Newbury
Wickham	*Hants* - Portsmouth
Wickham	*Norfolk* - Kings Lynn
Wickham Bishops	*Essex* - Maldon
Wickhambreaux	*Kent* - Canterbury
Wickhambrook	*Suffolk* - Bury St. Edmunds
Wickham Bushes	*Kent* - Dover
Wickham, East	*Kent* - Dartford
Wickhamford	*Worcester* - Evesham
Wickham Market	*Suffolk* - Woodbridge
Wickhampton	*Norfolk* - Great Yarmouth
Wickham St. Paul's	*Suffolk* - Sudbury
Wickham Skeith	*Suffolk* - Stowmarket
Wickham, West	*Cambridge* - Cambridge
Wickhill	*Wilts* - Chippenham
Wicklewood	*Norfolk* - Norwich
Wick, Lower	*Worcester* - Worcester
Wickmere	*Norfolk* - Norwich
Wick Rock	*Gloucester* - Bristol
Wick St. Lawrence	*Somerset* - Weston Super Mare
Wick, Upper	*Worcester* - Worcester
Wickwar	*Gloucester* - Bristol
Wick Wick	*Gloucester* - Bristol
Wicor	*Hants* - Portsmouth
Wicton	*Hereford* - Leominster
Widbrook	*Wilts* - Trowbridge
Widbury Hill	*Herts* - Hertford
Widcombe	*Somerset* - Bath
Widdington	*Essex* - Bishop's Stortford

WID - WIL

Widdington	*York, W.R.* - Harrogate
Widdrington	*Northumberland* - Morpeth
Widecombe in the Moor	*Devon* - Newton Abbot
Widegates	*Cornwall* - Liskeard
Wide Open	*Northumberland* - Newcastle upon Tyne
Widford	*Essex* - Chelmsford
Widford	*Herts* - Hertford
Widford	*Oxford* - Witney
Widley	*Hants* - Portsmouth
Widmerpool	*Notts* - Nottingham
Widmore End	*Bucks* - High Wycombe
Widnes	*Lancaster* - St. Helens
Widworthy	*Devon* - Axminster
Wield, Lower	*Hants* - Winchester
Wield, Upper	*Hants* - Winchester
Wigan	*Lancaster* - Wigan
Wiganthorpe	*York, N.R.* - Malton
Wigfair	*Denbigh* - Rhyl
Wiggaton	*Devon* - Exeter
Wiggenhall St. Germans	*Norfolk* - King's Lynn
Wiggenhall St. Mary The Virgin	*Norfolk* - King's Lynn
Wiggenhall St. Mary Magdalen	*Norfolk* - King's Lynn
Wiggenhall St. Peter	*Norfolk* - King's Lynn
Wigginton	*Herts* - Hemel Hempstead
Wigginton	*Oxford* - Banbury
Wigginton	*Stafford* - Tamworth
Wigginton	*York, N.R.* - York
Wigglesworth	*York, W.R.* - Skipton
Wiggold	*Gloucester* - Cheltenham
Wiggonby	*Cumberland* - Carlisle
Wiggonholt	*Sussex* - Chichester
Wighill	*York, W.R.* - York
Wighton	*Norfolk* - King's Lynn
Wightwick	*Stafford* - Wolverhampton
Wigland	*Cheshire* - Whitchurch
Wigley	*Derby* - Chesterfield
Wigmore	*Hereford* - Ludlow
Wigmore	*Kent* - Rochester
Wigmore	*Salop* - Shrewsbury
Wigmore	*Stafford* - West Bromwich
Wigpool	*Gloucester* - Gloucester
Wigsley	*Notts* - Newark
Wigsthorpe	*Northampton* - Peterborough
Wigston	*Leicester* - Leicester
Wigston, Great	*Leicester* - Leicester
Wigston, Magna	*Leicester* - Leicester
Wigston Parva	*Leicester* - Hinckley
Wigston, South	*Leicester* - Leicester
Wigthorpe	*Notts* - Worksop
Wigtoft	*Lincoln* - Boston
Wigtoft Fen	*Lincoln* - Boston
Wigton	*Cumberland* - Carlisle
Wigtwizzle	*York, W.R.* - Sheffield
Wigwell	*Derby* - Matlock
Wigwig	*Salop* - Bridgnorth
Wike	*York, W.R.* - Otley
Wilbarston	*Northampton* - Corby
Wilberfoss	*York, E.R.* - York
Wilbraham, Great	*Cambridge* - Cambridge
Wilbraham, Little	*Cambridge* - Cambridge
Wilbrighton	*Stafford* - Stafford
Wilburton	*Cambridge* - Ely
Wilbury	*Herts* - Hitchin
Wilby	*Norfolk* - Norwich
Wilby	*Northampton* - Wellingborough
Wilby	*Suffolk* - Halesworth
Wilcot	*Oxford* - Witney
Wilcot	*Wilts* - Swindon
Wilcote	*Oxford* - Oxford
Wilcott	*Salop* - Shrewsbury
Wilcott Marsh	*Salop* - Shrewsbury
Wilcove	*Cornwall* - Plymouth
Wilcrick	*Monmouth* - Newport (Mon.)
Wilday Green	*Derby* - Chesterfield
Wildbearclough	*Cheshire* - Macclesfield
Wild Duck	*Lancaster* - Barrow-in-Furness
Wilden	*Beds* - Bedford

Wilden	*Worcester* - Kidderminster
Wilden Top	*Worcester* - Kidderminster
Wilden Tump	*Hereford* - Worcester
Wilderhope	*Salop* - Ludlow
Wilderley	*Salop* - Shrewsbury
Wildhern	*Hants* - Andover
Wild Hill	*Herts* - St. Albans
Wildmoor	*Hants* - Basingstoke
Wildmoor	*Worcester* - Bromsgrove
Wildmore	*Lincoln* - Boston
Wildsworth	*Lincoln* - Gainsborough
Wilford	*Notts* - Nottingham
Wilfholme	*York, E.R.* - Beverley
Wilkings Green	*Herts* - St. Albans
Wilksby	*Lincoln* - Boston
Willand	*Devon* - Tiverton
Willaston	*Cheshire* - Birkenhead
Willaston	*Cheshire* - Crewe
Willen	*Bucks* - Bletchley and Leighton Buzzard
Willenhall	*Stafford* - Walsall
Willenhall	*Warwick* - Coventry
Willerby	*York, E.R.* - Kingston-upon-Hull
Willerby	*York, E.R.* - Scarborough
Willersey	*Gloucester* - Evesham
Willersley	*Hereford* - Hereford
Willersley Lane	*Derby* - Matlock
Willesborough	*Kent* - Ashford
Willesden	*London, N.W.10* - Willesden
Willesden Green	*London, N.W.2* - Willesden
Willesden Green	*London, N.W.10* - Willesden
Willesley	*Leicester* - Ashby-de-la-Zouch
Willesley	*Wilts* - Malmesbury
Willett	*Somerset* - Minehead
Willey	*Hereford* - Knighton
Willey	*Salop* - Bridgnorth
Willey	*Warwick* - Rugby
Willey Green	*Surrey* - Aldershot and Farnham
Williamoteswick	*Northumberland* - Hexham
Williamscote	*Oxford* - Banbury
Williamston	*Northumberland* - Hexham
Williamston, East	*Pembroke* - Haverfordwest
Williamston, West	*Pembroke* - Haverfordwest
Williamstown	*Glamorgan* - Pontypridd
Williamwood	*Notts* - Mansfield
Willian	*Herts* - Hitchin
Willicote	*Warwick* - Stratford-on-Avon
Willingale Doe	*Essex* - Chelmsford
Willingale Spain	*Essex* - Chelmsford
Willingdon	*Sussex* - Eastbourne
Willingham	*Cambridge* - Cambridge
Willingham	*Lincoln* - Gainsborough
Willingham	*Suffolk* - Lowestoft
Willingham, North	*Lincoln* - Louth
Willingham, South	*Lincoln* - Louth
Willington	*Beds* - Bedford
Willington	*Cheshire* - Chester
Willington	*Derby* - Derby
Willington	*Durham* - Bishop Auckland
Willington	*Flint* - Whitchurch
Willington	*Warwick* - Stratford on Avon
Willington-on-Tyne	*Northumberland* - North Shields
Willington Quay	*Northumberland* - North Shields
Willisham	*Suffolk* - Ipswich
Willitoft	*York, E.R.* - Goole
Williton	*Somerset* - Minehead
Willoughbridge	*Stafford* - Stoke-on-Trent
Willoughby	*Warwick* - Rugby
Willoughby Holes	*Cambridge* - Ely
Willoughby-with-Sloothby	*Lincoln* - Skegness
Willoughby on the Wolds	*Notts* - Loughborough
Willoughby Waterless	*Leicester* - Leicester
Willoughby, West	*Lincoln* - Grantham
Willoughton	*Lincoln* - Gainsborough
Willow Hall	*Cambridge* - Peterborough
Willow Holme	*Cumberland* - Carlisle
Willow Park	*York, W.R.* - Pontefract
Willsbridge	*Gloucester* - Bristol

Will's Pastures	*Warwick* - Warwick
Willsworthy	*Devon* - Plymouth
Willtown	*Devon* - Launceston
Wilmcote	*Warwick* - Stratford on Avon
Wilmingham	*I. of W.* - Newport (I.W.)
Wilmington	*Devon* - Axminster
Wilmington	*Kent* - Dartford
Wilmington	*Somerset* - Bath
Wilmington	*Sussex* - Eastbourne
Wilminstone	*Devon* - Plymouth
Wilmorton	*Derby* - Derby
Wilmslow	*Cheshire* - Macclesfield
Wilne	*Derby* - Derby
Wilnecote	*Stafford* - Tamworth
Wilpshire	*Lancaster* - Blackburn
Wilsden	*York, W.R.* - Keighley
Wilsford	*Lincoln* - Sleaford
Wilsford	*Wilts* - Devizes
Wilshamstead	*Beds* - Bedford
Wilsic	*York, W.R.* - Doncaster
Wilsill	*York, W.R.* - Harrogate
Wilson	*Hereford* - Monmouth
Wilson	*Leicester* - Loughborough
Wilstead	*Beds* - Bedford
Wilsthorpe	*Derby* - Nottingham
Wilsthorpe	*Lincoln* - Stamford
Wilsthorpe	*York, E.R.* - Bridlington
Wilstone	*Herts* - Aylesbury
Wilstone	*Salop* - Shrewsbury
Wilton	*Cumberland* - Whitehaven
Wilton	*Hereford* - Monmouth
Wilton	*Somerset* - Taunton
Wilton	*Wilts* - Salisbury
Wilton	*York, N.R.* - Malton
Wilton	*York, N.R.* - Middlesbrough
Wimbish	*Essex* - } Bishop's Stortford
Wimbish Green	*Essex* - } Bishop's Stortford
Wimblebury	*Stafford* - Walsall
Wimbledon	*London, S.W.19* - Kingston-upon-Thames
Wimbledon Park	*London, S.W.19* - Wandsworth
Wimbledon, South	*London, S.W.19* - Croydon
Wimblington	*Cambridge* - March
Wimboldsley	*Cheshire* - Northwich
Wimbolds Trafford	*Cheshire* - Chester
Wimborne Minster	*Dorset* - Wimborne Minster
Wimborne St. Giles	*Dorset* - Wimborne Minster
Wimbotsham	*Norfolk* - King's Lynn
Wimpole	*Cambridge* - Cambridge
Wincanton	*Somerset* - Yeovil
Winceby	*Lincoln* - Skegness
Wincham	*Cheshire* - Northwich
Winchcomb	*Gloucester* - Cheltenham
Winch, East	*Norfolk* - King's Lynn
Winchelsea	*Sussex* - Hastings
Winchester	*Hants* - Winchester
Winchestown	*Monmouth* - Blackwood
Winchett Hill	*Kent* - Cranbrook
Winchfawr	*Glamorgan* - Merthyr Tydfil
Winchfield	*Hants* - Basingstoke
Winch Hill	*Herts* - Hitchin
Winchmore Hill	*Bucks* - Amersham
Winchmore Hill	*London, N.21* - Edmonton
Winchwen	*Glamorgan* - Swansea
Winch, West	*Norfolk* - King's Lynn
Wincle	*Cheshire* - Macclesfield
Wincobank	*York, W.R.* - Sheffield
Windbrook	*Worcester* - Cheltenham
Windcross	*Gloucester* - Gloucester
Windermere	*Westmorland* - Kendal
Winderton	*Warwick* - Banbury
Windfallwood	*Sussex* - Chichester
Windhill	*York, W.R.* - Bradford
Windle	*Lancaster* - St. Helens
Windlehurst	*Cheshire* - Stockport
Windlehurst	*Lancaster* - St. Helens
Windlesham	*Surrey* - Aldershot and Farnham
Windlestone Hall	*Durham* - Bishop Auckland
Windlestone, New	*Durham* - Durham

Windley	*Derby* - Derby
Windmill	*Derby* - Buxton
Windmill	*Durham* - Bishop Auckland
Windmill	*York, W.R.* - Sheffield
Windmill End	*Worcester* - Dudley
Windmill Hill	*Worcester* - Evesham
Windrush	*Gloucester* - Cheltenham
Windsor	*Berks* - Slough
Windsor Forest	*Berks* - Slough
Windsor Great Park	*Berks* - Slough
Windsor, Old	*Berks* - Slough
Windy Arbour	*Stafford* - Stoke-on-Trent
Windy Arbour	*Warwick* - Warwick
Windyhaugh	*Northumberland* - Morpeth
Windy Hill	*Denbigh* - Wrexham
Windy Nook	*Durham* - Gateshead
Windyside	*Durham* - Bishop Auckland
Wineham	*Sussex* - Haywards Heath
Winestead	*York, E.R.* - Kingston-upon-Hull
Winewall	*Lancaster* - Nelson
Winfarthing	*Norfolk* - Norwich
Winford	*Somerset* - Bristol
Winforton	*Hereford* - Hereford
Winfrith, Newburgh	*Dorset* - Dorchester
Wing	*Bucks* - Bletchley and Leighton Buzzard
Wing	*Rutland* - Melton Mowbray
Wingate	*Durham* - Durham
Wingate Grange	*Durham* - Durham
Wingate Lane	*Durham* - Durham
Wingates	*Lancaster* - Bolton
Wingates	*Northumberland* - Morpeth
Wingate, South	*Durham* - Durham
Wingbury	*Bucks* - Bletchley and Leighton Buzzard
Wingerworth	*Derby* - Chesterfield
Wingfield	*Beds* - Luton
Wingfield	*Suffolk* - Halesworth
Wingfield	*Wilts* - Trowbridge
Wingfield, North	*Derby* - Chesterfield
Wingfield Park	*Derby* - Alfreton
Wingfield, South	*Derby* - Alfreton
Wingham	*Kent* - Canterbury
Wingham Well	*Kent* - Canterbury
Wingland (part)	*Lincoln* - Spalding
Wingland Marsh (part)	*Lincoln* - Spalding
Wingmore	*Kent* - Folkestone
Wingrave	*Bucks* - Aylesbury
Winkburn	*Notts* - Newark
Winkfield	*Berks* - Slough
Winkfield Row	*Berks* - Slough
Winkfield Street	*Berks* - Slough
Winkhill	*Stafford* - Leek
Winklebury	*Hants* - Basingstoke
Winkleigh	*Devon* - Barnstaple
Winksley	*York, W.R.* - Harrogate
Winkton	*Hants* - Bournemouth
Winkton Common	*Hants* - Bournemouth
Winlaton	*Durham* - Newcastle upon Tyne
Winlaton Mill	*Durham* - Newcastle upon Tyne
Winllan	*Montgomery* - Machynlleth
Winmarleigh	*Lancaster* - Lancaster
Winnall	*Hants* - Winchester
Winnall Common	*Hereford* - Hereford
Winnersh	*Berks* - Reading
Winning Colliery, Esh	*Durham* - Durham
Winnington	*Cheshire* - Northwich
Winnington	*Salop* - Shrewsbury
Winnington	*Stafford* - Market Drayton
Winnoth Dale (part)	*Stafford* - Stoke-on-Trent
Winnoth Dale (part)	*Stafford* - Uttoxeter
Winscales	*Cumberland* - Workington
Winscombe	*Somerset* - Weston Super Mare
Winsford	*Cheshire* - Northwich
Winsford	*Somerset* - Minehead and Chard
Winsham	*Somerset* - Axminster
Winshields	*Northumberland* - Hexham
Winskill	*Cumberland* - Penrith
Winslade	*Hants* - Basingstoke

Winsley	*Salop* - Shrewsbury
Winsley	*Wilts* - Trowbridge
Winsley	*York, W.R.* - Harrogate
Winslow	*Bucks* - Aylesbury
Winslow	*Hereford* - Hereford
Winson	*Gloucester* - Cheltenham
Winson Green	*Warwick* - Birmingham
Winsor	*Hants* - Southampton
Winstanley	*Lancaster* - Wigan
Winstanstow	*Salop* - Ludlow
Winster	*Derby* - Matlock
Winster	*Westmorland* - Kendal
Winston	*Durham* - Darlington
Winston	*Suffolk* - Ipswich
Winstone	*Gloucester* - Cheltenham
Winterborne Abbas	*Dorset* - Dorchester
Winterborne Came	*Dorset* - Dorchester
Winterborne Clenstone	*Dorset* - Dorchester
Winterborne Herringtone	*Dorset* - Dorchester
Winterborne Houghton	*Dorset* - Dorchester
Winterborne Kingston	*Dorset* - Wimborne Minster
Winterborne Monkton	*Dorset* - Dorchester
Winterborne Quarlestone	*Dorset* - Dorchester
Winterborne St. Martin	*Dorset* - Dorchester
Winterborne Steepleton	*Dorset* - Dorchester
Winterborne Stickland	*Dorset* - Dorchester
Winterborne Tomson	*Dorset* - Wimborne Minster
Winterborne Whitechurch	*Dorset* - Dorchester
Winterborne Zelstone	*Dorset* - Wimborne Minster
Winterbottom	*Cheshire* - Altrincham
Winterbourne	*Berks* - Newbury
Winterbourne	*Gloucester* - Bristol
Winterbourne Bassett	*Wilts* - Swindon
Winterbourne Dauntsey	*Wilts* - Salisbury
Winterbourne Earls	*Wilts* - Salisbury
Winterbourne Gunner	*Wilts* - Salisbury
Winterbourne Monkton	*Wilts* - Swindon
Winterbourne Stoke	*Wilts* - Salisbury
Winterburn	*York, W.R.* - Skipton
Winteringham	*Lincoln* - Scunthorpe
Winterley	*Cheshire* - Crewe
Winters Cross	*Hereford* - Monmouth
Wintersett	*York, W.R.* - Wakefield
Winterslow	*Wilts* - Salisbury
Winterton	*Lincoln* - Scunthorpe
Winterton	*Norfolk* - Great Yarmouth
Winterwell	*York, W.R.* - Rotherham
Winthill	*Somerset* - Weston Super Mare
Winthorpe	*Lincoln* - Skegness
Winthorpe	*Notts* - Newark
Wintles Hill	*Gloucester* - Gloucester
Winton	*Hants* - Bournemouth
Winton	*Lancaster* - Salford
Winton	*Westmorland* - Penrith
Wintringham	*Yorks, E.R.* - Malton
Wintringham, Lower	*Hunts* - Huntingdon
Wintringham, Upper	*Hunts* - Huntingdon
Winwick	*Hunts* - Huntingdon
Winwick	*Lancaster* - Warrington
Winwick	*Northampton* - Rugby
Winyates	*Worcester* - Redditch
Wirksworth	*Derby* - Matlock
Wirksworth Moor	*Derby* - Matlock
Wirswall	*Cheshire* - Whitchurch
Wisbech	*Cambridge* - Wisbech
Wisbech St. Mary	*Cambridge* - Wisbech
Wisborough Green	*Sussex* - Chichester
Wiseton	*Notts* - East Retford
Wisewood	*York, W.R.* - Sheffield
Wishaw	*Warwick* - Birmingham
Wishford	*Wilts* - Salisbury
Wishmore	*Hereford* - Worcester
Wisley	*Surrey* - Guildford

Wispington	*Lincoln* - Lincoln
Wissett	*Suffolk* - Halesworth
Wissington	*Suffolk* - Colchester
Wistanstow	*Salop* - Ludlow
Wistanswick	*Salop* - Market Drayton
Wistaston	*Cheshire* - Crewe
Wiston	*Pembroke* - Haverfordwest
Wiston	*Suffolk* - Colchester
Wiston	*Sussex* - Worthing
Wistow	*Hunts* - Huntingdon
Wistow	*Leicester* - Leicester
Wistow	*York, W.R.* - York
Wiswell	*Lancaster* - Blackburn
Witcham	*Cambridge* - Ely
Witcham Gravel	*Cambridge* - Ely
Witchampton	*Dorset* - Wimborne Minster
Witchcot	*Salop* - Ludlow
Witchford	*Cambridge* - Ely
Witchingham, Great	*Norfolk* - Norwich
Witchingham, Little	*Norfolk* - Norwich
Witcombe (Martock)	*Somerset* - Yeovil
Witcombe, Great	*Gloucester* - Cheltenham
Witcombe, Little	*Gloucester* - Cheltenham
Witham	*Essex* - Braintree
Witham Friary	*Somerset* - Frome
Witham, North	*Lincoln* - Grantham
Witham-on-the-Hill	*Lincoln* - Spalding
Witham, South	*Lincoln* - Grantham
Withcall	*Lincoln* - Louth
Withcote	*Leicester* - Melton Mowbray
Withdean	*Sussex* - Brighton
Witheridge	*Devon* - Tiverton
Witheridge Hill	*Oxford* - Reading
Witherley	*Leicester* - Nuneaton
Withernsea	*York, E.R.* - Kingston-upon-Hull
Withernwick	*York, E.R.* - Kingston-upon-Hull
Withern with Stain	*Lincoln* - Louth
Withersdale	*Suffolk* - Norwich
Withersdane	*Kent* - Ashford
Withersfield	*Suffolk* - Cambridge
Witherslack	*Westmorland* - Kendal
Withey Bridge	*Gloucester* - Cheltenham
Withiel	*Cornwall* - Bodmin
Withiel Florey	*Somerset* - Tiverton
Withington	*Gloucester* - Cheltenham
Withington	*Hereford* - Hereford
Withington	*Lancaster* - Manchester
Withington	*Salop* - Wellington (Salop)
Withington	*Stafford* - Uttoxeter
Withington, Lower	*Cheshire* - Macclesfield
Withleigh	*Devon* - Tiverton
Withnell	*Lancaster* - Chorley
Withybed Green	*Worcester* - Redditch
Withybrook	*Warwick* - Coventry
Withycombe	*Somerset* - Minehead
Withycombe Raleigh	*Devon* - Exeter
Withyham	*Sussex* - East Grinstead
Withypool	*Somerset* - Minehead
Withy Stakes	*Stafford* - Stoke-on-Trent
Witley	*Surrey* - Guildford
Witley, Great	*Worcester* - Worcester
Witley, Little	*Worcester* - Worcester
Witnesham	*Suffolk* - Ipswich
Witney	*Oxford* - Witney
Wittenham, Little	*Berks* - Didcot
Wittenham, Long	*Berks* - Didcot
Wittering	*Huntingdon and Peterborough* - Stamford
Wittering, East	*Sussex* - Chichester
Wittering, West	*Sussex* - Chichester
Wittersham	*Kent* - Cranbrook
Witton	*Cheshire* - Northwich
Witton	*Norfolk* - Norwich
Witton	*Warwick* - Birmingham
Witton	*Worcester* - Worcester
Witton, East	*York, N.R.* - Northallerton
Witton Gilbert	*Durham* - Durham
Witton Junction	*Durham* - Bishop Auckland
Witton-le-Wear	*Durham* - Bishop Auckland
Witton, Long	*Northumberland* - Morpeth

Witton Park	*Durham* - Bishop Auckland
Witton Shields	*Northumberland* - Morpeth
Witton, West	*Durham* - Bishop Auckland
Witton, West	*York, N.R.* - Northallerton
Wiveliscombe	*Somerset* - Taunton
Wivelsfield	*Sussex* - Haywards Heath
Wivelsfield Green	*Sussex* - Haywards Heath
Wivenhoe	*Essex* - Colchester
Wiveton	*Notts* - Nottingham
Wiverton	*Norfolk* - Norwich
Wix	*Essex* - Harwich
Wixford	*Warwick* - Redditch
Wixhill-under-Redcastle	*Salop* - Whitchurch
Wixoe	*Suffolk* - Sudbury
Woburn	*Beds* - Bletchley and Leighton Buzzard
Woburn Sands	*Beds and Bucks* - Bletchley and Leighton Buzzard
Wokefield	*Berks* - Reading
Woking	*Surrey* - Guildford
Wokingham	*Berks* - Reading
Wold	*Northampton* - Northampton
Woldingham	*Surrey* - Croydon
Wold Newton	*Lincoln* - Great Grimsby
Wold Newton	*York, E.R.* - Bridlington
Wolf Cleugh	*Northumberland* - Hexham
Wolferlow	*Hereford* - Leominster
Wolfe Rock Lighthouse	*Cornwall* - Penzance
Wolfhampcote	*Warwick* - Rugby
Wolford, Great	*Warwick* - Stratford on Avon
Wolford, Little	*Warwick* - Stratford on Avon
Wolforton	*Norfolk* - King's Lynn
Wolfscastle	*Pembroke* - Haverfordwest
Wolfsdale	*Pembroke* - Haverfordwest
Wollaston	*Northampton* - Wellingborough
Wollaston	*Salop* - Shrewsbury
Wollaston	*Worcester* - Stourbridge
Wollaston, Great	*Salop* - Shrewsbury
Wollaton	*Notts* - Nottingham
Wollerton	*Salop* - Market Drayton
Wollerton Wood	*Salop* - Market Drayton
Wollescote	*Worcester* - Stourbridge
Wolseley Bridge	*Stafford* - Stafford
Wolsingham	*Durham* - Bishop Auckland
Wolsingham St. John	*Durham* - Bishop Auckland
Wolstanton	*Stafford* - Stoke-on-Trent
Wolstenholme	*Lancaster* - Rochdale
Wolston	*Warwick* - Rugby
Wolsty	*Cumberland* - Carlisle
Wolterton	*Norfolk* - Norwich
Wolvercote	*Oxford* - Oxford
Wolverham	*Cheshire* - Ellesmere Port
Wolverhampton	*Stafford* - Wolverhampton
Wolverley	*Salop* - Shrewsbury
Wolverley	*Worcester* - Kidderminster
Wolvershill	*Somerset* - Weston Super Mare
Wolverton	*Bucks* Bletchley and Leighton Buzzard
Wolverton	*Hants* - Basingstoke
Wolverton	*Kent* - Dover
Wolverton	*Salop* - Shrewsbury
Wolverton	*Warwick* - Warwick
Wolverton	*Worcester* - Worcester
Wolves Newton	*Monmouth* - Chepstow
Wolveton	*Dorset* - Dorchester
Wolvey	*Warwick* - Nuneaton
Wolvey Heath	*Warwick* - Nuneaton
Wolviston	*Durham* - Stockton on Tees
Wombleton	*York, N.R.* - Malton
Wombourne	*Stafford* - Wolverhampton
Wombourne Common	*Stafford* - Wolverhampton
Wombridge	*Salop* - Wellington (Salop)
Wombridge Hill	*Salop* - Wellington (Salop)
Wombwell	*York, W.R.* - Barnsley
Womenswould	*Kent* - Canterbury
Womersley	*York, W.R.* - Pontefract
Wonersh	*Surrey* - Guildford
Wonston	*Hants* - Winchester
Wonston	*Dorset* - Blandford
Wooburn	*Bucks* - High Wycombe

Wooburn Common (Wooburn)	*Bucks* - High Wycombe
Wooburn Common (Taplow)	*Bucks* - Slough
Wooburn Green	*Bucks* - High Wycombe
Wooburn Moor	*Bucks* - High Wycombe
Woodall	*York, W.R.* - Worksop
Woodbasnk	*Cheshire* - Chester
Woodbatwick	*Norfolk* - Norwich
Woodbatch	*Salop* - Shrewsbury
Woodbatch	*Somerset* - Bath
Woodbatch	*Somerset* - Weston Super Mare
Woodbeck	*Notts* - East Retford
Woodberry Down	*London, N.4* - Shoreditch
Woodbine	*Lancaster* - Barrow-in-Furness
Woodborough	*Notts* - Nottingham
Woodborough	*Somerset* - Weston Super Mare
Woodborough	*Wilts* - Devizes
Woodbridge	*Suffolk* - Woodbridge
Woodbrook	*Hereford* - Hereford
Woodbrook	*York, W.R.* - Oldham
Wood Burcote	*Northampton* - Northampton
Woodburn, East	*Northumberland* - Hexham
Woodburn, West	*Northumberland* - Hexham
Woodbury	*Devon* - Exeter
Woodbury Salterton	*Devon* - Exeter
Woodchester	*Gloucester* - Stroud
Woodchurch	*Cheshire* - Birkenhead
Woodchurch	*Kent* - Cranbrook
Woodchurch	*Kent* - Margate
Woodcock Heath	*Stafford* - Uttoxeter
Woodcock Hill	*Herts* - Barnet
Woodcot	*Hants* - Newbury
Woodcote	*Oxford* - Didcot
Woodcote	*Salop* - Shrewsbury
Woodcote	*Salop* - Wellington (Salop)
Woodcote	*Sussex* - Chichester
Woodcote	*Worcester* - Bromsgrove
Woodcote Green	*Worcester* - Bromsgrove
Woodcroft	*Gloucester* - Chepstow
Woodcroft	*Northampton* - Peterborough
Wood Cross	*Stafford* - Wolverhampton
Woodcutts	*Dorset* - Salisbury
Wood Dalling	*Norfolk* - Norwich
Woodditton	*Cambridge* - Newmarket
Wood Eaton	*Oxford* - Oxford
Wood Eaton	*Stafford* - Stafford
Woodeaves	*Derby* - Uttoxeter
Wooden	*Pembroke* - Haverfordwest
Wood End	*Berks* - Oxford
Wood End	*Bucks* - Reading
Wood End	*Cumberland* - Workington
Wood End	*Herts* - Hitchin
Wood End	*Middlesex* - Uxbridge
Wood End	*Northampton* - Northampton
Woodend	*Notts* - Workson
Wood End	*Stafford* - Walsall
Wood End	*Stafford* - Wolverhampton
Wood End	*Warwick* - Tamworth
Wood End	*Warwick* - Birmingham
Wood Enderby	*Lincoln* - Boston
Wood End Green	*Middlesex* - Uxbridge
Woodfalls	*Wilts* - Salisbury
Wood Fen	*Cambridge* - Ely
Woodford	*Cheshire* - Stockport
Woodford	*Devon* - Kingsbridge
Woodford	*Gloucester* - Stroud
Woodford	*London, E.18* - Bow
Woodford	*Northampton* - Kettering
Woodford Bridge	*Essex* - Bow
Woodford Green	*Essex* - Bow
Woodford Halse	*Northampton* - Banbury
Woodford, Lower	*Wilts* - Salisbury
Woodford, Middle	*Wilts* - Salisbury
Woodford, South	*London, E.18* - Bow
Woodford, Upper	*Wilts* - Salisbury
Woodgate	*Salop* - Shrewsbury
Woodgate	*Sussex* - Chichester
Woodgate	*Warwick* - Birmingham
Woodgate	*Worcester* - Bromsgrove

Woodgreen	*Hants* - Salisbury
Wood Green	*London, N.22* - Edmonton
Wood Green	*Stafford* - Dudley
Woodhall	*York, W.R.* - Harrogate
Woodhall Hills	*York, W.R.* - Bradford
Woodhall, Old	*Lincoln* - Lincoln
Woodhall Spa	*Lincoln* - Lincoln
Woodham	*Bucks* - Aylesbury
Woodham	*Durham* - Bishop Auckland
Woodham Ferrers	*Essex* - Maldon
Woodham Mortimer	*Essex* - Maldon
Woodhampton	*Hereford* - Leominster
Woodham, South	*Essex* - Maldon
Woodham Walter	*Essex* - Maldon
Woodhatch	*Surrey* - Reigate
Woodhay, East	*Hants* - Newbury
Wood Hayes	*Stafford* - Wolverhampton
Woodhay, West	*Berks* - Newbury
Woodhead	*Derby* - Hyde
Woodhill	*Essex* - Chelmsford
Wood Hill	*Hereford* - Leominster
Woodhorn	*Northumberland* - Morpeth
Woodhorn Demesne	*Northumberland* - Morpeth
Woodhouse	*Cambridge* - Ely
Woodhouse	*Hants* - Andover
Woodhouse	*Northumberland* - Alnwick
Woodhouse	*Salop* - Shrewsbury
Woodhouse	*Salop* - Kidderminster
Woodhouse (Shelley)	*York, W.R.* - Huddersfield
Woodhouse	*York, W.R.* - Leeds
Woodhouse	*York, W.R.* - Sheffield
Woodhouse Close Colliery	*Durham* - Bishop Auckland
Woodhouse Down	*Gloucester* - Thornbury
Woodhouse Eaves	*Leicester* - Loughborough
Woodhouse Grange	*York, W.R.* - Leeds
Woodhouse Hill (Bierley)	*York, W.R.* - Bradford
Woodhouse Mill (part)	*York, W.R.* - Rotherham
Woodhouse Mill (part)	*York, W.R.* - Sheffield
Woodhouse Moor	*York, W.R.* - Wakefield
Woodhouses	*Cheshire* - Runcorn
Woodhouses	*Durham* - Bishop Auckland
Woodhouses	*Lancaster* - Oldham
Woodhouses	*Salop* - Whitchurch
Woodhouses	*Salop* - Wolverhampton
Woodhouses	*Stafford* - Uttoxeter
Woodhouses (Burntwood)	*Stafford* - Lichfield
Woodhouses (Yoxall)	*Stafford* - Lichfield
Woodhurst	*Hunts* - Huntingdon
Woodifield Colliery	*Durham* - Bishop Auckland
Woodifield Farm	*Durham* - Bishop Auckland
Woodifield, Old	*Durham* - Bishop Auckland
Woodingdean	*Sussex* - Brighton
Woodkirk	*York, W.R.* - Dewsbury
Woodland	*Devon* - Plymouth
Woodland	*Durham* - Bishop Auckland
Woodland	*Lancaster* - Barrow-in-Furness
Woodland Huts	*Durham* - Bishop Auckland
Woodlands	*Cornwall* - Truro
Woodlands	*Dorset* - Wimborne Minster
Woodlands	*Durham* - Durham
Woodlands	*Gloucester* - Thornbury
Woodlands (Swanwick)	*Hants* - Portsmouth
Woodlands (Eling)	*Hants* - Southampton
Woodlands	*York, W.R.* - Bradford
Woodlands	*York, W.R.* - Doncaster
Woodlands Westmeon	*Hants* - Petersfield
Wood Lane	*Stafford* - Stoke-on-Trent
Woodleigh	*Devon* - Kingsbridge
Woodlesford	*York, W.R.* - Leeds
Woodley	*Berks* - Reading
Woodley	*Cheshire* - Stockport
Woodley	*Hants* - Southampton
Wood Linkin	*Derby* - Ilkeston
Woodloes	*Warwick* - Warwick
Woodmancote	*Gloucester* - Cheltenham
Woodmancote (North Cerney)	*Gloucester* - Cheltenham

Woodmancote	*Gloucester* - Stroud
Woodmancote	*Sussex* - Brighton
Woodmancote	*Sussex* - Chichester
Woodmancote	*Worcester* - Worcester
Woodmancott	*Hants* - Basingstoke
Woodmansey	*York, E.R.* - Beverley
Woodman's Green	*Sussex* - Petersfield
Woodmansterne	*Surrey* - Croydon
Woodman Wray	*York, W.R.* - Harrogate
Woodmarsh	*Wilts* - Trowbridge
Woodnesborough	*Kent* - Deal
Woodnewton	*Northampton* - Peterborough and Oundle
Woodnook	*Lincoln* - Grantham
Wood Nook	*York, W.R.* - Huddersfield
Wood Norton	*Norfolk* - King's Lynn
Wood Plumpton	*Lancaster* - Preston
Wood Rising	*Norfolk* - East Dereham
Woodrow (Amersham)	*Bucks* - Amersham
Woodrow	*Dorset* - Blandford
Woodrow	*Worcester* - Kidderminster
Woodrow North	*Worcester* - Redditch
Woodrow South	*Worcester* - Redditch
Woodseats	*York, W.R.* - Sheffield
Woodseaves	*Salop* - Market Drayton
Woodseaves	*Stafford* - Stafford
Woodsetton	*Stafford* - Dudley
Woodsetts	*York, W.R.* - Worksop
Woodsfield	*Worcester* - Great Malvern
Woodsford	*Dorset* - Dorchester
Woodside	*Beds* - Luton
Woodside	*Berks* - Slough
Woodside	*Durham* - Bishop Auckland
Woodside	*Durham* - Newcastle upon Tyne
Woodside	*Herts* - Watford
Woodside	*Northumberland* - Morpeth
Woodside	*Salop* - Bridgnorth
Woodside	*Salop* - Ludlow
Woodside	*Salop* - Wellington (Salop)
Woodside	*Surrey* - Croydon
Woodside	*Worcester* - Dudley
Woodside	*Worcester* - Kidderminster
Woodside, East	*Cumberland* - Carlisle
Woodside, Green	*Essex* - Bishop's Stortford
Woodside Hedley	*Northumberland* - Hexham
Woodside Park	*London, N.12* - Barnet
Woodside, West	*Cumberland* - Carlisle
Woods Moor	*Cheshire* - Stockport
Wood Speen	*Berks* - Newbury
Woodspring	*Somerset* - Weston Super Mare
Woodstanley	*Gloucester* - Cheltenham
Woodstock	*Oxford* - Oxford
Woodstock	*Pembroke* - Haverfordwest
Woodstock, Old	*Oxford* - Oxford
Woodston	*Hunts* - Peterborough
Woodston Village	*Durham* - Durham
Woodthorpe	*Derby* - Chesterfield
Woodthorpe	*Leicester* - Loughborough
Woodthorpe	*Lincoln* - Louth
Woodthorpe	*Notts* - Nottingham
Woodthorpe	*York, W.R.* - Wakefield
Woodton	*Norfolk* - Norwich
Woodvale	*Lancaster* - Southport
Woodville	*Derby* - Ashby-de-la-Zouch
Woodhall Green	*Stafford* - Stafford
Woodwalton	*Hunts* - Huntingdon
Woodyates, East	*Dorset* - Salisbury
Woodyates, West	*Dorset* - Salisbury
Woody Bay	*Devon* - Barnstaple
Woofferton	*Salop* - Ludlow
Wofferwood	*Hereford* - Worcester
Wookey	*Somerset* - Wells
Wookey Hole	*Somerset* - Wells
Wool	*Dorset* - Swanage
Woolacombe	*Devon* - Barnstaple
Woolage Green	*Kent* - Canterbury
Woolaston	*Gloucester* - Chepstow
Woolavington	*Somerset* - Bridgwater
Woolavington	*Sussex* - Chichester

Woolbeding	*Sussex* - Petersfield
Woolcombe	*Dorset* - Dorchester
Wooldale	*York, W.R.* - Huddersfield
Wooler	*Northumberland* - Alnwick
Wooley	*Northumberland* - Hexham
Wooley Pit	*Durham* - Durham
Wooley Terrace P.O. Crook	*Durham* - Bishop Auckland
Woolfardisworthy	*Devon* - Bideford
Woolfardisworthy	*Devon* - Tiverton
Woolfold	*Lancaster* - Bury
Woolgarston	*Stafford* - Stafford
Woolhampton	*Berks* - Newbury
Woolhope	*Hereford* - Hereford
Wooland	*Dorset* - Dorchester
Woollard	*Somerset* - Bath
Woollard	*Somerset* - Bristol
Woolashill	*Worcester* - Worcester
Woollaston	*Stafford* - Stafford
Woollens Brook	*Herts* - Hertford
Woolley	*Derby* - Alfreton
Woolley	*Hunts* - Huntingdon
Woolley	*Somerset* - Bath
Woolley	*Wilts* - Trowbridge
Woolley Bridge	*Derby* - Hyde
Woolley Moor	*Derby* - Alfreton
Wooliscroft	*Stafford* - Stafford
Woolmer Green	*Herts* - Hertford
Woolminstone (Crewkerne)	*Somerset* - Yeovil
Woolpit	*Suffolk* - Stowmarket
Woolridge	*Gloucester* - Gloucester
Woolsbridge	*Dorset* - Wimborne Minster
Woolscott	*Salop* - Oswestry
Woolscott	*Warwick* - Rugby
Woolsery	*Devon* - Bideford
Woolsington	*Northumberland* - Newcastle upon Tyne
Woolstaston	*Salop* - Shrewsbury
Woolsthorpe-by-Belvoir	*Lincoln* - Grantham
Woolsthorpe-by-Colsterworth	*Lincoln* - Grantham
Woolston	*Devon* - Kingsbridge
Woolston	*Hants* - Southampton
Woolston	*Lancaster* - Warrington
Woolston	*Salop* - Ludlow
Woolston	*Salop* - Oswestry
Woolston	*Somerset* - Yeovil
Woolstone	*Berks* - Didcot
Woolstone	*Gloucester* - Cheltenham
Woolstone, Great	*Bucks* - Bletchley and Leighton Buzzard
Woolstone Hill	*Gloucester* - Cheltenham
Woolstone, Little	*Bucks* - Bletchley and Leighton Buzzard
Woolston Green	*Devon* - Newton Abbott
Woolston Moor	*Somerset* - Minehead
Woolstrop	*Gloucester* - Gloucester
Woolton Hill	*Hants* - Newbury
Woolton	*Lancaster*- Liverpool
Woolverton	*Somerset* - Frome
Woolvestone	*Suffolk* - Ipswich
Woolwich	*London, S.E.18* - Woolwich
Woolwich, North	*London, E.16* - Bow
Woontley	*Gloucester* - Cheltenham
Woonton	*Hereford* - Hereford
Woonton Ash	*Hereford* - Hereford
Wooperton	*Northumberland* - Alnwick
Woore	*Salop* - Market Drayton
Woore Hall	*Salop* - Market Drayton
Wootton	*Beds* - Bedford
Wootton	*Berks* - Oxford
Wootton	*Hants* - Lymington
Wootton	*I. of W.* - Newport (I.W.)
Wootton	*Kent* - Dover
Wootton	*Lincoln* - Great Grimsby
Wootton	*Northampton* - Northampton
Wootton	*Oxford* - Oxford
Wootton	*Salop* - Bridgnorth
Wootton	*Salop* - Oswestry

WOO - WOR

Wootton	*Stafford* - Ashbourne
Wootton	*Stafford* - Stafford
Wootton Bassett	*Wilts* - Swindon
Wootton Courtney	*Somerset* - Minehead
Wootton Fitzpaine	*Dorset* - Axminster and Chard
Wootton Glanville	*Dorset* - Dorchester
Wootton Green	*Suffolk* - Halesworth
Wootton, North	*Dorset* - Yeovil
Wootton, North	*Norfolk* - King's Lynn
Wootton, North	*Somerset* - Wells
Wootton Rivers	*Wilts* - Swindon
Wootton St. Lawrence	*Hants* - Basingstoke
Wootton, South	*Norfolk* - King's Lynn
Wootton Upper	*Hants* - Basingstoke
Wootton Wawen	*Warwick* - Stratford on Avon
Worbarrow	*Dorset* - Swanage
Worcester	*Worcester* - Worcester
Worcester Park	*Surrey* - Epsom
Wordsley	*Stafford* - Stourbridge
Wordwell	*Suffolk* - Bury St. Edmunds
Worfield	*Salop* - Bridgnorth
Worgret	*Dorset* - Swanage
Workington	*Cumberland* - Workington
Worksop	*Notts* - Worksop
Worlaby	*Lincoln* - Scunthorpe
Worlaby (Maidenwell)	*Lincoln* - Louth
Worldham, East	*Hants* - Aldershot and Farnham
Worldham, West	*Hants* - Aldershot and Farnham
World's End	*Berks* - Newbury
World's End (Denmead)	*Hants* - Portsmouth
World's End	*Warwick* - Birmingham
Worle	*Somerset* - Weston Super Mare
Worlebury	*Somerset* - Weston Super Mare
Worlingham	*Suffolk* - Lowestoft
Worlington	*Suffolk* - Newmarket
Worlington, East	*Devon* - Tiverton
Worlington, West	*Devon* - Tiverton
Worlingworth	*Suffolk* - Halesworth
Wormald Green	*York, W.R* - Ripon
Wormbridge	*Hereford* - Hereford
Wormegay	*Norfolk* - King's Lynn
Wormelow	*Hereford* - Hereford
Wormhill	*Derby* - Buxton
Wormingford	*Essex* - Colchester
Worminghall	*Bucks* - Thame
Wormington	*Gloucester* - Cheltenham
Wormleighton	*Warwick* - Banbury
Wormley	*Herts* - Hertford
Wormley	*Surrey* - Guildford
Worms Ash	*Worcester* - Bromsgrove
Wormshill	*Kent* - Sittingbourne
Wormsley	*Hereford* - Hereford
Wormsley	*Oxford* - High Wycombe
Wormwood	*Wilts* - Bath
Wormwood Scrubs	*London, N.W.10* - Bloomsbury and Marylebone
Wormwood Scrubs	*London, W.10* - Bloomsbury and Marylebone
Wormwood Scrubs	*London, W.12* - Willesden
Wornditch (Kimbolton)	*Hunts* - Huntingdon
Worplesdon	*Surrey* - Guildford
Worrall	*York, W.R.* - Sheffield
Worsall, High	*York, N.R.* - Stockton on Tees
Worsall, Low	*York, N.R.* - Stockton on Tees
Worsborough	*York, W.R.* - Barnsley
Worsborough Bridge	*York, W.R.* - Barnsley
Worsborough Dale	*York, W.R.* - Barnsley
Worsley	*Lancaster* - Salford
Worsley Hall	*Lancaster* - Wigan
Worsley Mesnes	*Lancaster* - Wigan
Worstead	*Norfolk* - Norwich
Worsthorne with Hurstwood	*Lancaster* - Burnley
Worston	*Lancaster* - Blackburn
Worston	*Stafford* - Stafford
Worth	*Cheshire* - Macclesfield
Worth	*Kent* - Deal
Worth	*Sussex* - East Grinstead
Wortham	*Suffolk* - Norwich

WOR - WRI

Worthen	*Salop* - Shrewsbury
Worthenbury	*Flint* - Wrexham
Worthing	*Norfolk* - East Dereham
Worthing	*Sussex* - Worthing
Worthington	*Lancaster* - Wigan
Worthington	*Leicester* - Ashby-de-la-Zouch
Worth Matravers	*Dorset* - Swanage
Worting	*Hants* - Basingstoke
Wortley	*Gloucester* - Stroud
Wortley	*York, W.R.* - Barnsley
Wortley	*York, W.R.* - Leeds
Worton	*Oxford* - Oxford
Worton	*Wilts* - Devizes
Worton, Nether	*Oxford* - Banbury
Worton, Over	*Oxford* - Banbury
Wortwell	*Norfolk* - Norwich
Wothersome	*York, W.R.* - Leeds
Wotherton (Chirbury)	*Salop* - Welshpool
Wothorpe	*Huntingdon and Peterborough* - Stamford
Wotter	*Devon* - Plymouth
Wotton	*Surrey* - Dorking
Wotton under Edge	*Gloucester* - Stroud
Wotton Underwood	*Bucks* - Aylesbury
Woughton	*Bucks* - Bletchley and Leighton Buzzard
Wouldham	*Kent* - Rochester
Wrabness	*Essex* - Harwich
Wrackleford	*Dorset* - Dorchester
Wrafton	*Devon* - Barnstaple
Wragby	*Lincoln* - Lincoln
Wragby	*York, N.R.* - Whitby
Wragby	*York, W.R.* - Pontefract
Wragg Marsh	*Lincoln* - Spalding
Wragholme	*Lincoln* - Louth
Wragmire	*Cumberland* - Carlisle
Wramplingham	*Norfolk* - Norwich
Wrangbrook	*York, W.R.* - Pontefract
Wrangham	*Northumberland* - Berwick-upon-Tweed
Wrangle	*Lincoln* - Boston
Wrangle Common	*Lincoln* - Boston
Wrangle Marsh	*Lincoln* - Boston
Wrangway	*Somerset* - Taunton
Wrantage	*Somerset* - Taunton
Wrawby	*Lincoln* - Scunthorpe
Wraxall	*Dorset* - Dorchester
Wraxall	*Somerset* - Bristol
Wraxall	*Somerset* - Wells
Wraxall, North	*Wilts* - Chippenham
Wraxall, South	*Wilts* - Trowbridge
Wray	*Lancaster* - Kendal
Wraysbury	*Bucks* - Slough
Wrayton	*Lancaster* - Lancaster
Wray with Botton	*Lancaster* - Lancaster
Wrea Green	*Lancaster* - Preston
Wreaks	*Lancaster* - Barrow-in-Furness
Wreay	*Cumberland* - Carlisle
Wreay	*Cumberland* - Penrith
Wrecclesham	*Surrey* - Aldershot and Farnham
Wreighill	*Northumberland* - Morpeth
Wrekenton	*Durham* - Gateshead
Wrekin, The	*Salop* - Wellington (Salop)
Wrelton	*York, N.R.* - Malton
Wrenbury cum Frith	*Cheshire* - Crewe
Wreningham	*Norfolk* - Norwich
Wrentham	*Suffolk* - Lowestoft
Wrenthorpe	*York, W.R.* - Wakefield
Wrentnall	*Salop* - Shrewsbury
Wressell	*York, E.R.* - Goole
Wressle Houses	*Lincoln* - Scunthorpe
Wressle Intake	*York, E.R.* - Goole
Wrestlingworth	*Beds* - Biggleswade
Wretton	*Norfolk* - King's Lynn
Wrexham	*Denbigh* - Wrexham
Wribbenhall	*Worcester* - Kidderminster
Wribbesford	*Worcester* - Kidderminster
Wright Green	*Cumberland* - Workington
Wrightington	*Lancaster* - Wigan
Wrinehill	*Stafford* - Crewe

Wrington	*Somerset* - Weston Super Mare
Writhlington	*Somerset* - Frome
Writtle	*Essex* - Chelmsford
Wrockwardine	*Salop* - Wellington (Salop)
Wrockwardine Bank	*Salop* - Wellington (Salop)
Wrockwardine Wood	*Salop* - Wellington (Salop)
Wroot	*Lincoln* - Thorne
Wrose Hill	*York, W.R.* - Bradford
Wrotham	*Kent* - Sevenoaks
Wrotham Heath	*Kent* - Sevenoaks
Wrottesley	*Stafford* - Wolverhampton
Wroughton	*Wilts* - Swindon
Wroxall	*I. of W.* - Newport (I.W.)
Wroxall	*Warwick* - Warwick
Wroxeter	*Salop* - Shrewsbury
Wroxham	*Norfolk* - Norwich
Wroxton	*Oxford* - Banbury
Wryde	*Northampton* - Peterborough
Wyaston	*Derby* - Derby
Wyatts Green	*Essex* - Brentwood
Wyberton	*Lincoln* - Boston
Wyberton Marsh	*Lincoln* - Boston
Wyberton Roads	*Lincoln* - Boston
Wyboston	*Beds* - Biggleswade
Wybourn	*York, W.R.* - Sheffield
Wybunbury	*Cheshire* - Crewe
Wycar Leys	*Notts* - Mansfield
Wychbold	*Worcester* - Bromsgrove
Wyche (part)	*Hereford* - Great Malvern
Wyche (part)	*Worcester* - Great Malvern
Wych, High	*Herts* - Bishop's Stortford
Wych, Higher	*Cheshire* - Whitchurch
Wychling	*Kent* - Sittingbourne
Wych, Lower	*Cheshire* - Whitchurch
Wychnor	*Stafford* - Burton-on-Trent
Wychwood	*Oxford* - Oxford
Wyckham	*Oxford* - Banbury
Wyck Rissington	*Gloucester* - Cheltenham
Wycliffe	*York, N.R.* - Darlington
Wycollar	*Lancaster* - Nelson
Wycomb	*Leicester* - Melton Mowbray
Wycombe Heath	*Bucks* - High Wycombe
Wycombe, High	*Bucks* - High Wycombe
Wycombe Marsh	*Bucks* - High Wycombe
Wycombe, West	*Bucks* - High Wycombe
Wyddial	*Herts* - Hitchin
Wydon	*Northumberland* - Hexham
Wydon Cleugh-side	*Northumberland* - Hexham
Wye	*Kent* - Ashford
Wyehead	*Derby* - Buxton
Wyesham	*Monmouth* - Monmouth
Wyfold Court	*Oxford* - Didcot
Wyfold Grange	*Oxford* - Reading
Wyfordby	*Leicester* - Melton Mowbray
Wyham	*Lincoln* - Louth
Wyke	*Devon* - Axminster and Chard
Wyke (Sherbourne)	*Dorset* - Yeovil
Wyke	*Hants* - Andover
Wyke	*Salop* - Bridgnorth
Wyke	*Surrey* - Aldershot and Farnham
Wyke	*York, W.R.* - Bradford
Wyke Champflower	*Somerset* - Yeovil
Wyke Green	*Middlesex* - Brentford
Wykeham	*Lincoln* - Spalding
Wykeham	*Lincoln* - Louth
Wykeham	*York, N.R.* - Scarborough
Wyken	*Salop* - Bridgnorth
Wyken	*Warwick* - Coventry
Wyke Regis	*Dorset* - Weymouth
Wykey	*Salop* - Oswestry
Wykin	*Leicester* - Hinckley
Wylam	*Northumberland* - Newcastle upon Tyne
Wylam, North	*Northumberland* - Newcastle upon Tyne
Wylam, West	*Northumberland* - Hexham
Wylde Green	*Warwick* - Birmingham
Wyley Moor	*Cumberland* - Carlisle
Wylfa	*Anglesey* - Llangefni
Wyllie	*Monmouth* - Blackwood

Wylye	*Wilts* - Salisbury
Wymering	*Hants* - Portsmouth
Wymeswold	*Leicester* - Loughborough
Wymington	*Beds* - Wellingborough
Wymondham	*Leicester* - Melton Mowbray
Wymondham	*Norfolk* - Norwich
Wymondley, Great	*Herts* - Hitchin
Wymondley, Little	*Herts* - Hitchin
Wyndford Mill	*Stafford* - Stafford
Wynford Eagle	*Dorset* - Dorchester
Wynnstay	*Montgomery* - Machynlleth
Wynyard	*Durham* - Stockton on Tees
Wyrardisbury	*Bucks* - Slough
Wyre Forest	*Worcester* - Kidderminster
Wyre Hill	*Worcester* - Kidderminster
Wyrs Piddle	*Worcester* - Evesham
Wyresdale, Nether	*Lancaster* - Lancaster
Wyresdale, Over	*Lancaster* - Lancaster
Wyrley, Great	*Stafford* - Walsall
Wyrley, Little	*Stafford* - Walsall
Wysall	*Notts* - Loughborough
Wyson	*Hereford* - Ludlow
Wythall	*Worcester* - Birmingham
Wytham	*Berks* - Oxford
Wythburn	*Cumberland* - Workington
Wytheford, Great	*Salop* - Shrewsbury
Wytheford, Little	*Salop* - Shrewsbury
Wythenshawe	*Lancaster* - Manchester
Wyther	*York, W.R.* - Leeds
Wythop	*Cumberland* - Workington
Wyton	*Hunts* - Huntingdon
Wyton	*York, E.R.* - Kingston-upon-Hull
Wyverstone	*Suffolk* - Stowmarket
Wyville	*Lincoln* - Grantham

Y

Yaddlethorpe	*Lincoln* - Scunthorpe
Yafford	*I. of W.* - Newport (I.W.)
Yafforth	*York, N.R.* - Northallerton
Yalding	*Kent* - Maidstone
Yantlett Creek, North	*Kent* - Rochester
Yanwath	*Westmorland* - Penrith
Yanworth	*Gloucester* - Cheltenham
Yapham	*York, E.R.* - York
Yapton	*Sussex* - Chichester
Yarburgh	*Lincs* - Louth
Yarcombe	*Devon* - Axminster
Yard Down	*Devon* - Barnstaple
Yardley	*Herts* - Hitchin
Yardley	*Warwick* - Birmingham
Yardley Gobion	*Northampton* - Northampton
Yardley Hastings	*Northampton* - Northampton
Yardley Wood	*Warwick* - Birmingham
Yarford	*Somerset* - Taunton
Yarkhill	*Hereford* - Hereford
Yarlet	*Stafford* - Stafford
Yarley	*Somerset* - Wells
Yarlington	*Somerset* - Yeovil
Yarm	*York, N.R.* - Stockton on Tees
Yarmouth	*I. of W.* - Newport (I.W,)
Yarmouth, Great	*Norfolk* - Great Yarmouth
Yarnbrook	*Wilts* - Trowbridge
Yarnfield	*Somerset* - Frome
Yarnfield	*Stafford* - Stoke-on-Trent
Yarningale Common	*Warwick* - Warwick
Yarnscombe	*Devon* - Barnstaple
Yarnton	*Oxford* - Oxford
Yarpole	*Hereford* - Leominster
Yarr	*Worcester* - Redditch
Yarrhampton	*Worcester* - Kidderminster
Yarrom	*Northumberland* - Hexham
Yarwell	*Northampton* - Peterborough
Yate	*Gloucester* - Bristol
Yate Common	*Gloucester* - Bristol
Yateley	*Hants* - Aldershot and Farnham

YAT - YOR

Yate Rocks	*Gloucester* - Bristol
Yatesbury	*Wilts* - Chippenham
Yattendon	*Berks* - Newbury
Yatt, New	*Oxford* - Witney
Yatton	*Hereford* - Leominster
Yatton	*Hereford* - Hereford
Yatton	*Somerset* - Weston Super Mare
Yatton Keynell	*Wilts* - Chippenham
Yawl Bottom	*Devon* - Axminster and Chard
Yawthorpe	*Lincoln* - Gainsborough
Yaxham	*Norfolk* - East Dereham
Yaxley	*Hunts* - Peterborough
Yaxley	*Suffolk* - Norwich
Yazor	*Hereford* - Hereford
Yeading	*Middlesex* - Uxbridge
Yeadon	*York, W.R.* - Otley
Yealand Conyers	*Lancaster* - Lancaster
Yealand Redmayne	*Lancaster* - Lancaster
Yealand Storrs	*Lancaster* - Lancaster
Yealmbridge	*Devon* - Plymouth
Yealmpton	*Devon* - Plymouth
Yearby	*York, N.R.* - Middlesbrough
Yearley	*Stafford* - Ashbourne
Yearsley	*York, N.R.* - York
Yeatman's Barn	*Dorset* - Dorchester
Yeaton	*Salop* - Shrewsbury
Yeatsall	*Stafford* - Uttoxeter
Yeaveley	*Derby* - Derby
Yeavering	*Northumberland* - Berwick-upon-Tweed
Yeddingham	*York, E.R.* - Malton
Yelden	*Beds* - Wellingborough
Yeldersley	*Derby* - Derby
Yeld, The	*Cheshire* - Northwich
Yelford	*Oxford* - Witney
Yelling	*Hunts* - Huntingdon
Yelsted	*Kent* - Sittingbourne
Yelvertoft	*Northampton* - Rugby
Yelverton	*Devon* - Plymouth
Yelverton	*Norfolk* - Norwich
Yenston	*Somerset* - Yeovil
Yeoford	*Devon* - Exeter
Yeolmbridge	*Devon* - Launceston
Yeo Mill	*Devon* - Tiverton
Yeovil	*Somerset* - Yeovil
Yeovilton	*Somerset* - Yeovil
Yerbeston	*Pembroke* - Haverfordwest
Yerngill	*Cumberland* - Carlisle
Yetlington	*Northumberland* - Alnwick
Yetminster	*Dorset* - Yeovil
Yetson	*Devon* - Kingsbridge
Yews	*York, W.R.* - Rotherham
Yewthwaite	*Cumberland* - Workington
Yewtree	*Stafford* - Stafford
Yew Tree Estate	*Stafford* - West Bromwich
Yew Tree Hill	*Worcester* - Worcester
Yielding Tree	*Worcester* - Stourbridge
Yiewsley	*Middlesex* - Uxbridge
Ynismeudw	*Glamorgan* - Neath
Ynisymond	*Glamorgan* - Neath
Ynysawdre	*Glamorgan* - Bridgend
Ynysddu	*Monmouth* - Blackwood
Ynysforgan	*Glamorgan* - Swansea
Ynyshir	*Glamorgan* - Pontypridd
Ynyslas	*Cardigan* - Aberystwyth
Ynyslas	*Glamorgan* - Bridgend
Ynystawe	*Glamorgan* - Swansea
Ynysybwl	*Glamorgan* - Pontypridd
Ynysyboeth	*Glamorgan* - Aberdare
Yockleton	*Salop* - Shrewsbury
Yokefleet	*York, E.R.* - Goole
York	*York, E.R.* - York
Yorkletts	*Kent* - Canterbury
Yorkley	*Gloucester* - Monmouth
York, New	*Durham* - Gateshead
York, New	*Lincoln* - Boston
York, New	*York, W.R.* - Harrogate
York Town (Camberley)	*Surrey* - Aldershot and Farnham
Yorton	*Salop* - Shrewsbury
Yorton Heath	*Salop* - Shrewsbury

YOU - ZOU

Youlgreave	*Derby* - Matlock
Youlthorpe	*York, E.R.* - York
Yoxall	*Stafford* - Lichfield
Yoxford	*Suffolk* - Woodbridge
Ysbytyl Ifan	*Denbigh* - Conway
Ysbyty	*Montgomery* - Oswestry
Ysceifiog	*Flint* - Holywell
Yscuborycoed	*Cardigan* - Machynlleth
Ystalyfera	*Glamorgan* - Neath
Ystrad	*Glamorgan* - Pontypridd
Ystradfellte	*Glamorgan* - Neath
Ystradgynlais	*Brecon* - Neath
Ystrad Mynach (part)	*Glamorgan* - Bargoed
Ystrad Mynach (part)	*Glamorgan* - Caerphilly
Ystradowen	*Glamorgan* - Bridgend
Ystradynod	*Montgomery* - Newtown
Ystumtuen	*Cardigan* - Aberystwyth
Ystymcolwyn	*Montgomery* - Oswestry
Ystymgynog	*Montgomery* - Oswestry

Z

Zealand, New	*Wilts* - Swindon
Zeal Monachorum	*Devon* - Okehampton
Zeals	*Wilts* - Shaftesbury
Zeal, South	*Devon* - Okehampton
Zelah	*Cornwall* - Truro
Zennor	*Cornwall* - Penzance
Zouch	*Notts* - Loughborough

Dd. 500245 K12 H.P.Ltd. 11/70

SBN 11 700361 1